The AMERICAN JOURNEY

A History of the United States

CONCISE EDITION SECOND EDITION

VOLUME 2

David Goldfield
UNIVERSITY OF NORTH CAROLINA, CHARLOTTE

Carl Abbott
PORTLAND STATE UNIVERSITY

Virginia DeJohn Anderson
UNIVERSITY OF COLORADO, BOULDER

Jo Ann E. Argersinger
SOUTHERN ILLINOIS UNIVERSITY

Peter H. Argersinger
SOUTHERN ILLINOIS UNIVERSITY

William L. Barney
UNIVERSITY OF NORTH CAROLINA, CHAPEL HILL

Robert M. Weir
UNIVERSITY OF SOUTH CAROLINA

PEARSON

Boston Columbus Indianapolis New York San Francisco Upper Saddle River
Amsterdam Cape Town Dubai London Madrid Milan Munich Paris Montréal Toronto
Delhi Mexico City São Paulo Sydney Hong Kong Seoul Singapore Taipei Tokyo

Editor-in-Chief: Dickson Musselwhite
Publisher: Charlyce Jones Owen
Editorial Assistant: Maureen Diana
Senior Manufacturing and Operations Manager for Arts & Sciences: Nick Sklitsis
Director of Marketing: Brady Dawson
Senior Marketing Manager: Maureen E. Prado Roberts
Marketing Assistant: Samantha Bennett
Editorial Project Manager: Emsal Hasan
Senior Managing Editor: Ann Marie McCarthy
Production Project Manager: Clara Bartunek
Cover Designer: Suzanne Behnke
Cover Photos: The American Journey, Concise Edition, Combined, 2/E – 0205214940 Credit: *The Library of Congress* The American Journey, Concise Edition, Volume 1, 2/E – 0205214959 Credit:

© *The Granger Collection, New York* The American Journey, Concise Edition, Volume 2- 2/E- 0205214967 Credit: *Diego Rivera, Mural depicting Detroit Industry, 1932-33. Fresco. The Detroit Institute of Arts. gift of Edsel B. Ford/The Bridgeman Art Library/(c) 2011 Banco de México Diego Rivera Frida Kahlo Museums Trust, Mexico, D.F./Artists Rights Society (ARS) New York.*
Media Director: Brian Hyland
Creative Art Director: Jayne Conte
Lead Media Project Manager: Andrea Messineo
Full-Service Project Management: Element/ Thomson North America
Printer/Binder: R.R. Donnelley/ Crawsfordsville
Cover Printer: Lehigh/Phoenix-Hagerstown
Text Font: Adobe Jenson Regular

Credits and acknowledgments borrowed from other sources and reproduced, with permission, in this textbook appear on appropriate page within text (or on page C1–C2).

Library of Congress Cataloging-in-Publication Data

The American journey : a history of the United States / David Goldfield . . . [et al.].—Concise ed. 2nd ed.
      p. cm.
   Includes index.
   ISBN-13: 978-0-205-21494-5 (combined vol.)
   ISBN-10: 0-205-21494-0 (combinded vol.)
   ISBN-13: 978-0-205-21495-2 (v. 1)
   ISBN-10: 0-205-21495-9 (v. 1)
   [etc.]
1. United States—History.   I. Goldfield, David R.,
   E178.1.A4925 2012
   973–dc23

                                                                    2011024440

10 9 8 7 6 5 4 3 2 1

Combined Volume:	Volume 1:
ISBN 10: 0-205-21494-0	ISBN 10: 0-205-21495-9
ISBN 13: 978-0-205-21494-5	ISBN 13: 978-0-205-21495-2
Examination Copy:	Volume 2:
ISBN 10: 0-205-21500-9	ISBN 10: 0-205-21496-7
ISBN 13: 978-0-205-21500-3	ISBN 13: 978-0-205-21496-9

CONTENTS

22 CREATING AN EMPIRE •• 1865–1917   654

23 AMERICA AND THE GREAT WAR •• 1914–1920   682

24 TOWARD A MODERN AMERICA •• *1920s* 710

27 THE COLD WAR AT HOME AND ABROAD •• *1946–1952*   806

28 THE CONFIDENT YEARS ·· *1953–1964*   838

31 COMPLACENCY, CRISIS AND GLOBAL REENGAGEMENT •• *1993–2010*   942

PREFACE

The path that led us to *The American Journey* began in the classroom with our students. Our primary goal is to make American history accessible to them. The key to that goal—the core of the book—is a strong, clear narrative. We chose our book's title because we believe the theme of *journey* offers an ideal way to give coherence to our narrative and yet fairly represent the complexities of our nation's past.

We employ this theme throughout the book, in its chapters, its pedagogical features, and its selection of primary source documents. The journeys we describe can be geographical, focusing on the movement of people, goods, ideas, or even germs from one place to another. They can also be ideological, political, or social—some eventually codified in our founding documents and institutions, others culminating in patterns of personal behavior and social relationships, still others reaching a dead end because of popular opposition, political or economic changes, or even war.

Not all journeys were straightforward in reaching their destinations. American history contains many examples of thwarted personal hopes and national promises that remained unfulfilled for generations. Americans debated the meaning of the liberty they hailed as their nation's founding principle and the extent of power they were willing to entrust to their government. Did the full measure of liberty apply to all its peoples irrespective of race, gender, or ethnicity? Were American freedoms defined only in the political terms set out in the Bill of Rights of 1791 or were they also to include freedom from economic insecurity and social injustice? Some of the journeys assumed a regional dimension as the environment and inherited cultural patterns imparted a distinctive approach to issues affecting the entire nation.

Most of all, the journeys have been those of individuals. We have tried to include as many of them as possible and to blend their stories into the larger national narrative of which they were and are a part. The voices of contemporaries open each chapter, describing their personal journeys—and detours—toward fulfilling their dreams, hopes, and ambitions as part of the broader American journey. These voices provide a personal window on our nation's history, and the themes they express resonate throughout the narrative. Embedding these individual stories within a broader narrative allows us to address questions of culture, identity, politics, and ideas as they shaped the lives of elites and common people alike.

By including stories from the perspectives of different individuals and groups in the text and Web-based features, we aim to provide students with a balanced overview of the American past. We do not shy away from controversial issues, such as the effects of early contacts between Native Americans and Europeans, why the political crisis of the 1850s ended in a bloody Civil War, how Populists fit into the American political spectrum, or why the United States used nuclear weapons against Japan. If our treatment of these topics provokes debate between students and instructors, we encourage such discussions as an important catalyst to learning.

We invite students and teachers to think about how their own stories and those of their families relate to the theme of our book. Most of all, we hope that *The American Journey* can guide students along their own intellectual paths toward a better understanding of American history and their own place in it.

APPROACH

In telling our story, we had some definite ideas about what we might include and emphasize that other texts do not—information we felt that the current and next generations of students will need to know about our past to function best in a new society.

CHRONOLOGICAL ORGANIZATION

A strong chronological backbone supports the book. We have found that jumping back and forth in time confuses students. They abhor dates but need to know the sequence of events in history. A chronological presentation is the best way to help students.

GEOGRAPHICAL LITERACY

We also want students to be geographically literate. We expect them not only to know what happened in American history, but where it happened as well. Physical locations and spatial relationships were often important in shaping historical events. The abundant maps in *The American Journey*—all numbered and called out in the text—are an integral part of our story.

REGIONAL BALANCE

The American Journey presents balanced coverage of all regions of the country. In keeping with this balance, the South and the West receive more coverage in this text than in comparable books.

RELIGION

This text stresses the importance of religion in American society as a cultural force and an influence on political action.

WHAT'S NEW IN THE SIXTH EDITION

- There is greater emphasis on the personal and collective journeys that have shaped America's history, from the personal documents that open each chapter to the narrative that defines the journey.
- Every chapter has been thoroughly revised and improved with new special features as well as updated scholarship.
- Throughout the text, there is an increased emphasis on environmental history in both the chapter narrative and special features.
- A new **MyHistoryLab Connections** section highlights documents, maps, audio, and video resources related to the content of each chapter that are available on the extensively revised MyHistoryLab Web site.

HIGHLIGHT OF CHANGES BY CHAPTER:

Chapter 16 The chapter stresses the violence against southern Republican governments, particularly blacks, as the key factor in ending Reconstruction. The new **American Journey** chapter opener is a poem by black poet Frances E. W. Harper.

Chapter 17 There is more emphasis on how "old" the New South was, particularly with respect to race relations. An expanded discussion is found in "Lynch Law." There is a new **American Views** feature, "An Account of a Lynching."

Chapter 18 A more nuanced portrait is given of the great entrepreneurs that stresses their innovative business techniques.

Chapter 19 A new discussion of the role of the army in the West emphasizes military tactics.

Chapter 21 The new **American Journey** chapter opening features the nearly mythical labor agitator Mother Jones and her crusade against child labor.

Chapter 22 A new section on U.S. relations with Europe in the early twentieth century before World War I helps to put into context America's ultimate involvement in that war.

Chapter 24 There is new material on ethnicity and immigration, including a discussion of Sacco and Vanzetti.

Chapter 25 A new **American Journey** chapter opener is drawn from one of FDR's "fireside chats."

Chapt er 26 Expanded coverage of the controversial Dresden bombing and expanded data on military and civilian deaths around the world.

Chapter 27 The treatment of the "second red scare" notes the bipartisan breadth of the anti-Communist efforts.

Chapter 28 A new **American Views** document on open space, shows the roots of the modern environmental movement as a reaction against suburban sprawl.

Chapter 29 A new **American Journey** on Dolores Huerta opens the chapter. The chapter reevaluates the Nixon-Kissinger diplomatic strategy.

Chapter 31 There is a new **American Journey** from a Katrina survivor and a new Overview table on Core Support for Republicans and Democrats in 2008. The new section "The Obama Phenomenon" covers the election of 2008 (including a map).

ACKNOWLEDGMENTS

All of us are grateful to our families, friends, and colleagues for their support and encouragement. Jo Ann and Peter Argersinger would like in particular to thank Anna Champe, Linda Hatmaker, and John Willits; William Barney thanks Pamela Fesmire and Rosalie Radcliffe; Virginia Anderson thanks Fred Anderson, Kim Gruenwald, Ruth Helm, Eric Hinderaker, and Chidiebere Nwaubani; and David Goldfield thanks Frances Glenn and Jason Moscato.

Finally, we would like to acknowledge the members of our Prentice Hall family. They are not only highly competent professionals but also pleasant people. We regard them with affection and appreciation. None of us would hesitate to work with this fine group again. We would especially like to thank our editorial team: Charlyce Jones Owen, Publisher, our marketing team: Maureen Prado Roberts, Senior Marketing Manager, and Brandy Dawson, Director of Marketing; our production team: Anne Marie McCarthy, Clara Bartunek, Editorial Director, and Yolanda deRooy, president of Prentice Hall's Humanities and Social Sciences division.

SUPPLEMENTARY INSTRUCTIONAL MATERIALS

For Instructors	For Students
myhistorylab www.myhistorylab.com **Save Time. Improve Results.** MyHistoryLab is a dynamic website that provides a wealth of resources geared to meet the diverse teaching and learning needs of today's instructors and students.	**myhistorylab** www.myhistorylab.com **Save Time. Improve Results.** MyHistoryLab is a dynamic website that provides a wealth of resources geared to meet the diverse teaching and learning needs of today's instructors and students.
Instructor's Resource Center www.pearsonhighered. com/irc This website provides instructors with additional text-specific resources that can be downloaded for classroom use. Resources include the Instructor's Resource Manual, PowerPoint presentations, and the test item file.	www.coursemart.com CourseSmart eTextbooks offer the same content as the printed text in a convenient online format—with highlighting, online search, and printing capabilities. You **save 60% over the list price** of the traditional book.
Instructor's Resource Manual Available for download at www.pearsonhighered.com/irc, *the* Instructor's Resource Manual contains chapter outlines, detailed chapter overviews, lecture outlines, topics for discussion, and information about audio-visual resources.	**Library of American Biography Series** www.pearson-highered.com/educator/series/Library-of-American-Biography/10493.page Pearson's renowned series of biographies spotlighting figures who had a significant impact on American history.
Test Item File Available for download at www.pearson-highered.com/irc, the Test Item File contains more than 1,5 00 multiple-choice, identification, matching, true-false, and essay test questions and 10–15 questions per chapter on the maps found in each chapter.	*American Stories: Biographies in United States History* This two-volume collection of sixty-two biographies provides insight into the lives and contributions of key figures as well as ordinary citizens to American history. **ISBN-10: 0131826549 ISBN-13: 9780131826540**; Volume 2 **ISBN-10: 0131826530 ISBN-13: 9780131826533**
PowerPoint Presentations Available for download at www.pearsonhighered.com/irc, the PowerPoints contain chapter outlines and full-color images of maps, figures, and images.	**Penguin Valuepacks** www.pearsonhighered.com/penguin A variety of Penguin-Putnam texts is available at discounted prices when bundled with *The American Journey, Concise Edition.* Texts include
MyTest www.pearsonmytest.com MyTest is a powerful assessment generation program that helps instructors easily create and print quizzes and exams. Instructors can easily access existing questions and edit, create, and store using simple drag-and-drop and Word-like controls.	*A Short Guide to Writing About History, 7/e* Written by Richard Marius, late of Harvard University, and Melvin E. Page, Eastern Tennessee State University, this text explores the writing and researching processes, identifies different modes of historical writing, including argument, and concludes with guidelines for improving style. **ISBN-10: 0205673708; ISBN-13: 9780205673704**
Retrieving the American Past (www.pearsoncustom. com, **keyword search | rtap**) Available through the Pearson Custom Library, the *Retrieving the American Past* (RTAP) program lets you create a textbook or reader *The American Journey, Brief 6/e*, in the depth and sequence you want, at the price you want your students to pay.	**Longman American History Atlas** This full-color historical atlas designed especially for college students, this atlas includes maps covering the scope of American history from the lives of the Native Americans to the 1990s. Produced by a renowned cartographic firm and a team of respected historians, the Longman American History Atlas will enhance any American history survey course. **ISBN: 0321004868; ISBN-13: 9780321004864**

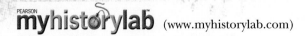 **PEARSON** **myhistorylab** (www.myhistorylab.com)

FOR INSTRUCTORS AND STUDENTS

Save TIME. Improve Results.
MyHistoryLab is a dynamic web-site that provides a wealth of resources geared to meet the diverse teaching and learning needs of today's instructors and students. MyHistoryLab's many accessible tools will encourage students to read their text and help them improve their grade in their course.

- **Pearson eText**—An e-book version of *The American Journey* is included in MyHistoryLab. Just as with the printed text, students can high-light and add their own notes as they read the book online.

- **Gradebook**—Students can follow their own progress and instructors can monitor the work of the class. Automated grading of quizzes and assignments helps both instructors and students save time and monitor their results throughout the course.

- **History Bookshelf**—Students may read, download, or print 100 of the most com-monly assigned history works like Homer's *The Iliad* or Machiavelli's *The Prince*.

- **Audio Files**—Full audio of the text is included to suit the varied learning styles of today's students.

- **MySearchLab**—This website provides students access to a number of reliable sources for online research, as well as clear guidance on the research and writing process.

16 Reconstruction • • 1865–1877

Hear the audio files for Chapter 16 at **www.myhistorylab.com.**

FOCUS QUESTIONS

HOW DID southerners remember the war?

HOW DID it shape their response to Reconstruction?

WHAT WERE African Americans' hopes for Reconstruction?

HOW DID Presidential Reconstruction differ from Congressional Reconstruction?

WHAT ROLE did violence play in Counter-Reconstruction?

WHY DID the federal government abandon African Americans after 1872?

HOW AND why did Reconstruction end?

An elderly man reads a newspaper with the headline "Presidential Proclamation, Slavery," which refers to the January 1863 Emancipation Proclamation in this painting by Henry Louis Stephens (1824–1882).

ONE AMERICAN JOURNEY
AN APPEAL TO THE AMERICAN PEOPLE (1871)

When a dark and fearful strife
Raged around the nation's life,
And the traitor plunged his steel
Where your quivering hearts could feel,
When your cause did need a friend,
We were faithful to the end.

With your soldiers, side by side,
Helped we turn the battle's tide,
Till o'er ocean, stream and shore,
Wave the rebel flag no more,
And above the rescued sod
Praises rose to freedom's God.

But to-day the traitor stands
With crimson on his hands,
Scowling 'neath his brow of hate,
On our weak and desolate,
With the blood-rust on the knife
Aimed at the nation's life.

Asking you to weakly yield
All we won upon the field,
To ignore, on land and flood,
All the offerings of our blood,
And to write above our slain
"They have fought and died in vain."

Maryemma Graham, ed., *Complete Poems of Frances E. W. Harper* (New York: Oxford University Press, 1988), pp. 81–83.

FRANCES ELLEN WATKINS HARPER, the author of this poem, pleaded with northerners not to abandon African Americans in their quest for full equality. She appealed both to their sense of fairness—that African Americans had fought side-by-side and laid down their lives for the Union cause—and to their self-interest to not allow their winning the war, and the sacrifices that entailed, to be betrayed by losing the peace.

At the time, 1871, Reconstruction was under full assault in the South by white paramilitary groups associated with the Democratic Party. Though violence against the freedmen and their aspirations had been persistent since the end of the Civil War, the growing political power of blacks in the South after 1867 provoked more organized and violent assaults on blacks and some of their white colleagues. The federal government attempted to quell these disturbances with troops and legislation, but these measures were largely ineffective. While a majority of northern whites had opposed slavery, a majority also opposed racial equality. By 1871, a consensus emerged in the North to allow southern whites a free hand in dealing with their political problems. Harper's appeal, therefore, fell on deaf ears. The nation's journey toward a more just society took a major detour in the decade after the Civil War.

Frances Harper's personal journey was more rewarding. She was born into a free black family in Maryland, a slave state, in 1825. Orphaned at the age of three and raised by her aunt and uncle, she attended a noted school for free blacks in Baltimore. By the time she was 25, she had become the first woman professor at a seminary in Ohio which later became Wilberforce University. In 1853, Harper moved to Philadelphia where she worked in the Underground Railroad and became one of the few black women lecturers on abolition. In 1860, she married Fenton Harper, and had a daughter with him. When he died in 1864, she took her daughter and resumed lecturing, becoming one of the first women of color to travel throughout the South in the days after emancipation, helping to educate former slaves.

Although she arrived in the South with considerable hope, Harper left after five frustrating years. Violence against African Americans and their white allies had escalated and threatened to reduce the former slaves to a permanent category of second-class citizenship. Her poem was one of her last attempts to reach a northern public already grown weary of the periodic racial disturbances in the South. Harper spent the rest of her life writing novels and poetry, and working for the causes of temperance and of racial and women's rights.

The position of African Americans in American society was one of the two great issues of the Reconstruction era. The other great issue was how and under what terms to readmit the former Confederate states. Between 1865 and 1867, under President Andrew Johnson's Reconstruction plan, white southerners pretty much had their way with the former slaves and with their own state governments. Congressional action between 1867 and 1870 attempted to balance black rights and home rule, with mixed results. After 1870, white southerners gradually regained control of their states and localities, often through violence and intimidation, denying black southerners their political gains while Republicans in Washington and white northerners lost interest in policing their former enemies.

By the time the last federal troops left the South in 1877, the white southerners had prevailed. The Confederate states had returned to the Union with all of

CHRONOLOGY

1861   Tsar Alexander II frees the serfs of Russia.

1863   Lincoln proposes his Ten Percent Plan.

1864   Congress proposes the Wade-Davis Bill.

1865   Sherman issues Field Order No. 15.
Freedmen's Bureau is established.
Andrew Johnson succeeds to the presidency, unveils his Reconstruction plan.
Massachusetts desegregates all public facilities.
Black citizens in several southern cities organize Union Leagues.
Former Confederate states begin to pass black codes.

1866   Congress passes Southern Homestead Act, Civil Rights Act of 1866.
Ku Klux Klan is founded.
Fourteenth Amendment to the Constitution is passed (ratified in 1868).
President Johnson goes on a speaking tour.

1867   Congress passes Military Reconstruction Acts, Tenure of Office Act.

1868   President Johnson is impeached and tried in the Senate for defying the Tenure of Office Act.
Republican Ulysses S. Grant is elected president.

1869   Fifteenth Amendment passed (ratified 1870).

1870   Congress passes Enforcement Act.
Republican regimes topple in North Carolina and Georgia.

1871   Congress passes Ku Klux Klan Act.

1872   Freedmen's Bureau closes down.
Liberal Republicans emerge as a separate party.
Ulysses S. Grant is reelected.

1873   Severe depression begins.
Colfax Massacre occurs.
U.S. Supreme Court's decision in the *Slaughterhouse* cases weakens the intent of the Fourteenth Amendment.
Texas falls to the Democrats in the fall elections.

1874   White Leaguers attempt a coup against the Republican government of New Orleans.
Democrats win off-year elections across the South amid widespread fraud and violence.

1875   Congress passes Civil Rights Act of 1875.

1876   Supreme Court's decision in *United States v. Cruikshank* nullifies Enforcement Act of 1870.
Outcome of the presidential election between Republican Rutherford B. Hayes and Democrat Samuel J. Tilden is contested.

1877   Compromise of 1877 makes Hayes president and ends Reconstruction.

their rights and many of their leaders restored. And the freed slaves remained in mostly subservient positions with few of the rights and privileges enjoyed by other Americans.

WHITE SOUTHERNERS AND THE GHOSTS OF THE CONFEDERACY, 1865

The casualties of war in the South continued long after the hostilities ceased. Cities such as Richmond, Atlanta, Savannah, Charleston, and Columbia lay in ruins; farmsteads were stripped of everything but the soil; infrastructure, especially railroads, was damaged or destroyed; factories and machinery were demolished; and at least 5 million bales of cotton, the major cash crop, had gone up in smoke. Add a worthless currency, and the loss was staggering, climbing into hundreds of billions of dollars in today's currency.

Their cause lost and their society destroyed, white southerners lived through the summer and fall of 1865 surrounded by ghosts, the ghosts of lost loved ones, joyful times, bountiful harvests, self-assurance, and slavery. Defeat shook the basic tenets of their religious beliefs. Some praised God for delivering the South from the sin of slavery. But many other white southerners refused to accept their defeat as a divine judgment.

This engraving shows southerners decorating the graves of rebel soldiers at Hollywood Memorial Cemetery in Virginia in 1867. Northerners and southerners alike honored their war dead. But in the South, the practice of commemorating fallen soldiers became an important element in maintaining the myth of the Lost Cause that colored white southerners' view of the war.

Instead, they insisted, God had spared the South for a greater purpose. They came to view the war as the **Lost Cause** and interpreted it, not as a lesson in humility, but as an episode in the South's journey to salvation. White southerners transformed the bloody struggle into a symbol of courage against great odds and piety against sin. Eventually, they believed, redemption would come.

The Lost Cause would not merely exist as a memory, but also as a three-dimensional depiction of southern history, in rituals and celebrations, and as the educational foundation for future generations. The statues of the Confederate common soldier erected typically on the most important site in a town, the courthouse square; the commemorations of Confederate Memorial Day, the birthdays of prominent Confederate leaders, and the reunions of veterans, all marked with flourishing oratory, brass bands, parades, and related spectacles; and the textbooks implanting the white history of the South in young minds and carrying the legacy down through the generations—all of these ensured that the Lost Cause would not only be an interpretation of the past, but also the basic reality of the present and the foundation for the future.

Most white southerners approached the great issues of freedom and reunification with unyielding views. They saw African Americans as adversaries whose attempts at self-improvement were a direct challenge to white people's belief in their own racial superiority. White southerners saw outside assistance to black southerners as another invasion. The Yankees might have destroyed their families, their farms, and their fortunes, but they would not destroy the racial order. The war may have ended slavery, but white southerners were determined to preserve strict racial boundaries.

More than Freedom: African American Aspirations in 1865

Black southerners had a quite different perspective on the Civil War and Reconstruction, seeing the former as a great victory for freedom and the latter as a time of great possibility. To black southerners the Civil War was a war of liberation, not a Lost Cause. The response of southern whites to black aspirations still stunned African Americans, who believed, naively perhaps, that what they sought—education, land, access to employment, and equality in law and politics—were basic rights and modest objectives. The former slaves did not initially even dream of social equality; far less did they plot murder and mayhem, as white people feared. They did harbor two potentially contradictory aspirations. The first was to be left alone, free of white supervision. But the former slaves also wanted land, voting and civil rights, and education. To secure these, they needed the intervention and support of the white power structure.

In 1865, African Americans had reason to hope that their dreams of full citizenship might be realized. They enjoyed a reservoir of support for their aspirations among some Republican leaders. The first step Congress took beyond emancipation was to establish the Bureau of Refugees, Freedmen, and Abandoned Lands in March 1865. Congress envisioned the **Freedmen's Bureau,** as it came to be called, as a multipurpose

The Freedmen's Bureau, northern churches, and missionary societies established more than 3,000 schools, attended by some 150,000 men, women, and children in the years after the Civil War. At first, mostly young white women from the Northeast staffed these schools.

agency to provide social, educational, and economic services, advice, and protection to former slaves and destitute white southerners. The bureau marked the federal government's first foray into social welfare legislation. Congress also authorized the bureau to rent confiscated and abandoned farmland to freedmen in 40-acre plots, with an option to buy. This auspicious beginning belied the great disappointments that lay ahead.

EDUCATION

The greatest success of the Freedmen's Bureau was in education. The bureau coordinated more than fifty northern philanthropic and religious groups, which, in turn, established 3,000 freedmen's schools in the South, serving 150,000 men, women, and children.

Initially, single young women from the Northeast comprised much of the teaching force. By 1871, black teachers outnumbered white teachers in the "colored" schools. The financial troubles of northern missionary societies and white northerners' declining interest in the freedmen's condition opened opportunities for black teachers. Support for them came from black churches, especially the African Methodist Episcopal (AME) Church.

At the end of the Civil War, only about 10 percent of black southerners were literate, compared with more than 70 percent of white southerners. Within a decade, black literacy had risen above 30 percent. Joseph Wilson, a former slave, attributed the rise to "this longing of ours for freedom of the mind as well as the body."

Some black southerners went on to one of the thirteen colleges established by the American Missionary Association and black and white churches. Between 1860 and 1880 more than 1,000 black southerners earned college degrees at institutions still serving students today, such as Howard University in Washington, DC, Fisk University in Nashville, Hampton Institute (now University), Tuskegee Institute, and Biddle Institute (now Johnson C. Smith University) in Charlotte.

Pursuing freedom of the mind involved challenges beyond those of learning to read and write. Many white southerners condemned efforts at "Negro improvement." They viewed the time spent on education as wasted, forcing the former slaves to catch their lessons in bits and pieces between work, often by candlelight or on Sundays. White southerners also harassed white female teachers, questioning their morals and threatening people who rented rooms to them. After the Freedmen's Bureau folded in 1872 and many of the northern societies that supported freedmen's education collapsed or cut back their involvement, education for black southerners became more haphazard.

"FORTY ACRES AND A MULE"

Although education was important to the freed slaves in their quest for civic equality, land ownership offered them the promise of economic independence. For generations, black people had worked southern farms and had received nothing for their labor.

An overwhelmingly agricultural people, freedmen looked to farm ownership as a key element in their transition from slavery to freedom. "Gib us our own land and we take care of ourselves," a Charleston freedman asserted to a northern visitor in 1865. "But without land, de ole massas can hire or starve us, as dey please." Even before the war's end, rumors circulated through black communities in the South that the government would provide each black family with 40 acres and a mule. These rumors were fueled by General William T. Sherman's **Field Order No. 15** in January 1865, which set aside a vast swath of abandoned land along the South Atlantic coast from the Charleston area to northern Florida for grants of up to 40 acres. The Freedmen's Bureau likewise raised expectations when it was initially authorized to rent 40-acre plots of confiscated or abandoned land to freedmen.

By June 1865, about 40,000 former slaves had settled on Sherman land along the southeastern coast. In 1866, Congress passed the **Southern Homestead Act,** giving black people preferential access to public lands in five southern states. Two years later, the Republican government of South Carolina initiated a land-redistribution program financed by the sale of state bonds. The state used proceeds from the bond sales to purchase farmland, which it then resold to freedmen, who paid for it with state-funded long-term low-interest loans. By the late 1870s, more than 14,000 African American families had taken advantage of this program.

Land ownership did not ensure financial success. Most black-owned farms were small and on marginal land. The value of these farms in 1880 was roughly half that of white-owned farms. Black farmers also had trouble obtaining credit to purchase or expand their holdings. A lifetime of fieldwork left some freedmen without the managerial skills to operate a farm. The hostility of white neighbors also played a role in thwarting black aspirations.

The vast majority of former slaves, however, especially those in the Lower South, never fulfilled their dreams of land ownership. Rumors to the contrary, the federal government never intended to implement a land-redistribution program in the South. General Sherman viewed his field order as a temporary measure to support freedmen for the remainder of the war. President Andrew Johnson nullified the order in September 1865, returning confiscated land to its former owners. Even Republican supporters of black land ownership questioned the constitutionality of seizing privately owned real estate. Most of the land-redistribution programs that emerged after the war, including government-sponsored programs, required black farmers to have capital. But in the impoverished postwar economy of the South, it was difficult for them to acquire it.

Republican Party rhetoric of the 1850s extolled the virtues and dignity of free labor over the degradation of slave labor. Free labor usually meant working for a wage or under some other contractual arrangement. After the war, many white northerners envisioned former slaves assuming the status of free laborers, not necessarily of independent landowners.

Most of the officials of the Freedmen's Bureau shared these views and therefore saw reviving the southern economy as a higher priority than helping former slaves acquire farms. They wanted both to get the crop in the field and start the South on the road to a free labor system. Thus, they encouraged freedmen to work for their former masters under contract and to postpone their quest for land.

At first, agents of the Freedmen's Bureau supervised labor contracts between former slaves and masters. But after 1867, bureau surveillance declined. Agents assumed that both black laborers and white landowners had become accustomed to the mutual obligations of contracts. The bureau, however, underestimated the power of white landowners to coerce favorable terms or to ignore those they did not like. Contracts implied a mutuality that most planters could not accept in their relations with former slaves.

By the late 1870s, most former slaves in the rural South had been drawn into a subservient position in a new labor system called **sharecropping.** The premise of this system was relatively simple: The landlord furnished the sharecroppers with a house, a plot of land to work, seed, some farm animals, and farm implements and advanced them credit at a store the landlord typically owned. In exchange, the sharecroppers promised the landlord a share of their crop, usually one-half. The croppers kept the proceeds from the sale of the other half to pay off their debts at the store and save or spend as they and their families saw fit. In theory, a sharecropper could save enough to secure economic independence.

But white landlords perceived black independence as both contradictory and subversive. With landlords keeping the accounts at the store, black sharecroppers found that the proceeds from their share of the crop never left them very far ahead. Some found themselves in perpetual debt and worked as virtual slaves. Not all white landlords cheated their tenants, but given the sharecroppers' innocence regarding accounting methods and crop pricing, the temptation to do so was great.

MIGRATION TO CITIES

Even before the hope of land ownership faded, African Americans looked for alternatives to secure their personal and economic independence. Before the war, the city had offered slaves and free black people a measure of freedom unknown in the rural South. After the war, African Americans moved to cities to find families, seek work, escape the tedium and supervision of farm life, or simply to test their right to move about.

Between 1860 and 1870, the African American population in every major southern city rose significantly. In Atlanta, for example, black people accounted for one in five residents in 1860 and nearly one in two by 1870.

Once in the city, freedmen had to find a home and a job. They usually settled on the outskirts of town, where building codes did not apply. Rather than developing one large ghetto, as happened in many northern cities, black southerners lived in small concentrations in and around cities. Sometimes armed with a letter of reference from their former masters, black people went door to door to seek employment. Many found work serving white families, as guards, laundresses, or maids, for very low wages. Both skilled and unskilled laborers found work rebuilding war-torn cities like Atlanta.

Most rural black southerners, however, worked as unskilled laborers. In both Atlanta and Nashville, black people comprised more than 75 percent of the unskilled workforce in 1870. Their wages were at or below subsistence level. A black laborer in Richmond admitted to a journalist in 1870 that he had difficulty making ends meet on $1.50 a day. "It's right hard," he reported. "I have to pay $15 a month rent, and only two little rooms." His family survived because his wife took in laundry, while her mother watched the children. Considering the laborer's struggle, the journalist wondered, "Were not your people better off in slavery?" The man replied, "Oh, no sir! We're a heap better off now.... We're men now, but when our masters had us we was only change in their pockets."

FAITH AND FREEDOM

Religious faith framed and inspired the efforts of African Americans to test their freedom on the farm and in the city. White southerners used religion to transform the Lost Cause from a shattering defeat to a premonition of a greater destiny. Black southerners, in contrast, saw emancipation in biblical terms as the beginning of an exodus from bondage to the Promised Land.

Some black churches in the postwar South had originated during the slavery era, but most split from white-dominated congregations after the war. White churchgoers deplored the expressive style of black worship, and black churchgoers were uncomfortable in congregations that treated them as inferiors. A separate church also reduced white surveillance.

The church became a primary focus of African American life. It gave black people the opportunity to hone skills in self-government and administration that white-dominated society denied them. Within the supportive confines of the congregation, they could assume leadership positions, render important decisions, deal with financial matters, and engage in politics. The church also operated as an educational institution. Local governments, especially in rural areas, rarely constructed public schools for black people; churches often served that function.

The desire to read the Bible inspired thousands of former slaves to attend the church school. The church also spawned other organizations that served the black community, such as burial societies, Masonic lodges, temperance groups, trade unions, and drama clubs. African Americans took great pride in their churches, which became visible measures of their progress. The church and the congregation were a cohesive force in black communities.

The efforts of former slaves in the classroom, on the farm, in cities, and in the churches reflect the enthusiasm and expectations with which black southerners greeted freedom, raising the hopes of those who came to help them, such as Frances Harper. But the majority of white southerners were unwilling to see those expectations fulfilled. For this reason, African Americans could not secure the fruits of their emancipation without the support and protection of the federal government. The issue of freedom was therefore inextricably linked to the other great issue of the era, the rejoining of the Confederacy to the Union, as expressed in federal Reconstruction policy.

FEDERAL RECONSTRUCTION, 1865–1870

When the Civil War ended in 1865, no acceptable blueprint existed for reconstituting the Union. President Lincoln believed that a majority of white southerners were Unionists at heart and that they could and should undertake the task of reconstruction. He favored a conciliatory policy toward the South in order, as he put it in one of his last letters, "to restore the Union, so as to make it... a Union of hearts and hands as well as of States." He counted on the loyalists to be fair with respect to the rights of the former slaves.

As early as 1863, Lincoln had proposed to readmit a seceding state if 10 percent of its prewar voters took an oath of loyalty to the Union, and it prohibited slavery in a new state constitution. But this Ten Percent Plan did not require states to grant equal civil and political rights to former slaves, and many Republicans in Congress thought it was not stringent enough. In 1864, a group of them responded with the Wade-Davis Bill, which required a majority of a state's prewar voters to pledge their loyalty to the Union and demanded guarantees of black equality before the law. The bill was passed at the end of a congressional session, but Lincoln kept it from becoming law by refusing to sign it (an action known as a "pocket veto"). Lincoln, of course, died before he could implement a Reconstruction plan.

The controversy over the plans introduced during the war reflected two obstacles to Reconstruction that would continue to plague the ruling Republicans after the war. First, neither the Constitution nor legal precedent offered any guidance on whether the president or Congress should take the lead on Reconstruction policy. Second, there was no agreement on what that policy should be. Proposals requiring various preconditions for readmitting a state, loyalty oaths, new constitutions with certain specific provisions, guarantees of freedmen's rights, all provoked vigorous debate.

President Andrew Johnson, some conservative Republicans, and most Democrats believed that because the Constitution made no mention of secession, the southern states had been in rebellion but had never left the Union, and therefore that there was no need for a formal process to readmit them. Moderate and radical Republicans disagreed, arguing that the defeated states had forfeited their rights. Moderates and radicals parted company, however, on the conditions necessary for readmission to the Union. The radicals wanted to treat the former Confederate states as territories, or "conquered provinces," subject to congressional legislation. Moderates wanted to grant the seceding states more autonomy and limit federal intervention in their affairs while they satisfied the conditions of readmission. Neither group held a majority in Congress, and legislators sometimes changed their positions (see the Overview table, Contrasting Views of Reconstruction).

PRESIDENTIAL RECONSTRUCTION, 1865–1867

When the Civil War ended in April 1865, Congress was not in session and would not reconvene until December. Thus, the responsibility for developing a Reconstruction policy initially fell on Andrew Johnson, who succeeded to the presidency upon Lincoln's assassination. Most northerners, including many Republicans, approved Johnson's Reconstruction plan when he unveiled it in May 1865. Johnson extended pardons and restored property rights, except in slaves, to southerners who swore an oath of allegiance to the Union and the Constitution. Southerners who had held prominent posts in the Confederacy, however, and those with more than $20,000 in taxable property, had to petition the president directly for a pardon. The plan said nothing about the voting rights or civil rights of former slaves.

Northern Democrats applauded the plan's silence on these issues and its promise of a quick restoration of the southern states to the Union. They expected the southern states to favor their party and expand its political power. Republicans approved the plan because it restored property rights to white southerners, although some wanted it to provide for black suffrage. Republicans also hoped that Johnson's conciliatory terms might attract some white southerners to the Republican Party.

On the two great issues of freedom and reunion, white southerners quickly demonstrated their eagerness to reverse the results of the Civil War. Although most states accepted President Johnson's modest requirements, several objected to one or more of them. Mississippi and Texas refused to ratify the Thirteenth Amendment, which abolished slavery. Alabama accepted only parts of the amendment. South Carolina declined to nullify its secession ordinance. No southern state authorized black voting. When Johnson ordered special congressional elections in the South in the fall of 1865, the all-white electorate returned many prominent Confederate leaders to office.

In late 1865, the newly elected southern state legislatures revised their antebellum slave codes. The updated **black codes** allowed local officials to arrest black people who could not document employment and residence or who were "disorderly" and sentence

"Selling a Freeman to Pay His Fine at Monticello, Florida." *This 1867 engraving shows how the black codes of the early Reconstruction era reduced former slaves to virtually their pre–Civil War status. Scenes like this convinced northerners that the white South was unrepentant and prompted congressional Republicans to devise their own Reconstruction plans.*

them to forced labor on farms or road crews. The codes also restricted black people to certain occupations, barred them from jury duty, and forbade them to possess firearms. Apprenticeship laws permitted judges to take black children from parents who could not, in the judges' view, adequately support them. Given the widespread poverty in the South in 1865, the law could apply to almost any freed black family. Northerners looking for contrition in the South found no sign of it. Worse, President Johnson did not seem perturbed about this turn of events.

The Republican-dominated Congress reconvened in December 1865 in a belligerent mood. When the radicals, who comprised nearly half of the Republican Party's strength in Congress, could not unite behind a program, their moderate colleagues took the first step toward a congressional Reconstruction plan. The moderates shared the radicals' desire to protect the former slaves' civil rights. But they would not support land-redistribution schemes or punitive measures against prominent Confederates, and

AMERICAN VIEWS

MISSISSIPPI'S 1865 BLACK CODES

*W*hite southerners, especially landowners and business owners, feared that emancipation would produce a labor crisis; freedmen, they expected, would either refuse to work or strike hard bargains with their former masters. White southerners also recoiled from the prospect of having to treat their former slaves as full social equals. Thus, beginning in late 1865, several southern states, including Mississippi, enacted laws designed to control black labor, mobility, and social status. Northerners responded to the codes as a provocation, a bold move to deny the result of the war and its consequences.

■ How did the black codes fit into President Andrew Johnson's Reconstruction program?

■ Some northerners charged that the black codes were a backdoor attempt at reestablishing slavery. Do you agree?

■ If southern states enacted black codes to stabilize labor relations, how did the provisions below effect that objective?

FROM AN ACT TO CONFER CIVIL RIGHTS ON FREEDMEN, AND FOR OTHER PURPOSES

Section 1. All freedmen, free negroes and mulattoes may sue and be sued, implead and be impleaded, in all the courts of law and equity of this State, and may acquire personal property, and choose in action, by descent or purchase, and may dispose of the same in the same manner and to the same extent that white persons may: Provided, That the provisions of this section shall not be so construed as to allow any freedman, free negro or mulatto to rent or lease any lands or tenements except in incorporated cities or towns, in which places the corporate authorities shall control the same.

Section 7. Every civil officer shall, and every person may, arrest and carry back to his or her legal employer any freedman, free negro, or mulatto who shall have quit the service of his or her employer before the expiration of his or her term of service without good cause; and said officer and person shall be entitled to receive for arresting and carrying back every deserting employee aforesaid the sum of five dollars, and ten cents per mile from the place of arrest to the place of delivery; and the same shall be paid by the employer, and held as a set off for so much against the wages of said deserting employee: Provided, that said arrested party, after being so returned, may appeal to the justice of the peace or member of the board of police of the county, who, on notice to the alleged employer, shall try summarily whether said appellant is legally employed by the alleged employer, and has good cause to quit said employer. Either party shall have the right of appeal to the county court, pending which the alleged deserter shall be remanded to the alleged employer or otherwise disposed of, as shall be right and just; and the decision of the county court shall be final.

FROM AN ACT TO AMEND THE VAGRANT LAWS OF THE STATE

Section 2. All freedmen, free negroes and mulattoes in this State, over the age of eighteen years, found on the second Monday in January, 1866, or thereafter, with no lawful employment or business, or found unlawfully assembling themselves together, either in the day or night time, and all white persons assembling themselves with freedmen, Free negroes or mulattoes, or usually associating with freedmen, free negroes or mulattoes, on terms of equality, or living in adultery or fornication with a freed woman, freed negro or mulatto, shall be deemed vagrants, and on conviction thereof shall be fined in a sum not exceeding, in the case of a freedman, free negro or mulatto, fifty dollars, and a white man two hundred dollars, and imprisonment at the discretion of the court, the free negro not exceeding ten days, and the white man not exceeding six months.

SOURCE: "Laws in Relation to Freedmen," 39 Congress, 2 Session, Senate Executive Document 6, Freedmen's Affairs, 182–86.

disagreed on extending voting rights to the freedmen. The moderates' first measure, passed in early 1866, extended the life of the Freedmen's Bureau and authorized it to punish state officials who failed to extend equal civil rights to black citizens. But President Johnson vetoed the legislation.

Undeterred, Congress passed the Civil Rights Act of 1866 in direct response to the black codes. The act specified the civil rights to which all U.S. citizens were entitled. In creating a category of national citizenship with rights that superseded state laws, the act changed federal-state relations (and in the process overturned the *Dred Scott* decision). President Johnson vetoed the act, but it became law when Congress mustered a two-thirds majority to override his veto, the first time in American history that Congress passed major legislation over a president's veto.

To keep freedmen's rights safe from presidential vetoes, state legislatures, and federal courts, the Republican-dominated Congress moved to incorporate some of the provisions of the 1866 Civil Rights Act into the Constitution. The **Fourteenth Amendment,** which Congress passed in June 1866, addressed the issues of civil and voting rights. It guaranteed every citizen equality before the law. The two key sections of the amendment prohibited states from violating the civil rights of their citizens, thus outlawing the black codes, and gave states the choice of enfranchising black people or losing representation in Congress. Some radical Republicans expressed disappointment that the amendment, in a reflection of northern ambivalence, failed to give the vote to black people outright.

The amendment also disappointed advocates of woman suffrage, for the first time using the word *male* in the Constitution to define who could vote. Susan B. Anthony, who had campaigned for the abolition of slavery before the war and helped mount a petition drive that collected 400,000 signatures for the Thirteenth Amendment, founded the American Equal Rights Association in 1866 with her colleagues to push for woman suffrage at the state level.

The Fourteenth Amendment had little immediate impact on the South. Although enforcement of black codes diminished, white violence against black people increased. In the 1870s, several decisions by the U.S. Supreme Court weakened the amendment's provisions. Eventually, however, it would play a major role in securing the civil rights of African Americans.

President Johnson encouraged southern white intransigence by openly denouncing the Fourteenth Amendment. In August 1866, at the start of the congressional election campaign, he undertook an unprecedented tour of key northern states to sell his message of sectional reconciliation to the public. Although listeners appreciated Johnson's desire for peace, they questioned his claims of southern white loyalty to the Union. The president's diatribes against the Republican Congress won him followers in those northern states with a reservoir of opposition to black suffrage. But the tone and manner of his campaign offended many as undignified. In the November elections, the Democrats suffered embarrassing defeats in the North as Republicans managed better than two-thirds majorities in both the House and Senate, sufficient to override presidential vetoes. Radical Republicans, joined by moderate colleagues buoyed by the election results and revolted by the president's and the South's intransigence, seized the initiative when Congress reconvened.

CONGRESSIONAL RECONSTRUCTION, 1867–1870

The radicals' first salvo in their attempt to take control of Reconstruction occurred with the passing over President Johnson's veto of the Military Reconstruction Acts.

The measures, passed in March 1867, inaugurated a period known as **Congressional Reconstruction** or Radical Reconstruction. With the exception of Tennessee, the only southern state that had ratified the Fourteenth Amendment and been readmitted to the Union, Congress divided the former Confederate states into five military districts, each headed by a general (see Map 16–1). The commanders' first order of business was to conduct voter-registration campaigns to enroll black people and bar white people who had held office before the Civil War and supported the Confederacy. The eligible voters would then elect delegates to a state convention to write a new constitution that guaranteed universal manhood suffrage. Once a majority of eligible voters ratified the new constitution and the Fourteenth Amendment, their state would be eligible for readmission to the Union.

The Reconstruction Acts fulfilled the radicals' three major objectives. First, they secured the freedmen's right to vote. Second, they made it likely that southern states would be run by Republican regimes that would enforce the new constitutions, protect former slaves' rights, and maintain the Republican majority in Congress. Finally, they set standards for readmission that required the South to accept the preeminence of the

MAP 16–1 • Congressional Reconstruction, 1865–1877 When Congress wrested control of Reconstruction policy from President Andrew Johnson, it divided the South into the five military districts depicted here. The commanding generals for each district held the authority both to hold elections and to decide who could vote.

▶ *What does the division of the South into military districts that included more than one state tell us about how northern Republicans saw the former Confederacy?*

federal government and the end of slavery. These measures seemed appropriate in view of the war's outcome and the freedmen's status, but white southerners, especially those barred from participation, perceived the state and local governments constructed upon the new basis as illegitimate. Many southern whites would never acknowledge the right of these governments and their officials to rule over them.

To limit presidential interference with their policies, Republicans passed the **Tenure of Office Act,** prohibiting the president from removing certain officeholders without the Senate's consent. Johnson, angered at what he believed was an unconstitutional attack on presidential authority, deliberately violated the act by firing Secretary of War Edwin M. Stanton, a leading radical, in February 1868. The House responded by approving articles of impeachment against a president for the first time in American history. That set the stage for the next step prescribed by the Constitution: a Senate trial to determine whether the president should be removed from office.

Johnson had indeed violated the Tenure of Office Act, a measure of dubious constitutionality even to some Republicans, but enough Republicans felt that his actions fell short of the "high crimes and misdemeanors" standard set by the Constitution for dismissal from office. Seven Republicans deserted their party, and Johnson was acquitted. The seven Republicans who voted against their party did so not out of respect for Johnson but because they feared that a conviction would damage the office of the presidency and violate the constitutional separation of powers. The outcome weakened the radicals and eased the way for Grant, a moderate Republican, to gain the party's nomination for president in 1868.

The Republicans viewed the 1868 presidential election as a referendum on Congressional Reconstruction. They supported black suffrage in the South but equivocated on allowing African Americans to vote in the North. Black northerners could vote in only eight of the twenty-two northern states, and between 1865 and 1869, white northerners rejected equal suffrage referendums in eight of eleven states. Republicans "waved the bloody shirt," reminding voters of Democratic disloyalty, the sacrifices of war, and the peace only Republicans could redeem. Democrats denounced Congressional Reconstruction as federal tyranny and, in openly racist appeals, warned white voters that a Republican victory would mean black rule. Grant won the election, but his margin of victory was uncomfortably narrow. Reflecting growing ambivalence in the North over issues of race and federal authority, New York's Horatio Seymour, the Democratic presidential nominee, probably carried a majority of the nation's white vote. Black voters' overwhelming support for Grant probably provided his margin of victory.

The Republicans retained a strong majority in both houses of Congress and managed to pass another major piece of Reconstruction legislation, the **Fifteenth Amendment,** in February 1869. In response to growing concerns about voter fraud and violence against freedmen, the amendment guaranteed the right of American men to vote, regardless of race. Although the amendment provided a loophole allowing states to restrict the right to vote based on literacy or property qualifications, it was nonetheless a milestone. It made the right to vote perhaps the most distinguishing characteristic of U.S. citizenship.

The Fifteenth Amendment allowed states to keep the franchise a male prerogative, angering many in the woman-suffrage movement more than had the Fourteenth Amendment. The resulting controversy severed the ties between the movement and Republican politics. Susan B. Anthony broke with her abolitionist colleagues and opposed the amendment. In an appeal brimming with ethnic and racial animosity, Elizabeth Cady Stanton warned that "if you do not wish the lower orders of Chinese, African, Germans and Irish, with their low ideas of womanhood to make laws for you and your daughters… awake to the danger… and demand that woman, too, shall be represented in the government!" Such language created a major rift in the nascent women's movement.

SOUTHERN REPUBLICAN GOVERNMENTS, 1867–1870

Away from Washington, the first order of business for the former Confederacy was to draft state constitutions. The documents embodied progressive principles new to the South. They mandated the election of numerous local and state offices. Self-perpetuating local elites could no longer appoint themselves or cronies to powerful positions. The constitutions committed southern states, many for the first time, to public education. Lawmakers enacted a variety of reforms, including social welfare, penal reform, legislative reapportionment, and universal manhood suffrage.

The Republican regimes that gained control in southern states promoted vigorous state government and the protection of civil and voting rights. Three Republican constituencies supported these governments: native whites, native blacks, and northern transplants. The small native white group was mostly made up of yeomen farmers. Residing mainly in the upland regions of the South and long ignored by lowland planters and merchants in state government, they were left devastated by the war. They struggled to keep their land and hoped for an easing of credit and for debt-stay laws to help them escape foreclosure. They wanted public schools for their children and good roads to get their crops to market. Some urban merchants and large planters also called themselves Republicans. They were attracted to the party's emphasis on economic development, especially railroad construction, and would become prominent in Republican leadership after 1867, forming a majority of the party's elected officials. Collectively, opponents called these native white southerners **scalawags.**

Northern transplants, or **carpetbaggers,** as many southern whites called them, constituted a second and smaller group of southern Republicans. Thousands of northerners came south during and after the war. Many were Union soldiers who simply enjoyed the climate and perhaps married a local woman. Most were drawn by economic opportunity. Land was cheap and the price of cotton high. Although most carpetbaggers had supported the Republican Party before they moved south, few became politically active until the cotton economy nosedived in 1866. Financial concerns were not all that motivated carpetbaggers to enter politics; some hoped to aid the freedmen.

Carpetbaggers never comprised more than 2 percent of any state's population. Most white southerners viewed them as an alien presence, instruments of a hated occupying force. Because many of them tended to support extending political and civil rights to black southerners, carpetbaggers were also often at odds with their fellow white Republicans, the scalawags.

African Americans constituted the Republican Party's largest southern constituency. In three states, South Carolina, Mississippi, and Louisiana, they also constituted the majority of eligible voters. They viewed the franchise as the key to civic equality and economic opportunity and demanded an active role in party and government affairs.

OVERVIEW CONTRASTING VIEWS OF RECONSTRUCTION: PRESIDENT AND CONGRESS

Politician or Group	Policy on Former Slaves	Policy on Readmission of Former Confederate States
President Johnson	Opposed to black suffrage	Maintained that rebellious states were already readmitted
	Silent on protection of black civil rights	Granted pardons and restoration of property to all who swore allegiance to the United States
	Opposed to land redistribution	
Radical Republicans	Favored black suffrage	Favored treating rebellious states as territories and establishing military districts*
	Favored protection of black civil rights	Favored limiting franchise to black people and loyal white people
	Favored land redistribution	
Moderate Republicans	Favored black suffrage*	Favored some restrictions on white suffrage**
	Favored protection of civil rights	Favored requiring states to meet various requirements before being readmitted*
	Opposed land redistribution	Split on military rule

*After 1866.
**True of most but not all members of the group.

Black people began to take part in southern politics even before the end of the Civil War, especially in cities occupied by Union forces. In February 1865, black people in Norfolk, Virginia, gathered to demand a say in the new government that Union supporters were forming in that portion of the state. In April, they created the Colored Monitor Union club, modeled after regular Republican Party organizations in northern cities, called **Union Leagues.** They demanded "the right of universal suffrage" for "all loyal men, without distinction of color." Black people in other southern cities held similar meetings, seeking inclusion in the democratic process to protect their freedom. Despite white threats, black southerners thronged to Union League meetings in 1867, even forging interracial alliances in states such as North Carolina and Alabama. Focusing on political education and recruitment, the leagues successfully mobilized black voters. In 1867, more than 90 percent of eligible black voters across the South turned out for elections. Black women, even though they could not vote, also played a role. During the 1868 presidential campaign, for example, black maids and cooks in the South wore buttons touting the candidacy of the Republican presidential nominee, Ulysses S. Grant.

Black southerners were not content just to vote; they also demanded political office. White Republican leaders in the South often took the black vote for granted. But on several occasions after 1867, black people threatened to run independent candidates, support rival Democrats, or simply stay home unless they were represented among Republican nominees. These demands brought them some success. The number of southern black congressmen in the U.S. House of Representatives increased from two in 1869 to seven in 1873, and more than 600 African Americans, most of them former slaves from plantation counties, were elected to southern state legislatures between 1867 and 1877.

White fears that black officeholders would enact vengeful legislation proved unfounded. African Americans generally did not promote race-specific legislation. Rather, they supported measures such as debt relief and state funding for education that benefited all poor and working-class people. Like all politicians, however, black officials in southern cities sought to enact measures beneficial to their constituents, such as roads and sidewalks.

During the first few years of Congressional Reconstruction, Republican governments walked a tightrope, attempting to lure moderate Democrats and unaffiliated white voters into the party without slighting the black vote. They used the lure of patronage power and the attractive salaries that accompanied public office. In 1868, for example, Louisiana's Republican governor, Henry C. Warmoth, appointed white conservatives to state and local offices, which he divided equally between Confederate veterans and black people, and repealed a constitutional provision disfranchising former Confederate officials.

Republicans also gained support by expanding the role of state government to a degree unprecedented in the South. Southern Republican administrations appealed to hard-pressed upland white constituents by prohibiting foreclosure and passing stay laws that allowed farm owners additional time to repay debts. They undertook building programs that benefited black and white citizens, erecting hospitals, schools, and orphanages. Stepping further into social policy than most northern states at the time, Republican governments in the South expanded women's property rights, enacted legislation against child abuse, and required child support from fathers of mulatto children. In South Carolina, the Republican government provided medical care for the poor; in Alabama, it provided free legal aid for needy defendants.

Despite these impressive policies, southern Republicans were unable to hold their diverse constituency together. The excesses of some state governments, high taxes, contests over patronage, and conflicts over the relative roles of white and black party members opened rifts in Republican ranks. Patronage triggered intraparty warfare. Every office secured by a Democrat created a disappointed Republican. Class tensions erupted in the party as economic development policies sometimes superseded relief and social service legislation supported by small farmers. The failure of Alabama Republicans to deliver on promises of debt relief and land redistribution eroded the party's support among upcountry white voters. There were differences among black voters too. In the Lower South, divisions that had developed in the prewar era between urban, lighter-skinned free black people and darker, rural slaves persisted into the Reconstruction era. In many southern states, black clergy, because of their independence from white support and their important spiritual and educational role, became leaders. But most preached salvation in the next world rather than equality in this one, conceding more to white people than their rank-and-file constituents.

COUNTER-RECONSTRUCTION, 1870–1874

Republicans might have survived battles over patronage, policy, expenditures, and taxes. But they could not overcome racism and the violence it generated. Racism killed Republican rule in the South because it deepened divisions within the party, encouraged white violence, and eroded support in the North. Southern Democrats discovered that they could use race baiting and racial violence to create solidarity among white people that overrode their economic and class differences. Unity translated into election victories.

Northerners responded to the persistent violence in the South, not with outrage, but with a growing sense of tedium. They came to accept the arguments of white southerners that it was folly to allow black people to vote and hold office, especially since most northern whites would not extend the franchise to African Americans in their own states.

By 1874, Americans were concerned with an array of domestic problems that overshadowed Reconstruction. A serious economic depression left them more preoccupied with survival than racial justice. Corruption convinced many that politics was part of the nation's problems, not a solution to them. With the rest of the nation thus distracted and weary, white southerners reclaimed control of the South.

THE USES OF VIOLENCE

Racial violence preceded Republican rule. As African Americans moved about, attempted to vote, haggled over labor contracts, and carried arms as part of the occupying Union forces, they tested the patience of white southerners, to whom any black assertion of equality seemed threatening. African Americans were the face of whites' defeat, of their world turned upside down. If the war was about slavery, then here was the visible proof of the Confederacy's defeat. Many white southerners viewed the term "free black" less as a status than as an oxymoron. The restoration of white supremacy meant the restoration of order and civilization, an objective southern whites would pursue with vengeance.

White paramilitary groups were responsible for much of the violence directed against African Americans. Probably the best-known of these groups was the **Ku Klux Klan.** Founded in Tennessee by six Confederate veterans in 1866, the Klan was initially a social club. Within a year, the Klan had spread throughout the South. In 1867, when black people entered politics in large numbers, the Klan unleashed a wave of terror against them. The Klan directed much of its violence toward subverting the electoral process. One historian has estimated that roughly 10 percent of all black delegates to the 1867 state constitutional conventions in the South became victims of political violence during the next decade.

By 1868, white paramilitary organizations permeated the South. Violence was particularly severe in election years in Louisiana, which had a large and active black electorate. The most serious example of political violence in Louisiana, occurred in Colfax in 1873, when a white Democratic mob attempted to wrest control of local

The Klan directed violence at African Americans primarily for engaging in political activity.
Here, a black man, John Campbell, vainly begs for mercy in Moore County, North Carolina,
in August 1871.

government from Republicans. For three weeks, black defenders held the town against the white onslaught. When the white mob finally broke through, they massacred the remaining black defenders, including those who had surrendered and laid down their weapons. It was the bloodiest peacetime massacre in nineteenth-century America.

Racial violence and the combative reaction it provoked both among black people and Republican administrations energized white voters. Democrats regained power in North Carolina, for example, after the state's Republican governor enraged white voters by calling out the militia to counter white violence during the election of 1870. That same year, the Republican regime in Georgia fell as well.

The federal government responded with a variety of legislation. One example was the Fifteenth Amendment. Another was the Enforcement Act of 1870, which authorized the federal government to appoint supervisors in states that failed to protect voting rights. When violence and intimidation persisted, Congress followed with a second, more sweeping measure, the Ku Klux Klan Act of 1871. This law permitted federal authorities, with military assistance, if necessary, to arrest and prosecute members of groups that denied a citizen's civil rights if state authorities failed to do so. The Klan Act was not successful in curbing racial violence, as the Colfax Massacre in 1873 made vividly clear. But with it, Congress, by claiming the right to override state authority to bring individuals to justice, established a new precedent in federal-state relations.

NORTHERN INDIFFERENCE

The success of political violence after 1871 reflected both a declining commitment on the part of northern Republicans to support southern Republican administrations and a growing indifference of northerners to the major issues of Reconstruction. That northern base grew increasingly skeptical about Reconstruction policy in general and assistance to the freedmen in particular. Northern Republicans looked around their cities and many saw the local political scene infested with unqualified immigrant voters and corruption. New York City's Democratic boss William M. Tweed and his associates bilked the city of an astounding $100 million. When white southerners charged that unqualified blacks and grasping carpetbaggers corrupted the political process in the South, northerners recognized the argument.

Changing perceptions in the North also indicated a convergence of racial views with white southerners. As a radical Republican congressman from Indiana, George W. Julian, admitted in 1865, white northerners *"hate the negro."* They expressed this hatred in their rejection of black suffrage, racial segregation of their African American population, and periodic violence against black residents, such as during the New York Draft Riots of 1863. Northerners' views were bolstered by prevailing scientific theories of race that "proved" blacks' limited capacities and, therefore, unfitness for either the ballot or skilled occupations.

Northerners also grew increasingly wary of federal power. The emerging scandals of the Grant administration, fueled, it seemed, by government subsidies to railroads and other private businesses, demanded a scaling back of federal power and discretion. When white southerners complained about federal meddling, again, they found resonance in the North.

The excesses and alleged abuses of federal power inspired a reform movement among a group of northern Republicans and some Democrats. In addition, business leaders decried the ability of wealthy lobbyists to influence economic decisions. An influential group of intellectuals and opinion makers lamented the inability of politicians to understand "natural" laws, particularly those related to race. And some Republicans joined the reform movement out of fear that Democrats would capitalize on the turmoil in the South and the political scandals in the North to reap huge electoral victories in 1872.

LIBERAL REPUBLICANS AND THE ELECTION OF 1872

Liberal Republicans, as the reformers called themselves, put forward an array of suggestions to improve government and save the Republican Party. They advocated civil service reform to reduce reliance on patronage and the abuses that accompanied office seeking. To limit government and reduce artificial economic stimuli, the reformers called for tariff reduction and an end to federal land grants to railroads. For the South, they recommended a general amnesty for white people and a return to "local self-government" by men of "property and enterprise."

When the Liberals failed to convince other Republicans to adopt their program, they broke with the party. Taking advantage of this split, the Democrats forged an alliance with the Liberals. Together, they nominated journalist Horace Greeley to challenge Ulysses S. Grant for the presidency in the election of 1872. Grant won resoundingly, helped by high turnout among black voters in the South, his continued popularity as a war hero, and Greeley's inept campaign.

ECONOMIC TRANSFORMATION

After 1873, the Republican Party in the South became a liability for the national party, especially as Americans fastened on to economic issues. The major story of the decade would not be equal rights for African Americans, but the changing nature of the American economy. An overextended banking and credit system generated the Panic of 1873 and caused extensive suffering, particularly among working-class Americans. But the depression masked a remarkable economic transformation as the nation moved toward a national industrial economy.

The depression and the economic transformation occupied center stage in the American mentality of the mid-1870s, at least in the North. Most Americans had mentally forsaken Reconstruction long before the Compromise of 1877 made its abandonment a political fact. The sporadic violence against black and white Republicans in the South, and the cries of help from freedmen as their rights and persons were abused by white Democrats, became distant echoes from another era, the era of the Civil War, now commemorated and memorialized, but no longer an active part of the nation's present and future. Of course, for white southerners, the past was not yet past. There was still work to do.

REDEMPTION, 1874–1877

For southern Democrats, the Republican victory in 1872 underscored the importance of turning out larger numbers of white voters and restricting the black vote. They accomplished these goals over the next four years with a surge in political violence, secure in the knowledge that federal authorities would rarely intervene against them. Preoccupied with corruption and economic crisis and increasingly indifferent, if not hostile, to African American aspirations, most Americans looked the other way. The elections of 1876 confirmed the triumph of white southerners.

In a religious metaphor that matched their view of the Civil War as a lost crusade, southern Democrats called their victory "Redemption" and depicted themselves as **Redeemers,** holy warriors who had saved the South from the hell of black Republican rule. Generations of American boys and girls would learn this interpretation of the Reconstruction era, and it would affect race relations for nearly a century.

THE DEMOCRATS' VIOLENT RESURGENCE

The violence between 1874 and 1876 differed in several respects from earlier attempts to restore white government by force. Attackers operated more openly and more closely identified themselves with the Democratic Party. Mounted, gray-clad ex-Confederate soldiers flanked Democratic candidates at campaign rallies and "visited" black neighborhoods afterward to discourage black men from voting. With black people intimidated and white people already prepared to vote, election days were typically quiet.

Democrats swept to victory across the South in the 1874 elections. "A perfect reign of terror" redeemed Alabama for the Democrats. The successful appeal to white supremacy inspired a massive white turnout to unseat Republicans in Virginia, Florida (legislature only), and Arkansas. Texas had fallen to the Democrats in 1873. Only South Carolina, Mississippi, and Louisiana, states with large black populations, survived the debacle. But the relentless tide of terror would soon overwhelm them as well.

Democratic leaders in those states announced a "white line" policy, inviting all white men, regardless of party affiliation, to "unite" and redeem the states. They all had the same objective: to eliminate African Americans as a political factor by any means. Black Republicans not only feared for their political future, but also for their lives.

A bold assault occurred in New Orleans in September 1874 when 8,500 White League troops, many of them leading citizens and Confederate veterans, attempted a coup to oust Republican Governor William P. Kellogg and members of his administration. The New Orleans Leaguers overwhelmed the city's racially mixed Metropolitan Police Force under the command of former Confederate general James B. Longstreet. The timely arrival of federal troops, ordered to the scene by President Grant, prevented the takeover. The League was more successful in the Louisiana countryside in the weeks preceding the Democratic victory in November 1874. League troops overthrew or murdered Republican officials in eight parishes.

The Democratic victory in Louisiana encouraged white paramilitarists in Mississippi. Blacks dominated the Warren County government headquartered in Vicksburg. Liners demanded the resignations of all black officials including the sheriff, Peter Crosby, a black Union veteran. Republican Governor Adelbert Ames, a native of Maine, ordered the Liners to disperse and granted Crosby's request to raise a protective militia to respond to future threats.

Peter Crosby's efforts to gather a militia force were too successful. An army of several hundred armed African Americans marched in three columns from the surrounding countryside to Vicksburg. Whites responded to the challenge, firing on the militia and tracking down and terrorizing blacks in the city and county over the next ten days. Leaguers killed at least twenty-nine blacks and wounded countless more. Democrats gained control of the county government.

The Vicksburg incident was a rehearsal for Democratic victories in statewide elections in 1875. Liners focused on the state's majority black counties and vowed to "overawe the negroes and exhibit to them the ocular proof of our power."

The intimidation worked and the Democrats swept to victory in Mississippi. They would not allow Governor Ames to finish his term, threatening him with impeachment. Fearing for his safety, Ames resigned and fled the state. The South's second war of independence was reaching its climax.

July Fourth, 1876. America's 100th birthday. A modest celebration unfolded in Hamburg, South Carolina, a small town in Edgefield County across the Savannah River from Augusta, Georgia. Blacks comprised more than 75 percent of the town's population. They held most of the political offices. An altercation occurred concerning the right of way between the black militia parading in the street and a passing wagon carrying several prominent white residents. When the aggrieved parties met four days later, more than 1,000 armed whites were milling in front of the wooden "armory" where 100 black militiamen had taken refuge. A shot rang out and shattered a second-floor window and soon a pitched battle was raging. The white attackers fired a cannon that turned most of the building into splinters. As blacks fled, whites tracked them down. The white men also burned homes and shops and robbed residents of the town.

Hamburg was part of a larger pattern of violence and intimidation in the state. In May 1876, South Carolina Democrats drafted *The Plan of the Campaign of 1876*, a manual on how to redeem the state. Some of the recommended strategies included: "Every Democrat must feel honor bound to control the vote of at least one negro, by intimidation, purchase, keeping him away or as each individual may determine how he may best accomplish it. Treat them as to show them, you are the superior race and that their natural position is that of subordination to the white man."

The November election went off in relative calm. In Edgefield County, out of 7,000 potential voters, 9,200 ballots were cast. Similar frauds occurred throughout the state. Still, the result hung in the balance. Both Democrats and Republicans claimed victory and set up rival governments. The following April after a deal brokered in Washington between the parties, federal troops were withdrawn from South Carolina and a Democratic government installed in Columbia. The victorious Democrats expelled twenty-four Republicans from the state legislature and elected Matthew C. Butler to the U.S. Senate. Butler had led the white attackers at Hamburg.

THE WEAK FEDERAL RESPONSE

When Governor Daniel H. Chamberlain could no longer contain the violence in South Carolina in 1876, he asked the president for help. Grant acknowledged the gravity of Chamberlain's situation but would offer him only the lame hope that South Carolinians would exercise "better judgment and cooperation" and assist the governor in bringing offenders to justice "without aid from the federal Government."

Congress responded to blacks' deteriorating status in the South with the Civil Rights Act of 1875. The act prohibited discrimination against black people in public accommodations, such as theaters, parks, and trains, and guaranteed freedmen's rights to serve on juries. It had no provision for voting rights, which Congress presumed the Fifteenth Amendment protected. Most judges, however, either interpreted the law narrowly or declared it unconstitutional. In 1883, the U.S. Supreme Court agreed and overturned the act, declaring that only the states, not Congress, could redress "a private wrong, or a crime of the individual."

THE ELECTION OF 1876 AND THE COMPROMISE OF 1877

Reconstruction officially ended with the presidential election of 1876, in which the Democrat Samuel J. Tilden ran against the Republican Rutherford B. Hayes. When the ballots were counted, it appeared that Tilden, a conservative New Yorker respectable enough for northern voters and Democratic enough for white southerners, had won. But despite a majority in the popular vote, disputed returns in three southern states left him with only 184 of the 185 electoral votes needed to win. The three states—Florida, South Carolina, and Louisiana—were the last in the South still to have Republican administrations.

Both camps maneuvered intensively in the following months to claim the disputed votes. Congress appointed a 15-member commission to settle the issue. Because the Republicans controlled Congress, they held a one-vote majority on the commission.

Southern Democrats wanted Tilden to win, but they wanted control of their states more. They were willing to deal. Hayes intended to remove federal support from the remaining southern Republican governments anyway. It thus cost him nothing to promise to do so in exchange for the contested electoral votes. The so-called **Compromise of 1877** installed Hayes in the White House and gave Democrats control of every state government in the South. Southern Democrats emerged the major winners from the Compromise of 1877. President Hayes and his successors into the next century left the South alone. In practical terms, the Compromise signaled the revocation of civil rights and voting rights for black southerners. The Fourteenth and Fifteenth Amendments would be dead letters in the South until well into the twentieth century. On the two great issues confronting the nation at the end of the Civil War, reunion and freedom, the white South had won. It reentered the Union largely on its own terms with the freedom to pursue a racial agenda consistent with its political, economic, and social interests.

THE MEMORY OF RECONSTRUCTION

Southern Democrats used the memory of Reconstruction to help maintain themselves in power. Reconstruction joined the Lost Cause as part of the glorious fight to preserve the civilization of the Old South. As white southerners elevated Civil War heroes into saints and battles into holy struggles, they equated Reconstruction with Redemption. White Democrats had rescued the South from a purgatory of black rule and federal oppression. The southern view of Reconstruction permeated textbooks, films, and standard accounts of the period. By the early 1900s, professional historians at the nation's finest institutions concurred in this view, ignoring contrary evidence and rendering the story of African Americans invisible. By that time, therefore, most Americans believed that the policies of Reconstruction had been misguided and had brought great suffering to the white South. The widespread acceptance of this view allowed the South to maintain its system of racial segregation and exclusion without interference from the federal government.

Memorialists did not deny the Redeemers' use of terror and violence. To the contrary; they praised it as necessary. South Carolina senator Benjamin R. Tillman, a participant in the Hamburg massacre, stood in front of his Senate colleagues in 1900 and asserted, "We were sorry we had the necessity forced upon us, but we could not help it, and as white men we are not sorry for it, and we do not propose to apologize for anything we have done in connection with it. We took the government away from them [African Americans] in 1876. We did take it.... We of the South have never recognized the right of the negro to govern white men, and we never will." The animosity of southern whites toward Republican governments had much less to do with alleged corruption and incompetence than the mere fact of African Americans casting ballots and making laws.

The national historical consensus grew out of a growing national reconciliation concerning the war, a mutual agreement that both sides had fought courageously and that it was time to move on. Hidden in all the goodwill was the tacit agreement between southern and northern whites that the South was now free to work out its own resolution to race relations. Reconstruction rested on a national consensus of African American inferiority.

Modest Gains

If the overthrow of Reconstruction elicited a resounding indifference from most white Americans, black southerners greeted it with frustration. Their dreams of land ownership faded as a new labor system relegated them to a lowly position in southern agriculture. Redemption reversed their economic and political gains and deprived them of most of the civil rights they had enjoyed under Congressional Reconstruction. Although they continued to vote into the 1890s, they had by 1877 lost most of the voting strength and political offices they held. Rather than becoming part of southern society, they were increasingly set apart from it, valued only for their labor.

Still, the former slaves were better off in 1877 than in 1865. They were free, however limited their freedom. Some owned land; some held jobs in cities. They raised their families in relative peace and experienced the spiritual joys of a full religious life. They socialized freely with relatives and friends, and they moved about. The Reconstruction amendments to the Constitution guaranteed an array of civil and political rights, and eventually these guarantees would form the basis of the civil rights revolution after World War II. But that outcome was long, too long, in the future.

Black southerners experienced some advances in the decade after the Civil War, but these owed little to Reconstruction. Black families functioned as economic and psychological buffers against unemployment and prejudice. Black churches played crucial roles in their communities. Self-help and labor organizations offered mutual friendship and financial assistance. All of these institutions had existed in the slavery era, although on a smaller scale. And some of them, such as black labor groups, schools, and social welfare associations, endured because comparable white institutions excluded black people.

Black people also scored some modest economic successes during the Reconstruction era, mainly from their own pluck. In the Lower South, black per capita income increased 46 percent between 1857 and 1879, compared with a 35 percent decline in white per capita income. Sharecropping, oppressive as it was, represented an advance over forced and gang labor. Collectively, black people owned more than $68 million worth of property in 1870, a 240 percent increase over 1860, but the average worth of each piece of property was only $408.

The Fourteenth and Fifteenth Amendments to the Constitution are among the few bright spots in Reconstruction's otherwise dismal legacy. But the benefits of these two landmark amendments did not accrue to African Americans until well into the twentieth century. White southerners effectively nullified the Reconstruction amendments, and the U.S. Supreme Court virtually interpreted them, and other Reconstruction legislation, out of existence.

OVERVIEW CONSTITUTIONAL AMENDMENTS AND FEDERAL LEGISLATION OF THE RECONSTRUCTION ERA

Amendment or Legislation	Purpose	Significance
Thirteenth Amendment (passed and ratified in 1865)	Prevented southern states from reestablishing slavery after the war	Final step toward full emancipation of slaves
Freedmen's Bureau Act (1865)	Oversight of resettlement, labor for former slaves	Involved the federal government directly in relief, education, and assisting the transition from slavery to freedom; worked fitfully to achieve this objective during its seven-year career
Southern Homestead Act (1866)	Provided black people preferential access to public lands in five southern states	Lack of capital and poor quality of federal land thwarted the purpose of the act
Civil Rights Act of 1866	Defined rights of national citizenship	Marked an important change in federal-state relations, tilting balance of power to national government
Fourteenth Amendment (passed 1866; ratified 1868)	Prohibited states from violating the rights of their citizens	Strengthened the Civil Rights Act of 1866 and guaranteed all citizens equality before the law
Military Reconstruction Acts (1867)	Set new rules for the readmission of former Confederate states into the Union and secured black voting rights	Initiated Congressional Reconstruction
Tenure of Office Act (1867)	Required congressional approval for the removal of any official whose appointment had required Senate confirmation	A congressional challenge to the president's right to dismiss cabinet members; led to President Andrew Johnson's impeachment trial
Fifteenth Amendment (passed 1869; ratified 1870)	Guaranteed the right of all American male citizens to vote regardless of race	The basis for black voting rights
Civil Rights Act of 1875	Prohibited racial discrimination in jury selection, public transportation, and public accommodations	Rarely enforced; Supreme Court declared it unconstitutional in 1883

In the ***Slaughterhouse* cases** (1873), the Supreme Court contradicted the intent of the Fourteenth Amendment by decreeing that most citizenship rights remained under state, not federal, control. In ***United States v. Cruikshank*** (1876), the Court overturned the convictions of some of those responsible for the Colfax Massacre, ruling that the Enforcement Act applied only to violations of black rights by states, not individuals. Within the next two decades, the Supreme Court would uphold the legality of racial segregation and black disfranchisement, in effect declaring that the Fourteenth and Fifteenth Amendments did not apply to African Americans.

CONCLUSION

White southerners robbed black southerners of their gains and sought to reduce them again to servitude and dependence, if not to slavery. But in the process, the majority of white southerners lost as well. Yeoman farmers missed an opportunity to break cleanly from the Old South and establish a more equitable society. Instead, they allowed the old elites to regain power and gradually ignore their needs. They preserved the social benefit of a white skin at the cost of almost everything else. Many lost their farms and sank into tenancy. Few had a voice in state legislatures or the U.S. Congress. A new South, rid of slavery and sectional antagonism, had indeed emerged—redeemed, regenerated, and disenthralled. But the old South lingered on.

The journey toward equality after the Civil War had aborted. Reconstruction had not failed. It was overthrown. In the weeks and months after Appomattox, white southerners launched a war against the freedmen and their allies to return white Democrats to power and African Americans to a position of permanent subordination in southern society. The indifferent and often hostile attitudes of white northerners toward blacks played a role in limiting the federal response and ensuring the success of the white South in prosecuting this war. As with the Civil War, the overthrow of Reconstruction was a national tragedy. By 1877, the "golden moment," an unprecedented opportunity for the nation to live up to its ideals by extending equal rights to all its citizens, black and white alike, had passed.

REVIEW QUESTIONS

1. Both Russia and America hoped to develop a free-labor agricultural class after their respective emancipations. Why didn't these governments follow through on their own objectives?

2. Given the different perspectives on the Civil War's outcome and what the social structure of a postwar South should be, was there any common ground between southern white and southern black on which to forge a Reconstruction policy?

3. Black people did achieve some notable gains during Reconstruction, despite its overall failure. What were those gains?

4. What prompted Frances Harper to write her pleading poem in 1871?

myhistorylab CONNECTIONS

Reinforce what you learned in this chapter by studying the many documents, images, maps, review tools, and videos available at **www.myhistorylab.com**.

READ AND REVIEW

✓●—**Study** and **Review** on **myhistorylab.com**   STUDY PLAN: CHAPTER 16

📖●—**Read** the **Document** on **myhistorylab.com**

A Sharecrop Contract (1882)

Carl Schurz, Report on the Condition of the South (1865)

Clinton B. Fisk, "Plain Counsels for Freedmen" (1865)

Albion W. Tourgee, Letter on Ku Klux Klan Activities (1870)

"Address of the Colored Citizens of Norfolk, Virginia" (1865)

Address of the Colored State Convention to the People of the State of South Carolina (1865)

Charlotte Forten, Life on the Sea Islands

Hannah Irwin Describes Ku Klux Klan Ride (Late 1860s)

Jourdon Anderson to His Former Master (1865)

President Johnson's Veto of the Civil Rights Act 1866

The Civil Rights Act of 1866

The Fourteenth Amendment (1868)

The Freedmen's Bureau Bill (1865)

The Mississippi Black Code (1865)

Thirteenth, Fourteenth, and Fifteenth Amendments

👁—**See** the **Map**

Congressional Reconstruction

RESEARCH AND EXPLORE

📖●—**Read** the **Document** on **myhistorylab.com**

Personal Journeys Online

From Then to Now Online: African American Voting Rights in the South

Exploring America: Did Reconstruction Work for the Freed People?

((●—**Listen** on **myhistorylab.com**

Free At Last

Remembering Slavery #2

Watch the **Video** on **myhistorylab.com**

The Promise and Failure of Reconstruction

Reconstruction in Texas

The Schools That the Civil War and Reconstruction Created

Trials of Racial Identity in Nineteenth-Century America

———————— (((•—**Listen** on **myhistorylab.com** ————————

Hear the audio files for Chapter 16 at
www.myhistorylab.com.

A New South: Economic Progress and Social Tradition • • 1877–1900

((●─Listen on **myhistorylab.com**

Hear the audio files for Chapter 17 at **www.myhistorylab.com.**

FOCUS QUESTIONS

HOW NEW was the New South?

WHAT WERE the origins and nature of southern Populism?

HOW DID traditional gender roles shape the opportunities available to women in the New South?

WHAT STEPS did southerners take in the late nineteenth century to limit the freedom of African Americans?

An interior view an African American business, "Dr. McDougal's Drug Store," in Georgia, circa 1899.

Collection of the New-York Historical Society negative number 51391.

One American Journey

The colored woman of to-day occupies . . . a unique position in this country. . . . She is confronted by both a woman question and a race problem. . . . While the women of the white race can with calm assurance enter upon the work they feel by nature appointed to do [including reform efforts both inside and outside the home], while their men give loyal support and appreciative countenance to [these] efforts, recognizing in most avenues of usefulness the propriety and the need of woman's distinctive co-operation, the colored woman too often finds herself hampered and shamed by a less liberal sentiment . . . on the part of those for whose opinion she cares most. . . .

You do not find the colored woman selling her birthright for a mess of pottage. . . . It is largely our women in the South to-day who keep the black men solid in the Republican Party. The black woman can never forget, however lukewarm the party may to-day appear, that it was a Republican president who struck the manacles from her own wrists and gave the possibilities of manhood to her helpless little ones; and to her mind a Democratic Negro is a traitor and a time-server.

To be a woman in a . . . [new] age carries with it a privilege and an opportunity never implied before. But to be a woman of the Negro race in America, and to be able to grasp the deep significance of the possibilities of the crisis, is to have a heritage, it seems to me, unique in the ages. In the first place, the race is young and full of the elasticity and hopefulness of youth. All its achievements are before it. . . . Everything to this race is new and strange and inspiring. There is a quickening of its pulses and a glowing of its self-consciousness. Aha, I can rival that! I can aspire to that! I can honor my name and vindicate my race! Something like this, it strikes me, is the enthusiasm which stirs the genius of young Africa in America; and the memory of past oppression and the fact of present attempted repression only serve to gather momentum for its irrepressible power. . . . What a responsibility then to have the sole management of the primal lights and shadows! Such is the colored woman's office. She must stamp weal or woe on the coming history of this people. May she see her opportunity and vindicate her high prerogative.

Anna J. Cooper,
A Voice from the South, 1892

Anna Julia Cooper, *A Voice from the South* (Xenia, OH: Aldine Printing House, 1892): pp. 134–135, 138–140, 142–145. The book may be accessed from the Internet: http://docsouth.unc.edu/church/cooper/cooper.html

A NNA J. COOPER undertook an incredible journey that took her from slavery at her birth in Raleigh, North Carolina, in 1858 to a doctoral degree at the Sorbonne in Paris, France, and to a prominent career as an educator. Throughout her life she remained a firm believer in the role women, especially black women, should play in striking down both white supremacy and male domination. In 1892, Dr. Cooper published *A Voice from the South,* excerpted here. The book appeared at a time when the first African American generation raised in freedom generated a relatively prosperous, educated middle class intent on challenging the limits of race in the New South. The assertiveness of this generation alarmed their white counterparts, who launched a campaign of violence and repression, mainly directed at black men.

By the early 1900s, Cooper was living in Washington, DC, and had immersed herself in the woman suffrage movement and the promotion of female education. She would live to see the dawn of a new racial and gender era in the South and in America, but the journey would take many years and many lives. Cooper died at the age of 106 in 1964.

THE "NEWNESS" OF THE NEW SOUTH

Anna J. Cooper's journey looked forward to a brighter, if elusive, future for African Americans, women in particular. White southerners marched backward toward an idealized past whose elements they hoped to restore as faithfully as possible, especially those related to race and gender. At the same time, they projected an image of progress, touting economic and technological advances, welcoming investment, and promoting benign race relations and a docile labor force. The progress was genuine, but only within the framework of white supremacy. When the idea of white supremacy proved insufficient to sustain order, white southerners resorted to legislation and violence. The New South, as one observer noted, was merely "the Old South under new conditions." By the early 1900s, the South had traveled further away from the American journey than at any time in its history.

On the surface, this did not seem to be the case. Southerners did what other Americans were doing between 1877 and 1900; they built railroads, erected factories, and moved to towns and cities, only on a smaller scale and with more modest results. But the factories did not dramatically alter the South's rural economy, and the towns and cities did not make it an urban region. The changes, nonetheless, brought political and social turmoil, emboldening black people like Cooper to assert their rights, encouraging women to work outside the home and pursue public careers, and frightening some white men. The backlash would be significant.

The New South's "newness" was to be found primarily in its economy, not in its social relations, although the two were complementary. After Reconstruction, new industries absorbed tens of thousands of first-time industrial workers from impoverished rural areas. Southern cities grew faster than those in any other region of the country. A burst of railroad construction linked these cities to one another and to the rest of the country, giving them increased commercial prominence. Growing in size and taking on new functions, cities extended their influence into the countryside with newspapers,

CHRONOLOGY

1872	Texas and Pacific Railway connects Dallas to eastern markets.
1880	First southern local of the Women's Christian Temperance Union is formed in Atlanta.
1881	Booker T. Washington establishes Tuskegee Institute.
1882	Agricultural Wheel is formed in Arkansas.
1883	Laura Haygood founds the home mission movement in Atlanta.
1884	James B. Duke automates his cigarette factory.
1886	Dr. John Pemberton creates Coca-Cola. Southern railroads conform to national track gauge standards.
1887	Charles W. Macune expands the Southern Farmers' Alliance from its Texas base to the rest of the South.
1888	The Southern Farmers' Alliance initiates a successful boycott of jute manufacturers.
1890	Mississippi becomes the first state to restrict black suffrage with literacy tests.
1892	The Populist Party forms.
1894	United Daughters of the Confederacy is founded.
1895	Booker T. Washington delivers his "Atlanta Compromise" address.
1895	Publication of Theodor Herzl's *The Jewish State* outlining his ideas for a Jewish homeland in Palestine in response to rising anti-Semitism in Europe.
1896	In *Plessy v. Ferguson,* the Supreme Court permits segregation by law.
1897	First Zionist Congress meets in Switzerland.
1898	North Carolina Mutual Life Insurance is founded.
1899	Publication of *Die Grundlagen des neunzehnten Jahrhunderts* ["The Foundations of the Nineteenth Century"] by British scientist Houston Stewart Chamberlain, promoting the superiority of the German "race."
1903	W.E.B. Du Bois publishes *The Souls of Black Folk*.
1905	James B. Duke forms the Southern Power Company. Thomas Dixon publishes *The Clansman.*
1906	Bloody race riots break out in Atlanta.
1907	Pittsburgh-based U.S. Steel takes over Birmingham's largest steel producer.

consumer products, and new values. But this urban influence had important limits. It did not bring electricity, telephones, public health services, or public schools to the rural South. It did not greatly broaden the rural economy with new jobs. And it left the countryside without the daily contact with the outside world that fostered a broader perspective.

The Democratic Party dominated southern politics after 1877, significantly changing the South's political system. Through various deceits, Democrats purged most black people and some white people from the electoral process and suppressed challenges to their leadership. The result was the emergence by 1900 of the **Solid South,** a period of white Democratic Party rule that lasted into the 1950s.

Although most southern women remained at home or in the farm, piecing together families shattered by war, some enjoyed new options after 1877. Middle-class women in the cities, both white and black, became increasingly active in civic work and reform. Tens of thousands of young white women from impoverished rural areas found work in textile mills, in city factories, or as servants. These new options posed a challenge to prevailing views about the role of women but ultimately did not change them.

The status of black southerners changed significantly between 1877 and 1900. The members of the first generation born after emancipation sought more than just freedom as they came of age. They also expected dignity and self-respect and the right to work, to vote, to go to school, and to travel freely. White southerners responded to the new challenge in the same manner they had responded immediately after the war, with violence and restrictive legislation. By 1900, black southerners found themselves more isolated from white southerners and with less political power than at any time since 1865. Despite these setbacks, they succeeded, especially in the cities, in building a rich community life and spawning a vibrant middle class, albeit in a restricted environment.

An Industrial and Urban South

Southerners manufactured very little in 1877, less than 10 percent of the national total. By 1900, however, they boasted a growing iron and steel industry, textile mills that rivaled those of New England, a world-dominant tobacco industry, and a timber-processing industry that helped make the South a leading furniture-manufacturing center. A variety of regional enterprises also rose to prominence, among them the maker of what would become the world's favorite soft drink, Coca-Cola.

Steel Mills and Textiles. Birmingham, barely a scratch in the forest in 1870, exemplified one aspect of what was new about the New South. Within a decade, its iron and steel mills were belching the smoke of progress across the northern Alabama hills. By 1889, Birmingham had surpassed the older southern iron center of Chattanooga, Tennessee, and was preparing to challenge Pittsburgh, the nation's preeminent steelmaking city.

The southern textile industry also experienced significant growth during the 1880s. Although the South had manufactured cotton products since the early decades of the nineteenth century, chronic shortages of labor and capital kept the

The face of southern industry. By the early 1900s, the South had become a national leader in textile production, relying on cheap labor, especially women and young children, such as this young girl in a Lewis Hine photograph at the Globe Cotton Mill in Augusta, Georgia, 1909. She stands in a grimy dress between two large looms. The floor is littered with cotton lint that is harmful to the lungs. Hine took such photographs to call attention to the evil of children labor. To hard-pressed southern families who could not sustain themselves on the farm, these industrial jobs were literally lifesaving, but at a terrible cost to the health, education, and welfare of their children.

industry small. In the 1870s, however, several factors drew local investors into textile enterprises. The population of the rural South was rising, but farm income was low, ensuring a steady supply of cheap labor. Cotton was plentiful and cheap. Mixing profit and southern patriotism, entrepreneurs promoted a strong textile industry as a way to make the South less dependent on northern manufactured products and capital. By 1900, the South had surpassed New England to become the nation's foremost textile-manufacturing center.

Tobacco and Coca-Cola. The South's tobacco industry, like its textile industry, predated the Civil War. Virginia was the dominant producer, and its main product was chewing tobacco. The discovery of bright-leaf tobacco, a strain suitable for smoking in the form of cigarettes, changed Americans' tobacco habits. In 1884, James B. Duke installed the first cigarette-making machine in his Durham, North Carolina, plant. By 1900, Duke's American Tobacco Company controlled 80 percent of all tobacco manufacturing in the United States.

Although not as important as textiles or tobacco in 1900, a soft drink developed by an Atlanta pharmacist, Dr. John Pemberton, eventually became the most renowned southern product worldwide. He called his concoction Coca-Cola. By the mid-1890s, Coca-Cola enjoyed a national market.

Railroads and Growth. Southern railroad construction boomed in the 1880s, outpacing the rest of the nation. Overall, southern track mileage doubled between 1880 and 1890, with the greatest increases in Texas and Georgia. In 1886, the southern railroads agreed to conform to a national standard for track width, firmly linking the region into a national transportation network and ensuring quick and direct access for southern products to the booming markets of the Northeast.

The railroads connected many formerly isolated small southern farmers to national and international agricultural markets. At the same time, it gave them access to a whole new range of products, from fertilizers to fashions. Drawn into commercial agriculture, the farmers were now subject to market fluctuations, their fortunes rising and falling with the market prices for their crops. To an extent unknown before the Civil War, the market now determined what farmers planted, how much credit they could expect, and on what terms. The railroad also opened new areas of the South to settlement and economic development.

THE LIMITS OF INDUSTRIAL AND URBAN GROWTH

These economic developments implied that the South was traveling on a new road. In fact, the journey was back to a very old place. Rapid as it was, urban and industrial growth in the South barely kept pace with that in the booming North (see Chapter 18). A weak agricultural economy and a high rural birthrate depressed wages in the South. Southern industrial workers earned roughly half the national average manufacturing wage during the late nineteenth century. Business leaders promoted the advantages of this cheap labor to northern investors. In 1904, a Memphis businessman boasted that his city "can save the northern manufacturer … who employs 400 hands, $50,000 a year on his labor bill."

Effects of Low Wages. Despite their attractiveness to industrialists, low wages undermined the southern economy in several ways. Poorly paid workers did not buy much, keeping consumer demand low and limiting the market for southern manufactured goods. They also could not provide much tax revenue, restricting the southern states' ability to fund services like public education. As a result, investment in education lagged in the South. Per-pupil expenditure in the region was at least 50 percent below that of the rest of the nation in 1900.

Finally, low wages kept immigrants, and the skills and energy they brought with them, out of the South. Between 1860 and 1900, during one of the greatest waves of immigration the United States has yet experienced, the foreign-born population of the South actually declined from about 10 percent to less than 2 percent.

Limited Capital. Why did the South not do better? Why did it not benefit more from the rapid expansion of the national economy in the last three decades of the nineteenth century? The simple answer is that, despite its growing links to the national economy, the South remained a region apart.

The Civil War had wiped out the South's capital resources, leaving it, in effect, an economic colony of the North. Northern goods flowed into the South, but northern capital, technology, and people did not. Northern-based national banks emerged in the wake of the Civil War to fund northern economic expansion. The South, in contrast, had few banks, and they lacked sufficient capital reserves to fuel an equivalent expansion. In 1880, Massachusetts alone had five times as much bank capital as the entire South.

With limited access to other sources of capital, the South's textile industry depended on thousands of small investors in towns and cities. These investors avoided risk and shunned innovation. Most textile operations remained small-scale. The average southern firm in 1900 was capitalized at $11,000, compared with an average of $21,000 elsewhere.

The lumber industry, the South's largest, typified the shortcomings of southern economic development in the late nineteenth century. It also reflected the lack of concern about the natural environment. As a nascent conservation movement took hold in the North, southerners continued to view the natural environment as a venue for economic exploitation. The lumber industry required little capital, relied on unskilled labor, and processed its raw materials on site. After clear-cutting (i.e., felling all the trees) in one region, sawmills moved quickly to the next stand of timber, leaving behind a bare landscape, rusting machinery, and a workforce no better off than before. This process, later repeated by the coal-mining industry, inflicted environmental damage on once remote areas such as Appalachia, and displaced their residents.

The tobacco industry, avoided the problems that plagued other southern enterprises. James B. Duke's American Tobacco Company was so immensely profitable that he became, in effect, his own bank. With more than enough capital to install the latest technology in his plants, Duke bought out his competitors. In the North, industrialization usually occurred in an urban context and promoted rapid urban growth. In the South, textile mills were typically located in the countryside, often in mill villages where employers could easily recruit families and keep them isolated from the distractions and employment alternatives of the cities. The timber industry similarly remained a rural-based enterprise. Tobacco manufacturing helped Durham and Winston, North Carolina, grow, but they remained small compared to northern industrial cities.

FARMS TO CITIES: IMPACT ON SOUTHERN SOCIETY

If industrialization in the South was limited compared to the North, it nonetheless had an enormous impact on southern society. In the southern Piedmont, for example, textile mills transformed a portion of the farm population into an industrial workforce. Failed farmers moved to textile villages to earn a living. Entire families secured employment and often a house in exchange for their labor. Widows and single young men also moved to the mills, usually the only option outside farm work in the South. Nearly one-third of the textile-mill labor force by 1900 consisted of children under the age of 14 and women.

In 1880, southern towns often did not differ much from the countryside in appearance, economy, religion, and outlook. Over the next twenty years, the gap between town and country widened. By 1900, a town in the New South would boast a business district and more elegant residences than before. It would have a relatively prosperous economy and more frequent contact with other parts of the country. Its influence would extend into the countryside. Mail, the telegraph, the railroad, and the newspaper brought city life to the attention of farm families. In turn, farm families visited nearby towns and cities more often.

The urban South drew the region's talented and ambitious young people. White men moved to cities to open shops or take jobs as bank clerks, bookkeepers, merchants, and salesmen. White women worked as retail clerks, telephone operators, and office personnel. Black women filled the growing demand for laundresses and domestic servants. And black men also found prospects better in towns than on the farm, despite a narrow and uncertain range of occupations available to them. The excitement that drew some southerners to their new cities repelled others. To them, urbanization and the emphasis on wealth, new technology, and display represented a second Yankee conquest. The cities, they feared, threatened to infect the South with northern values, undermining southern grace, charm, faith, and family.

White southerners in town and country, who not long before had lived similar lives, grew distant. Small landholding white farmers and their families had fallen on hard times. The market that lured them into commercial agriculture threatened to take away their independence. They faced the loss of their land and livelihood. Their way of life no longer served as the standard for the South. New South spokesmen promoted cities and industries and ordered farmers to get on board the train of progress before it left the station without them.

The Southern Agrarian Revolt

Even more than before the Civil War, cotton dominated southern agriculture between 1877 and 1900. And the economics of cotton brought despair to cotton farmers. The size of the cotton crop continued to set annual records after 1877. Fertilizers revived supposedly exhausted soils in North and South Carolina, turning them white with cotton. The railroad opened new areas for cultivation in Mississippi and eastern Texas. But the price of cotton fell while the price of fertilizers, agricultural tools, food, and most other necessities went up. As a result, the more cotton the farmers grew, the less money they made.

Cotton and Credit

The solution to this agrarian dilemma seemed simple: Grow less cotton. But that course was not possible for several reasons. In a cash-poor economy, credit ruled. Cotton was the only commodity instantly convertible into cash and thus the only commodity accepted for credit. Food crops generated less income per acre than cotton. Local merchants, themselves bound in a web of credit to merchants in larger cities, accepted cotton as collateral. As cotton prices plummeted, the merchants required their customers to grow more cotton to make up the difference. Trapped in debt by low cotton prices and

Black sharecroppers in Georgia cotton fields, 1898; the scene is reminiscent of the slavery era. Southern agriculture contradicted New South rhetoric both in social and economic terms.

Cook Collection, Valentine Museum/Richmond History Center.

high interest rates, small landowning farmers lost their land in record numbers. Just after the Civil War, less than one-third of white farmers in the South were tenants or sharecroppers. By the 1890s, nearly half were.

SOUTHERN FARMERS ORGANIZE, 1877–1892

As their circumstances deteriorated, southern farmers fought back. They had lived a communal life of church, family, and kin. Now they would widen the circle of their community to include other farmers sharing the same plight. These were not naive country folk; most owned their own land and participated in the market economy. They just wanted to make the market fairer, to lower interest rates and ease credit, to regulate railroad freight rates, and to keep the prices of necessities in check.

But these goals required legislation that neither the federal government nor southern state governments were inclined to support. Therefore, southern farmers joined their colleagues nationwide to address common grievances related to pricing, credit, and tax policies. Although some of the southern farmers' problems resulted from conditions peculiar to the South, agricultural distress became widespread after 1870. By 1875, nearly 250,000 southern landowners had joined the National

Grange of the Patrons of Husbandry or, more popularly, simply the **Grange** (see Chapter 20). The leaders of the Grange, however, were large landowners. They did not have the same interests as the small farmers who made up the organization's rank and file.

Salvation and Cooperation. The most powerful agricultural reform organization, the **Southern Farmers' Alliance**, originated in Texas in the late 1870s. Alliance-sponsored farmers' cooperatives provided their members with discounts on supplies and credit. Members also benefited from marketing their cotton crops collectively.

The Alliance was still very much a Texas organization in 1887 when Charles W. Macune, a Wisconsin native, became its driving force. Macune sent a corps of speakers to create a network of southern cooperatives. Within two years, the Alliance had spread throughout the South and into the North and West. By 1890, it claimed more than a million members. With the exception of a few large landowners and some tenant farmers, almost all were small farmers who owned their own land. The success of the Alliance reflected both the desperate struggle of these small farmers to keep their land and the failure of other organizations to help them.

The Alliance operated like a religious denomination. Its leaders preached a message of salvation through cooperation to audiences of as many as 20,000 people at huge revival-like rallies. Qualifications for membership included a belief in the divinity of Jesus and the literal truth of the Bible. Alliance speakers, many of them rural ministers, often held meetings in churches. In their talks, they stressed the importance of doing good as much as good farming. The Alliance lobbied state legislatures to fund rural public schools. To increase the sense of community, the Alliance sponsored picnics, baseball games, and concerts.

The Alliance became for many small farmers a surrogate government and church in a region where public officials and many mainline Protestant ministers ignored their needs. It imposed strict morality on its members, prohibiting drinking, gambling, and sexual misconduct. Alliance leaders criticized many Baptist, Methodist, and Presbyterian ministers who had strayed from the traditional emphasis on individual salvation and were defending a status quo that benefited large planters and towns.

The Alliance, however, did not accept black members. Black farmers formed the first **Colored Farmers' Alliance** in Texas in 1886. The Colored Alliance had fewer landowners and more tenants and sharecroppers in its ranks than the white organization. It concerned itself with issues relevant to this constituency, such as higher wages for cotton pickers. In 1891, the Colored Alliance attempted a region-wide strike over farm wages but was unable to enforce it in the worsening southern economy.

The white Alliance had better results with a protest over price fixing. To protect cotton shipped to market, farmers wrapped it in a burlap-like material called jute. In 1888, jute manufacturers combined to raise the price from 7 cents to as much as 14 cents a yard. The Alliance initiated a jute boycott throughout the South, telling farmers to use cotton bagging as an alternative. The protest worked, forcing the chastened jute manufacturers to offer farmers their product at a mere 5 cents per yard.

Storing Cotton. This success encouraged Macune to pursue a more ambitious project. Low cotton prices and a lack of cash kept farmers poor. To address these problems, Macune proposed his **subtreasury plan**. Alliance members were to store their crops in a subtreasury (i.e., warehouse), keeping their cotton off the market until the price rose. In the meantime, the government would loan the farmers up to 80 percent of the value of the stored crops at a low interest rate of 2 percent per year. This arrangement would free farmers from merchants' high interest rates and crop liens. Macune urged Alliance members to endorse political candidates who supported the subtreasury scheme. Many Democratic candidates for state legislatures throughout the South did endorse it and were elected, with Alliance backing, in 1890. Once in office, however, they failed to deliver.

The failure of the subtreasury plan, combined with a steep drop in cotton prices after 1890, undermined the Alliance. Alliance membership declined by two-thirds in Georgia that year. Desperate Alliance leaders merged their organization with a new national political party in 1892, the People's Party, better known as the **Populist Party**. The Populists appropriated the Alliance program and challenged Democrats in the South and Republicans in the West. The merger reflected desperation more than calculation. As we will see in Chapter 20, the Populists stirred up national politics between 1892 and 1896. In the South, they challenged the Democratic Party, sometimes courting Republicans, including black voters.

WOMEN IN THE NEW SOUTH

Because the antebellum reform movements included abolitionism, they had made little headway in the South. As a result, southern women had a meager reform tradition to build on. The war also left them ambivalent about independence. With husbands, fathers, and brothers dead or incapacitated, many women had to care for themselves and their families in the face of defeat and deprivation. Some determined never again to depend on men. Others, responding to the stress of running a farm or business, would have preferred less independence.

The response of southern white men to the war also complicated women's efforts to improve their status. Southern men had been shaken by defeat. They had lost the war and placed their families in peril. Many responded with alcoholism and violence. To regain their self-esteem, they recast the war as a noble crusade rather than a defeat. And they imagined southern white women as paragons of virtue and purity who required men to defend them. Demands for even small changes in traditional gender roles would threaten this image. Southern women understood this and never mounted an extensive reform campaign like their sisters in the North. Some middle-class women were openly hostile to reform, and others adopted conservative causes more inclined to reinforce the role of men in southern society than to challenge it.

Despite such limitations, middle-class southern women found opportunities to broaden their social role and enter the public sphere in the two decades after 1880. They found these opportunities primarily in the cities, where servants, stores, and schools freed them of many of the productive functions, such as making clothing, cooking, and childcare, that burdened their sisters in the country and kept them tied to the home.

CHURCH WORK AND PRESERVING MEMORIES

Southern women waded warily into the public arena, using channels men granted them as natural extensions of the home, such as church work. By the 1880s, evangelical Protestant churches had become prominent in many aspects of southern life. Women took advantage of the church's prominence to build careers using the moral gravity of church affiliation to political advantage. Most of the major reform efforts in the South during this era emanated from the church, and from the women for whom church work was an approved role for their gender.

The movement to found home mission societies, for example, was led by single white women in the Methodist Church. Home missions promoted industrial education among the poor and helped working-class women become self-sufficient. The home mission movement reflected an increased interest in missionary work in white southern evangelical churches. Lily Hammond extended the mission concept when she opened settlement houses in black and white neighborhoods in Atlanta in the 1890s. **Settlement houses**, pioneered in New York in the 1880s, promoted middle-class values in poor neighborhoods and provided them with a permanent source of services. In the North, they were privately sponsored. In the South, they were supported by the Methodist Church and known as Wesley Houses, after John Wesley, the founder of Methodism.

Religion also prompted southern white women to join the **Women's Christian Temperance Union (WCTU)**. Temperance reform, unlike other church-inspired activities, involved women directly in public policy. WCTU members visited schools to educate children about the evils of alcohol, addressed prisoners, and blanketed men's meetings with literature. As a result, they became familiar with the South's abysmal school system and its archaic criminal justice system. They soon began advocating education and prison reform as well as legislation against alcohol.

By the 1890s, many WCTU members realized that they could not achieve their goals unless women had the vote. Rebecca Latimer Felton, an Atlanta suffragist and WCTU member, reflected the frustration of her generation of southern women in an address to working women in 1892: "But some will say, you women might be quiet, you can't vote, you can't do anything! Exactly so, we have kept quiet for nearly a hundred years hoping to see relief come to the women of this country, and it hasn't come."

Rebecca Felton's own career highlighted the essentially conservative nature of the reform movement among middle-class white women in the New South. She fought for childcare facilities and sex education, as well as compulsory school attendance, and she pushed for the admission of women to the University of Georgia. But she strongly supported textile operators over textile workers and defended white supremacy. She had no qualms about the lynching of black men, executing them without trial "a thousand times a week if necessary" to preserve the purity of white women. In 1922, she became the first woman member of the U.S. Senate. By any definition, Felton was a reformer, but like most middle-class southern women, she had no interest in challenging the class and racial inequities of the New South.

The dedication of southern women to commemorating the memory of the Confederate cause also indicates the conservative nature of middle-class women's reform in the New South. Ladies' Memorial Associations formed after the war to ensure the proper burial of Confederate soldiers and suitable markings for their graves. The associations joined with men to erect monuments to Confederate leaders

Southern white women played a major role in memorializing the Civil War and Confederate veterans. Here, a float prepared for a Confederate Veterans parade includes the major symbols of the Lost Cause, including the prominent pictures of Robert E. Lee, Thomas "Stonewall" Jackson, and Jefferson Davis, as well as the Confederate Battle Flag. The sponsorship of a casket company affords some irony to the photograph.

and, by the 1880s, to the common soldier. These activities reinforced white solidarity and constructed a common heritage for all white southerners regardless of class or location.

WOMEN'S CLUBS

A broader spectrum of southern middle-class women joined women's clubs than joined church-sponsored organizations or memorial associations. Most women's clubs began in the 1880s as literary or self-improvement societies that had little interest in reform. By 1890, most towns and cities boasted at least several women's clubs and perhaps a federated club organization. But by that time, some clubs and their members had also begun to discuss political issues, such as child labor reform, educational improvement, and prison reform.

The activities of black women's clubs paralleled those of white women's clubs. Most African American women in southern cities worked as domestics or laundresses. Black women's clubs supported daycare facilities for working mothers and settlement houses in poor black neighborhoods modeled after those in northern cities. Atlanta's Neighborhood Union, founded by Lugenia Burns Hope in 1908, provided playgrounds and a health center and obtained a grant from a New York foundation to improve black education in the city. Black women's clubs also established homes for single black working women to protect them from sexual exploitation, and they worked for woman suffrage.

Only rarely, however, as at some meetings of the Young Women's Christian Association (YWCA) or occasional meetings in support of prohibition, did black and white club members interact. Some white clubwomen expressed sympathy for black women privately, but publicly they maintained white solidarity. Most were unwilling to sacrifice their own reform agenda to the cause of racial reconciliation.

SETTLING THE RACE ISSUE

The assertiveness of a new generation of African Americans in the 1880s and 1890s, especially in urban areas, provided the impetus and opportunity for white leaders to secure white solidarity. To counter black aspirations, white leaders enlisted the support of young white southerners, convincing them that the struggle for white supremacy would place them beside the larger-than-life heroes of the Civil War generation. African Americans resisted the resulting efforts to deprive them of their remaining freedoms. Although some left the South, many more built new lives and communities within the restricted framework white southerners allowed them.

THE FLUIDITY OF SOUTHERN RACE RELATIONS, 1877–1890

Race relations remained remarkably fluid in the South between the end of Reconstruction and the early 1890s. Despite the departure of federal troops and the end of Republican rule, many black people continued to vote and hold office. Some Democrats even courted the black electorate. Although segregation ruled in churches, schools, and in some organizations and public places after the Civil War, black people and white people continued to mingle, do business with each other, and often maintain cordial relations.

In 1885, T. McCants Stewart, a black journalist from New York, traveled to his native South Carolina, expecting a rough reception once his train headed south from Washington, DC. To his surprise, the conductor allowed him to remain in his seat while white riders sat on baggage or stood. He provoked little reaction among white passengers when he entered the dining car. Some of them struck up a conversation with him. In Columbia, South Carolina, Stewart found that he could move about with no restrictions. "I can ride in first-class cars. . . . I can go into saloons and get refreshments even as in New York. I can stop in and drink a glass of soda and be more politely waited upon than in some parts of New England."

Lynching became a public spectacle, a ritual designed to reinforce white supremacy. Note the matter-of-fact satisfaction of the spectators at this gruesome murder of a black man.

Other black people corroborated Stewart's experiences in different parts of the South. During the 1880s, black people joined interracial labor unions and continued to be active in the Republican Party. They engaged in business with white people. In the countryside, African Americans and white people hunted and fished together, worked side by side at sawmills, and traded with each other. Cities were segregated more by class than by race, and people of both races sometimes lived in the same neighborhoods. To be sure, black people faced discrimination in employment and voting and random retaliation for perceived violations of racial barriers. But the barriers were by no means fixed.

THE WHITE BACKLASH

The black generation that came of age in this environment demanded full participation in American society. For many in the generation of white southerners who came of age in the same period, this assertiveness rankled. These young white people, raised on the myth of the Lost Cause, were continually reminded of the heroism and sacrifice of their fathers during the Civil War. For them, black people replaced the Yankees as the enemy; they saw it as their mission to preserve white purity and dominance. The South's deteriorating rural economy and the volatile politics of the late 1880s and early 1890s exacerbated the growing tensions between assertive black people and threatened white people. So too did the growth of industry and cities in the South. In the cities, black and white people came into close contact, competing for jobs and jostling each other for

seats on streetcars and trains. Racist rhetoric and violence against black people accelerated in the 1890s.

LYNCH LAW

In 1892, three prominent black men, Tom Moss, Calvin McDowell, and William Stewart,
opened a grocery on the south side of Memphis, an area with a large African American
population. The People's Grocery prospered, while a white-owned store across the
street struggled. The proprietor of the white-owned store, W. H. Barrett, was incensed.
He obtained an indictment against Moss, McDowell, and Stewart for maintaining a public nuisance. Outraged black community leaders called a protest meeting at the grocery,
during which two people made threats against Barrett. Barrett learned of the threats,
notified the police, and warned the gathering at the People's Grocery that white people
planned to attack and destroy the store. Nine sheriff's deputies, all white, approached
the store to arrest the men who had threatened Barrett. Fearing Barrett's threatened
white assault, the people in the grocery fired on the deputies, unaware who they were,
and wounded three. When the deputies identified themselves, thirty black people
surrendered, including Moss, McDowell, and Stewart, and were imprisoned. Four days
later, deputies removed the three owners from jail, took them to a deserted area, and
shot them dead.

The men at the People's Grocery had violated two of the unspoken rules that
white southerners imposed on black southerners to maintain racial barriers: They
had prospered, and they had forcefully challenged white authority. During 1892, a
year of political agitation and economic depression, 235 **lynchings** occurred in the
South. White mobs lynched nearly 2,000 black southerners between 1882 and 1903.
Most lynchers were working-class whites with rural roots, who were struggling in the
depressed economy of the 1890s and enraged at the fluidity of urban race relations.
The most common justification for lynching was the presumed threat posed by black
men to the sexual virtue of white women. Sexual "crimes" could include remarks,
glances, and gestures. Yet only 25 percent of the lynchings that took place in thirty
years after 1890 had an alleged sexual connection. Certainly, the men of the People's
Grocery had committed no sex crime. Lynchers did not carry out their grisly crimes to
end a rape epidemic; they killed to keep black men in their place and to restore their
own sense of manhood and honor.

Ida B. Wells, who owned a black newspaper in Memphis, used her columns to
publicize the People's Grocery lynchings. The great casualty of the lynchings, she noted,
was her faith that education, wealth, and upright living guaranteed black people the
equality and justice they had long sought. The reverse was true. The more black people
succeeded, the greater was their threat to white people. She investigated other lynchings, countering the claim that they were the result of assaults on white women. When
she suggested that, on the contrary, perhaps some white women were attracted to black
men, the white citizens of Memphis destroyed her press and office. Exiled to Chicago,
Wells devoted herself to the struggle for racial justice.

What is striking about this carnival of lynching from the 1890s onward was its orchestrated cruelty and the involvement of large segments of the white community. Postcards
and bootlegged photographs of the events showed men, women, and even children gathering as if for a Sunday picnic, surrounding the mutilated corpse. The elevation of white men

Ida B. Wells, an outspoken critic of lynching, fled to Chicago following the People's Grocery lynchings in Memphis in 1892 and became a national civil rights leader.

as the protector for weak women was one reason for the spectacle, but, more important, lynching reinforced white solidarity and reiterated (especially to blacks) that white supremacy ruled the South with impunity. (See American Views: An Account of a Lynching.)

SEGREGATION BY LAW

Southern white lawmakers sought to cement white solidarity and ensure black subservience in the 1890s by instituting **segregation** by law and the **disfranchisement** of black voters. Racial segregation restricting black Americans to separate and rarely equal public facilities had prevailed nationwide before the Civil War. After 1870, the custom spread rapidly in southern cities.

During the same period, many northern cities and states, often in response to protests by African Americans, were ending segregation. Roughly 95 percent of the nation's black population, however, lived in the South. Integration in the North, consequently, required white people to give up very little to black people. And as African American aspirations increased in the South during the 1890s while their political power waned, they became more vulnerable to segregation by law at the state level. At the same time, migration to cities, industrial development, and technologies such as railroads and elevators increased the opportunities for racial contact and muddled the rules of racial interaction.

Much of the new legislation focused on railroads, a symbol of modernity and mobility in the New South. Local laws and customs could not control racial interaction on interstate railroads. White passengers objected to black passengers' implied assertion of economic and social equality when they sat with them in dining cars and first-class compartments. Black southerners, by contrast, viewed equal access to railroad facilities as a sign of respectability and acceptance. When southern state legislatures required railroads to provide segregated facilities, black people protested.

Segregation laws required the railroads to provide "separate but equal" accommodations for black passengers. Railroads balked at the expense involved in doing so and provided black passengers with distinctly inferior facilities. Many lines refused to sell first-class tickets to black people and treated them roughly if they sat in first-class seats or tried to eat in the dining car. In 1890, Homer Plessy, a black Louisianan, refused to leave the first-class car of a railroad traveling through the state. Arrested, he filed suit, arguing that his payment of the first-class fare entitled him to sit in the same first-class accommodations as white passengers.

The U.S. Supreme Court ruled on the case, ***Plessy v. Ferguson***, in 1896. In a seven-to-one decision, the Court held that Louisiana's railroad segregation law did not violate the Constitution as long as the railroads or the state provided equal accommodations for black passengers. The decision left unclear what "equal" meant. In the Court's view, "Legislation is powerless to eradicate racial instincts," meaning that segregation of the races was natural and transcended constitutional considerations. The only justice to vote against the decision was John Marshall Harlan, a Kentuckian and former slave owner. He predicted that the decision would result in an all-out assault on black rights.

Harlan's was a prophetic dissent. Both northern and southern states enacted new segregation laws in the wake of *Plessy v. Ferguson*. In practice, the separate facilities for black people these laws required, if provided at all, were rarely equal.

The segregation statutes came to be known collectively as **Jim Crow laws**, after the blackface stage persona of Thomas Rice, a white northern minstrel-show performer in the 1820s. Reflecting white stereotypes of African Americans, Rice had caricatured Crow as a foolish, elderly, lame slave who spoke in an exaggerated dialect. The purpose of these laws was not only to separate the races, but also to humiliate blacks and reinforce white supremacy. Separation was never equal.

Economic segregation followed social segregation. Before the Civil War, black men had dominated such crafts as carpentry and masonry. By the 1890s, white men were replacing them in these trades and excluding them from new ones, such as plumbing and electrical work. Trade unions, composed primarily of craft workers, began systematically to exclude African Americans. Although the steel and tobacco industries hired black workers, most other manufacturers turned them away. Confined increasingly to low or unskilled positions in railroad construction, the timber industry, and agriculture, black people underwent deskilling, a decline in workforce expertise, after 1890. With lower incomes from unskilled labor, they faced reduced opportunities for better housing and education.

OVERVIEW THE MARCH OF DISFRANCHISEMENT ACROSS THE SOUTH, 1889–1908

Year	State	Strategies
1889	Florida	Poll tax
1889	Tennessee	Poll tax
1890	Mississippi	Poll tax, literacy test, understanding clause
1891	Arkansas	Poll tax
1893, 1901	Alabama	Poll tax, literacy test, grandfather clause
1894, 1895	South Carolina	Poll tax, literacy test, understanding clause
1894, 1902	Virginia	Poll tax, literacy test, understanding clause
1897, 1898	Louisiana	Poll tax, literacy test, grandfather clause
1899, 1900	North Carolina	Poll tax, literacy test, grandfather clause
1902	Texas	Poll tax
1908	Georgia	Poll tax, literacy test, understanding clause, grandfather clause

DISFRANCHISEMENT

With economic and social segregation came political isolation. The authority of post-Reconstruction Redeemer governments had rested on their ability to limit and control the black vote. Following the political instability of the late 1880s and the 1890s, however, white leaders determined to disfranchise black people altogether, thereby reinforcing white solidarity and eliminating the need to consider black interests. Support for disfranchisement was especially strong among large landowners in the South's plantation districts, where heavy concentrations of black people threatened their political domination. Urban leaders, especially after the turmoil of the 1890s, looked on disfranchisement as a way to stabilize politics and make elections more predictable.

The movement to reduce or eliminate the black vote in the South began in the 1880s and continued through the early 1900s (see Overview, The March of Disfranchisement Across the South, 1889–1908). Democrats enacted a variety of measures to attain their objectives without violating the letter of the Fifteenth Amendment. They complicated

AMERICAN VIEWS

AN ACCOUNT OF A LYNCHING

*L*uther Holbert allegedly murdered a white plantation owner in Doddsville, Mississippi, in February 1904 after he refused the owner's demand to leave the property. Holbert and his wife fled, but a mob of 1,000 whites tracked them down. Although there was no evidence to link Holbert's wife to the crime, she was taken into custody as well. Six hundred people gathered, fortified by deviled eggs, lemonade, and whiskey. Following is an account from a local newspaper of what happened next.

■ What was the purpose of visiting such extreme cruelty upon the victims?

■ The lynching occurred without a proper trial. Do you think any of the perpetrators were ever arrested or tried for the lynching?

■ Why did a party atmosphere prevail?

They were tied to trees, and while the funeral pyres were being prepared they were forced to suffer the most fiendish tortures. The blacks were forced to hold out their hands while one finger at a time was chopped off. The fingers were distributed as souvenirs. The ears of the murderers were cut off. Holbert was beaten severely, his skull was fractured, and one of his eyes, knocked with the stick, hung by a shred from the socket. . . . The most excruciating form of punishment consisted in the use of a large corkscrew in the hands of some of the mob. This instrument was bored into the flesh of the man and woman, in the arms, legs, and body, and then pulled out, the spirals tearing out big pieces of raw, quivering flesh every time it was withdrawn.

SOURCE: *Vicksburg Evening Post*, February 8, 1904.

the registration and voting processes. States enacted **poll taxes**, requiring citizens to pay to vote. They adopted the secret ballot, which confused and intimidated illiterate black voters accustomed to using ballots with colors to identify parties. States set literacy and educational qualifications for voting or required prospective registrants to "interpret" a section of the state constitution. To avoid disfranchising poor, illiterate white voters with these measures, states enacted **grandfather clauses**, granting the vote automatically to anyone whose grandfather could have voted prior to 1867 (the year Congressional Reconstruction began). The grandfathers of most black men in the 1890s had been slaves, ineligible to vote.

Lawmakers sold white citizens on franchise restrictions with the promise that they would apply only to black voters and would scarcely affect white voters. This promise proved untrue. Alarmed by the Populist uprising, Democratic leaders used disfranchisement to gut dissenting parties. During the 1880s, minority parties in the South consistently polled an average of 40 percent of the statewide vote; by the mid-1890s, the figure had diminished to 30 percent despite the Populist insurgency.

Turnout dropped even more dramatically. In Mississippi, for example, voter turnout in gubernatorial races during the 1880s averaged 51 percent; during the 1890s, it was 21 percent. Black turnout in Mississippi, which averaged 39 percent in the 1880s, plummeted to near zero in the 1890s. Overall turnout, which averaged 64 percent during the 1880s, fell to only 30 percent by 1910.

Black people protested disfranchisement vigorously. When 160 South Carolina delegates gathered to amend the state constitution in 1895, the six black delegates among them mounted a passionate but futile defense of their right to vote. Black delegate W. J. Whipper noted the irony of white people clamoring for supremacy when they already held the vast majority of the state's elected offices. Robert Smalls, the state's leading black politician, urged delegates not to turn their backs on the state's black population. Such pleas fell on deaf ears.

HISTORY AND MEMORY

Whites codified white supremacy in laws, enforced it with violence, and institutionalized it on the landscape and in the history books. History not only immortalized the Lost Cause and the Redemption, but it also served a more contemporary purpose. It endorsed white supremacy and justified actions carried out in its name. By the early 1900s, a statue of a Confederate soldier stood guard over courthouse squares throughout the South, silent witness to sacrifice and restoration. In Richmond, the capital of the Confederacy became a shrine. Down the wide boulevard of Monument Avenue, the statues of the war heroes marched. By 1900, only three monuments paid tribute to black soldiers—none in the South. African Americans were as absent in the landscape as they were in the textbooks.

A NATIONAL CONSENSUS ON RACE

White southerners openly segregated, disfranchised, and lynched African Americans, and twisted the historical record beyond recognition without a national outcry for the same reasons they were able to overthrow Reconstruction. The majority of Americans in the 1890s subscribed to the notion that black people were inferior to white people and deserved to be treated as second-class citizens. Contemporary depictions of black people show scarcely human stereotypes: black men with bulbous lips and bulging eyes, fat black women wearing turbans and smiling vacuously, and black children contentedly eating watermelon or romping with jungle animals. Among the widely read books of the era was *The Clansman,* a glorification of the rise of the Ku Klux Klan. D. W. Griffith transformed *The Clansman* into an immensely popular motion picture epic under the title *Birth of a Nation.*

Intellectual and political opinion in the North bolstered southern policy. So-called scientific racism purported to establish white superiority and black inferiority on biological grounds. Northern-born professional historians reinterpreted the Civil War and Reconstruction in the white South's favor. Respected national journals openly supported disfranchisement and segregation. The *New York Times,* summarizing this national consensus in 1903, noted that "practically the whole country" supported the "southern solution" to the race issue, because "there was no other possible settlement."

These views permeated Congress, which made no effort to block the institutionalization of white supremacy in the South after 1890, and the courts, which upheld discriminatory legislation. As the white consensus on race emerged, the status of African Americans slipped in the North as well as the South. Although no northern states threatened to deny black citizens the right to vote, they did increase segregation. The booming industries of the North generally did not hire black workers. Antidiscrimination laws on the books since the Civil War went unenforced. In 1904, 1906, and 1908, race riots erupted in Springfield, Ohio; Greensburg, Indiana; and Springfield, Illinois, matching similar disturbances in Wilmington, North Carolina; and Atlanta, Georgia.

RESPONSE OF THE BLACK COMMUNITY

American democracy had, it seemed, hung out a "whites only" sign. How could African Americans respond to the growing political, social, and economic restrictions on their lives? Given white American's hostility, protest proved ineffective, even dangerous. African Americans organized more than a dozen boycotts of streetcar systems in the urban South between 1896 and 1908 in an effort to desegregate them, but not one succeeded. The Afro-American Council, formed in 1890 to protest the deteriorating conditions of black life, accomplished little and disbanded in 1908. W. E. B. Du Bois organized an annual Conference on Negro Problems at Atlanta University beginning in 1896, but it produced no effective plan of action.

A few black people chose to leave the South. Most black people who moved in the 1890s stayed within the South, settling in places like Mississippi, Louisiana, and Texas, where they could find work with timber companies or farming new lands that had opened to cotton and rice cultivation.

An Urban Middle Class. More commonly, black people withdrew to develop their own rich community life within the restricted confines white society permitted them. Particularly in the cities of the South, they could live relatively free of white surveillance and even white contact. In 1890, fully 70 percent of black city dwellers lived in the South; and between 1860 and 1900, the proportion of black people in the cities of the South rose from one in six to more than one in three. The institutions, businesses, and families that black people had begun painstakingly building during Reconstruction continued to grow, and in some cases flourished, after 1877.

By the 1880s, a new black middle class had emerged in the South. Urban-based, professional, business-oriented, and serving a primarily black clientele, its members fashioned an interconnected web of churches, fraternal and self-help organizations, families, and businesses. Black Baptists, AME, and AME Zion churches led reform efforts that sought to eliminate drinking, prostitution, and other vices in black neighborhoods.

African American fraternal and self-help groups, led by middle-class black people, functioned as surrogate welfare organizations for the poor. Fraternal orders also served as the seedbed for such business ventures as the North Carolina Mutual Life Insurance Company, founded in Durham in 1898. Within two decades,

North Carolina Mutual became the largest black-owned business in the nation and helped transform Durham into the "capital of the black middle class." Durham's thriving black business district included several black-owned insurance firms, banks, and a textile mill. Most southern cities boasted active black business districts by the 1890s.

The African American middle class worked especially hard to improve black education. Declining black political power encouraged white leaders to reduce funding for black public education. Black students in cities had only makeshift facilities; those in the countryside had almost no facilities. By the early 1900s, the student-teacher ratio in Nashville's segregated school system was 33 to 1 for white schools but 71 to 1 for black schools. To improve these conditions, black middle-class leaders solicited educational funds from northern philanthropic organizations.

Black Women's Roles. After disfranchisement, middle-class black women assumed an even more pivotal role in the black community. They often used their relations with prominent white women and organizations such as the WCTU and the Young Women's Christian Association (YWCA) to press for public commitments to improve the health and education of African Americans. Absent political pressure from black men, and given the danger of African American males asserting themselves in the tense racial climate after 1890, black women became critical spokespersons for their race.

The extension of black club work into rural areas of the South, where the majority of the African American population lived, to educate families about hygiene, nutrition, and childcare, anticipated similar efforts among white women after 1900. But unlike their white counterparts, these middle-class black women worked with limited resources in a context of simmering racial hostility and political and economic impotence. In response, they nurtured a self-help strategy to improve the conditions of the people they sought to help. One of the most prominent African American leaders of the late nineteenth and early twentieth century, Booker T. Washington, adopted a similar approach to racial uplift.

Booker T. Washington's Accommodation. Born a slave in Virginia in 1856, Washington and his family worked in the salt and coal mines of West Virginia after the Civil War. Ambitious and flushed with the postwar enthusiasm for advancement that gripped freedmen, he enrolled in Hampton Normal and Agricultural Institute, the premier black educational institution in the South. Washington worked his way through Hampton, graduated, taught for a time, and then, in 1881, founded the Tuskegee Institute for black students in rural Alabama. Washington thought that his students would be best served if they learned a trade and workplace discipline. By learning industrial skills, he maintained, black people could acquire self-respect and economic independence. As a result, Tuskegee emphasized vocational training over the liberal arts.

Washington argued that African Americans should accommodate themselves to segregation and disfranchisement until they could prove their economic worth to American society. In exchange for this accommodation, however, white people should help provide black people with the education and job training they would need to gain their independence. Washington articulated this position, known as the **Atlanta**

Compromise, in a speech at the Atlanta Cotton States and International Exposition in 1895. Despite his conciliatory public stance, Washington secretly helped to finance legal challenges to segregation and disfranchisement. The social and economic realities of the South, meanwhile, frustrated his educational mission. Increasingly, black people were shut out of the kinds of jobs for which Washington hoped to train them. Facing a depressed rural economy and growing racial violence, they had little prospect of advancement.

W. E. B. Du Bois Attacks the Atlanta Compromise. Another prominent African American leader, W. E. B. Du Bois, challenged Washington's acceptance of black social inequality. Born in Massachusetts in 1868, Du Bois was the first African American to earn a doctorate at Harvard. Du Bois promoted self-help, education, and black pride. In *The Souls of Black Folk*, published in 1903, he described the strengths of black culture and attacked Washington's Atlanta Compromise. Du Bois was a cofounder, in 1910, of the **National Association for the Advancement of Colored People (NAACP)**, an interracial organization dedicated to restoring African American political and social rights.

Despite their differences, which reflected their divergent backgrounds, Washington and Du Bois agreed on many issues. Both had reservations about

Booker T. Washington at his desk, Tuskegee Institute, 1902.

allowing illiterate black people to vote, and both believed that black success in the South required some white assistance. But it became apparent to Du Bois that white people did not care to elevate black southerners. In 1906, after a bloody race riot in Atlanta, Du Bois left the South, a decision millions of black southerners would make over the next two decades.

CONCLUSION

On the surface, the South was more like the rest of the nation in 1900 than at any other time since 1860. Southern cities hummed with activity, and industries from textiles to steel dotted the southern interior. Young men and women migrated to southern cities to pursue opportunities unavailable to their parents. Advances in the production and marketing of cigarettes and soft drinks would soon make southern entrepreneurs and their products household names. Southerners ordered fashions from Sears, Roebuck catalogs and enjoyed electric lights, electric trolleys, and indoor plumbing as much as other urban Americans.

Americans idealized the South—not the urban industrial South, but a mythical South of rural grace and hospitality. National magazines and publishers rushed to print stories about this land of moonlight and magnolias, offering it as a counterpoint to the crowded, immigrant-infested, factory-fouled, money-grubbing North. It was this fantasy South that white people in both the North and the South imagined as they came to a common view on race and reconciled their differences. White southerners cultivated national reconciliation but remained fiercely dedicated to preserving the peculiarities of their region: a one-party political system, disfranchisement of African Americans, and segregation by law. The region's urban and industrial growth, impressive from the vantage of 1865, paled before that of the North. The South remained a colonial economy characterized more by deep rural poverty than urban prosperity.

How one viewed the New South depended on one's vantage point. White northerners accepted at face value the picture white southerners painted for them of a chastened and prosperous, yet still attractive, region. Middle-class white people in the urban South enjoyed the benefits of a national economy and a secure social position. Middle-class white women enjoyed increased influence in the public realm, but not to the extent of their northern sisters. And the institutionalization of white supremacy gave even poor white farmers and factory workers a place in the social hierarchy a rung or two above the bottom.

For black people, the New South proved a crueler ruse than Reconstruction. No one now stepped forward to support their cause and stem the erosion of their economic independence, political freedom, and civil rights. Yet they did not give up the American dream, nor did they give up the South for the most part. They built communities and worked as best they could to challenge restrictions on their freedom.

The New South was thus both American and southern. It shared with the rest of the country a period of rapid urban and industrial growth. But the legacy of war and slavery still lay heavily on the South, manifesting itself in rural poverty, segregation, and black disfranchisement. The burdens of this legacy would limit the attainments of both black and white southerners for another half-century, until Americans finally rejected racial inequality as an affront to their national ideals. America allowed the South to take another path and the South took the nation on a long detour until the despised African righted the way.

REVIEW QUESTIONS

1. In what ways did the growing activism of white middle-class women, the increasing assertiveness of young urban black people, and the persistence of the agricultural depression affect the politics of the South in the late 1880s and early 1890s?

2. We associate segregation and disfranchisement with reactionary political and social views. Yet many white people who promoted both seriously believed them to be reforms. How could white people hold such a view?

3. What strategies did black southerners employ in response to the narrowing of economic and political opportunities in the New South?

4. What accounted for Anna J. Cooper's optimism for African American women in the South at a time when southern whites were beginning an extensive legal and physical assault on black civil rights?

5. Why did racial "problems" emerge as a major issue in Europe and the United States in the late nineteenth century?

PEARSON myhistorylab CONNECTIONS

Reinforce what you learned in this chapter by studying the many documents, images, maps, review tools, and videos available at **www.myhistorylab.com.**

READ AND REVIEW

✔— **Study** and **Review** on **myhistorylab.com** STUDY PLAN: CHAPTER 17

Read the **Document** on **myhistorylab.com**

The Nation, "The State of the South" (1872)

John Hill, Testimony on Southern Textile Industry (1883)

Ida B. Wells-Barnett, False Accusations (1895)

Opinion of the Supreme Court for Plessy v. Ferguson (1896)

Booker T. Washington, Atlanta Exposition Address (1895)

RESEARCH AND EXPLORE

Read the **Document** on **myhistorylab.com**

Personal Journeys Online

From Then to Now Online: The Confederate Battle Flag

Exploring America: Racism in America

Listen on **myhistorylab.com**

Address at the Atlanta Exposition by Booker T. Washington

Lynch Law in Georgia

A Republican Textbook for Colored Voters

Watch the **Video** on **myhistorylab.com**

The Lives of Southern Women

Moonlight and Magnolias: Creating the Old South

The Conflict between Booker T. Washington and W. E. B. Du Bois

---

Listen on **myhistorylab.com**

Hear the audio files for Chapter 17 at
www.myhistorylab.com.

18 Industry, Immigrants, and Cities •• 1870–1900

Hear the audio files for Chapter 18 at **www.myhistorylab.com.**

FOCUS QUESTIONS

HOW DID workers respond to the changing demands of the workplace in the late nineteenth century?

WHAT KINDS of communities did new immigrants create in America?

HOW DID the new cities help create the new middle class?

A young boy is at work amid shabby equipment in a dingy glass factory.
Courtesy of the Library of Congress

ONE AMERICAN JOURNEY

We were homeless, houseless, and friendless in a strange place. We had hardly money enough to last us through the voyage for which we had hoped and waited for three long years. We had suffered much that the reunion we longed for might come about; we had prepared ourselves to suffer more in order to bring it about, and had parted with those we loved, with places that were dear to us in spite of what we passed through in them, never again to see them, as we were convinced, all for the same dear end. With strong hopes and high spirits that hid the sad parting, we had started on our long journey. And now we were checked so unexpectedly but surely. . . . When my mother had recovered enough to speak, she began to argue with the gendarme, telling him our story and begging him to be kind. The children were frightened and all but I cried. I was only wondering what would happen. . . . Here we had been taken to a lonely place; . . . our things were taken away, our friends separated from us; a man came to inspect us, as if to ascertain our full value; strange- looking people driving us about like dumb animals, helpless and unresisting; children we could not see crying in a way that suggested terrible things; ourselves driven into a little room where a great kettle was boiling on a little stove; our clothes taken off, our bodies rubbed with a slippery substance that might be any bad thing; a shower of warm water let down on us without warning. . . . We are forced to pick out our clothes from among all the others, with the steam blinding us; we choke, cough, entreat the women to give us time; they persist, "Quick! Quick!, or you'll miss the train!", Oh, so we really won't be murdered! They are only making us ready for the continuing of our journey, cleaning us of all suspicions of dangerous sickness. Thank God! . . .

Oh, what solemn thoughts I had! How deeply I felt the greatness, the power of the scene! The immeasurable distance from horizon to horizon; . . . the absence of any object besides the one ship; . . . I was conscious only of sea and sky and something I did not understand. And as I listened to its solemn voice, I felt as if I had found a friend, and knew that I loved the ocean.

Mary Antin

Mary Antin, *The Promised Land* (Boston: Houghton Mifflin Co., 1912), chap. VIII.

MARY ANTIN, a 13-year-old Jewish girl describes her family's perilous journey from persecution in tsarist Russia to the ship that would take her from Hamburg, Germany, to faraway America. In 1894, Mary and her mother and sisters set out from their village to join her father in Boston.

Millions of European immigrants made similar journeys across the Atlantic (as did Chinese and Japanese immigrants, across the Pacific), a trip fraught with danger, unpredictable detours, occasional heartbreak, the sundering of family ties, and the fear of the unknown. So powerful was the promise of American life for the migrants that they willingly risked these obstacles to come to the United States.

For Mary, America did indeed prove to be *The Promised Land*, as she titled her emigration memoir, published in 1912. At the age of 15, she published her first poem in the *Boston Herald* and, after attending Barnard College in New York City, she wrote on immigrant issues, lectured widely, and worked for Theodore Roosevelt's Progressive Party. She fought against immigration- restriction legislation and promoted public education as the main channel of upward mobility for immigrants.

Mary and her family were part of a major demographic and economic transformation in the United States between 1870 and 1900. Rapid industrial development changed the nature of the workforce and the workplace. Large factories staffed by semiskilled laborers displaced the skilled artisans and small shops that had dominated American industry before 1870. Industrial development also accelerated urbanization. Between the Civil War and 1900, the proportion of the nation's population living in cities, swelled by migrants from the countryside and immigrants from Europe and Asia, increased from 20 to 40 percent, a rate of growth twice that of the population as a whole. During the 1880s alone, more than 5 million immigrants came to the United States, twice as many as in any previous decade.

The changes in American life were exhilarating for some, tragic for others. New opportunities opened as old opportunities disappeared. Vast new wealth was created, but poverty increased. New technologies eased life for some but left others untouched. It would be the great dilemma of early-twentieth-century America to reconcile these contradictions and satisfy the American quest for a decent life for all within the new urban industrial order.

Late-nineteenth-century America is often called the **Gilded Age.** The term is taken from the title of a novel by Mark Twain that satirizes the materialistic excesses of the day. It serves as a shorthand description of the shallow worship of wealth, and the veneer of respectability and prosperity covering deep economic and social divisions, that characterized the period. Even so, an array of opportunities opened for more Americans than at any previous time in the nation's history.

NEW INDUSTRY

Between 1870 and 1900, the United States transformed itself from an agricultural nation, a nation of farmers, merchants, and artisans, into the world's foremost industrial power, producing more than one-third of the world's manufactured goods. By the early twentieth century, factory workers made up one-fourth of the workforce, and agricultural workers had dropped from a half to less than a third.

Although the size of the industrial workforce increased dramatically, the number of firms in any given industry shrank. Mergers, changes in corporate management and the organization of the workforce, and a compliant government left a few companies in control of vast segments of the American economy. Workers, reformers, and eventually government challenged this concentration of economic power.

INVENTING TECHNOLOGY: THE ELECTRIC AGE

Technology played a major role in transforming factory work and increasing the scale of production. Steam engines and, later, electricity, freed manufacturers from dependence on water power. Factories no longer had to be located by rivers. Technology also enabled managers to substitute machines for workers, skewing the balance of power in the workplace toward employers. And it transformed city life, making available a host of new conveniences. By the early twentieth century, electric lights, appliances, ready-made clothing, and store-bought food eased middle-class life. Electric trolleys whisked clerks, salespeople, bureaucrats, and bankers to new urban and suburban subdivisions. Electric streetlights lit up city streets at night.

CHRONOLOGY

1869   The Knights of Labor is founded in Philadelphia.

1870   John D. Rockefeller organizes the Standard Oil Company.
Congress passes the Naturalization Act barring Asians from citizenship.

1871   Unification of Germany in the wake of rising nationalism following the
Franco-Prussian War.

1876   The Centennial Exposition opens in Philadelphia.
Beginning of the rule of dictator Porfirio Diaz in Mexico, whose regime is
ended by the Mexican Revolution.

1877   Execution of ten Molly Maguires in Pennsylvania.
The Great Uprising railroad strike, the first nationwide work stoppage in
the United States, provokes violent clashes between workers and federal
troops.

1879   Thomas Edison unveils the electric light bulb.

1880   Founding of the League of American Wheelmen helps establish bicycling as
one of urban America's favorite recreational activities.

1881   Assassination of Tsar Alexander II begins a series of pogroms that triggers a
wave of Russian Jewish immigration to the United States.

1882   Congress passes the Chinese Exclusion Act.
First country club in the United States founded in Brookline, Massachusetts.

1883   National League merges with the American Association and opens baseball
to working-class fans.

1884   Berlin Conference on Africa to set rules for competing European powers
annexing African territory.

1886   The Neighborhood Guild, the nation's first settlement house, opens in New
York City.
Riot in Chicago's Haymarket Square breaks the Knights of Labor.
American Federation of Labor is formed.

1887   Anti-Catholic American Protective Association is formed.

1888   Wanamaker's department store introduces a "bargain room," and
competitors follow suit.

1889   Jane Addams opens Hull House, the nation's most celebrated
settlement house, in Chicago.

1890   Jacob A. Riis publishes *How the Other Half Lives*.

1891   African American Chicago physician Daniel Hale Williams establishes
Provident Hospital, the nation's first interracially staffed hospital.

1892	General Electric opens the first corporate research and development division in the United States.
	Strike at Andrew Carnegie's Homestead steelworks fails.
1894	Pullman Sleeping Car Company strike fails.
	Immigration Restriction League is formed.
1895	American-born Chinese in California form the Native Sons of the Golden State to counter nativism.
1897	George C. Tilyou opens Steeplechase Park on Coney Island in Brooklyn, New York.
	First Zionist Congress meets in Switzerland, proclaiming its aim to create a home in Palestine for the Jewish people.
1898	Congress passes the Erdman Act to provide for voluntary mediation of railroad labor disputes.

For much of the nineteenth century, the United States was dependent on the industrial nations of Europe for technological innovation. In the late nineteenth century, the United States changed from a technology borrower to a technology innovator. By 1910, a million patents had been issued in the United States, 900,000 of them after 1870.

Nothing represented this shift better than Thomas A. Edison's development of a practical electric light bulb and electric generating system. Edison's invention transformed electricity into a new and versatile form of industrial energy. It also reflected a change in the relationship between science and technology. Until the late nineteenth century, advances in scientific theory usually followed technological innovation, rather than the other way around. Techniques for making steel, for example, developed before scientific theories emerged to explain how they worked. In contrast, scientists had developed a theoretical understanding of electricity long before Edison unveiled his light bulb in 1879. Edison's research laboratory at Menlo Park, New Jersey, also established a model for corporate-sponsored research and development that would rapidly increase the pace of technological innovation.

Edison's initial success touched off a wave of research and development in Germany, Austria, Great Britain, France, and the United States. Whoever could light the world cheaply and efficiently held the key to an enormous fortune. Ultimately, the prize fell not to Edison but to Elihu Thomson. Thomson purchased Edison's General Electric Company in 1892 and established the country's first corporate research and development division. His scientists produced what was then the most efficient light bulb design, and by 1914, General Electric was producing 85 percent of the world's light bulbs.

Following this precedent, other American companies established research and development laboratories. Standard Oil, U.S. Rubber, the chemical giant Du Pont, and the photographic company Kodak all became world leaders in their respective industries because of innovations their laboratories developed.

The process of invention that emerged in the United States gave the country a commanding technological lead. But the modernization of industry that made the United States the world's foremost industrial nation after 1900 reflected organizational as well as technological innovation. As industries sought efficient ways to apply technology and expand their markets within and beyond national borders, their workforces expanded, and their need for capital mounted. Coping with these changes required significant changes in corporate management.

THE CORPORATION AND ITS IMPACT

The modern corporation provided the structural framework for the transformation of the American economy. A corporation is an association of individuals that is legally authorized to act as a fictional "person" and thus relieves its individual members of certain legal liabilities. A key feature of a corporation is the separation of ownership from management. A corporation can raise capital by selling ownership shares, or stock, to people who have no direct role in running it.

The corporation had two major advantages over other forms of business organization that made it attractive to investors. First, unlike a partnership, which dissolves when a partner dies, a corporation can outlive its founders. This durability permits long-term planning. Second, a corporation's officials and shareholders are not personally liable for its debts. If it goes bankrupt, they stand to lose only what they have invested in it.

As large corporations emerged in major American industries, they had a ripple effect on the economy. To build plants, merge with or acquire other companies, develop new technology, and hire workers, large corporations needed huge supplies of capital. They turned to the banks to help meet these needs, and the banks grew in response. The corporations stimulated technological change as they looked for ways to speed production, improve products, and lower costs. As they grew, they generated jobs.

Large industrial corporations also changed the nature of work. By the early twentieth century, control of the workplace was shifting to managers, and semiskilled and unskilled workers were replacing skilled artisans. These new workers, often foreign-born, performed repetitive tasks for low wages.

Because corporations usually located factories in cities, they stimulated urban growth. Large industrial districts sprawled along urban rivers and rail lines. By 1900, fully 90 percent of all manufacturing occurred in cities.

Two organizational strategies, vertical integration and horizontal integration, helped successful corporations reduce competition and dominate their industries. **Vertical integration** involved the consolidation of all functions related to a particular industry, from the extraction and transport of raw materials to manufacturing and finished-product distribution and sales. Vertical integration reduced a company's dependence on outside suppliers, cutting costs and delays.

Horizontal integration involved the merger of competitors in the same industry. John D. Rockefeller's Standard Oil Company pioneered horizontal integration in the 1880s. He began investing in Cleveland oil refineries by his mid-twenties and formed Standard Oil in 1870. Using a variety of tactics, including threats, deceit, and price wars, Rockefeller rapidly acquired most of his competitors. Supported by investment bankers like J. P. Morgan, Standard Oil controlled 90 percent of the nation's oil refining by

Electricity conquered space and the night. The yellow glow of incandescent bulbs, the whiz of trolleys, and the rumble of elevated railways energize the Bowery, an emerging entertainment district in lower Manhattan at the end of the nineteenth century.

1890. Acquiring oil fields and pipelines as well as refineries, it achieved both vertical and horizontal integration.

Other entrepreneurs achieved similar dominance in other industries and amassed similarly enormous fortunes. The concentration of industry in the hands of a few powerful corporate monopolies or **trusts**, as they came to be known, alarmed many Americans. Giant corporations set prices, influenced politicians, and threatened to restrict opportunities for small entrepreneurs like the shopkeepers, farmers, and artisans who abounded at mid-century. Impersonal and governed by profit, the modern corporation challenged the ideal of the self-made man and the belief that success and advancement would reward hard work. These concerns eventually prompted the federal and state governments to respond with antitrust and other regulatory laws (see Chapters 20 and 21).

The entrepreneurs operated in an environment that allowed them free rein. They had access to capital, markets, and technology. And when they did not, they created it. Above all, they were innovators. The integration of the nation's transportation and communication infrastructure, the managerial revolution that rationalized the operation of geographically distant units and large and diverse work forces, and the application of continuous flow production pioneered in flour mills long before Henry Ford adapted it to car manufacturing, were a few of the innovations entrepreneurs devised to make their operations more efficient and profitable in the postwar years.

The large corporation changed how Americans lived their daily lives. People moved to cities in unprecedented numbers. They purchased goods that did not exist or that had limited distribution prior to the Civil War. They worked in an environment where management and labor became ever more distinct. And they established new consumption patterns in purchasing and furnishing their dwellings and in their leisure activities. Their lives revolved around family, work, and leisure. They were modern Americans.

THE CHANGING NATURE OF WORK

The growth of giant corporations was a mixed blessing. The corporations provided abundant jobs, but they firmly controlled working conditions, especially for those who worked with their hands instead of their brains.

As late as the 1880s, shops of skilled artisans were responsible for most manufacturing in the United States. Since the mid-century, however, industrialists had been introducing ways to simplify manufacturing processes so that they could hire low-skilled workers. This deskilling process accelerated in the 1890s in response to new technologies, new workers, and workplace reorganization.

Mechanization and technological innovation did not reduce employment, although they did eliminate some jobs, most of them skilled. On the contrary, the birth of whole new industries—steel, automobiles, electrical equipment, cigarettes, food canning, and machine tools— created a huge demand for workers. Innovations in existing industries, like railroads, similarly spurred job growth.

Ironically, it was a shortage of skilled workers as much as other factors that encouraged industrialists to mechanize. Unskilled workers cost less than the scarce artisans. And with massive waves of immigrants arriving from Europe and Asia between 1880 and 1920 (joined after 1910 by migrants from the American South), the supply of unskilled workers seemed limitless.

Low Salaries and Long Hours. The new workers shared little of the wealth generated by industrial expansion and enjoyed few of the gadgets and products generated by the new manufacturing. Nor did large corporations put profits into improved working conditions. In 1881, on-the-job accidents maimed or killed 30,000 railroad workers. Safety equipment existed that could have prevented many of these injuries, but the railroads refused to purchase it. At a U.S. Steel plant in Pittsburgh, injuries or death claimed one out of every four workers between 1907 and 1910.

Factory workers typically worked 10 hours a day, six days a week in the 1880s. Steel workers put in 12 hours a day. The mills operated around the clock, so once every two weeks, when the workers changed shifts, one group had to take a "long turn" and stay on the job for 24 hours.

Long hours affected family life. By Sunday, most factory workers were too tired to do more than sit around home. During the week, they had time only to eat and sleep. Workers lived as close to the factory as possible, to reduce the time and expense of getting to work.

Big factories were not characteristic of all industries after 1900. In some, like the "needle," or garment, trade, operations remained small scale. But salaries and working conditions in these industries were, if anything, worse than in the big factories. The garment industry was dominated by small manufacturers who assembled clothing for retailers from cloth provided by textile manufacturers. The manufacturers squeezed workers into small, cramped, poorly ventilated **sweatshops.** These might be in attics or lofts or even in the workers' own dwellings. Workers pieced together garments on the manufacturer's sewing machines. A government investigator in Chicago in the 1890s described one sweatshop in a three-room tenement where the workers, a family of eight, both lived and worked: "The father, mother, two daughters, and a cousin work together making trousers at seventy-five cents a dozen pairs. … They work seven days a week. … Their destitution is very great."

CHILD LABOR

Child labor was common in the garment trade and other industries. Industries that employed many children were often dangerous, even for adults. In the gritty coal mines of Pennsylvania, breaker boys, youths who stood on ladders to pluck waste matter from coal tumbling down long chutes, breathed harmful coal dust all day. Girls under 16 made up half the workforce in the silk mills of Scranton and Wilkes-Barre, Pennsylvania. Girls with missing fingers from mill accidents were a common sight in those towns.

By 1900, under pressure from reformers, Pennsylvania and a few other states had passed legislation regulating child labor, but enforcement of these laws was lax. Parents desperate for income often lied about their children's age, and government officials were usually sympathetic toward mill or mine owners, who paid taxes and provided other civic benefits.

WORKING WOMEN

Women accompanied children into the workforce outside the home in increasing numbers after 1870. The comparatively low wages of unskilled male workers often required women family members to work as well. Between 1870 and 1920, the number of women and children in the workforce more than doubled.

Like child labor, the growing numbers of women in the workforce alarmed middle-class reformers. They worried about the impact on family life and on the women themselves. Streets in working-class districts teemed with unsupervised children. Working-class men were also concerned. The trend toward deskilling favored women. Employers, claiming that women worked only for supplemental money, paid them less than men. In one St. Louis factory in 1896, women received $4 a week for work for which men were paid $16 a week.

Most women worked out of economic necessity. In 1900, fully 85 percent of wage-earning women were unmarried and under the age of 25. They supported siblings and contributed to their parents' income. A typical female factory worker earned $6 a week in 1900. On this wage, a married woman might help pull her family up to subsistence level. For a single woman on her own, however, it allowed little more, in the writer O. Henry's words, "than marshmallows and tea." Her lodging rarely consisted of more than one room.

Over time, more work options opened to women, but low wages and poor working conditions persisted. Women entered the needle trades after widespread introduction of the sewing machine in the 1870s. Factories gradually replaced sweatshops in the garment industry after 1900, but working conditions improved little.

Noted urban and labor photographer Lewis Hine's crusade against child labor included this photo of breaker boys at a Pennsylvania coal mine, 1910. The boys worked in a constant cloud of coal dust picking out refuse from coal coming down chutes. Note the overseer with a stick at right.

On the factory floor, young women had less room for negotiation because the customer was far removed from the manufacturing process, but they banded together, sometimes in labor unions after 1900, to demand and receive concessions from management. Working women, no less than working men, refused to be inanimate recipients of bosses' decrees and working conditions. And if a young woman could obtain some basic skills, other opportunities loomed as well.

The introduction of the typewriter transformed office work, dominated by men until the 1870s, into a female preserve. Women were alleged to have the dexterity and tolerance for repetition that the new technology required. But they earned only half the salary of the men they replaced. Middle-class parents saw office work as clean and honorable compared with factory or sales work. Consequently, clerical positions drew growing numbers of native-born women into the urban workforce after 1890.

By the turn of the century, women were gaining increased access to higher education. Coeducational colleges were rare, but by 1900 there were many women-only institutions. By 1910, women comprised 40 percent of all American college students, compared to 20 percent in 1870. Despite these gains, many professions, including those of physician and attorney, remained closed to women. Men still accounted for more than 95 percent of all doctors in 1900. Women also were rarely permitted to pursue doctoral degrees.

Most women college graduates found employment in such "nurturing" professions as nursing, teaching, and library work. Between 1900 and 1910, the number of trained women nurses increased sevenfold. In response to the growing problems of urban society, a relatively new occupation, social work, opened to women. There were

1,000 women social workers in 1890 and nearly 30,000 by 1920. Reflecting new theories on the nurturing role of women, school boards after 1900 turned exclusively to female teachers for the elementary grades. Despite these gains, women's work remained segregated. More than 90 percent of all wage-earning women in 1900 worked at occupations in which women comprised the great majority of workers. Some reforms meant to improve working conditions for women reinforced this state of affairs. Protective legislation restricted women to "clean" occupations and limited their ability to compete with men in other jobs.

Women also confronted negative stereotypes. Most Americans in 1900 believed a woman's proper role was to care for home and family. The single working woman faced doubts about her virtue. The system of "treating" on dates reinforced stories about loose salesgirls, flirtatious secretaries, and easy factory workers. Newspapers and magazines published exposes of working girls descending into prostitution. These images encouraged sexual harassment at work, which was rarely punished. Still, for a girl growing up after the Civil War, many more possibilities were open to her than before. Louisa May Alcott's *Little Women* appeared in 1868 and became the biggest selling novel since Harriet Beecher Stowe's *Uncle Tom's Cabin*. If any indicator summarized the difference between the overheated 1850s with its imagery of sin and salvation and the postwar era of promise and economic prosperity, it was the transition from Stowe to Alcott. Of the four March girls in Alcott's novel, Josephine, who preferred the masculine-sounding "Jo," became a writer. Meg, a governess, dreamed of acting; Amy, a schoolgirl, hoped to become a great painter. Beth, the only March girl who did not imagine a career outside the home, died prematurely of unknown causes.

RESPONSES TO POVERTY AND WEALTH

Concerns about working women merged with larger anxieties about the growing numbers of impoverished workers in the nation's cities during the 1890s and the widening gap between rich and poor. While industrial magnates flaunted their fabulous wealth, working men and women led hard lives on meager salaries and in crowded dwellings.

Inadequate housing was the most visible badge of poverty. Crammed into four- to six-story buildings on tiny lots, **tenement** apartments in urban slums were notorious for their lack of ventilation and light. Authorities did nothing to enforce laws prohibiting overcrowding for fear of leaving people homeless.

One early attempt to deal with these conditions was the settlement house. The settlement house movement, which originated in England, sought to moderate the effects of poverty through neighborhood reconstruction. New York's Neighborhood Guild, established in 1886, was the first settlement house in the country; Chicago's **Hull House,** founded in 1889 by Jane Addams, a young Rockford (Illinois) College graduate, became the most famous. Addams had visited settlement houses in England and thought the idea would work well in American cities.

The Gospel of Wealth. Late-nineteenth-century political ideology discouraged more comprehensive efforts to remedy urban poverty until the Progressive Era (discussed in Chapter 21). According to the Gospel of Wealth, a theory popular among industrialists, intellectuals, and some politicians, any intervention on behalf of the poor was of doubtful benefit. Hard work and perseverance, in this view, led to wealth. Poverty, by implication, resulted from the faulty character of the poor.

The new industrial age created great wealth and abject poverty, and the city became the stage upon which these hard economic lessons played out. Here a "modest" Fifth Avenue mansion in turn-of-the-century New York City; farther downtown, Jacob Riis found this tenement courtyard.

A flawed attempt to apply Charles Darwin's theory of biological evolution to human society emerged as a more common justification than the Gospel of Wealth for the growing gap between rich and poor. According to the theory of **Social Darwinism,** the human race evolves only through competition. The fit survive, the weak perish, and humanity moves forward. Wealth reflects fitness; poverty, weakness. For governments or private agencies to interfere with this natural process is futile. Thus, Columbia University president Nicholas Murray Butler, claiming that "nature's cure for most social and political diseases is better than man's," warned against charity for the poor in 1900.

WORKERS ORGANIZE

Wild swings in the business cycle, the fluctuation between periods of growth and contraction in the economy, aggravated tensions between labor and management. Two prolonged depressions, one beginning in 1873 and the other in 1893, threw as many as 2 million laborers out of work. Skilled workers, their security undermined by deskilling, were hit particularly hard. Their hopes of becoming managers or starting their own businesses disappearing, they saw the nation "drifting," as a carpenter put it in 1870, "to that condition of society where a few were rich, and the many very poor."

Beginning after the Civil War and continuing through World War I, workers fought their loss of independence to industrial capital by organizing and striking (see the Overview table, Workers Organize). Violence often accompanied these actions.

Such was the case with the railroad strike of 1877, sometimes referred to as the **Great Uprising.** The four largest railroads, in the midst of a depression and in the wake of a series of pay cuts over the preceding four years, agreed to slash wages yet again. When Baltimore & Ohio Railroad workers struck in July to protest the cut, President Rutherford B. Hayes dispatched federal troops to protect the line's property. The use of federal troops infuriated railroad workers throughout the East and Midwest, and they stopped work. Violence erupted in Pittsburgh when the state militia opened fire on strikers and their families, killing 25, including a woman and three children. As news of the violence spread, so did the strike, as far as Galveston, Texas, and San Francisco. Over the next two weeks, police and federal troops continued to clash with strikers. By the time this first nationwide work stoppage in American history ended, more than 100 had been killed. The wage cuts remained.

The **Knights of Labor,** a union of craft workers founded in Philadelphia in 1869, grew dramatically after the Great Uprising under the leadership of Terence V. Powderly. Reflecting the views of many skilled workers, the Knights saw "an inevitable … conflict between the wage system of labor and [the] republican system of government." Remarkably inclusive for its time, the Knights welcomed black workers and women to its ranks. Victories in several small railroad strikes in 1884 and 1885 boosted its membership to nearly 1 million workers by 1886.

In that year, the Knights led a movement for an eight-hour workday. Ignoring the advice of the national leadership to avoid strikes, local chapters staged more than 1,500 strikes involving more than 340,000 workers. Employers fought back. They persuaded the courts to order strikers back to work and used local authorities to arrest strikers for trespassing or obstructing traffic. In early May 1886, police killed four unarmed workers during a skirmish with strikers in Chicago. Rioting broke out when a bomb exploded at a meeting in Haymarket Square to protest the slayings. The bomb killed seven policemen and four strikers and left 100 people wounded. Eight strike leaders were tried for the deaths, and despite the lack of evidence linking them to the bomb, four were executed.

The Haymarket Square incident, and a series of disastrous walkouts that followed it, weakened the Knights of Labor. By 1890, it had fewer than 100,000 members. Thereafter, the **American Federation of Labor** (AFL), founded in 1886, became the major organizing body for skilled workers.

The AFL was much less ambitious, and less inclusive, than the Knights of Labor. Led by a British immigrant, Samuel Gompers, it emphasized **collective bargaining,** negotiations between management and union representatives, to secure workplace concessions. The AFL also discouraged political activism. With this business unionism, the AFL proved more effective than the Knights of Labor at meeting the needs of skilled workers, but it left out the growing numbers of unskilled workers, black workers, and women workers, to whom the Knights had given a glimmer of hope.

Rather than including all workers in one large union, the AFL organized skilled workers by craft. It then focused on a few basic workplace issues important to each craft. The result was greater cohesion and discipline. In 1889 and 1890, more than 60 percent of AFL-sponsored strikes were successful, a remarkable record in an era when most strikes failed. Responding to this success, employers determined to break the power of craft unions just as they had destroyed the Knights. In 1892, Andrew Carnegie dealt the steelworkers' union a major setback in the Homestead strike. Carnegie's manager,

OVERVIEW WORKERS ORGANIZE

Organization	History	Strategies
Knights of Labor	Founded in 1869; open to all workers; declined after 1886	Disapproved of strikes; supported an array of labor reforms, including cooperatives; favored broad political involvement
American Federation of Labor	Founded in 1886; open only to craft workers and organized by craft; hostile to blacks and women; became the major U.S. labor organization after 1880s	Opposed political involvement; supported a limited number of labor reforms; approved of strikes

Henry Clay Frick, announced to workers at Carnegie's Homestead plant in Pennsylvania that he would not renew the union's collective bargaining contract. Expecting a strike, Frick locked the union workers out of the plant and hired 300 armed guards to protect the nonunion ("scab") workers he planned to hire in their place. Union workers, with the help of their families and unskilled workers, seized control of Homestead's roads and utilities. In a bloody confrontation, they drove back Frick's forces. Nine strikers and seven guards died. But Pennsylvania's governor called out the state militia to open the plant and protect the nonunion workers. After four months, the union capitulated. With this defeat, skilled steelworkers lost their power on the shop floor. Eventually, mechanization cost them their jobs.

In 1894, workers suffered another setback in the Pullman strike, against George Pullman's Palace Sleeping Car Company. The strike began when the company cut wages for workers at its plant in the "model" suburb it had built outside Chicago, without a corresponding cut in the rent it charged workers for their company-owned housing. When Pullman rejected their demands, the workers appealed for support to the American Railway Union (ARU), led by Eugene V. Debs. On behalf of the Pullman strikers, Debs ordered a boycott of any trains with Pullman cars, disrupting train travel in several parts of the country. The railroads claimed to be innocent victims of a local dispute, and with growing public support, they fired workers who refused to handle trains with Pullman cars. Debs called for all ARU members to walk off the job, crippling rail travel nationwide. When Debs refused to honor a federal court injunction against the strike, President Cleveland, at the railroads' request, ordered federal troops to enforce it. Debs was arrested, and the strike and the union were broken.

These setbacks, and the depression that began in 1893, left workers and their unions facing an uncertain future. But growing public opposition to the use of troops, the high-handed tactics of industrialists, and the rising concerns of Americans about the power of big business sustained the unions. Workers would call more than 22,000 strikes over the next decade, the majority of them union-sponsored. Still, no more than 7 percent of the American workforce was organized by 1900. By that time, a dramatic change in the industrial workforce was afoot. As the large factories installed labor- and time-saving machinery, unskilled foreign-born labor flooded into the shop floor.

Immigrants transformed not only the workplace, but also the cities where they settled and the nation many eventually adopted. In the process, they changed themselves.

New Immigrants

The late nineteenth century was a period of unprecedented worldwide population movements. The United States was not the only New World destination for the migrants of this period. Many also found their way to Brazil, Argentina, and Canada. The scale of overseas migration to the United States after 1870, however, dwarfed all that preceded it. Between 1870 and 1910, the country received more than 20 million immigrants. Before the Civil War, most immigrants came from northern Europe. Most of the new immigrants, by contrast, came from southern and eastern Europe. Swelling their ranks were migrants from Mexico and Asia, as well as internal migrants moving from the countryside to American cities (see Map 18–1).

Old World Backgrounds

The people of southern and eastern Europe had long been accustomed to migrating within Europe on a seasonal basis to find work to support their families. In the final quarter of the nineteenth century, however, several factors drove migrants beyond the borders of Europe and into the Western Hemisphere.

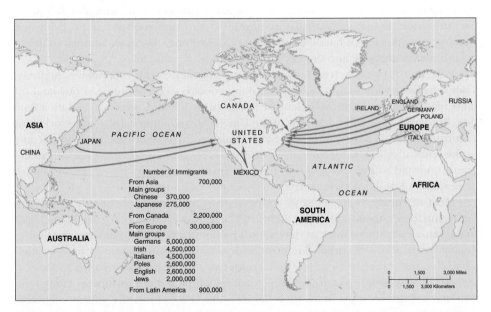

MAP 18–1 • Patterns of Immigration, 1820–1914 The migration to the United States was part of a worldwide transfer of population that accelerated with the industrial revolution and the accompanying improvement in transportation.

▶ *What forces propelled so many people to emigrate from European countries? How did conditions in the United States in the late nineteenth century differ from those in south and central Europe?*

A growing rural population combined with unequal land distribution to create economic distress in late-nineteenth-century Europe. With land ownership concentrated in increasingly fewer hands, more and more people found themselves working ever smaller plots as laborers rather than owners.

For Russian Jews, religious persecution compounded economic hardship. After the assassination of Tsar Alexander II in 1881, which was falsely blamed on Jews, the government sanctioned a series of violent attacks on Jewish settlements; these attacks were known as **pogroms.** At the same time, the government forced Jews into fewer towns, deepening their poverty and making them easier targets for violence.

Chinese and Japanese immigrants also came to the United States in appreciable numbers for the first time during the late nineteenth century. Most Chinese immigrants came from Canton in South China, a region of great rural poverty. They worked on railroads and in mines throughout the West and as farm laborers in California. Many eventually settled in cities such as San Francisco, where they established residential enclaves referred to as Chinatowns. The Chinese population in the United States peaked at about 125,000 in 1882.

Japanese began immigrating to the United States in the late 1880s, driven by a land shortage even more acute than the one in Europe. The first wave came by way of Hawaii to work on farms in California, taking the place of Chinese workers who had moved to the cities. By 1900, there were some 50,000 Japanese immigrants in the United States, nearly all on the West Coast.

Some immigrants came from right on our borders. In the late nineteenth century, Mexicans came across the border to work on the ranches and cotton farms of south and west Texas. Unlike their counterparts from Asia and Europe, these migrants settled primarily in rural areas. Whether on farms, in squalid quarters in the *barrios* of El Paso or San Antonio, or in the smaller urban centers in South Texas, such as Laredo, living and working conditions were harsh. By the turn of the century, Mexican laborers in urban areas began to organize into unions.

Wherever they came from, most migrants saw their route as a two-way highway. They intended to stay only a year or two, long enough to earn money to buy land or, more likely, to start a business back home and improve life for themselves and their families. Roughly half of all immigrants to the United States between 1880 and World War I returned to their country of origin. Some made several round trips. Jews, unwelcome in the lands they left, were the exception. No more than 10 percent of Jewish immigrants returned to Europe, and very few Jews from Russia, who accounted for almost 80 percent of Jewish immigrants after 1880, went back home.

Most of the newcomers were young men. (Jews, again, were the exception: Reflecting their intention to stay in their new home, they tended to migrate in families.) Immigrants easily found work in the nation's booming cities. The quickest way to make money was in the large urban factories, with their voracious demands for unskilled labor. Except for the Japanese, few immigrants came to work on farms after 1880.

By 1900, women began to equal men among all immigrant groups as young men who had decided to stay sent for their families. In a few cases, entire villages migrated, drawn by the good fortune of one or two compatriots, a process called **chain migration.** The success of Francesco Barone, a Buffalo tavern owner, induced 8,000 residents of his former village in Sicily to migrate to that city, many arriving on tickets Barone purchased.

Immigrants tended to live in neighborhoods among people from the same homeland. The desire of the new immigrants to retain their cultural traditions led contemporary observers to doubt their ability to assimilate into American society. Even sympathetic observers, such as social workers, marveled at the utterly foreign character of immigrant districts.

CULTURAL CONNECTIONS IN A NEW WORLD

Immigrants maintained their cultural traditions through the establishment of religious and communal institutions. Charitable organizations were frequently connected to religious institutions. The church or synagogue became the focal point for immigrant neighborhood life. Much more than a place of worship, it was a school for transmitting Old World values and language to American-born children. The church or synagogue also functioned as a recreational facility and a gathering place for community leaders. In Jewish communities, associations called *landsmanshaften* arranged for burials, jobs, housing, and support for the sick, poor, and elderly. Because religious institutions were so central to their lives, immigrant communities insisted on maintaining control over them.

Religious institutions played a less formal role among Chinese and Japanese neighborhoods. For them, the family functioned as the source of religious activity and communal organization. Chinatowns were organized in clans of people with the same surname. An umbrella organization called the Chinese Consolidated Benevolent Association emerged; it functioned like the Jewish *landsmanshaften*. A similar association, the Japanese Association of America, governed the Japanese community in the

Mulberry Street, New York, 1905. The vibrant, predominantly Russian-Jewish Lower East Side of New York at first reflected more the culture of the homeland than of the United States. Language, dress, and ways of doing business, keeping house, and worshiping, all followed Old World patterns. Gradually, thanks especially to the influence of school-age children, a blend of Russian Jewish and American traditions emerged.

United States. This organization was sponsored by the Japanese government, which was sensitive to mistreatment of its citizens abroad and anxious that immigrants set a good example. The Japanese Association, unlike other ethnic organizations, actively encouraged assimilation and stressed the importance of Western dress and learning English.

Ethnic newspapers, theaters, and schools supplemented associational life for immigrants. These institutions reinforced Old World culture while informing immigrants about American ways. Thus, the *Jewish Daily Forward,* first published in New York in 1897, reminded readers of the importance of keeping the Sabbath while admonishing them to adopt American customs.

THE JOB

If immigrant culture provided newcomers with a supportive environment, work offered the ultimate reward for coming to America. All immigrants perceived the job as the way to independence and as a way out, either back to the Old World or into the larger American society.

Immigrants typically got their first job with the help of a countryman. Italian, Chinese, Japanese, and Mexican newcomers worked with contractors who placed them in jobs. These middlemen often provided housing, loans, and other services for recent arrivals. Other immigrant groups, such as Poles and Russian Jews, often found work through their ethnic associations or village or family connections. Family members sometimes exchanged jobs with one another.

The type of work available to immigrants depended on their skills, the local economy, and local discrimination. Mexican migrants to southern California, for example, concentrated in railroad construction. Mostly unskilled, they replaced Chinese laborers when the federal government prohibited Chinese immigration after 1882. Mexicans built the interurban rail lines of Los Angeles in 1900 and established communities at their construction camps. Los Angeles businessmen barred Mexicans from other occupations. Similarly, Chinese immigrants were confined to work in laundries and restaurants within the boundaries of Los Angeles's Chinatown.

The Japanese who came to Los Angeles around 1900 were forced into sectors of the economy that native-born white people had either shunned or failed to exploit. The Japanese turned this discrimination to their benefit when they transformed the cultivation of market-garden crops into a major agricultural enterprise. By 1904, Japanese farmers owned more than 50,000 acres in California.

Stereotypes also channeled immigrants' work options, sometimes benefiting one group at the expense of another. Jewish textile entrepreneurs, for example, sometimes hired only Italians because they thought them less prone to unionization than Jewish workers. Other Jewish bosses hired only Jewish workers, hoping that ethnic loyalty would overcome the lure of the unions. Pittsburgh steelmakers preferred Polish workers to the black workers who began arriving in northern cities in appreciable numbers after 1900. This decision began the decades-long tradition of handing down steel mill jobs through the generations in Polish families.

Jews, alone among European ethnic groups, found work almost exclusively with one another. Among the factors contributing to this pattern may have been the discrimination Jews faced in eastern Europe, the existence of an established Jewish community when they arrived, and their domination of the needle trades. Jews comprised three-quarters of the more than a half-million workers in New York City's garment industry in 1910. Jews were also heavily concentrated in the retail trade.

Like their native-born counterparts, few married immigrant women worked outside the home, but unlike the native-born, many Italian and Jewish women did piecework for the garment industry in their apartments. Unmarried Polish women often worked in factories or as domestic servants. Japanese women, married and single, worked with their families on farms. Until revolution in China in 1911 began to erode traditional gender roles, married Chinese immigrant women typically remained at home.

The paramount goal for many immigrants was to work for themselves rather than for someone else. Most new arrivals, however, had few skills, and no resources beyond their wits, with which to realize their dreams. Major banks at the time were unlikely to extend even a small business loan to a budding ethnic entrepreneur. Family members and small ethnic-based community banks provided the initial stake for most immigrant businesses.

Immigrants could not fully control their own destinies in the United States, any more than native-born Americans could. The vagaries of daily life, including death, disease, and bad luck, thwarted many immigrants' dreams. Hard work did not always ensure success. Add to these the difficulty of cultural adjustment to an unfamiliar environment, and the newcomer's confident hopes could fade quickly. Almost all immigrants, however, faced an obstacle that white native-born Americans did not: the antiforeign prejudice of American nativism.

NATIVISM

Despite the openness of America's borders in the nineteenth century, and contrary to the nation's reputation as a refuge from foreign persecution and poverty, immigrants

"Throwing Down the Ladder by Which They Rose," Thomas Nast's 1870 attack on nativism. White workers, many of them immigrants themselves, objected to labor competition from Chinese immigrants and eventually helped to persuade Congress to pass the Chinese Exclusion Act in 1882.

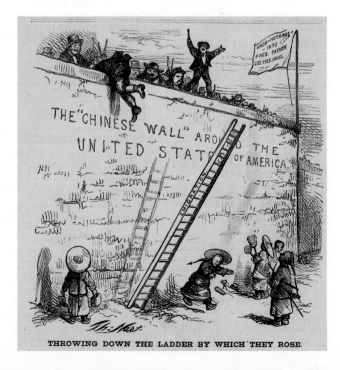

THROWING DOWN THE LADDER BY WHICH THEY ROSE.

AMERICAN VIEWS

TENEMENT LIFE

I n 1890, the Danish immigrant Jacob A. Riis published How the Other Half Lives, an exposé of living conditions among immigrants in New York City's Lower East Side neighborhood. The book, complete with vivid photographs, caused a sensation. At a time when newspapers and magazines competed for readers with lurid tales of urban life, Riis's detailed and gruesome depictions shocked readers and provided an impetus for housing reform in New York and, eventually, across the urban nation. Riis's scientific tone, devoid of sensationalism, rendered the scenes that much more dramatic. For a nation that valued family life and the sanctity of childhood, Riis's accounts of how the environment, inside and outside the tenement, destroyed young lives provided moving testimony that for some and perhaps many immigrants, the "promise" had been taken out of the Promised Land.

- **What** is Jacob Riis's attitude toward the tenement dwellers?
- **Considering** the destitute character of the family Riis describes, what sort of assistance do you think they receive?
- **Why** do you suppose the authorities were reluctant to enforce sanitary, capacity, and building regulations in these neighborhoods?

Look into any of these houses, everywhere the same piles of rags, of malodorous bones and musty paper all of which the sanitary police flatter themselves they have banished. . . . Here is a "parlor" and two pitch-dark coops called bedrooms. Truly, the bed is all there is room for. The family teakettle is on the stove, doing duty for the time being as a wash-boiler. By night it will have returned to its proper use again, a practical illustration of how poverty . . . makes both ends meet. One, two, three beds are there, if the old boxes and heaps of foul straw can be called by that name; a broken stove with crazy pipe from which the smoke leaks at every joint, a table of rough boards propped up on boxes, piles

did not always receive a warm reception. From the 1830s to 1860, nativist sentiment, directed mainly at Irish Catholic immigrants, expressed itself in occasional violence and job discrimination. Anti-immigrant sentiment gave rise to an important political party, the Know-Nothings, in the 1850s.

When immigration revived after the Civil War, so did antiforeign sentiment. But late-nineteenth-century **nativism** differed in two ways from its antebellum predecessor. First, the target was no longer Irish Catholics, but the even more numerous Catholics and Jews of southern and eastern Europe, people whose languages and usually darker complexions set them apart from the native-born majority. Second, late-nineteenth-century nativism had a pseudoscientific underpinning. As we saw in Chapter 17, the "scientific" racism of the period maintained that some people are inherently inferior to others. Social Darwinism, which justified the class hierarchy, reinforced scientific racism.

of rubbish in the corner. The closeness and smell are appalling. . . .

Well do I recollect the visit of a health inspector to one of these tenements on a July day when the thermometer outside was climbing high in the nineties; but inside, in that awful room, with half a dozen persons washing, cooking, and sorting rags, lay the dying baby alongside the stove, where the doctor's thermometer ran up to 115 degrees! Perishing for the want of a breath of fresh air in this city of untold charities! . . .

A message came one day last spring summoning me to a Mott Street tenement in which lay a child dying from some unknown disease. With the "charity doctor" I found the patient on the top floor, stretched upon two chairs in a dreadfully stifling room. She was gasping in the agony of peritonitis [abdominal infection] that had already written its death-sentence on her wan and pinched face. The whole family, father, mother, and four ragged children, sat around looking on with the stony resignation of helpless despair that had long since given up the fight against fate as useless. A glance around the wretched room left no doubt as to the cause of the children's condition. "Improper nourishment," said the doctor, which translated to suit the place, meant starvation. The father's hands were crippled from lead poisoning. He had not been able to work for a year. A contagious disease of the eyes, too long neglected, had made the mother and one of the boys nearly blind. The children cried with hunger. . . . For months the family had subsisted on two dollars a week from the priest, and a few loaves and a piece of corned beef which the sisters sent them on Saturday. The doctor gave direction for the treatment of the child, knowing that it was possible only to alleviate its sufferings until death should end them, and left some money for food for the rest. An hour later, when I returned, I found them feeding the dying child with ginger ale, bought for two cents a bottle at the pedlar's cart down the street. A pitying neighbor had proposed it as the one thing she could think of as likely to make the child forget its misery.

Source: Jacob A. Riis, *How the Other Half Lives: Studies Among the Tenements of New York* (New York: Charles Scribner's Sons, 1890).

When the "inferior" races began to arrive in the United States in significant numbers after 1880, nativists sounded the alarm. A prominent Columbia University professor wrote in 1887 that Hungarians and Italians were "of such a character as to endanger our civilization." Nine years later, the director of the U.S. census warned that eastern and southern Europeans were "beaten men from beaten races. They have none of the ideas and aptitudes which fit men to take up readily and easily the problem of self-care and self-government." The result of unfettered migration would be "race suicide."

The popular press translated these scientific pronouncements into blunter language. In the mid-1870s, a Chicago newspaper described recently arrived immigrants from Bohemia (the present-day Czech Republic) as "depraved beasts, harpies, decayed physically and spiritually, mentally and morally, thievish and licentious." The rhetoric of the scientific press was scarcely less extreme. *Scientific American* magazine warned immigrants to "assimilate" quickly or "share the fate of the native Indians" and face "a quiet but sure extermination."

Such sentiments generated proposals to restrict foreign immigration. The treatment of the Chinese provided a precedent. Chinese immigrants had long worked for low wages, under harsh conditions, in mining and railroad construction in the West. Their different culture and their willingness to accept low wages provoked resentment among native- and European-born workers. Violence against Chinese laborers increased during the 1860s and 1870s. In 1870, the Republican-dominated Congress passed the Naturalization Act, which limited citizenship to "white persons and persons of African descent." The act was specifically intended to prevent Chinese from becoming citizens, a ban not lifted until 1943, but it affected other Asian groups also. The Chinese Exclusion Act of 1882, passed following another decade of anti-Chinese pressure, made the Chinese the only ethnic group in the world that could not immigrate freely into the United States.

Labor competition also contributed to the rise of new anti-immigrant organizations. A group of skilled workers and small businessmen formed the American Protective Association (APA) in 1887 and claimed half a million members a year later. The APA sought to limit Catholic civil rights in the United States to protect the jobs of Protestant workingmen.

The Immigration Restriction League (IRL), formed in 1894 in the midst of a depression, took a more modest and indirect approach. The IRL proposed to require prospective immigrants to pass a literacy test that most southern and eastern Europeans would presumably fail. The IRL ultimately failed to have its literacy requirement enacted. The return of prosperity and the growing preference of industrialists for immigrant labor put an end to calls for formal restrictions on immigration for the time being. Less than 30 years later, however, Congress would enact major restrictive legislation aimed at southern and eastern European immigrants. In the meantime, IRL propaganda encouraged northern universities to establish quotas limiting the admission of new immigrants, especially Jews.

Immigrants and their communal associations fought attempts to restrict immigration. The Japanese government even hinted at violent retaliation if Congress ever enacted restrictive legislation on Japanese similar to that imposed on the Chinese. But most immigrants believed that the more "American" they became, the less prejudice they would encounter. Accordingly, leaders of immigrant groups stressed the importance of assimilation.

Assimilation connotes the loss of one culture in favor of another. The immigrant experience of the late nineteenth and early twentieth century might better be described as a process of adjustment between old ways and new. It was a dynamic process that resulted in entirely new cultural forms. The Japanese, for example, had not gone to Los Angeles to become truck farmers, but circumstances led them to that occupation, and they used their cultural heritage of hard work, strong family ties, and sober living to make a restricted livelihood successful. Sometimes economics and the availability of alternatives resulted in modifications of traditions that nonetheless maintained their spirit. In the old country, Portuguese held *festas* every Sunday honoring a patron saint. In New England towns, they confined the tradition to their churches instead of parading through the streets. And instead of baking bread themselves, Portuguese immigrant women were happy to buy all the bread they needed from local bakers.

Despite the antagonism of native-born white people toward recent immigrants, the greatest racial divide in America remained that between black and white. Newcomers quickly caught on to this distinction and sought to assert their "whiteness" as a common bond with other European immigrant groups and a badge of acceptance into the larger society. For immigrants, therefore, becoming "white," distancing themselves from African American culture and people, was often part of the process of adjusting to American life, especially as increasing numbers of black southerners began moving to northern cities.

ROOTS OF THE GREAT MIGRATION

Nearly 90 percent of African Americans still lived in the South in 1900, most in rural areas. Between 1880 and 1900, however, black families began to move into the great industrial cities of the Northeast and Midwest. They were drawn by the same economic promise that attracted overseas migrants and were pushed by growing persecution in the South. Job opportunities probably outweighed all other factors in motivating what became known as the **Great Migration.**

In most northern cities in 1900, black people typically worked as common laborers or domestic servants. They competed with immigrants for jobs, and in most cases they lost. Immigrants even claimed jobs that black workers had once dominated, such as barbering and service work in hotels, restaurants, and transportation.

Black women had very few options in the northern urban labor force outside of domestic service, although they earned higher wages than they had for similar work in southern cities. The retail and clerical jobs that attracted young working-class white women remained closed to black women. Employers rejected them for any job involving direct contact with the public.

The lack of options black migrants confronted in the search for employment matched similar frustrations in their quest for a place to live. Even more than foreign immigrants, they were restricted to segregated urban ghettos. Small black ghettos existed in antebellum northern cities. As black migration to northern cities accelerated after 1900, the pattern of residential isolation became more pronounced. The black districts in northern cities were more diverse than those in southern cities. Migration brought rural southerners, urban southerners, and West Indians together with the black northerners already living there. People of all social classes lived in these districts.

The difficulties that black families faced to make ends meet paralleled in some ways those of immigrant working-class families. Restricted job options, however, limited the income of black families, even with black married women five times more likely to work than married white women. In black families, moreover, working teenage children were less likely to stay home and contribute their paychecks to the family income.

Popular culture reinforced the marginalization of African Americans. Vaudeville and minstrel shows, popular urban entertainments around 1900, featured songs belittling black people and black characters with names like Useless Peabody and Moses Abraham Highbrow. Immigrants frequented these shows and absorbed the culture of racism from them. The new medium of film perpetuated the negative stereotypes.

In the North as in the South, African Americans sought to counter the hostility of the larger society by building their own communal institutions. An emerging middle-class leadership sought to develop black businesses. Despite these efforts, chronic lack of capital kept black businesses mostly small and confined to the ghetto. Immigrant groups often pooled extended-family capital resources or tapped ethnic banks. With few such resources at their disposal, black businesses failed at a high rate. Most black people worked outside the ghetto for white employers. Economic marginalization often

An African American religious meeting, New York City, early 1900s. Black migrants from the South found vibrant communities in northern cities typically centered around black churches and their activities. Like immigrants from Asia and Europe, who sought to transplant the culture of their homelands within the urban United States, black migrants reestablished southern religious and communal traditions in their new homes.

attracted unsavory businesses—dance halls, brothels, and bars—to black neighborhoods. One recently arrived migrant from the South complained that in his Cleveland neighborhood, his family was surrounded by loafers, "gamblers [and] pocket pickers; I can not raise my children here like they should be."

Other black institutions proved more lasting than black businesses. In Chicago in 1891, black physician Daniel Hale Williams established Provident Hospital, the nation's first interracially staffed hospital, with the financial help of wealthy white Chicagoans. Although it failed as an interracial experiment, the hospital thrived, providing an important training ground for black physicians and nurses.

Black branches of the Young Men's and Young Women's Christian Association provided living accommodations, social facilities, and employment information for black young people. Many black migrants to northern cities, perhaps a majority, were single, and the Y provided them with guidance and a "home." White people funded many black Y projects but did not accept black members in their chapters. By 1910, black settlement houses modeled on the white versions appeared in several cities.

NEW CITIES

Immigration from abroad and migration from American farms to the cities resulted in an urban explosion during the late nineteenth century. In 1850, six cities had a population exceeding 100,000; by 1900, thirty-eight did. In 1850, only 5 percent of the nation's population lived in cities of more than 100,000 inhabitants; by 1900, the figure was 19 percent. The nation's population tripled between 1860 and 1920, but the urban population increased ninefold.

In Europe, a few principal cities, such as Paris and Berlin, absorbed most of the urban growth during this period. In the United States, by contrast, growth was more evenly distributed among many cities. Despite the relative evenness of growth, a distinctive urban system had emerged by 1900, with New York and Chicago anchoring an urban-industrial core extending in a crescent from New England to the cities bordering the Great Lakes. This region included nine of the nation's ten largest cities in 1920. Western cities like Denver, San Francisco, and Los Angeles emerged as dominant urban places in their respective regions but did not challenge the urban core for supremacy. Southern cities, limited in growth by low consumer demand, low wages, and weak capital formation, were drawn into the orbit of the urban core (see Chapter 17).

Urban growth highlighted the growing divisions in American society. The crush of people and the emergence of new technologies expanded the city outward and upward as urban dwellers sorted themselves by social class and ethnic group. While the new infrastructure of water and sewer systems, bridges, and trolley tracks kept steel mills busy, it also fragmented the urban population by allowing settlements well beyond existing urban boundaries. The way people satisfied their needs for food, clothing, and shelter stimulated the industrial economy while distinguishing one class from another. Although urban institutions emerged to counter these divisive trends, they could not overcome them completely.

CENTERS AND SUBURBS

The centers of the country's great cities changed in scale and function in this era, achieving a prominence they would eventually lose in the twentieth century. Downtowns expanded up and out as tall buildings arose, monuments to business and finance, creating towering urban skylines. Residential neighborhoods were pushed out, leaving the center dominated by corporate headquarters and retail and entertainment districts.

Corporate heads administered their empires from downtown, even if their factories were located on the urban periphery or in other towns and cities. Banks and insurance companies clustered in such financial centers. Department stores and shops clustered in retail districts in strategic locations along electric trolley lines.

As retail and office uses crowded out dwellings from the city center, a new phenomenon emerged: the residential neighborhood. Advances in transportation technology, first the horsedrawn street railway and, by the 1890s, the electric trolley, eased commuting for office workers. Some in the growing and increasingly affluent middle class left the crowded, polluted city altogether to live in new residential suburbs. These people did not abandon the city; they still looked to it for its jobs, schools, libraries, and entertainment, but they rejected it as a place to live, leaving it to the growing ranks of working-class immigrants and African Americans.

The suburb emerged as the preferred place of residence for the urban middle class after 1870. As early as 1873, Chicago boasted nearly 100 suburbs with a combined population of more than 50,000. The ideals that had promoted modest suburban growth earlier in the nineteenth century—privacy, aesthetics, and home ownership—became increasingly important to the growing numbers of middle-class families after 1880. Consider the Russells of Short Hills, New Jersey. Short Hills lay 18 miles by railroad from New York City. William Russell; his wife, Ella Gibson Russell; and their six children moved there from Brooklyn in the late 1880s, seeking a "pleasant, cultured people whose society we could enjoy" and a cure for Russell's rheumatism. Russell owned and managed a small metal brokerage in New York. Ella Russell cared for their six children with the help of a servant and also found time for several clubs and charities.

The design of the Russell home reflected the principles Catharine Beecher and Harriet Beecher Stowe outlined in their suburban home bible, *American Woman's Home* (1869). The kitchen, according to Beecher and Stowe, should be organized for expedience and hygiene. The home's utilities should be confined to a central core, freeing wall areas for other functions. The new technology of central heating made it unnecessary to divide a house into many small rooms, each with its own fireplace or stove. Taking advantage of this change, Beecher and Stowe recommended that a home's ground floor have fewer but larger rooms, to encourage the family to pursue their individual activities in a common space. Parlors and reception rooms disappeared, along with such former standards as the children's wing, the male "smoking room," and the female parlor.

The once-prevailing view that women were too frail for vigorous exercise was changing. Thus, the entire Russell family was to be found enjoying the tennis, swimming, and skating facilities at the Short Hills Athletic Club. Because the community bordered on undeveloped woodland traversed by trails, "wheel clubs" appeared in the 1880s to organize families for bicycle outings. The emphasis on family togetherness also reflected the changing role of men in late-nineteenth-century society. Women's roles also broadened, as Ella Russell's club work attested.

Suburbs differed, not only from the city, but also from one another. With the growth after 1890 of the electric trolley, elevated rail lines, and other relatively inexpensive forms of commuter travel, suburbs became accessible to a broader spectrum of the middle class. The social structure, architecture, and amenities of suburbs varied, depending on the rail service and distance from the city. The commuter railroad remained popular among people like the Russells who could afford the time and expense of commuting to and from the city center.

The suburb underscored the growing fragmentation of life in and around American cities in the late nineteenth century. Residence, consumer habits, and leisure activities reflected growing social and class divisions. Yet, at the same time, the growing materialism of American society promised a common ground for its disparate ethnic, racial, and social groups.

THE NEW MIDDLE CLASS

From the colonial era, America's urban middle class had included professionals, physicians, lawyers, ministers, educators, editors, as well as merchants, shopkeepers, and skilled artisans (until they dropped from the middle class in the late nineteenth century).

In the late nineteenth century, industrial technology and urban growth expanded the urban middle class to include salespeople, factory supervisors, managers, civil servants, technicians, and a broad range of "white-collar" office workers, such as insurance agents, bank tellers, and legal assistants. This newer middle class set national trends in residential patterns, consumption, and leisure.

The more affluent members of the new middle class, like the Russells, repaired to new subdivisions within and outside the city limits. Simple row houses sheltered the growing numbers of clerks and civil servants who remained in the city. These dwellings contrasted sharply with the crowded one- or two-room apartments that confined the working class. Rents for these apartments ran as much as $3 a week, at a time when few workers made more than $9 or $10.

A CONSUMER SOCIETY

The new middle class transformed America into a consumer society. In earlier times, land had been a symbol of prestige. Now it was consumer goods. And the new industries obliged with a dazzling array of merchandise and technologies. By 1910, the new middle class lived in all-electric homes with indoor plumbing. A typical kitchen might include an electric coffeepot, a hot plate, a chafing dish, and a toaster. The modern city dweller worked by the clock, not by the sun. Eating patterns changed: Cold packaged cereals replaced hot meats at breakfast; fast lunches of Campbell's soup, "a meal in itself," or canned stews weaned Americans from the heavy lunch.

The middle class liked anything that saved time: trolleys, trains, electric razors, vacuum cleaners. The telephone replaced the letter for everyday communication; it was quicker and less formal. By 1900, some 1.4 million phones were in service, and many middle-class homes had one. Observers wondered if the telephone would eventually make written communication obsolete.

The middle class liked its news in an easy-to-read form. Urban tabloids multiplied after 1880, led by Joseph Pulitzer's *New York World* and William Randolph Hearst's *New York Journal.* The newspapers organized the news into topical sections, used bold headlines and graphics to catch the eye, ran human interest stories to capture the imagination, inaugurated sports pages to attract male readers, and offered advice columns for women. And they opened their pages to a wide range of attractive advertising, much of it directed to women, who did about 90 percent of the shopping in American cities by 1900.

As the visual crowded out the printed in advertising, newspapers, and magazines, these materials became accessible to a wider urban audience. Although mainly middle class in orientation, the tabloid press drew urban society together with new features such as the comic strip, which first appeared in the 1890s, and heart-rending personal sagas drawn from real life. Immigrants, who might have had difficulty reading small-type newspapers, received their initiation into the mainstream of American society through the tabloids.

In a similar manner, the department store, essentially a middle-class retail establishment, became one of the city's most democratic forums and the focus of the urban downtown after 1890. Originating in the 1850s and 1860s with the construction of retail palaces such as Boston's Jordan Marsh, Philadelphia's Wanamaker & Brown, New York's Lord & Taylor, and Chicago's Marshall Field, the department store came to epitomize the bounty of the new industrial capitalism. They exuded limitless abundance with their extensive inventories, items for every budget, sumptuous surroundings, and efficient, trained personnel.

At first, most department-store customers were middle-class married women. Not expected to work and with disposable income and flexible schedules, these women had the means and time to wander department store aisles. The stores catered to their tastes, and the current emphasis on home and domesticity, with such items as prefabricated household furnishings, ready-made clothing, toys, and stationery. Department stores maintained consumers' interest with advertising campaigns arranged around holidays like Easter and Christmas, the seasons, and the school calendar. Each event required new clothing and accessories, and the ready-made clothing industry changed fashions accordingly.

Soon the spectacle and merchandise of the department store attracted shoppers from all social strata, not just the middle class. Although many less affluent women came merely to "window-shop," some came to buy. After 1890, department stores increasingly hired young immigrant women to cater to their growing foreign-born clientele.

The department store, the turn-of-the-century shopping mall, provided inexpensive amusement for young working-class people, especially immigrants. Mary Antin recalled how she and her teenage friends and sister would spend their Saturday nights patrolling "a dazzlingly beautiful palace called a 'department store.'" It was there that Mary and her sister "exchanged our hateful homemade European costumes … for real American machine-made garments, and issued forth glorified in each other's eyes."

THE GROWTH OF LEISURE ACTIVITIES

By 1900, department stores had added sporting goods and hardware sections and were attracting customers from a wide social spectrum. The expanding floor space devoted to sporting goods reflected the growth of leisure in urban society. And like other aspects of that society, leisure and recreation both separated and cut across social classes. The leisure activities of the wealthy increasingly removed them from the rest of urban society. As such sports as football became important extracurricular activities at Harvard, Yale, and other elite universities, intercollegiate games became popular occasions for the upper class to congregate and, not incidentally, to discuss business. The elite also gathered at the athletic clubs and country clubs that emerged as open spaces disappeared in the city. High fees and strict membership criteria kept these clubs exclusive. The clubs offered a suburban retreat, away from the diverse middle- and working-class populations, where the elite could play in privacy.

Middle-class urban residents could not afford country clubs, but they rode electric trolleys to the end of the line to enjoy suburban parks and bicycle and skating clubs. Reflecting the emphasis on family togetherness in late-nineteenth-century America, both men and women participated in these sports. Bicycling in particular became immensely popular.

If college football was the rage among the elite, baseball was the leading middle-class spectator sport. Organized baseball originated among the urban elite before the Civil War. The middle class took over the sport after the war. Baseball epitomized the nation's transition from a rural to an urban industrial society. Reflecting rural tradition, it was played on an expanse of green, usually on the outskirts of the city. It was leisurely; unlike other games, it had no time limit. Reflecting industrial society, however, it had clearly defined rules and was organized into leagues. Professional leagues were profit-making enterprises, and, like other enterprises, they frequently merged. Initially, most professional baseball games were played on weekday afternoons, making it hard for working-class spectators to attend. After merging with the American Association in 1883, the

National League adopted some of its innovations to attract more fans, including beer sales, cheap admission, and, despite the objections of Protestant churches, Sunday games.

The tavern, or saloon, was the workingman's club. Typically an all-male preserve, the saloon provided drink, cheap food, and a place to read a newspaper, socialize, and learn about job opportunities. Alcoholism was a severe problem in cities, especially, though not exclusively, among working-class men, fueling the prohibition movement of the late nineteenth century.

Amusement parks, with their mechanical wonders, were another hallmark of the industrial city. Declining trolley fares made these parks accessible to the working class around 1900. Unlike taverns, they provided a place for working-class men and women to meet and date.

The most renowned of these parks was Brooklyn's Coney Island. In 1897, George C. Tilyou opened Steeplechase Park on Coney Island. Together with such attractions as mechanical horses and 250,000 of Thomas Edison's light bulbs, Steeplechase dazzled patrons with its technological wonders. It was quickly followed by Luna Park and Dreamland, and the Coney Island attractions became collectively known as "the poor man's paradise." Immigrant entrepreneurs, seeing a good thing, flocked to Coney Island to set up sideshows, pool halls, taverns, and restaurants.

After 1900, the wonders of Coney Island began to lure people from all segments of an increasingly diverse city. Sightseers came from around the world. In much the same manner, baseball was becoming a national pastime as games attracted a disparate crowd of people with little in common but their devotion to the home team.

Increasing materialism had revealed great fissures in American urban society by 1900. Yet places like department stores, baseball parks, and amusement parks provided democratic spaces for some interaction. Newspapers and schools also offered diverse groups the vicarious opportunity to share similar experiences.

THE IDEAL CITY

For all its problems, the American city was undeniably the locus of the nation's energy; in some ways, with the passing of the frontier, it competed with the West in the national imagination as the environment where possibility was boundless. John Dewey, on his first encounter with Chicago in 1894, sensed this energy, writing to his wife back home, "Chicago is the place to make you appreciate at every turn the absolute opportunity which chaos affords. . . . I had no conception that things could be so much more phenomenal & objective than they are in a country village." This sense of limitless energy and innovation appeared most notably in urban skylines where skyscrapers reached heavenward as graceful cathedrals of commerce. The tall buildings bespoke a confidence that declared even the sky was not the limit.

There was great interest in creating clean cities, harmonious with nature, and with aesthetic and cultural amenities. The advent of planned towns with these qualities coincided with a growing conservation movement that also included protecting the natural environment from the sprawl of urban growth. Few landscapes expressed this new urban ideal better than the 1893 World's Columbian Exposition in Chicago, a World's Fair to celebrate the 400th anniversary of the European discovery of America. The fair demonstrated how with foresight, planning, and copious funds, it was possible to create a safe and aesthetic urban environment, quite different from the gritty industrial city just beyond its borders. Dubbed the White City, the exposition epitomized cleanliness, grandeur, beauty, and order in its architecture. That it was sheer fantasy, a temporary respite from the reality beyond the gates, did not faze the millions who attended. The White City represented the possibility, and in America, anything was possible.

CONCLUSION

The new industrial order, the changing nature of work, the massive migrations of populations from the countryside and abroad, and the rise of great cities changed the American landscape in the late nineteenth century. By 1900, the factory worker and the department store clerk were more representative of the new America than the farmer and small shopkeeper. Industry and technology had created thousands of new jobs, but they also eliminated the autonomy many workers had enjoyed and limited their opportunities to advance. The individual journey from farms and small towns to large cities, and from Europe, Asia, and Latin America to the United States, became a collective journey, moving America further toward becoming a modern urban and industrial nation, with all of the accompanying ills, but also with all of its possibilities.

Immigrants thronged to the United States to realize their dreams of economic and religious freedom. They found both to varying degrees but also discovered a darker side to the promise of American life. The great cities thrilled newcomers with their possibilities and their abundance of goods and activities. But the cities also bore witness to the growing divisions in American society. As the new century dawned, the prospects for urban industrial America seemed limitless, yet the stark contrasts that had appeared so vividly inside and outside the Centennial Exposition persisted and deepened.

Still, it would be wrong to depict the nation in 1900 as merely a larger and more divided version of what it had been in 1876. Although sharp ethnic, racial, and class differences persisted, the nation seemed better poised to address them in 1900 than it had a quarter-century earlier. Labor unions, ethnic organizations, government legislation, and new urban institutions promised ways to remedy the worst abuses of the new urban, industrial economy.

REVIEW QUESTIONS

1. Were there ways to achieve the benefits of industrialization without its social costs, or did the nation's political and economic systems make that impossible?

2. How did working-class women respond to the new economy? How did their participation and responses differ from that of working-class men?

3. What factors accounted for immigration becoming a global phenomenon during the late nineteenth century?

4. The growing fragmentation of urban life reflected deep divisions in modern urban industrial society. At the same time, there were forces that tended to overcome these divisions. What were these forces, and were they sufficient to bridge the divisions?

5. How did Old World conditions influence Mary Antin's adjustment to American life? Would individuals from other immigrant groups have expressed similar sentiments, or was Mary's reaction specific to her Jewish background?

myhistorylab CONNECTIONS

Reinforce what you learned in this chapter by studying the many documents, images, maps, review tools, and videos available at **www.myhistorylab.com**.

READ AND REVIEW

✓• **Study** and **Review** on **myhistorylab.com** STUDY PLAN: CHAPTER 18

📖• **Read** the **Document** on **myhistorylab.com**

Mark Twain, from The Gilded Age (1873)

Thomas Edison, The Success of the Electric Light (1880)

Upton Sinclair, The Jungle (1906)

Andrew Carnegie, Wealth and Its Uses (1907)

George Engel, Address by a Condemned Haymarket Anarchist (1886)

Lee Chew, "Life of a Chinese Immigrant" (1903)

Chinese Exclusion Act (1882)

Richard K. Fox, from Coney Island Frolics (1883)

William Graham Sumner, from What the Social Classes Owe to Each Other (1883)

🔍• **View** the **Map** on **myhistorylab.com**

Foreign-Born Population, 1890

Organizing American Labor in the Late Nineteenth Century

RESEARCH AND EXPLORE

📖• **Read** the **Document** on **myhistorylab.com**

Personal Journeys Online

From Then to Now Online: Green Cities

Exploring America: The Unwelcome Mat

((•• **Listen** on **myhistorylab.com**

Hungarian Rag

👁• **Watch** the **Video** on **myhistorylab.com**

Ellis Island Immigrants, 1903

The Great Migration

———— ((•• **Listen** on **myhistorylab.com** ————

Hear the audio files for Chapter 18 at
www.myhistorylab.com.

CHAPTER

19 Transforming the West •• 1865–1890

Hear the audio files for Chapter 19 at **www.myhistorylab.com.**

FOCUS QUESTIONS

WHAT WERE the main objectives of federal Indian policy in the late nineteenth century?

HOW DID mining in the West change over the course of the second half of the nineteenth century?

WHAT FACTORS contributed to the development of the range cattle industry?

HOW DID new technology contribute to the growth of western agriculture?

Chinese miners in Idaho operate the destructive water cannons used in hydraulic mining.
Idaho State Historical Society.

ONE AMERICAN JOURNEY

After a pleasant ride of about six miles we attained a very high elevation, and, passing through a gorge of the mountains, we entered a level, circular valley, about three miles in diameter, surrounded on every side by mountains. The track is on the eastern side of the plain, and at the point of junction extends in nearly a southwest and northeast direction. Two lengths of rails are left for today's work. . . . At a quarter to nine A.M. the whistle of the C.P. [Central Pacific Railroad] is heard, and soon arrives, bringing a number of passengers. . . . Two additional trains arrive from the East. At a quarter to eleven the Chinese workmen commenced leveling the bed of the road with picks and shovels, preparatory to placing the ties. . . . At 12 M. the rails were laid, and the iron spikes driven. The last tie . . . is of California laurel, finely polished, and is ornamented with a silver escutcheon bearing the following inscription: "The last tie laid on the Pacific Railroad, May 10th, 1869." . . .

The point of contact is 1,085 4/5 miles from Omaha, leaving 690 miles for the C.P. portion of the work. The engine Jupiter, of the C.P., and engine 119, of the U.P.R.R. [Union Pacific Railroad] moved up within thirty feet of each other. . . . Three cheers were given for the Government of the United States, for the railroad, for the President, for the Star Spangled Banner, for the laborers, and for those who furnished the means respectively. The four spikes, two gold and two silver, were furnished by Montana, Idaho, California, and Nevada. Dr. Harkness, of Sacramento, on presenting to Governor Stanford a spike of pure gold, delivered a short and appropriate speech. The Hon. F.A. Tuttle, of Nevada, presented Dr. Durant with a spike of silver, saying: 'To the iron of the East, and the gold of the West, Nevada adds her link of silver to span the continent and wed the oceans.' . . . The two locomotives then moved up until they touched each other, . . . and at one P.M., under an almost cloudless sky . . . the completion of the greatest railroad on earth was announced.

Andrew J. Russell, "The Completion of the Pacific Railroad," *Frank Leslie's Illustrated Newspaper,* June 5, 1869.

ANDREW J. RUSSELL'S short journey on the morning of May 10, 1869, from Ogden to Promontory Summit, Utah, enabled him, in his capacity as the official Union Pacific photographer, to document what he called "the completion of the greatest work of the age, by which this vast continent is spanned, from ocean to ocean, by the iron path of travel and commerce." The construction of the transcontinental railroad set a precedent for western development. The two railroads that met in a desolate sagebrush basin were huge corporate enterprises, not individual efforts, and corporations would dominate western growth as much as they did eastern industrialization. The crowd of onlookers had good reason to give three cheers for the federal government, for it played a crucial role in railroad construction, as in virtually all aspects of western development. Congress had authorized the Union Pacific and Central Pacific to build the railroad link, given them the right-of-way for their tracks, and provided huge land grants and financial subsidies.

The railroads' dependence on capital investment, engineering knowledge, technological innovations, and labor skills also typified western development. Their labor forces both reflected and reinforced the region's racial and ethnic diversity. European immigrants, Mexicans, Paiute Indians, both male and female, and especially Chinese, recruited in California and Asia, chiseled the tunnels through the mountains, built the bridges over the gulches, and laid the ties and rails across the plains. But Russell had the Chinese workers step back so as not to appear in the famous photographs he took at Promontory, an indication of the racism that marred so many western achievements.

Laying track as quickly as possible to collect the subsidies awarded by the mile, the railroad corporations adopted callous and reckless construction tactics, resulting in waste, deaths (perhaps as many as a thousand Chinese), and environmental destruction, all consequences that would similarly characterize other forms of economic development in the West. And as with most American undertakings in the West, the construction provoked conflict with the Cheyenne, Sioux, and other tribes.

The most important feature of the railroad, however, was that traffic moved in both directions. The transcontinental and subsequent railroads helped move soldiers, miners, cattle raisers, farmers, merchants, and other settlers into the West, but they also enabled the West to send precious metals, livestock, lumber, and wheat to the growing markets in the East. Thus the railroad both integrated the West into the rest of the nation and made it a crucial part of the larger economic revolution that transformed America after the Civil War.

Subjugating Native Americans

The initial obstacle to exploiting the West was the people already living there, who used its resources in their own way and held different concepts of progress and civilization. As whites pressed westward, they attempted to subjugate the Indians, displace them from their lands, and strip them of their culture.

Tribes and Cultures

Throughout the West, Indians had adapted to their environment, developing subsistence economies ranging from simple gathering to complex systems of irrigated agriculture. Each activity encouraged their sensitivity to the natural world, and each had social and political implications.

In the Northwest, abundant food from rich waters and dense forests gave rise to complex and stable Indian societies. Tillamooks, Chinooks, and other tribes developed artistic handicrafts, elaborate social institutions, and a satisfying religious life. At the opposite environmental extreme, in the dry and barren Great Basin of Utah and Nevada, Shoshones and Paiutes ate grasshoppers and other insects to supplement their diet of rabbits, mice, and other small animals. Such harsh environments restricted the size, strength, and organizational complexity of societies. In the Southwest, the Pueblos dwelled in permanent towns of adobe buildings and practiced intensive agriculture. Because tribal welfare depended on maintaining complex irrigation systems, the Zunis, Hopis, and other Pueblos emphasized community solidarity rather than individual ambition. Town living encouraged social stability and the development of effective governments, elaborate religious ceremonies, and creative arts.

The most numerous Indian groups lived on the Great Plains. The largest of these tribes were the Lakotas, or Sioux, who ranged from western Minnesota through the Dakotas; the

CHRONOLOGY

1858	Gold is discovered in Colorado, Nevada, and British Columbia.
1860	Gold is discovered in Idaho.
1862	Homestead Act is passed. Gold is discovered in Montana.
1864	Militia slaughters Cheyennes at Sand Creek, Colorado.
1867	Cattle drives make Abilene the first cow town.
1868	Fort Laramie Treaty is signed.
1869	First transcontinental railroad is completed.
1872	Canada enacts homestead law.
1874	Gold is discovered in the Black Hills. Turkey Red wheat is introduced in Kansas. Barbed wire is patented.
1876	Indians devastate U.S. troops in the Battle of the Little Bighorn.
1879	Defeat of Araucanian Indians opens the pampas to settlement in Argentina. "Exodusters" migrate to Kansas.
1885	Chinese massacred at Rock Springs, Wyoming.
1887	Dawes Act is passed.
1890	Government troops kill 200 Sioux at Wounded Knee, South Dakota.
1892	Mining violence breaks out at Coeur d'Alene, Idaho.
1893	Western Federation of Miners is organized.

Cheyennes and Arapahos, who controlled much of the central plains between the Platte and Arkansas rivers; and the Comanches, preeminent on the southern plains. Two animals dominated the lives of these peoples: the horse, which enabled them to move freely over the plains and to use the energy stored in the valuable grasses, and the buffalo, which provided meat, hides, bones and horns for tools, and a focus for spiritual life.

Clashing Values. Despite their diversity, all tribes emphasized community welfare over individual interest. They based their economies on subsistence rather than profit. They tried to live in harmony with nature to ward off sickness, injury, death, or misfortune. And they were intensely religious, absorbed with the need to establish proper relations with supernatural forces that linked human beings with all other living things. These connections also shaped Indians' attitude toward land, which they regarded, like air and water, as part of nature to be held and used communally, not as an individual's personal property from which others could be excluded.

This photograph, taken by A. J. Russell, records the celebration at the joining of the Central Pacific and Union Pacific railroads on May 10, 1869, at Promontory Summit, Utah. Railroads transformed the American West, linking the region to outside markets, spurring rapid settlement, and threatening Indian survival.

White and Indian cultural values were incompatible. Disdaining Native Americans and their religion, white people condemned them as "savages" to be converted or exterminated. Rejecting the concept of communal property, most settlers demanded land for the exclusive use of ambitious individuals. Ignoring the need for natural harmony, they followed their own culture's goal of extracting wealth from the land for a market economy.

FEDERAL INDIAN POLICY

The government had in the 1830s adopted the policy of separating whites and Indians (see Chapter 10). Eastern tribes were moved west of Missouri and resettled on land then scorned as "the Great American Desert," unsuitable for white habitation and development. This division presumed a permanent frontier with perpetual Indian ownership of western America. It collapsed in the 1840s, when the United States acquired Texas, California, and Oregon, and migrants crossed Indian lands to reach the West Coast. Rather than curbing white entry into Indian country, the government built forts along the overland trails and ordered the army to punish Indians who threatened travelers.

White migration devastated the Indians, already competing among themselves for the limited resources of the Plains. Migrants' livestock destroyed crucial timber and pastures along streams in the semiarid region; trails disrupted buffalo grazing patterns and eliminated buffalo from tribal hunting ranges. The Plains Indians also suffered from diseases the white migrants introduced. Smallpox, cholera, measles, whooping cough,

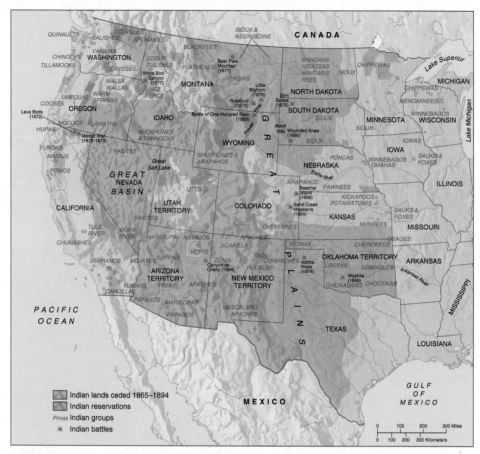

MAP 19–1 • Indian Land Cessions, 1860–1894 As white people pushed into the West to exploit its resources, Indians were steadily forced to cede their lands. By 1900 they held only scattered parcels, often in areas considered worthless by white people. Restricted to these reservations, tribes endured official efforts to suppress Indian customs and values.

▶ *What does* this map tell you about federal Indian policy in the decades after the Civil War? What forces shaped post–Civil War policy?

and scarlet fever, for which Indians had no natural immunity, swept through the tribes, killing up to 40 percent of their population. Emigrants along the Platte River routes came across "villages of the dead."

By the early 1850s, white settlers sought to occupy Indian territory. Recognizing that the Great Plains could support agriculture, they demanded the removal of the Indians. Simultaneously, railroad companies developed plans to lay tracks across the plains. To promote white settlement, the federal government decided to relocate the tribes to separate specific reserves. In exchange for accepting such restrictions, the tribes were promised annual payments of livestock, clothing, and other materials. To implement this policy, the government negotiated treaties extinguishing Indian rights to millions of acres (see Map 19–1) and ordered the army to keep Indians on their assigned reservations.

But the treaties, often coerced or misleading, so disadvantaged the tribes that one historian has termed them "instruments of chicanery and weapons of aggression." White negotiators sometimes omitted from the formal documents provisions that Indians had insisted upon, or included others specifically rejected, and at times Congress sharply reduced the annual payments or the size of the reservations promised in the treaties.

WARFARE AND DISPOSSESSION

Most smaller tribes accepted the government's conditions, realizing that their survival depended upon accommodation to American power. Many larger tribes resisted. From the 1850s to the 1880s, warfare engulfed the advancing frontier. Indians sometimes initiated conflict, especially in the form of small raids, but invading Americans bore ultimate responsibility for these wars. As General Philip Sheridan declared of the Indians: "We took away their country and their means of support, broke up their mode of living, their habits of life, introduced disease and decay among them, and it was for this and against this that they made war. Could anyone expect less?"

One notorious example of white aggression occurred in 1864, at Sand Creek, Colorado. Gold discoveries had attracted a flood of white settlers onto land only recently guaranteed to the Cheyennes and Arapahos. Rather than enforcing the Indians' treaty rights, however, the government compelled the tribes to relinquish their lands, except for a small tract designated as the Sand Creek reservation. But white settlers wanted to eliminate the Indian presence altogether. John Chivington, a Methodist minister who had organized Denver's first Sunday school, led a militia force to the Sand Creek camp of a band of Cheyennes under Black Kettle, an advocate of peace and accommodation. The militia attacked Black Kettle's sleeping camp without warning. With howitzers and rifles, the soldiers fired into the camp and then assaulted any survivors with swords and knives. One white trader later described the helpless Indians: "They were scalped, their brains knocked out; the [white] men used their knives, ripped open women, clubbed little children, knocked them in the head with their guns, beat their brains out, mutilated their bodies in every sense of the word."

The **Sand Creek Massacre** appalled many easterners. The Cheyennes, protested the commissioner of Indian affairs, were "butchered in cold blood by troops in the service of the United States." Westerners, however, justified the brutality as a means to secure their own opportunities. One western newspaper demanded, "Kill all the Indians that can be killed. Complete extermination is our motto."

Other tribes were more formidable. None was more powerful than the Sioux, whose military skills had been honed in conflicts with other tribes. An army offensive against the Sioux in 1866 failed completely. Entire units deserted in fear and frustration; others were crushed by the Sioux. General William T. Sherman, who had marched through Georgia against Confederates, knew that the odds were different in the West. Fifty Plains Indians, he declared, could "checkmate" 3,000 soldiers. General Philip Sheridan calculated that the army suffered proportionately greater losses fighting Indians than either the Union or the Confederacy had suffered in the Civil War.

With the army unable to defeat the Sioux and their allies, and with many easterners shocked by both the military's indiscriminate aggression and the expense of the fighting, the government sued for peace. Describing white actions as "uniformly unjust," a federal peace commission in 1868 negotiated the **Treaty of Fort Laramie,** in which the United States abandoned the Bozeman Trail and other routes and military posts on Sioux territory, one of the few times Indians forced whites to retreat. The United States also guaranteed the Sioux permanent ownership of the western half of South Dakota and the right to inhabit and hunt in the Powder River country in Wyoming and Montana, an area to be henceforth closed to all white people.

The army was a key institution in developing the West. It built roads, undertook scientific activities, distributed rations and clothing to destitute settlers, settled civil disputes, and even supervised the earliest national parks. Government contracts to supply military posts with food, building materials, uniforms, grain, and horses promoted freight companies, commercial development, and agriculture.

But the army's primary role was military, and its leaders were bitter about the Sioux victory. Turning to the southern plains, they adopted a devastating new strategy: winter campaigns directed at villages. Winter impaired Indian mobility by depleting food sources for both people and ponies, while the army could draw upon stocks of supplies, equipment, and animals. And attacks on villages, inevitably causing heavy casualties among women and children, might demoralize warriors. The Seventh Cavalry initiated the strategy in a surprise attack on a Cheyenne winter camp on the Washita River in Oklahoma. Colonel George A. Custer reported that his troops killed 103 men and, "in the excitement," many women and children as well. They then destroyed the tribe's 875 horses, its lodges and clothing, and its "whole supply" of food. Any survivors would be impoverished and starving in the bitter weather. By such offensives, the army secured the southern plains by 1875.

Momentum soon shifted on the northern plains as well. Peace had prevailed for several years after the Fort Laramie treaty, but in 1872, the Northern Pacific Railroad began to build westward on a route that would violate Sioux territory. Rather than stopping the railroad, the government sent an army to protect the surveyors. Sherman drew up plans for the war that he expected the construction to provoke. He regarded railroad expansion as the most important factor in defeating the Indians, for it would allow troops to travel as far in a day as they could march in weeks. Other technological developments, from the telegraph to rapid-fire weapons, also undercut the skills of the Indian warrior.

The destruction of the buffalo also threatened Native Americans. From 1872 to 1874, white hunters killed 4 million buffalo. Railroad survey and construction parties disrupted grazing areas, and hunters working for the railroads killed hordes of buffalo, both to feed construction crews and to prevent the animals from obstructing rail traffic. Hide hunters slaughtered even more of the beasts for their skins, leaving the bodies to rot. Federal officials encouraged the buffalo's extermination because it would destroy the Indians' basis for survival.

The climactic provocation of the Sioux began in 1874, when Colonel George A. Custer led an invasion to survey the Black Hills for a military post and to confirm the presence of gold. Thousands of white miners then illegally poured onto Sioux land. Ignoring Sioux demands that the government enforce the Fort Laramie treaty, the army insisted that the Indians leave their Powder River hunting grounds. When the Sioux refused, the army attacked. The Oglala Sioux under Crazy Horse repulsed one prong of this offensive at the Battle of the Rosebud in 1876 and then joined a larger body of Sioux under Sitting Bull and their Cheyenne and Arapaho allies to overwhelm a second American column, under Custer, at the **Battle of the Little Bighorn.**

But the Indians could not follow up their dramatic victory. They had to divide their forces to find fresh grass for their horses and to hunt for food. Not similarly handicapped but supplied and equipped by an industrializing nation, the U.S. Army relentlessly pursued the separate bands to exhaustion. In the end, the conquest of the northern plains came, not through any decisive victory, but through attrition and the inability of the traditional Indian economy to support resistance to the technologically and numerically superior white forces.

In the Southwest, the Navajos and the Comanches were subdued, as the Sioux had been, by persistent pursuit that prevented them from obtaining food. The last to submit were the Apaches, under Geronimo. In 1886, he and 36 followers, facing 5,000 U.S. troops, finally surrendered. Geronimo and other Apaches were sent to a military prison in Florida; the tribes were herded onto barren reservations. The Oglala chief Red Cloud concluded of the white invasion: "They made us many promises, more than I can remember, but they never kept but one. They promised to take our land, and they took it."

LIFE ON THE RESERVATION: AMERICANIZATION

Conquering the tribes and seizing their land were only the initial objectives of government policy. The next goal was to require Indians to adopt white ways, instilled by education and religion and enforced when necessary by the military. This goal did not involve assimilation but merely "Americanization," an expression of cultural conquest.

The government received aid from many Christian denominations, which had long proposed nonviolent methods of controlling Indians. Reformers wanted to change Indian religious and family life, train Indian children in Protestant beliefs, and force Indians to accept private ownership and market capitalism.

Confined to reservations, Indians were a captive audience for white reformers. Furthermore, with their very survival dependent on government rations and annual payments stipulated by treaties, Indians were "compelled by sheer necessity," as one federal official said, to accept government orders "or starve." Government agents of the Bureau of Indian Affairs used their power to undermine tribal authority and destroy traditional Indian government, prohibiting tribal councils from meeting and imprisoning tribal leaders.

White activists sought to destroy Indian religion because it was "pagan" and because it helped Indians resist assimilation. Protestant religious groups persuaded the Bureau of Indian Affairs to frame a criminal code prohibiting tribal religious practices. Established in 1884, the code remained in effect until 1933. To enforce the ban, the government withheld rations and disrupted the religious ceremonies that transmitted traditional values. In 1890, to suppress the Ghost Dance religion, the army even used artillery and killed at least 200 Sioux men, women, and children at Wounded Knee, South Dakota, in what became known as the **Wounded Knee Massacre.**

The government and religious groups also used education to eliminate Indian values and traditions. They isolated Indian children from tribal influences at off-reservation boarding schools. Troops often seized Indian children for these schools, where they were confined until after adolescence. The schoolchildren were forced to speak English, attend Christian services, and profess white American values (see American Views: Zitkala-Sa's View of Americanization).

Dressed in their school uniforms, Indian children sit under the U.S. flag. Government and missionary schools sought to promote "Americanization" and suppress native cultures. Such education, said one member of Congress, "is the solution of the vexed Indian problem." Western History Collections, University of Oklahoma Library, "Phillips #436."

Finally, the government and the religious reformers imposed the economic practices and values of white society on Indians. Government agents taught Indian men how to farm and distributed agricultural implements, but Indians could not farm successfully on reservation lands that whites had already rejected as unproductive. Whites, however, believed that the real obstacle to economic prosperity for the Indians was their rejection of private property. The Indians' communal values, the reformers argued, inhibited the pursuit of personal success that lay at the heart of capitalism.

To force such values on Indians, Congress in 1887 passed the **Dawes Act,** which divided tribal lands among individual Indians. Western settlers who had no interest in the Indians supported the law because it provided that reservation lands not allocated to individual Indians would be opened to white settlers. Under this "reform," the amount of land held by Indians declined by more than half by 1900. White acquisition and exploitation of Indian land seemed to be the only constant in the nation's treatment of Native Americans.

Certainly assimilation scarcely succeeded. Some Indians did accept Christianity, formal education, and new job skills in attempting to adapt to their changing world. But often they employed such knowledge in another strategy of resistance, lecturing and lobbying to reform Indian policies or working to curtail the economic exploitation of their tribes. Other Indians, when they returned from school to their reservations, simply went "back to the blanket," as disgusted white critics called their reversion to traditional ways. Most Indians resented assimilationist efforts, clinging to their own values and rejecting as selfish, dishonorable, and obsessively materialistic those favored by whites. As Big Bear, a chief of the Otoe-Missouria, defiantly declared, "You cannot make white men of us. That is one thing you can't do." But if it was not yet clear what place Native Americans would have in America, it was at least clear by 1900 that they would no longer stand in the way of western development.

EXPLOITING THE MOUNTAINS: THE MINING BONANZA

In the late nineteenth century, the West experienced several stages of economic development that transformed the environment, produced economic and social conflict, and integrated the region into the modern national economy. The first stage of development centered on mining, which attracted eager prospectors into the mountains and deserts in search of gold and silver. They founded communities, stimulated the railroad construction that brought further development, and contributed to the disorderly heritage of the frontier. But few gained the wealth they expected.

RUSHES AND MINING CAMPS

The first important gold rush in the Rocky Mountains came in Colorado in 1859. More than 100,000 prospectors crowded into Denver and nearby mining camps. Simultaneously, the discovery of the famous Comstock Lode in Nevada produced an eastward rush of miners from California and booming mining camps like Virginia City. Strikes in the northern Rockies followed in the 1860s. The last of the frontier gold rushes came in 1874 on the Sioux reservation in the Black Hills of South Dakota, where the roaring mining camp of Deadwood flourished. Later, other minerals shaped frontier development: silver in Nevada, silver and lead in Colorado and Idaho, silver and copper in Arizona and Montana.

Mining camps were often isolated by both distance and terrain. They frequently consisted only of flimsy shanties, saloons, crude stores, dance halls, and brothels, all hastily built by entrepreneurs. Such towns reflected the speculative, exploitive, and transitory character of mining. And yet they did contribute to permanent settlement by encouraging agriculture, industry, and transportation in the surrounding areas.

The camps had an unusual social and economic structure. Their population was overwhelmingly male. In 1860, for example, about 2,300 men and only 30 women lived in the Nevada camps of Virginia City and Gold Hill. Women found far fewer economic opportunities than men did on the mining frontier. Some became prospectors, but most stayed within conventional domestic spaces. Several opened lodging houses or hotels. Those with less capital worked as seamstresses and cooks and took in washing. The few married women often earned more than their husbands by boarding other miners willing to pay for the trappings of family life.

Prostitution. But the largest source of paid employment for women was prostitution, a flourishing consequence of the gender imbalance and the limited economic options for women. Many who entered brothels already suffered from economic hardship or a broken family. Some Chinese women were virtually sold into prostitution. By the 1890s,

AMERICAN VIEWS

ZITKALA-SA'S VIEW OF AMERICANIZATION

Zitkala-Sa, or Red Bird, was an 8-year-old Sioux girl when she was taken from her South Dakota reservation in 1884 and placed in a midwestern missionary school, where she encountered what she called the "iron routine" of the "civilizing machine." Here she recalls her first day at the school.

■ What lessons were the missionaries trying to teach Zitkala-Sa by their actions?

■ What lessons did Zitkala-Sa learn?

Soon we were being drawn rapidly away by the white man's horses. When I saw the lonely figure of my mother vanish in the distance, a sense of regret settled heavily upon me. . . . I no longer felt free to be myself, or to voice my own feelings. The tears trickled down my cheeks, and I buried my face in the folds of my blanket. Now the first step, parting me from my mother, was taken, and all my belated tears availed nothing. . . . Trembling with fear and distrust of the palefaces . . . I was as frightened and bewildered as the captured young of a wild creature. . . .

[At the missionary school,] the constant clash of harsh noises, with an undercurrent of many voices murmuring an unknown tongue, made a bedlam within which I was securely tied. And though my spirit tore itself in struggling for its lost freedom, all was useless. . . .

We were placed in a line of girls who were marching into the dining room. . . . A small bell was tapped, and each of the pupils drew a chair from under the table. Supposing this act meant they were to be seated, I pulled out mine and at once slipped into it from one side. But when I turned my head, I saw that I was the only one seated, and all the rest at our table remained standing. Just as I began to rise, looking shyly around to see how chairs were to be used, a second bell was sounded. All were seated at last, and I had to crawl back into my chair again. I heard a man's voice at one end of the hall, and I looked around to see him. But all others hung their heads over their plates. As I glanced at the long chain of tables, I caught the eyes of a paleface woman upon me. Immediately I dropped my eyes, wondering why I was so keenly watched

---

as men gained control of the vice trade from the madams, violence, suicide, alcoholism, disease, drug addiction, and poverty overcame most prostitutes.

Public authorities showed little concern for the abuse and even murder of prostitutes, although they fined and taxed "sporting women" to raise revenue. Condemning such moral indifference, middle-class Protestant women in Denver and other cities established "rescue homes" to protect or rehabilitate prostitutes and dance-hall girls from male vice and violence. But their attempts to impose piety and purity had little success; male community leaders valued social order less than they did economic opportunity.

Saloon Society. The gender imbalance in the mining camps also made saloons prevalent among local businesses. An 1879 business census of Leadville, Colorado, reported 10 dry-goods stores, 4 banks, and 4 churches, but 120 saloons, 19 beer halls, and 118 gambling

by the strange woman. The man ceased his mutterings, and then a third bell was tapped. Every one picked up his knife and fork and began eating. I began crying instead, for by this time I was afraid to venture anything more.

But this eating by formula was not the hardest trial in that first day. Late in the morning, my friend Judewin gave me a terrible warning. Judewin knew a few words of English; and she had overheard the paleface woman talk about cutting our long, heavy hair. Our mothers had taught us that only unskilled warriors who were captured had their hair shingled by the enemy. Among our people, short hair was worn by mourners, and shingled hair by cowards!

. . . I remember being dragged out, though I resisted by kicking and scratching wildly. In spite of myself, I was carried downstairs and tied fast in a chair. I cried aloud, shaking my head all the while until I felt the cold blades of the scissors against my neck, and heard them gnaw off one of my thick braids. Then I lost my spirit. . . . My long hair was shingled like a coward's. In my anguish I moaned for my mother, but no one came to comfort me. Not a soul reasoned quietly with me, as my own mother used to do; for now I was only one of many little animals driven by a herder. . . .

I blamed the hard-working, well-meaning, ignorant [missionary] woman who was inculcating in our hearts her superstitious ideas. Though I was sullen in all my little troubles, as soon as I felt better I was . . . again actively testing the chains which tightly bound my individuality like a mummy for burial. . . .

Many specimens of civilized peoples visited the Indian school. The city folks with canes and eyeglasses, the countrymen with sunburnt cheeks and clumsy feet, forgot their relative social ranks in an ignorant curiosity. Both sorts of these Christian palefaces were alike as at seeing the children of savage warriors so docile and industrious. . . .

In this fashion many [whites] have passed idly through the Indian schools during the last decade, afterward to boast of their charity to the North American Indian. But few there are who have paused to question whether real life or long-lasting death lies beneath this semblance of civilization.

SOURCE: Zitkala-Sa, "The School Days of an Indian Girl" (1900). Reprinted in *American Indian Stories* (Glorieta, NM: Rio Grande Press, 1976).

houses. Saloons were social centers in towns where most miners lived in crowded and dirty tents and rooming houses.

The male-dominated saloon society of the mining camps generated social conflict. Disputes over mining claims could become violent, adding to the disorder. The California mining town of Bodie experienced 29 killings between 1877 and 1883, a homicide rate higher than that of any U.S. city a century later. But such killings occurred only within a small group of males, young, single, surly, and armed, who were known as the Badmen of Bodie. Daily life for most people was safe.

Collective Violence. Indeed, personal and criminal violence, which remains popularly associated with the West, was less pervasive than collective violence. This, too, affected mining camps and was aggravated by their ethnic and racial diversity. Irish, Germans,

English, Chinese, Australians, Italians, Slavs, and Mexicans, among others, rushed into the mining regions. In many camps, half the population was foreign-born. The European immigrants who sometimes encountered nativist hostility in the East experienced less animosity in the West, but nonwhite minorities often suffered. Whites frequently drove Mexicans and Chinese from their claims or refused to let them work in higher-paid occupations in the mining camps. The Chinese had originally migrated to the California gold fields and thereafter spread to the new mining areas of the Rockies and the Great Basin, where they worked in mining when possible, operated laundries and restaurants, and held menial jobs like hauling water and chopping wood. In 1870, more than a quarter of Idaho's population and nearly 10 percent of Montana's were Chinese. Where they were numerous, the Chinese built their own communities and maintained their customs.

But racism and fear of economic competition sparked hostility and violence against the Chinese almost everywhere. The worst anti-Chinese violence occurred in Rock Springs, Wyoming, in 1885 when whites killed 28 Chinese workers and drove away all 700 residents from the local Chinatown. Although the members of the mob were well known, the grand jury, speaking for the white majority, found no cause for legal action. Such community sanction for violence against racial minorities made mob attacks one of the worst features of the mining camps.

LABOR AND CAPITAL

New technology had dramatic consequences for both miners and the mining industry. Initially, mining was an individual enterprise in which miners used simple tools, such as picks, shovels, and wash pans, to work shallow surface deposits known as placers. Placer mining attracted prospectors with relatively little capital or expertise, but surface deposits were quickly exhausted. More complex and expensive operations were needed to reach the precious metal buried in the earth.

Hydraulic mining, for example, required massive capital investment to build reservoirs, ditches, and troughs to power high-pressure water cannons that would pulverize hillsides and uncover the mineral deposits. Quartz, or lode, mining, sometimes called hard-rock mining, required still more money, technology, and time to sink a shaft into the earth, timber underground chambers and tunnels, install pumps to remove underground water and hoists to lower men and lift out rock, and build stamp mills and smelters to treat the ore.

Such complex, expensive, and permanent operations necessarily came under corporate control. Often financed with eastern or British capital, the new corporations integrated the mining industry into the larger economy. Hard-rock mining produced more complex ores than could be treated in remote mining towns. With the new railroad network, they were shipped to smelting plants as far away as Kansas City and St. Louis and then to refineries in eastern cities. Western ores thus became part of national and international business.

Effects of Corporate Mining. Although corporate mining helped usher the mining frontier into a more stable period, it had disturbing effects. Its impact on the environment was horrendous. Hydraulic mining washed away hillsides, depositing debris in canyons and valleys to a depth of 100 feet or more, clogging rivers and causing floods, and burying thousands of acres of farmland. Such damage provoked an outcry and eventually led to government regulation. Fewer westerners worried about sterile slag heaps or the toxic fumes that

Opening restaurants and boarding houses, some women earned money from their domestic skills in the mining camps.

belched from smelters and killed vegetation. They were the signs of progress. "The thicker the fumes," declared one proud Butte newspaper, "the greater our financial vitality."

Corporate mining also hurt miners, transforming them into wageworkers with restricted opportunities. Miners' status declined as new machinery, such as power drills, reduced the need for skilled laborers and enabled employers to hire cheaper workers from eastern and southern Europe. Mining corporations, moreover, did little to protect miners' health or safety. Miners died in cave-ins, explosions, and fires or from the great heat and poisonous gases in underground mines. Others contracted silicosis, lead poisoning, or other diseases or were crippled or killed by machines.

Unions and Union Busting. To protect themselves, miners organized unions. These funtioned as benevolent societies, aiding injured miners or their survivors, establishing hospitals and libraries, and providing an alternative to the saloons with union halls serving as social and educational centers. Unions also promoted miners' interests by striking against wage cuts and campaigning for mine safety. They convinced states to pass mine safety laws and, beginning in the 1880s, to appoint mine inspectors. The chief role of these state officials was, in the words of a Colorado inspector, to decide "How far should an industry be permitted to advance its material welfare at the expense of human life?"

The industry itself, however, often provided the answer to this question, for mining companies frequently controlled state power and used it to crush unions. Thus, in 1892, in the Coeur d'Alene district of Idaho, mining companies locked out strikers and imported a private army, which battled miners in a bloody gunfight. Management next persuaded the governor and the president to send in the state militia and the U.S. Army. State officials then suppressed the strike and the union by confining all union members and their sympathizers in stockades.

Strikes, union busting, and violence continued for years. When mining companies in Utah, Colorado, and Montana pursued the same aggressive tactics of lockouts and wage cuts, the local miners' unions in the West united for strength and self-protection. In 1893, they formed one of the nation's largest and most militant unions, the Western Federation of Miners.

Violence and conflict were attributable not to frontier lawlessness but to the industrialization of the mines. Both management's tactics—blacklisting union members, locking out strikers, obtaining court injunctions against unions, and using soldiers against workers—and labor's response mirrored conditions in the industrial East. In sum, western mining, reflecting the industrialization of the national economy, had been transformed from a small-scale prospecting enterprise characterized by individual initiative and simple tools into a large-scale corporate business characterized by impersonal management, outside capital, advanced technology, and wage labor.

USING THE GRASS: THE CATTLE KINGDOM

The development of the range-cattle industry opened a second stage of exploitation of the late-nineteenth-century West. It reflected the needs of an emerging eastern urban society, the economic possibilities of the grasslands of the Great Plains, the technology of the expanding railroad network, and the requirements of corporations and capital. It also brought "cow towns" and urban development to the West. The fabled cowboy, though essential to the story, was only a bit player.

CATTLE DRIVES AND COW TOWNS

The cattle industry originated in southern Texas, where the Spanish had introduced cattle in the eighteenth century. Developed by Mexican ranchers, "Texas longhorns" proved well adapted to the plains grasslands. By the 1860s, they numbered about 5 million head. As industrial expansion in the East and Midwest enlarged the urban market for food, the potential value of Texas steers increased. And the extension of the railroad network into the West opened the possibility of tapping that market. The key was to establish a shipping point on the railroads west of the settled farming regions, a step first taken in 1867 by Joseph McCoy, an Illinois cattle shipper. McCoy selected Abilene, Kansas. Abilene was the western railhead of the Kansas Pacific Railroad and was ringed by lush grasslands for cattle. Texans opened the **Chisholm Trail** through Indian Territory to drive their cattle northward to Abilene. Within three years, a million and a half cattle reached Abilene, divided into herds of several thousand, each directed by a dozen cowhands on a "long drive" taking two to three months.

Cow Town Life. The cattle trade attracted other entrepreneurs who created a bustling town. As both railroads and settlement advanced westward, a series of other cow towns—Ellsworth, Wichita, Dodge City, Cheyenne—attracted the long drives, cattle herds, and urban development.

As with the mining camps, the cow towns' reputation for violence was exaggerated. They adopted gun-control laws, prohibiting the carrying of handguns within city limits, and established police forces to maintain order. The primary duties of law officers were arresting drunks, fixing sidewalks, and collecting fines. The cow towns regulated, rather than prohibited, prostitution and gambling, for merchants viewed these vices as necessary to attract the cattle trade. Thus, the towns taxed prostitutes and gamblers and charged high fees for liquor licenses. By collecting such "sin taxes," Wichita was able to forgo general business taxes, thereby increasing its appeal to prospective settlers.

Not all cow towns became cities like Wichita; most, like Abilene, dwindled into small towns serving farm populations. But cow towns, again like mining camps, contributed to the growth of an urban frontier. Railroads often determined the location and growth of western cities, providing access to markets for local products, transporting supplies and machinery for residents, and attracting capital for commercial and industrial development. The West, in fact, had become the most urban region in the nation by 1890, with two-thirds of its population living in communities of at least 2,500 people.

RISE AND FALL OF OPEN-RANGE RANCHING

The significance of the long drive to the cow towns faded as cattle raising expanded beyond Texas. Indian removal and extension of the railroads opened land for ranching in Kansas, Nebraska, Wyoming, Colorado, Montana, and the Dakotas. Cattle reaching Kansas were increasingly sold to stock these northern ranges rather than for shipment to the packinghouses. Ranches soon spread across the Great Plains and into the Great Basin, the Southwest, and even eastern Oregon and Washington. This expansion was helped by the initially low investment that ranching required. Calves were cheap, labor costs low, and grazing lands the open range of the public domain.

Cowboys gather around the chuck wagon at the XIT Ranch in Texas. Poor pay and arduous work defined the lives of most cowboys.

By the early 1880s, the high profits from this enterprise and an expanding market for beef attracted speculative capital and reshaped the industry. Eastern and European capital flooded the West, with British investors particularly prominent. Some investors went into partnership with existing ranchers, providing capital in exchange for expertise and management. On a larger scale, British and American corporations acquired, expanded, and managed huge ranches.

Effects of Corporate Control. Large companies soon dominated the industry, just as they had gained control of mining. Cattle companies often worked together to enhance their power, especially by restricting access to the range and by intimidating small competitors. Some large companies illegally enclosed the open range, building fences to exclude newcomers and minimize labor costs by reducing the number of cowboys needed to control the cattle. One Wyoming newspaper complained: "Some morning we will wake up to find that a corporation has run a wire fence about the boundary lines of Wyoming, and all within the same have been notified to move."

Such tensions sometimes exploded in instances of social violence as serious as those that disrupted the mining frontier. Attempts by large ranchers to fence off public lands in Texas provoked the Fence-Cutters War of 1883–84. Montana's largest cattlemen organized an armed force known as "Stuart's Stranglers" and, in America's worst vigilante violence, killed over a hundred people they viewed as challenging their power.

The corporate cattle boom overstocked the range and threatened the industry itself. Overgrazing replaced nutritious grasses with sagebrush, Russian thistle, and other plants that livestock found unpalatable. Droughts in the mid-1880s further withered vegetation and enfeebled the animals. Millions of cattle starved or froze to death in terrible blizzards in 1886 and 1887. These ecological and financial disasters destroyed the open-range cattle industry. The surviving ranchers reduced their operations, restricted the size of their herds, and tried to ensure adequate winter feed by growing hay. To further reduce their dependence on natural vegetation, they introduced drought-resistant sorghum and new grasses; to reduce their dependence on rainfall, they drilled wells and installed windmills to pump water.

COWHANDS AND CAPITALISTS

One constant in the cattle industry was the cowboy, but his working conditions and opportunities changed sharply over time and corresponded little to the romantic image of a dashing individual free of social constraints. Cowboys' work was hard, dirty, seasonal, tedious, sometimes dangerous, and poorly paid. Many early cowboys were white southerners unwilling or unable to return home after the Civil War. Black cowhands made up perhaps 25 percent of the trail-herd outfits. Many others, especially in Texas and the Southwest, were Mexicans. Indeed, Mexicans developed most of the tools, techniques, and trappings that characterized the cattle industry, from boots, chaps, and the "western" saddle to roundups and roping. As the industry expanded northward, more cowboys came from rural Kansas, Nebraska, and neighboring states.

Initially, in the frontier-ranching phase dominated by the long drive, cowboys were seasonal employees who worked closely with owners. Often the sons or neighbors of ranchers, they frequently expected to become stock raisers themselves. They typically enjoyed the rights to "maverick" cattle, or put their own brand on unmarked animals they encountered, and to "run a brand," or to own their own cattle while working for a ranch. These informal rights provided opportunities to acquire property and move up the social ladder.

As ranching changed with the appearance of large corporate enterprises, so did the work and work relationships of cowhands. The power and status of employer and employees diverged, and the cowboys' traditional rights disappeared. Employers redefined mavericking as rustling and prohibited cowhands from running a brand of their own. One cowboy complained that these restrictions deprived a cowhand of his one way "to get on in the world." But that was the purpose: Cowboys were to be workers, not potential ranchers and competitors. To increase labor efficiency, some companies prohibited their cowboys from drinking, gambling, and carrying guns.

Unions and Strikes. Cowboys sometimes responded to these structural transformations the same way skilled workers in the industrial East did, by forming unions and striking. The first strike occurred in Texas in 1883, when the Panhandle Stock Association, representing large operators, prohibited ranch hands from owning their own cattle and imposed a standard wage. More than 300 cowboys struck seven large ranches for higher wages and the right to brand mavericks for themselves and to run small herds on the public domain. Ranchers evicted the cowboys, hired scabs, and used the Texas Rangers to drive the strikers from the region.

Other strikes also failed because corporate ranches and their stock associations had great influence and cowhands faced long odds in their efforts to organize. They were isolated across vast spaces and had little leverage in the industry. After asking employers for "what we are worth after many years' experience," they conceded, "We are dependent on you."

The transformation of the western cattle industry and its integration into a national economy dominated by corporations thus made the cherished image of cowboy independence and rugged individualism more myth than reality. One visitor to America in the late 1880s commented: "Out in the fabled West, the life of the 'free' cowboy is as much that of a slave as is the life of his Eastern brother, the Massachusetts mill-hand. And the slave-owner is in both cases the same, the capitalist."

Working the Earth: Homesteaders and Agricultural Expansion

Even more than ranching and mining, agricultural growth boosted the western economy and bound it tightly to national and world markets. In this process, the government played a significant role, as did the railroads, science and technology, eastern and foreign capital, and the dreams and hard work of millions of rural settlers. The development of farming produced remarkable economic growth, but it left the dreams of many unfulfilled.

Settling the Land

To stimulate agricultural settlement, Congress passed the most famous land law, the **Homestead Act** of 1862 (see the Overview table, Government Land Policy). The measure offered 160 acres of land free to anyone who would live on the plot and farm it for five years. The act promised opportunity and independence to ambitious farmers.

Limits of the Homestead Act. Despite the apparently liberal land policy, however, prospective settlers found less land open to public entry than they expected. Federal land laws did not apply in much of California and the Southwest, where Spain and Mexico had previously transferred land to private owners. Elsewhere, the government had given away millions of acres to railroads or authorized selling millions more for educational and other purposes. Moreover, other laws provided for easy transfer of public lands to cattle companies, to other corporations exploiting natural resources, and to land speculators.

Thus, settlers in Kansas, Nebraska, Minnesota, and the Dakotas in the late 1860s and early 1870s often found most of the best land unavailable for homesteading and much of the rest remote from transportation facilities and markets. Although 375,000 farms were claimed by 1890 through the Homestead Act, a success by any measure, most settlers had to purchase their land.

The Homestead Act also reflected traditional eastern conceptions of the family farm, which were inappropriate in the West. A farm of 160 acres would have suited conditions in eastern Kansas or Nebraska, but farther west, larger-scale farming was necessary. And the law ignored the need for capital—for machinery, buildings, livestock, and fencing—that was required for successful farming.

Promoting Settlement. Nevertheless, many interests promoted settlement. Newspaper editors trumpeted the prospects of their region. Land companies, eager to sell their speculative holdings, sent agents through the Midwest and Europe to encourage migration. Steamship companies, hoping to sell transatlantic tickets, advertised the opportunities in the American West across Europe. Religious and ethnic groups encouraged immigration.

Most important, railroad advertising and promotional campaigns attracted people to the West. Promotion of the West was in the railroads' financial interest. Not only would they profit from selling their huge land reserves to settlers, but a successful agricultural economy would produce crops to be shipped east and a demand for manufactured goods to be shipped west on their lines. The railroads therefore advanced credit to prospective farmers, provided transportation assistance, and extended technical and agricultural advice.

Thus encouraged, migrants poured into the West, occupying and farming more acres between 1870 and 1900 than Americans had in the previous 250 years. Farmers settled in every region. Most, however, streamed into the Great Plains states, from the Dakotas to Texas.

White migrants predominated in the mass migration, but African Americans initiated one of its most dramatic episodes, a millenarian folk movement they called the Exodus. Seeking to escape the misery and repression of the post- Reconstruction South, these poor "Exodusters" established several dozen black communities in 1879 in Kansas and Nebraska on the agricultural frontier.

Many of the new settlers came from Europe, bringing with them not only their own attitudes toward the land but also special crops, skills, settlement patterns, and agricultural practices. Peasants from Norway, Sweden, and Denmark flocked to Minnesota. Germans, Russians, and Irish put down roots across Texas, Kansas, Nebraska, and the Dakotas. French, Germans, and Italians developed vineyards, orchards, and nurseries in California, where laborers from Japan and Mexico arrived to work in fields and canneries. Many Mexicans also entered Texas, some as temporary harvest labor, others as

Mexican-American ranch family, Mora Valley, New Mexico Territory, 1895. Anglo-dominated develop-
ment often displaced such families from their traditional lands and turned them into wage-laborers.
Courtesy: Photographic Archives, Palace of the Governors, Museum of New Mexico, Santa Fe, New Mexico /DCA Negative
No: 22468.

permanent residents. By 1890, many western states had substantial foreign-born populations; North Dakota's exceeded 40 percent, California's was nearly as high. Immigrants
often settled together in separate ethnic communities, held together by their church,
and attempted to preserve their language and customs rather than be assimilated.

Hispanic Losses. Migrants moved into the West in search of opportunity, which they
sometimes seized at the expense of others already there. In the Southwest, Hispanics
had long lived in village communities largely outside a commercial economy, farming
small tracts of irrigated land and herding sheep on communal pastures. As Anglos, or
white Americans, arrived, their political and economic influence undermined traditional Hispanic society. Congress restricted the original Hispanic land grants to only
the villagers' home lots and irrigated fields, throwing open most of their common lands
to newcomers. Hispanic title was confirmed to only 2 million of the 37.5 million acres
at stake. Anglo ranchers and settlers manipulated the federal land system to control
these lands.

Spanish Americans resisted these losses in court or through violence. One militant group, organized as *Las Gorras Blancas* ("the White Caps"), staged night raids
to cut fences erected by Anglo ranchers and farmers and to attack the property of
railroads, the symbol of the encroaching new order. Such resistance, however, had
little success.

OVERVIEW GOVERNMENT LAND POLICY

Legislation	Result
Railroad land grants (1850–1871)	Granted 181 million acres to railroads to encourage construction and development
Homestead Act (1862)	Gave 80 million acres to settlers to encourage settlement
Morrill Act (1862)	Granted 11 million acres to states to sell to fund public agricultural colleges
Other grants	Granted 129 million acres to states to sell for other educational and related purposes
Dawes Act (1887)	Allotted some reservation lands to individual Indians to promote private property and weaken tribal values among Indians and offered remaining reservation lands for sale to whites (by 1906, some 75 million acres had been acquired by whites)
Various laws	Permitted direct sales of 100 million acres by the Land Office

As their landholdings shrank, Hispanic villagers could not maintain their pastoral economy. Few turned to homesteading, for that would have required dispersed settlement and abandoning the village and its church, school, and other cultural institutions. Thus many Hispanics became seasonal wage laborers in the Anglo-dominated economy, sometimes working as stoop labor in the commercial sugar-beet fields that emerged in the 1890s, sometimes working on the railroads or in the mines. Such seasonal labor enabled Hispanics to maintain their villages and provided sufficient income to adopt some Anglo technology, such as cook stoves and sewing machines. But if Hispanics retained some cultural autonomy, they had little influence over the larger processes of settlement and development that restricted their opportunities and bound them to the western and national economy.

HOME ON THE RANGE

In settling the West, farm families encountered many difficulties, especially on the Great Plains, where they had to adapt to a radically new environment. The scarcity of trees on the plains meant that there was little wood for housing, fuel, and fencing. Until they had reaped several harvests and could afford to import lumber, pioneer families lived in houses made of sod. Though inexpensive and sturdy, sod houses were also dark and dirty. Snakes, mice, and insects often crawled out of the walls and roofs.

Women's Work. Within these rough houses, women worked to provide food, clothing, and medicine to ensure the family's survival. Their efforts were greatly constrained by the harsh environment. For fuel, families often had to rely on buffalo or cattle "chips," dried dung. The scarcity of water also complicated women's domestic labor. They often had to transport water over long distances, pulling barrels on "water sleds" or carrying pails on neck yokes. They melted snow for wash water and used the same water over again for different chores. Where possible, they also helped to dig wells by hand.

Some women farmed the land themselves. Single women could claim land under the Homestead Act, and in some areas, women claimants made up 18 percent of the total and succeeded more frequently than men in gaining final title. At times, married women operated the family farm by themselves while their husbands worked elsewhere to earn the money needed for seeds, equipment, and building supplies.

Isolation and Community. Isolation and loneliness troubled many early settlers on the plains. Women especially suffered because they frequently had less contact with other people than farm men, who conducted their families' business in town and participated in such public activities as political meetings.

Over time, conditions improved. As population increased, women in particular worked to bind isolated households into communities by organizing social activities and institutions. They held fairs, dances, and picnics and established churches, schools, and libraries, thereby gaining both companionship and a sense of purpose.

Churches, in turn, also promoted community. Indeed, many were "union" churches, open to people of all denominations. In addition to holding religious services, revivals, and camp meetings, churches were often the center of social life, especially by sponsoring socials and children's organizations. Nondenominational Sunday schools helped bind together differing nationalities and church preferences, and because they did not require the services of an ordained minister they often enabled women to initiate and lead community activities.

Other institutions also encouraged community action. Rural families created their own agricultural cooperatives and other economic and social organizations, like local Grange lodges. External developments also served the rural population. Rural Free Delivery, for example, eventually brought letters, newspapers, magazines, and advertisements to farm families' doorsteps; mail-order companies made available to farm people such helpful goods as stoves, sewing machines, and shoes. Such changes helped incorporate westerners into the larger society.

FARMING THE LAND

Pioneer settlers had to make daunting adjustments to develop the agricultural potential of their new land. Advances in science, technology, and industry made such adjustments possible. The changes not only reshaped the agricultural economy but also challenged traditional rural values and expectations.

Growing Crops. Fencing was an immediate problem, for crops needed protection from livestock. But without timber, farmers could not build wooden fences. Barbed wire, developed in the mid-1870s, solved the problem. By 1900, farmers were importing nearly 300 million pounds of barbed wire each year from eastern and midwestern factories.

The aridity of most of the West also posed difficulties. In California, Colorado, and a few other areas, settlers used streams fed by mountain snow packs to irrigate land. Elsewhere, enterprising farmers developed variants of the "dry farming" practices that the Mormons had introduced in Utah to maximize the limited rainfall. Some farmers erected windmills to pump underground water. The scarce rainfall also discouraged the cultivation of many of the crops that supported traditional general agriculture and encouraged farmers to specialize in a single cash crop for market. Government agencies and agricultural colleges contributed to the success of such adaptations, and private engineers and inventors also fostered agricultural development. Related technological advancements included grain elevators that would store grain for shipment and load it into rail cars mechanically and mills that used corrugated, chilled-iron rollers rather than millstones to process the new varieties of wheat.

Mechanization and technological innovations made possible the large-scale farming practiced in semiarid regions. Farmers required special plows to break the tough sod, new harrows to prepare the soil for cultivation, grain drills to plant the crop, and harvesting and threshing machines to bring it in. Thanks to more and better machines, agricultural efficiency and productivity shot up. By the 1890s, machinery permitted the farmer to produce 18 times more wheat than hand methods had. Nearly 1,000 corporations were manufacturing agricultural machinery to meet the demands of farmers, who purchased implements in steadily mounting quantities.

Growing Tensions. These developments reflected both the expansion of agriculture and its increasing dependence on the larger society. Western commercial farmers needed the high demand of eastern and midwestern cities and the expanding world market. The rail network provided essential transportation for their crops; the nation's industrial sector produced necessary agricultural machinery. Banks and loan companies extended the credit and capital that allowed farmers to take advantage of mechanization and other new advances; and many other businesses graded, stored, processed, and sold their crops. In short, because of its market orientation, mechanization, and specialization, western agriculture relied on other people or impersonal forces as it was incorporated into the national and international economy.

When conditions were favorable—good weather, good crops, and good prices—western farmers prospered. Too often, however, they faced adversity. The early years of settlement were unusually wet, but even then periodic droughts brought crop failures. Other natural hazards also disrupted production. Especially alarming were plagues of grasshoppers. Grasshoppers ate crops, clothing, and bedding; they attacked sod houses and chewed woodwork and furniture.

In the late 1880s, drought coincided with a slump in crop prices. The large European market that had encouraged agricultural expansion in the 1870s and early 1880s contracted after 1885, when several nations erected trade barriers to U.S. commodities. More important, America's production competed with that from Argentina, Canada, Australia, and Russia, and a world surplus of grain drove prices steadily downward.

Squeezed between high costs for credit, transportation, and manufactured goods and falling agricultural prices, western farmers faced disaster. They responded by lashing back at their points of contact with the new system. They especially condemned the railroads, believing that the companies charged excessive and discriminatory freight rates.

Farm workers harvested grain with a horse-drawn Marsh harvester, manufactured by a Chicago company. Such machinery increased farm productivity but made farming more expensive.

Farmers censured the grain elevators in the local buying centers. Often owned by eastern corporations, including the railroads, elevators allegedly exploited their local monopoly to cheat farmers by fixing low prices or misrepresenting the quality of wheat. A Minnesota state investigation found that systematic fraud by elevators cost farmers collectively a massive sum. Farmers also denounced the bankers and mortgage lenders who had provided the credit for them to acquire land, equipment, and machinery. Much of the money had come from eastern investors seeking the higher interest rates in the West. With failing crops and falling prices, however, the debt burden proved calamitous for many farmers. Beginning in 1889, many western farms were foreclosed.

Stunned and bitter, western farmers concluded that their problems arose because they had been incorporated into the new system, an integrated economy directed by forces beyond their control. And it was a system that did not work well. "There is," one of them charged, "something radically wrong in our industrial system. There is a screw loose."

CONCLUSION

The farmers' complaints indicted the major processes by which the West was developed and exploited in the late nineteenth century. Railroad expansion, population movements, eastern investment, corporate control, technological innovations, and government policies had incorporated the region fully into the larger society. Indians experienced this incorporation most thoroughly and most tragically, losing their lands, their traditions, and often their lives.

Cowboys and miners also learned that the frontier merely marked the cutting edge of eastern industrial society. Both groups were wageworkers, often for corporations controlled by eastern capital, and if industrial technology directly affected miners more than cowhands, neither could escape integration into the national economy by managerial decisions, transportation links, and market forces. Most settlers in the West were farmers, but they too learned that their distinctive environment did not insulate them from assimilation into larger productive, financial, and marketing structures.

Western developments, in short, reflected and interacted with those of eastern industrial society. The processes of incorporation drained away westerners' hopes along with their products, and many of the discontented would demand a serious reorganization of relationships and power. Led by angry farmers, they turned their attention to politics and government, where they encountered new obstacles and opportunities.

REVIEW QUESTIONS

1. Why was the completion of the first transcontinental railroad, described by Andrew J. Russell, celebrated from Boston to San Francisco? How did western railroads shape the settlement and development of the West and affect the East as well?

2. What factors were most influential in the subjugation of American Indians?

3. What were the major goals of federal Indian policy, and how did they change?

4. How did technological developments affect Indians, miners, and farmers in the West?

5. How did the federal government help transform the West?

6. In what ways did European investors, markets, and migrants influence the development of the American West?

PEARSON myhistorylab CONNECTIONS

Reinforce what you learned in this chapter by studying the many documents, images, maps, review tools, and videos available at **www.myhistorylab.com.**

READ AND REVIEW

✓•─Study and Review on myhistorylab.com STUDY PLAN: CHAPTER 19

▯•─Read the Document on myhistorylab.com

Helen Hunt Jackson, From A Century of Dishonor (1881)

Accounts of the Wounded Knee Massacre (1890s)

John Lester, "Hydraulic Mining" (1873)

Joseph G. McCoy, Historic Sketches of the Cattle Trade of the West and Southwest (1874)

Perspectives on the American Cowboy (1884, 1886)

Advice on Keeping Children on the Farm (1881)

Frederick Jackson Turner, Rise of the New West (1906)

Secretary of Interior's Congressional Report on Indian Affairs (1887)

The Homestead Act of 1862

👁─See the Map

Resources and Conflict in the West

RESEARCH AND EXPLORE

▯•─Read the Document on myhistorylab.com

Personal Journeys Online

From Then to Now Online: The Legacy of Americanization

Exploring America: Dakota Sioux Conflict

Exploring America: Americanization

👁─Watch the Video on myhistorylab.com

Sioux Ghost Dance

Cowboys and Cattle

The Real West Is an Urban West

(((•─Listen on myhistorylab.com

Hear the audio files for Chapter 19 at
www.myhistorylab.com.

20 Politics and Government • • 1877–1900

Hear the audio files for Chapter 20 at **www.myhistorylab.com.**

FOCUS QUESTIONS

HOW DID parties shape late-nineteenth-century politics?

WHAT EXPLAINS the weakness and inefficiency of late-nineteenth-century government?

HOW EFFECTIVE was government in addressing the problems of America's industrializing economy?

WHAT FACTORS contributed to the rise and fall of the Populist Party?

In the late nineteenth century, parades like this Republican one in Canton, Ohio, in 1896 were popular features of a participatory political culture dominated by political parties and intense partisanship.

ONE AMERICAN JOURNEY

The largest political procession of the season in Fort Wayne, so far, was that of the Republicans Saturday night. They turned out in very large numbers and paraded on the principal streets preparatory to the speaking which came later at the Rifles' armory. The following were in line:

First Regiment Band
Railroad Men's Club
Soldiers' and Sons' Union Club
Tippecanoe Club
Chase Club
Lincoln Club
McKinley Club
Colored Drum Corps
Colored Republicans' Club
Republican Voters

The McKinley Club wore tin hats and the Tippecanoe club carried torches that spouted fire at intervals. One of the prettiest illuminations was the railroad lantern light of the Railroad Men's Republican club. The numerous lights of the colors used in the railway service make as pretty a sight as can be seen anywhere.

Most of the clubs were in fine uniforms and made a grand appearance. Numerous banners and transparencies announcing mottoes of the campaign were carried. One banner bore the words, "Cleveland's record—Glad Lincoln was shot—Pronounced the war a failure."

The great parade was viewed by thousands of people who thronged the streets all along the line of march.

The hall was crowded and the meeting was most enthusiastic. Music was furnished by the band and Emerson quartette of Huntington. . . . The quartette just took the cake. Anything more enjoyable and mirth-provoking than their glees rendered as they render them would be hard to find. After music by the quartette, which was enthusiastically encored, Dr. Stemen, the presiding officer, introduced the speaker of the evening, Hon. L. R. Stookey, of Warsaw, Ind. Mr. Stookey is a ready and rapid speaker. He paid a glowing tribute to the soldiers, and referred in scathing terms to Grover Cleveland's treatment of them and his insulting vetoes of pension bills. He spoke . . . [of a law providing for election supervisors at the polls] and what we ask is that it shall apply without limitation north and south whenever there is an attempt or danger of attempt, to deny equal rights of all to cast their free ballot and have it counted as cast.

When he concluded the Emerson quartette gave another selection and responded to an encore. The audience then began to call loudly for "You," "You." Mr. A. J. You, our candidate for congress, was then introduced and made a stirring address. Mr. You has been speaking nearly every day and evening and is holding out first rate and proving himself one of the most popular candidates in the field.

He was repeatedly and enthusiastically cheered during his speech. Another selection by the quartette, and the house resounded with calls for "Brown," "Brown." Rev. W. H. Brown, for years the pastor of the A. M. E. church, of this city, took the platform and though he protested that the hour was too late to permit another speech made it clearly evident in the course of a twenty minute speech that the colored people of the country understand the situation and intend to stand by the party that broke the chains and gave freedom to the slave. The meeting then adjourned to music by the Glee club.

Fort Wayne (Ind.) *Weekly Gazette,* October 20, 1892.

T**HE** *Fort Wayne Weekly Gazette,* a fiercely Republican newspaper, proudly reported on the activities of the local Republicans in Indiana during the political campaign in 1892. The pageantry and hoopla made politics a major source of popular entertainment for Republicans and Democrats alike. But the extreme campaign rhetoric and outright misrepresentation of opponents indicated the intensity of partisan emotions. So did the military-style campaign, with uniformed marchers organized into companies, brigades, and divisions; with signs, slogans, and speeches referring to soldiers and the Civil War; with rallies held in armories. These campaign features also pointed to the enduring importance of the Civil War as a basis for partisan divisions and loyalties and marked electoral politics as a rough-and-tumble masculine business.

At the same time, contemporary issues did matter. Stookey's stump appeal for election supervisors to protect voters' rights at the polls pointed to an important policy issue while hinting at the sometimes violent nature of elections, including the suppression of voters. It also emphasized that suffrage was often a contested issue.

The prominent role of Rev. Brown, the content of his speech, and the participation of the Colored Drum Corps and the Colored Republicans' Club in the parade show that partisan divisions in the United States overlapped with racial, religious, and other social divisions. Black voters, for instance, would "stand by the party that broke the chains and gave freedom to the slave."

While the *Gazette* lavished praise on the Republican campaign, its Democratic counterpart, the *Fort Wayne Sentinel,* extolled the success of the Democratic campaign. Such partisanship permeated journalism as well as nearly all aspects of public life, including government agencies.

These features of late-nineteenth-century politics would eventually be transformed in significant ways. But while they endured, they shaped not only campaigns and elections but also the form and role of government. Only a national crisis in the 1890s would finally cause some Americans to demand more of their political leaders and institutions.

THE STRUCTURE AND STYLE OF POLITICS

Politics in the late nineteenth century was an absorbing activity. Campaigns and elections expressed social values as they determined who held the reins of government. Political parties dominated political life. They organized campaigns, controlled balloting, and held the unswerving loyalty of most of the electorate. While the major parties

CHRONOLOGY

1867   Patrons of Husbandry (the Grange) is founded.

1869   Massachusetts establishes the first state regulatory commission.

1873   Silver is demonetized in the "Crime of '73."

1874   Woman's Christian Temperance Union is organized.

1875   U.S. Supreme Court, in *Minor v. Happersett,* upholds denial of suffrage to women.

1876   Greenback Party runs presidential candidate.

1877   Rutherford B. Hayes becomes president after disputed election.
Farmers' Alliance is founded.
Supreme Court, in *Munn v. Illinois,* upholds state regulatory authority over private property.

1878   Bland-Allison Act requires the government to buy silver.

1880   James A. Garfield is elected president.

1881   Garfield is assassinated; Chester A. Arthur becomes president.

1883   Pendleton Civil Service Act is passed.

1884   Grover Cleveland is elected president.

1886   Supreme Court, in *Wabash v. Illinois,* rules that only the federal government, not the states, can regulate interstate commerce.

1887   Interstate Commerce Act is passed.

1888   Benjamin Harrison is elected president.

1890   Sherman Antitrust Act is passed.
McKinley Tariff Act is passed.
Sherman Silver Purchase Act is passed.
National American Woman Suffrage Association is organized.
Wyoming enters the Union as the first state with woman suffrage.

1892   People's Party is organized.
Cleveland is elected to his second term as president.

1893   Depression begins.
Sherman Silver Purchase Act is repealed.

1894   Coxey's Army marches to Washington.
Pullman strike ends in violence.

1895   Supreme Court, in *Pollock v. Farmers' Loan and Trust Company,* invalidates the federal income tax.
Supreme Court, in *United States v. E. C. Knight Company,* limits the Sherman Antitrust Law to commerce, excluding industrial monopolies.

| 1896 | William Jennings Bryan is nominated for president by Democrats and Populists. William McKinley is elected president. |
| 1900 | Currency Act puts U.S. currency on the gold standard. |

worked to maintain a sense of unity and tradition among their followers, third parties sought to activate those the major parties left unserved. Other Americans looked outside the electoral arena to achieve their political goals.

CAMPAIGNS AND ELECTIONS

Political campaigns and elections generated remarkable public participation and enthusiasm. They constituted a major form of entertainment at a time when recreational opportunities were limited. Attending party meetings and conventions, listening to lengthy speeches appealing to group loyalties and local pride, gathering at the polls to watch the voting and the counting, celebrating victory and drowning the disappointment of defeat—all these provided social enjoyment and defined popular politics.

Virtually all men participated in politics. In many states, even immigrants not yet citizens were eligible to vote and flocked to the polls. African Americans voted regularly in the North and irregularly in the South before being disfranchised at the end of the century. Overall, turnout was remarkably high, averaging nearly 80 percent of eligible voters in presidential elections between 1876 and 1900, a figure far greater than ever achieved thereafter.

Political parties mobilized this huge electorate. With legal regulations and public machinery for elections negligible, parties dominated the campaigns and elections. Until the 1890s, most states had no laws to ensure secrecy in voting, and balloting often took place in open rooms or on sidewalks. Election clerks and judges were not public officials but partisans chosen by the political parties.

Nor did public authorities issue official ballots. Instead voters used party tickets—strips of paper printed by the parties—listing only the names of the candidates of the party issuing them and varying in size and color. Casting a ballot thus revealed the voter's party allegiance. Fighting and intimidation were so commonplace at the polls that one state supreme court ruled in 1887 that they were "acceptable" features of elections.

As the court recognized, the open and partisan aspects of the electoral process did not necessarily lead to election fraud, however much they shaped the nature of political participation. In these circumstances, campaigns and elections provided opportunities for men to demonstrate publicly their commitment to their party and its values, thereby reinforcing their partisan loyalties.

Although not permitted to vote, women, too, often exhibited their partisanship in this exciting political environment. Women wrote partisan literature and gave campaign speeches. Sometimes they acted together with men; other times they worked through separate women's organizations. In these partisan groups women discussed and circulated party literature and devised plans to influence elections.

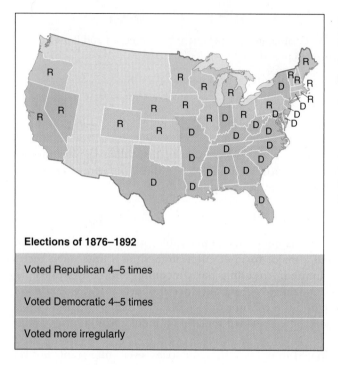

MAP 20–1 • **The Two-Party Stalemate of the Late Nineteenth Century** Strong parties, staunch loyalties, and an evenly divided electorate made for exciting politics but often stalemated government in the late nineteenth century. Most states voted consistently for one of the major parties, leaving the few swing states like New York and Indiana the scenes of fierce partisan battles.

Elections of 1876–1892

Voted Republican 4–5 times

Voted Democratic 4–5 times

Voted more irregularly

PARTISAN POLITICS

A remarkably close balance prevailed between the two major parties in the elections of this era. Democrats and Republicans had virtually the same level of electoral support, one reason they worked so hard to get out the vote (see Map 20–1). Control of the presidency and Congress shifted back and forth. Rarely did either party control both branches of government at once.

The party balance gave great influence to New York, New Jersey, Ohio, and Indiana, whose evenly divided voters controlled electoral votes that could swing an election either way. Both parties tended to nominate presidential and vice presidential candidates from those states to woo their voters. The parties also concentrated campaign funds and strategy on the swing states.

Party Loyalty. Interrelated regional, ethnic, religious, and local factors determined the party affiliations of most Americans. Economic issues, although important to the politics of the era, generally did not decide party ties. Farmers, for example, despite their many shared economic concerns, affiliated with both major parties. Like religious belief and ethnic identity, partisan loyalty was largely a cultural trait passed from parents to children, a situation that helps to explain the electoral stability of most communities.

Republicans were strongest in the North and Midwest, where they benefited from their party's role as the defender of the Union in the Civil War. But not all northerners voted for the Grand Old Party, or GOP. The Republican Party appealed primarily to old-stock Americans and other Protestants, including those of German and Scandinavian descent. African Americans, loyal to the party that had emancipated and enfranchised the slaves of the South, also supported the GOP where they could vote. Democrats were strongest in the South, where they stood as the defenders of the traditions of the region's white population. But Democrats also drew support in the urban Northeast, especially from Catholics and recent immigrants.

Party Identities. Each major party consisted of a complex coalition of groups with differing traditions and interests. This internal diversity often provoked conflict and threatened party stability. To hold its coalition together, each party identified itself with a theme that appealed broadly to all its constituents, while suggesting that it was menaced by the members and objectives of the opposing party.

Republicans identified their party with nationalism and national unity and attacked the Democrats as an "alliance between the embittered South and the slums of the northern cities." They combined a "bloody shirt" appeal to the memories of the Civil War with campaigns for immigration restriction and cultural uniformity. Seeing a threat to American society in efforts by Catholic immigrants to preserve their ethnic and cultural traditions, for example, Republican legislatures in several states in the 1880s and 1890s enacted laws regulating parochial schools, the use of foreign languages, and alcohol consumption.

Democrats portrayed themselves as the party of limited government and "personal liberties," a theme that appealed to both the racism of white southerners and the resentment immigrants felt about the nativist meddling of Republicans. The Democrats' commitment to personal liberties had limits. They supported the disfranchisement of African Americans, the exclusion of Chinese immigrants, and the dispossession of American Indians. Nevertheless, their emphasis on traditional individualism and localism proved popular.

The partisan politics of both major parties culminated in party machines, especially at the local level. Led by powerful bosses, the machines controlled not only city politics but also municipal government. Party activists used well-organized ward clubs to mobilize working-class voters, who were rewarded with municipal jobs and baskets of food or coal doled out by the machine. Such assistance was often necessary, given the lack of public welfare systems, but to buy votes the machine also sold favors. Public contracts and franchises were peddled to businesses whose high bids covered kickbacks to the machine.

Third Parties. The partisan politics of the era left room for several third parties, organized around specific issues or groups. The **Prohibition Party** persistently championed the abolition of alcohol but also supported electoral reforms such as woman suffrage, economic reforms such as railroad regulation and income taxes, and social reforms including improved race relations. The **Greenback Party** of the 1870s denounced "the infamous financial legislation which takes all from the many to enrich the few." Its policies of labor reform and currency inflation (to stimulate and democratize the economy) attracted supporters from Maine to Texas. Other significant third parties included the Anti-Monopoly Party, the Union Labor Party, and, most important, the People's or **Populist Party** of the 1890s. Although third parties often won temporary success at the local or regional level, they never permanently displaced the major parties or undermined traditional voter allegiances.

ASSOCIATIONAL POLITICS

Much political activity was neither partisan nor electoral. Associations of like-minded citizens, operating as pressure groups, played an increasingly important role in late-nineteenth-century politics. These organizations worked to achieve public policies beneficial to their members. Farmers organized many such groups, most notably the Patrons of Husbandry, known familiarly as the Grange (see Chapter 17). Its campaign for public regulation of the rates charged by railroads and grain elevators helped convince midwestern states to pass the so-called **Granger laws.**

Industrialists also formed pressure groups. Organizations such as the American Iron and Steel Association and the American Protective Tariff League lobbied Congress for high tariff laws and made campaign contributions to friendly politicians of both parties. At the state level, business groups used their political clout to block the reform efforts of farmers and workers, sometimes in the legislatures but otherwise in the courts.

A small group of conservative reformers known derisively as **Mugwumps** (the term derives from the Algonquian word for "chief") devoted most of their effort to campaigning for honest and efficient government through civil service reform. Other pressure groups focused on cultural politics. The rabidly anti-Catholic American Protective Association, for example, agitated for laws restricting immigration, taxing church property, and inspecting Catholic religious institutions.

Christian lobbyists committed their political energies to demanding laws imposing their view of personal moral behavior. They campaigned to require Bible reading in schools, restrict divorces, and prohibit gambling and other "sinful" practices. Their greatest success was the Comstock Law, passed by Congress in 1873, which outlawed the possession or sale of "obscene" materials, including any contraceptive information or devices. Directly affecting the lives of many Americans, the Comstock Law clearly revealed the importance of this type of political activism.

Women as Activists. Women also sought power and influence through associational politics. The **National American Woman Suffrage Association** lobbied Congress and state legislatures for constitutional amendments extending the vote to women. Despite the opposition of male politicians of both major parties, suffragists succeeded by the mid-1890s in gaining full woman suffrage in four western states, Wyoming, Colorado, Idaho, and Utah, and partial suffrage (the right to vote in school elections) in several other states, east and west.

Other women shaped public issues through social service organizations. Although the belief that women belonged in the domestic sphere limited their involvement in electoral politics, it furnished a basis for political action focused on welfare and moral reform. With petition campaigns, demonstrations, and lobbying, women's social service organizations sought to remedy poverty and disease, improve education and recreation, and provide day nurseries for the children of working women.

Women combined domesticity and politics in the temperance movement. Alcoholism, widespread in U.S. society, was regarded as a major cause of crime, wife abuse, and broken homes. The temperance movement thus invoked women's presumed moral superiority to address a real problem that fell within their accepted sphere. The Woman's Christian Temperance Union (WCTU) gained a massive membership by campaigning for restrictive liquor laws.

Women lobbying a Congressional committee to support woman suffrage. Susan B. Anthony noted with regret that "to all men women suffrage is only a side issue."

Under the leadership of Frances Willard, the WCTU built on traditional women's concerns to develop an important critique of American society. Reversing the conventional view, Willard argued that alcohol abuse was a result, not a cause, of poverty and social disorder. Under the slogan of "Home Protection," the WCTU inserted domestic issues into the political sphere with a campaign for social and economic reforms far beyond temperance. It pushed for improved health conditions, reached out to the Knights of Labor to support workplace reforms, and lobbied for federal aid to education, particularly as a means to provide schooling for black children in the South. It eventually supported woman suffrage as well, on the grounds that women needed the vote to fulfill their duty to protect home, family, and morality.

THE LIMITS OF GOVERNMENT

Despite the popular enthusiasm for partisan politics and the persistent pressure of associational politics, government in the late nineteenth century was neither active nor productive by present standards. The receding governmental activism of the Civil War and Reconstruction years coincided with a resurgent belief in localism and **laissez-faire** policies. In addition, a Congress and presidency divided between the two major parties, a small and inefficient bureaucracy, and judicial restraints joined powerful private interests to limit the size and objectives of the federal government.

THE WEAK PRESIDENCY

The presidency was a weak and restricted institution. The impeachment of President Johnson at the outset of Reconstruction had undermined the office. President Grant clearly subordinated it to the legislative branch by deferring to Congress on

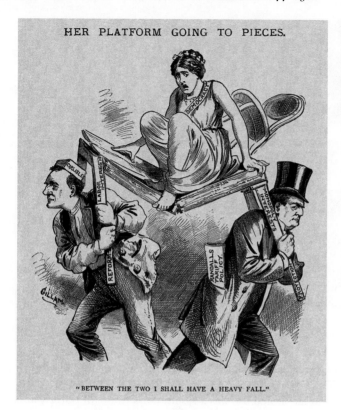

HER PLATFORM GOING TO PIECES.

"BETWEEN THE TWO I SHALL HAVE A HEAVY FALL."

Political divisions over public policies often occurred within rather than between the major parties. Here the platform of the Democratic Party ("Democracy") is splintering because of conflicting interests.

appointments and legislation. Other factors contributed as well. The men who filled the office between 1877 and 1897 were all honest and generally capable. Each had built a solid political record at the state or federal level. But they were all conservatives, with a narrow view of the presidency, and proposed few initiatives. The presidents of this era viewed their duties as chiefly administrative. They made little effort to reach out to the public or to exert legislative leadership. The presidency was also hampered by its limited control over bureaus and departments, which responded more directly to Congress, and by its small staff, consisting of no more than a half-dozen secretaries, clerks, and telegraphers.

THE INEFFICIENT CONGRESS

Congress was the foremost branch of the national government. It exercised authority over the federal budget, oversaw the cabinet, debated public issues, and controlled legislation. Its members were often state and national party leaders, who were strong-willed and, as one senator conceded, "tolerated no intrusion from the President or from anybody else."

But Congress was scarcely efficient. Its chambers were noisy and chaotic, and members rarely devoted their attention to the business at hand. The repeated shifts in party control impeded effective action. So, too, did the loss of experienced legislators to rapid turnover. In some Congresses, a majority of members were first-termers. Procedural rules, based on precedents from a simpler time and manipulated by determined partisans, hindered congressional action. Some rules restricted the introduction of legislation; others prevented its passage. The most notorious rule required that a quorum be not only present but voting. When the House was narrowly divided along party lines, the minority could block all business simply by refusing to answer when the roll was called.

But as a nationalizing economy required more national legislation, the amount of business before Congress grew relentlessly. The expanding scale of congressional work prompted a gradual reform of procedures and the centralization of power in the Speaker of the House and the leading committees. These changes did not, however, create a coherent program for government action.

THE FEDERAL BUREAUCRACY AND THE SPOILS SYSTEM

Reflecting presidential weakness and congressional inefficiency, the federal bureaucracy remained small and limited in the late nineteenth century. There were little more than 50,000 government employees in 1871, and three-fourths of them were local postmasters scattered across the nation.

The system for selecting and supervising federal officials had developed gradually in the first half of the century. Known as the spoils system, its basic principle was that victorious politicians awarded government jobs to party workers, often with little regard for qualifications, and ousted the previous employees. The spoils system played a crucial role in all aspects of politics. It enabled party leaders to strengthen their organizations, reward loyal party service, and attract the political workers needed to mobilize the electorate. Supporters described it as a democratic system that offered opportunities to many citizens and prevented the emergence of an entrenched bureaucracy.

Critics, however, charged that the system was riddled with corruption, abuse, and inefficiency. Rapid turnover bred instability; political favoritism bred incompetence. Certainly, the spoils system was ineffective for filling positions that required special clerical skills or scientific expertise. Even worse, the spoils system absorbed the president and Congress in unproductive conflicts over patronage.

INCONSISTENT STATE GOVERNMENT

State governments were more active than the federal government. Considered closer and more responsible to the people, they had long exercised police power and regulatory authority. They collected taxes for education and public works, and they promoted private enterprise and public health. Still, they did little by today's standards. Few people thought it appropriate for government at any level to offer direct help to particular social groups. Some state governments contracted in the 1870s and 1880s, following the wartime activism of the 1860s, and new state constitutions restricted the scope of public authority.

Nonetheless, state governments gradually expanded their role in response to the stresses produced by industrialization. Following the lead of Massachusetts in 1869, most states had by the turn of the century created commissions to investigate and regulate industry. Public intervention in other areas of the economy soon followed. In Minnesota, for example, the state helped farmers by establishing a dairy commission, prohibiting the manufacture or sale of margarine, creating a bureau of animal industry, and employing state veterinarians.

Not all such agencies and laws were effective, nor were all state governments as diligent as Minnesota's. Southern states, especially, lagged, and one midwesterner complained that his legislature "meets in ignorance, sits in corruption, and dissolves in disgrace every two years." Still, the widening scope of state action represented a growing acceptance of public responsibility for social welfare and economic life and laid the foundation for more effective steps in the early twentieth century.

PUBLIC POLICIES AND NATIONAL ELECTIONS

Several great issues dominated the national political arena in the late nineteenth century, including civil service reform, tariffs, and business and financial regulation. Rarely, however, did these issues clearly and consistently separate the major political parties. Instead, they divided each party into factions along regional, interest, and economic lines. As a consequence, these leading issues often played only a small role in determining elections and were seldom resolved by government action.

CIVIL SERVICE REFORM

Reform of the spoils system emerged as a prominent issue during the 1870s. The Mugwumps and other reformers wanted a professional civil service, based on merit and divorced from politics. They wanted officeholders to be selected on the basis of competitive written examinations and protected from removal on political grounds. They expected such a system to promote efficiency, economy, and honesty in government. But they also expected it to increase their own influence and minimize that of "mere politicians."

President Rutherford B. Hayes favored civil service reform but did not fully renounce the spoils system. He rewarded those who had helped to elect him, permitted party leaders to name or veto candidates for the cabinet, and insisted that his own appointees contribute funds to Republican election campaigns. But he rejected the claims of some machine leaders and office seekers and struck a blow for change when he fired Chester A. Arthur from his post as New York customs-house collector after an investigation pronounced Arthur's patronage system "unsound in principle, dangerous in practice," and characterized by "ignorance, inefficiency, and corruption."

The weakness of the civil service reformers was dramatically underscored in 1880 when the Republicans, to improve their chances of carrying the crucial state of New York, nominated Chester A. Arthur for vice president on a ticket headed by James Garfield of Ohio. They won, and Garfield immediately found himself enmeshed in the demands of the unreformed spoils system. Within a few months of his inauguration in 1881, Garfield was assassinated by a disappointed and crazed office seeker, and Arthur became president.

Public dismay over this tragedy finally spurred changes in the spoils system. In 1883 Congress passed the **Pendleton Civil Service Act,** prohibiting federal employees from soliciting or receiving political contributions from government workers and creating the Civil Service Commission to administer competitive examinations to applicants for government jobs. The act gave the commission jurisdiction over only about 10 percent of federal positions but provided that presidents could extend its authority. A professional civil service free from partisan politics gradually emerged,

In the 1880s many Americans feared that corporate power had too much influence in government and was endangering popular liberty. The question, as posed by this cartoon, was "What are you going to do about it?"

strengthening the executive branch's ability to handle its increasing administrative responsibilities.

The new emphasis on merit and skill rather than party ties opened new opportunities to women. Federal clerks were nearly exclusively male as late as 1862, but by the early 1890s, women held a third of the clerical positions in the executive departments in Washington. These workers constituted the nation's first substantial female clerical labor force. Their work in public life challenged the conventional belief that a woman's ability and personality limited her to the domestic sphere.

THE POLITICAL LIFE OF THE TARIFF

Americans debated heatedly over tariff legislation throughout the late nineteenth century. This complex issue linked basic economic questions to partisan, ideological, and regional concerns. Tariffs on imported goods provided revenue for the federal government and protected American industry from European competition. They promoted industrial growth but often allowed favored industries to garner high profits. By the 1880s, tariffs covered 4,000 items and generated more revenue than the government needed to carry on its limited operations.

Reflecting its commitment to industry, the Republican Party vigorously championed protective tariffs. Party leaders also claimed that American labor benefited from tariff protection. Most Democrats, by contrast, favored tariff reduction, a position that reflected their party's relatively laissez-faire outlook. They argued that lower tariffs would encourage foreign trade and, by reducing the treasury surplus, minimize the temptation for the government to pursue activist policies. They pointed out the discriminatory effects of high tariffs, which benefited some interests, such as certain manufacturers, but hurt others, such as some farmers, while raising the cost of living for all (see the Overview, Arguments in the Tariff Debates).

The differences between the parties, however, were often more rhetorical than substantial. They disagreed only about how high tariffs should be and what interests they should protect. Congressmen of both parties voted for tariffs that would benefit their districts.

In the 1884 campaign, the Republican presidential candidate, James G. Blaine, maintained that prosperity and high employment depended on high tariffs. The Democrats' platform endorsed a lowered tariff, but their candidate, New York governor Grover Cleveland, generally ignored the issue. Unable to address this and other important issues, both parties resorted to scandal mongering. One observer called the election "a more bitter, personal, and disgusting campaign than we have ever seen."

Cleveland continued to avoid the tariff issue for three years after his election, until the growing treasury surplus and rising popular pressure for tariff reduction prompted him to act. He devoted his entire 1887 annual message to attacking the "vicious, inequitable, and illogical" tariff, apparently making it the dominant issue of his 1888 reelection campaign. Once again, however, the distinctive political attribute of the period—intense and organized campaigning between closely balanced parties—forced both Democrats and Republicans to blur their positions. Cleveland proposed a Democratic platform that ignored his recent message and did not even use the word *tariff*. Cleveland won slightly more popular votes than his Republican opponent, Benjamin Harrison of Indiana, but Harrison carried the electoral college, indicating the decisive importance of strategic campaigning, local issues, and large campaign funds rather than great national issues.

The triumphant Republicans raised tariffs to prohibitive levels with the McKinley Tariff Act of 1890. William McKinley praised the law as "protective in every paragraph and American on every page," but it provoked a popular backlash that helped return the Democrats to power. Still, the Democrats made little effort to push tariff reform.

THE BEGINNINGS OF FEDERAL REGULATION

While business leaders pressed for protective tariffs and other public policies that promoted their interests, they otherwise used their great political influence to ensure governmental laissez-faire. Popular pressure nonetheless compelled Congress to take the first steps toward the regulation of business with the passage of the Interstate Commerce Act in 1887 and the Sherman Antitrust Act in 1890.

Popular concern focused first on the railroads, the preeminent symbol of big business. Both farm groups and business shippers complained of discriminatory rates levied by railroads. Consumers condemned the railroads' use of pooling arrangements to suppress competition and raise rates. The resulting pressure was responsible for the Granger laws enacted in several midwestern states in the 1870s to regulate railroad freight and storage rates. At first, the Supreme Court upheld this legislation, ruling in *Munn v. Illinois* (1877) that state governments had the right to regulate private property when it was "devoted to a public use." But in 1886, the Court ruled in *Wabash, St. Louis, and Pacific Railway Company v. Illinois* that only the federal government could regulate interstate commerce. This decision effectively ended state regulation of railroads but simultaneously increased pressure for congressional action. With the support of both major parties, Congress in 1887 passed the **Interstate Commerce Act.**

OVERVIEW ARGUMENTS IN THE TARIFF DEBATES

Area Affected	High-Tariff Advocates	Low-Tariff Advocates
Industry	Tariffs promote industrial growth.	Tariffs inflate corporate profits.
Employment	Tariffs stimulate job growth.	Tariffs restrict competition.
Wages and prices	Tariffs permit higher wages.	Tariffs increase consumer prices.
Government	Tariffs provide government revenue.	Tariffs violate the principle of laissez-faire and produce revenues that tempt the government to activism.
Trade	Tariffs protect the domestic market.	Tariffs restrict foreign trade.

The act prohibited rebates, discriminatory rates, and pooling and established the **Interstate Commerce Commission (ICC)** to investigate and prosecute violations. The ICC was the first federal regulatory agency. But its powers were too limited to be effective. Railroads continued their objectionable practices and frustrated the commission by refusing to provide required information and endlessly appealing its orders to a conservative judiciary. In its first 15 years, only one court case was decided in favor of the ICC.

Many people saw railroad abuses as indicative of the dangers of corporate power in general and demanded a broader federal response. As with railroad regulation, the first antitrust laws—laws intended to break up or regulate corporate monopolies—were passed by states. Exposes of the monopolistic practices of such corporations as Standard Oil forced both major parties to endorse national antitrust legislation during the campaign of 1888. In 1890, Congress enacted the **Sherman Antitrust Act** with only a single vote in opposition. But this near unanimity concealed real differences over the desirability and purpose of the law. Although it emphatically prohibited any combination in restraint of trade (any attempt to restrict competition), the law was vaguely written and too weak to prevent abuses. The courts further weakened the act, and presidents of both parties made little effort to enforce it. Essentially still unfettered, large corporations remained a threat in the eyes of many Americans.

THE MONEY QUESTION

Persistent wrangling over questions of currency and coinage made monetary policy the most divisive political issue. Despite the sometimes arcane and difficult nature of the money question, millions of Americans adopted positions on it and defended them with religious ferocity.

Creditors, especially bankers, as well as conservative economists and many business leaders favored limiting the money supply. They called this a **sound money** policy and insisted that it would ensure economic stability, maintain property values, and retain investor confidence. Farmers and other debtors complained that this deflationary monetary policy would depress already low crop prices, drive debtors further into debt, and restrict economic opportunities. They favored expanding the money supply to match the country's growing population and economy. They expected this inflationary policy to raise prices, stimulate the economy, reduce debt burdens, and increase opportunities.

The conservative leadership of both major parties supported the sound money policy, but their rank-and-file membership, especially in the West and the South, included many inflationists. As a result, the parties avoided confronting each other on the money issue.

The conflict between advocates of sound money and inflation centered on the use of paper money, or "greenbacks," and silver coinage. In 1875, sound money advocates in Congress enacted a deflationary law that withdrew some greenbacks from circulation and required that the remainder be convertible into gold after 1878. This action forced the money issue into electoral politics. Outraged inflationists organized the Greenback Party. The Greenbackers polled more than a million votes in 1878 and elected 14 members of Congress, nearly gaining the balance of power in the House. As the depression faded, however, so did interest in the greenback issue, and the party soon withered.

The Silver Issue. Inflationists then turned to the silver issue, which would prove more enduring and disruptive. Historically, the United States had been on a bimetallic standard, using both gold and silver as the basis of its currency. But after the 1840s, the market price of silver rose above the currency value assigned to it by the government. Silver miners and owners began to sell the metal for commercial use rather than to the government for coinage, and little silver money circulated. In 1873, Congress passed a law "demonetizing" silver, thereby making gold the only standard for U.S. currency. Gold-standard supporters hoped that the law would promote international trade by aligning U.S. financial policy with that of Great Britain, which insisted on gold-based currency. But they also wanted to prevent new silver discoveries in the American West from expanding the money supply.

Indeed, silver production soon boomed, flooding the commercial market and dropping the value of the metal. Dismayed miners wanted the Treasury Department to purchase their surplus silver on the old terms and demanded a return to the bimetallic system. More important, the rural debtor groups seeking currency inflation joined in this demand, seeing renewed silver coinage as a means to reverse the long deflationary trend in the economy. (See Global Connections: The Money Issue and the World.)

Again, both major parties equivocated. Eastern conservatives of both parties denounced silver; southerners and westerners demanded **free silver,** meaning unlimited silver coinage. By 1878, a bipartisan coalition succeeded in passing the Bland-Allison Act. This compromise measure required the government to buy and coin at least $2 million of silver a month. However, the government never exceeded the minimum, and the law had little inflationary effect.

After hard times hit rural regions in the late 1880s, inflationists secured passage of the Sherman Silver Purchase Act of 1890. The Treasury now had to buy a larger volume of silver and pay for it with treasury notes redeemable in either gold or silver. But this, too, produced little inflation, because the government did not coin the silver it purchased, redeemed the notes only with gold, and, as western silver production increased further, had to spend less and less to buy the stipulated amount of silver. Debtors of both parties remained convinced that the government favored the "classes rather than the masses." Gold-standard advocates (again, of both parties) were even less happy with the law and planned to repeal it at their first opportunity. The division between the two groups was deep and bitter.

THE CRISIS OF THE 1890S

In the 1890s, social, economic, and political pressures created a crisis for both the political system and the government. A third-party political challenge generated by agricultural discontent disrupted traditional party politics. A devastating depression spawned social misery and labor violence. Changing public attitudes led to new demands on the government and a realignment of parties and voters. These developments, in turn, set the stage for important political, economic, and social changes in the new century.

FARMERS PROTEST INEQUITIES

The agricultural depression that engulfed the Great Plains and the South in the late 1880s brought misery and despair to millions of rural Americans. Falling crop prices and rising debt overwhelmed many people already exhausted from overwork and alarmed by the new corporate order. "At the age of 52 years, after a long life of toil, economy, and self-denial, I find myself and family virtual paupers," lamented one Kansan. His family's farm, rather than being "a house of refuge for our declining years, by a few turns of the monopolistic crank has been rendered valueless." To a large extent, the farmers' plight stemmed from bad weather and international overproduction of farm products. Seeking relief, however, the farmers naturally focused on the inequities of railroad discrimination, tariff favoritism, a restrictive financial system, and apparently indifferent political parties.

Credit Inequities. Angry farmers particularly singled out the systems of money and credit that worked so completely against agricultural interests. Government rules for national banks directed credit into the urbanized North and East at the expense of the rural South and West and prohibited loans on farm property and real estate. As a result, farmers had to turn to other sources of credit and pay higher interest rates. In the West, farmers borrowed from mortgage companies to buy land and machinery, but declining crop prices made it difficult for them to pay their debts, and mortgage foreclosures then crushed the hopes of many. In the South, the credit shortage interacted with the practices of cotton marketing and retail trade to create the sharecropping system, which trapped more and more farmers, black and white, in a vicious pattern of exploitation. Moreover, the government's policies of monetary deflation worsened the debt burden for all farmers.

Freight Rates and Tariffs. Farmers protested other features of the nation's economic system as well. Railroad freight rates were two or three times higher in the West and South than in the North and East. The near-monopolistic control of grain elevators and cotton brokerages in rural areas left farmers feeling exploited. Protective tariffs on agricultural machinery and other manufactured goods further raised their costs. The failure of political parties and the government to devise effective regulatory and anti-trust measures or to correct the inequities in the currency, credit, and tariff laws capped the farmers' anger. By the 1890s, many were convinced that the nation's economic and political institutions were aligned against them.

Farmers Organize. In response, farmers turned to the **Farmers' Alliance,** the era's greatest popular movement of protest and reform. Originating in Texas, the Southern Farmers' Alliance spread throughout the South and across the Great Plains to the Pacific coast. African American farmers organized the Colored Farmers' Alliance. The Northwestern Farmers' Alliance reached westward and northward from Illinois to Nebraska and Minnesota. In combination, these groups constituted a massive grassroots movement committed to economic and political reform.

The Farmers' Alliance restricted membership to men and women of the "producing class" and urged them to stand "against the encroachments of monopolies and in opposition to the growing corruption of wealth and power." At first, the Alliance organized farmers' cooperatives to market crops and purchase supplies. Although some co-ops worked well, most soon failed because of the opposition of established business interests. In Leflore County, Mississippi, when members of the Colored Farmers' Alliance shifted their trade to an Alliance store, local merchants provoked a conflict in which state troops killed 25 black farmers, including the local leaders of the Colored Alliance.

The Alliance also developed ingenious proposals to remedy rural credit and currency problems. In the South, the Alliance pushed the sub-treasury system, which called on the government to warehouse farmers' cotton and advance them credit based on its value (see Chapter 17). In the West, the Alliance proposed a system of federal loans to farmers, using land as security. These proposals were immensely popular among farmers, but the major parties and Congress rejected them. The Alliance also took up earlier calls for free silver, government control of railroads, and banking reform, again to no avail.

THE PEOPLE'S PARTY

In the West, discontented agrarians organized independent third parties to achieve reforms the major parties had ignored. State-level third parties appeared in the elections of 1890 under many names. All eventually adopted the labels "People's" or "Populist," which were first used by a Kansas party formed by members of the Farmers' Alliance, the Knights of Labor, the Grange, and the old Greenback Party. The new party's campaign, marked by grim determination and fierce rhetoric, set the model for Populist politics.

The Populist parties proved remarkably successful. They gained control of the legislatures of Kansas and Nebraska and won congressional elections in Kansas, Nebraska, and Minnesota. Their victories came at the expense of the Republicans, who had traditionally controlled politics in these states, and contributed to a massive defeat of the GOP in the 1890 midterm elections. Thereafter, Populists won further victories throughout the West. In the mountain states, where their support came more from miners than from farmers, they won governorships in Colorado and Montana. On the Pacific coast, angry farmers found allies among urban workers in Seattle, Tacoma, Portland, and San Francisco, where organized labor had campaigned for reform since the 1880s. The Populists elected a governor in Washington, congressmen in California, and legislators in all three states.

With their new political power, farmers enacted reform legislation in many western states. New laws regulated banks and railroads and protected debtors by capping interest rates and restricting mortgage foreclosures. Others protected unions and mandated

Established interests ridiculed the Populists unmercifully. This hostile cartoon depicts the People's Party as an odd assortment of radical dissidents committed to a "Platform of Lunacy."

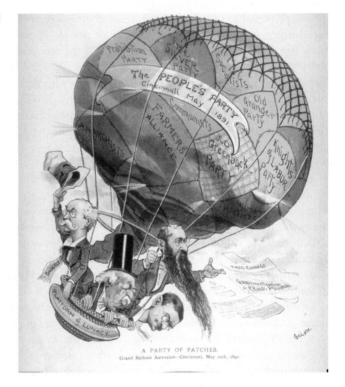

A PARTY OF PATCHES.
Grand Balloon Ascension—Cincinnati, May 20th, 1891.

improved workplace conditions. Still others made the political system more democratic. Populists were instrumental, for example, in winning woman suffrage in Colorado and Idaho, although the united opposition of Democrats and Republicans blocked their efforts in other states.

In the South, the angry farmers did not initially form third parties but instead attempted to seize control of the dominant Democratic Party by forcing its candidates to pledge support to the Alliance platform. The rural southern electorate then swept these "Alliance Democrats" into office. But most of these Democrats then repudiated their Alliance pledges and remained loyal to their party and its traditional opposition to governmental activism. Betrayed again by the political system, disgruntled Alliance members began organizing their own Populist parties, but they faced obstacles that western farmers did not. A successful challenge to the entrenched Democrats would require the political cooperation of both white and black farmers, but that would expose Populists to demagogic attacks from Democrats for undermining white supremacy, frightening away potential white supporters.

Some southern Populists, black and white, did appeal for racial cooperation in political if not social action. In Georgia, the Populist leader Tom Watson supported a biracial party organization and counseled white people to accept black people as partners in their common crusade. "You are kept apart," Watson told black and white southerners, "that you may be separately fleeced of your earnings. You are made to hate each other because upon that hatred is rested the keystone of the arch of financial despotism which enslaves you both."

But steeped in racism, most white southerners recoiled from the prospect of inter-racial unity. And for their part, most black people remained loyal to the Republican Party for its role in abolishing slavery and for the few patronage crumbs the party still threw their way. Moreover, primarily tenants and farm laborers, their interests were not identical to those of white landowning farmers who formed the core of the Populist Party. Unwilling or unable to mobilize black voters and largely unsuccessful in dislodging white voters from the Democratic Party, Populists in the South achieved but limited political success, making significant inroads only in the legislatures of Texas, Alabama, and Georgia, and sending Tom Watson to Congress.

National Action. Populists soon realized that successful reform would require national action. They met in Omaha, Nebraska, on July 4, 1892, to organize a national party and nominated former Greenbacker James B. Weaver for president. The party platform, known as the **Omaha Platform,** rejected the laissez-faire policies of the old parties: It demanded government ownership of the railroads and the telegraph and telephone systems, a national currency issued by the government rather than by private banks, the sub-treasury system, free silver, a graduated income tax, and the redistribution to settlers of land held by railroads and speculative corporations. Accompanying resolutions endorsed the popular election of senators, the secret ballot, and other electoral reforms to make government more democratic and responsive to popular wishes.

The Populists left Omaha to begin an energetic campaign. Weaver toured the western states and with movement leader Mary Lease invaded the Democratic stronghold of the South where some Populists tried to mobilize black voters. Southern Democrats, however, used violence and fraud to intimidate Populist voters and cheat Populist candidates out of office. Some local Populist leaders were murdered, and Weaver was driven from the South. Southern Democrats also appealed effectively to white supremacy, undermining the Populist effort to build a biracial reform coalition.

Elsewhere, too, Populists met disappointment. Midwestern farmers unfamiliar with Alliance ideas and organization ignored Populist appeals and stood by their traditional political allegiances. So did most eastern working-class voters, who learned little of the Populist program beyond its demand for inflation, which they feared would worsen their own conditions.

The Populists lost the election but showed impressive support. They garnered more than a million votes, carried several western states, and won hundreds of state offices throughout the West and in pockets of the South. Populist leaders immediately began working to expand their support, to the alarm of both southern Democrats and northern Republicans.

THE CHALLENGE OF THE DEPRESSION

The emergence of a significant third-party movement was but one of many developments that combined by the mid-1890s to produce a national political crisis. A harsh and lengthy depression began in 1893, cruelly worsening conditions not only for farmers but for most other Americans. Labor unrest and violence engulfed the nation, reflecting workers' distress but frightening more comfortable Americans. The persistent failure of the major parties to respond to serious problems contributed mightily to the growing popular discontent. Together these developments constituted an important challenge to America's new industrial society and government.

Although the Populists lost in 1892, the election nonetheless reflected the nation's spreading dissatisfaction. Voters decisively rejected President Harrison and the incumbent Republicans in Congress, putting the Democrats in control of Congress and Grover Cleveland back in the White House. But the conservative Cleveland was almost oblivious to the mounting demand for reform. He delivered an inaugural address championing laissez-faire and rejecting government action to solve social or economic problems.

Cleveland's resolve was immediately tested when the economy collapsed in the spring of 1893. Railroad overexpansion, a weak banking system, tight credit, and plunging agricultural prices all contributed to the disaster. So too did a depression in Europe, which reduced American export markets and prompted British investors to sell their American investments for gold. Hundreds of banks closed, and thousands of businesses, including the nation's major railroads, went bankrupt. By winter, 20 percent of the labor force was unemployed, and the jobless scavenged for food in a country that had no public unemployment or welfare programs.

Churches, local charity societies, and labor unions tried to provide relief but were overwhelmed. Most state governments offered little relief beyond encouraging private charity to the homeless.

Appeals for Federal Action. If Cleveland and Congress had no idea how the federal government might respond to the depression, other Americans did. Jacob Coxey, a Populist businessman from Ohio, proposed a government public-works program for the unemployed to be financed with paper money. This plan would improve the nation's infrastructure, create jobs for the unemployed, and provide an inflationary stimulus to counteract the depression's deflationary effects. In short, Coxey advocated positive government action to combat the depression.

Coxey organized a march of the unemployed to Washington as "a petition with boots on" to support his ideas. **Coxey's Army** of the unemployed, as the excited press dubbed it, marched through the industrial towns of Ohio and Pennsylvania and into Maryland, attracting attention and support. Other armies formed in eastern cities from Boston to Baltimore, and some of the largest organized in the western cities of Denver, San Francisco, and Seattle. All set out for the capital.

The sympathy and assistance with which Americans greeted these industrial armies reflected more than anxiety over the depression and unemployment. As one economist noted, what distinguished the Populists and Coxeyites from earlier reformers was their appeal for federal action. Their substantial public support suggested a deep dissatisfaction with the failure of the government to respond to social and economic needs.

Nonetheless, the government acted to suppress Coxey. When he reached Washington with 600 marchers, police and soldiers arrested him and his aides, beat sympathetic bystanders in a crowd of 20,000, and herded the marchers into detention camps. Unlike the lobbyists for business and finance, Coxey was not permitted to reach Congress to deliver his statement urging the government to assist "the poor and oppressed."

Protecting Big Business. The depression also provoked labor turmoil. In 1894, there were some 1,400 industrial strikes, involving nearly 700,000 workers, the largest number of strikers in any year in the nineteenth century. Cleveland had no response except to

Jacob Coxey's "Army" of the unemployed marches to Washington, DC, in 1894. Many such "industrial armies" were organized during the depressed 1890s, revealing dissatisfaction with traditional politics and limited government.

call for law and order. One result was the government's violent suppression of the Pullman strike (see Chapter 18).

In a series of decisions in 1895, the Supreme Court strengthened the bonds between business and government. First, it upheld the use of a court-ordered injunction to break the Pullman strike. As a result, injunctions became a major weapon for courts and corporations against labor unions, until Congress finally limited their use in 1932. Next, in *United States v. E. C. Knight Company,* the Court gutted the Sherman Antitrust Act by ruling that manufacturing, as opposed to commerce, was beyond the reach of federal regulation. Finally, the Court invalidated an income tax that agrarian Democrats and Populists had maneuvered through Congress. Not until 1913, and then only with an amendment to the Constitution, would it be possible to adopt an equitable system of taxation.

Surveying these developments, farmers and workers increasingly concluded that the government protected powerful interests while ignoring the plight of ordinary Americans. Certainly the callous treatment shown workers contrasted sharply with Cleveland's concern for bankers as he managed the government's monetary policy in the depression. Cleveland blamed the economic collapse on the Sherman Silver Purchase Act, which he regarded as detrimental to business confidence and a threat to the nation's gold reserve. He persuaded Congress in 1893 to repeal the law, enraging southern and western members of his own party. These Silver Democrats condemned Cleveland for betraying the public good to "the corporate interests."

Cleveland's policy failed to end the depression. By 1894, the Treasury began borrowing money from Wall Street to bolster the gold reserve. These transactions benefited a syndicate of bankers headed by J. P. Morgan. It seemed to critics that an indifferent Cleveland was helping rich bankers profit from the nation's economic agony.

THE BATTLE OF THE STANDARDS AND THE ELECTION OF 1896

The government's unpopular actions, coupled with the unrelenting depression, alienated workers and farmers from the Cleveland administration and the Democratic Party. In the off-year elections of 1894, the Democrats suffered the greatest loss of congressional seats in American history. Populists increased their vote by 42 percent, making especially significant gains in the South. But the real beneficiaries of the popular hatred of Cleveland and his policies were the Republicans. They gained solid control of Congress as well as state governments across the North and West. All three parties began to plan for the presidential election of 1896.

As hard times persisted, the silver issue came to overshadow all others. Some Populist leaders, hoping to broaden the party's appeal, began to emphasize silver rather than the more radical but divisive planks of the Omaha Platform. Many southern and western Democrats, who had traditionally favored silver inflation, also decided to stress the issue, both to undercut the Populists and to distance themselves and their party from the despised Cleveland.

McKinley and the Republicans. William McKinley, governor of Ohio and author of the McKinley Tariff Act of 1890, emerged as the front-runner of a crowd of hopeful

William Jennings Bryan in 1896. A powerful orator of great human sympathies, Bryan was adored by his followers as "the majestic man who was hurling defiance in the teeth of the money power." Nominated three times for the presidency by the Democrats, he was never elected.

AMERICAN VIEWS

A POPULIST VIEWS AMERICAN GOVERNMENT

*A*n educator, merchant, and former editor, Lorenzo D. Lewelling became one of the most articulate champions of the Populist Party and its principles. Elected governor of Kansas in 1892, he headed what was heralded as "The First People's Party Government on Earth." On January 9, 1893, Lewelling delivered his inaugural address, in which he declared, "I appeal to the people of this great commonwealth to array themselves on the side of humanity and justice." The following passages from the speech sketch out Lewelling's views of the 1890s and his "dream of the future."

- How does Lewelling's rhetoric reflect the deep divisions of the 1890s?
- What is Lewelling's view of the proper role of government?
- For what does Lewelling criticize the government of the 1890s?
- What does Lewelling mean by his statement that "the rich have no right to the property of the poor"?

The survival of the fittest is the government of brutes and reptiles, and such philosophy must give place to a government which recognizes human brotherhood. It is the province of government to protect the weak, but the government today is resolved into a struggle of the masses with the classes for supremacy and bread, until business, home, and personal integrity are trembling in the face of possible want in the family. Feed a tiger regularly and you tame and make him harmless, but hunger makes tigers of men. If it be true that the poor have no right to the property of the rich let it also be declared that the rich have no right to the property of the poor.

It is the mission of Kansas to protect and advance the moral and material interests of all its citizens. It is its especial duty at the present time to protect the producer from the ravages of combined wealth. National legislation has for twenty years fostered and protected the interests of the few, while it has left the South and West to supply the products with which to feed and clothe the world, and thus to become the servants of wealth.

The demand for free coinage has been refused. The national banks have been permitted to withdraw their circulation, and thus the interests of the East and West have been diverged until the passage of the McKinley bill culminated in their diversement. The purchasing power of the dollar has become so great [that] corn, wheat, beef, pork, and cotton have scarcely commanded a price equal to the cost of production.

The instincts of patriotism have naturally rebelled against these unwarranted encroachments of the power of money. Sectional hatred has also been kept alive

Republican presidential candidates. The Republicans nominated McKinley on the first ballot at their 1896 convention. Their platform called for high tariffs but also endorsed the gold standard, placating eastern delegates but prompting several western Silver Republicans to withdraw from the party.

Bryan and the Silverites. When the Democratic convention met, embattled supporters of the gold standard soon learned that the silver crusade had made them a minority in

by the old powers, the better to enable them to control the products and make the producer contribute to the millionaire; and thus, while the producer labors in the field, the shop, and the factory, the millionaire usurps his earnings and rides in gilded carriages with liveried servants. . . .

The problem of today is how to make the State subservient to the individual, rather than to become his master. Government is a voluntary union for the common good. It guarantees to the individual life, liberty, and the pursuit of happiness. The government then must make it possible for the citizen to enjoy liberty and pursue happiness. If the government fails of these things, it fails in its mission. . . . If old men go to the poor-house and young men go to prison, something is wrong with the economic system of the government.

What is the State to him who toils, if labor is denied him and his children cry for bread? What is the State to the farmer who wearily drags himself from dawn till dark to meet the stern necessities of the mortgage on the farm? What is the State to him if it sanctions usury and other legal forms by which his home is destroyed and his innocent ones become a prey to the fiends who lurk in the shadow of civilization? What is the State to the business man, early grown gray, broken in health and spirit by successive failures; anxiety like a boding owl his constant companion by day and the disturber of his dreams by night? How is life to be sustained, how is liberty to be enjoyed, how is happiness to be pursued under such adverse conditions as the State permits if it does not sanction? Is the State powerless against these conditions?

This is the generation which has come to the rescue. Those in distress who cry out from the darkness shall not be heard in vain. Conscience is in the saddle. We have leaped the bloody chasm and entered a contest for the protection of home, humanity, and the dignity of labor.

The grandeur of civilization shall be emphasized by the dawn of a new era in which the people shall reign, and if found necessary they will "expand the powers of government to solve the enigmas of the times." The people are greater than the law or the statutes, and when a nation sets its heart on doing a great and good thing it can find a legal way to do it.

I have a dream of the future. I have the evolution of an abiding faith in human government, and in the beautiful vision of a coming time I behold the abolition of poverty. A time is foreshadowed when the withered hand of want shall not be outstretched for charity; when liberty, equality, and justice shall have permanent abiding places in the republic.

SOURCE: *People's Party Paper* (Atlanta), January 20, 1893.

the party. With a fervor that conservatives likened to "scenes of the French Revolution," the Silver Democrats revolutionized their party. They adopted a platform repudiating Cleveland and his policies and endorsing free silver, the income tax, and tighter regulation of trusts and railroads. A magnificent speech supporting this platform by William Jennings Bryan helped convince the delegates to nominate him for president.

Holding their convention last, the Populists faced a terrible dilemma. The Democratic nomination of Bryan on a silver platform undercut their hopes of attracting disappointed reformers from the major parties. Bryan, moreover, had already worked closely with Nebraska Populists, who now urged the party to endorse him rather than split the silver vote and ensure the victory of McKinley and the gold standard. Other Populists argued that fusing—joining with the Democrats—would cost the Populists their separate identity and subordinate their larger political principles to the issue of free silver. After anguished discussion, the Populists nominated Bryan for president.

Money and Oratory. The campaign was intense and dramatic, with each side demonizing the other. Eastern financial and business interests contributed millions of dollars to McKinley's campaign. Standard Oil alone provided $250,000, about the same amount as the Democrats' total national expenses. Republicans used these funds to organize an unprecedented campaign. Shifting the emphasis from parades to information, they issued 250 million campaign documents in a dozen languages, warning of economic disaster should Bryan be elected and the bimetallic standard be restored, but promising that McKinley's election would finally end the depression. Republicans were aided by a national press so completely sympathetic that many newspapers not only shaped their editorials but distorted their news stories to Bryan's disadvantage. Lacking the Republicans' superior resources, the Democrats relied on Bryan's superb speaking ability and youthful energy. Bryan was the first presidential candidate to campaign systematically, speaking hundreds of times to millions of voters. But as the Democratic candidate, Bryan was, ironically, burdened with the legacy of the hated Cleveland administration.

The intense campaign brought a record voter turnout, but McKinley won decisively by capturing the East and Midwest as well as Oregon and California (see Map 20–2).

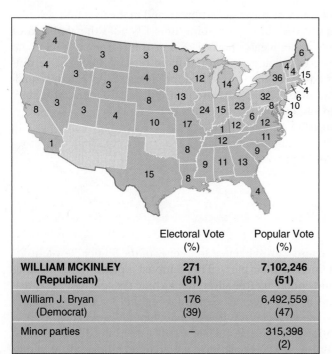

	Electoral Vote (%)	Popular Vote (%)
WILLIAM MCKINLEY (Republican)	**271 (61)**	**7,102,246 (51)**
William J. Bryan (Democrat)	176 (39)	6,492,559 (47)
Minor parties	–	315,398 (2)

MAP 20–2 · The Election of 1896 William Jennings Bryan carried most of the rural South and West, but his free silver campaign had little appeal to more urban and industrial regions, which swung strongly to Republican candidate William McKinley.

▶ *Was the election of 1896 closer than the electoral vote would suggest?*

Bryan carried the traditionally Democratic South and the mountain and plains states, where Populists and silverites dominated. He failed to gain support in either the Midwest or the cities of the East, where his silver campaign had little appeal to industrial workers.

The elections of 1894 and 1896 ended the close balance between the major parties. Cleveland's failures, coupled with an economic recovery in the wake of the election of 1896, gained the Republicans a reputation as the party of prosperity and industrial progress, firmly establishing them in power for years to come. By contrast, the Democratic Party receded into an ineffectual sectional minority dominated by southern conservatives, despite Bryan's liberal views.

The People's Party simply dissolved. Demoralized by fusion with the Democrats, who had earlier violently repressed them, many southern Populists dropped out of politics. The Democrats' disfranchisement laws, directed at discontented poor white southerners as well as poor black southerners, further undermined the Populists in the South. In the West, the silver tide of 1896 carried many Populists into office, but with their party collapsing, they had no hope of reelection. By 1898, the Populist Party had virtually disappeared. Its reform legacy, however, proved more enduring. The issues it raised would continue to shape state and national politics.

McKinley plunged into his presidency. Unlike his predecessors, he had a definite, if limited, program, consisting of tariff protection, sound money, and overseas expansion. He worked actively to see it through Congress and to shape public opinion, thereby helping establish the model of the modern presidency. He had promised prosperity, and it returned, although not because of the record high tariff his party enacted in 1897 or the Currency Act of 1900, which firmly established the gold standard. Prosperity returned, instead, because of reviving markets and a monetary inflation that resulted from the discovery of vast new deposits of gold in Alaska, Australia, and South Africa. The silverites had recognized that an expanding industrial economy required an expanding money supply. Ironically, the new inflation was greater than the inflation that would have resulted from free silver. With the return of prosperity and the decline of social tensions, McKinley easily won reelection in 1900, defeating Bryan a second time.

CONCLUSION

In late-nineteenth-century America, politics and government often seemed at cross-purposes. Political contests were exciting events, absorbing public attention, attracting high voter turnout, and often raising issues of symbolic or substantive importance. Closely balanced political parties commanded the zealous support of their constituents and wielded power and influence. The institutions of government, by contrast, were limited in size, scope, and responsibility. A weakened presidency and an inefficient Congress, hampered by a restrictive judiciary, were often unable to resolve the very issues that were so dramatically raised in the political arena. The persistent disputes over tariff and monetary policy illustrate this impasse. But the issue that most reflected it was civil service reform. The patronage system provided the lifeblood of politics but also disrupted government business.

Localism, laissez-faire, and other traditional principles that shaped both politics and government were becoming increasingly inappropriate for America's industrializing society. New challenges were emerging that state and local governments could not effectively solve on their own. The national nature of the railroad network, for example, finally brought the federal government into the regulatory arena, however imperfectly, with the Interstate Commerce Act of 1887. Both the depression of the 1890s and the popular discontent articulated most clearly by the Populist rejection of laissez-faire underscored the need for change and discredited the limited government of the Cleveland administration.

By the end of the decade, the political system had changed. The Republicans had emerged as the dominant party, ending the two-party stalemate of previous decades. Campaign hoopla in local communities, like the elaborate parade and ceremonies in Fort Wayne described at the beginning of this chapter, had given way to information-based campaigns directed by and through national organizations. A new, activist presidency was emerging. And the disruptive currency issue faded with the hard times that had brought it forth. Still greater changes were on the horizon. The depression and its terrible social and economic consequences undermined traditional ideas about the responsibilities of government and increased public support for activist policies. The stage was set for the Progressive Era.

REVIEW QUESTIONS

1. What social and institutional factors shaped the disorderly nature of elections in the late nineteenth century? How did they operate in U.S. politics?

2. What social and institutional factors determined the role of government? How and why did the role of government change during this period?

3. What factors determined the party affiliation of American voters? Why did so many third parties develop during this era?

4. How might the planks of the Omaha Platform have helped solve farmers' troubles?

5. What factors shaped the conduct and outcome of the election of 1896? How did that contest differ from earlier elections?

PEARSON
myhistorylab CONNECTIONS

Reinforce what you learned in this chapter by studying the many documents, images, maps, review tools, and videos available at www.myhistorylab.com.

READ AND REVIEW

✔•─ **Study** and **Review** on **myhistorylab.com** STUDY PLAN: CHAPTER 20

▢•─ **Read** the **Document** on **myhistorylab.com**

Pendleton Civil Service Act (1883)

Workingman's Amalgamated Sherman Anti-Trust (1893)

William Jennings Bryan, "Cross of Gold" Speech (1896)

The People's Party Platform (1892)

Henry Cabot Lodge, "The Business World vs. the Politicians" (1895)

Proceedings of the Thirteenth Session of the National Grange of the Patrons of Husbandry (1879)

Jacob S. Coxey, "Address of Protest" (1894)

RESEARCH AND EXPLORE

Read the **Document** on **myhistorylab.com**

Personal Journeys Online

From Then to Now Online. Political Parties

Listen on **myhistorylab.com**

Hear the audio files for Chapter 20 at
www.myhistorylab.com.

21 The Progressive Era •• 1900–1917

Hear the audio files for Chapter 21 at **www.myhistorylab.com.**

FOCUS QUESTIONS

WHAT VALUES and beliefs bound progressives together?

HOW DID progressives respond to the social challenges of industrializing America?

HOW DID progressives change American politics and government?

HOW DID Theodore Roosevelt envision the power of the president?

HOW DID Woodrow Wilson's vision of reform differ from Theodore Roosevelt's?

Women march in support of Mother Jones in Trinidad, Colorado. Dramatic tactics and careful organizing like those that marked this parade often helped secure reform in the Progressive Era.

ONE AMERICAN JOURNEY

In the spring of 1903 I went to Kensington, Pennsylvania, where 75,000 textile workers were on strike. Of this number at least 10,000 were little children. The workers were striking for more pay and shorter hours. Every day little children came into Union Headquarters, some with their hands off, some with the thumb missing, some with their fingers off at the knuckle. They were stooped little things, round shouldered and skinny. Many of them were not over ten years of age. . . .

We assembled a number of boys and girls one morning in Independence Park and from there we arranged to parade with banners to the court house where we would hold a meeting.

A great crowd gathered in the public square in front of the city hall. I put the little boys with their fingers off and hands crushed and maimed on a platform. I held up their mutilated hands and showed them to the crowd and made the statement that Philadelphia's mansions were built on the broken bones, the quivering hearts, and drooping heads of these children. . . .

I [then] decided to go with the children to see President Roosevelt to ask him to have Congress pass a law prohibiting the exploitation of childhood. I thought that President Roosevelt might see these mill children and compare them with his own little ones spending the summer at the seashore at Oyster Bay. . . .

Everywhere [en route] we had meetings, showing with little children the horrors of child labor. . . . [In New York City] I told an immense crowd of the horrors of child labor in the mills . . . and I showed them Gussie Rangnew, a little girl from whom all the childhood had gone. Her face was like an old woman's. Gussie packed stockings in a factory, eleven hours a day for a few cents a day. . . . [I said,] "Fifty years ago there was a cry against slavery and men gave up their lives to stop the selling of black children on the block. Today the white child is sold for two dollars a week to the manufacturers."

. . . We marched down to Oyster Bay but the president refused to see us and he would not answer my letters. But our march had done its work. We had drawn the attention of the nation to the crime of child labor. And while the strike of the textile workers in Kensington was lost and the children driven back to work, not long afterward the Pennsylvania legislature passed a child labor law that kept thousands of children home from the mills.

The Autobiography of Mother Jones, 3rd ed. (Chicago: Kerr Publishing Co., 1977).

SWEET-FACED, WHITE-HAIRED "MOTHER" JONES was nearly 70 years old when she led "the children's crusade" in 1903. Born Mary Harris in Ireland, she had survived famine, emigration, hard labor, and the horrible deaths of her husband and their four children. Indomitable, she had become a celebrated union organizer and powerful orator against what she saw as the economic injustices of America.

The journey of Mother Jones, with Gussie Rangnew and other maimed children, from Kensington, Pennsylvania, to Oyster Bay, New York, was thus just part of her legendary life journey. But it also illustrated critical features of life in the **Progressive Era**. Important movements challenged traditional relationships and attitudes—here involving working conditions, unregulated industrial development, concepts of opportunity and childhood itself—and often met strong resistance and only limited success. "Progressives" seeking change investigated problems, proposed solutions, organized their supporters, and attempted to mobilize public opinion—just as Mother Jones sought to do. And rather than rely only on traditional partisan politics, reformers adopted new political techniques, including lobbying and demonstrating as nonpartisan pressure groups. Reform work begun at the local and state levels—where the campaign against child labor had already met some success—inexorably moved to the national level as the federal government expanded its authority and became the focus of political interest. Finally, Mother Jones's march reveals the exceptional diversity of the progressive movement, for she and her followers were marching, in part, against the seemingly indifferent Theodore Roosevelt, perhaps the most prominent progressive.

The issue of child labor, then, did not define progressivism. Indeed, in a sense, there was no "progressive movement," for progressivism had no unifying organization, central leadership, or consensus on objectives. Instead, it represented the coalescing of different and sometimes even contradictory movements that sought changes in the nation's social, economic, and political life. But reformers did share certain convictions. They believed that industrialization and urbanization had produced serious social disorders, from city slums to corporate abuses. They believed that new ideas and methods were required to correct these problems. In particular, they rejected the ideology of individualism in favor of broader concepts of social responsibility, and they sought to achieve social order through organization and efficiency. Finally, most progressives believed that government itself, as the organized agent of public responsibility, should address social and economic problems.

THE FERMENT OF REFORM

The diversity of progressivism reflected the diverse impulses of reform. Reformers responded to the tensions of industrialization and urbanization by formulating programs according to their own interests and priorities. Nearly every movement for change encountered fierce opposition. But in raising new issues and proposing new ideas, progressives helped America grapple with the problems of industrial society. (See Overview, Major Progressive Organizations and Groups.)

THE CONTEXT OF REFORM: INDUSTRIAL AND URBAN TENSIONS

The origins of progressivism lay in the crises of the new urban-industrial order that emerged in the late nineteenth century. The severe depression and mass suffering of the 1890s, the labor violence and industrial armies, the political challenges of Populism and an obviously ineffective government shattered the complacency many middle-class Americans had felt about their nation and made them aware of social and economic inequities that rural and working-class families had long recognized. Many Americans began to question the validity of Social Darwinism and the laissez-faire policies that had justified unregulated industrial growth. They began to reconsider the responsibilities of government and, indeed, of themselves for social order and betterment.

By 1900, returning prosperity had eased the threat of major social violence, but the underlying problems intensified. Big business, which had disrupted traditional economic relationships in the late nineteenth century, suddenly became bigger in a series of mergers between 1897 and 1903, resulting in huge new business combinations. Such

CHRONOLOGY

1893–1898	Depression grips the nation.
1893	New Zealand establishes woman suffrage.
1894	New Zealand establishes maximum hours and compulsory arbitration.
1898	South Dakota adopts initiative and referendum. New Zealand initiates old age pensions. National Consumers' League is organized.
1899	Anti-Cigarette League of America is established.
1900	Robert La Follette is elected governor of Wisconsin.
1901	United States Steel Corporation is formed. President William McKinley is assassinated; Theodore Roosevelt becomes president. Socialist Party of America is organized. New York Tenement House Law is enacted. Galveston, Texas, initiates the city commission plan.
1902	Antitrust suit is filed against Northern Securities Company. *McClure's* initiates muckraking journalism. Mississippi enacts the first direct-primary law. National Reclamation Act is passed. Roosevelt intervenes in coal strike.
1903	Women's Trade Union League is organized.
1904	National Child Labor Committee is formed. Roosevelt is elected president.
1905	Industrial Workers of the World is organized.
1906	Hepburn Act strengthens the Interstate Commerce Commission. Meat Inspection Act extends government regulation. Pure Food and Drug Act is passed.
1908	*Muller v. Oregon* upholds maximum workday for women. William Howard Taft is elected president.
1910	National Association for the Advancement of Colored People is organized. Ballinger-Pinchot controversy erupts.
1912	Children's Bureau is established. Progressive Party organizes and nominates Roosevelt. Woodrow Wilson is elected president.
1913	Sixteenth and Seventeenth Amendments are ratified. Underwood-Simmons Tariff Act establishes an income tax. Federal Reserve Act creates the Federal Reserve System.

1914	Federal Trade Commission is established.
	Harrison Act criminalizes narcotics.
1915	National Birth Control League is formed.
1916	Keating-Owen Act prohibits child labor.
1917	Congress enacts literacy test for immigrants.
1918	Woman Suffrage is adopted in England.
1919	Eighteenth Amendment is ratified.
1920	Nineteenth Amendment is ratified.

gigantic corporations threatened to squeeze opportunities for small firms and workers, dominate markets, and raise social tensions. They also inspired calls for public control.

Industrial growth affected factory workers most directly. Working conditions were difficult and often dangerous. Wages were minimal; an economist in 1905 calculated that 60 percent of all adult male breadwinners made less than a living wage. Family survival, then, often required women and children to work, often in the lowest paid, most exploited positions. Poor ventilation, dangerous fumes, open machinery, and the absence of safety programs threatened not only workers' health but their lives as well. Such conditions were gruesomely illustrated in 1911, when a fire killed 146 workers, most of them young women, trapped inside the factory of the Triangle Shirtwaist Company in New York because management had locked the exits. The United States had the highest rate of industrial accidents in the world. Half a million workers were injured and 30,000 killed at work each year. These terrible conditions cried out for reform.

Other Americans saw additional social problems in the continuing flood of immigrants who were transforming America's cities. From 1900 to 1917, more than 14 million immigrants entered the United States. Most of the arrivals were so-called new immigrants from southern and eastern Europe, rather than the British, Irish, Germans, and Scandinavians who had arrived earlier. Several hundred thousand Japanese also arrived, primarily in California, as did increasing numbers of Mexicans. Crowding into urban slums, immigrants overwhelmed municipal sanitation, education, and fire protection services.

CHURCH AND CAMPUS

Many groups, drawing from different traditions and inspirations, responded to these economic and social issues. Reform-minded Protestant ministers were especially influential, creating the **Social Gospel movement,** which sought to introduce religious ethics into industrial relations and appealed to churches to meet their social responsibilities. Washington Gladden, a Congregational minister in Columbus, Ohio, was one of the earliest Social Gospelers. Shocked in 1884 by a bloody strike crushed by wealthy members of his own congregation, Gladden began a ministry in working-class neighborhoods that most churches ignored. He endorsed unions and workers' rights and proposed replacing a cruelly competitive wage system with profit sharing.

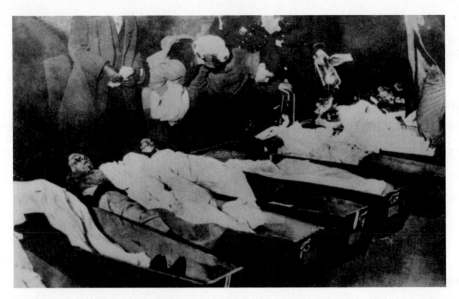

Families of the victims of the Triangle Shirtwaist fire later received from the factory owners $75 for each life lost. Still mourning, family members asked, "Justice, what justice?"

The Social Gospel was part of an emerging liberal movement in American religion. Scholars associated with this movement discredited the literal accuracy of the Bible and emphasized instead its general moral and ethical lessons. As modernists, they abandoned theological dogmatism for a greater tolerance of other faiths and became more interested in social problems. By linking reform with religion, the Social Gospel movement gave progressivism a powerful moral drive that affected much of American life.

The Social Gospel movement provided an ethical justification for government intervention to improve the social order. Scholars in the social sciences also gradually helped turn public attitudes in favor of reform by challenging the laissez-faire views of the Social Darwinists and traditional academics. In *Applied Sociology* (1906), Lester Ward called for social progress through rational planning and government intervention rather than through unrestrained and unpredictable competition. Economists rejected laissez-faire principles in favor of state action to accomplish social evolution. Industrialization, declared economist Richard T. Ely, "has brought to the front a vast number of social problems whose solution is impossible without the united efforts of church, state, and science."

MUCKRAKERS

Journalists also spread reform ideas by developing a new form of investigative reporting known as **muckraking.** Technological innovations had recently made possible the mass circulation of magazines, and editors competed to attract an expanding urban readership. Samuel S. McClure sent his reporters to uncover political and corporate corruption for *McClure's Magazine*. Sensational exposes sold magazines, and soon *Cosmopolitan,*

OVERVIEW MAJOR PROGRESSIVE ORGANIZATIONS AND GROUPS

Group	Activity
Social Gospel movement	Urged churches and individuals to apply Christian ethics to social and economic problems
Muckrakers	Exposed business abuses, public corruption, and social evils through investigative journalism
Settlement House movement	Attempted through social work and public advocacy to improve living and working conditions in urban immigrant communities
National Consumers' League (1898)	Monitored businesses to ensure decent working conditions and safe consumer products
Women's Trade Union League (1903)	United workingwomen and their middle-class allies to promote unionization and social reform
National Child Labor Committee (1904)	Campaigned against child labor
Country Life movement	Attempted to modernize rural social and economic conditions according to urban-industrial standards
National American Woman Suffrage Association	Led the movement to give women the right to vote
Municipal reformers	Sought to change the activities and structure of urban government to promote efficiency and control
Conservationists	Favored efficient management and regulation of natural resources rather than uncontrolled development or preservation

Everybody's, and other journals began publishing investigations of business abuses, dangerous working conditions, and the miseries of slum life.

Muckraking novels also appeared. *The Octopus* (1901), by Frank Norris, dramatized the Southern Pacific Railroad's stranglehold on California's farmers, and *The Jungle* (1906), by Upton Sinclair, exposed the nauseating conditions in Chicago's meatpacking industry. Such muckraking aroused indignant public demands for reform.

THE GOSPEL OF EFFICIENCY

Many progressive leaders believed that efficiency and expertise could control or resolve the disorder of industrial society. President Theodore Roosevelt praised the "gospel of efficiency." Like many other progressives, he admired the success of corporations in applying management techniques to guide economic growth. Drawing from science and technology as well as from the model of the corporation, many progressives attempted to manage or direct change efficiently. They used scientific methods to collect extensive data and relied on experts for analysis and recommendations. "Scientific management," a concept often used interchangeably with "sound business management," seemed the key to eliminating waste and inefficiency in government, society, and industry.

Business leaders especially advocated efficiency, order, and organization. Industrialists were drawn to the ideas of Frederick Taylor, a proponent of scientific management, for cutting factory labor costs. Taylor proposed to increase worker efficiency through imposed work routines, speedups, and mechanization. Workers, Taylor insisted, should "do what they are told promptly and without asking questions.... It is absolutely necessary for every man in our organization to become one of a train of gear wheels." By assigning workers simple and repetitive tasks on machines, Taylorization made their skills expendable and enabled managers to control the production, pace of work, and hiring and firing of personnel. Stripped of their influence and poorly paid, factory workers shared little of the wealth generated by industrial expansion and scientific management.

Sophisticated managers of big business saw some forms of government intervention as another way to promote order and efficiency. In particular, they favored regulations that could bring about safer and more stable conditions in society and the economy. Government regulations, they reasoned, could reassure potential consumers, open markets, mandate working conditions that smaller competitors could not provide, or impose systematic procedures that competitive pressures would otherwise undercut.

LABOR DEMANDS ITS RIGHTS

Industrial workers with different objectives also hastened the ferment of reform. Workers resisted the new rules of efficiency experts and called for improved wages and working conditions and reduced work hours. They and their middle-class sympathizers sought to achieve some of these goals through state intervention, demanding laws to compensate workers injured on the job, curb child labor, and regulate the employment of women.

Workers also organized unions to improve their lot. The American Federation of Labor (AFL) claimed 4 million members by 1920, recruiting mainly skilled workers, particularly native-born white males. New unions organized the factories and sweatshops where most immigrants and women worked. Despite strong employer resistance, the International Ladies Garment Workers Union (1900) and the Amalgamated Clothing Workers (1914) organized the garment trades, developed programs for social and economic reforms, and led their members—mostly young Jewish and Italian women—in spectacular strikes.

A still more radical union tried to organize miners, lumberjacks, and Mexican and Japanese farm workers in the West, black dockworkers in the South, and immigrant factory hands in New England. Founded in 1905, the Industrial Workers of the World (IWW), whose members were known as **"Wobblies,"** used sit-down strikes, sit-ins, and mass rallies, tactics adopted by other industrial unions in the 1930s and the civil rights movement in the 1960s.

EXTENDING THE WOMAN'S SPHERE

Women reformers and their organizations played a key role in progressivism. Women responded not merely to the human suffering caused by industrialization and urbanization but also to related changes in their own status and role. By the early twentieth century, more women than before were working outside the home—in the factories, mills, and sweatshops of the industrial economy and as clerks in stores and offices. In 1910, more than one-fourth of all workers were women, increasing numbers of them married. Their importance in the workforce and participation in unions and strikes challenged assumptions that woman's "natural" role was to be a submissive housewife.

The women's clubs that had begun multiplying in the late nineteenth century became seed-beds of progressive ideas in the early twentieth century. Often founded for cultural purposes, women's clubs soon adopted programs for social reform and gave their members a route to public influence.

Women also joined or created other organizations that pushed beyond the limits of traditional domesticity. "Woman's place is in the home," observed one progressive, but "no longer is the home encompassed by four walls." By threatening healthy and happy homes, urban problems required that women become "social housekeepers" in the community.

Although most progressive women stressed women's special duties and responsibilities as social housekeepers, others began to demand women's equal rights. In 1914, for example, critics of New York's policy of dismissing women teachers who married

Women's activism was critically important in reconstructing American life during the Progressive Era. Busily engaged in social housekeeping, Mother America uses corrective legislation to clean the dirty laundry of industrialization and injustice.

Greene, in New York (N. Y.) Telegram

A WOMAN'S WORK IS NEVER DONE

formed a group called the Feminist Alliance and demanded "the removal of all social, political, economic and other discriminations which are based upon sex, and the award of all rights and duties in all fields on the basis of individual capacity alone." With these new organizations and ideas, women gave important impetus and direction to the reform sentiments of the early twentieth century.

TRANSATLANTIC INFLUENCES

A major source of America's progressive impulse lay outside its borders. European nations were already grappling with many of the problems that stemmed from industrialization and urbanization, and they provided guidance, examples, and possible solutions. Progressive reformers soon learned that America's political, economic, and social structures made it necessary to modify, adapt, or even abandon these imported ideas, but their influence was obvious.

International influences were especially strong in the Social Gospel movement, symbolized by William T. Stead, a British social evangelist, whose idea of a "Civic Church" (a partnership of churches and reformers) captured great attention in the United States. Muckrakers not only exposed American problems but looked for foreign solutions. *Everybody's* sent Charles E. Russell around the world in 1905 to describe the social advances in Europe and New Zealand. (See Global Connections, The New Zealand Way.)

By 1912, American consumer activists, trade unionists, factory inspectors, and feminists regularly participated in international conferences on labor legislation, child welfare, social insurance, and housing reform and returned home with new ideas and strategies. State governments organized commissions to analyze European policies and agencies for lessons that might be applicable in the United States.

SOCIALISM

The growing influence of socialist ideas also promoted the spirit of progressivism. Socialism never attracted a large following in the United States, but its criticism of the industrial economy gained increasing attention in the early twentieth century. American socialists condemned social and economic inequities, criticized limited government, and demanded public ownership of railroads, utilities, and communications. They also campaigned for tax reforms, better housing, factory inspections, and recreational facilities for all.

The most prominent socialist was the dynamic and engaging Eugene V. Debs. An Indiana labor leader who had converted to socialism while imprisoned for his role in the 1894 Pullman strike, Debs had evangelical energy and a generous spirit. He decried what he saw as the dehumanization produced by industrial capitalism and hoped for an egalitarian society where everyone would have the opportunity "to develop the best there is in him for his own good as well as the good of society."

In 1901, Debs helped organize the Socialist Party of America; thereafter, he worked tirelessly to attract followers to a vision of socialism deeply rooted in American political and religious traditions. In the next decade, the party won many local elections, especially in Wisconsin and New York, where it drew support from German and Russian immigrants, and in Oklahoma, where it attracted poor tenant farmers.

Most progressives considered socialist ideas too drastic. Nevertheless, socialists contributed importantly to the reform ferment, not only by providing support for reform initiatives but often also by prompting progressives to push for changes to undercut increasingly attractive radical alternatives.

OPPONENTS OF REFORM

Not all Americans supported progressive reforms. Social Gospelers faced opposition from Protestant traditionalists emphasizing what they termed fundamental beliefs. Particularly strong among evangelical denominations with rural roots, these **fundamentalists** stressed personal salvation rather than social reform. Indeed, the urban and industrial crises that inspired Social Gospelers to preach reform drove many evangelical leaders to endorse social and political conservatism. The evangelist Billy Sunday condemned the Social Gospel as "godless social service nonsense."

Business interests, angered by exposes of corporate abuse and corruption, attacked the muckrakers. Business groups such as the American Bankers' Association accused muckrakers of promoting socialism. Major corporations like Standard Oil created public relations bureaus to improve their image and identify business, not its critics, with the public interest. Advertising boycotts discouraged magazines from running critical stories, and credit restrictions forced some muckraking journals to suspend publication. By 1910, the heyday of muckraking was over.

Labor unions likewise encountered resistance. Led by the National Association of Manufacturers, business groups denounced unions as corrupt and radical, hired thugs to disrupt them, organized strikebreaking agencies, and used blacklists to eliminate union activists. The antiunion campaign peaked in Ludlow, Colorado, in 1914, when John D. Rockefeller's Colorado Fuel and Iron Company used armed guards and the state militia to shoot and burn striking workers and their families. The courts aided employers by issuing injunctions against strikes and prohibiting unions from using boycotts, one of their most effective weapons.

Progressives campaigning for government intervention and regulation also met stiff resistance. Many Americans objected to what they considered unwarranted interference in private economic matters. Again, the courts often supported these attitudes. In *Lochner v. New York* (1905), the Supreme Court even overturned a maximum-hours law on the grounds that it deprived employers and employees of their "freedom of contract." Progressives continually struggled against such opponents, and progressive achievements were limited by the persistence and influence of their adversaries.

REFORMING SOCIETY

With their varied motives and objectives, progressives worked to transform society by improving living conditions, educational opportunities, family life, and social and industrial relations. (See Overview, Major Laws and Constitutional Amendments of the Progressive Era.) They sought what they called social justice, but their plans for social reform sometimes also smacked of social control. Organized women dominated the movement to reform society, but they were supported, depending on the goal, by Social Gospel ministers, social scientists, urban immigrants, labor unions, and even some conservatives eager to regulate personal behavior.

SETTLEMENT HOUSES AND URBAN REFORM

The spearheads for social reform were settlement houses—community centers in urban immigrant neighborhoods. Reformers created 400 settlement houses, largely modeled after Hull House in Chicago, founded in 1889 by Jane Addams. Most were led and staffed primarily by middle-class young women, seeking to alleviate poverty and do useful professional work when most careers were closed to them. Settlement work did not immediately violate prescribed gender roles because it initially focused on the "woman's sphere"—family, education, domestic skills, and cultural "uplift."

However, settlement workers soon saw that the root problem for immigrants was widespread poverty that required more than changes in individual behavior. Unlike earlier reformers, they regarded many of the evils of poverty as products of the social environment rather than of moral weakness. Thus, settlement workers campaigned for stricter building codes to improve slums, better urban sanitation systems to enhance public health, public parks to revive the urban environment, and laws to protect women and children.

Their crusades for sanitation and housing reform demonstrated the impact that social reformers often had on urban life. Settlement worker Mary McDowell became known as the "Garbage Lady" for her success in improving Chicago's massive environmental problems. Similarly, Lawrence Veiller was convinced by his work at the University Settlement in New York City that "the improvement of the homes of the people was the starting point for everything." Based on the findings of settlement workers, Veiller drafted a new housing code limiting the size of tenements and requiring toilet facilities, ventilation, and fire protection. In 1901, the New York Tenement House Law became a model for other cities.

PROTECTIVE LEGISLATION FOR WOMEN AND CHILDREN

While settlement workers initially undertook private efforts to improve society, many reformers eventually concluded that only government intervention could achieve social justice. The National Child Labor Committee, organized in 1904, led the campaign to curtail child labor. Reformers documented the problem with extensive investigations and also benefited from the public outrage stirred by Mother Jones's "children crusade" and by socialist John Spargo's muckraking book *The Bitter Cry of the Children* (1906). In 1900, most states had no minimum working age; by 1914, every state but one had such a law. Effective regulation, however, required national action, for many state laws were weak or poorly enforced.

Social reformers also lobbied for laws regulating the wages, hours, and working conditions of women and succeeded in having states from New York to Oregon pass maximum-hours legislation. After the Supreme Court upheld such laws in *Muller v. Oregon* (1908), 39 states enacted new or stronger laws on women's maximum hours between 1909 and 1917. Eight midwestern and western states authorized commissions to set minimum wages for women, but few other states followed.

Protective legislation for women posed a troubling issue for reformers. In California, for example, middle-class clubwomen favored protective legislation on the grounds of women's presumed weakness. They wanted to preserve "California's potential motherhood." More radical progressives, as in the socialist-led Women's Trade Union League of Los Angeles, supported such legislation to help secure economic

OVERVIEW MAJOR LAWS AND CONSTITUTIONAL AMENDMENTS OF THE PROGRESSIVE ERA

Legislation	Effect
New York Tenement House Law (1901)	Established a model housing code for safety and sanitation
Newlands Act (1902)	Provided for federal irrigation projects
Hepburn Act (1906)	Strengthened the Interstate Commerce Commission
Pure Food and Drug Act (1906)	Regulated the production and sale of food and drug products
Meat Inspection Act (1906)	Authorized federal inspection of meat products
Sixteenth Amendment (1913)	Authorized a federal income tax
Seventeenth Amendment (1913)	Mandated the direct popular election of senators
Underwood-Simmons Tariff Act (1913)	Lowered tariff rates and levied the first regular federal income tax
Federal Reserve Act (1913)	Established the Federal Reserve System to supervise banking and provide a national currency
Federal Trade Commission Act (1914)	Established the FTC to oversee business activities
Harrison Act (1914)	Regulated the distribution and use of narcotics
Smith-Lever Act (1914)	Institutionalized the county agent system
Keating-Owen Act (1916)	Indirectly prohibited child labor
Eighteenth Amendment (1919)	Instituted prohibition
Nineteenth Amendment (1920)	Established woman suffrage

independence and equality in the labor market for women, increase the economic strength of the working class, and serve as a precedent for laws improving conditions for all workers.

Progressive Era lawmakers adopted the first viewpoint. They limited protective legislation to measures reflecting the belief that women needed paternalist protection, even by excluding them from certain occupations. Laws establishing a minimum wage for women, moreover, usually set a wage level below subsistence rates. Rather than ensuring women's economic independence, then, protective legislation in practice reinforced women's subordinate place in the labor force.

Social justice reformers forged the beginnings of the welfare state in further legislation. Prompted by both humanitarian and paternalistic urgings, many states began in 1910 to provide "mothers' pensions" to indigent widows with dependent children. Twenty-one states, led by Wisconsin in 1911, enacted workers' compensation programs, ending the custom of holding workers themselves liable for injuries on the job.

Compared to the social insurance programs in Western Europe, however, these were feeble responses to the social consequences of industrialization. Proposals for health insurance, unemployment insurance, and old-age pension programs went nowhere. Business groups and other conservative interests curbed the movement toward state responsibility for social welfare.

RESHAPING PUBLIC EDUCATION

Concerns about child labor overlapped with increasing attention to the public schools. The rapid influx of immigrants, as well as the demands of the new corporate workplace, generated interest in education not only as a means of advancement but also as a tool for assimilation and the training of future workers.

Between 1880 and 1920, compulsory school attendance laws, kindergartens, age-graded elementary schools, professional training for teachers, vocational education, parent-teacher associations, and school nurses became standard elements in American education. School reformers believed these measures to be both educationally sound and important for countering slum environments. Others supported the kindergarten as "the earliest opportunity to catch the little Russian, the little Italian, the little German, Pole, Syrian, and the rest and begin to make good American citizens of them."

The famous photographer Lewis Hine used his camera to document child labor. The 11-year-old boys at this North Carolina textile mill in 1908 earned sixty cents a day.

Public education in the South lagged behind the North. Northern philanthropy and southern reformers brought some improvements after 1900, as per capita expenditures for education doubled, school terms were extended, and high schools spread across the region. But the South frittered away its limited resources on a segregated educational system that shortchanged both races. Black southerners particularly suffered, for the new programs increased the disparity in funding for white and black schools. South Carolina spent 12 times as much per white pupil as per black pupil.

Racism also underlay important changes in the schooling of Native Americans. The earlier belief that education would promote equality and facilitate assimilation gave way to a conviction that Indians were inferior and fit merely for manual labor. Educators now rejected the notion of a common school education for Indian children in favor of manual training that would enable Indians to fill menial jobs and whites to "turn their attention to more intellectual employments." Educators also renounced the practice of integrating Indian children into previously all-white classrooms, a policy begun in 1891.

CHALLENGING GENDER RESTRICTIONS

Most reformers held fairly conservative, moralistic views about sexuality and gender roles, but a small group of influential women sharply challenged conventional ideas about the social role of women. In critiquing women's subordinate status in society and articulating the case for full female equality, these women began self-consciously to refer to themselves as "feminists."

In *Women and Economics* (1898) and subsequent writings, Charlotte Perkins Gilman maintained that a communally organized society, with cooperative kitchens, nurseries, laundries, and housekeeping run by specialists, would free women from domestic drudgery and enable them to fulfill productive roles in the larger society while being happier wives and better mothers.

Emma Goldman, a Russian immigrant, was more of an activist in seeking woman's emancipation. A charismatic speaker (and celebrated anarchist), she delivered lectures attacking marriage as legalized prostitution rather than a partnership of independent equals and advocating birth control as a means to willing and "healthy motherhood and happy child-life."

Margaret Sanger succeeded where Goldman could not in establishing the modern birth control movement. A public-health nurse and an IWW organizer, she soon made the struggle for reproductive rights her personal crusade. Sanger saw in New York's immigrant neighborhoods the plight of poor women worn out from repeated pregnancies or injured or dead from self-induced knitting-needle abortions. Despite federal and state laws against contraceptives, Sanger began promoting birth control as a way to avert such tragedies. Prohibiting contraceptives meant "enforced motherhood," Sanger declared. "Women cannot be on an equal footing with men until they have full and complete control over their reproductive function."

Sanger's crusade attracted support from many women's and labor groups, but it also infuriated those who regarded birth control as a threat to the family and morality. Indicted for distributing information about contraception, Sanger fled to Europe. Other women took up the cause, forming the National Birth Control League in 1915 to campaign for the repeal of laws restricting access to contraceptive information and devices.

REFORMING COUNTRY LIFE

Although most progressives focused on the city, others sought to reform rural life, both to modernize its social and economic conditions and to integrate it more fully into the larger society. They worked to improve rural health and sanitation, to replace inefficient one-room schools with modern consolidated ones under professional control, and to extend new roads and communication services into the countryside. To further these goals, President Theodore Roosevelt created the Country Life Commission in 1908. The country lifers had a broad program for social and economic change, involving expanded government functions, activist government agencies staffed by experts, and the professionalization of rural social services.

Agricultural scientists, government officials, and many business interests also sought to promote efficient, scientific, and commercial agriculture. A key innovation was the county-agent system: The U.S. Department of Agriculture and business groups placed an agent in each county to teach farmers new techniques and to encourage changes in the rural social values that had previously spawned the Populist radicalism that most progressives decried. Few farmers, however, welcomed these efforts. Most farmers believed that their problems stemmed, not from rural life, but from industrial society and its nefarious trusts, banks, and middlemen. Rural Americans did not want their lives revolutionized.

Even so, rural people were drawn into the larger urban-industrial society during the Progressive Era. Government agencies, agricultural colleges, and railroads and banks steadily tied farmers to urban markets. Telephones and rural free delivery of mail lessened countryside isolation but quickened the spread of city values. Improved roads and the coming of the automobile eliminated many rural villages and linked farm families directly with towns and cities. Consolidated schools wiped out the social center of rural neighborhoods and carried children out of their communities, eventually encouraging an ever-growing migration to the city.

MORAL CRUSADES AND SOCIAL CONTROL

Moral reform movements, although often appearing misguided or unduly coercive today, generally reflected the progressive hope to protect people in a debilitating environment. In practice, however, these efforts to shape society tended toward social control. Moreover, these efforts often meshed with the restrictive attitudes that conservative Americans held about race, religion, immigration, and morality. The result was widespread attempts to restrict certain groups and control behavior.

Controlling Immigrants. Many Americans wanted to limit immigration for racist reasons. Nativist agitation in California prompted the federal government to secure restrictions on Japanese immigration in 1907. Californians, including local progressives, also hoped to curtail the migration of Mexicans.

Nationally, public debate focused on restricting the flow of new immigrants from southern and eastern Europe. Some labor leaders believed that immigration held down wages and impeded unionization; many sociologists thought it created serious social problems; other Americans disliked the newcomers on religious, cultural, or ethnic grounds. Many backed their prejudice with a distorted interpretation of Darwinism, labeling the Slavic and Mediterranean peoples "inferior races."

Other nativists demanded the "Americanization" of immigrants already in the country. The Daughters of the American Revolution sought to inculcate loyalty, patriotism, and conservative values. Settlement workers and Social Gospelers promoted a gentler kind of Americanization through English classes and home mission campaigns, but they too attempted to transfer their own values to the newcomers.

Prohibition. Closely linked to progressives' worries about immigrants was their campaign for **prohibition.** This movement engaged many of the progressives' basic impulses. Social workers saw liquor as a cause of crime, poverty, and family violence; employers blamed it for causing industrial accidents and inefficiency; Social Gospel ministers condemned the "spirit born of hell" because it impaired moral judgment and behavior. But also important was native-born Americans' fear of new immigrants—"the dangerous classes, who are readily dominated by the saloon." Many immigrants, in fact, viewed liquor and the neighborhood saloon as vital parts of daily life, and so prohibition became a focus of nativist hostility, cultural conflict, and Americanization pressures. In the South, racism also figured prominently. Alexander McKelway, the southern secretary for the National Child Labor Committee, endorsed prohibition as a way to maintain social order and white supremacy.

Protestant fundamentalists also stoutly supported prohibition, working through the Anti-Saloon League, founded in 1893. Their nativism and antiurban bias surfaced in demands for prohibition to prevent the nation's cities from lapsing into "raging mania, disorder, and anarchy."

With these varied motivations, prohibitionists campaigned for local and state laws against the manufacture and sale of alcohol. Beginning in 1907, they proved increasingly successful, especially in the South, Midwest, and Far West. By 1917, 26 states had prohibition laws. Congress then approved the **Eighteenth Amendment,** which made prohibition the law of the land by 1920.

Less controversial were drives to control or prohibit narcotics and cigarettes. Patent (over-the-counter) medicines commonly contained opium, heroin, and cocaine (popularly used for hay fever), and physicians known as "dope doctors" openly dispensed drugs to paying customers. Fears that addiction was spreading in "the fallen and lower classes"—and particularly among black people and immigrants—prompted Congress in 1914 to pass the Harrison Act, prohibiting the distribution and use of narcotics for other than medicinal purposes. The Anti-Cigarette League of America, organized in 1899 and having 300,000 members by 1901, led the charge against cigarettes. Many states soon restricted cigarettes, but such laws were rarely enforced and often repealed within a few years.

Suppressing Prostitution. Reformers also sought to suppress the "social evil" of prostitution. Like crowded slums, sweatshops, and child labor, the "vice districts" where prostitution flourished were seen as part of the exploitation and disorder in the industrial cities. Women's low wages as factory workers and domestic servants explained some of the problem, as a muckraking article entitled "The Daughters of the Poor" pointed out. But nativism spurred public concern, as when New York officials insisted that most prostitutes and brothel owners, some of whom "have been seducers of defenseless women all their lives," were foreign-born.

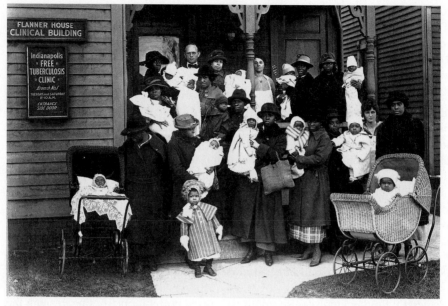

The Flanner House, a black settlement house in Indianapolis, provided the black community with many essential services, including health care. In addition to this baby clinic, pictured in 1918, it established a tuberculosis clinic at a time when the city's public hospitals refused to treat black citizens afflicted with the disease.
INDIANA HISTORICAL SOCIETY, M0513

   The response to prostitution was typical of progressivism: investigation and exposure, a reliance upon experts—boards of health, medical groups, clergy—for recommendations, and enactment of new laws. The progressive solution emerged in state and municipal action abolishing the "red light" districts previously tolerated and in a federal law, the Mann Act of 1910, prohibiting the interstate transport of women "for immoral purposes."

FOR WHITES ONLY?

Racism permeated the Progressive Era. In the South, progressivism was built on black disfranchisement and segregation. Like most white southerners, progressives believed that racial control was necessary for social order and that it enabled reformers to address other social problems. Such reformers also invoked racism to gain popular support for their objectives. In Georgia, for instance, child labor reformers warned that while white children worked in the Piedmont textile mills, black children were going to school: Child labor laws and compulsory school attendance laws were necessary to maintain white supremacy.

   Governors Hoke Smith of Georgia and James Vardaman, "the White Chief," of Mississippi typified the link between racism and reform in the South. These men supported progressive reforms but also viciously attacked black rights. Their racist demagogy incited antiblack violence throughout the South.

   Even in the North, race relations deteriorated. Civil rights laws went unenforced, restaurants and hotels excluded black customers, and schools were segregated. A reporter in Pennsylvania found that "this disposition to discriminate against Negroes has greatly increased within the past decade." Antiblack race riots exploded in New York in 1900 and in Springfield, Illinois—Abraham Lincoln's hometown—in 1908.

Black Activism. Although most white progressives promoted or accepted racial discrimination, and most black southerners had to adapt to it, black progressive activism was growing. Even in the South, some African Americans struggled to improve conditions. In Atlanta, for example, black women created progressive organizations and established settlement houses, kindergartens, and daycare centers.

In the North, African Americans more openly criticized discrimination and rejected Booker T. Washington's philosophy of accommodation. Ida Wells-Barnett, the crusading journalist who had fled the South for Chicago (see Chapter 17), became nationally prominent for her militant protests. She fought fiercely against racial injustices, especially school segregation, agitated for woman suffrage, and organized kindergartens and settlement houses for Chicago's black migrants.

Still more important was W. E. B. Du Bois, who campaigned tirelessly against all forms of racial discrimination. In 1905, Du Bois and other black activists met in Niagara Falls, Canada, to make plans to promote political and economic equality. In 1910, this **Niagara Movement** joined with a small group of white reformers, including Jane Addams, to organize the National Association for the Advancement of Colored People. The NAACP sought to overthrow segregation and establish equal justice and educational opportunities. As its director of publicity and research, Du Bois launched an influential magazine, *The Crisis,* to shape public opinion. "Agitate," he counseled, "protest, reveal the truth, and refuse to be silenced." By 1918, the NAACP had 44,000 members in 165 branches.

REFORMING POLITICS AND GOVERNMENT

Progressives of all kinds worked to reform politics and government. But their political activism was motivated by different concerns, and they sometimes pursued competing objectives. Many wanted to change procedures and institutions to promote greater democracy and responsibility. Others hoped to improve the efficiency of government, eliminate corruption, or increase their own influence. All justified their objectives as necessary to adapt the political system to the nation's new needs.

WOMAN SUFFRAGE

One of the most important achievements of the era was woman suffrage. The movement had begun in the mid-nineteenth century, but suffragists had been frustrated by the prevailing belief that women's proper sphere was the home and the family. Males dominated the public sphere, including voting. Woman suffrage, especially when championed as a step toward women's equality, seemed to challenge the natural order of society, and it generated much opposition, not only among men but among traditionalist-minded women as well.

Most women progressives viewed suffrage as the key issue of the period. Already taking active leadership in broad areas of public affairs—especially by confronting and publicizing social problems and then lobbying legislators and other officials to adopt their proposed solutions—they thought it ridiculous to be barred from the ballot box.

Carrying ballot boxes on a stretcher to ridicule American pretensions to a healthy democracy without woman suffrage, these activists marched in a dramatic parade in New York City in 1915. Combining such tactics with traditional appeals to patriotism and women's moral purity, woman suffragists eventually achieved the greatest democratic reform of the Progressive Era.

But most of all, the vote meant power, both to convince politicians to take seriously their demands for social reforms and to participate fully in electoral as in other forms of politics, thereby advancing the status of women.

In the early twentieth century, suffragists began to outflank their traditional opposition. Under a new generation of leaders, such as Carrie Chapman Catt and Harriot Stanton Blatch, they adopted activist tactics, including parades, mass meetings, and "suffrage tours" by automobile. They also organized by political districts and attracted workingwomen and labor unions. By 1917, the National American Woman Suffrage Association had over 2 million members.

Some suffrage leaders adopted new arguments to gain more support. Rather than insisting on the justice of woman suffrage or emphasizing equal rights, they spoke of the special moral and maternal instincts women could bring to politics if allowed to vote. Many suffragists, particularly among working-class groups, remained committed to the larger possibilities they saw in suffrage, but the new image of the movement increased public support by appealing to conventional views of women.

Gradually, the suffrage movement began to prevail (see Map 21–1). In 1910, Washington became the first state since the mid-1890s to approve woman suffrage, followed by California in 1911 and Arizona, Kansas, and Oregon in 1912. Suffragists also mounted actions to revive interest in a federal constitutional amendment to grant women the vote, and women sent petitions and organized pilgrimages to Washington from across the country. By 1919, thirty-nine states had established full or partial woman suffrage, and Congress finally approved an amendment. Ratified by the states in 1920, the **Nineteenth Amendment** marked a critical advance in political democracy.

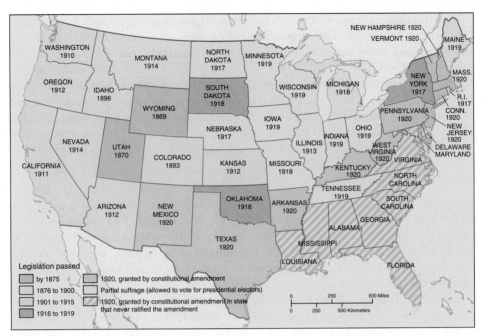

MAP 21–1 • Woman Suffrage in the United States Before the Ratification of the Nineteenth Amendment Beginning with Wyoming in 1869, woman suffrage slowly gained acceptance in the West, but women in the South and much of the East got the ballot only when the Nineteenth Amendment was ratified in 1920.

▶ *How might you explain the relatively early dates at which women in the West got the right to vote? Why was woman suffrage slower in coming to the East and South?*

ELECTORAL REFORM

Other electoral reforms changed the election process and the meaning of political participation. The so-called **Australian ballot** adopted by most states during the 1890s provided for secret voting, freeing voters from intimidation and discouraging vote buying and other corruption.

Government responsibility for the ballot soon led to public regulation of other parts of the electoral process previously controlled by parties. Beginning with Mississippi in 1902, nearly every state provided for direct primaries to remove nominations from the boss-ridden caucus and convention system. Many states also reformed campaign practices.

These reforms weakened the influence of political parties. Their decreasing ability to mobilize voters was reflected in a steady decline in voter participation, from 79 percent in 1896 to 49 percent in 1920. These developments had ominous implications, for parties and voting had traditionally linked ordinary Americans to their government. As parties slowly contracted, nonpartisan organizations and pressure groups, promoting narrower objectives, gained influence. Many of these special-interest groups represented the same middle- or upper-class interests that had led the attack on parties. Their organized lobbying would steadily give them greater influence over government and contribute to the declining popular belief in the value of voting or participation in politics.

Disfranchisement more obviously undermined American democracy. In the South, Democrats—progressive and conservative alike—eliminated not only black voters but also many poor white voters from the electorate through poll taxes, literacy tests, and other restrictions. Republicans in the North adopted educational or literacy tests in ten states, enacted strict registration laws, and gradually abolished the right of aliens to vote. These restrictions reflected both the progressives' anti-immigrant prejudices and their obsessions with social control and with purifying politics and "improving" the electorate. Such electoral reforms reduced the political power of ethnic and working-class Americans, often stripping them of their political rights and means of influence.

MUNICIPAL REFORM

Antiparty attitudes also affected progressives' efforts to reform municipal government, which they regarded as inefficient and corrupt, at least partly because of the power of urban political machines. Muckrakers had exposed crooked alliances between city bosses and business leaders that resulted in wasteful or inadequate municipal services. In some cities, urban reformers attempted to break these alliances and improve conditions for those suffering most from municipal misrule.

More elitist progressives changed the structure of urban government by replacing ward elections, which could be controlled by the neighborhood-based city machine, with at-large elections. To win citywide elections required greater resources and therefore helped swell middle-class influence at the expense of the working class. So did nonpartisan elections, which reformers introduced to weaken party loyalties.

Urban reformers developed two other structural innovations: the city commission and the city manager. Both attempted to institutionalize efficient, businesslike government staffed by professional administrators. By 1920, hundreds of cities had adopted one of the new plans, which business groups often promoted. Again, then, reform often shifted political power from ethnic and working-class voters, represented however imperfectly by partisan elections, to smaller groups with greater resources.

PROGRESSIVE STATE GOVERNMENT

Progressives also reshaped state government. Some tried to democratize the legislative process, regarding the legislature—the most important branch of state government in the nineteenth century—as ineffective and even corrupt, dominated by party bosses and corporate influences. The Populists had first raised such charges in the 1890s and proposed two novel solutions. The **initiative** enabled reformers to propose legislation directly to the electorate, bypassing an unresponsive legislature; the **referendum** permitted voters to approve or reject legislative measures. South Dakota Populists established the first system of "direct legislation" in 1898, and progressives adopted these innovations in 20 other states between 1902 and 1915.

Other innovations also expanded the popular role in state government. The **Seventeenth Amendment,** ratified in 1913, provided for the election of U.S. senators directly by popular vote instead of by state legislatures. Beginning with Oregon in 1908, ten states adopted the **recall,** enabling voters to remove unsatisfactory public officials from office.

As state legislatures and party machines were curbed, dynamic governors such as Robert La Follette in Wisconsin, Charles Evans Hughes in New York, and Hiram Johnson in California pushed progressive programs into law. Elected governor in 1900, "Fighting Bob" La Follette turned Wisconsin into "the laboratory of democracy." Overcoming fierce opposition from "stalwart" Republicans, La Follette established direct primaries, railroad regulation, the first state income tax, workers' compensation, and other important measures before being elected to the U.S. Senate in 1906. La Follette also stressed efficiency and expertise. The Legislative Reference Bureau that he created to advise on public policy was staffed by university professors. He used regulatory commissions to oversee railroads, banks, and other interests. Most states followed suit, and expert commissions became an important feature of state government, gradually gaining authority at the expense of elected local officials.

THEODORE ROOSEVELT AND THE PROGRESSIVE PRESIDENCY

When an anarchist assassinated William McKinley in 1901, Theodore Roosevelt entered the White House, and the progressive movement gained its most prominent leader. The son of a wealthy New York family, Roosevelt had pursued a career in Republican politics, serving as a New York legislator, U.S. civil service commissioner, and assistant secretary of the navy. After his exploits in the Spanish-American War (see Chapter 22), he was elected governor of New York in 1898 and vice president in 1900. Roosevelt's flamboyance and ambitions made him the most popular politician of the time and enabled him to dramatize the issues of progressivism and to become the first modern president.

TR AND THE MODERN PRESIDENCY

Roosevelt rejected the limited role of Gilded Age presidents. He believed that the president could do anything to meet national needs that the Constitution did not specifically prohibit. Indeed, the expansion of government power and its consolidation in the executive branch were among his most significant accomplishments.

Rather than defer to Congress, Roosevelt exerted legislative leadership. He spelled out his policy goals in more than 400 messages to Congress, sent drafts of bills to Capitol Hill, and intervened to win passage of "his" measures. Roosevelt generally avoided direct challenges to the conservative Old Guard Republicans who controlled Congress, but his activities helped shift the balance of power within the national government.

Roosevelt also reorganized the executive branch. He believed in efficiency and expertise, which he attempted to institutionalize in special commissions and administrative procedures. To promote rational policymaking and public management, he staffed the expanding federal bureaucracy with able professionals.

Finally, Roosevelt encouraged the development of a personal presidency by exploiting the public's interest in their exuberant young president. He established the first White House press room and skillfully handled the mass media. His endless and well-reported activities, from playing with his children in the White House to wrestling, hiking, and horseback-riding with various notables, made him a celebrity, known as TR or Teddy. The publicity not only kept TR in the spotlight but also enabled him to mold public opinion.

ROOSEVELT AND LABOR

One sign of TR's vigorous new approach to the presidency was his handling of a coal strike in 1902. Members of the United Mine Workers Union walked off their jobs, demanding higher wages, an eight-hour day, and recognition of their union. The mine owners closed the mines and waited for the union to collapse. But led by John Mitchell, the strikers held their ranks. The prospect of a freezing winter frightened consumers. Management's stubborn arrogance contrasted with the workers' orderly conduct and willingness to negotiate and hardened public opinion against the owners.

Although his legal advisers told him that the government had no authority to intervene, Roosevelt invited both the owners and the union leaders to the White House and declared that the national interest made government action necessary. Mitchell agreed to negotiate with the owners or to accept an arbitration commission appointed by the president. The owners, however, refused even to speak to the miners and demanded that Roosevelt use the army to break the union, as Cleveland had done in the Pullman strike in 1894.

Roosevelt was not a champion of labor, and he had favored shooting the Pullman strikers. But as president, he believed his role was to mediate social conflict for the public good. Roosevelt announced that he would use the army to seize and operate the mines, not to crush the union. Reluctantly, the owners accepted the arbitration commission they had previously rejected. The commission gave the miners a 10 percent wage increase and a nine-hour day, but not union recognition, and permitted the owners to raise coal prices by 10 percent. Roosevelt's intervention set important precedents for an active government role in labor disputes and a strong president acting as a steward of the public.

MANAGING NATURAL RESOURCES

Federal land policy had helped create farms and develop transportation, but it had also ceded to speculators and business interests much of the nation's forests, mineral deposits, waterpower sites, and grazing lands. Reckless exploitation of these resources alarmed a new generation that believed the public welfare required the **conservation** of natural resources through efficient and scientific management. Conservationists achieved early victories in the Forest Reserve Act (1891) and the Forest Management Act (1897), which authorized the federal government to withdraw timberlands from development and to regulate grazing, lumbering, and hydroelectric sites in the forests.

Roosevelt built on these beginnings and on his friendship with Gifford Pinchot to make conservation a major focus of his presidency. Appointed in 1898 to head the new Division of Forestry (renamed the Forest Service in 1905), Pinchot brought rational management and regulation to resource development. With his advice, TR used presidential authority to triple the size of the forest reserves to 150 million acres, set aside another 80 million acres valuable for minerals and petroleum, and establish dozens of wildlife refuges. In 1908, Roosevelt held a White House conference of state and federal officials that led to the creation of the National Conservation Commission, 41 state conservation commissions, and widespread public support for the conservation movement.

Not everyone, of course, agreed with TR's conservationist policies. Some favored **preservation,** hoping to set aside land as permanent wilderness, whereas Roosevelt favored a scientific and efficient rather than uncontrolled use of resources. Preservationists won some victories, saving a stand of California's giant redwoods and helping create the National Park Service in 1916, but more Americans favored the utilitarian emphasis of the early conservationists.

Other interests opposed conservation completely. While some of the larger timber and mineral companies supported conservation as a way to guarantee long-run profits, smaller western entrepreneurs often cared only about quick returns. Many westerners, moreover, resented having easterners make key decisions about western growth and saw conservation as a perpetuation of this colonial subservience.

But westerners were happy to take federal money for expensive irrigation projects that private capital would not underwrite. They favored the 1902 National Reclamation Act, which established what became the **Bureau of Reclamation.** Its engineers were to construct dams, reservoirs, and irrigation canals, and the government was to sell the irrigated lands in tracts no larger than 160 acres. With massive dams and networks of irrigation canals, it reclaimed fertile valleys from the desert, but by not enforcing the 160-acre limitation it helped create powerful corporate farms in the West.

Theodore Roosevelt and John Muir, here on a 1903 camping trip in Yosemite, championed public responsibility for the nation's scenic and other natural resources.

Westerners also welcomed Roosevelt's conservationist emphasis on rational development when it restricted Indian control of land and resources. He favored policies breaking up many reservations to open the land to whites for "efficient" development and diverting Indian waters to growing cities like Phoenix. Tribal protests were ignored.

CORPORATE REGULATION

Nothing symbolized Roosevelt's active presidency better than his popular reputation as a "trust buster." TR regarded the formation of large business combinations favorably, but he realized he could not ignore the public anxiety about corporate power. Rather than invoking "the foolish antitrust law," he favored government regulation to prevent corporate abuses and defend the public interest. "Misconduct," not size, was the issue.

But Roosevelt did file lawsuits against some "bad trusts," including the Northern Securities Company, a holding company organized by J. P. Morgan to control the railroad network of the Northwest. For TR, this suit was an assertion of government power that reassured a worried public and encouraged corporate responsibility. In 1904, the Supreme Court ordered the dissolution of the Northern Securities Company. Ultimately, Roosevelt brought 44 antitrust suits against business combinations, but except for a few like Standard Oil, he avoided the giant firms. Many of the cases had inconclusive outcomes, but Roosevelt was more interested in establishing a regulatory role for government than in breaking up big businesses.

Elected president in his own right in 1904 over the colorless and conservative Democratic candidate, Judge Alton B. Parker, Roosevelt responded to the growing popular demand for reform by pushing further toward a regulatory government. In 1906, Congress passed the Hepburn Act to extend the authority of the Interstate Commerce

Commission over railroads, the Pure Food and Drug Act, and the Meat Inspection Act. All three were compromises between reformers seeking serious government control of the industries involved and political defenders and lobbyists of the industries themselves.

Despite the compromises and weaknesses in the three laws, TR contended that they marked "a noteworthy advance in the policy of securing federal supervision and control over corporations." In 1907 and 1908, he pushed for an eight-hour workday, stock market regulation, and inheritance and income taxes. Republican conservatives in Congress blocked such reforms, and tensions increased between the progressive and conservative wings of the party.

TAFT AND THE INSURGENTS

TR handpicked his successor as president: a loyal lieutenant, William Howard Taft. If Roosevelt thought that Taft would be a successful president, continuing his policies and holding the Republican Party together, he was wrong. Taft's election in 1908, over Democrat William Jennings Bryan in his third presidential campaign, led to a Republican political disaster.

Taft did preside over important progressive achievements. His administration pursued a more active and successful antitrust program than Roosevelt's. He supported the Mann-Elkins Act (1910), which extended the ICC's jurisdiction to telephone and telegraph companies. Taft set aside more public forest lands and oil reserves than Roosevelt had. He also supported a constitutional amendment authorizing an income tax, which went into effect in 1913 under the **Sixteenth Amendment.** One of the most important accomplishments of the Progressive Era, the income tax would provide the means for the government to expand its activities and responsibilities.

Nevertheless, Taft soon alienated progressives and floundered into a political morass. His problems were twofold. First, the Republicans were divided. Midwestern reform Republicans, led by La Follette, clashed with conservative Republicans, led by Senator Nelson Aldrich of Rhode Island. Second, Taft was politically inept. He was unable to mediate between the two Republican factions, and the party split apart.

Reformers wanted to restrict the power of the Speaker of the House, "Uncle Joe" Cannon, a reactionary who systematically blocked progressive measures and loudly declared, "I am goddamned tired of listening to all this babble of reform." After seeming to promise support, Taft backed down when conservatives threatened to defeat important legislation. The insurgents in Congress eventually restricted the speaker's powers, but they never forgave what they saw as Taft's betrayal. The tariff also alienated progressives from Taft. He had campaigned in 1908 for a lower tariff to curb inflation, but when they introduced tariff reform legislation, the president failed to support them, and Aldrich's Senate committee added 847 amendments, many of which raised tariff rates. Progressives concluded that Taft had sided with the Old Guard against real change.

This perception solidified when Taft stumbled into a controversy over conservation. Gifford Pinchot had become embroiled in a complex struggle with Richard Ballinger, Taft's secretary of the interior. Ballinger, who was closely tied to western mining and lumbering interests, favored private development of public lands. When Pinchot challenged Ballinger's role in a questionable sale of public coal lands in Alaska to a J. P. Morgan syndicate, Taft upheld Ballinger and fired Pinchot. Progressives concluded that Taft had repudiated Roosevelt's conservation policies.

The progressives determined to replace Taft, whom they now saw as an obstacle to reform. In 1911, the National Progressive League organized to champion La Follette for the Republican nomination in 1912. Roosevelt rejected an appeal for support, convinced that a challenge to the incumbent president was both doomed and divisive. Besides, his own position was closer to Taft's than to what he called "the La Follette type of fool radicalism." But Taft's political blunders increasingly angered Roosevelt. Condemning Taft as "disloyal to our past friendship," TR began to campaign for the Republican nomination himself. In 13 state primaries, he won 278 delegates, to only 46 for Taft. But most states did not then have primaries; as a result, Taft was able to dominate the Republican convention and win renomination. Roosevelt's forces formed a third party—the Progressive Party—and nominated the former president. The Republican split almost guaranteed victory for the Democratic nominee, Woodrow Wilson.

WOODROW WILSON AND PROGRESSIVE REFORM

The pressures for reform called forth many new leaders. The one who would preside over progressivism's culmination, and ultimately its collapse, was Woodrow Wilson. Elected president in 1912 and 1916, he mediated among differing progressive views to achieve a strong reform program, enlarge the power of the executive branch, and make the White House the center of national politics.

THE ELECTION OF 1912

Despite the prominence of Roosevelt and La Follette, progressivism was not simply a Republican phenomenon. As the Republicans quarreled during Taft's administration, Democrats pushed progressive remedies and achieved major victories in the state and congressional elections of 1910. To improve the party's chances in 1912, William Jennings Bryan announced that he would step aside. The Democratic spotlight shifted to the governor of New Jersey, Woodrow Wilson.

Wilson first entered public life as a conservative, steeped in the limited-government traditions of his native South. As president of Princeton University, beginning in 1902, he became a prominent representative of middle-class respectability and conservative causes. In 1910, New Jersey's Democratic bosses selected him for governor to head off the progressives. But once in office, Wilson championed popular reforms and immediately began to campaign as a progressive for the party's 1912 presidential nomination.

Wilson's progressivism differed from that of Roosevelt in 1912. TR emphasized a strong government to promote economic and social order. He defended big business as inevitable and healthy provided that government control ensured that it would benefit the entire nation. Roosevelt called this program the **New Nationalism,** reflecting his belief in a powerful state and a national interest. He also supported demands for social welfare, including workers' compensation and the abolition of child labor.

Wilson was horrified by Roosevelt's vision. His **New Freedom** program rejected what he called TR's "regulated monopoly." Wilson wanted "regulated competition," with the government's role limited to breaking up monopolies through antitrust action and preventing artificial barriers like tariffs from blocking free enterprise. Wilson opposed social-welfare legislation as paternalistic, reaching beyond the proper scope of the federal government, which he hoped to minimize.

Roosevelt's endorsement of social legislation attracted many women into political action. As Jane Addams observed, "their long concern for the human wreckage of industry has come to be considered politics." (See American Views: The Need for Woman Suffrage.)

The Progressive Party also endorsed woman suffrage, accepted women as convention delegates, and pledged to give women equal representation on party committees.

Despite his personal popularity, however, TR was unable to add progressive Democrats to the Republicans who followed him into the Progressive Party, and thus was doomed to defeat. Other reform voters embraced the Socialist candidate, Eugene V. Debs, who captured 900,000 votes—6 percent of the total. Taft played little role in the campaign.

Wilson won an easy electoral college victory, though he received only 42 percent of the popular vote and fewer popular votes than Bryan had won in any of his three campaigns (see Map 21–2). Roosevelt came in second, Taft third. The Democrats also gained control of Congress, giving Wilson the opportunity to enact his New Freedom program.

IMPLEMENTING THE NEW FREEDOM

As president, Wilson built on Roosevelt's precedent to strengthen executive authority. He proposed a full legislative program and worked forcefully to secure its approval. When necessary, he appealed to the public for support, ruthlessly used patronage, or compromised with conservatives. With such methods and a solid Democratic majority, Wilson gained approval of important laws.

Wilson turned first to the traditional Democratic goal of reducing the high protective tariff, the symbol of special privileges for industry. He forced through the **Underwood-Simmons Tariff Act** of 1913, the first substantial reduction in duties since before the Civil War. The act also levied the first income tax under the recently ratified Sixteenth Amendment. Conservatives condemned the "revolutionary" tax, but it was designed simply to compensate for lower tariff rates. The top tax rate paid by the wealthiest was a mere 7 percent.

MAP 21–2 • **The Election of 1912** The split within the Republican Party enabled Woodrow Wilson to carry most states and become president even though he won only a minority of the popular vote.

▶ *How is it possible that Woodrow Wilson received 82 percent of the electoral vote but only 42 percent of the popular vote?*

	Electoral Vote (%)	Popular Vote (%)
WOODROW WILSON (Democrat)	**435** **(82)**	**6,296,547** **(42)**
Theodore Roosevelt (Progressive)	88 (17)	4,118,571 (27)
William Taft (Republican)	8 (1)	3,486,720 (23)
Eugene Debs (Socialist)	–	900,672 (6)

Wilson next reformed the nation's banking and currency system, which was inadequate for a modernizing economy. Wilson skillfully maneuvered a compromise measure through Congress, balancing the demands of agrarian progressives for government control with the bankers' desires for private control. The **Federal Reserve Act** of 1913 created 12 regional Federal Reserve banks that, although privately controlled, were to be supervised by the Federal Reserve Board, appointed by the president. The law also provided for a flexible national currency and improved access to credit.

Wilson's third objective was new legislation to break up monopolies. Initially, he supported the Clayton antitrust bill, which prohibited unfair trade practices and sharply restricted holding companies. But when business leaders and other progressives strenuously objected, Wilson reversed himself. Opting for continuous federal regulation rather than for the dissolution of trusts, Wilson endorsed the creation of the **Federal Trade Commission** **(FTC)** to oversee business activity and prevent illegal restrictions on competition.

The Federal Trade Commission Act of 1914 dismayed many of Wilson's early supporters because it embraced the New Nationalism's emphasis on positive regulation. Roosevelt's 1912 platform had proposed a federal trade commission; Wilson now accepted what he had earlier denounced as a partnership between trusts and the government that the trusts would dominate. Indeed, Wilson's conservative appointments to the FTC ensured that the agency would not seriously interfere with business, and by the 1920s, the FTC had become virtually a junior partner of the business community.

The fate of the Clayton antitrust bill after Wilson withdrew his support reflected his new attitude toward big business. Congressional conservatives gutted the bill with crippling amendments before permitting it to become law in 1914.

These measures indicate the limited nature of Wilson's vision of reform. In fact, he now announced that no further reforms were necessary—astonishing many progressives whose objectives had been completely ignored. Wilson refused to support woman suffrage and helped kill legislation abolishing child labor and expanding credits to farmers. He demonstrated his indifference to issues of social justice by supporting the introduction of racial segregation within the government itself. Government offices, shops, restrooms, and restaurants were all segregated; employees who complained were fired. Federal officials in the South discharged black employees.

THE EXPANSION OF REFORM

Wilson had won in 1912 only because the Republicans had split. By 1916, Roosevelt had returned to the GOP, and Wilson realized that he had to attract some of TR's former followers. Wilson therefore abandoned his opposition to social and economic reforms and promoted measures he had previously condemned. But he had also grown in the White House and now recognized that some problems could be resolved only by positive federal action.

To assist farmers, Wilson in 1916 convinced Congress to pass the Federal Farm Loan Act. This law, which Wilson himself had earlier rejected twice, provided farmers with federally financed long-term agricultural credits. The Warehouse Act of 1916 improved short-term agricultural credit. The Highway Act of 1916 provided funds to construct and improve rural roads through the adoption of the dollar-matching principle by which the federal government would expand its power over state activities in the twentieth century.

Wilson and the Democratic Congress also reached out to labor. Wilson signed the Keating-Owen Act prohibiting the interstate shipment of products made by child labor.

AMERICAN VIEWS

THE NEED FOR WOMAN SUFFRAGE

*T*he movement for woman suffrage was one of the most important components of progressivism, and it gained increasing numbers of adherents, who created new organizations, adopted new tactics, and crafted new arguments for the reform. The task remained the same: persuading first legislative committees and then electorates to approve a fundamental change in the political system. In 1912 Caroline A. Lowe, of Kansas City, Missouri, delivered the following remarks to a hearing of a joint committee formed by the Judiciary Committee and the Woman Suffrage Committee of the U.S. Senate.

■ **What** arguments does Lowe advance to support the need for woman suffrage?

■ **How** does Lowe attempt to counteract objections to the reform?

■ **How** does Lowe's rhetoric reflect the varied impulses underlying progressive reform?

Gentlemen of the committee, it is as a wage earner and on behalf of the 7,000,000 wage-earning women in the United States that I wish to speak.

I entered the ranks of the wage earners when 18 years of age. Since then I have earned every cent of the cost of my own maintenance, and for several years was a potent factor in the support of my widowed mother.

The need of the ballot for the wage-earning women is a vital one. No plea can be made that we have the protection of the home or are represented by our fathers and brothers. We need the ballot that we may broaden our horizon and assume our share in the solution of the problems that seriously affect our daily lives. . . .

We need the ballot for the purpose of self-protection. . . . Does the young woman cashier in Marshall Field's need any voice in making the law that sets the hours of labor that shall constitute a day's work?. . . . Has the young woman whose scalp was torn from her head at the Lawrence mill any need of a law demanding that safety appliances be placed upon all dangerous machinery? And what of the working girls who, through unemployment, are denied the opportunity to sell the labor of their hands and are driven to the sale of their virtue?

. . . . We wage earners know it to be almost universal that the men in the industries receive twice the wage granted to us, although we may be doing the same work and should have the same pay. We women work side by side with our brothers. We are children of the same parents, reared

In 1902, Wilson had denounced Roosevelt's intervention in the coal strike, but in 1916 he broke a labor-management impasse and averted a railroad strike by helping pass the Adamson Act establishing an eight-hour day for railroad workers. Wilson also pushed the Kern-McGillicuddy Act, which achieved the progressive goal of a workers' compensation system for federal employees. Together, these laws marked an important advance toward government regulation of the labor market.

Wilson also promoted activist government when he nominated Louis Brandeis to the Supreme Court. Known as "the people's lawyer," Brandeis had successfully defended

in the same homes, educated in the same schools, ride to and fro on the same early morning and late evening streetcars, work together the same number of hours in the same shops, and we have equal need of food, clothing, and shelter. But at 21 years of age our brothers are given a powerful weapon for self-defense, a larger means for growth and self-expression. We working women, even because we are women and find our sex not a source of strength but a source of weakness and offering a greater opportunity for exploitation, are denied this weapon.

Gentlemen of the committee, is there any justice underlying such a condition? If our brother workingmen are granted the ballot with which to protect themselves, do you not think that the working women should be granted this same right?

What of the working girl and her employer? Why is the ballot given to him while it is denied to us? Is it for the protection of his property, that he may have a voice in the governing of his wealth, of his stocks and bonds and merchandise?

The wealth of the working woman is of far greater value to the State. From nature's raw products the working class can readily replace all of the material wealth owned by the employing class, but the wealth of the working woman is the wealth of flesh and blood, of all her physical, mental, and spiritual powers. It is the wealth, not only of today, but that of future generations, that is being bartered away so cheaply. Have we no right to a voice in the disposal of our wealth, the greatest wealth that the world possesses—the priceless wealth of its womanhood?

Is it not the cruelest injustice that the man whose material wealth is a source of strength and protection to him and of power over us should be given the additional advantage of an even greater weapon which he can use to perpetuate our condition of helpless subjection?

. . . Mr. Chairman and gentlemen of the committee, the time is ripe for the extension of the franchise to women. We do not come before you to beg you to grant us a favor; we come presenting to you a glorious opportunity to place yourselves abreast of the current of this great evolutionary movement. You can refuse to accept this opportunity, and you may, for a moment, delay the movement, but only as the old woman who, with her tiny broom, endeavored to sweep back the incoming tide from the sea.

If today, taking your places as men of affairs in the world's progress, you step out in unison with the eternal upward trend toward true democracy, you will support the suffrage amendment now before your committee.

SOURCE: U.S. Congress, Senate, Joint Committee, 62nd Cong., 2nd sess., S. Document 601, pp. 16–19.

protective labor legislation before the conservative judiciary. The nomination outraged conservatives, including William Howard Taft and the American Bar Association. Brandeis was the first Jew nominated to the court, and anti-Semitism motivated some of his opponents. Wilson overcame a vicious campaign against Brandeis and secured his confirmation.

By these actions, Wilson brought progressivism to a culmination of sorts and consolidated reformers behind him for a second term. Less than a decade earlier, Wilson the private citizen had assailed government regulation and social legislation; by 1916, he had guided an unprecedented expansion of federal power. His own personal and political journey symbolized the development of progressivism.

CONCLUSION

Progressivism had its ironies and paradoxes. It called for democratic reforms—and did achieve woman suffrage, direct legislation, and popular election of senators—but helped disfranchise black southerners and northern immigrants. It advocated social justice but often enforced social control. It demanded responsive government but helped create bureaucracies largely removed from popular control. It endorsed the regulation of business in the public interest but forged regulatory laws and commissions that tended to aid business.

Both the successes and the failures of progressivism revealed that the nature of politics and government had changed significantly. Americans had come to accept that government action could resolve social and economic problems, and the role and power of government expanded accordingly. The emergence of an activist presidency, capable of developing programs, mobilizing public opinion, directing Congress, and taking forceful action, epitomized this key development.

These important features would be crucial when the nation fought World War I, which brought new challenges and dangers to the United States. The Great War would expose many of the limitations of progressivism and the naivete of the progressives' optimism.

REVIEW QUESTIONS

1. How and why did the presidency change during the Progressive Era?

2. How did the progressive concern for efficiency affect social reform efforts, public education, government administration, and rural life?

3. How and why did the relationship between business and government change during this time?

4. Why did social reform and social control often intermingle in the Progressive Era? Can such objectives be separate?

5. What factors, old and new, stimulated the reform movements of progressivism?

6. How did the role of women change during the Progressive Era? How did the changes affect progressivism?

7. Why did the demand for woman suffrage provoke such determined support and such bitter opposition?

PEARSON myhistorylab CONNECTIONS

Reinforce what you learned in this chapter by studying the many documents, images, maps, review tools, and videos available at www.myhistorylab.com.

READ AND REVIEW

✓•⌐Study and Review on myhistorylab.com STUDY PLAN: CHAPTER 21

⌐•⌐Read the Document on myhistorylab.com

Herbert Croly, Progressive Democracy (1914)

Charlotte Perkins Gilman, "If I Were a Man" (1914)

Emma Goldman, Anarchism and Other Essays (1917)

Eugene V. Debs, "The Outlook for Socialism in America" (1900)

Frederick W. Taylor, The Principles of Scientific Management (1911)

Jane Addams, from Twenty Years at Hull House (1910)

Gifford Pinchot, The Fight for Conservation (1910)

Helen M. Todd, "Getting Out the Vote" (1911)

Jane Addams, "Ballots Necessary for Women" (1906)

Louis Brandeis, Other People's Money and How the Bankers Use It (1913)

Mary Church Terrell, The Progress of Colored Women (1898)

Mother Jones, "The March of the Mill Children" (1903)

Platform Adopted by the National Negro Committee (1909)

The Niagara Movement, Declaration of Principles (1905)

Theodore Roosevelt, "The New Nationalism" (1910)

Woodrow Wilson, from The New Freedom (1913)

View the **Map** on **myhistorylab.com**

Woman Suffrage before the Nineteenth Century

RESEARCH AND EXPLORE

Read the **Document** on **myhistorylab.com**

Personal Journeys Online

From Then to Now Online: The Environmental Movement

Exploring America: Americanization

Listen on **myhistorylab.com**

Crisis Magazine by W. E. B. Du Bois

The Primary Needs of the Negro Race by Kelly Miller

The Progress of Colored Women by Mary Church Terrell

Watch the **Video** on **myhistorylab.com**

Bull Moose Campaign Speech

Punching the Clock

Women in the Workplace, 1904

What Was the Progressive Education Movement?

Listen on **myhistorylab.com**

Hear the audio files for Chapter 21 at
www.myhistorylab.com.

Hear the audio files for Chapter 22 at **www.myhistorylab.com.**

FOCUS QUESTIONS

WHAT ARGUMENTS were made in favor of American expansion in the late nineteenth century?

WHAT STEPS did the United States take to expand its global influence in the decades before the Spanish-American War?

WHAT WERE the most important consequences of the Spanish-American War?

WHAT WAS the nature of U.S. involvement in Asia?

HOW DID Latin Americans respond to U.S. intervention in the region?

WHY DID the United States take a larger role in Europe at the beginning of the twentieth century?

A jubilant Uncle Sam celebrates victory in the Spanish-American War and anticipates the building of an American empire.

ONE AMERICAN JOURNEY

Havana, Cuba October 1901

When the Spanish-American war was declared the United States … assumed a position as protector of the interests of Cuba. It became responsible for the welfare of the people, politically, mentally, and morally. The mere fact of freeing the island from Spanish rule has not ended the care which this country should give…. The effect will be to uplift the people, gaining their permanent friendship and support and greatly increasing our own commerce. At present there are two million people requiring clothing and food, for but a small proportion of the necessaries of life are raised on the island. It is folly to grow food crops when sugar and tobacco produce such rich revenues in comparison. The United States should supply the Cubans with their breadstuffs, even wine, fruit, and vegetables, and should clothe the people…. The money received for their crops will be turned over in a great measure in buying supplies from the United States….

Naturally the manufacturers of the United States should have precedence in furnishing machinery, locomotives, cars, and rails, materials for buildings and bridges, and the wide diversity of other supplies required, as well as fuel for their furnaces. With the present financial and commercial uncertainty at an end the people of the island will … come into the American market as customers for products of many kinds.

The meeting of the Constitutional Convention on November 5th will be an event in Cuban history of the greatest importance, and much will depend upon the action and outcome of this convention as to our future control of the island…. I considered it unwise to interfere, and I have made it a settled policy to permit the Cubans to manage every part of their constitution-making. This has been due to my desire to prevent any possible charge of crimination being brought against the United States in the direction of their constitutional affairs….

There is no distrust of the United States on the part of the Cubans, and I know of no widespread antipathy to this country, its people, or its institutions. There are, of course, a handful of malcontents, as there must be in every country….

I could not well conceive how the Cubans could be otherwise than grateful to the United States for its efforts in their behalf…. In the brief time since the occupation of the island by American troops the island has been completely rehabilitated—agriculturally, commercially, financially, educationally, and governmentally. This improvement has been so rapid and so apparent that no Cuban could mistake it. To doubt in the face of these facts that their liberators were not still their faithful friends would be impossible.

Major-General Leonard Wood, "The Future of Cuba," *The Independent* 54 (January 23, 1902): 193–194; idem, "The Cuban Convention," *The Independent* 52 (November 1, 1900): 265–266.

GENERAL LEONARD WOOD'S reports on Cuba, then under his control as military governor, captured the complex mixture of attitudes and motives that underlay the journey of the United States from a developing nation to a world power. Plans for economic expansion, a belief in national mission, a sense of responsibility to help others, scarcely hidden religious impulses and racist convictions—all combined in an uneasy mixture of self-interest and idealism.

The tension between what a friend of Wood's called the "righteous" and the "selfish" aspects of expanding American influence lay beneath the surface in Wood's reports. His claim that he was not interfering with Cuba's constitutional convention was disingenuous, for he had already undertaken to limit those who could participate as voters or delegates and was even then devising means to restrict the convention's autonomy. And in his repeated insistence that the Cubans were grateful for the intervention of "their faithful friends," the Americans, Wood obviously protested too much: Cubans, as well as Filipinos, Puerto Ricans, and others, rarely perceived American motives or American actions as positively as did Wood and other proponents of American expansion. Victory in the Spanish-American War had provided the United States with an extensive empire, status as a world power, and opportunities and problems that would long shape U.S. foreign policy.

THE ROOTS OF IMPERIALISM

The United States had a long-established tradition of expansion across the continent. Indeed, by the 1890s, Republican Senator Henry Cabot Lodge of Massachusetts boasted that Americans had "a record of conquest, colonization, and territorial expansion unequalled by any people in the nineteenth century." Lodge now urged the country to build an overseas empire, emulating the European model of **imperialism** based on the acquisition and exploitation of colonial possessions. Other Americans favored a less formal empire, in which United States interests and influence would be ensured through extensive trade and investments rather than through military occupation. Still others advocated a cultural expansionism in which the nation exported its ideals and institutions. All such expansionists could draw from many sources to support their plans. (See Overview, Rationales for Imperialism).

IDEOLOGICAL AND RELIGIOUS ARGUMENTS

Scholars, authors, politicians, and religious leaders provided interlocking ideological arguments for the new imperialism. Some intellectuals, for example, invoked Social Darwinism, maintaining that the United States should engage in a competitive struggle for wealth and power with other nations. "The survival of the fittest," declared one writer, was "the law of nations as well as a law of nature." As European nations expanded into Asia and Africa in the 1880s and 1890s, seeking colonies, markets, and raw materials, these advocates argued, the United States had to adopt similar policies to ensure national success.

Related to Social Darwinism was a pervasive belief in racial inequality and in the superiority of people of English, or Anglo-Saxon, descent. To many Americans, the industrial progress, military strength, and political development of England and the United States were proof of an Anglo-Saxon superiority that carried with it a responsibility to extend the blessings of their rule to less able people. As a popular expression put it, colonialism was the "white man's burden," carrying with it a duty to aid and uplift other peoples. Such attitudes led some expansionists to favor imposing American ideas and practices on other cultures regardless of their own values and customs.

CHRONOLOGY

1861–1869	Seward serves as secretary of state.
1867	United States purchases Alaska from Russia.
1870	Annexation of the Dominican Republic is rejected.
1879	France conquers Algeria.
1881	Naval Advisory Board is created.
1882	Great Britain occupies Egypt.
1887	United States gains naval rights to Pearl Harbor.
1890	Alfred Thayer Mahan publishes *The Influence of Sea Power upon History*.
1893	Harrison signs but Cleveland rejects a treaty for the annexation of Hawaii.
1893–1897	Depression increases interest in economic expansion abroad.
1894–1895	Sino-Japanese War is fought.
1895	United States intervenes in Great Britain–Venezuelan boundary dispute.
	Cuban insurrection against Spain begins.
1896	William McKinley is elected president on an imperialist platform.
1898	Spanish-American War is fought.
	Hawaii is annexed.
	Anti-Imperialist League is organized.
	Treaty of Paris is signed.
1899–1902	Filipino-American War is fought.
1899	Open Door note is issued.
	First Hague Peace Conference creates Court of Arbitration.
1900	Boxer Rebellion against foreign influence breaks out in China.
1901	Theodore Roosevelt becomes president.
1903	Platt Amendment restricts Cuban autonomy.
	Panama "revolution" is abetted by the United States.
1904	United States acquires the Panama Canal Zone.
	Roosevelt Corollary is announced.
1904–1905	Russo-Japanese War is fought.
1905	Treaty of Portsmouth ends the Russo-Japanese War through U.S. mediation.
1906–1909	United States occupies Cuba.
1907–1908	Gentlemen's Agreement restricts Japanese immigration.
1909	United States intervenes in Nicaragua.

1912–1933	United States occupies Nicaragua.
1914	Panama Canal opens.
1914–1917	United States intervenes in Mexico.
1915–1934	United States occupies Haiti.
1916–1924	United States occupies the Dominican Republic.
1917	Puerto Ricans are granted U.S. citizenship.
1917–1922	United States occupies Cuba.

Reflecting this aggressiveness, as well as Darwinian anxieties, some Americans endorsed expansion as consistent with their ideals of masculinity. Forceful expansion would be a manly course, relying upon and building strength and honor among American males. Men who confronted the challenges of empire would thereby improve their ability to compete in the international arena. "Pride of race, courage, manliness," predicted one enthusiast, would be both the causes and the consequences of an assertive foreign policy.

American missionaries also promoted expansionist sentiment. Hoping to evangelize the world, American religious groups increased the number of Protestant foreign missions sixfold from 1870 to 1900. Women in particular organized foreign missionary societies and served in the missions. Missionaries publicized their activities throughout the United States, generating interest in foreign developments and support for what one writer called the "imperialism of righteousness." Abroad they pursued a religious transformation that often resembled a cultural conversion, for they promoted trade, developed business interests, and encouraged westernization through technology and education as well as religion. Sometimes, as in the Hawaiian Islands, American missionaries even promoted annexation by the United States.

Indeed, the American religious press endlessly repeated the themes of national destiny, racial superiority, and religious zeal. Missionaries contributed to the imperial impulse by describing their work in terms of the conquest of enemy territory. Thus, while missionaries were motivated by what they considered to be idealism and often brought real benefits to other lands, especially in education and health, religious sentiments reinforced the ideology of American expansion.

STRATEGIC CONCERNS

Other expansionists were motivated by strategic concerns, shaped by what they saw as the forces of history and geography. America's location in the Western Hemisphere, its coastlines on two oceans, and the ambitions and activities of other nations, particularly Germany and Britain, convinced some Americans that the United States had to develop new policies to protect and promote its national security and interests. Alfred Thayer Mahan, president of the Naval War College, emphasized the importance of a strong navy for national greatness in his book *The Influence of Sea Power upon History*. To complement the navy, Mahan proposed that the United States build a canal across the isthmus of Panama to link its

OVERVIEW RATIONALES FOR IMPERIALISM

Category	Beliefs
Racism and Social Darwinism	The conviction that Anglo-Saxons were racially superior and should dominate other peoples, either to ensure national success, establish international stability, or benefit the "inferior" races by imposing American ideas and institutions on them
Righteousness	The conviction that Christianity, and a supporting American culture, should be aggressively spread among the benighted peoples of other lands
Mahanism	The conviction, following the ideas advanced by Alfred Thayer Mahan, that U.S. security required a strong navy and economic and territorial expansion
Economics	A variety of arguments holding that American prosperity depended on acquiring access to foreign markets, raw materials, and investment opportunities

coasts, acquire naval bases in the Caribbean and the Pacific to protect the canal, and annex Hawaii and other Pacific islands to promote trade and service the fleet.

Mahanism found a receptive audience. President Benjamin Harrison declared in 1891 that "as to naval stations and points of influence, we must look forward to a departure from the too conservative opinions which have been held heretofore." Still more vocal advocates of Mahan's program were a group of nationalistic Republicans, predominantly from the Northeast. They included politicians like Henry Cabot Lodge and Theodore Roosevelt, journalists like Whitelaw Reid and Albert Shaw, and diplomats and lawyers like John Hay and Elihu Root.

Even so, Mahan was not solely responsible for the large-navy policy popular among imperialists. Its origins went back to 1881, when Congress established the Naval Advisory Board, which successfully lobbied for larger naval appropriations. An extensive program to replace the navy's obsolete wooden ships with modern cruisers and battleships was well under way by 1890, when Mahan's book appeared. The United States soon possessed the formidable navy the expansionists wanted. This larger navy, in turn, demanded strategic bases and coaling stations.

ECONOMIC DESIGNS

One reason for the widespread support for a larger navy was its use to expand and protect America's international trade. Nearly all Americans favored economic expansion through foreign trade. Such a policy promised national prosperity: more markets for manufacturers and farmers, greater profits for merchants and bankers, more jobs for workers. Far fewer favored the acquisition of colonies that was characteristic of European imperialism.

The United States had long aggressively fostered American trade, especially in Latin America and East Asia. As early as 1844, the United States had negotiated a trade treaty with China, and ten years later a squadron under Commodore Matthew Perry had forced the Japanese to open their ports to American products. In the late nineteenth

Emily Hartwell, an American missionary, and her Chinese converts ("Bible Women") in the Foochow Mission in 1902. American missionaries wanted to spread the Gospel abroad but inevitably spread American influence as well. Hartwell used the ethnocentric and militant rhetoric of the imperialism of righteousness in appealing to Americans for money and prayers for her "picket duty on the very outskirts of the army of the Lord."

century, the dramatic expansion of the economy caused many Americans to favor more government action to open foreign markets to American exports.

Exports, especially of manufactured goods, which grew ninefold between 1865 and 1900, did increase greatly in the late nineteenth century. Still, periodic depressions fed fears of overproduction. The massive unemployment and social unrest that accompanied these economic crises also provided social and political arguments for economic relief through foreign trade.

In the depression of the 1890s, with the secretary of state seeing "symptoms of revolution" in the Pullman strike and Coxey's Army of unemployed workers (see Chapter 20), the interest in foreign trade became obsessive. More systematic government efforts to promote trade seemed necessary, a conclusion strengthened by new threats to existing American markets. In that tumultuous decade, European nations raised tariff barriers against American products, and Japan and the European imperial powers began to restrict commercial opportunities in the areas of China that they controlled. Many American leaders decided that the United States had to adopt decisive new policies or face economic catastrophe.

FIRST STEPS

Despite the growing ideological, strategic, and economic arguments for imperialism, the government only fitfully interested itself in foreign affairs before the mid-1890s. It did not pursue a policy of isolationism from international affairs, for the nation maintained normal diplomatic and trade ties and at times vigorously intervened in Latin America and East Asia. But in general the government deferred to the initiative of private interests, reacted haphazardly to outside events, and did little to create a professional foreign service. In a few bold if inconsistent steps, however, the United States moved to expand its influence.

SEWARD AND BLAINE

Two secretaries of state, William H. Seward, secretary under Presidents Abraham Lincoln and Andrew Johnson (1861–1869), and James G. Blaine, secretary under Presidents James Garfield and Benjamin Harrison (1881, 1889–1892), laid the foundation for a larger and more aggressive U.S. role in world affairs. Seward possessed an elaborate imperial vision, based on his understanding of commercial opportunities, strategic necessities, and national destiny. His interest in opening East Asia to American commerce and establishing American hegemony over the Caribbean anticipated the subsequent course of American expansion. Seward purchased Alaska from Russia in 1867, approved the navy's occupation of the Midway Islands in the Pacific, pushed American trade on a reluctant Japan, and repeatedly tried to acquire Caribbean naval bases (see Map 22–1).

Blaine was an equally vigorous, if inconsistent, advocate of expansion. He worked to extend what he called America's "commercial empire" in the Pacific. In an effort to induce Latin American nations to import manufactured products from the United

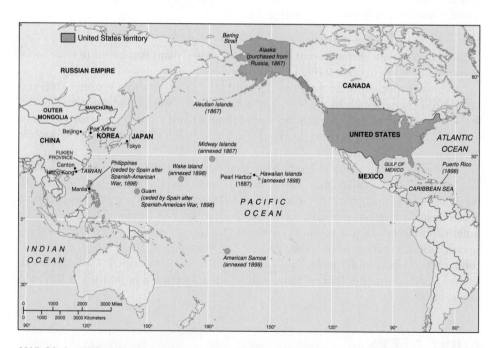

MAP 22–1 • United States Expansion in the Pacific, 1867–1899 Pursuing visions of a commercial empire in the Pacific, the United States steadily expanded its territorial possessions as well as its influence there in the late nineteenth century.

▶ *How did a desire to expand American economic activity in China motivates and shape U.S. expansion in the Pacific? What light does this map shed on this question?*

States rather than Europe, Blaine proposed a customs union to reduce trade barriers, expecting it to strengthen U.S. control of hemispheric markets. Wary of economic subordination to the colossus of the north, however, the Latin American nations rejected Blaine's plan but did agree to establish what eventually came to be known as the **Pan American Union.** Based in Washington, it helped to promote hemispheric understanding and cooperation.

If U.S. officials were increasingly assertive toward Latin America and Asia, however, they remained little involved in Europe and wholly indifferent to Africa, which the European powers were then carving up into colonies. In short, despite some important precedents for the future, much of American foreign policy remained undeveloped, sporadic, and impulsive.

HAWAII

Blaine regarded Hawaii as "indispensably" part of "the American system." As early as 1842, the United States had announced its opposition to European control of Hawaii, a key way-station in the China trade and where New England missionaries and whalers were already active. Although Hawaii continued to be ruled by native monarchs, American influence grew, particularly as other Americans arrived to establish sugar plantations and eventually dominate the economy. Treaties in 1875 and 1887 integrated the islands into the American economy and gave the United States control over Pearl Harbor on the island of Oahu. In 1887, the United States rejected a proposal from Britain and France for a joint guarantee of Hawaii's independence and endorsed a new Hawaiian constitution that gave political power to wealthy white residents. The obvious next step was U.S. annexation, which Blaine endorsed in 1891.

A combination of factors soon impelled American planters to bid for annexation. The McKinley Tariff Act of 1890 effectively closed the U.S. market to Hawaiian sugar producers, threatening their economic ruin. At the same time, Queen Liliuokalani moved to restore native control of Hawaiian affairs. To ensure market access and protect their political authority, the American planters decided to seek annexation to the United States. In 1893, they overthrew the queen. John Stevens, the American diplomatic representative, ordered U.S. marines to help the rebels and then declared an American protectorate over the new Hawaiian government. A delegation from the new provisional government, which did not include any native Hawaiians, went to Washington to draft a treaty for annexation. President Harrison signed the pact but could not get Senate approval before the new Cleveland administration took office.

Grover Cleveland immediately called for an investigation of the whole affair. Soon convinced that "the undoubted sentiment of the people is for the Queen, against the provisional Government, and against annexation," Cleveland apologized to the queen for the "flagrant wrong" done her by the "reprehensible conduct" of U.S. diplomats and troops. But the American-dominated provisional government refused to step down, and Cleveland's rejection of annexation set off a noisy debate in the United States.

Many Republicans strongly supported annexation, which they regarded as merely part of a larger plan of expansion. Democrats generally opposed annexation. They doubted, as Missouri senator George Vest declared, whether the United States should desert its traditional principles and "venture upon the great colonial system of the European powers." The Hawaiian episode of 1893 thus foreshadowed the arguments over imperialism at the end of the century and emphasized the policy differences between Democrats and the increasingly expansionist Republicans.

CHILE AND VENEZUELA

American reactions to developments in other countries in the 1890s also reflected an increasingly assertive national policy and excitable public opinion. In 1891, American sailors on shore leave in Chile became involved in a drunken brawl that left two of them dead, 17 injured, and dozens in jail. Encouraged by a combative navy, President Harrison threatened military retaliation against Chile, provoking an outburst of bellicose nationalism in the United States. Harrison relented only when Chile apologized and paid an indemnity.

A few years later, the United States again threatened war over a minor issue but against a more formidable opponent. In 1895, President Cleveland intervened in a boundary dispute between Great Britain and Venezuela over British Guiana. Cleveland was motivated not only by the long-standing U.S. goal of challenging Britain for Latin American markets but also by ever more expansive notions of the Monroe Doctrine and the authority of the United States. Secretary of State Richard Olney sent Britain a blunt note demanding arbitration of the disputed territory and stoutly asserting American supremacy in the Western Hemisphere. Cleveland urged Congress to establish a commission to determine the boundary and enforce its decision by war if necessary. As war fever swept the United States, Britain agreed to arbitration, recognizing the limited nature of the issue that so convulsed Anglo-American relations.

Cleveland's assertion of U.S. hemispheric dominance angered Latin Americans, and their fears deepened when the United States decided arbitration terms with Britain without consulting Venezuela, which protested before bowing to American pressure. The United States had intervened less to protect Venezuela from the British bully than to advance its own hegemony. The further significance of the Venezuelan crisis, Captain Mahan noted, lay in its "awakening of our countrymen to the fact that we must come out of our isolation ... and take our share in the turmoil of the world."

THE SPANISH-AMERICAN WAR

The forces pushing the United States toward imperialism and international power came to a head in the Spanish-American War. Cuba's quest for independence from the oppressive colonial control of Spain activated Americans' long-standing interest in the island. Many sympathized with the Cuban rebels' yearning for freedom, others worried that disorder in Cuba threatened their own economic and political interests, and some thought that intervention would increase the influence of the United States in the Caribbean and along key Pacific routes to Asian markets. But few foresaw that the war that finally erupted in 1898 would dramatically change U.S. relationships with the rest of the world and give the United States a colonial empire.

THE CUBAN REVOLUTION

The last major European colony in Latin America, Cuba held an economic potential that attracted American business interests and a strategic significance for any Central American canal. In the late nineteenth century, American investors expanded their economic influence in Cuba, while Cubans themselves rebelled repeatedly but unsuccessfully against increasingly harsh Spanish rule. Cuban discontent erupted again in 1895, when the Cuban patriot José Martí launched another revolt.

The rebellion was a classic guerrilla war, with the rebels controlling the countryside and the Spanish army the towns and cities. American economic interests were seriously affected, for both Cubans and Spaniards destroyed American property and disrupted American trade. But the brutality with which Spain attempted to suppress the revolt promoted American sympathy for the Cuban insurgents. Determined to cut the rebels off from their peasant supporters, the Spanish herded most civilians into "reconcentration camps," where tens of thousands died of starvation and disease.

American sympathy was further aroused by the sensationalist **yellow press.** To attract readers and boost advertising revenues, the popular press of the day adopted bold headlines, fevered editorials, and real or exaggerated stories of violence, sex, and corruption. A circulation war helped stimulate interest in a Cuban war. Failure to intervene to protect the innocent from Spanish lust and cruelty, insisted the yellow journalists, would be dishonorable and cowardly.

The nation's religious press, partly because it reflected the prejudice of many Protestants against Catholic Spain, also advocated American intervention. The *Catholic Herald* of New York sarcastically referred to the "bloodthirsty preachers" of the Protestant churches, but such preachers undeniably influenced American opinion against Spain.

As the Cuban rebellion dragged on, more and more Americans advocated intervention to stop the carnage, protect U.S. investments, or uphold various principles. In the election of 1896, both major parties endorsed Cuban independence.

GROWING TENSIONS

In his 1897 inaugural address, President William McKinley outlined an expansionist program ranging from further enlargement of the navy to the annexation of Hawaii and the construction of a Central American canal in Nicaragua, but his administration soon focused on Cuba. McKinley's principal complaint was that chronic disorder in Cuba disrupted American investments and agitated public opinion. Personally opposed to military intervention, McKinley first used diplomacy to press Spain to adopt reforms that would settle the rebellion. In late 1897, Spain modified its brutal military tactics and offered limited autonomy to Cuba. But Cubans insisted on complete independence, a demand that Spain rejected.

Relations between the United States and Spain deteriorated. On February 15, 1898, the U.S. battleship *Maine* blew up in Havana harbor, killing 260 men. The Spanish were not responsible for the tragedy, which a modern naval inquiry has attributed to an internal accident. But many Americans agreed with Theodore Roosevelt, the assistant secretary of the navy, who called it "an act of dirty treachery on the part of the Spaniards" and told McKinley that only war was "compatible with our national honor."

Popular anger was inflamed, but the sinking of the *Maine* by itself did not bring war, though it did restrict McKinley's options and pressure him to be more assertive toward Spain. Other pressures soon began to build on the president. Increasingly, business interests favored war as less disruptive than a volatile peace that threatened their investments. Further, McKinley feared that a moderate policy would endanger Republican congressional candidates.

At the end of March 1898, McKinley sent Spain an ultimatum. He demanded an armistice in Cuba, an end to the reconcentration policy, and the acceptance of American arbitration, which implied Cuban independence. Again, Spain made concessions, abolishing reconcentration and declaring a unilateral armistice. But McKinley had already begun war preparations. He submitted a war message to Congress on April 11, asking for authority to use force against Spain. Congress declared war on Spain on April 25, 1898.

A few national leaders welcomed the war as a step toward imperialism, but there was little popular support for an imperialist foreign policy. Most interventionists were not imperialists, and Congress added the **Teller Amendment** to the war resolution, disclaiming any intention of annexing Cuba and promising that Cubans would govern themselves. Congress also refused to approve either a canal bill or the annexation of Hawaii. Nevertheless, the Spanish-American War did turn the nation toward imperialism.

WAR AND EMPIRE

The decisive engagement of the war took place not in Cuba but in another Spanish colony, the Philippines, and it involved the favored tool of the expansionists, the new navy. Once war was declared, Commodore George Dewey led the U.S. Asiatic squadron into Manila Bay and destroyed the much weaker Spanish fleet on May 1, 1898. This dramatic victory galvanized expansionist sentiment in the United States. With Dewey's triumph, exulted one expansionist, "We are taking our proper rank among the nations of the world. We are after markets, the greatest markets now existing in the world." To expand this foothold in Asia, McKinley ordered troops to the Philippines, postponing the military expedition to Cuba itself.

Dewey's victory also precipitated the annexation of Hawaii, which had seemed unlikely only weeks before. Annexationists now pointed to the islands' strategic importance as stepping stones to Manila. In July, Congress approved annexation, a decision welcomed by Hawaii's white minority. Native Hawaiians solemnly protested this step taken "without reference to the consent of the people of the Hawaiian Islands." Filipinos would soon face the same American imperial impulse.

Military victory also came swiftly in Cuba, once the U.S. Army finally landed in late June. Victory came despite bureaucratic bungling in the War Department, which left the American army poorly led, trained, and supplied. More than 5,000 Americans died of diseases and accidents brought on by such mismanagement; only 379 were killed in battle. State militias supplemented the small regular army, as did volunteer units, such as the famous Rough Riders, a cavalry regiment of cowboys and eastern dandies organized by Leonard Wood and Theodore Roosevelt.

While the Rough Riders captured public attention, other units were more effective. The 10th Negro Cavalry, for example, played the crucial role in capturing San Juan Hill, a battle popularly associated with the Rough Riders. Nevertheless, the Rough Riders gained the credit, thanks in part to Roosevelt's self-serving and well-promoted account of the conflict.

U.S. naval power again proved decisive. In a lopsided battle on July 3, the Spanish squadron in Cuba was destroyed, isolating the Spanish army and guaranteeing its defeat. U.S. forces then seized the nearby Spanish colony of Puerto Rico without serious opposition. Humbled, Spain signed an armistice ending the war on August 12.

THE TREATY OF PARIS

The armistice required Spain to accept Cuban independence, cede Puerto Rico and Guam (a Pacific island between Hawaii and the Philippines) to the United States, and allow the Americans to occupy Manila, pending the final disposition of the Philippines at a formal peace conference. The acquisition of Puerto Rico and Guam indicated the expansionist nature the conflict had assumed for the United States. So did the postponement of the Philippine issue. McKinley knew that delay would permit the advocates of expansion to build public support for annexation.

McKinley defended his decision to acquire the Philippines with self-righteous imperialist rhetoric, promising to extend Christian influence and American values. But he was motivated primarily by a determination to use the islands to strengthen America's political and commercial position in East Asia. Moreover, he believed the Filipinos poorly suited to self-rule, and he feared that Germany or Japan might seize the Philippines if the United States did not. Meeting in Paris in December, American and Spanish negotiators settled the final terms for peace. Spain agreed—despite Filipino demands for independence—to cede the Philippines to the United States.

The decision to acquire the Philippines sparked a dramatic debate over the ratification of the Treaty of Paris. Imperialists invoked the familiar arguments of economic expansion, national destiny, and strategic necessity, while asserting that Americans had religious and racial responsibilities to advance civilization by uplifting backward peoples.

Opponents of the treaty raised profound questions about national goals and ideals (see American Views: A Southern Senator Opposes Annexation). Opponents included such prominent figures as the civil service reformer Carl Schurz, the steel baron Andrew Carnegie, the social reformer Jane Addams, the labor leader Samuel Gompers, and the author Mark Twain. Their organizational base was the Anti-Imperialist League, which campaigned against the treaty, distributing pamphlets,

Theodore Roosevelt and the Rough Riders. Ironically, their horses were left behind in Florida and TR complained of the army's "confusion and lack of system and general mismanagement."

American Views

A Southern Senator Opposes Annexation

*I*n the Senate's debate over the ratification of the Treaty of Paris, ending the Spanish-American War and ceding the Philippines to the United States, both supporters and opponents appealed to noble ideals, invoked base motives, and expressed anxiety for the future. Senator James H. Berry, a conservative Democrat from Arkansas, delivered a particularly forceful attack upon the treaty. The following passages from his speech outline some of his views of what he termed President McKinley's "wild scheme of colonization and acquisition of territory."

- In what ways did Berry regard the treaty as a repudiation of the war itself?
- What were the dangers that Berry saw for the United States in approving the treaty?
- What forces did Berry believe were directing the development of American foreign policy?

When the protocol for peace was signed on the 12th day of last August, I think it could have been truthfully said that there had never been a time since the organization of the Government when the American Republic commanded so much respect from the nations of the world, and never a time when its own citizens felt for that Republic so much love, so much devotion, and so much admiration. Less than six months have passed and there are thousands and tens of thousands of intelligent and patriotic citizens who sincerely believe that the danger of the destruction and overthrow of our institutions has never been so great as it is today.

What has been the cause of the remarkable change in the policy of our Government? What has been the mighty influence that has caused us to depart from the teachings of our fathers and to enter upon a course of action directly opposed to all that we have professed? ...

The cause for the universal rejoicing of our people at the close of the war can be easily understood.... The pride and glory that the American people felt in the Army and Navy was greatly enhanced by the fact that all felt and knew that the war had been waged by us from unselfish and disinterested motives. We had fought to make others free as we ourselves were free; we had fought to enable the Cuban people to throw off their colonial dependence upon Spain and establish a free and independent government for themselves; we had disclaimed, in the act declaring war,

petitioning Congress, and holding rallies. The League's criticisms reflected a conviction that imperialism was a repudiation of the moral and political traditions embodied in the Declaration of Independence. The acquisition of overseas colonies, they argued, conflicted with the nation's commitment to liberty and its claim to moral superiority.

But other arguments were less high-minded. Many anti-imperialists objected to expansion on the racist grounds that Filipinos were inferior and unassimilable. Gompers feared that cheap Asian labor would undercut the wages and living standards of American workers. The *San Francisco Call*, representing California-Hawaiian sugar interests, wanted no competition from the Philippines.

any intention of acquiring territory in the island. The President himself had said that the forcible acquisition of territory would not be tolerated by the American people, and that such an attempt would be criminal aggression. The American people were proud because they had done a brave and generous and unselfish deed, which would be a gratification to them and to their children in all the years to come.

They had no thought then that the great combinations of wealth and greed would be able thereafter to unite and bring to bear such a mighty influence as would control the public press, to a large extent public sentiment, the President, and the Senate of the United States, and secure the adoption of a policy that would hereafter forever dim and obscure the glory that they had fairly won. We fought Spain in order to free the Cubans from her control. We can not, in my opinion, without placing a blot upon the fair name of the Republic, without dishonor to ourselves, fight the inhabitants of the Philippine Islands in order to subject them to our control. But such is the proposition made to us today.

... We are told that we must conquer these people in the interest of humanity and for their own good, that we must entail enormous expense upon our own people, that we must drag our youth to that far-off land, and kill and slaughter hundreds and, it may be, thousands of these people in order that we may civilize and Christianize the remainder... .

[But] the plea of humanity is not the true cause of this movement. It doubtless has controlled the judgment of many, but the all-powerful force behind it is the desire of extending trade and commerce. It is the desire for gain, and not to relieve suffering... .

But it is not the people of these far-off islands that concern me most; it is the effect upon our own country, our own Government, and our own institutions; ... it is the regret that I feel for the great demoralization of our people which must come when all their ideals are shattered and when we adopt a line of action which we have for more than a hundred years denounced as unjust and wicked... .

We are entering upon a dangerous field. We are doing it on the pretense, it may be, of humanity and Christianity, but behind it all, I repeat, is the desire for trade and commerce; and whenever and wherever considerations of money making are placed above the honor and fair fame of this Republic, the men who are doing it are undermining the very foundations of the Government under which we live.

SOURCE: *Congressional Record,* 55th Cong., 3rd sess., pp. 1297–99 (January 31, 1899).

Finally, on February 6, 1899, the Senate narrowly ratified the treaty. All but two Republicans supported the pact; most Democrats opposed it, although several voted in favor after William Jennings Bryan suggested that approval was necessary to end the war and detach the Philippines from Spain. Thereafter, he hoped, a congressional resolution would give the Filipinos their independence. But by a single vote, the Republicans defeated a Democratic proposal for Philippine independence once a stable government had been established; the United States would keep the islands.

Bryan attempted to make the election of 1900 a referendum on "the paramount issue" of imperialism, promising to free the Philippines if the Democrats won. But other issues determined the outcome. Some of the most ardent anti-imperialists were conservatives who remained loyal to McKinley because they could not tolerate Bryan's economic policies. Republicans also benefited from the prosperity the country experienced under McKinley after the hard 1890s, and they played on the nationalist emotions evoked by the war, especially by nominating the "hero of San Juan Hill," Theodore Roosevelt, for vice president. Bryan lost again, as in 1896, and under Republican leadership, the United States became an imperial nation.

IMPERIAL AMBITIONS: THE UNITED STATES AND EAST ASIA, 1899–1917

In 1899, as the United States occupied its new empire, Assistant Secretary of State John Bassett Moore observed that the nation had become "a world power…. Where formerly we had only commercial interests, we now have territorial and political interests as well." American policies to promote these expanded interests focused first on East Asia and Latin America, where the Spanish-American War had provided the United States with both opportunities and challenges. In Asia, the first issue concerned the fate of the Philippines, but looming beyond it were American ambitions in China, where other imperial nations had their own goals.

THE FILIPINO-AMERICAN WAR

Filipino nationalists, like the Cuban insurgents, were already fighting Spain for their independence before the sudden American intervention. The Filipino leader, Emilio Aguinaldo, welcomed Dewey's naval victory as the sign of a *de facto* alliance with the United States; he then issued a declaration of independence and proclaimed the Philippine Republic. His own troops captured most of Luzon, the Philippines' major island, before the U.S. Army arrived. When the Treaty of Paris provided for U.S. ownership rather than independence, Filipinos felt betrayed. Mounting tensions erupted in a battle between American and Filipino troops outside Manila on February 4, 1899, sparking a long and brutal war.

Ultimately, the United States used nearly four times as many soldiers to suppress the Filipinos as it had to defeat Spain in Cuba and, in a tragic irony, employed many of the same brutal methods for which it had condemned Spain. U.S. military commanders adopted ever harsher measures, often directed at civilians, who were crowded into concentration camps in which perhaps 200,000 died. American troops often made little effort to distinguish between soldiers and noncombatants, viewing all Filipinos with racial antagonism. After reporting one massacre of a thousand men, women, and children, an American soldier declared, "I am in my glory when I can sight my gun on some dark skin and pull the trigger."

A California newspaper defended such actions with remarkable candor: "There has been too much hypocrisy about this Philippine business…. Let us all be frank. WE DO NOT WANT THE FILIPINOS. WE DO WANT THE PHILIPPINES. All of our troubles in this annexation matter have been caused by the presence in the Philippine Islands of the Filipinos…. The more of them killed the better. It seems harsh. But they must yield before the superior race."

Other Americans denounced the war. The Anti-Imperialist League revived, citing the war as proof of the corrosive influence of imperialism on the nation's morals and principles. Women figured prominently in mass meetings and lobbying efforts to have the troops returned, their moral stature further undercutting the rationale for colonial wars. By 1902, the realities of imperial policy—including American casualties far exceeding those of the Spanish-American War—disillusioned most of those who had clamored to save Cuba.

By that time, however, the American military had largely suppressed the rebellion, and the United States had established a colonial government headed by an American governor general appointed by the president. Filipino involvement in the government was limited on educational and religious grounds. Compared to the brutal war policies, U.S. colonial rule was relatively benign, though paternalistic. William Howard Taft, the first governor general, launched a program that brought the islands new schools and roads, a public health system, and an economy tied closely to both the United States and a small Filipino elite. Independence would take nearly half a century.

CHINA AND THE OPEN DOOR

America's determined involvement in the Philippines reflected its preoccupation with China. By the mid-1890s, other powers threatened prospects for American commercial expansion in China. Japan, after defeating China in 1895, annexed Formosa (Taiwan) and secured economic privileges in the mainland province of Fukien (Fujian); the major European powers then competed aggressively to claim other areas of China as their own **spheres of influence.**

These developments alarmed the American business community. It was confident that, given an equal opportunity, the United States would prevail in international trade because of its efficient production and marketing systems. But the creation of exclusive spheres of influence limited the opportunity to compete. In early 1898, business leaders organized the Committee on American Interests in China to lobby Washington to promote American trade in the shrinking Chinese market. The committee persuaded the nation's chambers of commerce to petition the McKinley administration to act. This campaign influenced McKinley's interest in acquiring the Philippines, but the Philippines, in the words of Mark Hanna, were only a "foothold"; China was the real target.

In 1899, the government moved to advance American interests in China. Without consulting the Chinese, Secretary of State John Hay asked the imperial powers to maintain an **Open Door** for the commercial and financial activities of all nations within their Chinese spheres of influence. Privately, Hay had already approved a plan to seize a Chinese port for the United States, if necessary to join in the partition of China, but equal opportunity for trade and investment would serve American interests far better. It would avoid the expense of military occupation, avert further domestic criticism of U.S. imperialism, and guarantee a wider sphere for American business.

The other nations replied evasively, except for Russia, which rejected the Open Door concept. In 1900, an antiforeign Chinese nationalist movement known as the Boxers laid siege to the diplomatic quarter in Beijing. The defeat of the Boxer Rebellion by a multinational military force, to which the United States contributed troops, again raised the prospect of a division of China among the colonial powers. Hay sent a second Open Door note, reaffirming "the principle of equal and impartial trade" and respect for China's territorial integrity.

Despite Hay's notes, China remained a tempting arena for imperial schemes. But the Open Door became a cardinal doctrine of American foreign policy in the twentieth century, a means by which the United States sought to dominate foreign markets. The

United States promoted an informal or economic empire, as opposed to the traditional territorial colonial empire identified with European powers. Henceforth, American economic interests expected the U.S. government to oppose any developments that threatened to close other nations' economies to American penetration and to advance "private enterprise" abroad.

RIVALRY WITH JAPAN AND RUSSIA

At the turn of the twentieth century, both the Japanese and the Russians were more deeply involved in East Asia than was the United States. Japan and Russia expressed little support for the Open Door, which they correctly saw as favoring American interests over their own. But in pursuing their ambitions in China, the two countries came into conflict with each other. Alarmed at the threat of Russian expansion in Manchuria and Korea, Japan in 1904 attacked the Russian fleet at Port Arthur and defeated the Russian army in Manchuria.

American sympathies in the Russo-Japanese War lay with Japan, for the Russians were attempting to close Manchuria to foreign trade. President Theodore Roosevelt privately complained that a reluctant American public opinion meant that "we cannot fight to keep Manchuria open." He welcomed the Japanese attack in the belief that "Japan is playing our game." But he soon began to fear that an overwhelming Japanese victory would threaten American interests as much as Russian expansionism did, so he skillfully mediated an end to the war. In the Treaty of Portsmouth in 1905, Japan won control of Russia's sphere of influence in Manchuria, half the Russian island of Sakhalin, and recognition of its domination of Korea.

The United States usually preferred the "annexation of trade" to the annexation of territory. The Open Door policy promised to advance American commercial expansion, but Uncle Sam had to restrain other imperialists with colonial objectives.

A FAIR FIELD AND NO FAVOR.
UNCLE SAM: "I'm out for commerce, not conquest."

The treaty marked Japan's emergence as a great power, but, ironically, it worsened relations with the United States. Anti-American riots broke out in Tokyo. The Japanese people blamed Roosevelt for obstructing further Japanese gains and blocking a Russian indemnity that would have helped Japan pay for the war. Tensions were further aggravated by San Francisco's decision in 1906 to segregate Asian and white schoolchildren. Japan regarded this as a racist insult, and Roosevelt worried that "the infernal fools in California" would provoke war. Finally, he persuaded the city to rescind the school order in exchange for his limiting Japanese immigration, which lay at the heart of California's hostility. Under the **Gentlemen's Agreement,** worked out through a series of diplomatic notes in 1907 and 1908, Japan agreed to deny passports to workers trying to come to the United States, and the United States promised not to prohibit Japanese immigration overtly or completely.

The United States and Japan entered into other agreements aimed at calming their mutual suspicions in East Asia but failed to mend the deteriorating relationship. Increasingly, Japan began to exclude American trade from its territories in East Asia and to press for further control over China. General Leonard Wood complained that the Japanese "intend to dominate Asia as we do the Americas." Elihu Root, Roosevelt's secretary of state, insisted that the Open Door and American access had to be maintained but asserted also that the United States did not want to be "a protagonist in a controversy in China with Russia and Japan or with either of them." The problem was that the United States could not sustain the Open Door without becoming a protagonist in China. This paradox, and the unwillingness to commit military force, would plague American foreign policy in Asia for decades.

IMPERIAL POWER: THE UNITED STATES AND LATIN AMERICA, 1899–1917

In Latin America, where no major powers directly challenged American objectives as Japan and Russia did in Asia, the United States was more successful in exercising imperial power. In the two decades after the Spanish-American War, the United States intervened militarily in Latin America no fewer than 20 times to promote its own strategic and economic interests (see Overview, U.S. Interventions in Latin America, 1891–1933). Intervention at times achieved American goals, but it often ignored the wishes and interests of Latin Americans, provoked resistance and disorder, and aroused lasting ill will.

U.S. RULE IN PUERTO RICO

Military invasion during the Spanish-American War and the Treaty of Paris brought Puerto Rico under American control, with mixed consequences. A military government improved transportation and sanitation and developed public health and education. But to the dismay of Puerto Ricans, who had been promised that American rule would bestow "the advantages and blessings of enlightened civilization," their political freedoms were curtailed.

In 1900, the United States established a civil government, but it was under U.S. control, with popular participation even less than under Spain. In the so-called Insular Cases (1901), the Supreme Court upheld the authority of Congress to establish an inferior status for Puerto Rico as an "unincorporated territory" without promise of

OVERVIEW U.S. INTERVENTIONS IN LATIN AMERICA, 1891–1933

Country	Type of Intervention	Year
Chile	Ultimatum	1891–1892
Colombia	Military intervention	1903
Cuba	Occupation	1898–1902, 1906–1909, 1912, 1917–1922
Dominican Republic	Military and administrative intervention	1905–1907
	Occupation	1916–1924
Haiti	Occupation	1915–1934
Mexico	Military intervention	1914, 1916–1917
Nicaragua	Occupation	1912–1925, 1927–1933
Panama	Acquisition of Canal Zone	1904
Puerto Rico	Military invasion and territorial acquisition	1898

statehood. Disappointed Puerto Ricans pressed to end this colonial status, some advocating independence, others statehood or merely greater autonomy. This division would continue for decades to come. In 1917, the United States granted citizenship and greater political rights to Puerto Ricans, but their island remained an unincorporated territory under an American governor appointed by the president.

Economic development also disappointed most islanders, for American investors quickly gained control of the best land and pursued large-scale sugar production for the U.S. market. The landless peasants struggled to survive as workers on large plantations. Increasingly, Puerto Ricans left their homes to seek work in the United States.

CUBA AS A U.S. PROTECTORATE

Despite the Teller Amendment, the Spanish-American War did not leave Cuba independent. McKinley opposed independence and distrusted the Cuban rebels. Accordingly, a U.S. military government was established in the island. Only in 1900, when the Democrats made an issue of imperialism, did the McKinley administration move toward permitting a Cuban government and withdrawing American troops. McKinley summoned a Cuban convention to draft a constitution under the direction of the American military governor, General Leonard Wood. Reflecting the continuing U.S. fear of Cuban autonomy, the constitution restricted suffrage on the basis of property and education, leaving few Cubans with the right to vote.

Even so, before removing its troops, the United States wanted to ensure its control over Cuba. It therefore made U.S. withdrawal contingent on Cuba's adding to its constitution the provisions of the **Platt Amendment,** drawn up in 1901 by the U.S. secretary of war. The Platt Amendment restricted Cuba's autonomy in diplomatic relations with other countries and in internal financial policies, required Cuba to lease naval bases to the

United States, and most important, authorized U.S. intervention to maintain order and preserve Cuban independence. As General Wood correctly observed, "There is, of course, little or no independence left Cuba under the Platt Amendment."

To preserve American influence, the United States sent troops into Cuba three times between 1906 and 1917. During their occupations of Cuba, the Americans modernized its financial system, built roads and public schools, and developed a public-health and sanitation program that eradicated the deadly disease of yellow fever. But most Cubans thought that these material benefits did not compensate for their loss of political and economic independence. The Platt Amendment remained the basis of U.S. policy toward Cuba until 1934.

The Panama Canal

The Spanish-American War intensified the long American interest in a canal through Central America to eliminate the lengthy and dangerous ocean route around South America. Its commercial value seemed obvious, but the war emphasized its strategic importance. McKinley declared that a canal was now "demanded by the annexation of the Hawaiian Islands and the prospective expansion of our influence and commerce in the Pacific."

Theodore Roosevelt moved quickly to implement McKinley's commitment to a canal after becoming president in 1901. First, Roosevelt persuaded Britain to renounce its treaty right to a joint role with the United States in any canal venture. Where to build the canal was a problem. One possibility was Nicaragua, where a sea-level canal could be built. Another was Panama, then part of Colombia. A canal through Panama would require an elaborate system of locks. But the French-owned Panama Canal Company had been unsuccessfully trying to build a canal in Panama and was now eager to sell its rights to the project before they expired in 1904.

In 1902, Congress directed Roosevelt to purchase the French company's claims for $40 million and build the canal in Panama if Colombia ceded a strip of land across the isthmus on reasonable terms. Otherwise, Roosevelt was to negotiate with Nicaragua for the alternative route. In 1903, Roosevelt pressed Colombia to sell a canal zone to the United States for $10 million and an annual payment of $250,000. Colombia, however, rejected the proposal, fearing the loss of its sovereignty in Panama and hoping for more money.

Roosevelt was furious. After threatening "those contemptible little creatures" in Colombia, he began writing a message to Congress proposing military action to seize the isthmus of Panama. Instead of using direct force, however, Roosevelt worked with Philippe Bunau-Varilla, a French official of the Panama Canal Company, to exploit long-smoldering Panamanian discontent with Colombia. Roosevelt ordered U.S. naval forces to Panama; from New York, Bunau-Varilla coordinated a revolt against Colombian authority directed by officials of the Panama Railroad, owned by Bunau-Varilla's canal company. The bloodless "revolution" succeeded when U.S. forces prevented Colombian troops from landing in Panama, although the United States was bound by treaty to maintain Colombian sovereignty in the region. Bunau-Varilla promptly signed a treaty accepting Roosevelt's original terms for a canal zone and making Panama a U.S. protectorate, which it remained until 1939. Panamanians themselves denounced the treaty for surrendering sovereignty in the zone to the United States, but the United States took formal control of the canal zone in 1904 and completed construction of the Panama Canal in 1914.

THE ROOSEVELT COROLLARY

To protect the security of the canal, the United States increased its authority in the Caribbean. The objective was to establish conditions there that would both eliminate any pretext for European intervention and promote American control over trade and investment. The inability of Latin American nations to pay their debts to foreign lenders raised the possibility of European intervention, as evidenced by a German and British blockade of Venezuela in 1903 to secure repayment of debts to European bankers. "If we intend to say hands off to the powers of Europe," Roosevelt concluded, "then sooner or later we must keep order ourselves."

Toward that end, in 1904, Roosevelt announced a new policy, the so-called **Roosevelt Corollary** to the Monroe Doctrine. "Chronic wrongdoing," he declared, would cause the United States to exercise "an international police power" in Latin America. The Monroe Doctrine had expressed American hostility to European intervention in Latin America; the Roosevelt Corollary attempted to justify U.S. intervention and authority in the region. Roosevelt invoked his corollary immediately, imposing American management of the debts and customs duties of the Dominican Republic in 1905. Commercial rivalries and political intrigue in that poor nation had created disorder, which Roosevelt suppressed for both economic and strategic reasons. Financial insolvency was averted, popular revolution prevented, and possible European intervention forestalled.

Latin Americans vigorously resented the United States' unilateral claim to authority. By 1907, the so-called Drago Doctrine (named after Argentina's foreign minister) was incorporated into international law, prohibiting armed intervention to collect debts. Still, the United States would continue to invoke the Roosevelt Corollary to advance its interests in the hemisphere.

DOLLAR DIPLOMACY

Roosevelt's successor as president, William Howard Taft, hoped to promote U.S. interests in less confrontational ways. He proposed "substituting dollars for bullets"— using government action to encourage private American investments in Latin America to supplant European interests, promote development and stability, and earn profits for American bankers. Under this **dollar diplomacy,** American investments in the Caribbean increased dramatically during Taft's presidency from 1909 to 1913, and the State Department helped arrange for American bankers to establish financial control over Haiti and Honduras.

But Taft did not shrink from employing military force to protect American property or to establish the conditions he thought necessary for American investments. In fact, Taft intervened more frequently than Roosevelt had, with Nicaragua a major target. In 1909, Taft sent U.S. troops there to aid a revolution fomented by an American mining corporation and to seize the Nicaraguan customs houses. Under the new government, American bankers then gained control of Nicaragua's national bank, railroad, and customs service. To protect these arrangements, U.S. troops were again dispatched in 1912. To control popular opposition to the American client government, the marines remained in Nicaragua for two decades.

Dollar diplomacy increased American power and influence in the Caribbean and tied underdeveloped countries to the United States economically and strategically. By 1913, American investments in the region reached $1.5 billion, and Americans had captured more than 50 percent of the foreign trade of Costa Rica, Cuba, the Dominican

Republic, Guatemala, Haiti, Honduras, Nicaragua, and Panama. But this policy failed to improve conditions for most Latin Americans. U.S. officials remained primarily concerned with promoting American control and extracting American profits from the region. Not surprisingly, dollar diplomacy proved unpopular in Latin America.

WILSONIAN INTERVENTIONS

Taking office in 1913, the Democrat Woodrow Wilson repudiated the interventionist policies of his Republican predecessors. He promised that the United States would "never again seek one additional foot of territory by conquest" but would instead work to promote "human rights, national integrity, and opportunity" in Latin America.

Nonetheless, Wilson soon became the most interventionist president in American history. Convinced that the United States had to expand its exports and investments abroad and that U.S. dominance of the Caribbean was strategically necessary, he also held the racist belief that Latin Americans were inferior and needed paternalistic guidance from the United States. In providing that guidance, through military force if necessary, Wilson came close to assuming that American principles and objectives were absolutes, and that different cultural traditions and national aspirations were simply wrong.

Caribbean Interventions. In 1915, Wilson ordered U.S. marines to Haiti to preserve "gravely menaced" American interests. The United States saved and even enhanced those interests

THE BIG STICK IN THE CARIBBEAN SEA

The Roosevelt Corollary proclaimed the intention of the United States to police Latin America. Enforcement came, as this cartoon shows, with Roosevelt and subsequent presidents sending the U.S. Navy to one Caribbean nation after another.

by establishing a protectorate over Haiti and drawing up a constitution that increased U.S. property rights and commercial privileges. The U.S. Navy selected a new Haitian president, granting him nominal authority over a client government. Real authority, however, rested with the American military, which controlled Haiti until 1934, protecting the small elite who cooperated with American interests and exploited their own people.

Wilson also intervened elsewhere in the Caribbean. In 1916, when the Dominican Republic refused to cede control of its finances to U.S. bankers, Wilson ordered the marines to occupy the country. The marines ousted Dominican officials, installed a military government to rule "on behalf of the Dominican government," and ran the nation until 1924. In 1917, the United States intervened in Cuba, which remained under American control until 1922.

Interfering with Mexico. Wilson also involved himself in the internal affairs of Mexico. The lengthy dictatorship of Porfirio Díaz had collapsed in 1911 in revolutionary disorder. The popular leader Francisco Madero took power and promised democratic and economic reforms that alarmed both wealthy Mexicans and foreign investors, particularly Americans. In 1913, General Victoriano Huerta seized control in a brutal counterrevolution backed by the landed aristocracy and foreign interests. Appalled by the violence of Huerta's power grab and aware that opponents had organized to reestablish constitutional government, Wilson refused to recognize the Huerta government.

Wilson authorized arms sales to the Constitutionalist forces led by Venustiano Carranza, pressured Britain and other nations to deprive Huerta of foreign support, and blockaded the Mexican port of Veracruz. In 1914 Wilson exploited a minor incident to have the marines attack and occupy Veracruz. This assault damaged his image as a promoter of peace and justice, and even Carranza and the Constitutionalists denounced the American occupation as unwarranted aggression. After Carranza toppled Huerta, Wilson shifted his support to Francisco ("Pancho") Villa, who seemed more susceptible to American guidance. But Carranza's growing popular support in Mexico and Wilson's preoccupation with World War I in Europe finally led the United States to grant de facto recognition to the Carranza government in 1915.

THE WHITE MAN'S BURDEN.

Racist attitudes about the "white man's burden" underlay many of Wilson's interventions in Mexico and elsewhere in Latin America.

Villa then began terrorizing New Mexico and Texas, hoping to provoke an American intervention that would undermine Carranza. In 1916, Wilson ordered troops under General John J. Pershing to pursue Villa into Mexico, leading Carranza to fear a permanent U.S. occupation of northern Mexico. Soon the American soldiers were fighting the Mexican army rather than Villa's bandits. On the brink of full-fledged war, Wilson finally ordered U.S. troops to withdraw in January 1917 and extended full recognition to the Carranza government. Wilson lamely defended these steps as showing that the United States had no intention of imposing on Mexico "an order and government of our own choosing." That had been Wilson's original objective, however. His aggressive tactics had not merely failed but also embittered relations with Mexico.

ENGAGING EUROPE: NEW CONCERNS, OLD CONSTRAINTS

While the United States expanded its power in Latin American and strove to increase its influence in Asia in the early twentieth century, it also took a larger role in Europe. Its traditional policy of noninvolvement, however, remained popular with many Americans and constituted an important restraint upon the new imperial nation.

Responding to the lopsided outcome of the Spanish-American War, European nations immediately began to adjust their policies to take into account the evident power of the United States. German officials even considered seeking an alliance in order to strengthen Germany in Europe. But Germany's rival, Great Britain, moved quickly to resolve all possible disputes with the United States and thereby establish a basis for long-term cooperation. Britain's support for the American annexation of the Philippines and its decision in 1901 to accede to American control of the projected Panama Canal were early examples of this policy. By 1905, only a decade after Britain and the United States seemed on the verge of war over Venezuela, British and American diplomats agreed that their nations' interests were "absolutely identical and that the more closely we can work together, the better it will be for us and the world at large."

Roosevelt also cautiously intervened in European affairs. The great European powers were aligning themselves into rival blocs: the Entente of Britain and France (and sometimes Russia) and the Alliance of Germany and Austria-Hungary (and sometimes Italy). When France and Germany quarreled over the control of Morocco in 1906, Roosevelt helped arrange an international conference at Algeciras, Spain, to resolve the crisis. While placating Germany, American diplomats then helped uphold France's claims, upon its pledge to maintain an open door in Morocco, a pledge the United States would later use to insist upon securing petroleum and commercial opportunities. Roosevelt had helped preserve the balance of power in Europe while advancing what he saw as America's own interests.

Eager to ensure stability, American leaders also engaged Europeans in efforts to promote arbitration of international disputes. In 1899, the United States participated in the First Hague Peace Conference, which created the Permanent Court of Arbitration. Roosevelt helped arrange a second Hague conference in 1907. It did not accept American proposals for compulsory arbitration, but it led to another conference in 1909 which issued the Declaration of London codifying international law for maritime war and establishing the rights of neutral nations. And Roosevelt, Taft, and Wilson negotiated dozens of arbitration or conciliation treaties providing for submitting international disputes to the Hague Court.

However, public opinion and Senate opposition, rooted in older perspectives toward involvement in world affairs, persistently restricted the effectiveness of these efforts. Although the treaties themselves had broad loopholes, the Senate insisted upon further restricting the possible questions to be arbitrated and reserved for itself the right to approve every particular decision to arbitrate. These restrictive views, grumbled Roosevelt and Taft, rendered the treaties ineffective; they would shortly cause Wilson still greater difficulty.

CONCLUSION

By the time of Woodrow Wilson's presidency, the United States had been expanding its involvement in world affairs for half a century. Several themes had emerged from this activity: increasing American domination of the Caribbean, continuing interest in East Asia, the creation of an overseas empire, and the evolution of the United States into a major world power. Underlying these developments was an uneasy mixture of ideas and objectives. The American involvement in the world reflected a traditional, if often misguided, sense of national rectitude and mission. Generous humanitarian impulses vied with ugly racist prejudices as Americans sought both to help other peoples and to direct them toward U.S. concepts of religion, sanitation, capitalist development, and public institutions. American motives ranged from ensuring national security and competing with European colonial powers to the conviction that the United States had to expand its economic interests abroad. But if imperialism, both informal and at times colonial, brought Americans greater wealth and power, it also increased tensions in Asia and contributed to anti-American hostility and revolutionary ferment in Latin America. It also entangled the United States in the Great Power rivalries that would ultimately result in two world wars.

REVIEW QUESTIONS

1. After the Spanish-American War, General Leonard Wood asserted that Cubans believed that their American "liberators" were "still their faithful friends." Why might Cubans not have agreed with Wood?

2. What factors, old and new, shaped American foreign policy in the late nineteenth century? How were they interrelated?

3. How were individual politicians and diplomats able to affect America's foreign policy? How were they constrained by governmental institutions, private groups, and public opinion?

4. To what extent was the United States' emergence as an imperial power a break from, as opposed to a culmination of, its earlier policies and national development?

5. How effective were U.S. interventions in Latin America? What were the objectives and consequences?

6. In what ways did the policies of other nations shape the development of American foreign policy?

myhistorylab CONNECTIONS

Reinforce what you learned in this chapter by studying the many documents, images, maps, review tools, and videos available at **www.myhistorylab.com.**

READ AND REVIEW

✓●─[Study and **Review** on **myhistorylab.com** STUDY PLAN: CHAPTER 22

▐●─[**Read** the **Document** on **myhistorylab.com**

The Teller Amendment (1898)

William Graham Sumner, "On Empire and the Philippines" (1898)

William McKinley, "Decision on the Philippines" (1900)

Rudyard Kipling, "The White Man's Burden" (1899)

Dollar Diplomacy (1912)

Carl Schurz, Platform of the American Anti-Imperialist League (1899)

Alfred Thayer Mahan, The Interest of America in Sea Power (1897)

Henry Cabot Lodge, Annex of Hawaii (1895)

Platt Amendment (1901)

Mark Twain, "Incident in the Philippines" (1924)

Theodore Roosevelt, Panama Canal Message to Congress (1903)

●─[**View** the **Map** on **myhistorylab.com**

Activities of the United States in the Caribbean, 1898–1930s

RESEARCH AND EXPLORE

▐●─[**Read** the **Document** on **myhistorylab.com**

Personal Journeys Online

From Then to Now Online: The Panama Canal

Exploring America: White Man's Burden

●─[**Watch** the **Video** on **myhistorylab.com**

Roosevelt's Rough Riders

───────── ((●─[**Listen** on **myhistorylab.com** ─────────

Hear the audio files for Chapter 22 at
www.myhistorylab.com.

23 America and the Great War •• 1914–1920

Hear the audio files for Chapter 23 at **www.myhistorylab.com.**

FOCUS QUESTIONS

WHY WERE Americans so reluctant to get involved in World War I?

HOW DID the war effort threaten civil liberties?

WHAT HOPES did Wilson have for the Treaty of Versailles?

WHAT CHALLENGES did America face in the aftermath of the war?

Women war workers in an engineering
shop, 1917.

ONE AMERICAN JOURNEY

Property can be paid for; the lives of peaceful and innocent people cannot be. The present German submarine warfare against commerce is a warfare against mankind. . . . It is a war against all nations. . . . Each nation must decide for itself how it will meet it. . . . There is one choice we cannot make, we are incapable of making: we will not choose the path of submission and suffer the most sacred rights of our nation and our people to be ignored or violated. . . . Neutrality is no longer feasible or desirable where the peace of the world is involved and the freedom of its peoples, and the menace to that peace and freedom lies in the existence of autocratic governments backed by organized force which is controlled wholly by their will, not the will of the people. The world must be made safe for democracy. Its peace must be planted upon the tested foundations of political liberty.

. . . It is a fearful thing to lead this great peaceful people into war, into the most terrible and disastrous of all wars, civilization itself seeming to be in the balance. But the right is more precious than the peace, and we shall fight for the things which we have always carried nearest our hearts. . . . To such a task we can dedicate our lives and our fortunes, everything that we are and everything that we have, with the pride of those who know that the day has come when America is privileged to spend her blood and her might for the principles that gave her birth and happiness and the peace she has treasured.

Excerpted from President Woodrow Wilson's Request for Declaration of War, April 2, 1917. Woodrow Wilson Presidential Library

ESCORTED BY THE U.S. CAVALRY on the evening of April 2, 1917, Woodrow Wilson drove through a misty rain eerily illuminated by searchlights down Pennsylvania Avenue to Capitol Hill to deliver his war address. Throughout the day, the Emergency Peace Federation had frantically lobbied Congress, but sentiment in both houses was growing for war. When Wilson promised to make the world "safe for democracy," many members of Congress, waving small American flags, broke into cheers, and pro-war Senator Henry Cabot Lodge personally congratulated Wilson.

On April 4, Senator Robert La Follette delivered a three-hour speech denouncing the president's call for war as a dangerous and reckless journey for the American nation. But La Follette's well-known oratorical talents proved unable to sway the forces for war in Congress. Indeed, his speech aroused such anger in the Senate chamber that he was handed a noose as he exited the room. Both the Senate and the House overwhelmingly supported Wilson's request and the United States entered the war on April 6. Denounced in the press, Senator La Follette and his family were ostracized for his antiwar views, providing a sobering indication of the treatment Americans would face who dared to oppose the war against Germany.

Two years later on July 10, 1919, Wilson made the same journey down Pennsylvania Avenue to Capitol Hill. He asked the Senate to ratify a peace treaty that most Americans favored and that he promised would prevent future wars. But Wilson's reception in the Senate was chilly; some even refused to stand when he entered the room and many others received the address in silence. The Senate ultimately rejected the treaty and Wilson's peace.

Between these two presidential appearances, Americans experienced the horrors of the Great War, confronting and overcoming challenges but also sacrificing some of their national ideals and aspirations. Not only was the war the United States' first major military conflict on foreign soil, but it also changed American life.

Many of the changes, from increased efficiency to Americanization, reflected prewar progressivism, and the war years did promote some reforms. But the war also diverted reform energies into new channels, subordinated generous impulses to attitudes that were more coercive, and strengthened the conservative opposition to reform. The results were often reactionary and contributed to a postwar mood that not only curtailed further reform but also helped defeat the peace treaty upon which so much had been gambled.

Waging Neutrality

Few Americans were prepared for the Great War that erupted in Europe in August 1914, but fewer still foresaw that their own nation might become involved in it. With near unanimity, they supported neutrality. But American attitudes, decisions, and actions, both public and private, undercut neutrality, and the policies of governments in Berlin, London, and Washington drew the United States into the war.

The Origins of Conflict

There had been plenty of warning. Since the 1870s, the competing imperial ambitions of the European powers had led to economic rivalries, military expansion, diplomatic maneuvering, and international tensions. A complex system of alliances divided the continent into two opposing blocs. In central Europe, the expansionist Germany of Kaiser Wilhelm II allied itself with the multinational Austro-Hungarian Empire. Confronting them, Great Britain and France entered into alliances with tsarist Russia. A succession of crises threatened this precarious balance of power, and in May 1914, an American diplomat reported anxiously, "There is too much hatred, too many jealousies." He predicted "an awful cataclysm."

The cataclysm began a month later. On June 28, a Serbian terrorist assassinated Archduke Franz Ferdinand, the heir to the Austro-Hungarian throne, in Sarajevo. With Germany's support, Austria declared war on Serbia on July 28. Russia then mobilized its army against Austria to aid Serbia, its Slavic client state. To assist Austria, Germany declared war on Russia and then on Russia's ally, France. Hoping for a quick victory, Germany struck at France through neutral Belgium; in response, Britain declared war on Germany on August 4. Soon Turkey and Bulgaria joined Germany and Austria to form the **Central Powers.** The **Allies**—Britain, France, and Russia—were joined by Italy and Japan.

Mass slaughter enveloped Europe as huge armies battled to a stalemate. The British and French faced the Germans along a line of trenches stretching across France and Belgium from the English Channel to Switzerland. Little movement occurred despite great efforts and terrible casualties from artillery, machine guns, and poison gas. The belligerents subordinated their economies, politics, and cultures to military demands. The Great War, said one German soldier, had become "the grave of nations."

CHRONOLOGY

1914   World War I begins in Europe.
President Woodrow Wilson declares U.S. neutrality.

1915   Germany begins submarine warfare.
Lusitania is sunk.
Woman's Peace Party is organized.

1916   Sussex Pledge is issued.
Preparedness legislation is enacted.
Woodrow Wilson is reelected president.

1917   Germany resumes unrestricted submarine warfare.
March uprisings end the tsarist regime in Russia.
The United States declares war on Germany.
Selective Service Act establishes the military draft.
Espionage Act is passed.
Committee on Public Information, War Industries Board, Food
Administration, and other mobilization agencies are established.
American Expeditionary Force arrives in France.
East St. Louis race riot erupts.
Bolshevik Revolution occurs in Russia.

1918   Wilson announces his Fourteen Points.
Sedition Act is passed.
Eugene Debs is imprisoned.
The United States intervenes militarily in Russia.
Armistice ends World War I.

1919   Paris Peace Conference is held.
Steel, coal, and other strikes occur.
Red Scare breaks out.
Prohibition amendment is adopted.
Wilson suffers a massive stroke.

1920   Palmer Raids round up radicals.
League of Nations is defeated in the U.S. Senate.
Woman suffrage amendment is ratified.
U.S. troops are withdrawn from Russia.
Warren Harding is elected president.

1921   United States signs a separate peace treaty with Germany.

AMERICAN ATTITUDES

Although the United States had also competed for markets, colonies, and influence, few Americans had expected this calamity. Most believed that the United States had no vital interest in the war and would not become involved. President Wilson issued a proclamation of neutrality and urged Americans to be "neutral in fact as well as in name . . . impartial in thought as well as in action."

However, neither the American people nor their president stayed strictly neutral. German Americans often sympathized with Germany, and many Irish Americans hoped for a British defeat that would free Ireland from British rule. But most Americans sympathized with the Allies. Ethnic, cultural, and economic ties bound most Americans to the British and French. Politically, too, most Americans felt a greater affinity for the democratic Western Allies—tsarist Russia repelled them—than for Germany's more authoritarian government and society.

Wilson himself admired Britain's culture and government and distrusted Germany's imperial ambitions. Like other influential Americans, Wilson believed that a German victory would threaten America's economic, political, and perhaps even strategic interests. Secretary of State William Jennings Bryan was genuinely neutral, but most officials favored the Allies. Robert Lansing, counselor of the State Department; Walter Hines Page, the ambassador to England; and Colonel Edward House, Wilson's closest adviser on foreign affairs—all assisted British diplomats, undercut official U.S. protests against British violations of American neutrality, and encouraged Wilson's suspicions of Germany.

British propaganda bolstered American sympathies. British writers, artists, and lecturers depicted the Allies as fighting for civilization against a brutal Germany that mutilated nuns and babies. Although German troops, like most other soldiers, did commit outrages, they were not guilty of the systematic barbarity claimed by Allied propagandists. Britain, however, shaped America's view of the conflict.

Sympathy for the Allies, however, did not mean that Americans favored intervention. Indeed, few Americans doubted that neutrality was the appropriate course and peace the proper goal. The carnage in France solidified their convictions. Wilson was determined to pursue peace as long as his view of national interests allowed.

THE ECONOMY OF WAR

Economic issues soon threatened American neutrality. International law permitted neutral nations to sell or ship war matériel to belligerents, and with the economy mired in a recession when the war began, many Americans looked to war orders to spur economic recovery. But the British navy prevented trade with the Central Powers. Only the Allies could buy American goods. Some Americans worried that this one-sided war trade undermined genuine neutrality. Congress even considered an embargo on munitions. But few Americans supported the idea.

A second economic issue complicated matters. To finance their war purchases, the Allies borrowed from American bankers. Initially, Secretary of State Bryan persuaded Wilson to prohibit loans to the belligerents as "inconsistent with the true spirit of neutrality." But as the importance of the war orders to both the Allies and the American economy became clear, Wilson ended the ban. By April 1917, American loans to the Allies exceeded $2 billion, nearly a hundred times the amount lent to Germany. These financial ties, like the war trade they underwrote, linked the United States to the Allies and convinced Germany that American neutrality was only a formality.

THE DIPLOMACY OF NEUTRALITY

The same imbalance characterized American diplomacy. Wilson insisted on American neutral rights but acquiesced in British violations of those rights, while sternly refusing to yield on German actions.

When the war began, the United States asked belligerents to respect the 1909 **Declaration of London** on neutral rights. Germany agreed to do so; the British refused. Instead, skirting or violating established procedures, Britain blockaded Germany, mined the North Sea, and forced neutral ships into British ports to search their cargoes and confiscate material deemed useful to the German war effort. Wilson branded Britain's blockade illegal and unwarranted, but by October he had conceded many of America's neutral rights in order to avoid conflict with Britain.

The British then prohibited food and other products that Germany had imported during peacetime, thereby interfering further with neutral shipping. Even the British admitted that these steps had no legal justification. But when the Wilson administration finally protested, it undermined its own position by noting that "imperative necessity" might justify a violation of international law. This statement virtually authorized the British to violate American rights. Wilson yielded further by observing that "no very important questions of principle" were involved in the Anglo-American quarrels over ship seizures and that they could be resolved after the war.

Submarine Warfare. This policy tied the United States to the British war effort and provoked a German response. With its army stalemated on land and its navy no match for Britain's, Germany decided in February 1915 to use its submarines against Allied shipping in a war zone around the British Isles. Neutral ships risked being sunk by mistake, partly because British ships illegally flew neutral flags. Germany maintained that the blockade and the acquiescence of neutral countries in British violations of international law made submarine warfare necessary.

In May 1915, a German submarine sank a British passenger liner, the *Lusitania*. It had been carrying arms, and the German embassy had warned Americans against traveling on the ship, but the loss of life—1,198 people, including 128 Americans— caused Americans to condemn Germany. Yet only six of a thousand editors surveyed called for war, and even the combative Theodore Roosevelt estimated that 98 percent of Americans still opposed war. Wilson saw that he had to "carry out the double wish of our people, to maintain a firm front in respect of what we demand of Germany and yet do nothing that might by any possibility involve us in the war."

This was a difficult stance. Wilson demanded that Germany abandon its submarine campaign. His language was so harsh that Bryan resigned, warning that by requiring more of Germany than of Britain, the president violated neutrality and threatened to draw the nation into war. Bryan protested Britain's use of American passengers as shields to protect contraband cargo and proposed prohibiting Americans from traveling on belligerent ships. His proposal gained support in the South and West and was introduced as a resolution in both the Senate and the House in February 1916.

Wilson moved to defeat the resolutions, insisting that they impinged on presidential control of foreign policy and on America's neutral rights. In truth, the resolutions abandoned no vital national interest and offered to prevent another provocative incident. Moreover, neither law nor tradition gave Americans the right to travel safely on belligerent ships. Wilson's assertion of such a right committed him to a policy that could only lead to conflict.

Arguments over submarine warfare climaxed in April 1916. A German submarine torpedoed the French ship *Sussex,* injuring four Americans. Wilson threatened to break diplomatic relations if Germany did not abandon unrestricted submarine warfare against all merchant vessels, enemy as well as neutral. This threat implied war. Germany promised not to sink merchant ships without warning but made its ***Sussex* Pledge** contingent on the United States' requiring Britain also to adhere to "the rules of international law universally recognized before the war." Peace for America would depend on the British adopting a course they had already rejected. Wilson's diplomacy had left the nation's future at the mercy of others.

The Battle over Preparedness

The threat of war sparked a debate over military policy. Theodore Roosevelt and a handful of other politicians, mostly northeastern Republicans convinced that Allied victory was in the national interest, advocated what they called **preparedness,** a program to expand the armed forces and establish universal military training. Conservative business groups also joined the agitation. The National Security League, consisting of eastern bankers and industrialists, combined demands for preparedness with attacks on progressive reforms.

But most Americans, certain that their nation would not join the bloody madness, opposed expensive military preparations. Many supported the peace movement. Most opponents agreed that military spending would undermine domestic reform and raise taxes while enriching arms merchants and financiers.

Wilson also opposed preparedness initially, but he reversed his position when the submarine crisis with Germany intensified. He also began to champion military expansion lest Republicans accuse him in the 1916 election of neglecting national defense.

The Election of 1916

Wilson's preparedness plans stripped the Republicans of one issue in 1916, and his renewed support of progressive reforms (see Chapter 21) helped to hold Bryan Democrats in line. Wilson continued his balancing act in the campaign itself, at first stressing Americanism and preparedness but then emphasizing peace. The slogan "He Kept Us Out of War" appealed to the popular desire for peace, and the Democratic campaign became one long peace rally.

The Republicans were divided. They had hoped to regain their progressive members after Roosevelt urged the Progressive Party to follow him back into the GOP. But many joined the Democratic camp instead, including several Progressive Party leaders, who endorsed Wilson for having enacted the party's demands of 1912. Roosevelt's frenzied interventionism had alienated many midwestern Republicans opposed to preparedness and cost him any chance of gaining the nomination for himself. Instead, the GOP nominated Charles Evans Hughes, a Supreme Court justice and former New York governor. The platform denounced Wilson's "shifty expedients" in foreign policy and promised "strict and honest neutrality." Unfortunately for Hughes, Roosevelt's attacks on Wilson for not pursuing a war policy persuaded many voters that the GOP was a war party.

The election was the closest in decades (see Map 23–1). When California narrowly went for Wilson, it decided the contest. The results reflected sectional differences, with the South and West voting for Wilson and most of the Northeast and Midwest for Hughes. The desire for peace, all observers concluded, had determined the election.

MAP 23–1 • **The Election of 1916** Woodrow Wilson won reelection in 1916, despite a reunified Republican Party, by sweeping the South and West on campaign appeals to peace and progressive reform.

▶ *How was Woodrow Wilson able to win reelection in 1916 despite the reunification of the Republican Party?*

	Electoral Vote (%)	Popular Vote (%)
WOODROW WILSON (Democrat)	**277** (52)	**9,127,695** (49.4)
Charles E. Hughes (Republican)	254 (48)	8,533,507 (46.2)
A.L. Benson (Socialist)	–	585,113 (3.2)
Other parties (Socialist Labor, Prohibition)	–	233,909 (1.3)

DESCENT INTO WAR

Still, Wilson knew that war loomed, and he made a last effort to avert it. In 1915 and 1916, he had tried to mediate the European conflict, using Colonel House as a secret intermediary. Now he again appealed for an end to hostilities. In January 1917, he sketched out the terms of what he called a "peace without victory." Anything else, he warned, would only lead to another war. The new world order should be based on national equality and **self-determination,** arms reductions, freedom of the seas, and an international organization to ensure peace. It was a distinctly American vision.

Neither the Allies nor the Central Powers were interested. Each side had sacrificed too much to settle for anything short of outright victory. To break the deadlock, Germany resumed unrestricted submarine warfare. German generals believed that even if the United States declared war, it could do little more in the short run to injure Germany than it was already doing. German submarines, they hoped, would end the war by cutting the Allies off from U.S. supplies before the United States could send an army to Europe. On January 31, Germany announced its decision to unleash its submarines in a broad war zone.

Wilson Commits to War. Wilson was now virtually committed to a war many Americans opposed. He broke diplomatic relations with Germany and asked Congress to arm American merchant vessels. When the Senate refused, Wilson invoked an antipiracy law of 1819 and armed the ships anyway. Although no American ships had yet been sunk, he also ordered the naval gun crews to fire at submarines on sight. The secretary of the navy warned Wilson that these actions violated international law and were a step toward war; Wilson called his policy "armed neutrality." Huge rallies across America demanded peace.

Several developments soon shifted public opinion. On March 1, Wilson released an intercepted message from the German foreign minister, Arthur Zimmermann, to the German minister in Mexico. It proposed that in the event of war between the United States and Germany, Mexico should ally itself with Germany; in exchange, Mexico would recover its "lost territory in Texas, New Mexico, and Arizona." The Zimmermann note produced a wave of hostility toward Germany and increased support for intervention in the war, especially in the Southwest, which had opposed involvement. When submarines sank four American freighters in mid-March, anti-German feeling broadened.

On April 2, 1917, Wilson delivered his war message, declaring that neutrality was no longer possible, given Germany's submarine "warfare against mankind." To build support for joining a war that most people had long regarded with revulsion and as alien to American interests, Wilson set forth the nation's war goals as simple and noble. The United States would not fight for conquest or domination but for "the ultimate peace of the world and for the liberation of its peoples." After vigorous debate, the Senate passed the war resolution 82 to 6 and the House 373 to 50. On April 6, 1917, the United States officially entered the Great War.

WAGING WAR IN AMERICA

Mobilizing for military intervention was a massive undertaking. The government reorganized the economy to emphasize centralized management, developed policies to control public opinion and suppress dissent, and transformed the role of government itself.

MANAGING THE WAR ECONOMY

To harness the nation's economic power for the war, federal and state governments developed a complex structure of agencies and controls for every sector of the economy, from industry and agriculture to transportation and labor (see Overview, Major Government Wartime Agencies). Supervised by the Council of National Defense, these agencies shifted resources to war-related enterprises, increased production of goods and services, and improved transportation and distribution.

Organizing Industry. The most important agency was the **War Industries Board (WIB)**, established in July 1917 to set industrial priorities, coordinate military purchasing, and supervise business. Led by financier Bernard Baruch, the WIB exercised unprecedented power over industry by setting prices, allocating scarce materials, and standardizing products and procedures to boost efficiency. Yet Baruch was not an industrial dictator; he aimed at business-government integration. The WIB promoted major business interests, helped suspend antitrust laws, and guaranteed huge corporate profits. Some progressives began to see the dangers, and business leaders the advantages, of government economic intervention.

The Railroad Administration also linked business ambitions to the war economy. Under William McAdoo, it operated the nation's railroads as a unified system to move supplies and troops efficiently. Centralized management eliminated competition, permitted improvements in equipment, and brought great profits to the owners but higher prices to the general public.

OVERVIEW MAJOR GOVERNMENT WARTIME AGENCIES

Agency	Purpose
War Industries Board	Reorganized industry to maximize wartime production
Railroad Administration	Modernized and operated the nation's railroads
Food Administration	Increased agricultural production, supervised food distribution and farm labor
National War Labor Board	Resolved labor-management disputes, improved labor conditions, and recognized union rights as means to promote production and efficiency
Committee on Public Information	Managed propaganda to build public support for the war effort

Ensuring Food Supplies. Equally effective and far more popular was the Food Administration, headed by Herbert Hoover. Hoover had organized relief supplies for war-torn Belgium and now controlled the production and distribution of food for the United States and its allies. He persuaded millions of Americans to accept meatless and wheatless days, so that the Food Administration could feed military and foreign consumers. Half a million women went door to door to secure food-conservation pledges from housewives. City residents planted victory gardens in parks and vacant lots, and President Wilson even pastured sheep on the White House lawn.

Hoover also worked closely with agricultural processors and distributors, ensuring profits in exchange for cooperation. Farmers profited from the war, too. To encourage production, Hoover established high prices for commodities, and agricultural income rose by 30 percent. State and federal governments provided commercial farmers with sufficient farm labor despite the military draft and competition from high-wage war industries.

Overseeing Labor Relations. The National War Labor Board supervised labor relations. In exchange for labor's cooperation, this agency guaranteed the rights of unions to organize and bargain collectively. With such support, unions sharply increased their membership. The labor board also encouraged improved working conditions, higher wages, and shorter hours. War contracts stipulated an eight-hour day, and by the end of the war, nearly half the nation's workers had achieved the 48-hour week. Wages rose, too, but often only as fast as inflation. These improvements limited labor disputes during the war, and Secretary of War Baker praised labor as "more willing to keep in step than capital." But when such unions as the Industrial Workers of the World did not keep in step, the government suppressed them.

Although these and other government regulatory agencies were dismantled when the war ended, their activities reinforced many long-standing trends in the American economy, from the consolidation of business to the commercialization of agriculture and the organization of labor. They also set a precedent for governmental activism that would prove valuable during the crises of the 1930s and 1940s.

WOMEN AND MINORITIES: NEW OPPORTUNITIES, OLD INEQUITIES

Women and War Work. The reorganization of the economy also had significant social consequences, especially for women and African Americans. In response to labor shortages, public officials and private employers exhorted women to join the work force. Women now took jobs previously closed to them. More than 100,000 women worked in munitions plants and 40,000 in the steel industry. Women constituted 20 percent or more of all workers making electrical machinery, leather and rubber goods, and food. They operated drills and lathes, controlled cranes in steel mills, and repaired equipment in machine shops.

Many working women simply shifted to other jobs, where their existing skills earned better wages and benefits. The reshuffling of jobs among white women opened new vacancies for black women in domestic, clerical, and industrial employment. As black women replaced white women in the garment and textile industries, social reformers spoke of "a new day for the colored woman worker" and African American women themselves celebrated their long-awaited industrial employment. But their optimism was unwarranted and their gains short-lived. Racial as well as gender segregation continued to mark employment. Federal efforts to prevent pay inequities and sexual harassment in the workplace were halfhearted and subordinated to the goals of efficiency and productivity. The policies of the government and employers ensured that women would be unable to sustain their wartime advances in the workplace. (See American Views: Reconstruction and the Colored Woman, January 1919.)

With women's labor crucial for the war effort, both government agencies and private industry recruited women for factory work. Here, four women, wearing "womanall" worksuits, pause at their jobs at the Westinghouse Electric Company in 1918. Hagley Museum and Library, Wilmington, Delaware.

Black women work in a brickyard for wartime construction. Mobilization opened new jobs for women, but racial subordination and segregation persisted. Black women often performed the hardest and least desirable work.

Woman Suffrage and Prohibition. The war did help middle-class women reformers achieve two long-sought objectives: woman suffrage and prohibition. Women's support for the war effort prompted more Americans to support woman suffrage. Congress approved the suffrage amendment, which was ratified in 1920. Convinced that abstaining from alcohol would save grain and make workers and soldiers more efficient, Congress also passed the Prohibition amendment, which was ratified in 1919.

African Americans and War Work. The war also changed the lives of African Americans. The demand for industrial labor caused a huge migration of black people from the rural South, where they had little opportunity, few rights, and no hope. In northern cities, they worked in shipyards, steel mills, and packing houses. Half a million African Americans moved north during the war, doubling and tripling the black populations of Chicago, Detroit, and other industrial cities.

Unfortunately, blacks often encountered the kind of racial discrimination and violence in the North that they had hoped to leave behind in the South. Fearful and resentful whites started race riots in northern cities. In East St. Louis, Illinois, where thousands of black southerners sought defense work, a white mob, in July 1917, murdered at least 39 black people, sparing, as an investigating committee reported, "neither age nor sex in their blind lust for blood."

FINANCING THE WAR

To finance the war, the government borrowed money and raised taxes. Business interests favored the first course, but southern and western progressives argued that taxation was more efficient and equitable and would minimize war profiteering. Despite conservative and business opposition to progressive taxation, the tax laws of 1917 and 1918 established a graduated tax structure with higher taxes on large incomes, corporate profits, and wealthy estates. Conservative opposition, however, would frustrate progressives' hopes for permanent tax reforms.

The government raised two-thirds of the war costs by borrowing. Most of the loans came from banks and wealthy investors, but the government also campaigned to sell **Liberty Bonds** to the general public. Celebrities went to schools, churches, and rallies to persuade Americans to buy bonds as their patriotic duty. Using techniques of persuasion and control from advertising and mass entertainment, the Wilson administration thus enlisted the emotions of loyalty, fear, patriotism, and obedience for the war effort.

CONQUERING MINDS

The government also tried to promote a war spirit among the American people by establishing propaganda agencies and enacting legislation to control social attitudes and behavior. This program drew from the restrictive side of progressivism: its impulses toward social control, behavior regulation, and nativism. It also reflected the interests of more conservative forces. The Wilson administration adopted this program of social mobilization because many Americans opposed the war.

Government Propaganda. To rally Americans behind the war effort, Wilson established the **Committee on Public Information (CPI)** under journalist George Creel. Despite its title, the CPI sought to manipulate, not inform, public opinion. The CPI flooded the country with press releases, advertisements, cartoons, and canned editorials. The CPI made newsreels and war movies to capture public attention. It scheduled 75,000 speakers, who delivered a million speeches to 400 million listeners. It hired artists to design posters, professors to write pamphlets in 23 languages, and poets to compose war poems for children.

Other government agencies launched similar campaigns. The Woman's Committee of the Council of National Defense established the Department of Educational Propaganda and Patriotic Education. The agency worked to win over women who opposed the war, particularly in the rural Midwest, West, and South. It formed women's speakers bureaus, developed programs for community meetings at country schools, and distributed millions of pamphlets.

Government propaganda had three themes: national unity, the loathsome character of the enemy, and the war as a grand crusade for liberty and democracy. Obsessed with national unity and conformity, Creel promoted fear, hatred, and prejudice in the name of a triumphant Americanism. Germans were depicted as brutal, even subhuman, rapists and murderers. The campaign suggested that any dissent was unpatriotic, if not treasonous, and dangerous to national survival. This emphasis on unreasoning conformity helped prompt hysterical attacks on German Americans, radicals, and pacifists.

SUPPRESSING DISSENT

The Wilson administration also suppressed dissent, now officially branded disloyalty. For reasons of their own, private interests helped shape a reactionary repression that tarnished the nation's professed idealistic war goals. The campaign also established unfortunate precedents for the future.

Congress rushed to stifle antiwar sentiment. The **Espionage Act** provided heavy fines and up to 20 years in prison for obstructing the war effort, a vague phrase but "omnipotently comprehensive," warned an Idaho senator who opposed the law. In fact, the Espionage Act became a weapon to crush dissent and criticism. Eventually, Congress

AMERICAN VIEWS

RECONSTRUCTION AND THE COLORED WOMAN, JANUARY 1919

I*n 1917, commentators throughout America noted the "mass exodus" of African Americans from the South to the North. Adversely affected by an agricultural depression in the South and attracted to wartime employment opportunities in the North, 500,000 blacks moved into northern cities. Black migrants made the journey to what they called the "promised land." And although conditions were better than they had endured in the South, they encountered white hostility and even violence at home and at work. Still, wartime mobilization required thousands of new workers, and even African American women found new opportunities as railroad workers and general laborers in a variety of fields. As railroad worker Helen Ross explained, "All the colored women like this work and want to keep it.... Of course we should like easier work than this if it were open to us, but this pays well and is no harder than other work open to us." Grateful for even the least desirable jobs, these black women workers were, however, ultimately forced to return to their former jobs after the war.*

Black social worker Forrester B. Washington of the Detroit Urban League wrote frequently about the injustices faced by black migrants, pointing up the particular hardships suffered by African American women.

■ What kinds of work did African American women do during the war?

■ How did the experiences faced by African American women at home correspond to the nation's wartime goals abroad?

■ How would you describe the impact of the Great War on African American women?

The history of the experiences of colored women in the present war should make fair-minded Americans blush with shame. They have been universally the last to be employed. They were the marginal workers of industry all through the war. They have been given, with few exceptions, the most undesirable and lowest

---

passed the still more sweeping **Sedition Act of 1918,** which provided severe penalties for speaking or writing against the draft, bond sales, and war production and for criticizing government personnel or policies.

Postmaster General Albert Burleson banned antiwar or radical newspapers and magazines from the mail. Even more zealous in attacking radicals and presumed subversives was the reactionary attorney general, Thomas Gregory, who made little distinction between traitors and pacifists, war critics, and radicals. Eugene Debs was sentenced to ten years in prison for a "treasonous" speech in which he declared it "extremely dangerous to exercise the right of free speech in a country fighting to make democracy safe in the world." By war's end, a third of the Socialist Party's national leadership was in prison, leaving the party in a shambles.

Gregory also enlisted the help of private vigilantes, including the several hundred thousand members of the reactionary American Protective League, which sought to purge radicals and reformers from the nation's economic and political life. They wiretapped telephones, intercepted private mail, burglarized union offices, broke up German-language newspapers, harassed immigrants, and staged mass raids, seizing thousands of people who they claimed were not doing enough for the war effort.

paid work, and now the war is over they are the first to be released.

It is especially significant that Chicago, which now has the third largest negro population in the country, should be the most inconsiderate in its treatment of the colored woman worker. As a matter of fact, the country as a whole has not treated the colored working woman according to the spirit of democracy. The essential difference between Chicago and elsewhere is that in other cities the colored woman made some little progress into the skilled and so-called semi-skilled industries. In Chicago, while she did get into many occupations in which she had never gained entrance before, they were only the marginal occupations. She became the bus girl in the dairy lunches, the elevator girl, the ironer in the laundry, etc. Now she is being discharged from even these menial and low-paid positions....

Detroit, perhaps, stands foremost among the cities of the country in the industrial opportunities offered colored women during the war. Here they were found working on machines in many of the big auto plants. . . . Colored women were also employed in Detroit as assemblers, inspectors and shippers in auto plants, as core makers and chippers in foundries, as shell makers in munition factories, as plate makers in dental laboratories, as garment makers and as armature winders in insulated wire factories. . . .

The American employer in his treatment of colored women wage-earners should square himself with the democratic ideal of which he made so much during the war. During those perilous times white and black women looked alike in the factory when they were striving to keep the industry of the country up to 100 per cent production, just as white and black soldiers looked alike going over the top to preserve the honor of the country....

If either the American employer or the American laborer continues to deny the colored woman an opportunity to make a decent living, the Bolshevik cannot be blamed for proclaiming their affirmation of democratic principles a sham.

SOURCE: *Life and Labor*, vol. 9 (January 1919): 3–7.

State and local authorities also suppressed what they saw as antiwar, radical, or pro-German activities. They established 184,000 investigative and enforcement agencies, known as councils of defense or public-safety committees. They encouraged Americans to spy on one another, required people to buy Liberty Bonds, and prohibited teaching German in schools or using the language in religious services and telephone conversations. Indeed, suppression of all things German reached extremes. Germanic names of towns, streets, and people were changed; sauerkraut became liberty cabbage, and the hamburger the liberty sandwich.

Members of the business community exploited the hysteria to promote their own interests at the expense of farmers, workers, and reformers. On the Great Plains from Texas to North Dakota, the business target was the Nonpartisan League, a radical farm group demanding state control or ownership of banks, grain elevators, and flour mills. Although the League supported the war, oversubscribed bond drives, and had George Creel affirm its loyalty, conservatives depicted it as seditious to block its advocacy of political and economic reforms, including the confiscation of large fortunes to pay for the war. Nebraska's council of defense barred League meetings. Public officials and self-styled patriots broke up the League's meetings and whipped and jailed its leaders.

"Beat Back the Hun," a poster to induce Americans to buy Liberty Bonds, demonizes the enemy in a raw, emotional appeal. Liberty bond drives raised the immense sum of $23 billion.

In the West, business interests targeted labor organizations, especially the Industrial Workers of the World. In Arizona, for example, the Phelps-Dodge Company broke a mine strike in 1917 by depicting the Wobblie miners as bent on war-related sabotage. A vigilante mob, armed and paid by the mining company, seized 1,200 strikers, many of them Wobblies and one-third of them Mexican Americans, and herded them into the desert without food or water.

The government itself assisted the business campaign. It used the army to break loggers' support for the IWW in the Pacific Northwest, and it raided IWW halls across the country in September 1917. The conviction of nearly 200 Wobblies on charges of sedition in three mass trials in Illinois, California, and Kansas crippled the nation's largest industrial union.

In the end, the government was primarily responsible for the war hysteria. It encouraged suspicion and conflict through inflammatory propaganda, repressive laws, and violation of basic civil rights, by supporting extremists who used the war for their own purposes, and by tolerating mob violence against German Americans. This ugly mood would infect the postwar world.

WAGING WAR AND PEACE ABROAD

While mobilizing the home front, the Wilson administration undertook an impressive military effort to help the Allies defeat the Central Powers. Wilson also struggled to secure international acceptance for his plans for a just and permanent peace.

The War to End All Wars

When the United States entered the war, the Allied position was dire. The losses from three years of trench warfare had sapped military strength and civilian morale. French soldiers mutinied and refused to continue an assault that had cost 120,000 casualties in five days; the German submarine campaign was devastating the British. On the eastern front, the Russian army had collapsed, and the Russian government had gradually disintegrated after the overthrow of the tsarist regime.

In May, Congress passed the **Selective Service Act of 1917,** establishing conscription. More than 24 million men eventually registered for the draft, and nearly 3 million entered the army when their numbers were drawn in a national lottery. Almost 2 million more men volunteered, as did more than 13,000 women, who served in the navy and marines. Nearly one-fifth of America's soldiers were foreign-born (Europeans spoke of the "American Foreign Legion"); 367,000 were black. Many Native Americans served with distinction as well; in recognition, Indian veterans were made citizens in 1919, a status extended to all Indians five years later.

Civilians were transformed into soldiers in hastily organized training camps, operated according to progressive principles. Prohibition prevailed in the camps; the poorly educated and largely working-class recruits were taught personal hygiene; worries about sin and inefficiency produced massive campaigns against venereal disease; and immigrants were taught English and American history. Some units were ethnically segregated: At Camp Gordon, Georgia, Italians and Slavs had separate units, with their own officers.

Racial segregation was more rigid, not only in training camps and military units but in assignments as well. The navy assigned black sailors to menial positions, and the army similarly used black soldiers primarily as gravediggers and laborers. But one black combat division was created, and four black regiments fought under French command. France decorated three of these units with its highest citations for valor. White American officers urged the French not to praise black troops, treat black officers as equals, or permit fraternization. But white racism could not diminish the extraordinary record of one of the most famous of the black units in France—the 369th Infantry Regiment, also known as the "Harlem Hellfighters." The 369th spent 191 days in combat and was the first Allied unit to reach the Rhine.

Women were recruited as noncombatant personnel, such as clerks, translators, and switchboard operators, thereby enabling more men to be assigned to combat duty. The navy awarded them equal rank with males performing the same tasks, and they were eligible after the war for veterans benefits. The army was a different story. Although they served in uniform and under military discipline, women had no formal military status, were ineligible for benefits, and often had their skills and contributions devalued.

Into Action in France. The first American troops, the American Expeditionary Force (AEF), landed in France in June 1917. Months of training, under French direction, then followed as the Americans learned about trench warfare: using bayonets, grenades, and machine guns and surviving poison-gas attacks. Finally in October, the 1st Division, the Big Red One, moved into the trenches.

Full-scale American intervention began in the late spring of 1918 (see Map 23–2). In June, the fresh American troops helped the French repulse a German thrust toward Paris at Château-Thierry. Further savage fighting at Belleau Wood blocked the Germans again, prompting a French officer to declare, "You Americans are our hope, our strength, our life." In July, the AEF helped defeat another German advance, at Rheims.

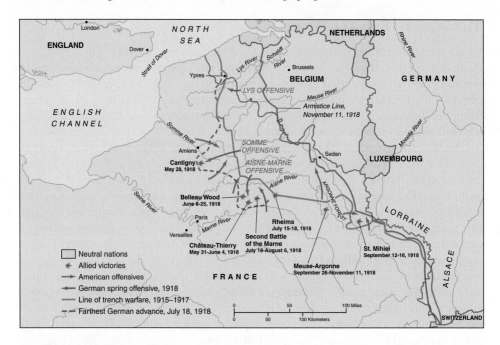

MAP 23–2 • The Western Front, 1918 After three years of trench warfare, the arrival of large numbers of American troops in 1918 enabled the Allies to launch an offensive that drove back the Germans and forced an armistice.

▶ *How did* the entry of American troops turn the tide of war on the western front?

The influx of American troops had tipped the balance toward Allied victory. By July 18, the German chancellor later acknowledged, "even the most optimistic among us knew that all was lost. The history of the world was played out in three days."

The Russian Front. In July, Wilson also agreed to commit 15,000 American troops to intervene in Russia. Russia's provisional government had collapsed when the radical **Bolshevik** faction of the communist movement had seized power in November 1917. Under V. I. Lenin, the Bolsheviks signed an armistice with Germany in early 1918, which freed German troops for the summer offensive in France. The Allied interventions were initially designed to reopen the eastern front and later to help overthrow the Bolshevik government.

Lenin's call for the destruction of capitalism and imperialism alarmed the Allied leaders. One Wilson adviser urged the "eradication" of the Russian government. Soon, American and British troops were fighting Russians in an effort to influence Russia's internal affairs. U.S. forces remained in Russia even after Germany surrendered in 1918. They did not leave until 1920. These military interventions failed, but they contributed to Russian distrust of the West.

The Western Front. The Allies were more successful on the western front. Having stopped the German offensive in July, they launched their own advance. The decisive battle began in late September when an American army over 1 million strong attacked German trenches in the Argonne Forest. Many Americans were still inexperienced; some had been drafted only in July and had spent more time traveling than training. Nevertheless, they advanced steadily, despite attacks with poison gas and heavy artillery.

The battle for the Argonne raged for weeks. A German general reported that his exhausted soldiers faced Americans who "were fresh, eager for fighting, and brave." But he found their sheer numbers most impressive. Eventually, this massive assault overwhelmed the Germans. Despite severe casualties, the AEF had helped the British and French to defeat the enemy. With its allies surrendering, its own army in retreat, and revolution breaking out among the war-weary residents of its major cities, Germany asked for peace. On November 11, 1918, an armistice ended the Great War. More than 115,000 Americans were among the 8 million soldiers and 7 million civilians dead.

THE FOURTEEN POINTS

The armistice was only a step toward final peace. President Wilson had already enunciated America's war objectives on January 8, 1918, in a speech outlining what became known as the Fourteen Points. In his 1917 war message, Wilson had advocated a more democratic world system, and this new speech spelled out how to achieve it. But Wilson also had a political purpose. The Bolsheviks had published the Allies' secret treaties dividing up the expected economic and territorial spoils of the war. Lenin had called for an immediate peace based on the liberation of all colonies, self-determination for all peoples, and the rejection of annexations and punitive indemnities. Wilson's Fourteen Points reassured the American and Allied peoples that they were fighting for more than imperialist gains and offered an alternative to what he called Lenin's "crude formula" for peace.

Eight of Wilson's points proposed creating new nations, shifting old borders, or ensuring self-determination for peoples previously subject to the Austrian, German, or Russian empire. The point about Russia would haunt Wilson after the Allied interventions there began, for it called on all nations to evacuate Russian territory and permit Russia "an unhampered and unembarrassed opportunity for the independent determination of her own political development" under "institutions of her own choosing." Another five points invoked principles to guide international relations: freedom of the seas, open diplomacy instead of secret treaties, reduction of armaments, free trade, and the fair settlement of colonial claims. Wilson's fourteenth and most important point proposed a league of nations to carry out these ideals and ensure international stability.

Wilson and the German government had these principles in mind when negotiating the armistice. The Allies, however, had never explicitly accepted the Fourteen Points, and framing a final peace treaty would be difficult. While Wilson favored a settlement that would promote international stability and economic expansion, he recognized that the Allies sought "to get everything out of Germany that they can." Indeed, after their human and economic sacrifices, Britain and France wanted tangible compensation, not pious principles.

Convinced of the righteousness of his cause, Wilson decided to attend the peace conference in Paris, although no president had ever gone to Europe while in office. But Wilson weakened his position before he even set sail. First, he urged voters to support Democratic candidates in the November 1918 elections to indicate approval of his peace plan. But the electorate, responding primarily to domestic problems like inflation, gave the Republicans control of both houses of Congress. This meant that any treaty would have to be approved by Senate Republicans angry that Wilson had tried to use war and peace for partisan purposes. Second, Wilson refused to consult with Senate Republicans on plans for the peace conference and failed to name important Republicans to the Paris delegation. It was going to be Wilson's treaty, and Republicans would feel no responsibility to approve it.

THE PARIS PEACE CONFERENCE

The peace conference opened on January 18, 1919. Meeting at the Palace of Versailles, the delegations were dominated by the principal Allied leaders: Wilson of the United States, David Lloyd George of Britain, Georges Clemenceau of France, and Vittorio Orlando of Italy. The Central Powers and Bolshevik Russia were excluded. The treaty would be one-sided except to the extent that Wilson could insist on the liberal terms of the Fourteen Points against French and British intransigence.

For months, the conference debated Wilson's other goals and the Allies' demands for compensation and security. Lloyd George later commented, with reference to the self-righteous Wilson and the assertive Clemenceau, "I think I did as well as might be expected, seated as I was between Jesus Christ and Napoleon Bonaparte." Under protest, Germany signed the **Treaty of Versailles** on June 28, 1919. Its terms were far more severe than Wilson had proposed or Germany had anticipated. Germany had to accept sole responsibility for starting the war, a stipulation that all Germans bitterly resented. It was required to pay huge reparations to the Allies, give up land to France, Poland, Belgium, and Denmark, cede its colonies, limit its army and navy to small self-defense forces, destroy military bases, and promise not to manufacture or purchase armaments.

Wilson gained some acceptance of self-determination. As the German, Austro-Hungarian, Turkish, and Russian empires had collapsed at the end of the war, nationalist groups had proclaimed their independence. On one hand, the peace settlement formally recognized these new nation-states: Poland, Finland, Estonia, Latvia, and Lithuania in eastern Europe and Austria, Hungary, Czechoslovakia, and Yugoslavia in central Europe. On the other hand, France, Italy, Romania, and Japan all annexed territory regardless of the wishes of the inhabitants. Germans were placed under Polish control in Silesia and Czech control in Bohemia. Austria was not allowed to merge with Germany. And the conference sanctioned colonialism by establishing a trusteeship system that enabled France, Britain, and Japan to take over German colonies and Turkish territory.

The Allied leaders endorsed the changes in eastern Europe in part because the new states there were anticommunist and would constitute a barrier against Bolshevism. Communist movements in early 1919 in Germany, Austria, and Hungary caused the Allies to fear that "the Russian idea was still rising in power," and they hoped to isolate and weaken Bolshevik Russia. Allied armies were in Russia during the peace conference, and Wilson and the other leaders agreed to provide further aid to fight the Bolsheviks. This hostility to Russia, like the punitive terms for Germany and the concessions to imperial interests, boded ill for a stable and just postwar order. (See Global Connections, War and Revolution: The Bolsheviks and the International Community.)

But Wilson hoped that the final section of the Versailles treaty would resolve the flaws of the agreement by establishing his great international organization to preserve peace: the **League of Nations.** The Covenant, or constitution, of the League was built into the treaty. Its crucial feature, Article Ten, bound the member nations to guarantee each other's independence—a provision that was Wilson's concept of collective security. "At least," he told an aide, "we are saving the Covenant, and that instrument will work wonders, bring the blessing of peace, and then when the war psychosis has abated, it will not be difficult to settle all disputes that baffle us now."

With the defeat of Germany, Americans wanted their soldiers home. And although many returning African American soldiers were denied celebratory homecomings and would face discrimination and hostility, their role in World War I brought fresh confidence and respect to the African American community. Few units stirred the patriotism and pride as did the valiant 369th Infantry Regiment, decorated by the French government for heroism and "gallantry under fire." Here African American friends and families turn out to welcome home the "Men of Bronze," as they were also called.

Waging Peace at Home

Wilson was determined to defeat the opposition to the peace treaty. But many Americans were engaged in their own struggles with the new conditions of a nation suddenly at peace but driven by economic, social, and political conflict. Wilson's battle for the League of Nations would fail tragically. The other conflicts would rage until the election of 1920 restored a normalcy of sorts.

Battle over the League

Most Americans favored the Versailles treaty. A survey of 1,400 newspapers found fewer than 200 opposed. Thirty-three governors and 32 state legislatures endorsed the League of Nations. But when Wilson called for the Senate to accept "the moral leadership . . . and confidence of the world" by ratifying the treaty, he met resistance. Some Republicans wanted to prevent the Democrats from campaigning in 1920 as the party responsible for a victorious war and a glorious peace. But most Republican opponents of the treaty raised serious questions, often reflecting national traditions in foreign relations. Nearly all Democrats favored the treaty, but they were a minority; some Republicans would have to be converted for the treaty to be approved.

Progressive Republican senators, such as Robert La Follette and Hiram Johnson, led one group of opponents. Called the **Irreconcilables,** they opposed participation in the League of Nations, which they saw as designed to perpetuate the power of imperialist countries. Article Ten, they feared, would require the United States to help suppress rebellions in Ireland against British rule or to enforce disputed European borders. Most of the Irreconcilables gave priority to restoring civil liberties and progressive reform at home. Many progressives also criticized the treaty's compromises on self-determination, reparations, and colonies. Linking these failures with Wilson's domestic policies, one former supporter concluded, "The administration has become reactionary, and deserves no support from any of us."

A larger group of opponents had reservations about the treaty's provisions. These **Reservationists** were led by Henry Cabot Lodge, the chair of the Senate Foreign Relations Committee. They regarded Article Ten as eroding congressional authority to declare war. They also fretted that the League might interfere with domestic questions, such as immigration laws.

Lodge's opposition was further shaped by both partisanship and deep personal hostility. Wilson reciprocated, and when Lodge proposed reservations or amendments to the treaty, Wilson refused to compromise. He proposed "a direct frontal attack" on his opponents. If they wanted war, he said, he would "give them a belly full." In early September 1919, Wilson set out across the country to win popular support for the League. In three weeks, he traveled 8,000 miles and delivered 37 speeches.

In poor health following a bout with influenza, Wilson collapsed in Pueblo, Colorado. Taken back to Washington, Wilson, on October 2, suffered a massive stroke that paralyzed his left side and left him psychologically unstable and temporarily blind. Wilson's physician and his wife, Edith Galt Wilson, kept the nature of his illness secret from the public, Congress, and even the vice president and cabinet. Rumors circulated that Edith Wilson was running the administration, but she was not. Instead, it was immobilized.

By February 1920, Wilson had partially recovered, but he remained suspicious and quarrelsome. Bryan and other Democratic leaders urged him to accept Lodge's reservations to gain ratification of the treaty. Wilson refused. Isolated and inflexible, he ordered Democratic senators to vote with the Irreconcilables against the treaty as amended by Lodge. On March 19, 1920, the Senate killed the treaty.

ECONOMIC READJUSTMENT AND SOCIAL CONFLICT

The League was not the only casualty of the struggle to conclude the war. Grave problems shook the United States in 1919 and early 1920. An influenza epidemic had erupted in Europe in 1918 among the massed armies. It now hit the United States, killing perhaps 700,000 Americans, far more than had died in combat. Frightened officials closed public facilities and banned public meetings in futile attempts to stop the contagion.

Meanwhile, the Wilson administration had no plans for an orderly reconversion of the wartime economy, and chaos ensued. The government canceled war contracts and dissolved the regulatory agencies. Noting that "the war spirit of cooperation and sacrifice"had disappeared with the Armistice, Bernard Baruch decided to "turn industry absolutely free" and abolished the War Industries Board as of January 1, 1919. Other agencies followed in such haste that turmoil engulfed the economy.

The government also demobilized the armed forces. With no planning or assistance, veterans were hustled back into civilian life. There they competed for scarce jobs with workers recently discharged from the war industries.

As unemployment mounted, the removal of wartime price controls brought runaway inflation. The cost of food, clothing, and other necessities more than doubled over prewar rates. The return of the soldiers caused a serious housing shortage, and rents skyrocketed. Democratic leaders urged Wilson to devote less time to the League of Nations and more to the cost of living and the tensions it unleashed. Farmers also suffered from economic readjustments. Net farm income declined by 65 percent between 1919 and 1921. Farmers who had borrowed money for machinery and land to expand production for the war effort were left impoverished and embittered.

Postwar Battles: Gender and Race. Women also lost their wartime economic advances. Returning soldiers took away their jobs. Male trade unionists insisted that women go back to being housewives. At times, male workers struck to force employers to fire women and barred women from unions in jobs where union membership was required for employment. Indeed, state legislatures passed laws prohibiting women from working in many of the occupations they had successfully filled during the war. By 1919, half of the women newly employed in heavy industry during the war were gone; by 1920, women constituted a smaller proportion of the workforce than they had in 1910.

The postwar readjustments also left African Americans disappointed. During the war, they had agreed with W. E. B. Du Bois to "forget our special grievances and close our ranks shoulder to shoulder with our own white fellow citizens." Participation in the war effort, they had hoped, might be rewarded by better treatment thereafter. Now, the meagerness of their reward became clear.

Housing shortages and job competition interacted with racism in 1919 to produce race riots in 26 towns and cities, resulting in at least 120 deaths. In Chicago, 38 people were killed and more than 500 injured in a five-day riot that began when white thugs stoned to death a black youth swimming too near "their" beach. White rioters then fired a machine gun from a truck hurtling through black neighborhoods. But black residents fought back, no longer willing, the *Chicago Defender* reported, "to move along the line of least resistance as did their sires." The new militancy reflected both their experiences in the military and in industry and their exposure to propaganda about freedom and democracy. Racial conflict was part of a postwar battle between Americans hoping to preserve the new social relations fostered by the war effort and those wanting to restore prewar patterns of power and control.

Fighting for Industrial Democracy. Even more pervasive discontents roiled as America adjusted to the postwar world. More than 4 million angry workers launched a wave of 3,600 strikes in 1919. They were reacting not only to the soaring cost of living, which undermined the value of their wages, but also to employers' efforts to reassert their authority and destroy the legitimacy labor had won by its participation in the war effort. The abolition of government controls on industry enabled employers not only to raise prices but also to rescind their recognition of unions and reimpose objectionable working conditions. Employers also protected their rising profits by insisting that wages remain fixed. In response, strikers demanded higher wages, better conditions, and recognition of unions and the right of collective bargaining.

The greatest strike involved the American Federation of Labor's attempt to organize steelworkers, who endured dangerous conditions and 12-hour shifts. When the steel companies refused to recognize the union or even discuss issues, 365,000 workers went out on strike in September 1919. Employers hired thugs to beat the strikers, used strikebreakers to take their jobs, and exploited ethnic and racial divisions. To undercut support for the workers, management portrayed the strikers as disruptive radicals influenced by Bolshevism. After four months, the strike failed.

Employers used the same tactic to defeat striking coal miners, whose wages had fallen behind the cost of living. Refusing to negotiate with the United Mine Workers, coal operators claimed that Russian Bolsheviks had financed the strike to destroy the American economy. Attorney General A. Mitchell Palmer secured an injunction against the strike under the authority of wartime legislation. Because the government no longer controlled coal prices or enforced protective labor rules, miners complained bitterly that the war had ended for corporations but not for workers.

Two municipal strikes in 1919 also alarmed the public when their opponents depicted them as revolutionary attacks on the social order. In Seattle, the Central Labor Council called a general strike to support 35,000 shipyard workers striking for higher wages and shorter hours. When 60,000 more workers from 110 local unions also walked out, the city ground to a halt. The strikers behaved peacefully and protected public health and safety by operating garbage and fire trucks and providing food, water, and electricity. Nevertheless, Seattle's mayor, business leaders, and newspapers attacked them as Bolsheviks and anarchists. Threatened with military intervention, the labor council called off the strike, but not before it had caused a public backlash against unions across the nation.

In Boston, the police commissioner fired police officers for trying to organize a union to improve their inadequate pay. In response, the police went on strike. As in Seattle, Boston newspapers, politicians, and business leaders attributed the strike to Bolshevism. Massachusetts Governor Calvin Coolidge gained nationwide acclaim when he mobilized the National Guard to break the strike. The entire police force was fired; many of their replacements were war veterans.

THE RED SCARE

The strikes contributed to an anti-Bolshevik hysteria that swept the country in 1919. The **Red Scare** reflected fears that the Bolshevik revolution in Russia might spread to the United States. Steeped in the antiradical propaganda of the war years, many Americans were appalled by Russian Bolshevism, described by the *Saturday Evening Post* as a "compound of slaughter, confiscation, anarchy, and universal disorder." But the Red Scare also reflected the willingness of antiunion employers, ambitious politicians, sensational journalists, zealous veterans, and racists to exploit the panic to advance their own purposes.

Fed by misleading reports about Russian Bolshevism and its influence in the United States, the Red Scare reached panic levels by mid-1919. Bombs mailed anonymously to several prominent people on May Day seemed proof enough that a Bolshevik conspiracy threatened America. The Justice Department, Congress, and patriotic organizations like the American Legion joined with business groups to suppress radicalism, real and imagined. Wilson and Attorney General Palmer called for more stringent laws and refused to release political prisoners jailed during the war. State governments harassed and arrested hundreds.

Palmer created a new agency, headed by J. Edgar Hoover, to suppress radicals and impose conformity. Its war on radicalism became the chief focus of the Justice Department. As an ambitious and ruthless bureaucrat, Hoover had participated in the government's assault on aliens and radicals during the war. Now he collected files on labor leaders and other "radical agitators" from Senator Robert La Follette to Jane Addams, issued misleading reports on communist influence in labor strikes and race riots, and contacted all major newspapers "to acquaint people like you with the real menace of evil-thinking, which is the foundation of the Red Movement."

In November 1919, Palmer and Hoover began raiding groups suspected of subversion. A month later, they deported 249 alien radicals, including the anarchist Emma Goldman, to Russia. In January 1920, Palmer and Hoover rounded up more than 4,000 suspected radicals in 33 cities. Often without warrants, they broke into union halls, club rooms, and private homes, assaulting and arresting everyone in sight. People were jailed without access to lawyers; some were beaten into signing false confessions. The *Washington Post* declared, "There is no time to waste on hairsplitting over infringement of liberty."

Other Americans began to recoil from the excesses and illegal acts. Support for the Red Scare withered. Palmer's attempt to inflame public emotion backfired. When his predictions of a violent attempt to overthrow the government on May 1, 1920, came to naught, most Americans realized that no menace had ever existed. They agreed with the *Rocky Mountain News:* "We can never get to work if we keep jumping sideways in fear of the bewhiskered Bolshevik." But if the Red Scare faded in mid-1920, the hostility to immigrants, organized labor, and dissent it reflected would endure for a decade.

THE ELECTION OF 1920

The Democratic coalition that Wilson had cobbled together on the issues of progressivism and peace came apart after the war. Workers resented the administration's hostility to the postwar strikes. Ethnic groups brutalized by the Americanization of the war years blamed Wilson for the war or condemned his peace settlement. Farmers grumbled about wartime price controls and postwar falling prices. Wartime taxes and the social and economic turmoil of 1919–1920 alienated the middle class. Americans were weary of great crusades and

Jailed for her antiwar speeches, Lithuanian-born anarchist and birth control advocate Emma Goldman (1869–1940) was deported to the Soviet Union on the *SS Buford*, known as the Red Ark. Her autobiography, entitled *Living My Life* (1931), traces her political activism from her arrival in the United States in 1885.

social sacrifices; in the words of Kansas journalist William Allen White, they were "tired of issues, sick at heart of ideals, and weary of being noble." They yearned for what the Republican presidential candidate, Warren Harding of Ohio, called "normalcy."

The Republican ticket in 1920 symbolized the reassurance of simpler times. Harding was a genial politician who devoted more time to golf and poker than to public policy. An Old Guard conservative, he had stayed with the GOP when Theodore Roosevelt led the progressives out in 1912. His running mate, Calvin Coolidge, governor of Massachusetts, owed his nomination to his handling of the Boston police strike.

Wilson called the election of 1920 "a great and solemn referendum" on the League of Nations, but such lofty appeals fell flat. Harding was ambiguous about the League, and the Democratic national platform endorsed it but expressed a willingness to accept amendments or reservations. The Democratic nominees, James Cox, former governor of Ohio, and the young Franklin D. Roosevelt, Wilson's assistant secretary of the navy, favored the League, but it was not a decisive issue in the campaign.

Harding won in a landslide reflecting the nation's dissatisfaction with Wilson and the Democratic Party. Not even his closest backers considered Harding qualified for the White House, but, as Lippmann said, the nation's "public spirit was exhausted" after the war years. The election of 1920 was "the final twitch" of America's "war mind."

CONCLUSION

Participation in the war had changed the U.S. government, economy, and society. Some of these changes, including the centralization of the economy and an expansion of the regulatory role of the federal government, were already under way; some offered opportunities to implement progressive principles or reforms. Woman suffrage and prohibition gained decisive support because of the war spirit. But other consequences of the war betrayed both progressive impulses and the democratic principles the war was allegedly fought to promote. The suppression of civil liberties, manipulation of human emotions, repression of radicals and minorities, and exploitation of national crises by narrow interests helped disillusion the public. The repercussions of the Great War would linger for years, at home and abroad.

REVIEW QUESTIONS

1. Why did Senator Robert La Follette oppose the war against Germany? How did many Americans regard the war and possible U.S. intervention?

2. What were the major arguments for and against U.S. entry into the Great War? What position do you find most persuasive? Why?

3. How and why did the United States shape public opinion in World War I? What were the consequences, positive and negative, of the propaganda of the Committee on Public Information, the Food Administration, and other government agencies?

4. How did the war affect women and minorities?

5. Evaluate the role of Woodrow Wilson at the Paris Peace Conference. What obstacles did he face? How successful was he in shaping the settlement?

6. Discuss the arguments for and against American ratification of the Treaty of Versailles.

myhistórylab Connections

Reinforce what you learned in this chapter by studying the many documents, images, maps, review tools, and videos available at **www.myhistorylab.com.**

READ AND REVIEW

✓● Study and Review on **myhistorylab.com** STUDY PLAN: CHAPTER 23

📖● Read the Document on **myhistorylab.com**

Letter from William Jennings (1915)

Newton D. Baker, "The Treatment of German-Americans" (1918)

The Espionage Act (1917)

Eugene V. Debs, Critique of World War I (1918)

Eugene Kennedy, A "Doughboy" Describes the Fighting Front (1918)

President Woodrow Wilson's Fourteen Points (1918)

Henry Cabot Lodge's Objections to Treaty of Versailles (1919)

F. J. Grimke, Address to African American Soldiers (1919)

RESEARCH AND EXPLORE

📖● Read the Document on **myhistorylab.com**

Personal Journeys Online

From Then to Now Online: Women and War

((●● Listen on **myhistorylab.com**

Immigrants and the Great War

The Speech That Sent Debs to Jail

If We Must Die; poem and reading by Claude McKay

👁●— Watch the Video on **myhistorylab.com**

American Entry into World WWI

Charles E. Hughes 1916 Presidential Campaign Speech

———— ((●● Listen on **myhistorylab.com** ————

Hear the audio files for Chapter 23 at
www.myhistorylab.com.

((•[Listen on **myhistorylab.com**

Hear the audio files for Chapter 24 at **www.myhistorylab.com.**

FOCUS QUESTIONS

WHAT CONTRIBUTED to the economic boom of the 1920s?

WHAT WAS the relationship between big business and government in the 1920s?

WHAT FACTORS contributed to the growth of America's cities and suburbs in the 1920s?

HOW DID new systems of distribution, marketing, and mass communication shape American culture?

WHAT FORCES fueled the culture wars of the 1920s?

WHAT ROLE did the United States play in international diplomacy in the decade after World War I?

WHAT FACTORS contributed to Herbert Hoover's victory in 1928 over his Democratic opponent, Alfred E. Smith? In what ways did Hoover epitomize the policies of the New Era?

Violinist Carroll Dickerson, at the Sunset Café in 1922, led one of the jazz bands that flourished in Chicago's many clubs, pointing up the central role of African Americans in the Jazz Age.

ONE AMERICAN JOURNEY

Happy times were here again. American industry, adopting Henry Ford's policy of mass pro-duction and low prices, was making it possible for everybody to have his share of everything. The newspapers, the statesmen, the economists, all agreed that American ingenuity had solved the age-old problem of poverty. There could never be another depression. . . .

The war had done something to Henry, it had taught him a new way to deal with his fellow men. . . . He became more abrupt in his manner, more harsh in his speech. "Gratitude?" he would say. "There's no gratitude in business. Men work for money." . . . From now on he was a business man, and held a tight rein on everything. This industry was his, he had made it himself, and what he wanted of the men he hired was that they should do exactly as he told them. . . .

Every worker had to be strained to the uttermost limit, every one had to be giving the last ounce of energy he had in his carcass. . . . They were tired when they started in the morning, and when they quit they were grey and staggering with fatigue, they were empty shells out of which the last drop of juice had been squeezed. . . .

Henry Ford was now getting close to his two million cars a year goal. . . . From the moment the ore was taken out of the ship at the River Rouge plant [in Detroit], through all the processes turning it into steel and shaping it into automobile parts with a hundred-ton press, and putting five thousand parts together into a car which rolled off the assembly line under its own power—all those processes were completed in less than a day and a half!

Some forty-five thousand different machines were now used in the making of Ford cars, in sixty establishments scattered over the United States. . . . Henry Ford was remaking the roads of America, and in the end he would remake the roads of the world—and line them all with filling stations and hot-dog stands of the American pattern.

Upton Sinclair, *The Flivver King: A Story of Ford-America* (Chicago: Charles H. Kerr, 1999).

UPTON SINCLAIR, one of America's most famous muckraking journalists, won his greatest recognition with the 1906 publication of his novel *The Jungle*, which graphically depicted the wretched conditions endured by Chicago's immigrant meat-packing workers. In *The Flivver King*, Sinclair demonstrates his extraordinary ability to weave together the dramatic and historical journey of industrial America, as embodied in the rise of the automobile industry and the revolutionizing vision of Henry Ford, the entrepreneur who captured the American mind and symbolized modern America to the world.

"Machinery," proclaimed Henry Ford, "is the new Messiah." Ford had introduced the assembly line at his automobile factory on the eve of World War I, and by 1925 it was turning out a Model T car every ten seconds. The term "mass production" originated in Henry Ford's 1926 description of the system of flow-production techniques popularly called "Fordism." The system symbolized the nation's booming economy: in the 1920s, Europeans used the word *Fordize* as a synonym for *Americanize*.

Henry Ford was conflicted about the progress he championed—the changes he saw and had helped facilitate. Launching a crusade against the new direction America was headed, Ford decided, according to Sinclair, that "what America needed was to be led back to its past." Embracing nativism and Protestantism, Ford, an ardent anti-Semite, targeted Jewish Americans in his diatribes, blaming them for radicalism and labor organization, and he singled out the "International Jew" for allegedly controlling the international financial community.

Henry Ford and Fordism reflected the complexity of the 1920s. Economic growth and technological innovation were paired with social conflict as traditions were destroyed, values were displaced, and new people were incorporated into a society increasingly industrialized, urbanized, and dominated by big business. Industrial production and national wealth soared, buoyed by new techniques and markets for consumer goods. Business values pervaded society, and government promoted business interests.

But not all Americans prospered. Many workers were unemployed, and the wages of still more were stagnant or falling. Farmers endured grim conditions and worse prospects. Social change brought pleasure to some and deep concern to others. City factories like the Ford Works attracted workers from the countryside, increasing urbanization; rapid suburbanization opened other horizons. Leisure activities flourished, and new mass media promoted modern ideas and stylish products. Workers would have to achieve personal satisfaction through consumption and not production. But such experiences often proved unsettling, and some Americans, like Ford, sought reassurance by imposing their cultural or religious values on everyone around them.

The Economy That Roared

Following a severe postwar depression in 1920 and 1921, the American economy boomed through the remainder of the decade. Gross domestic product soared nearly 40 percent; output per worker-hour, or productivity, rose 72 percent in manufacturing; average per capita income increased by a third. Although the prosperity was not evenly distributed and some sectors of the economy were deeply troubled, most Americans welcomed the industrial expansion and business principles of the New Era.

Boom Industries

Many factors spurred the economic expansion of the 1920s. The huge wartime and postwar profits provided investment capital that enabled business to mechanize. Mass production spread quickly in American industry; machine-made standardized parts and the assembly line increased efficiency and production. Businesses steadily adopted the scientific management principles of Frederick W. Taylor (see Chapter 21). The nation more than doubled its capacity to generate electricity during the decade, further bolstering the economy.

The automobile industry drove the economy. Its productivity increased constantly, and sales rose from about 1.9 million vehicles in 1920 to nearly 5 million by 1929, when 26 million vehicles were on the road. The automobile industry also employed one of every 14 manufacturing workers and stimulated other industries, from steel to rubber and glass. It created a huge new market for the petroleum industry and fostered oil drilling in Oklahoma, Texas, and Louisiana. It launched new businesses, from service stations (over 120,000 by 1929) to garages. It also encouraged the construction industry, a mainstay of the 1920s economy. Large increases in road building and residential housing, prompted by growing automobile ownership and migration to cities and suburbs, provided construction jobs, markets for lumber and other building materials, and profits.

CHRONOLOGY

1915	Ku Klux Klan is founded anew.
1919	Volstead Act is passed.
1920	Urban population exceeds rural population for the first time.
	Warren Harding is elected president.
	Prohibition takes effect.
	First commercial radio show is broadcast.
	Sinclair Lewis publishes *Main Street*.
1921	Sheppard-Towner Maternity and Infancy Act is passed.
	Washington Naval Conference limits naval armaments.
1922	Fordney-McCumber Act raises tariff rates.
	Sinclair Lewis publishes *Babbitt*.
	Country Club Plaza in Kansas City opens.
1923	Harding dies; Calvin Coolidge becomes president.
1924	National Origins Act sharply curtails immigration.
	Coolidge is elected president.
1925	Scopes trial is held in Dayton, Tennessee.
	F. Scott Fitzgerald publishes *The Great Gatsby*.
1927	Charles A. Lindbergh flies solo across the Atlantic.
1928	Kellogg-Briand Pact is signed.
	Herbert Hoover is elected president.
1929	Ernest Hemingway publishes *A Farewell to Arms*.

The Great War also stimulated the chemical industry. The government confiscated chemical patents from German firms that had dominated the field and transferred them to U.S. companies like DuPont. With this advantage, DuPont in the 1920s became one of the nation's largest industrial firms, a chemical empire producing plastics, finishes, dyes, and organic chemicals. Led by such successes, the chemical industry became a $4 billion giant employing 300,000 workers by 1929.

The new radio and motion picture industries also flourished. Commercial broadcasting began with a single station in 1920. By 1927, there were 732 stations, and Congress created the Federal Radio Commission to prevent wave-band interference. The rationale for this agency, which was reorganized as the Federal Communications Commission (FCC) in 1934, was that the airwaves belong to the American people and not to private interests. Nevertheless, corporations quickly dominated the new industry.

The motion-picture industry became one of the nation's five largest businesses, with 20,000 movie theaters selling 100 million tickets a week. Hollywood studios were huge factories, hiring directors, writers, camera crews, and actors to produce films on an assembly-line basis. While Americans watched Charlie Chaplin showcase his comedic genius in such films as *The Gold Rush* (1925), corporations like Paramount were integrating production with distribution and exhibition to maximize control and profit and eliminate independent producers and theaters. The advent of talking movies later in the decade brought still greater profits and power to the major studios, which alone could afford the increased engineering and production costs.

CORPORATE CONSOLIDATION

A wave of corporate mergers, rivaling the one at the turn of the century, swept over the 1920s economy. Great corporations swallowed up thousands of small firms. Particularly significant was the spread of **oligopoly**—the control of an entire industry by a few giant firms. The number of automobile manufacturers dropped from 108 to 44, while only three companies—Ford, General Motors, and Chrysler—produced 83 percent of the nation's cars. In the electric light and power industry, nearly 4,000 local utility companies were merged into a dozen holding companies. By 1929, the nation's 200 largest corporations controlled nearly half of all nonbanking corporate wealth.

OPEN SHOPS AND WELFARE CAPITALISM

Business also launched a vigorous assault on labor. In 1921, the National Association of Manufacturers organized an **open-shop** campaign to break union-shop contracts, which required all employees to be union members. Denouncing collective bargaining as un-American, businesses described the open shop, in which union membership was not required and usually prohibited, as the "American plan." They forced workers to sign so-called **yellow-dog contracts** that bound them to reject unions to keep their jobs. Business also used boycotts to force employers into a uniform antiunion front. Bethlehem Steel, for example, refused to sell steel to companies employing union labor. Where unions existed, corporations tried to crush them, using spies or hiring strikebreakers.

Some companies advocated a paternalistic system called **welfare capitalism** as an alternative to unions. Eastman Kodak, General Motors, U.S. Steel, and other firms provided medical services, insurance programs, pension plans, and vacations for their workers and established employee social clubs and sports teams. These policies were designed to undercut labor unions and persuade workers to rely on the corporation. Welfare capitalism, however, covered scarcely 5 percent of the workforce and often benefited only skilled workers already tied to the company through seniority.

Corporations in the 1920s also promoted company unions, management-sponsored substitutes for labor unions. But company unions were usually forbidden to handle wage and hour issues. Their function was to implement company policies and undermine real unionism.

Partly because of these pressures, membership in labor unions fell from 5.1 million in 1920 to 3.6 million in 1929. But unions also contributed to their own decline. Conservative union leaders neglected ethnic and black workers in mass-production industries. Nor did they try to organize women, by 1930 nearly one-fourth of all workers. And they failed to respond effectively to other changes in the labor market. The growing numbers of white-collar workers regarded themselves as middle class and beyond the scope of union action.

With increasing mechanization and weak labor unions, workers suffered from job insecurity and stagnant wages. Unemployment reached 12 percent in 1921 and remained a persistent concern of many working-class Americans during the decade. And despite claims to the contrary, hours were long: The average workweek in manufacturing remained more than 50 hours.

An Assembly Line
of the
Ford Motor Company

Ford Motor Company's assembly line at the River Rouge plant in Detroit. The increasing mechanization of work, linked to managerial and marketing innovations, boosted productivity in the 1920s and brought consumer goods within the reach of far more Americans than before.
State Historical Society of Wisconsin.

The promise of business to pay high wages proved hollow. Real wages (purchasing power) did improve, but most of the improvement came before 1923 and reflected falling prices more than rising wages. The failure to raise wages when productivity was increasing threatened the nation's long-term prosperity. In short, rising national income largely reflected salaries and dividends, not wages.

Some workers fared worse than others. Unskilled workers, especially southern and eastern Europeans, black migrants from the rural South, and Mexican immigrants, saw their already low wages decline relative to those of skilled workers. Southern workers earned much less than northerners, even in the same industry, and women were paid much less than men even for the same jobs. Overall, the gap between rich and poor widened during the decade. By 1929, fully 71 percent of American families earned less than what the U.S. Bureau of Labor Statistics regarded as necessary for a decent living standard. The maldistribution of income meant that eventually Americans would be unable to purchase the products they made.

Consumer credit, rare before the 1920s, expanded during the decade. Credit offered temporary relief by permitting consumers to buy goods on time. General Motors introduced consumer credit on a national basis to create a mass market for expensive automobiles. By 1927, two-thirds of automobiles were purchased on the installment plan. By 1929, providing consumer credit had become the nation's tenth-largest business. Nevertheless, installment loans did not in the long run raise the purchasing power of an income; they simply added interest charges to the price of products.

SICK INDUSTRIES

Despite the general appearance of prosperity, several "sick" industries dragged on the economy. Coal mining, textile and garment manufacturing, and railroads suffered from excess capacity (too many mines and factories), shrinking demand, low returns, and management-labor conflicts. For example, U.S. coal mines had a capacity of a billion tons, but scarcely half of that amount was needed because of increasing use of oil, natural gas, and hydroelectricity. Using company police, strikebreakers, and injunctions, mine operators broke the United Mine Workers and slashed wages by up to one-third. Unemployment in the industry approached 30 percent.

Similarly, the textile industry coped with overcapacity and declining demand by shifting operations from New England to the cheap-labor South, employing girls and young women for 56-hour weeks at 18 cents an hour. Textile companies, aided by local authorities, suppressed strikes in Tennessee and North Carolina. Despite substandard wages and repressive policies, the textile industry remained barely profitable.

American agriculture never recovered from the 1921 depression. Agricultural surpluses and shrinking demand forced down prices. After the war, foreign markets dried up, and domestic demand for cotton slackened. Moreover, farmers' wartime expansion left them heavily mortgaged in the 1920s. Small farmers, unable to compete with larger, better-capitalized farmers, suffered most. Many lost their land and became tenants or farm hands.

Racial discrimination worsened conditions for black and Hispanic tenants, sharecroppers, and farm workers. In the South, African American sharecroppers trapped in grinding poverty endured segregation, disfranchisement, and violence. Mexican immigrants and Hispanic Americans labored as migrant farm workers in the Southwest and California. Exploited by the contract-labor system pervasive in large-scale agriculture, they suffered from poor wages, miserable living conditions, and racism.

THE BUSINESS OF GOVERNMENT

The Republican surge in national politics also shaped the economy. In the 1920 election, the Republican slogan was "Less government in business, more business in government." By 1924, Calvin Coolidge, the decade's second Republican president, proclaimed, "This is a business country . . . and it wants a business government." Under such direction, the federal government advanced business interests at the expense of other objectives.

REPUBLICAN ASCENDANCY

Republicans in 1920 had retained control of Congress and put Warren Harding in the White House. Harding was neither capable nor bright, but he recognized his own limitations and promised to appoint "the best minds" to his cabinet. Some of his appointees were highly accomplished, and two of them, Secretary of Commerce Herbert Hoover and Secretary of the Treasury Andrew Mellon, shaped economic policy throughout the 1920s.

A self-described progressive dedicated to efficiency, Hoover made the Commerce Department the government's most dynamic office. He cemented its ties with the leading sectors of the economy, expanded its collection and distribution of industrial information, pushed to exploit foreign resources and markets, and encouraged innovation. Hoover's goal was to foster prosperity by making business efficient, responsive, and profitable.

Andrew Mellon had a narrower goal. A wealthy banker and industrialist, he pressed Congress to reduce taxes on businesses and the rich. He argued that lower taxes would enable wealthy individuals and corporations to increase their capital investments, thereby creating new jobs and general prosperity. But Mellon's hope that favoring the rich would cause prosperity to trickle down to the working and middle classes proved ill-founded. Nevertheless, despite the opposition of progressives in Congress, Mellon succeeded in lowering maximum tax rates and eliminating wartime excess-profits taxes in 1921.

The Harding administration promoted business interests in other ways, too. The tariff of 1922 raised import rates to protect industry from foreign competition. But high tariffs made it difficult for European nations to earn the dollars to repay their war debts to the United States. High rates also impeded American farm exports and raised consumer prices.

The Harding administration aided the business campaign against unions and curtailed government regulation. By appointing advocates of big business to the Federal Trade Commission and the Federal Reserve Board, among others, Harding made government the collaborator rather than the regulator of business.

Finally, Harding reshaped the Supreme Court into a still more aggressive champion of business. He named the conservative William Howard Taft as chief justice and matched him with three other justices. All were, as one of them proclaimed, sympathetic to business leaders "beset and bedeviled with vexatious statutes, prying commissions, and government intermeddling of all sorts." The Court struck down much of the government economic regulation adopted during the Progressive Era, invalidated restraints on child labor and a minimum wage law for women, and approved restrictions on labor unions.

GOVERNMENT CORRUPTION

The green light that Harding Republicans extended to private interests led to corruption and scandals. Harding appointed many friends and cronies who saw public service as an opportunity for graft. Attorney General Harry Daugherty's associates in the Justice Department took bribes in exchange for pardons and government jobs. The head of the Veterans Bureau went to prison for cheating disabled veterans of $200 million. Albert Fall, the secretary of the interior, leased petroleum reserves set aside by progressive conservationists to oil companies in exchange for cash, bonds, and cattle for his New Mexico ranch. Exposed for his role in the Teapot Dome scandal, named after a Wyoming oil reserve, Fall became the first cabinet officer in history to go to jail. Daugherty escaped a similar fate by destroying records and invoking the Fifth amendment.

Harding was appalled by the scandals. "My God, this is a hell of a job!" he told William Allen White. "I have no trouble with my enemies. . . . But my damned friends, . . . they're the ones that keep me walking the floor nights!" Harding died shortly thereafter, probably of a heart attack.

COOLIDGE PROSPERITY

On August 3, 1923, Vice President Calvin Coolidge was sworn in as president. Coolidge's calm appearance hid a furious temper and a mean spirit. Coolidge supported business with ideological conviction. He opposed the activist presidency of the Progressive Era, cultivating instead a deliberate inactivity calculated to lower expectations of government.

Like Harding, Coolidge installed business supporters in the regulatory agencies. To chair the Federal Trade Commission he appointed an attorney who had condemned the agency as "an instrument of oppression and disturbance and injury instead of help to business." Under this leadership, the FTC described its new goal as "helping business to help itself," which meant approving trade associations and agreements to suppress competition. This attitude, endorsed by the Supreme Court, aided the mergers that occurred after 1925. The *Wall Street Journal* crowed, "Never before, here or anywhere else, has a government been so completely fused with business."

"Coolidge prosperity" determined the 1924 election. The Democrats, hopelessly divided, took 103 ballots to nominate the colorless, conservative Wall Street lawyer John W. Davis. A more interesting opponent for Coolidge was Robert La Follette, nominated by discontented farm and labor organizations that formed a new Progressive Party. La Follette campaigned against "the power of private monopoly over the political and economic life of the American people." The Republicans, backed by immense contributions from business, denounced La Follette as an agent of Bolshevism. The choice, Republicans insisted, was "Coolidge or Chaos." Thus instructed, Americans chose Coolidge, although barely half the electorate bothered to vote.

The Fate of Reform

But progressive reform was not completely dead. A small group in Congress, led by La Follette and George Norris, attacked Mellon's regressive tax policies and supported measures regulating agricultural processors, protecting workers' rights, and maintaining public ownership of a hydroelectric dam at Muscle Shoals, Alabama, that conservative Republicans wanted to privatize. Yet the reformers' successes were few and often temporary.

The fate of women's groups illustrates the difficulties reformers faced in the 1920s. At first, the adoption of woman suffrage prompted politicians to champion women's reform issues. In 1920, both major parties endorsed many of the goals of the new **League of Women Voters.** Within a year, many states had granted women the right to serve on juries, several enacted equal-pay laws, and Wisconsin adopted an equal-rights law. Congress passed the **Sheppard-Towner Maternity and Infancy Act,** the first federal social-welfare law, in 1921. It provided federal funds for infant and maternity care, precisely the type of protective legislation that the suffragists had described as women's special interest. Women also ran for political office and by 1922 there were fifteen women mayors of small towns throughout the nation.

But thereafter women reformers gained little. As it became clear that women did not vote as a bloc but according to their varying social and economic backgrounds, Congress lost interest in women's issues. In 1929, Congress killed the Sheppard-Towner Act. Nor could reformers gain ratification of a child-labor amendment after the Supreme Court invalidated laws regulating child labor. Conservatives attacked women reformers as "Bolsheviks."

Cities and Suburbs

The 1920 census was the first to report that more Americans lived in urban than in rural areas. The trend toward urbanization accelerated in the 1920s as millions of Americans fled the depressed countryside for the booming cities. This massive population movement interacted with technological innovations to reshape cities, build suburbs, and transform urban life (see Map 24–1).

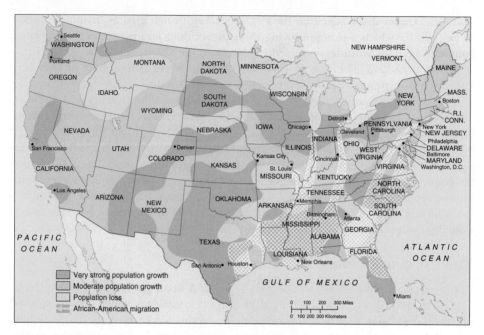

MAP 24–1 • Population Shifts, 1920–1930 Rural Americans fled to the cities during the 1920s, escaping a declining agricultural economy to search for new opportunities. African Americans in particular left the rural South for eastern and midwestern cities, but the urban population also jumped in the West and in the South itself.

▶ *Why did certain states and areas gain population during this period and why did others see population decreases?*

EXPANDING CITIES

Urbanization affected every region of the country. In absolute terms, the older industrial cities of the Northeast and upper Midwest grew the most, attracting migrants from the rural South and distressed Appalachia. New York remained the nation's foremost metropolis.

Rural southerners also headed for southern cities. In fact, the South was the nation's most rapidly urbanizing region. Migrants from the countryside poured into Atlanta, Birmingham, Memphis, and Houston. Little more than jungle before 1914, Miami became the fastest growing city in the United States during the 1920s—"the Magic City."

In the West, Denver, Portland, and Seattle (each a regional economic hub) and several California cities grew rapidly. Los Angeles grew by 115 percent and by 1930 was the nation's fifth-largest city, with over 1.2 million people.

The population surge transformed the urban landscape. As land values soared, developers built skyscrapers, giving Cleveland, Kansas City, San Francisco, and many other cities modern skylines. By the end of the decade, American cities had nearly 400 skyscrapers taller than 20 stories.

THE GREAT BLACK MIGRATION

A significant feature of the rural-to-urban movement was the **Great Migration** of African Americans from the South. Like other migrants, they were responding chiefly to economic factors. Southern segregation and violence made migration attractive, but job opportunities made it possible. Prosperity created jobs, and with the decline in European immigration, black workers filled the positions previously given to new immigrants. Although generally the lowest paid and least secure jobs, they were better than sharecropping in the rural South. The migrants often found adjustment to their new environment difficult. Southern rural black culture clashed with industrial work rhythms and discipline and with urban living. Still, more than 1.5 million African Americans moved to northern cities in the 1920s.

There black ghettos usually developed, more because of prejudice than the wishes of the migrants. Although African Americans, like European immigrants, often wanted to live together to sustain their culture, racist restrictions meant that segregation, not congregation, most shaped their urban community. With thousands of newcomers limited to certain neighborhoods, housing shortages developed. High rents and low wages forced black families to share inferior and unsanitary housing that threatened their health and safety.

However, the Great Migration also increased African Americans' racial consciousness, autonomy, and power. In 1928, for instance, black Chicagoans, using the ballot denied to African Americans in the South, elected the first black man to Congress since the turn of the century. Mutual-aid societies and fraternal orders proliferated. Churches were particularly influential. A reporter in 1926 counted 140 black churches in a 150-block area of Harlem.

Zora Neale Hurston, folklorist, anthropologist, and novelist, wrote with wit and verve about the African American South she so closely studied. Part of the dynamic community known as the Harlem Renaissance, Hurston won recognition in 1925 for her short story "Spunk." Her collective work, especially her later novel, *Their Eyes Were Watching God,* both reflected and advanced the creative pulse of what one black intellectual regarded as the first opportunity for African Americans to realize "group expression and self-determination."

Another organization also appealed to poor black ghetto dwellers. The Universal Negro Improvement Association (UNIA), organized by Marcus Garvey, a Jamaican immigrant to New York, rejected the NAACP's goal of integration. A black nationalist espousing racial pride, Garvey exhorted black people to migrate to Africa to build a "free, redeemed, and mighty nation." In the meantime, he urged them to support black businesses. UNIA organized many enterprises, including groceries, restaurants, laundries, a printing plant, and the Black Star Steamship Line, intended as a commercial link between the United States, the West Indies, and Africa. UNIA attracted half a million members, the first black mass movement in American history. When Garvey was convicted of mail fraud and deported, however, the movement collapsed.

Racial pride also found expression in the **Harlem Renaissance,** an outpouring of literature, painting, sculpture, and music. Inspired by African American culture and black urban life, writers and artists created works of power and poignancy. The poetry of Langston Hughes reflected the rhythm and mood of jazz and the blues. Other leading authors of the Harlem Renaissance who asserted their independence included Claude McKay, who wrote of the black working class in *Home to Harlem* (1928), Zora Neale Hurston, James Weldon Johnson, and Dorothy West.

BARRIOS

Hispanic migrants also entered the nation's cities in the 1920s, creating their own communities, or barrios. Fifty thousand Puerto Ricans settled in New York, mostly in East ("Spanish") Harlem, where they found low-paying jobs. Far more migrants arrived from Mexico. Although many worked as migrant farm laborers, they often lived in cities in the off-season. Others permanently joined the expanding urban economy in industrial and construction jobs. The barrios, with their own businesses, churches, and cultural organizations, created a sense of permanency.

These communities enabled the newcomers to preserve their cultural values and build social institutions, such as *mutualistas* (mutual aid societies), that helped them obtain credit, housing, and healthcare. But the barrios also reflected the hostility that Hispanics encountered in American cities. Los Angeles maintained separate schools for Mexicans, and a social worker reported that "America has repulsed the Mexican immigrant in every step he has taken" toward integration. As new migrants streamed in, conditions in the barrios deteriorated, for few cities provided adequate public services for them.

Some Hispanics fought discrimination. La Orden de Hijos de America ("The Order of the Sons of America"), organized in San Antonio in 1921, campaigned against inequities in schools and the jury system. In 1929, it helped launch the larger League of United Latin American Citizens (LULAC), which would help advance civil rights for all Americans.

THE ROAD TO SUBURBIA

As fast as the cities mushroomed in the 1920s, the suburbs grew twice as fast. Automobiles created the modern suburb. Nineteenth-century suburbs were small and linear, stretching along the street railway system. The new developments were sprawling and dispersed, for the automobile enabled people to live in formerly remote areas. A single-family house surrounded by a lawn became the social ideal, a pastoral escape from the overcrowded and dangerous city. Many suburbs excluded African Americans, Hispanics, Jews, and working-class people.

Suburbanization and the automobile brought other changes. The government provided federal money to states to build highways, and by the end of the decade, road construction was the largest single item in the national budget. Autos and suburbs also stimulated the growth of new industries. In 1922, J. C. Nichols opened the Country Club Plaza, the first suburban shopping center, in Kansas City; it provided free off-street parking. Department stores and other large retailers began leaving the urban cores for the suburbs, where both parking and more affluent customers were waiting. Drive-in restaurants began with Royce Hailey's Pig Stand in Dallas in 1921. That same year, the first fast-food franchise chain, White Castle, appeared, with its standardized menu and building, serving hamburgers "by the sack" to Americans in record numbers.

Mass Culture in the Jazz Age

The White Castle chain symbolized a new society and culture. Urbanization and the automobile joined with new systems of distributing, marketing, and communications to mold a mass culture of standardized experiences and interests. Not all Americans participated equally in the new culture, however, and some attacked it.

Advertising the Consumer Society

Advertising and its focus on increasing consumption shaped the new society. Advertisers exhorted consumers via newspapers, billboards, streetcar signs, junk mail, radio, movies, and even skywriting. They sought to create a single market where everyone, regardless of region and ethnicity, consumed brand-name products. Advertisers attempted to stimulate new wants by ridiculing previous models or tastes as obsolete, acclaiming the convenience of a new brand, or linking the latest fashion with status or sex appeal.

The home, in particular, became a focus of consumerism. Middle- and upper-class women purchased mass-produced household appliances, such as electric irons, toasters, vacuum cleaners, washing machines, and refrigerators. Working-class women bought packaged food, ready-made clothing, and other consumer goods to lighten their workload. Advertisers attempted to redefine the housewife's role as primarily that of a consumer, purchasing goods for her family.

A shifting labor market also promoted mass consumption. The increasing number of white-collar workers had more time and money for leisure and consumption. Factory workers, whose jobs often provided little challenge, less satisfaction, and no prospect for advancement, found in consumption not only material rewards but, thanks to advertisers' claims, some self-respect and fulfillment as stylish and attractive people worthy of attention.

Under the stimulus of advertising, consumption increasingly displaced the traditional virtues of thrift, prudence, and avoidance of debt. Installment buying became common. By 1928, fully 85 percent of furniture, 80 percent of radios, and 75 percent of washing machines were bought on credit. But with personal debt rising more than twice as fast as incomes, even aggressive advertising and the extension of credit could not indefinitely prolong the illusion of a healthy economy.

The soup for men
who eat to win!

MEN with the success-habit eat wisely and well, both. They enjoy Campbell's Tomato Soup regularly and they get from it a sparkle and zest, which tell in the day's work. All of the rich, tonic goodness. All of the famous tomato healthfulness. 12 cents a can.

Advertisements for brand-name products, like this 1929 ad for Campbell's tomato soup, often tried to link simple consumption with larger issues of personal success and achievement.

LEISURE AND ENTERTAINMENT

During the 1920s, Americans also spent more on recreation and leisure, important features of the new mass society. Millions of people packed into movie theaters whose ornate style symbolized their social importance.

Movies helped to spread common values and to set national trends in dress, language, and behavior. Studios made films to attract the largest audiences and fit prevailing stereotypes. Cecil B. De Mille titillated audiences while reinforcing conventional standards with religious epics like *The Ten Commandments* (1923) and *The King of Kings* (1927). Set in ancient times, such movies depicted both sinful pleasures and the eventual triumph of moral order.

Radio also helped to mold popular culture. The first radio network, the National Broadcasting Company (NBC), was formed in 1926. Soon it was charging $10,000 to broadcast a commercial to a national market. Networks provided standardized entertainment, personalities, and news to Americans across the nation. Radio incorporated listeners into a national society.

The phonograph, another popular source of entertainment, allowed families to listen to music of their choice in their own homes. The phonograph business boomed.

Manufacturers turned out more than 2 million phonographs and 100 million records annually. The popularity of the trumpet player Louis Armstrong and other jazz greats gave the decade its nickname, the **Jazz Age.**

Jazz derived from African American musical traditions. The Great Migration spread it from New Orleans and Kansas City to cities throughout the nation. Its improvisational and rhythmic characteristics differed sharply from older and more formal music and were often condemned by people who feared that jazz would undermine conventional restraints on behavior.

Professional sports also became more commercialized. Millions of Americans, attracted by the popularity of such celebrities as Babe Ruth of the New York Yankees, crowded into baseball parks to follow major league teams. Ruth treated himself as a commercial commodity, hiring an agent, endorsing Cadillacs and alligator shoes, and defending a salary in 1932 that dwarfed that of President Hoover by declaring, "I had a better year than he did."

Large crowds turned out to watch boxers Jack Dempsey and Gene Tunney pummel each other; those who could not get tickets listened to radio announcers describe each blow. College football attracted frenzied followers among people with no interest in higher education. By 1929, the Carnegie Commission noted that the commercialization of college sports had "overshadowed the intellectual life for which the university is assumed to exist."

THE NEW MORALITY

The promotion of consumption and immediate gratification weakened traditional self-restraint and fed a desire for personal fulfillment. The failure of wartime sacrifices to achieve promised glories deepened Americans' growing disenchantment with traditional values. The social dislocations of the war years and growing urbanization accelerated moral and social change. Sexual pleasure became an increasingly open objective. Popularization of Sigmund Freud's ideas weakened prescriptions for sexual restraint; the growing availability of birth control information enabled women to enjoy sex with less fear of pregnancy. Traditionalists worried as divorce rates, cigarette consumption, and hemlines went up while respect for parents, elders, and clergy went down.

Young people seemed to embody the new morality. Rejecting conventional standards, they embraced the era's frenzied dances, bootleg liquor, smoking, more revealing clothing, and sexual experimentation. They welcomed the freedom from parental control that the automobile afforded. The "flapper"—a frivolous young woman with short hair and a skimpy skirt who danced, smoked, and drank in oblivious self-absorption—was a major obsession in countless articles bearing such titles as "These Wild Young People" and "The Uprising of the Young."

But the new morality was neither as new nor as widespread as its advocates and critics believed. Signs of change had appeared before the Great War in the popularity of new clothing fashions, social values, and public amusements among working-class and ethnic groups. And if it now became fashionable for the middle class to adopt such attitudes and practices, most Americans still adhered to traditional beliefs and values. Moreover, the new morality offered only a limited freedom. It certainly did not promote social equality for women, who remained subject to traditional double standards, with marriage and divorce laws, property rights, and employment opportunities biased against them.

THE SEARCHING TWENTIES

Many writers rejected what they considered the materialism, conformity, and provincialism of mass culture. Their criticism made the postwar decade one of the most creative periods in American literature. The brutality and hypocrisy of the war stimulated the critics' disillusionment and alienation. What Gertrude Stein called the Lost Generation considered, in the words of F. Scott Fitzgerald, "all Gods dead, all wars fought, all faiths in man shaken." Ernest Hemingway, wounded as a Red Cross volunteer during the war, rejected idealism in his novel *A Farewell to Arms* (1929), declaring that he no longer saw any meaning in "the words sacred, glorious, and sacrifice."

Novelists also turned their attention to American society. In *The Great Gatsby* (1925), Fitzgerald traced the self-deceptions of the wealthy. Sinclair Lewis ridiculed middle-class society and its narrow business culture in *Babbitt* (1922), whose title character provided a new word applied to the smug and shallow. In 1930, Lewis became the first American to win the Nobel Prize in literature.

Other writers condemned the mediocrity and intolerance of mass society. The critic Harold Stearns edited *Civilization in the United States* (1922), a book of essays. Its depiction of a repressive society sunk in hypocrisy, conformity, and materialism prompted his departure for Paris, where he lived, like Hemingway and Fitzgerald, as an expatriate, alienated from America. H. L. Mencken made his *American Mercury* the leading magazine of cultural dissenters. Conventional and conservative himself, Mencken heaped vitriol on the "puritans," "peasants," and "prehensile morons" he saw everywhere in American life.

CULTURE WARS

Despite the blossoming of mass culture and society in the 1920s, conflicts divided social groups. Some of these struggles involved reactions against the new currents in American life, including technological and scientific innovations, urban growth, and materialism. But movements to restrict immigration, enforce prohibition, prohibit the teaching of evolution, and even sustain the Ku Klux Klan did not have simple origins, motives, or consequences. The forces underlying the culture wars of the 1920s would surface repeatedly in the future (see Overview, Issues in the Culture Wars of the 1920s).

NATIVISM AND IMMIGRATION RESTRICTION

For years, many Americans, from racists to reformers, had campaigned to restrict immigration. In 1917, Congress required immigrants to pass a literacy test. But renewed immigration after the war revived the anti-immigration movement, and the propaganda of the war and the Red Scare years generated public support for more restriction. Depicting immigrants as radicals, racial inferiors, religious subversives, or criminals, nativists clamored for congressional action. The arrests of two Italian-born anarchists, Nicola Sacco and Bartolomeo Vanzetti, in May 1920 fueled the controversy over radicalism and immigration. Charged with armed robbery and murder, they proclaimed their innocence and insisted that they were on trial solely for their political beliefs. Convicted in 1921, they were executed in 1927. Opponents of the verdict saw the trial and execution as a result of public hysteria, but defenders, like evangelist Billy Sunday, championed it as a vindication of American justice.

The passage of the Emergency Quota Act in 1921 responded to popular concerns by reducing immigration by about two-thirds and establishing quotas for nationalities on the basis of their numbers in the United States in 1910. Restrictionists, however, demanded more stringent action, especially against the largely Catholic and Jewish immigrants from southern and eastern Europe. Coolidge himself urged that America "be kept American," by which he meant white, Anglo-Saxon, and Protestant. Congress adopted this racist rationale in the **National Origins Act of 1924,** which proclaimed its objective to be the maintenance of the "racial preponderance" of "the basic strain of our population." This law restricted immigration quotas to 2 percent of the foreign-born population of each nationality as recorded in the 1890 census, which was taken before the mass immigration from southern and eastern Europe. Another provision, effective in 1929, restricted total annual immigration to 150,000, with quotas that nearly eliminated southern and eastern Europeans. The law also completely excluded Japanese immigrants.

Other actions targeted Japanese residents in America. California, Oregon, Washington, Arizona, and other western states prohibited them from owning or leasing land, and in 1922, the Supreme Court ruled that, as nonwhites, they could never become naturalized citizens. Dispirited by the prejudice of the decade, Japanese residents hoped for fulfillment through their children, the *Nisei,* who were American citizens by birth.

Ironically, the Philippines, as a U.S. territory, was not subject to the National Origins Act, and Filipino immigration increased ninefold during the 1920s. Most Filipino newcomers became farm laborers, especially in California, or worked in Alaskan fisheries. Similarly, because the law did not apply to immigrants from the Western Hemisphere, Mexican immigration also grew. Nativists lobbied to exclude Mexicans, but agribusiness interests in the Southwest blocked any restrictions on low-cost migrant labor.

THE KU KLUX KLAN

Nativism was also reflected in the popularity of the revived Ku Klux Klan, the goal of which, according to its leader, was to protect "the interest of those whose forefathers established the nation." Founded in Georgia in 1915 and modeled on its Reconstruction predecessor, the new Klan was a national, not only a southern, movement and claimed several million members by the mid-1920s. Admitting only native-born white Protestants, the Klan embodied the fears of a traditional culture threatened by social change. Ironically, its rapid spread owed much to modern business and promotional techniques as hundreds of professional recruiters raked in hefty commissions selling Klan memberships to those hoping to defend their way of life.

In part, the Klan was a fraternal order, providing entertainment, assistance, and community for its members. Its picnics, parades, charity drives, and other social and family-oriented activities—perhaps a half-million women joined the Women of the Ku Klux Klan—sharply distinguished the organization from both the small, secretive Klan of the nineteenth century and the still smaller, extremist Klan of the later twentieth century. Regarding themselves as reformers, Klan members supported immigration restriction and Prohibition.

But the Klan also exploited racial, ethnic, and religious prejudices and campaigned against many social groups and what it called "alien creeds." It attacked African Americans in the South, Mexicans in Texas, Japanese in California, and Catholics and Jews everywhere. A twisted religious impulse ran through much of the Klan's organization and activities. It hired itinerant Protestant ministers to spread its message, erected altars and flaming crosses at its meetings, and sang Klan lyrics to the tunes of well-known hymns. The Klan also resorted to violence. In 1921, for example, a Methodist minister

OVERVIEW ISSUES IN THE CULTURE WARS OF THE 1920S

Issue	Proponent view	Opponent view
The new morality	Promotes greater personal freedom and opportunities for fulfillment	Promotes moral collapse
Evolutionism	A scientific advance linked to notions of progress	A threat to religious belief
Jazz	Modern and vital	Unsettling, irregular, vulgar, and primitive
Immigration	A source of national strength from ethnic and racial diversity	A threat to the status and authority of old-stock white Protestants
Great Migration	A chance for African Americans to find new economic opportunities and gain autonomy and pride	A threat to traditional white privilege, control, and status
Prohibition	Promotes social and family stability and reduces crime	Restricts personal liberty and increases crime
Fundamentalism	An admirable adherence to traditional religious faith and biblical injunctions	A superstitious creed given to intolerant interference in social and political affairs
Ku Klux Klan	An organization promoting community responsibility, patriotism, and traditional social, moral, and religious values	A group of religious and racial bigots given to violent vigilantism and fostering moral and public corruption
Mass culture	Increases popular participation in national culture; provides entertainment	Promotes conformity, materialism, mediocrity, spectacle, and relaxation
Consumerism	Promotes material progress and higher living standards	Promotes waste, sterility, and self-indulgence

who belonged to the Klan murdered a Catholic priest on his own doorstep, and other Klansmen burned down Catholic churches. The leader of the Oregon Klan insisted that "the only way to cure a Catholic is to kill him."

To the Klan, Catholics and Jews symbolized not merely subversive religions but also the ethnic diversity and swelling urban population that challenged traditional Protestant culture. To protect that culture, the Klan attempted to censor or disrupt "indecent" entertainment, assaulted those it accused of adultery, and terrorized doctors who performed abortions.

While the Klan's appeal seemed rooted in the declining countryside, it also attracted urban residents. Chicago had the largest Klan organization in the nation, with

50,000 members, and Houston, Dallas, Portland, Indianapolis, Denver, and the satellite communities ringing Los Angeles were also Klan strongholds. Urban Klansmen were largely lower or lower middle class, many recently arrived from the country and retaining its attitudes; others were long-term urban residents who feared being marginalized by social changes, especially by competition from immigrants and new ideas.

The Klan also ventured into politics, with some success. But eventually it encountered resistance. In the North, Catholic workers disrupted Klan parades. In the South, too, Klan excesses provoked a backlash. After the Klan in Dallas flogged 68 people in a "whipping meadow" along the Trinity River in 1922, respect turned to outrage. Newspapers demanded that the Klan disband, district attorneys began to prosecute Klan thugs, and in 1924 Klan candidates were defeated by a ticket headed by Miriam "Ma" Ferguson, whose gubernatorial campaign called for anti-Klan laws and for the loss of tax exemptions for churches used for Klan meetings. Elsewhere the Klan was stung by revelations of criminal behavior and corruption by Klan leaders, who had been making fortunes pocketing membership fees and selling regalia to followers. The Klan crusade to purify society had bred corruption and conflict everywhere. By 1930, the Klan had nearly collapsed.

PROHIBITION AND CRIME

Like the Klan, Prohibition both reflected and provoked social tensions in the 1920s. Reformers had long believed that prohibiting the sale of alcohol would improve social conditions, reduce crime and family instability, increase economic efficiency, and

To entertain families and friends, the KKK held "Klan Day at the Races," pictured here at Denver's Overland Park Race Track.

purify politics. They rejoiced in 1920 when the Eighteenth Amendment, prohibiting the manufacture, sale, or transportation of alcoholic beverages, took effect. Congress then passed the **Volstead Act,** which defined the forbidden liquors and established the Prohibition Bureau to enforce the law. But many social groups, especially in urban ethnic communities, opposed Prohibition, and the government could not enforce the law where public opinion did not endorse it.

Evasion was easy. By permitting alcohol for medicinal, sacramental, and industrial purposes, the Volstead Act gave doctors, priests, and druggists a huge loophole through which to satisfy their friends' needs. City-dwellers made "bathtub gin," and rural people distilled "moonshine." Scofflaws frequented the speakeasies that replaced saloons or bought liquor from bootleggers and rumrunners, who imported it from Canada, Cuba, or Mexico. The limited resources of the Prohibition Bureau often allowed bootleggers to operate openly.

The ethics and business methods of bootleggers soon shocked Americans, however. The huge profits encouraged organized crime, which had previously concentrated on gambling and prostitution, to develop elaborate liquor-distribution networks. Operating outside the law, crime "families" used violence to enforce contracts, suppress competition, and attack rivals. In Chicago, Al Capone's army of nearly a thousand gangsters killed hundreds. Using the profits from bootlegging and new tools like the automobile and the submachine gun, organized crime corrupted city governments and police forces.

Gradually, even many "drys"—people who had initially favored Prohibition—dropped their support, horrified by the boost the amendment gave organized crime and worried about the general disrespect for law that it promoted. A 1926 poll found that four-fifths of Americans wanted to repeal or modify Prohibition. Yet it remained in force because it was entangled in party politics and social conflict. Democrats called for repeal in their 1928 and 1932 platforms, and in 1933, 36 states ratified an amendment repealing what Herbert Hoover had called a "noble experiment."

OLD-TIME RELIGION AND THE SCOPES TRIAL

Religion provided another fulcrum for traditionalists attempting to stem cultural change. Protestant fundamentalism, which emphasized the infallibility of the Bible, including the creation story, emerged at the turn of the century as a conservative reaction to religious modernism and the social changes brought by the mass immigration of Catholics and Jews, the growing influence of science and technology, and the secularization of public education. But the fundamentalist crusade to reshape America became formidable only in the 1920s. Evangelists like Billy Sunday and Aimee Semple McPherson attracted thousands to their revivals across America. (See American Views: Evangelism and the Search for Salvation.)

Fundamentalist groups, colleges, and publications sprang up throughout the nation, especially in the South. The anti-Catholic sentiment exploited by the Klan was but one consequence of fundamentalism's insistence on strict biblical Christianity. A second was the assault on Darwin's theory of evolution, which contradicted literal interpretations of biblical Creation. Fundamentalist legislators tried to prevent the teaching of evolution in public schools in at least 20 states. In 1923, Oklahoma banned textbooks based on Darwinian theory, and Florida's legislature denounced teaching evolution as "subversive." In 1925, Tennessee forbade teaching any idea contrary to the biblical account of human origins.

Social or political conservatism, however, was not an inherent part of old-time religion. The most prominent antievolution politician, William Jennings Bryan, contin-

Evangelist Aimee Semple McPherson Evangelist Aimee Semple McPherson delivering her "Foursquare Gospel" that offered all sinners salvation.

ued to campaign for political, social, and economic reforms. Never endorsing the Klan, he served on the American Committee on the Rights of Religious Minorities and condemned anti-Semitism and anti-Catholicism. Bryan feared that Darwinism promoted political and economic conservatism.

The controversy over evolution came to a head when the American Civil Liberties Union (ACLU) responded to Tennessee's violation of the constitutional separation of church and state by offering to defend any teacher who tested the antievolution law. John Scopes, a high school biology teacher in Dayton, Tennessee, did so and was arrested. The Scopes trial attracted national attention after Bryan agreed to assist the prosecution and Clarence Darrow, a famous Chicago lawyer and prominent atheist, volunteered to defend Scopes.

Millions of Americans tuned their radios to hear the first trial ever broadcast. The judge, a fundamentalist, sat under a sign urging people to "Read Your Bible Daily." He ruled that scientists could not testify in support of evolution: Because they were not present at the Creation, their testimony would be "hearsay." But he did allow Darrow to put Bryan on the stand as an expert on the Bible. Bryan insisted on the literal truth of every story in the Bible, allowing Darrow to ridicule his ideas and force him to concede that some biblical passages had to be construed symbolically. Although the local jury took only eight minutes to convict Scopes, fundamentalists suffered public ridicule from reporters.

But fundamentalism was hardly destroyed, and antievolutionists continued their campaign. New organizations, such as the Bryan Bible League, lobbied for state laws and an antievolution amendment to the Constitution. Three more states forbade teaching evolution, but by 1929 the movement had faltered. Even so, fundamentalism retained religious influence and would again challenge science and modernism in American life.

EVANGELISM AND THE SEARCH FOR SALVATION

*A*imee Semple McPherson defied traditional roles for women in becoming one of the most famous evangelical leaders in the United States. Traveling in her "Gospel Car," she crisscrossed the nation reminding her followers that "Jesus Is Coming Soon" and advising them to "Get Ready." In 1923, she opened the Angelus Temple in Los Angeles—a white-domed building large enough for 5,000 followers of what McPherson called the "Foursquare Gospel." A lighted rotating cross on top of the dome could be seen from fifty miles away—a beacon for those who journeyed to her center of "spiritual energy." A charismatic orator, McPherson embraced the theatrics of Hollywood to stir her crowds and raised vast sums of money, or "love gifts," to finance the Temple and its activities. Playing upon the phrase shareholder, McPherson sold doll-house chairs for $25 each, enabling purchasers to be "chair-holders" in the Temple. Though tainted by a mysterious disappearance in 1926, she remained extraordinarily popular, attracting crowds of thousands who sought salvation during times of change and uncertainty. McPherson died in 1944 from an accidental overdose of sleeping pills.

In this excerpt from one of her autobiographies, McPherson describes the growth of the Angelus Temple and her pioneering use of radio to advance her "success in soul winning."

■ **Why** was Aimee Semple McPherson so popular in the 1920s?

■ **What** does her success suggest about the role of religion in American life?

■ **How** do you think evangelicals like McPherson might have viewed the cult of business that also characterized the decade?

From the days the doors opened on January 1, 1923, a mighty spiritual revival surged into Angelus Temple with ever-increasing power and fervor. Eight thousand converts knelt at the altars in the first

A NEW ERA IN THE WORLD?

Abroad and at home, Americans in the 1920s sought peace and economic order. Rejection of the Treaty of Versailles and the League of Nations did not foreshadow isolationism. Indeed, in the 1920s, the United States became more deeply involved in international matters than ever before in peacetime. This involvement both produced important successes and sowed the seeds for serious future problems.

WAR DEBTS AND ECONOMIC EXPANSION

The United States was the world's dominant economic power in the 1920s, changed by the Great War from a debtor to a creditor nation. The loans the United States had made to its allies during the war troubled the nation's relations with Europe throughout the decade. American insistence on repayment angered Europeans, who saw the money as a U.S. contribution to the joint war effort against Germany. Moreover, high American tariffs blocked Europeans from exporting goods to the United States and earning dollars to repay their debts. Eventually, the United States readjusted the terms for repayment, and American bank-

six months and fifteen hundred believers were immersed in the baptistry. Hundreds were healed and baptized with the Holy Spirit. One thousand young people covenanted together to serve as the Angelus Temple Foursquare Crusaders. And as the weeks and months passed, new outreaches commenced.

In February, the Prayer Tower opened, where prayer has not ceased as men gather in two-hour shifts during the night and women pray during the day, bringing God thousands of requests which come by mail, telephone, and telegraph from all over the world.

Then came the challenge of the radio! . . . My soul was thrilled with the possibilities this media offered for the spread of gospel. We secured time on a radio station and began broadcasting a few services. But the thought persisted that if Angelus Temple had her own radio station we could broadcast almost all of the meetings!

And God provided through the love gifts of his people for the radio station. In February 1924, KFSG— Kall Four Square Gospel—went on the air, broadcasting the glorious song, "Give the winds a mighty voice, Jesus saves!" . . . Time and time again converted gamblers, dope addicts, bootleggers, and white-slavery victims rose from knees to send thrilling testimonies out over radio station KFSG as well as to the Temple audience.

. . . For three years I stayed close by Angelus Temple, preaching and teaching many times a week, conducting a daily "Sunshine Hour" broadcast, writing, editing, publishing, and praying for the sick. . . . The revival swept on and out. Branch churches sprang up in cities and towns. [And the Foursquare gospel] message has become well known around the world.

SOURCE: *Aimee Semple McPherson: The Story of My Life* (Waco, TX: Word Books, 1973).

---

ers extended large loans to Germany, which used the money to pay reparations to Britain and France, whose governments then used the same money to repay the United States. This unstable system depended on a continuous flow of money from the United States.

America's global economic role expanded in other ways as well. Exports, especially of manufactured goods, soared. To expand their markets and avoid foreign tariffs, many U.S. companies became **multinational corporations,** establishing branches or subsidiaries abroad. Ford built assembly plants in England, Japan, Turkey, and Canada. International Telephone and Telegraph owned two dozen factories in Europe and employed more overseas workers than any other U.S. corporation.

Other companies gained control of foreign supply sources. American oil companies invested in foreign oil fields, especially in Latin America, where they controlled more than half of Venezuelan production. The United Fruit Company developed such huge operations in Central America that it often dominated national economies. In Costa Rica, the company had a larger budget than the national government.

Europeans and Latin Americans alike worried about this economic invasion; even Secretary of Commerce Herbert Hoover expressed concerns. Multinationals, he warned, might eventually take markets from American manufacturers and jobs from American workers. Business leaders, however, dismissed such reservations.

Hoover's concerns, moreover, did not prevent him from promoting economic expansion abroad. The government worked to open doors for American businesses in foreign countries, helping them to secure access to trade, investment opportunities, and raw materials. Hoover's Bureau of Foreign Commerce opened 50 offices around the world to boost American business. Hoover also pressed the British to give U.S. corporations access to rubber production in the British colony of Malaya. Secretary of State Charles Evans Hughes negotiated access to Iraqi oil fields for U.S. oil companies. The government also authorized bankers and manufacturers to form combinations, exempt from antitrust laws, to exploit foreign markets.

REJECTING WAR

Although government officials cooperated with business leaders to promote American strategic and economic interests, they had little desire to use force abroad. Popular reaction against the Great War, strengthened by a strong peace movement, constrained policymakers. Having repudiated collective security as embodied in the League of Nations, the United States nonetheless sought to minimize international conflict and promote its national security. In particular, the State Department sought to restrict the buildup of armaments among nations.

At the invitation of President Harding, delegations from nine nations met in Washington at the Washington Naval Conference in 1921 to discuss disarmament. The conference drafted a treaty to reduce battleship tonnage and suspend the building of new ships for a decade. Japan and the United States also agreed not to fortify their possessions in the Pacific any further and to respect the Open Door in East Asia. Public opinion welcomed the treaty; the U.S. Senate ratified it with only one dissenting vote, and the 1924 Republican platform hailed it as "the greatest peace document ever drawn."

The United States made a more dramatic gesture in 1928, when it helped draft the **Kellogg-Briand Pact.** Signed by 64 nations, the treaty renounced aggression and outlawed war. Without provisions for enforcement, however, it was little more than symbolic. The Senate reserved the right of self-defense, repudiated any responsibility for enforcing the treaty, and maintained U.S. claims under the Monroe Doctrine.

MANAGING THE HEMISPHERE

Senate insistence on the authority of the Monroe Doctrine reflected the U.S. claim to a predominant role in Latin America. The United States continued to dominate the hemisphere to promote its own interests. It exerted its influence through investments, control of the Panama Canal, invocation of the Monroe Doctrine, and, when necessary, military intervention.

In response to American public opinion, the peace movement, and Latin American nationalism, the United States retreated from the extreme gunboat diplomacy of the Progressive Era, withdrawing troops from the Dominican Republic and Nicaragua. But Haiti remained under U.S. occupation throughout the decade, American troops stayed in Cuba and Panama, and the United States directed the financial policies of other Latin American countries. Moreover, it sent the marines into Honduras in 1924 and back to Nicaragua in 1926. Such interventions could establish only temporary stability while provoking further Latin American hostility.

Latin American resentment led to a resolution at the 1928 Inter-America Conference denying the right of any nation "to intervene in the internal affairs of another." The U.S. delegation rejected the measure, but the anger of Latin Americans prompted the Hoover administration to rescind support for the Roosevelt Corollary (see Chapter), and J. Reuben Clark, chief legal officer of the State Department, drafted the Clark Memorandum. Not published until 1930, this document stated that the Roosevelt Corollary was not a legitimate extension of the Monroe Doctrine and thereby helped prepare the way for the so-called Good Neighbor Policy toward Latin America. Still, the United States did not pledge nonintervention and retained the means, both military and economic, to dominate the hemisphere.

HERBERT HOOVER AND THE FINAL TRIUMPH OF THE NEW ERA

As the national economy steamed ahead in 1928, the Republicans chose as their presidential candidate Herbert Hoover, a man who symbolized the policies of prosperity and the New Era. Hoover was not a politician—he had never been elected to office—but a successful administrator who championed rational and efficient economic development.

The Democrats, by contrast, chose a candidate who evoked the cultural conflicts of the 1920s. Alfred E. Smith, a four-term governor of New York, was a Catholic, an opponent of Prohibition, and a Tammany politician tied to the immigrant constituency of New York City. His nomination plunged the nation into the cultural strife that had divided the Democrats in 1924. Rural fundamentalism, anti-Catholicism, Prohibition, and nativism were crucial factors in the campaign.

But Hoover was, in certain ways, the more progressive candidate. Sympathetic to labor, sensitive to women's issues, hostile to racial segregation, and favorable to the League of Nations, Hoover had always distanced himself from what he called "the reactionary group in the Republican party." By contrast, despite supporting factory reform and state welfare legislation to benefit his urban working-class constituents, Smith was as parochial as his most rural adversaries. He responded to a question about the needs of the states west of the Mississippi by asking, "What states *are* west of the Mississippi?"

Although many Americans voted against Smith because of his social background, the same characteristics attracted others. Millions of urban and ethnic voters, previously Republican or politically uninvolved, voted for Smith and laid the basis for the new Democratic coalition that would emerge in the 1930s. In 1928, however, with the nation still enjoying the economic prosperity so closely associated with Hoover and the Republicans, the Democrats were routed.

CONCLUSION

The New Era of the 1920s changed America. Technological and managerial innovations produced giant leaps in productivity, new patterns of labor, a growing concentration of corporate power, and high corporate profits. Government policies, from protective tariffs and regressive taxation to the relaxation of regulatory laws, reflected and reinforced the triumphs of the business elite over traditional cautions and concerns.

The decade's economic developments, in turn, stimulated social change, drawing millions of Americans from the countryside to the cities, creating an urban nation, and fostering a new ethic of materialism, consumerism, and leisure and a new mass culture based on the automobile, radio, the movies, and advertising. This social transformation swept up many Americans but left others unsettled by the erosion of traditional practices and values. Henry Ford, who as Upton Sinclair observed, remade the "roads of America," was also disturbed by America's new direction and reflected the ambivalence others shared about modern society. The concerns of many traditionalists found expression in campaigns for prohibition and against immigration, the revival of the Ku Klux Klan, and the rise of religious fundamentalism. Intellectuals denounced the materialism and conformity they saw in the new social order and fashioned new artistic and literary trends.

But the impact of the decade's trends was uneven. Mechanization increased the productivity of some workers but cost others their jobs; people poured into the cities while others left for the suburbs; Prohibition, intended to stabilize society, instead produced conflict, crime, and corruption; government policies advanced some economic interests but injured others. Even the notion of a "mass" culture obscured the degree to which millions of Americans were left out of the New Era. With no disposable income and little access to electricity, rural Americans scarcely participated in the joys of consumerism; racial and ethnic minorities were often isolated in ghettos and barrios; and many workers faced declining opportunities. Most ominous was the uneven prosperity undergirding the New Era. Although living standards rose for many Americans and the rich expanded their share of the national wealth, more than 40 percent of the population earned less than $1,500 a year and fell below the established poverty level. The unequal distribution of wealth and income made the economy unstable and vulnerable to a disastrous collapse.

REVIEW QUESTIONS

1. How did the automobile industry affect the nation's economy and society in the 1920s? In the excerpt from *The Flivver King*, how does Upton Sinclair illustrate the tension between workers and technology even as they both served Henry Ford's vision of mass production and mass consumerism?

2. What factors characterized the boom industries of the 1920s? The sick industries? How accurate is it to label the 1920s the decade of prosperity?

3. What were the underlying issues in the election of 1924? Of 1928? What role did politics play in the public life of the 1920s?

4. What were the chief points of conflict in the culture wars of the 1920s? What were the underlying issues in these clashes? Why were they so hard to compromise?

5. In what ways did World War I experience shape developments in the 1920s?

6. What were the chief features of American involvement in world affairs in the 1920s? To what extent did that involvement constitute a new role for the United States?

PEARSON
myhistorylab CONNECTIONS

Reinforce what you learned in this chapter by studying the many documents, images, maps, review tools, and videos available at **www.myhistorylab.com**.

READ AND REVIEW

✔•─ **Study** and **Review** on **myhistorylab.com** STUDY PLAN: CHAPTER 24

📖•─ **Read** the **Document** on **myhistorylab.com**

Calvin Coolidge, Inaugural Address (1925)

Edward Earle Purinton, "Big Ideas from Big Business" (1921)

Carter G. Woodson, A Century of Negro Migration (1918)

1924 Immigration Law

Advertisements (1925, 1927)

Margaret Sanger, "Happiness in Marriage" (1926)

Court Statements Nicola Sacco and Bartolomeo Vanzetti (1927)

Creed of Klanswomen (1924)

Hiram Evans, The Klan's Fight for Americanism (1926)

Letters from the Great Migration (1916–1917)

Charles S. Johnson, The City Negro (1925)

🔍─ **View** the **Map** on **myhistorylab.com**

African American Population, 1910 and 1950

The Expansion of Black Harlem, 1911–1930

RESEARCH AND EXPLORE

📖•─ **Read** the **Document** on **myhistorylab.com**

Personal Journeys Online

From Then to Now Online: The Culture Wars

Exploring America: Harlem Renaissance

((•─ **Listen** on **myhistorylab.com**

Prohibition is a Failure

"I Too"; poem and reading by Langston Hughes

👁•─ **Watch** the **Video** on **myhistorylab.com**

The Great Migration

The Harlem Renaissance

The Rise and Fall of the Automobile Economy

Warren C. Harding

─────── ((•─ **Listen** on **myhistorylab.com** ───────

Hear the audio files for Chapter 24 at
www.myhistorylab.com.

Hear the audio files for Chapter 25 at **www.myhistorylab.com**.

FOCUS QUESTIONS

WHAT TRIGGERED the Great Depression?

HOW DID Herbert Hoover respond to the depression? Why did his policies fail?

WHAT WERE the goals of the early New Deal?

WHAT WERE the major accomplishments of the Second New Deal?

WHAT IMPACT did the New Deal have on American social and economic life?

WHY DID the New Deal lose momentum after 1936?

HOW DID Roosevelt respond to the rise of fascism in Europe?

Hands in their pockets, hungry men stand numbly in one of New York City's 82 breadlines.

One American Journey

We are bringing order out of the old chaos with a greater certainty of labor at a reasonable wage and of more business at a fair profit. These governmental and industrial developments hold promise of new achievements for the nation.

Our first problem was, of course, the banking situation because, as you know, the banks had collapsed. Some banks could not be saved but the great majority of them, either through their own resources or with government aid, have been restored to complete public confidence. This has given safety to millions of depositors in these banks.

The second step we have taken in the restoration of normal business enterprise has been to clean up thoroughly unwholesome conditions in the field of investment. . . . The country now enjoys the safety of bank savings under the new banking laws, the careful checking of new securities under the Securities Act and the curtailment of rank stock speculation through the Securities Exchange Act. . . .

Those, fortunately few in number, who are frightened by boldness and cowed by the necessity for making decisions, complain that all we have done is unnecessary and subject to great risks. Now that these people are coming out of their storm cellars, they forget that there ever was a storm. [But] nearly all Americans are sensible and calm people. We do not get greatly excited nor is our peace of mind disturbed, whether we be businessmen or workers or farmers, by awesome pronouncements concerning the unconstitutionality of some of our measures of recovery and relief and reform. We are not frightened by reactionary lawyers or political editors. All these cries have been heard before.

I still believe in ideals. I am not for a return to that definition of Liberty under which for many years a free people were being gradually regimented into the service of the privileged few. I prefer and I am sure you prefer that broader definition of Liberty under which we are moving forward to greater freedom, to greater security for the average man than he has ever known before in the history of America.

Excerpted from President Franklin D. Roosevelt's radio address entitled "On Moving Forward to Greater Freedom and Greater Security," September 30, 1934.

A S PRESIDENT FRANKLIN D. ROOSEVELT acknowledged in his 1934 radio address, the U.S. economy had utterly collapsed. Men, women, children everywhere saw their families and dreams shattered, watched their life savings vanish in faulty banks, and felt the sting of humiliation as they stood in bread lines or begged for clothes or food scraps. The winter of 1932–1933 had been particularly cruel: Unemployment soared and stories of malnutrition and outright starvation made headlines in newspapers throughout the nation.

The election of Franklin D. Roosevelt in 1932 had, however, lifted the spirits and hopes of jobless Americans throughout the nation. They enthusiastically responded to his "new deal for the American people" and particularly embraced his use of the radio to address the nation. In these "fireside chats," the president offered reassurance about the economic crisis, compassionately explaining his decisions and policies, as he did in this 1934 address. And he promised a brighter future, charting a new journey, he predicted, that he would restore confidence among despairing Americans and provide greater economic security for the nation's citizens. "Among our objectives," Roosevelt insisted, "I place the security of the men, women, and children of the Nation first."

To be sure, FDR's bold rhetoric occasionally outdistanced his legislative agenda, and certain programs hardly worked against what he termed the "privileged few." Moreover, his policies often failed to challenge the racism and sexism that precluded a new deal for all Americans. Still, the unprecedented federal activism of the 1930s, even while achieving neither full recovery nor systematic reform, effectively restored confidence to many Americans and permanently transformed the nation's responsibility for the welfare of its citizens.

HARD TIMES IN HOOVERVILLE

The prosperity of the 1920s ended in a stock-market crash that revealed the flaws honeycombing the economy. As the nation slid into a catastrophic depression, factories closed, employment and incomes tumbled, and millions lost their homes, hopes, and dignity. Some protested and took direct action; others looked to the government for relief.

CRASH!

The buoyant prosperity of the New Era, more apparent than real by the summer of 1929, collapsed in October, when the stock market crashed. During the preceding two years, the market had hit record highs, stimulated by optimism, easy credit, and speculators' manipulations. But after peaking in September, it suffered several sharp checks, and on October 29, "Black Tuesday," panicked investors dumped their stocks, wiping out the previous year's gains in one day. Confidence in the economy disappeared, and the slide continued for months, and then years. The market hit bottom in July 1932. Much of the paper wealth of America had evaporated, and the nation sank into the **Great Depression**.

The Wall Street Crash marked the beginning of the depression, but it did not cause it. The depression stemmed from weaknesses in the New Era economy. Most damaging was the unequal distribution of wealth and income. Workers' wages and farmers' incomes had fallen far behind industrial productivity and corporate profits; by 1929, the richest 0.1 percent of American families had as much total income as the bottom 42 percent. With more than half the nation's people living at or below the subsistence level, there was not enough purchasing power to maintain the economy.

A second factor was that oligopolies dominated American industries. By 1929, the 200 largest corporations (out of 400,000) controlled half the corporate wealth. Their power led to "administered prices," prices kept artificially high and rigid rather than determined by supply and demand. Because it did not respond to purchasing power, this system not only helped bring on economic collapse but also dimmed prospects for recovery.

Weaknesses in specific industries had further unbalanced the economy. Agriculture suffered from overproduction, declining prices, and heavy debt; so did the coal and textile industries. These difficulties left the economy dependent on a few industries for expansion and employment, and these industries could not carry the burden. Banking presented other problems. Poorly managed and regulated banks had contributed to the instability of prosperity; they now threatened to spread panic and depression.

CHRONOLOGY

1929   Stock market crashes.

1932   Farmers' Holiday Association organizes rural protests in the Midwest.
Reconstruction Finance Corporation is created to assist financial institutions.
Bonus Army is routed in Washington, DC.
Franklin D. Roosevelt is elected president.

1931   Japan invades Manchuria.

1933   Adolf Hitler comes to power in Germany.
Emergency Banking Act is passed.
The United States recognizes the Soviet Union.
Agricultural Adjustment Administration (AAA) is created to regulate farm production.
National Recovery Administration (NRA) is created to promote industrial cooperation and recovery.
Federal Emergency Relief Act provides federal assistance to the unemployed.
Civilian Conservation Corps (CCC) is established to provide work relief in conservation projects.
Public Works Administration (PWA) is created to provide work relief on large public construction projects.
Civil Works Administration (CWA) provides emergency winter relief jobs.
Tennessee Valley Authority (TVA) is created to coordinate regional development.

1934   Securities and Exchange Commission (SEC) is established.
Indian Reorganization Act reforms Indian policy.
Huey Long organizes the Share-Our-Wealth Society.
Democrats win midterm elections.

1935   Supreme Court declares NRA unconstitutional.
Italy attacks Ethiopia.
National Labor Relations Act (Wagner Act) guarantees workers' rights to organize and bargain collectively.
Social Security Act establishes a federal social insurance system.
Banking Act strengthens the Federal Reserve.
Revenue Act establishes a more progressive tax system.
Resettlement Administration is created to aid dispossessed farmers.
Rural Electrification Administration (REA) is created to help provide electric power to rural areas.
Soil Conservation Service is established.
Emergency Relief Appropriation Act authorizes public relief projects for the unemployed.
Works Progress Administration (WPA) is created.
Huey Long is assassinated.

1936	Supreme Court declares AAA unconstitutional.
	Roosevelt is reelected president.
	Hitler remilitarizes the Rhineland.
	Roosevelt sails to South America as part of Good Neighbor Policy.
	Sit-down strikes begin.
1937	Chicago police kill workers in Memorial Day Massacre.
	FDR tries but fails to expand the Supreme Court.
	Farm Security Administration (FSA) is created to lend money to small farmers to buy and rehabilitate farms.
	National Housing Act is passed to promote public housing projects.
	"Roosevelt Recession" begins.
1938	Congress of Industrial Organizations (CIO) is founded.
	Germany annexes Austria.
	Fair Labor Standards Act establishes minimum wage and maximum hours rules for labor.
	Roosevelt fails to "purge" the Democratic Party.
	Republicans make gains in midterm elections.
	Munich agreement reached, appeasing Hitler's demand for Sudetenland.
	Kristallnacht, violent pogrom against Jews, occurs in Germany.

International economic difficulties spurred the depression as well. Shut out from U.S. markets by high tariffs, Europeans had depended on American investments to manage their debts and reparation payments from the Great War. The stock market crash dried up the flow of American dollars to Europe, causing financial panics and industrial collapse and making the Great Depression global. In turn, European nations curtailed their imports of American goods and defaulted on their debts, further debilitating the U.S. economy. (See Global Connections, The Worldwide Collapse.)

Government policies also bore some responsibility for the crash and depression. Failure to enforce antitrust laws had encouraged oligopolies and high prices; failure to regulate banking and the stock market had permitted financial recklessness and irresponsible speculation. Reducing tax rates on the wealthy had also encouraged speculation and contributed to the maldistribution of income. Opposition to labor unions and collective bargaining helped keep workers' wages and purchasing power low. The absence of an effective agricultural policy and the high tariffs that inhibited foreign trade and reduced markets for agricultural products hurt farmers. In short, the same governmental policies that shaped the booming 1920s economy also led to economic disaster.

State and local fiscal policies also pointed to economic problems for the 1930s. The expansion of public education and road construction led to higher property taxes in communities throughout the nation, and although per capita tax collection at the federal level actually declined between 1920 and 1929, the tax burden in states and cities increased dramatically. Indeed, state and local taxes rose faster than personal incomes in the 1920s. The real estate industry reported a decline as early as 1926, and homeowners steadily protested their higher property taxes.

But the crash did more than expose the weaknesses of the economy. Business lost confidence and refused to make investments that might have brought recovery. Instead, banks called in loans and restricted credit, and depositors tried to withdraw their savings, which were uninsured. The demand for cash caused banks to fail, dragging the economy down further. And the Federal Reserve Board prolonged the depression by restricting the money supply.

THE DEPRESSION SPREADS

By early 1930, the effects of financial contraction were painfully evident. Factories shut down or cut back, and industrial production plummeted. By 1932, one-fourth of the labor force was out of work. Personal income dropped by more than half between 1929 and 1932. Moreover, the depression began to feed on itself in a vicious circle: Shrinking wages and employment cut into purchasing power, causing business to slash production again and lay off workers, thereby further reducing purchasing power.

The depression particularly battered farmers. Commodity prices fell by 55 percent between 1929 and 1932, stifling farm income. Unable to pay their mortgages, many farm families lost their homes and fields. The dispossessed roamed the byways, highways, and railways of a troubled country.

Urban families were also evicted when they could not pay their rent. Some moved in with relatives; others lived in **Hoovervilles**—the name reflects the bitterness directed at the president—shacks where people shivered, suffered, and starved. Oklahoma City's vast Hooverville covered 100 square miles.

Soup kitchens became standard features of the urban landscape, with lines of the hungry stretching for blocks. But charities and local communities could not meet the massive needs, and neither the states nor the federal government had welfare or unemployment compensation programs.

"WOMEN'S JOBS" AND "MEN'S JOBS"

The depression affected wage-earning women in complex ways. Although they suffered 20 percent unemployment by 1932, women were less likely than men to be fired. Gender segregation had concentrated women in low-paid service, sales, and clerical jobs that were less vulnerable than the heavy industries where men predominated. But while traditional attitudes somewhat insulated working women, they also reinforced opposition to female employment, especially that of married women. Three-fourths of the nation's school systems refused to hire married women as teachers, and two-thirds dismissed female teachers who were married. Many private employers, especially banks and insurance companies, also fired married women. Nonetheless, the proportion of married women in the workforce increased in the 1930s as women took jobs to help their families survive, and about one-third of working married women provided the sole support for their families.

FAMILIES IN THE DEPRESSION

"I have watched fear grip the people in our neighborhood around Hull House," wrote Jane Addams as the depression deepened in 1931 and family survival itself seemed threatened. Divorce declined because it was expensive, but desertion increased, and people postponed marriage. Birthrates fell. Husbands and fathers, the traditional

Squalid Hoovervilles sprang up in towns like Centerville, Ohio during the Depression. Many farm families like this one lost their homes and gravitated to towns, which were unable to house this new influx of population.

breadwinners, were often humiliated and despondent when laid off from work. Unemployed men, sociologists reported, "lost much of their sense of time and dawdled helplessly and dully about the streets," dreading to return home.

Women's responsibilities, by contrast, often grew. The number of female-headed households increased sharply. Not only did some women become wage earners, but their traditional role as homemakers also gained new significance. To make ends meet, many women sewed their own clothing and raised and canned vegetables, reversing the trend toward consumerism. Some also took on extra work at home.

The depression also affected children. Some parents sacrificed their own well-being to protect their children. But children felt the tension and fear, and many went without food. In New York City, 139 people, most of them children, died of starvation and malnutrition in 1933. Boys and girls stayed home from school and church because they lacked shoes or clothing; others gave up their plans for college. As hope faded, family conflicts increased. The California Unemployment Commission concluded that the depression had left the American family "morally shattered. There is no security, no foothold, no future."

"LAST HIRED, FIRST FIRED"

The depression particularly harmed racial minorities. With fewer resources and opportunities, they were less able than other groups to absorb the economic pain. African Americans were caught in a double bind, reported a sociologist at Howard University in 1932: They were "the last to be hired and the first to be fired." Black unemployment rates were more than twice the white rate, reflecting increased job competition and persistent racism.

Racism also limited the assistance African Americans received. Religious and charitable organizations often refused to care for black people. Local and state governments set higher relief eligibility requirements for blacks than for whites and provided them with less aid. Out of work for longer periods of time and without even modest relief assistance, African Americans were forced to crowd together in already cramped apartments, while still paying exorbitant rents to white landlords. By 1932, most African Americans were suffering acute privation. "At no time in the history of the Negro since slavery," reported the Urban League, "has his economic and social outlook seemed so discouraging."

Hispanic Americans also suffered. As mostly unskilled workers, they faced increasing competition for decreasing jobs paying declining wages. They were displaced even in the California agricultural labor force, which they had dominated. By the mid-1930s, they made up only a tenth of the state's migratory labor force, which increasingly consisted of white people who had fled the South and the Great Plains. Other jobs were lost when Arizona, California, and Texas barred Mexicans from public works and highway construction jobs. Vigilantes threatened employers who hired Mexicans rather than white Americans.

Economic woes and racism drove nearly half a million Mexican immigrants and their American-born children from the United States. Local authorities in the Southwest, with the blessing of the Department of Labor, urged all Mexicans, regardless of their citizenship status, to return to Mexico and free up jobs and relief assistance for white Americans. To intimidate Mexican residents, the U.S. Immigration Service conducted several raids, rounding up people and demanding immediate proof of citizenship.

PROTEST

Bewildered and discouraged, most Americans reacted to the crisis without protest. Influenced by traditional individualism, many blamed themselves for their plight. But others did act, especially to protect their families. Protests ranged from small desperate gestures like stealing food and coal to more dramatic deeds. In Louisiana, women seized a train to call attention to the needs of their families; in New Jersey, in the "bloodless battle of Pleasantville," 100 women held the city council hostage to demand assistance.

Communists, socialists, and other radicals organized more formal protests. Communists led the jobless into "unemployment councils" that staged hunger marches, demonstrated for relief, and blocked evictions. Socialists built similar organizations, including the People's Unemployment League in Baltimore, which had 12,000 members. Groups of this kind provided protection and assistance. However, local officials often suppressed their protests. In 1932, police fired on the Detroit Unemployment Council as it marched to demand food and jobs, killing four marchers and wounding many more.

Rural protests also broke out. Again, communists organized some of them, as in Alabama, where the Croppers' and Farm Workers' Union mobilized black agricultural laborers in 1931 to demand better treatment. In the Midwest, the Farmers' Holiday Association, organized among family farmers in 1932, stopped the shipment of produce to urban markets, hoping to drive up prices. A guerrilla war broke out as farmers blocked roads and halted freight trains, dumped milk in ditches, and fought bloody battles with deputy sheriffs. Midwestern farmers also tried to prevent foreclosure of their farms. In Iowa, farmers beat sheriffs and mortgage agents and nearly lynched a judge conducting foreclosure proceedings; in Nebraska, a Farmers' Holiday leader warned that if the state did not halt foreclosures, "200,000 of us are coming to Lincoln and we'll tear that new State Capitol Building to pieces."

HERBERT HOOVER AND THE DEPRESSION

The Great Depression challenged the optimism, policies, and philosophy that Herbert Hoover had carried into the White House in 1929. The president took unprecedented steps to resolve the crisis but shrank back from the interventionist policies activists urged. His failures, personal as well as political and economic, led to his repudiation and to a major shift in government policies.

THE FAILURE OF VOLUNTARISM

Hoover fought economic depression more vigorously than any previous president, but he believed that voluntary private relief was preferable to federal intervention. The role of the national government, he thought, was to advise and encourage the voluntary efforts of private organizations, individual industries, or local communities.

Hoover obtained pledges from business leaders to maintain employment and wage levels. But most corporations soon repudiated these pledges, slashed wages, and laid off workers. Hoover himself said, "You know, the only trouble with capitalism is capitalists; they're too damn greedy." Still, he rejected government action.

Hoover also depended on voluntary efforts to relieve the misery caused by massive unemployment. He created the President's Organization for Unemployment Relief to help raise private funds for voluntary relief agencies. Charities and local authorities, he believed, should help the unemployed; direct federal relief would expand government power and undermine the recipients' character. He vetoed congressional attempts to aid the unemployed.

The depression rendered Hoover's beliefs meaningless. Private programs to aid the unemployed scarcely existed. Only a few unions, such as the Amalgamated Clothing Workers, had unemployment funds, and these were soon spent. Company plans for unemployment compensation covered less than 1 percent of workers, revealing the charade of the welfare capitalism of the 1920s. Private charitable groups like the Salvation Army, church associations, and ethnic societies quickly exhausted their resources.

Nor could local governments cope, and their efforts declined as the depression deepened. By 1932, more than 100 cities made no relief appropriations at all, and the commissioner of charity in Salt Lake City reported that people were sliding toward starvation. Only eight state governments provided even token assistance.

As the depression worsened, Hoover adopted more activist policies. He persuaded Congress to cut taxes to boost consumers' buying power, and he increased the public works budget. The Federal Farm Board lent money to cooperatives and spent millions trying to stabilize crop prices. Unable to control production, however, the board conceded failure by late 1931. More successful was the Reconstruction Finance Corporation (RFC).

Established in January 1932, the RFC lent federal funds to banks, insurance companies, and railroads so that their recovery could "trickle down" to ordinary Americans. Hoover still opposed direct aid to the general public, although he finally allowed the RFC to lend small amounts to state and local governments for unemployment relief.

Far more action was necessary, but Hoover remained committed to voluntarism and a balanced budget. Hoover's ideological limitations infuriated Americans who saw him as indifferent to their suffering and a reactionary protector of privileged business interests—an image his political opponents encouraged.

REPUDIATING HOOVER: THE 1932 ELECTION

Hoover's treatment of the **Bonus Army** symbolized his unpopularity and set the stage for the 1932 election. In 1932, unemployed veterans of World War I gathered in Washington, demanding payment of service bonuses not due until 1945. Hoover refused to meet with them, and Congress rejected their plan. But 10,000 veterans erected a shantytown at the edge of Washington and camped in vacant public buildings. Hoover decided to evict the veterans, but General Douglas MacArthur exceeded his cautious orders and on July 28 led cavalry, infantry, and tanks against the ragged Bonus Marchers. The troops cleared the buildings and assaulted the shantytown, dispersing the veterans and their families and setting their camp on fire.

This assault provoked widespread outrage. The administration tried to brand the Bonus Marchers as communists and criminals, but subsequent investigations refuted such claims. The incident confirmed Hoover's public image as harsh and insensitive.

In the summer of 1932, with no prospects for victory, Republicans renominated Hoover. Confident Democrats selected Governor Franklin D. Roosevelt of New York, who promised "a new deal for the American people."

The 1932 campaign gave scant indication of what Roosevelt's **New Deal** might involve. The Democratic platform differed little from that of the Republicans, and Roosevelt spoke in vague or general terms. Still, observers found clues in Roosevelt's record as governor of New York, where he had created the first state system of unem-

Bonus Marchers battling police in Washington, DC, in 1932. Police and military assaults on these homeless veterans infuriated Americans and prompted Democratic presidential nominee Franklin D. Roosevelt to declare, "Well, this will elect me."

ployment relief and supported social welfare and conservation. More important was his outgoing personality, which radiated warmth and hope in contrast to Hoover's gloom.

FDR carried every state south and west of Pennsylvania. Yet Hoover would remain president for four more months, as the Constitution then required. And in those four months, the depression worsened, spreading misery throughout America. The final blow came in February 1933, when panic struck the banking system. Nearly 6,000 banks had already failed, robbing 9 million depositors of their savings. Desperate Americans rushed to withdraw their funds from the remaining banks, pushing them to the brink. With the federal government under Hoover immobilized, state governments shut the banks to prevent their failure. By March, an eerie silence had descended on the nation. Hoover concluded, "We are at the end of our string."

LAUNCHING THE NEW DEAL

In the midst of this national anxiety, Franklin D. Roosevelt pushed forward an unprecedented program to resolve the crises of a collapsing financial system, crippling unemployment, and agricultural and industrial breakdown and to promote reform. The early New Deal achieved successes and attracted support, but it also had limitations and generated criticism that suggested the need for still greater innovations.

ACTION NOW!

On March 4, 1933, Franklin Delano Roosevelt became president and immediately reassured the American people. He insisted that "the only thing we have to fear is fear itself" and he promised "action, and action now!" Summoning Congress, Roosevelt pressed forward on a broad front. In the first three months of his administration, the famous Hundred Days of the New Deal, the Democratic Congress passed many important laws (see Overview, Major Laws of the Hundred Days).

Roosevelt's program reflected a mix of ideas, some from FDR himself, some from a diverse group of advisers, including academic experts dubbed the "brain trust," politicians, and social workers. It also incorporated principles from the progressive movement, precedents from the Great War mobilization, and even plans from the Hoover administration. Above all, the New Deal was a practical response to the depression. FDR had set its tone in his campaign when he declared, "The country needs, and, unless I mistake its temper, the country demands bold, persistent experimentation. . . . Above all, try something."

FDR first addressed the banking crisis. On March 5, he proclaimed a national bank holiday, closing all remaining banks. Congress then passed his Emergency Banking Act, a conservative measure that extended government assistance to sound banks and reorganized weak ones. Prompt government action, coupled with a reassuring **fireside chat** over the radio by the president, restored popular confidence in the banks. When they reopened on March 13, deposits exceeded withdrawals. In June, Congress created the **Federal Deposit Insurance Corporation (FDIC)** to guarantee bank deposits up to $2,500.

The financial industry was also reformed. The Glass-Steagall Act separated investment and commercial banking to curtail risky speculation. The Securities Act reformed the sale of stocks to prevent the insider abuses that had characterized Wall Street, and in 1934 the

OVERVIEW MAJOR LAWS OF THE HUNDRED DAYS

Law	Objective
Emergency Banking Act	Stabilized the private banking system
Agricultural Adjustment Act	Established a farm recovery program based on production controls and price supports
Emergency Farm Mortgage Act	Provided for the refinancing of farm mortgages
National Industrial Recovery Act	Established a national recovery program and authorized a public works program
Federal Emergency Relief Act	Established a national system of relief
Home Owners Loan Act	Protected homeowners from mortgage foreclosure by refinancing home loans
Glass-Steagall Act	Separated commercial and investment banking and guaranteed bank deposits
Tennessee Valley Authority Act	Established the TVA and provided for the planned development of the Tennessee River Valley
Civilian Conservation Corps Act	Established the CCC to provide work relief on reforestation and conservation projects
Farm Credit Act	Expanded agricultural credits and established the Farm Credit Administration
Securities Act	Required full disclosure from stock exchanges
Wagner-Peyser Act	Created a U.S. Employment Service and encouraged states to create local public employment offices

Securities and Exchange Commission (SEC) was created to regulate the stock market. Two other financial measures in 1933 created the Home Owners Loan Corporation and the Farm Credit Administration, which enabled millions to refinance their mortgages.

CREATING JOBS

Roosevelt also provided relief for the unemployed. The Federal Emergency Relief Administration (FERA) furnished funds to state and local agencies. Harry Hopkins, who had headed Roosevelt's relief program in New York, became its director and one of the New Deal's most important members. FERA spent over $3 billion before it ended in 1935, and by then Hopkins and FDR had developed new programs that provided work rather than just cash. Work relief, they believed, preserved both the skills and the morale of recipients. In the winter of 1933–1934, Hopkins spent nearly $1 billion to create jobs for 4 million men and women through the Civil Works Administration (CWA). The CWA hired laborers to build roads and airports, teachers to staff rural schools, and singers and artists to give public performances. The Public Works Administration (PWA) provided work relief on useful projects to stimulate the economy through public expenditures. Directed by Harold Ickes, the PWA spent billions from 1933 to 1939 to build schools, hospitals, courthouses, dams, and bridges.

One of FDR's personal ideas, the Civilian Conservation Corps (CCC), combined work relief with conservation. Launched in 1933, the CCC employed 2.5 million young men to work on reforestation and flood-control projects, build roads and bridges in national forests and parks, restore Civil War battlefields, and fight forest fires.

HELPING SOME FARMERS

Besides providing relief, the New Deal promoted economic recovery. In May 1933, Congress established the Agricultural Adjustment Administration (AAA) to combat the depression in agriculture caused by crop surpluses and low prices. The AAA subsidized farmers who agreed to restrict production. The objective was to boost farm prices to parity, a level that would restore farmers' purchasing power to what it had been in 1914.

Agricultural conditions improved. Farm prices rose from 52 percent of parity in 1932 to 88 percent in 1935, and gross farm income rose by 50 percent. Not until 1941, however, would income exceed the level of 1929, a poor year for farmers. Moreover, some of the decreased production and increased prices stemmed from devastating droughts and dust storms on the Great Plains. The AAA itself harmed poor farmers while aiding larger commercial growers. As southern planters restricted their acreage, they dismissed tenants and sharecroppers, and with AAA payments, they bought new farm machinery, reducing their need for farm labor.

A coal miner greeting Franklin D. Roosevelt in West Virginia in 1932. Roosevelt's promise of a New Deal revived hope among millions of Americans trapped in hard times.

AMERICAN VIEWS

THE COMMISSIONER OF THE BUREAU OF INDIAN AFFAIRS ON THE NEW DEAL FOR NATIVE AMERICANS

*J*ohn Collier, reformer and social worker, served as commissioner of the Bureau of Indian Affairs (BIA) from 1933 until 1945. During his tenure, he radically transformed the agency—long known to be corrupt and hostile to Native Americans—into an organization committed to the preservation of tribal cultures and the restoration of Indian lands. Like other New Dealers, Collier attempted to use the power of the federal government to protect those with limited political power and economic influence—in this case Native Americans.

Collier was extraordinarily successful in promoting the restoration of tribal rights and autonomy and helped ensure that future generations of Indians could reclaim their lands. Yet he was frustrated by Congress's unwillingness to fund the programs he believed necessary for a genuine New Deal for Native Americans. In his 1938 annual report, he calls for greater economic support, arguing that it would be a good investment for the nation. Most important, even as he acknowledges that real changes have occurred since 1933, he points out that there is still much to be done to achieve political autonomy and economic self-sufficiency for American Indians.

- How did Collier describe the treatment of Native Americans, and why did white Americans regard Indians as a "problem" to be eliminated?
- What were the new goals of the Bureau of Indian Affairs?
- How did Collier regard the role of land in Native American society? Why?
- What was the greatest challenge Collier saw for Native Americans in 1938?

For nearly 300 years white Americans, in our zeal to carve out a nation made to order, have dealt with the Indians on the erroneous, yet tragic, assumption that the Indians were a dying race—to be liquidated. We took away their best lands;

THE FLIGHT OF THE BLUE EAGLE

The New Deal attempted to revive U.S. industry with the National Industrial Recovery Act (NIRA), which created the National Recovery Administration (NRA). The NRA sought to halt the slide in prices, wages, and employment by suspending antitrust laws and authorizing industrial and trade associations to draft codes setting production quotas, price policies, wages and working conditions, and other business practices. The codes promoted the interests of business generally and big business in particular, but Section 7a of the NIRA guaranteed workers the rights to organize unions and bargain collectively—a provision that John L. Lewis of the United Mine Workers called an Emancipation Proclamation for labor.

Hugh Johnson became director of the NRA. He persuaded business leaders to cooperate in drafting codes and the public to patronize participating companies. The NRA Blue Eagle insignia and its slogan "We Do Our Part" covered workplaces, storefronts, and billboards. Blue Eagle parades marched down the nation's main streets and climaxed in a massive demonstration in New York City.

broke treaties, promises; tossed them the most nearly worthless scraps of a continent that had once been wholly theirs. But we did not liquidate their spirit. The vital spark which kept them alive was hardy. So hardy, indeed, that we now face an astounding and heartening fact.

Actually, the Indians, on the evidence of federal census rolls of the past eight years, are increasing almost twice the rate of the population as a whole.

With this fact before us, our whole attitude toward the Indians has necessarily undergone a profound change. Dead is the centuries-old notion that the sooner we eliminate this doomed race, preferably humanely, the better. . . . No longer can we naively talk of or think of the "Indian problem."

We, therefore, define our Indian policy somewhat as follows: So productively to use the moneys appropriated by the Congress for Indians as to enable them, on good, adequate land of their own, to earn decent livelihoods and lead self-respecting, organized lives in harmony with their own aims and ideals, as an integral part of American life. This will not happen tomorrow; perhaps not in our lifetime; but with the revitalization of Indian hope due to the actions and attitudes of this government during the last few years, that aim is a probability, and a real one. . . . So intimately is all of Indian life tied up with the land and its utilization that to think of Indians is to think of land. The two are inseparable. Upon the land and its intelligent use depends the main future of the American Indian.

The Indian feels toward his land, not a mere ownership but a devotion and veneration befitting that what is not only a home but a refuge. . . . Not only does the Indian's major source of livelihood derive from the land but his social and political organizations are rooted in soil.

Since 1933, the Indian Service has made a concerted effort—an effort which is as yet but a mere beginning—to help the Indian to build back his landholdings to a point where they will provide an adequate basis for a self-sustaining economy, a self-satisfying social organization.

SOURCE: John Collier. Annual Report of the Secretary of the Interior for the Fiscal Year Ended June 30, 1938. From http://historymatters.gmu.edu/.

Support for the NRA waned, however. Corporate leaders used it to advance their own goals and to discriminate against small producers, consumers, and labor. Businesses also violated the labor rights specified in Section 7a. Defiant employers viewed collective bargaining as infringing their authority. Employers even used violence to smother unions. The NRA did little to enforce Section 7a, and Johnson, strongly pro-business, denounced all strikes. Workers felt betrayed. Roosevelt tried to reorganize the NRA, but the act remained controversial until the Supreme Court declared it unconstitutional in 1935.

CRITICS RIGHT AND LEFT

The early New Deal did not end the depression. Recovery was fitful and uneven; millions of Americans remained unemployed. Nevertheless, the New Deal's efforts to grapple with problems, its successes in reducing suffering and fear, and Roosevelt's own skills carried the Democratic Party to victory in the 1934 elections. But New Deal policies also

New Deal agricultural programs stabilized the farm economy, but not all farmers benefited. Landowners who received AAA payments evicted these black sharecroppers huddled in a makeshift roadside camp in Missouri in 1935.

provoked criticism, from both those convinced that too little had been achieved and those alarmed that too much had been attempted.

Despite the early New Deal's pro-business character, conservatives complained that the expansion of government activity and its regulatory role weakened the autonomy of American business. They also condemned the efforts to aid nonbusiness groups as socialistic, particularly the "excessive" spending on unemployment relief and the "instigation" of labor organizing. These critics attracted little popular support, however, and their selfishness antagonized Roosevelt.

More realistic criticism came from the left. In 1932, FDR had campaigned for "the forgotten man at the bottom of the economic pyramid," and some radicals argued that the early New Deal had forgotten the forgotten man. Communists and socialists focused public attention on the poor, especially in the countryside. In California, communists organized Mexican, Filipino, and Japanese farm workers into the Cannery and Agricultural Workers Union; in Arkansas and Tennessee, socialists in 1934 helped organize sharecroppers into the Southern Tenant Farmers Union, protesting the "Raw Deal" they had received from the AAA. Even without the involvement of socialists or communists, labor militancy in 1934 pressed Roosevelt. The number of workers participating in strikes leaped from 325,000 in 1932 (about the annual average since 1925) to 1.5 million in 1934.

Rebuffing FDR's pleas for fair treatment, employers moved to crush the strikes, often using complaisant police and private strikebreakers. In Minneapolis, police shot 67 teamsters, almost all in the back, as they fled an ambush arranged by employers; in Toledo, company police and National Guardsmen attacked autoworkers with tear gas, bayonets, and rifle fire; in the textile strike, police killed six picketers in South Carolina, and soldiers wounded another 50 in Rhode Island. Against such powerful opponents, workers needed help to achieve their rights. Harry Hopkins and other New Dealers realized that labor's demands could not be ignored.

Four prominent individuals mobilized popular discontent to demand government action to assist groups neglected by the New Deal. Representative William Lemke of North Dakota, an agrarian radical leader of the Nonpartisan League, called attention to rural distress. Lemke objected to the New Deal's limited response to farmers crushed by the depression. In his own state, nearly two-thirds of the farmers had lost their land through foreclosures.

Francis Townsend, a California physician, proposed to aid the nation's elderly, many of whom were destitute. The Townsend Plan called for a government pension to every American over the age of 60, provided that the recipient retired from work and spent the entire pension. This scheme promised to extend relief to the elderly, open jobs for the unemployed, and stimulate economic recovery. Over 5,000 Townsend Clubs lobbied for government action to help the elderly poor.

Father Charles Coughlin, a Catholic priest in the Detroit suburb of Royal Oak, threatened to mobilize another large constituency against the limitations of the early New Deal. Thirty million Americans listened eagerly to his weekly radio broadcasts, which mixed religion with anti-Semitism and demands for social justice and financial reform. Coughlin had condemned Hoover for assisting banks but ignoring the unemployed, and initially he welcomed the New Deal as "Christ's Deal." But after concluding that FDR's policies favored "the virile viciousness of business and finance," Coughlin organized the National Union for Social Justice to lobby for his goals. With support among lower-middle-class, heavily Catholic, urban ethnic groups, Coughlin posed a real challenge to Roosevelt's Democratic Party.

Roosevelt found Senator Huey P. Long of Louisiana still more worrisome. Alternately charming and autocratic, Long had modernized his state with taxation and educational reforms and an extensive public-works program after his election as governor in 1928. Moving to the Senate and eyeing the White House, Long proposed more comprehensive social-welfare policies than the New Deal had envisaged. In 1934, he organized the Share-Our-Wealth Society. His plan to end poverty and unemployment called for confiscatory taxes on the rich to provide every family with a decent income, health coverage, education, and old-age pensions. Long's appeal was enormous. Within months, his organization claimed more than 27,000 clubs and 7 million members.

These dissident movements raised complex issues and simple fears. They built on concerns about the New Deal, both demanding government assistance and fretting about government intrusion. Their programs were often ill-defined or impractical—Townsend's plan would cost more than half the national income; and some of the leaders, like Coughlin and Long, approached demagoguery. Nevertheless, their popularity warned Roosevelt that government action was needed to satisfy reform demands and ensure his reelection in 1936.

The New Deal enabled photographers and artists to take to the road to capture images of the nation's dispossessed. This photograph by Dorothea Lange of an 18-year-old mother and her child in a migrant labor camp in 1937 illustrates both despair and detachment and conveys the hardship of homelessness and deprivation in the Great Depression.

CONSOLIDATING THE NEW DEAL

Responding to the persistence of the depression and political pressures, Roosevelt in 1935 undertook economic and social reforms that some observers have called the Second New Deal. The new measures shifted government action more toward reform even as they still addressed relief and recovery. Nor did FDR's interest in reform simply reflect cynical politics. He had frequently championed progressive measures in the past, and many of his advisers had deep roots in reform movements. After the 1934 elections gave the president an even more Democratic Congress, Harry Hopkins exulted: "Boys—this is our hour. We've got to get everything we want—a works program, social security, wages and hours, everything—now or never."

WEEDING OUT AND LIFTING UP

"In spite of our efforts and in spite of our talk," Roosevelt told the new Congress in 1935, "we have not weeded out the overprivileged and we have not effectively lifted up the underprivileged." To do so, he developed "must" legislation. One of the new laws protected labor's rights to organize and bargain collectively. The Wagner National Labor Relations Act, dubbed "Labor's Magna Carta," guaranteed workers the right to organize unions and prohibited employers from adopting unfair labor practices, such

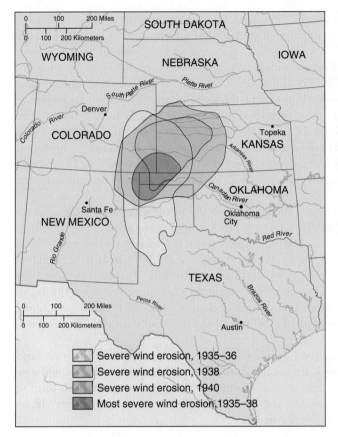

MAP 25–1 • The Dust Bowl
Years of overcultivation, drought, and high winds created the Dust Bowl, which most severely affected the southern Great Plains. Federal relief and conservation programs provided assistance, but many residents fled the area, often migrating to California.

▶ *Why were farmers on the Great Plains particularly vulnerable to environmental disaster?*

as firing union activists and forming company unions. The law also set up the National Labor Relations Board (NLRB) to enforce these provisions, protect workers from coercion, and supervise union elections.

Social Security. Of greater long-range importance was the Social Security Act. Other industrial nations had established national social-insurance systems much earlier, but only the Great Depression moved the United States to accept the idea that the federal government should protect the poor and unemployed. Even so, the law was a compromise, framed by a nonpartisan committee of business, labor, and public representatives and then weakened by congressional conservatives. It provided unemployment compensation, old-age pensions, and aid for dependent mothers and children and the blind.

The conservative nature of the law appeared in its stingy benefit payments, its lack of health insurance, and its exclusion of more than one-fourth of all workers, including many in desperate need of protection, such as farm laborers and domestic servants. Moreover, unlike in other nations, the old-age pensions were financed through a regressive payroll tax on both employees and employers rather than through general tax revenues. Thus the new system was more like a compulsory insurance program.

Despite its weaknesses, the Social Security Act was one of the most important laws in American history and Roosevelt was justifiably proud. It provided, he pointed out, "at least some measure of protection to the average citizen and to his family against the loss of a job and against poverty-ridden old age." Moreover, by establishing federal responsibility for social welfare, it inaugurated a welfare system that subsequent generations would expand.

Money, Tax, and Land Reform. Another reform measure, the Banking Act of 1935, increased the authority of the Federal Reserve Board over the nation's currency and credit system and decreased the power of the private bankers whose irresponsible behavior had contributed to the depression and the appeal of Father Coughlin. The Revenue Act of 1935 provided for graduated income taxes and increased estate and corporate taxes. Opponents called it Soak the Rich Tax, but with its many loopholes, it was scarcely that and was certainly not a redistributive measure such as Huey Long had proposed. Nevertheless, it set a precedent for progressive taxation and attracted popular support.

The Second New Deal also responded belatedly to the environmental catastrophe that had turned much of the Great Plains from Texas to the Dakotas into a Dust Bowl (see Map 25–1). Since World War I, farmers had stripped marginal land of its native grasses to plant wheat. When drought and high winds hit the plains in 1932, crops failed, and nothing was left to hold the soil. Dust storms blew away millions of tons of topsoil, despoiling the land and darkening the sky a thousand miles away. Families abandoned their farms in droves. Many of these poor "Okies" headed for California, their plight captured in John Steinbeck's novel, *The Grapes of Wrath* (1939).

In 1935, Roosevelt established the Resettlement Administration to focus on land reform and help poor farmers. Under Rexford Tugwell, this agency initiated soil erosion projects and attempted to resettle impoverished farmers on better land, but the problem exceeded its resources. Congress moved to save the land, if not its people, by creating the Soil Conservation Service in 1935.

EXPANDING RELIEF

If reform gained priority in the Second New Deal, relief remained critical. With millions still unemployed, Roosevelt pushed through Congress in 1935 the Emergency Relief Appropriation Act, authorizing $5 billion—at the time the largest single appropriation in American history—for emergency public employment. Roosevelt created the Works Progress Administration (WPA) under Hopkins, who set up work relief programs to assist the unemployed and boost the economy. Before its end in 1943, the WPA gave jobs to 9 million people (more than a fifth of the labor force) and spent nearly $12 billion. Three-fourths of its expenditures went on construction projects that could employ manual labor: The WPA built 125,000 schools, post offices, and hospitals; 8,000 parks; nearly 100,000 bridges; and enough roads and sewer systems to circle the earth 30 times. The WPA laid much of the basic infrastructure on which the nation still relies.

The WPA also developed work projects for unemployed writers, artists, musicians, and actors. "Why not?" said FDR. "They are human beings. They have to live." WPA programs allowed people to use their talents while surviving the depression, increased popular access to cultural performances, and established a precedent for federal support of the arts.

The National Youth Administration (NYA), another WPA agency, gave part-time jobs to students, enabling 2 million high school and college students to stay in school, learn skills, and do productive work. At the University of Nebraska, NYA students built an observatory; at Duke University, law student Richard M. Nixon earned 35 cents an hour doing research in the library. Lyndon Johnson, a Texas NYA official, believed that "if the Roosevelt administration had never done another thing, it would have been justified by the work of this great institution for salvaging youth."

THE ROOSEVELT COALITION AND THE ELECTION OF 1936

The 1936 election gave Americans an opportunity to judge FDR and the New Deal. Conservatives alarmed at the expansion of government, businesspeople angered by regulation and labor legislation, and wealthy Americans furious with tax reform decried the New Deal. But they were a minority. Even the presidential candidate they supported, Republican Governor Alf Landon of Kansas, endorsed much of the New Deal, criticizing merely the inefficiency and cost of some of its programs.

The programs and politicians of the New Deal had created an invincible coalition behind Roosevelt. Despite ambivalence about large-scale government intervention, the New Deal's agricultural programs reinforced the traditional Democratic allegiance of white southerners while attracting many western farmers. Labor legislation clinched the active support of the nation's workers. Middle-class voters, whose homes had been saved and whose hopes had been raised, also joined the Roosevelt coalition.

So did urban ethnic groups, who had benefited from welfare programs and appreciated the unprecedented recognition Roosevelt's administration gave them. African Americans voted overwhelmingly Democratic for the first time. Women, too, were an important part of the Roosevelt coalition, and Eleanor Roosevelt often attracted their support as much as Franklin did.

This political realignment produced a landslide. Roosevelt polled 61 percent of the popular vote and the largest electoral vote margin ever recorded, 523 to 8. Democrats also won huge majorities in Congress. Roosevelt's political coalition reflected a mandate for himself and the New Deal; it would enable the Democrats to dominate national elections for three decades.

THE NEW DEAL AND AMERICAN LIFE

The landslide of 1936 revealed the impact of the New Deal on Americans. Industrial workers mobilized to secure their rights, women and minorities gained increased, if still limited, opportunities to participate in American society, and southerners and westerners benefited from government programs they turned to their own advantage. Government programs changed daily life, and ordinary people often helped shape the new policies.

LABOR ON THE MARCH

The labor revival in the 1930s reflected both workers' determination and government support. Workers wanted to improve their wages and benefits as well as to gain union recognition and union contracts that would allow them to limit arbitrary managerial authority and achieve some control over the workplace. This larger goal provoked opposition from employers and their allies and required workers to organize, strike, and become politically active. Their achievement was remarkable.

The Second New Deal helped. By guaranteeing labor's rights to organize and bargain collectively, the Wagner Act sparked a wave of labor activism. But if the government ultimately protected union rights, the unions themselves had to form locals, recruit members, and demonstrate influence in the workplace.

At first, those tasks overwhelmed the American Federation of Labor (AFL). Its reliance on craft-based unions and reluctance to organize immigrant, black, and women workers left it unprepared for the rush of industrial workers seeking unionization. More progressive labor leaders saw that industry-wide unions were more appropriate for unskilled workers in mass-production industries. Forming the Committee for Industrial Organization (CIO) within the AFL, they campaigned to unionize workers in the steel, auto, and rubber industries, all notoriously hostile to unions. AFL leaders insisted that the CIO disband and then in 1937 expelled its unions. The militants reorganized as the separate **Congress of Industrial Organizations**. (In 1955, the two groups merged as the AFL-CIO.)

The split roused the AFL to increase its own organizing activities, but it was primarily the new CIO that put labor on the march. It inspired workers previously neglected by organized labor. The CIO's interracial union campaign in the Birmingham steel mills, said one organizer, was "like a second coming of Christ" for black workers, who welcomed the union as a chance for social recognition as well as economic opportunity. The CIO also employed new and aggressive tactics, particularly the sit-down strike, in which workers, rather than picketing outside the factory, simply sat inside the plant, thereby blocking both production and the use of strikebreakers.

The CIO won major victories despite bitter opposition from industry and its allies. The issue was not wages but labor's right to organize and bargain with management. Sit-down strikes paralyzed General Motors in 1937 after it refused to recognize the United Auto Workers. GM tried to force the strikers out of its Flint, Michigan, plants by turning off the heat, using police and tear gas, threatening strikers' families, and obtaining court orders to clear the plant by military force. But the governor refused to order National Guardsmen to attack, and the strikers held out, aided by the Women's Emergency Brigade, working-class women who picketed the building, heckled the police, and smuggled food to the strikers. After six weeks, GM signed a contract with the UAW. Chrysler soon followed suit. Ford refused to recognize the union until 1941, often violently disrupting organizing efforts.

Steel companies also used violence against unionization. In the Memorial Day Massacre in Chicago in 1937, police guarding a plant of the Republic Steel Company fired on strikers and their families, killing ten people as they tried to flee. A Senate investigation found that Republic and other companies had hired private police to attack workers seeking to unionize, stockpiled weapons and tear gas, and corrupted officials. Federal court orders finally forced the companies to bargain collectively.

New Deal labor legislation, government investigations and court orders, and the federal refusal to use force against strikes helped the labor movement secure basic rights for American workers. Union membership leaped from under 3 million in 1932 to 9 million by 1939, and workers won higher wages, better working conditions, and more economic democracy.

With an appointment in the National Youth Administration, the educator Mary McLeod Bethune was the highest-ranking African American woman in the Roosevelt administration. She advised FDR on all racial matters and envisioned "dozens of Negro women coming after me, filling positions of trust and strategic importance."

WOMEN AND THE NEW DEAL

New Deal relief programs had a mixed impact on working women. Formal government policy required equal consideration for women and men, but local officials flouted this requirement. Women on relief were restricted to women's work—more than half worked on sewing projects, regardless of their skills—and were paid scarcely half what men received. WPA training programs also reinforced traditional ideas about women's work; black women, for example, were trained to be maids, dishwashers, and cooks. Although women constituted nearly one-fourth of the labor force, they obtained only 19 percent of the jobs created by the WPA, 12 percent of those created by the FERA, and 7 percent of those created by the CWA. The CCC excluded women altogether. Still, relief agencies provided crucial assistance to women during the depression.

Other New Deal programs also had mixed benefits for women. Many NRA codes mandated lower wage scales for women than for men, which officials justified as reflecting long-established customs. But by raising minimum wages, the NRA brought relatively greater improvement to women, who were concentrated in the lowest paid occupations, than to male workers. The Social Security Act did not cover domestic servants, waitresses, or women who worked in the home, but it did help mothers with dependent children.

Still more significant, the Social Security Act reflected and reinforced prevailing notions about proper roles for men and women. The system was based on the idea that men should be wage earners and women should stay at home as wives and mothers.

Accordingly, if a woman worked outside the home and her husband was eligible for benefits, she would not receive her own retirement pension. And if a woman had no husband but had children, welfare authorities would remove her from work-relief jobs regardless of whether she wanted to continue to work, and would give her assistance from the Aid to Dependent Children (ADC) program, which was also created under the Social Security Act. These new programs, then, while providing much-needed assistance, also institutionalized a modern welfare system that segregated men and women in separate spheres and reaffirmed the then popular belief that the success of the family depended on that separation.

Women also gained political influence under the New Deal. Molly Dewson, the director of the Women's Division of the Democratic Party, exercised considerable political power and helped to shape the party's campaigns. Around Dewson revolved a network of women, linked by friendships and experiences in the National Consumers' League, Women's Trade Union League, and other progressive reform organizations. Appointed to many positions in the Roosevelt administration, they helped develop and implement New Deal social legislation. Secretary of Labor Frances Perkins was the first woman cabinet member and a key member of the network; other women were in the Treasury Department, the Children's Bureau, and relief and cultural programs.

Eleanor Roosevelt was their leader. Described by a Washington reporter as "a cabinet member without portfolio," she roared across the social and political landscape of the 1930s, pushing for women's rights, demanding reforms, traveling across the country, writing newspaper columns and speaking on the radio, developing plans to help unemployed miners in West Virginia and abolish slums in Washington, and lobbying both Congress and her husband. FDR used her as his eyes and ears and sometimes his conscience. Indeed, Eleanor Roosevelt had become not merely the most prominent first lady in history but a force in her own right and a symbol of the growing importance of women in public life.

MINORITIES AND THE NEW DEAL

Despite the move of African Americans into the Democratic Party, the New Deal's record on racial issues was limited. Although Roosevelt deplored racial abuses, he never pushed for civil rights legislation, fearing to antagonize southern congressional Democrats whose support he needed. For similar reasons, many New Deal programs discriminated against African Americans. And racist officials discriminated in allocating federal relief. Atlanta, for instance, provided average monthly relief checks of $32.66 to white people but only $19.29 to black people.

Nonetheless, disproportionately poor and unemployed African Americans did benefit from the New Deal's welfare and economic programs. W. E. B. Du Bois asserted that "large numbers of colored people in the United States would have starved to death if it had not been for the Roosevelt policies," adding that the New Deal served to sharpen their sense of the value of citizenship by making clear the "direct connection between politics and industry, between government and work, [and] between voting and wages." And key New Dealers campaigned against racial discrimination. Eleanor Roosevelt prodded FDR to appoint black officials, wrote articles supporting racial equality, and flouted segregationist laws. Attacked by white racists, she was popular in the black community. Harry Hopkins and Harold Ickes also promoted equal rights. As black votes in northern cities became important, pragmatic New Dealers also began to pay attention to black needs.

African Americans themselves pressed for reforms. Civil rights groups protested discriminatory policies, including the unequal wage scales in the NRA codes and the CCC's limited enrollment of black youth. African Americans demonstrated against racial discrimination in hiring and their exclusion from federally financed construction projects.

In response, FDR took more interest in black economic and social problems. He prohibited discrimination in the WPA in 1935, and the NYA adopted enlightened racial policies. Roosevelt also appointed black people to important positions, including the first black federal judge. Many of these officials began meeting regularly at the home of Mary McLeod Bethune of the National Council of Negro Women. Dubbed the Black Cabinet, they worked with civil rights organizations, fought discrimination in government, influenced patronage, and stimulated black interest in politics.

The New Deal improved economic and social conditions for many African Americans. Black illiteracy dropped because of federal education projects, and the number of black college students and graduates more than doubled, in part because the NYA provided student aid to black colleges. New Deal relief and public health programs reduced black infant mortality rates and raised life expectancy rates. Conditions for black people continued to lag behind those for white people, and discrimination persisted, but the black switch to the Roosevelt coalition reflected the New Deal's benefits.

Native Americans also benefited from the New Deal. The depression had imposed further misery on a group already suffering from poverty, wretched health conditions, and the nation's lowest educational level. Many New Deal programs had limited applicability to Indians, but the CCC appealed to their interests and skills. More than 80,000 Native Americans received training in agriculture, forestry, and animal husbandry, along with basic academic subjects. CCC projects, together with those undertaken by the PWA and the WPA, built schools, hospitals, roads, and irrigation systems on reservations.

New Deal officials also refocused government Indian policy, which had undermined tribal authority and promoted assimilation by reducing Indian landholding and attacking Indian culture. Appointed commissioner of Indian affairs in 1933, John Collier prohibited interference with Native American religious or cultural life, directed the Bureau of Indian Affairs to employ more Native Americans, and prevented Indian schools from suppressing native languages and traditions.

Collier also persuaded Congress to pass the Indian Reorganization Act of 1934, often called the Indians' New Deal. The act guaranteed religious freedom, reestablished tribal self-government, and halted the sale of tribal lands. It also provided funds to expand Indian landholdings, support Indian students, and establish tribal businesses. But social and economic problems persisted on the isolated reservations, and white missionaries and business interests attacked Collier's reforms as atheistic and communistic. And not all Native Americans supported Collier's reforms, asserting that he, too, stereotyped Indians and their culture, and labeling his efforts as "back-to-the-blanket" policies designed to make Native American cultures historical commodities. (See American Views, The Commissioner of the Bureau of Indian Affairs on the New Deal for Native Americans.)

Hispanic Americans received less assistance from the New Deal. Relief programs aided many Hispanics in California and the Southwest but ignored those who were not citizens. Moreover, local administrators often discriminated against Hispanics, especially by providing higher relief payments to Anglos. Finally, by excluding agricultural workers, neither the Social Security Act nor the Wagner Act gave Mexican Americans much protection or hope. Farm workers remained largely unorganized, exploited, and at the mercy of agribusinesses.

THE NEW DEAL: NORTH, SOUTH, EAST, AND WEST

"We are going to make a country," President Roosevelt declared, "in which no one is left out." And with that statement, along with his belief that the federal government must take the lead in building a new "economic constitutional order," FDR ensured that his New Deal programs and policies fanned out throughout the nation.

The New Deal in the South. The New Deal's agricultural program boosted farm prices and income more in the South than any other region. By controlling cotton production, it also promoted diversification; its subsidies financed mechanization. The resulting modernization helped replace an archaic sharecropping system with an emergent agribusiness. The rural poor were displaced, but the South's agricultural economy advanced.

The New Deal also improved southern cities. FERA and WPA built urban sewer systems, airports, bridges, roads, and harbor facilities. Whereas northern cities had already constructed such facilities themselves—and were still paying off the debts these had incurred—the federal government largely paid for such modernization in the South, giving its cities an economic advantage.

Federal grants were supposed to be awarded to states in proportion to their own expenditures, but while southern politicians welcomed New Deal funds, they refused to contribute their share of the costs. Nationally, the federal proportion of FERA expenditures was 62 percent; in the South, it was usually 90 percent and never lower than 73 percent.

Federal money enabled southern communities to balance their budgets, preach fiscal orthodoxy, and maintain traditional claims of limited government. Federal officials complained about the South's "parasitic" behavior in accepting aid but not responsibility, and even southerners acknowledged the hypocrisy of the region's invocation of states' rights. "We recognize state boundaries when called on to give," noted the *Houston Press*, "but forget them when Uncle Sam is doing the giving."

The federal government had a particularly powerful impact on the South with the **Tennessee Valley Authority (TVA)**, launched in 1933. Coordinating activities across seven states, the TVA built dams to control floods and generate hydroelectric power, produced fertilizer, fostered agricultural and forestry development, encouraged conservation, improved navigation, and modernized school and health systems. Private utility companies denounced the TVA as socialistic, but most southerners supported it. Its major drawback was environmental damage that only became apparent later. Over a vast area of the South, it provided electricity for the first time.

The New Deal further expanded access to electricity by establishing the Rural Electrification Administration (REA) in 1935. Private companies had refused to extend power lines into the countryside because it was not profitable, consigning 90 percent of the nation's farms to drudgery and darkness. The REA revolutionized farm life by sponsoring rural nonprofit electric cooperatives. By 1941, 35 percent of American farms had electricity; by 1950, 78 percent.

The New Deal in the West. The New Deal also changed the West. Westerners received the most federal money per capita in welfare, relief projects, and loans. Like southerners, they accepted federal aid and clamored for more.

The Bureau of Reclamation, established in 1902, emerged as one of the most important government agencies in the West. It built huge dams to control the western river systems and promote large-scale development. By furnishing capital and expertise, the government subsidized and stimulated western economic development, particularly the growth of agribusiness.

Westerners welcomed such assistance but rarely shared the federal goals of rational resource management. Instead, they often wanted to continue to exploit the land and resented federal supervision as colonial control. In practice, however, the government worked in partnership with the West's agribusinesses and timber and petroleum industries.

THE NEW DEAL AND PUBLIC ACTIVISM

Despite Hoover's fear that government responsibility would discourage local initiative, the 1930s witnessed an upsurge in activism. New Deal programs, in fact, often encouraged or empowered groups to shape public policy. Moreover, because the administration worried about centralization, some federal agencies fostered what New Dealers called "grassroots democracy." The AAA set up committees that ultimately included more than 100,000 people to implement agricultural policy and held referendums on crop controls; local advisory committees guided the various federal arts projects; federal management of the West's public grasslands mandated cooperation with associations of livestock raisers.

At times, local administration of national programs enabled groups to exploit federal policy for their own advantage. Wealthy planters shaped AAA practices at the expense of poor tenant farmers; local control of TVA projects excluded black people. But federal programs often allowed previously unrepresented groups to contest traditionally dominant interests. Often seeing greater opportunities for participation and influence in federal programs than in city and state governments, community groups campaigned to expand federal authority. In short, depression conditions and New Deal programs actually increased citizen involvement in public affairs.

EBBING OF THE NEW DEAL

After his victory in 1936, Roosevelt committed himself to further reforms. But determined opponents, continuing economic problems, and the president's own misjudgments blocked his reforms and deadlocked the New Deal.

CHALLENGING THE COURT

Roosevelt regarded the Supreme Court as his most dangerous opponent. During his first term, the Court had declared several important measures unconstitutional. Indeed, most of the justices were elderly conservatives, appointed by Republicans and unsympathetic to an activist federal government. It seemed that the Court would also strike down the Second New Deal.

Emboldened by the 1936 landslide, Roosevelt decided to restructure the federal judiciary. In early 1937, he proposed legislation authorizing the president to name a new justice for each one serving past the age of 70. Additional justices, he said, would increase judicial efficiency. But his real goal was to appoint new justices more sympathetic to the New Deal.

His Court plan led to a divisive struggle. The proposal was perfectly legal: Congress had the authority, which it had used repeatedly, to change the number of justices on the Court. But Republicans and conservative Democrats attacked the plan as a scheme to "pack" the Court and subvert the separation of powers among the three branches of government. Some conservatives called the president a dictator, but even many liberals expressed reservations about the plan or FDR's lack of candor in proposing it.

The Court itself undercut support for FDR's proposal by upholding the Social Security and Wagner acts and minimum-wage legislation. Moreover, the retirement of a conservative justice allowed Roosevelt to name a sympathetic successor. Congress rejected Roosevelt's plan.

Roosevelt's challenge to the Court hurt the New Deal. It worried the public, split the Democratic Party, and revived conservatives. Opponents promptly attacked other New Deal policies, from support for unions to progressive taxation. Henceforth, a conservative coalition of Republicans and southern Democrats in Congress blocked FDR's reforms.

MORE HARD TIMES

A sharp recession, beginning in August 1937, added to Roosevelt's problems. The New Deal's deficit spending had reflected his desire to alleviate suffering, not a conviction that it would stimulate economic recovery. As the economy improved in 1936, Roosevelt decided to cut federal expenditures and balance the budget. But private investment and employment remained stagnant, and the economy plunged.

In 1938, Roosevelt reluctantly increased spending. New appropriations for the PWA and other government programs revived the faltering economy, but neither FDR nor Congress would spend what was necessary to end the depression. Only the vast expenditures for World War II would bring full recovery.

POLITICAL STALEMATE

The recession interrupted the momentum of the New Deal and strengthened its opponents. In late 1937, their leaders in Congress issued a "conservative manifesto" decrying New Deal fiscal, labor, and regulatory policies. Holding seniority in a Congress malapportioned in their favor, they blocked most of Roosevelt's reforms. None of his must legislation passed a special session of Congress in December. In 1938, Congress rejected tax reforms and reduced corporate taxes. The few measures that passed were heavily amended.

To protect the New Deal, Roosevelt turned again to the public, with whom he remained immensely popular. In the 1938 Democratic primaries, he campaigned against the New Deal's conservative opponents. But FDR could not transfer his personal popularity to the political newcomers he supported. What his foes attacked as a purge failed. Roosevelt lost further political leverage when the Republicans gained 75 seats in the House and seven in the Senate and 13 governorships.

The 1938 elections did not repudiate the New Deal, for the Democrats retained majorities in both houses of Congress. But the Republican revival and the survival of the conservative southern Democrats guaranteed that the New Deal had gone as far as it ever would. With Roosevelt in the White House and his opponents controlling Congress, the New Deal ended in political stalemate.

Good Neighbors and Hostile Forces

Even before FDR's conservative opponents derailed the New Deal, the president felt their impact in the area of foreign policy. Isolationists in Congress counseled against any U.S. involvement in world affairs and appealed to the growing national disillusionment with America's participation in the Great War to support their position. Moreover, Roosevelt himself, although not an isolationist, believed that the gravity of the nation's economic depression warranted a primary focus on domestic recovery, and in the early years of his presidency, took few international initiatives.

The actions he did take related directly to salvaging America's desperate economy. As the depression worsened in 1933, American businesses searched for new markets throughout the world, and key business leaders informed FDR that they would welcome the opportunity to expand trade to the Soviet Union. Moscow was also eager to renew ties to the United States, and President Roosevelt extended formal recognition of the Soviet Union in November 1933.

Enhancing trade opportunities and rescuing the economy from the damage wrought by high tariffs figured prominently in Roosevelt's policies in the Western Hemisphere. In large measure, Roosevelt merely extended the Good Neighbor policy begun by his predecessor. Hoover had abandoned the U.S. policy of interventionism, and by the time he left office in March 1933, all U.S. troops had been removed from Latin America. Still, the Great Depression strained U.S.-Latin American relations, sending economic shock waves throughout Central and South America and, in several instances, helping propel to power ruthless dictators who ruled with iron fists and U.S. support.

To symbolize that the United States was a "good neighbor," FDR visited the Caribbean in 1934, receiving an enthusiastic reception, and in 1936, he broke new ground by becoming the first U.S. president to sail to South America. He also worked to encourage trade by reducing tariffs.

Neutrality and Fascism

Outside the hemisphere, during his first term as president, Roosevelt generally followed the policy of avoiding involvement in Europe's political, economic, and social problems. But the aggressive actions of Adolf Hitler in Germany ultimately led Roosevelt to a different position, and in the latter part of the decade, he faced the task of educating the American public, still resentful of U.S. participation in World War I, about the fascist danger that was spreading in Europe.

Hitler came to power in 1933, shortly before FDR entered the White House, and he pledged to restore German pride and nationalism in the aftermath of the Versailles Treaty. As the leader of the National Socialist Workers Party, or Nazis, Hitler established a **fascist government**—a one-party dictatorship closely aligned with corporate interests, committed to a "biological world evolution," and determined to establish a new empire, the Third Reich. He vowed to eliminate Bolshevik radicalism and purify the German "race" through the elimination of those he deemed undesirable, especially targeting Jews, the group Hitler blamed for most, if not all, Germany's ills.

Others aided the spread of fascism. Italian leader Benito Mussolini, who had assumed power in 1922 and envisaged emulating the power and prestige of the Roman Empire, brutally attacked Ethiopia in 1935. The following year, a young fascist military officer, Francisco Franco, led an uprising in Spain, and with the assistance of Italy and Germany, successfully ousted the Spanish Republic and its loyalist supporters by 1939 to create an authoritarian government. Meanwhile, Hitler implemented his plan of conquest: He remilitarized the Rhineland in 1936, and in 1938 he annexed Austria.

The aggressive actions of Germany and Italy failed to eclipse U.S. fears of becoming involved in another European war. Congress passed Neutrality Acts designed to continue America's trade with its world partners but prohibit the president from taking sides in the mounting European crisis.

Appeasement and More Neutrality. After annexing Austria, Hitler pushed again in 1938 when he demanded the Sudetenland from Czechoslovakia. The French and the British refused to stand up to Hitler, following instead a policy of appeasement. Meeting in Munich in September 1938, the leaders of England and France abandoned their security obligations to the Czechs, yielding the Sudetenland to Hitler in exchange for a weak promise of no more annexations. In America, too, the sentiment was for peace at all costs, and isolationism permeated the halls of Congress.

Isolationism compounded by anti-Semitism and by the divisions between the leaders of the American Jewish community combined to ensure that the United States would not become a haven for Jews suffering under Nazi brutality. News of Nazi atrocities

On November 9, 1938, Nazi Germany launched an attack on Jews, destroying their businesses and burning their synagogues. This street scene in Berlin shows the shattered windows of Jewish businesses. Nazi leader Joseph Goebbels recorded the event, known as Kristallnacht, in his diary: "Yesterday: Berlin. There, all proceeded fantastically. One fire after another. It is good that way. . . . 100 dead. But no German property damaged."

against Austrian Jews in 1938 shocked the American press, and Hitler's violent pogrom, known as *Kristallnacht* ("Night of the Broken Glass"), conducted against Jews throughout Germany in November 1938, added fresh proof of Nazi cruelty. Although the United States recalled its ambassador from Berlin to protest the pogrom (in response, Germany recalled its ambassador from Washington), it did not alter its restrictive immigration-quota system, the 1924 National Origins Act, to provide refuge for German Jews.

As Europe edged closer to war, the relationship between the United States and Japan, periodically tense in the twentieth century, became more strained. Japan resented U.S. economic interests in East Asia and was offended by the policy of excluding Japanese immigrants. The United States regarded Japan's desires for empire as threatening but also needed Japan as a trading partner, especially in the economically depressed 1930s. Consequently, in September 1931, when Japan seized Manchuria, the United States did little more than denounce the action. Again in 1937, after Japanese troops attacked Chinese forces north of Beijing and outright war began between Japan and China, the United States merely condemned the action.

EDGING TOWARD INVOLVEMENT

After the Munich agreement, President Roosevelt moved away from domestic reform toward preparedness for war, fearful that conflict in Europe was unavoidable and determined to revise the neutrality laws. In his State of the Union address in January 1939, FDR explained that America's neutrality laws might "actually give aid to an aggressor and deny it to the victim." By the fall of that year, he had won support for changes in the laws that would enable the United States to provide important assistance to Britain and France in the winter of 1939–1940. Hitler's defiance of the Munich agreement in Czechoslovakia, overrunning Prague by March 1939, merely anticipated his next move toward Poland and also convinced the British and the French that war was imminent.

CONCLUSION

The Great Depression and the New Deal mark a major divide in American history. The depression cast doubt on the traditional practices, policies, and attitudes that underlay not only the nation's economy but also its social and political institutions and relationships. The New Deal brought only partial economic recovery. However, its economic policies, from banking and securities regulation to unemployment compensation, farm price supports, and minimum wages, created barriers against another depression. The gradual adoption of compensatory spending policies expanded the government's role in the economy. Responding to the failures of private organizations and state and local governments, the federal government assumed the obligation to provide social welfare.

Roosevelt also expanded the role of the presidency. As his White House took the initiative for defining public policy, drafting legislation, lobbying Congress, and communicating with the nation, it became the model for all subsequent presidents. Not only was the president's power increased, but Roosevelt made the federal government, rather than state or local governments, the focus of public interest and expectations.

By the end of the 1930s, as international relations deteriorated, FDR was already considering a shift, as he later said, from Dr. New Deal to Dr. Win-the-War. Reluctant to move beyond public opinion that did not want war and limited by neutrality legislation, FDR cautiously led the nation toward war—this time against an enemy far more threatening than the Great Depression. Ironically, only then would President Roosevelt end the depression that had ravaged the nation for nearly a decade.

REVIEW QUESTIONS

1. Why did President Hoover's emphasis on voluntarism fail to resolve the problems of the Great Depression in the United States?

2. Describe the relief programs of the New Deal. What were they designed to accomplish? What were their achievements and their limitations?

3. What were the major criticisms of the early New Deal? How accurate were those charges?

4. How did the policies of the New Deal shape the constituency and the prospects of the Democratic Party in the 1930s?

5. Describe the conflict between management and labor in the 1930s. What were the major issues and motivations? How did the two sides differ in resources and tactics, and how and why did these factors change over time?

6. How did the role of the federal government change in the 1930s? What factors were responsible for the changes?

myhistörylab CONNECTIONS

Reinforce what you learned in this chapter by studying the many documents, images, maps, review tools, and videos available at **www.myhistorylab.com.**

READ AND REVIEW

✔● Study and Review on myhistorylab.com STUDY PLAN: CHAPTER 25

📖● Read the Document on myhistorylab.com

Franklin D. Roosevelt, First Inaugural Address (1932)

Luther C. Wandall, A Negro in the CCC (1935)

Tennessee Valley Authority Act (1933)

E. E. Lewis, Black Cotton Farmers and the AAA (1935)

An Attack on New Deal Farm Policies (1936)

Frances Perkins and the Social Security Act (1935, 1960)

Caroline Manning, The Immigrant Woman and Her Job (1930)

Richard Wright, Are We Solving America's Race Problem? (1945)

Mrs. Henry Weddington, Letter to President Roosevelt (1938)

View the **Map** on **myhistorylab.com**

The Great Depression

RESEARCH AND EXPLORE

Read the **Document** on **myhistorylab.com**

Personal Journeys Online

From Then to Now Online: Social Security

Dealing with Hard Times: The Great Depression

Listen on **myhistorylab.com**

"I've Known Rivers"; poem and reading by Langston Hughes

FDR's First Inaugural Address

Watch the **Video** on **myhistorylab.com**

Dorothea Lange and Migrant Mother

Responding to the Great Depression: Whose New Deal?

President Roosevelt Focuses on America's Youth

Jesse Owens and the 1936 Olympics

Listen on **myhistorylab.com**

Hear the audio files for Chapter 25 at
www.myhistorylab.com.

26 World War II •• 1939–1945

Hear the audio files for Chapter 26 at **www.myhistorylab.com.**

FOCUS QUESTIONS

WHY WERE most Americans reluctant to get involved in World War II?

HOW DID the Allies fare in 1941 and 1942?

WHAT STEPS did the U.S. government take to organize the economy for war?

HOW DID the war alter American society?

WHY DID the Allies win the war?

American soldiers landing on the coast of France at Normandy on June 6, 1944 (D-Day).

ONE AMERICAN JOURNEY

December, 1942

The scene [under the stadium] at The University of Chicago would have been confusing to an outsider, if he could have eluded the security guards and gained admittance. He would have seen only what appeared to be a crude pile of black bricks and wooden timbers. . . .

Finally, the day came when we were ready to run the experiment. We gathered on a balcony about 10 feet above the floor of the large room in which the structure had been erected. Beneath us was a young scientist, George Weil, whose duty it was to handle the last control rod that was holding the reaction in check. . . .

Finally, it was time to remove the control rods. Slowly, Weil started to withdraw the main control rod. On the balcony, we watched the indicators which measured the neutron count and told us how rapidly the disintegration of the uranium atoms under their neutron bombardment was proceeding.

At 11:35 A.M., the counters were clicking rapidly. Then, with a loud clap, the automatic control rods slammed home. The safety point had been set too low. . . .

At 2:30, Weil pulled out the control rod in a series of measured adjustments. Shortly after, the intensity shown by the indicators began to rise at a slow but ever-increasing rate. At this moment we knew that the self-sustaining [nuclear] reaction was under way.

The event was not spectacular, no fuses burned, no lights flashed. But to us it meant that release of atomic energy on a large scale would be only a matter of time.

Enrico Fermi, in *The First Reactor* (Washington, DC: U.S. Department of Energy, 1982).

ENRICO FERMI was describing the first controlled nuclear chain reaction—the critical experiment from which atomic weapons and atomic power would soon develop. Fermi had emigrated to escape the growing political repression of Fascist Italy. In 1942, after the United States joined the ongoing global conflict of World War II, Fermi was put in charge of nuclear fission research at the University of Chicago and played a leading role in efforts to develop an atomic bomb. The following year found Fermi, other atomic scientists, and their families at Los Alamos, a science city that the government built hurriedly on a high plateau in northern New Mexico, where isolation was supposed to ensure secrecy and help the United States win the race with Nazi Germany to develop atomic weapons.

The Fermis were not the only family to give Los Alamos a multinational flavor. Laura remembered that it was "all one big family and all one big accent. . . . Everybody in science was there, both from the United States and from almost all European countries." The internationalism of Los Alamos mirrored the larger war effort. Japan's attack on Pearl Harbor in December 1941 thrust the United States into a war that spanned the globe. America's allies against Japan in the Pacific and East Asia included Great Britain, Australia, and China. In Europe, its allies against Nazi Germany and Fascist Italy included Great Britain, the Soviet Union, and more than 20 other nations. The scientists racing to perfect the atomic bomb knew that victory was far from certain. Germany and Japan had piled one conquest on another since the late 1930s, and they continued to seize new territories in 1942. Allied defeat in a few key battles could have resulted in a standoff or an Axis victory. A new weapon might end the war more quickly or make the difference between victory and defeat.

The war's domestic impacts were as profound as its international consequences. The race to build an atomic bomb was only one part of a vast effort to harness the resources of the United States to the war effort. The war highlighted racial inequalities, gave women new opportunities, and fostered growth in the South and West. By devastating the nation's commercial rivals, compelling workers to retrain and factories to modernize, World War II left the United States dominant in the world economy. It also increased the size and scope of the federal government and built an alliance among the armed forces, big business, and science that helped shape postwar America.

THE DILEMMAS OF NEUTRALITY

Americans in the 1930s wanted no part of another overseas war. Despite two years of German victories and a decade of Japanese aggression against China, opinion polls in the fall of 1941 showed that a majority of voters still hoped to avoid war. President Roosevelt's challenge was to lead the United States toward rearmament and support for Great Britain and China without alarming a reluctant public.

THE ROOTS OF WAR

The roots of World War II can be found in the aftereffects of World War I. The peace settlement created a set of small new nations in eastern Europe that were vulnerable to aggression by their much larger neighbors, Germany and the Soviet Union (more formally, the Union of Soviet Socialist Republics, or USSR). Italy and Japan thought that the Treaty of Versailles had not recognized their stature as world powers. Many Germans were convinced that Germany had been betrayed rather than defeated in 1918. In the 1930s, economic crisis undermined an already shaky political order. Economic hardship and political instability fueled the rise of right-wing dictatorships that offered territorial expansion by military conquest as the way to redress old rivalries, dominate trade, and gain access to raw materials.

Japanese nationalists believed that the United States, Britain, and France had treated Japan unfairly after World War I, despite its participation against Germany. They believed that Japan should expel the French, British, Dutch, and Americans from Asia and create a **Greater East Asia Co-Prosperity Sphere,** in which Japan gave the orders and other Asian peoples complied. Seizing the Chinese province of Manchuria to expand an East Asian empire that already included Korea and Taiwan emboldened Japan's military in 1931. A full-scale invasion of China followed in 1937. Japan took many of the key cities and killed tens of thousands of civilians in the "rape of Nanking," but failed to dislodge the government of Jiang Jieshi (Chiang Kai-shek) and settled into a war of attrition.

Italian aggression embroiled Africa and the Mediterranean. The Fascist dictator Benito Mussolini had sent arms and troops to aid General Francisco Franco's right-wing rebels in Spain. The three-year civil war, which ended with Franco's victory in 1939, became a bloody testing ground for new German military tactics and German and Italian ambitions against democratic Europe.

In Germany, Adolf Hitler mixed the desire to reassert national pride and power after the defeat of World War I with an ideology of racial hatred. Coming to power by

CHRONOLOGY

1931   Japan invades Manchuria.

1933   Hitler takes power in Germany.

1935   Congress passes first of three neutrality acts.
Italy invades Ethiopia.

1936   Germany and Italy form the Rome-Berlin Axis.
Civil war erupts in Spain.

1937   Japan invades China.

1938   Germany absorbs Austria.
Munich agreement between Germany, Britain, and France.

1939   Germany and the Soviet Union sign a nonaggression pact.
Germany absorbs Czechoslovakia.
Germany invades Poland; Great Britain and France declare war on Germany.

1940   Germany conquers Denmark, Norway, Belgium, the Netherlands, and France.
Japan, Germany, and Italy sign the Tripartite Pact.
Germany bombs England in the Battle of Britain.
The United States begins to draft men into the armed forces.
Franklin Roosevelt wins an unprecedented third term.

1941   The United States begins a lend-lease program to make military equipment
available to Great Britain and later the Soviet Union.
The Fair Employment Practices Committee is established.
Germany invades the Soviet Union.
Roosevelt and Churchill issue the Atlantic Charter.
Japan attacks U.S. military bases in Hawaii.

1942   American forces in the Philippines surrender to Japan.
President Roosevelt authorizes the removal and internment of Japanese
Americans living in four western states.
Naval battles in the Coral Sea and off the island of Midway blunt Japanese
expansion. U.S. forces land in North Africa.
Soviet forces encircle a German army at Stalingrad.
The first sustained and controlled nuclear chain reaction takes place at the
University of Chicago.

1943   U.S. and British forces invade Italy, which makes terms with the Allies.
Race conflict erupts in riots in Detroit, New York, and Los Angeles.
The landing of Marines on Tarawa initiates the island-hopping strategy.
U.S. war production peaks.
Roosevelt, Churchill, and Stalin confer at Tehran.

1944   Allied forces land in Normandy.
The U.S. Navy destroys Japanese sea power in the battles of the
Philippine Sea and Leyte Gulf.
The Battle of the Bulge is the last tactical setback for the Allies.

1945	Roosevelt, Stalin, and Churchill meet at Yalta to plan the postwar world.
	The United States takes the Pacific islands of Iwo Jima and Okinawa.
	Franklin Roosevelt dies; Harry S. Truman becomes president.
	Germany surrenders to the United States, Great Britain, and the Soviet Union.
	The United Nations is organized at an international meeting in San Francisco.
	Potsdam Conference.
	Japan surrenders after the detonation of atomic bombs over Hiroshima and Nagasaki.

constitutional means in 1933, Hitler quickly consolidated his grip by destroying opposition parties and made himself the German Führer, or absolute leader. Proclaiming the start of a thousand-year Reich ("empire"), he combined the historic German interest in eastward expansion with a long tradition of racialist thought about German superiority.

Special targets of Nazi hatred were the Jews, who were prominent in German business and professional life but soon faced persecution aimed at driving them from the country. In 1935, the Nuremberg Laws denied civil rights to Jews and the campaign against them intensified. On November 9, 1938, in vicious attacks across Germany that became known as *Kristallnacht* ("Night of the Broken Glass"), Nazi thugs rounded up, beat, and murdered Jews, smashed property, and burned synagogues. The Nazi government began expropriating Jewish property and excluded Jews from most employment.

Germany and Italy formed the Rome-Berlin Axis in October 1936 and the Tripartite Pact with Japan in 1940, leading to the term **Axis Powers** to describe the aggressor nations. Hitler's Germany was the most repressive. The Nazi concentration camp began as a device for political terrorism, where socialists and other dissidents and "antisocials"—homosexuals and beggars—could be separated from "pure" Germans. Soon the systematic discrimination and concentration camps would evolve into massive forced-labor camps and then into hellish extermination camps.

HITLER'S WAR IN EUROPE

After annexing Austria through a coup and seizing and slicing up Czechoslovakia, Germany demonstrated the worthlessness of the Munich agreement by invading Poland on September 1, 1939. Britain and France, Poland's allies, declared war on Germany but could not stop the German war machine. Western journalists covering the three-week conquest of Poland coined the term *Blitzkrieg,* or "lightning war," to describe the German tactics. Armored divisions with tanks and motorized infantry punched holes in defensive positions and raced forward 30 or 40 miles per day.

Hitler's greatest advantage was the ability to attack when and where he chose. From September 1939 to October 1941, Germany marched from victory to victory. Striking from a central position against scattered enemies, Hitler chose the targets and timing of each new front: eastward to smash Poland in September 1939; northward to conquer Denmark and Norway in April and May 1940; westward to defeat the Netherlands, Belgium, and France in May and June 1940, an attack that Italy also joined; southward into the Balkans, enlisting Hungary, Romania, and Bulgaria as allies and conquering Yugoslavia and Greece in April and May 1941. Hitler also launched the Battle of Britain in the second half of 1940. German planes bombarded Britain mercilessly, in an unsuccessful effort to pound the British into submission.

Hitler gambled once too often in June 1941. Having failed to knock Britain out of the war, he invaded the Soviet Union. The attack caught the Red Army off guard. Germany and the USSR had signed a nonaggression pact in 1939, and the Soviets had helped to dismember Poland. Hitler hoped that smashing the USSR and seizing its vast resources would make Germany invincible. Before desperate Soviet counterattacks and a bitter winter stopped the German columns, they had reached the outskirts of Moscow and expected to finish the job in the spring.

TRYING TO KEEP OUT

For more than two years after the invasion of Poland, strong sentiment against intervention shaped public debate and limited President Roosevelt's ability to help Britain and its allies. Much of the emotional appeal of neutrality came from disillusionment with the American crusade in World War I, which had failed to make the world safe for democracy. Many opponents of intervention wanted the United States to protect its traditional spheres of interest in Latin America and the Pacific. Noninterventionists spanned the political spectrum from left-leaning labor unions to conservative business tycoons like Henry Ford. The country's ethnic variety also complicated U.S. responses. Nazi aggression ravaged the homelands of Americans of Polish, Czech, Greek, and Norwegian ancestry. More than 5 million German Americans remembered the anti-German sentiment of World War I, while many of the 4.6 million Italian Americans admired Mussolini. Any move to intervene in Europe had to take these different views into account, meaning that Roosevelt had to move slowly and carefully in his effort to align the United States on the side of Britain.

The raspy-voiced Adolf Hitler had a remarkable ability to stir the German people. He and his inner circle made skillful use of propaganda, exploiting German resentment over the country's defeat in World War I and, with carefully staged mass rallies, such as this event in 1938, inspiring an emotional conviction of national greatness.

EDGING TOWARD INTERVENTION

Still, Roosevelt's appeals to democratic values gained support in 1939 and 1940. Radio broadcasts from England describing London under German bombing heightened the sense of imperiled freedom. The importance of open markets also bolstered interventionism. U.S. business leaders had little doubt that Axis victories would bring economic instability and require crushing defense budgets to protect Fortress America.

Because 85 percent of the American people agreed that the nation should fight only if it was directly attacked, Roosevelt had to chip away at neutrality, educating, arguing, and taking one step at a time. The first step came in October 1939. A month-long congressional debate inspired millions of letters and telegrams in favor of keeping an arms embargo in place against warring nations. Nevertheless, the lawmakers reluctantly allowed arms sales to belligerent nations on a "cash-and-carry" basis, to avoid expanding European debts. In control of the Atlantic, France and Britain were the only expected customers.

Isolationism and anti-Semitism help to explain why the United States accepted only a few thousand Jewish refugees. American law strictly limited the numbers of Europeans who could enter the United States, and Congress in 1939 declined to authorize the entry outside the quotas of 20,000 Jewish children. Bureaucrats at the State Department blocked entry to "undesirables," such as left-wing opponents of Hitler, and were unsympathetic to Jewish refugees. In 1939, officials turned the passenger ship *St. Louis* away from Miami and forced its 950 German Jewish refugees back to Europe. The consequences of these restrictions would prove tragic later in the war, as the Nazis began systematic genocide of European Jews.

The Collapse of France and U.S. Rearmament. Despite the efforts of non interventionists, in 1940 the United States edged closer to involvement in the war. In May, the Roosevelt administration established the National Defense Advisory Commission and the Council of National Defense to deal with strategic planning for war. The sudden defeat of France, which had survived four years of German attacks in World War I, made the new war seem far more serious. The United States no longer had the option of standing on the sidelines while European nations fought to a standstill. In the summer of 1940, Congress voted to expand the army to 2 million men, build 19,000 new warplanes, and add 150 ships to the navy. Lawmakers approved the nation's first peacetime draft in September, requiring 16.5 million men between the ages of 21 and 35 to register for military service on October 16.

In the same month, the United States concluded a destroyer deal with Britain. The British were desperate for small, maneuverable warships to guard imports of food and war materials against German submarines. The Americans had long wanted additional air and naval bases to guard the approaches to North America. Roosevelt met both needs by trading 50 old destroyers for the use of bases on British territories in the Caribbean, Bermuda, and Newfoundland.

The Election of 1940. In the presidential election of 1940, the big campaign issue was whether FDR's unprecedented try for a third term represented arrogance or a legitimate concern for continuity in a time of peril. The election was tighter than in 1932 or 1936, but Roosevelt received 55 percent of the vote. The president pledged that no Americans would fight in a foreign war. But if the United States were attacked, he said privately, the war would no longer be "foreign."

THE BRINK OF WAR

After the election, FDR and his advisers edged the United States toward stronger support of Britain and put pressure on Japan. In January 1941, Roosevelt proposed the lend-lease program, which allowed Britain to "borrow" military equipment for the duration of the war.

The **Lend-Lease Act** triggered intense political debate. Charles Lindbergh, the spokesperson for the America First Committee, protested that the United States should not give away weapons it might need to defend itself. Congress finally passed the measure in March 1941, authorizing the president to lease, lend, or otherwise dispose of arms and other equipment to any country whose defense was considered vital to the security of the United States. The program proved invaluable in aiding Great Britain and later in assisting the Soviet Union.

FDR soon began an undeclared war in the North Atlantic, instructing the navy to report sightings of German submarines to the British. In September, the U.S. destroyer *Greer* clashed with a German submarine. Portraying the incident as German aggression, Roosevelt proclaimed a "shoot on sight" policy for German subs and ordered American ships to escort British convoys to within 400 miles of Britain. In reply, German submarines torpedoed the destroyer *Kearny* on October 17 and sank the destroyer *Reuben James,* with the loss of more than 100 lives, on October 30. The United States was now approaching outright naval war with Germany.

The Atlantic Charter. With U.S. ships on a war footing in the North Atlantic, Roosevelt and the British prime minister, Winston Churchill, met secretly off Newfoundland in August 1941 to map out military strategy and postwar goals. They agreed that the defeat of Germany was their first priority, and Japan was secondary. Their joint proclamation, known as the **Atlantic Charter**, provided a political umbrella for American involvement in the war. Echoing Woodrow Wilson, Roosevelt insisted on a commitment to oppose territorial conquest, support self-government, promote freedom of the seas, and create a system of economic collaboration. Churchill signed to keep Roosevelt happy, but the document papered over sharp differences between U.S. and British expectations about the future of world trade and European colonial possessions.

Events in the Pacific. The final shove came in the Pacific rather than the Atlantic. In 1940, as part of its rearmament program, the United States decided to build a "two-ocean navy." This decision antagonized Japan, prodding it toward a war that most U.S. leaders hoped to postpone or avoid. Through massive investment and national sacrifice, Japan had achieved roughly 70 percent of U.S. naval strength by late 1941. However, America's buildup promised to reduce the ratio to only 30 percent by 1944. Furthermore, the United States was restricting Japan's vital imports of steel, iron ore, and aluminum in an effort to curb its military aggression. In July 1941, after Japan occupied French Indochina, Roosevelt froze Japanese assets in the United States, blocked shipments of petroleum products, and began to build up U.S. forces in the Philippines. These actions caused Japan's rulers to consider war against the United States while Japan still had a petroleum reserve. Both militarily and economically, it looked in Tokyo as if 1942 was Japan's last chance for victory.

Japanese war planners never seriously considered an invasion of the United States or expected a decisive victory. They hoped that attacks on American Pacific bases would shock the United States into letting Japan have its way in Asia or at least win time to create impenetrable defenses in the central Pacific.

DECEMBER 7, 1941

On December 7, 1941, the Japanese navy launched a surprise attack on American bases in Hawaii. The Japanese fleet sailed a 4,000-mile loop through the empty North Pacific, avoiding merchant shipping and American patrols. Before dawn on December 7, six Japanese aircraft carriers launched 351 planes in two bombing strikes against Pearl Harbor. When the smoke cleared, Americans counted their losses: eight battleships, eleven other warships, and nearly all military aircraft damaged or destroyed, and 2,403 people killed. They could also count their good fortune. Dockyards, drydocks, and oil storage tanks remained intact because the Japanese admiral had refused to order a third attack. And the American aircraft carriers, at sea on patrol, were unharmed. They proved far more important than battleships as the war developed. Within hours, the Japanese attacked U.S. bases at Guam, Wake Island, and in the Philippines.

Speaking to Congress the following day, Roosevelt proclaimed December 7, 1941, "a date which will live in infamy." He asked for and got a declaration of war against Japan. Hitler and Mussolini declared war on the United States on December 11, supporting their Tripartite Pact ally. On January 1, 1942, the United States, Britain, the Soviet Union, and 23 other nations subscribed to the principles of the Atlantic Charter and pledged not to negotiate a separate peace.

HOLDING THE LINE

Japan's armies quickly conquered most of Southeast Asia; its navy forced the United States onto the defensive in the central Pacific. As it turned out, Japan's conquests reached their limit after six months, but in early 1942, this was far from clear. At the same time, in Europe, Allied fortunes went from bad to worse. Again, no one knew that German and Italian gains would peak at midyear. Decisive turning points did not come until November 1942, a year after the United States entered the war, and not until the middle of 1943 could the **Allies**—the United States, Britain, the Soviet Union, China, and other nations at war with Germany, Japan, and Italy with confidence to plan for victory.

STOPPING GERMANY

In December 1941, the United States plunged into a truly global war that was being fought on six distinct fronts. In North Africa, the British were battling Italian and German armies that were trying to seize the Suez Canal, a critical transportation link to Asia. Along the 1,000-mile **Eastern Front**, Soviet armies held defensive positions as German forces, pushing deeply into Soviet territory, reached the outskirts of Moscow and Leningrad (now St. Petersburg). In the North Atlantic, German submarines stalked merchant ships carrying supplies to Britain. In China, Japan controlled the most productive provinces but could not crush Chinese resistance. In Southeast Asia, Japanese troops attacked the Philippines, the Dutch East Indies (now Indonesia), New Guinea, Malaya, and Burma. In the central Pacific, the Japanese fleet confronted the U.S. Navy. With the nation facing danger across both the Atlantic and Pacific oceans, Roosevelt helped Americans understand the global nature of the conflict by calling it the "second world war."

Despite the popular desire for revenge against Japan, the Allies had already decided to defeat Germany first. The reasoning was simple: Germany was far stronger than Japan. Defeat of Japan would not ensure the defeat of Germany, especially if the

Germans crushed the Soviet Union or starved Britain into submission. By contrast, a strategy that helped the Soviets and British survive and then destroyed German military power would doom Japan.

The Eastern Front and the Battle of Stalingrad. The Eastern Front held the key to Allied hopes in Europe. In 1941, Germany had seized control of 45 percent of the Soviet population, 47 percent of its grain production, and more than 60 percent of its coal, steel, and aluminum industries. Hitler next sought to destroy the Soviet capacity to wage war, targeting southern Russia, an area rich in grain and oil. The German thrust in 1942 was also designed to eliminate the British from the Middle East.

The turning point of the war in Europe came at Stalingrad (present-day Volgograd), an industrial center on the western bank of the Volga River. After initially aiming at the city, German armies turned south toward the Russian oil fields, leaving a dangerous strongpoint on their flank that the German command decided to capture. In September and October 1942, German, Italian, and Romanian soldiers fought their way house by house into the city. For both Hitler and Stalin, the city became a test of will that outweighed even its substantial military importance.

The Red Army delivered a counterstroke on November 18 that cut off 290,000 Axis soldiers. Airlifts kept the Germans fighting for more than two additional months, but

The Japanese attack on Pearl Harbor shocked the American people. Images of burning battleships confirmed the popular image of Japan as sneaky and treacherous and stirred a desire for revenge. The attack rendered the United States incapable of resisting Japanese aggression in Southeast Asia in early 1942, but it failed to achieve its goal of destroying U.S. naval power in the Pacific.

they surrendered in February 1943. This was the first German mass capitulation, and it came at immense human cost to both sides. The Soviet army suffered more deaths in this battle than the United States did in the entire war.

Behind the victory was an extraordinary revival of the Soviet capacity to make war. In the desperate months of 1941, the Soviets dismantled nearly 3,000 factories and rebuilt them far to the east of the German advance in the midst of Siberian winter. By the time the two armies clashed at Stalingrad, the Soviets were producing four times as many tanks and warplanes as the Germans, portending the outcome of the battles to come.

THE SURVIVAL OF BRITAIN

After the failure of German air attacks in 1940, the British struggled to save their empire and supply themselves with food and raw materials. In World War I, German submarines (known as U-boats, from *Unterseeboot*) had nearly isolated Great Britain. In 1940 and 1941, they tried again. Through the end of 1941, German "tonnage warfare" sank British, Allied, and neutral merchant vessels faster than they could be replaced.

The Battle of the Atlantic. The British fought back in what came to be known as the **Battle of the Atlantic**. Between 1939 and 1944, planning and rationing cut Britain's need for imports in half. At sea, the British organized protected convoys. Merchant ships sailing alone were defenseless against submarines. Grouping the merchant ships with armed escorts "hardened" the targets and made them more difficult to find in the wide ocean. Roosevelt's destroyer deal of 1940 and U.S. naval escorts in the western Atlantic in 1941 contributed directly to Britain's survival.

Nevertheless, German submarines dominated the Atlantic in 1942. The balance shifted only when Allied aircraft began to track submarines with radar, spot them with searchlights as they maneuvered to the surface, track them with new sonar systems, and attack them with depth charges. By the spring of 1943, American shipyards were launching ships faster than the Germans could sink them.

North Africa. British ground fighting in 1942 centered in North Africa, where the British operated out of Egypt and the Italians and Germans from the Italian colony of Libya. By October 1942, Field Marshal Erwin Rommel's German and Italian forces were within striking distance of the Suez Canal. At El Alamein, however, General Bernard Montgomery forced the enemy to retreat in early November and lifted the danger to the Middle East.

RETREAT AND STABILIZATION IN THE PACIFIC

Reports from eastern Asia after Pearl Harbor were appalling. The Japanese attack on the Philippines (see Map 26–1) had been another tactical surprise that destroyed most American air power on the ground and isolated U.S. forces. In February, a numerically inferior Japanese force seized British Singapore, until then considered an anchor of Allied strength, and then pushed the British out of Burma. In a three-month siege, they overwhelmed Filipino and U.S. defensive positions on the Bataan peninsula outside Manila; thousands of their captives died of maltreatment on their way to prisoner-of-war camps in what is remembered as the Bataan Death March. On May 6, the last American bastion, the island fortress of Corregidor in Manila Bay, surrendered. The Japanese fleet was virtually undamaged at the end of April, and the Japanese army was triumphant in its conquest of European and American territories in Southeast Asia.

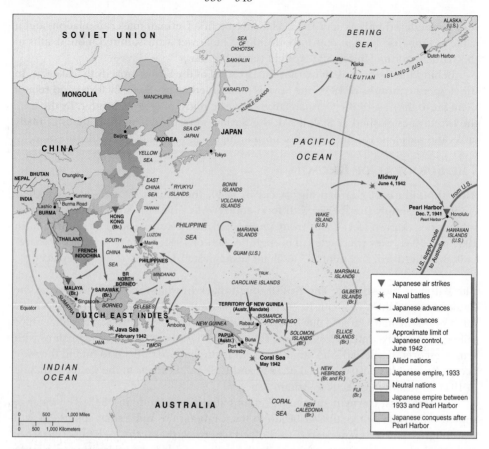

MAP 26–1 • World War II in the Pacific, from Pearl Harbor to Midway The first six months after the Japanese attack on Pearl Harbor brought a string of Japanese victories and conquests in the Pacific, the islands southeast of Asia, and the British colonies of Malaya and Burma. Japan's advance was halted by a standoff battle in the Coral Sea, a decisive U.S. naval victory at Midway, and the length and vulnerability of Japanese supply lines to the most distant conquests.

▶ *What challenges* did Japan face as it attempted to hold onto control of the eastern Pacific? How did the geography of the region aid the Allies and shape their strategy?

The Battles of the Coral Sea and Midway. The first check to Japanese expansion came on May 7–8, 1942, in the Battle of the Coral Sea, where U.S. aircraft carriers halted a Japanese thrust toward Australia and confirmed that the U.S. Navy could fight effectively. In June, the Japanese struck at the island of Midway, 1,500 miles northwest of Honolulu. Their goal was to destroy American carrier forces. Having cracked Japanese radio codes, U.S. forces were aware of the plan. On the morning of June 4, the Japanese and American carrier fleets faced off across 175 miles of ocean, each sending planes to search out the other. U.S. Navy dive bombers found the Japanese fleet and sank or crippled three aircraft carriers in five minutes; another damaged Japanese carrier sank later in the day. The Battle of Midway ended Japanese efforts to expand in the Pacific.

MOBILIZING FOR VICTORY

War changed the lives of most Americans. Millions of men and women served in the armed forces, and millions more worked in defense factories. In order to keep track of this staggering level of activity, the number of civilian employees of the federal government quadrupled to 3.8 million, a much greater increase than during the New Deal. The breadth of involvement in the war effort gave Americans a common purpose that softened the divisions of region, class, and national origin while calling attention to continuing inequalities of race.

ORGANIZING THE ECONOMY

The need to fight a global war brought a huge expansion of the federal government. Congress authorized the president to reorganize existing government departments and create new agencies. The War Manpower Commission allocated workers among vital industries and the military. The War Production Board invested $17 billion for new factories and managed $181 billion in war-supply contracts, favoring existing corporations because they had experience in large-scale production.

The Office of Price Administration (OPA) fought inflation with price controls and rationing. By slowing price increases, the OPA helped convince Americans to buy the war bonds that financed half the war spending. Americans also felt the bite of the first payroll deductions for income taxes as the government secured a steady flow of revenues and soaked up some of the high wages that would have pushed inflation. In total, the federal budget in 1945 was $98 billion, eleven times as large as in 1939, and the national debt had increased more than sixfold.

Industry had reluctantly begun to convert from consumer goods to defense production in 1940 and 1941. Existing factories retooled to make war equipment, and huge new facilities turned out thousands of planes and ships.

Most defense contracts went to such established industrial states as Michigan, New York, and Ohio, but the relative impact was greatest in the South and West, where the war marked the takeoff of what Americans would later call the Sunbelt. Millions of Americans moved back and forth across the country to war jobs. Washington, DC, teemed with staff officers, stenographers, and other office workers who helped to coordinate the war effort. Local leaders in cities from Charlotte to Fort Worth to Phoenix saw the war as an economic opportunity and campaigned for defense factories and military bases.

The output of America's war industries was staggering. One historian estimates that 40 percent of the world's military production was coming from the United States by 1944. Equally impressive is the 30 percent increase in the productivity of U.S. workers between 1939 and 1945. Surging farm income pulled agriculture out of its long slump. Organized labor offered a no-strike pledge for the duration, ensuring that no one could accuse unions of undermining the war effort but limiting the economic gains of some workers and damping the militancy of the CIO. Nevertheless, overall per capita income doubled, and the poorest quarter of Americans made up some of the ground lost during the Great Depression.

THE ENLISTMENT OF SCIENCE

The war reached into scientific laboratories as well as shops and factories. At the center of the scientific enterprise was Vannevar Bush, former dean at the Massachusetts Institute of Technology. As head of the newly established Office of Scientific Research and

Development, Bush guided spending to develop new drugs such as antibiotics, blood-transfusion procedures, weapons systems, radar, sonar, and dozens of other military technologies. The scale of research and development dwarfed previous scientific work and set the pattern of massive postwar federal support for science.

The most costly scientific effort was the development of radar, or radio detection and ranging devices. Building on British research on microwaves, the United States put $3 billion into the Radiation Laboratory at MIT. Increasingly compact and sophisticated radar systems helped to defeat the German and Japanese navies and to give the Allies control of the air over Europe. Radar research and engineering laid the basis for microwave technology, transistors, and integrated circuits after the war.

In the summer of 1945, *Time* magazine planned a cover story on radar as the weapon that won the war. However, the *Time* story was upstaged by the atomic bomb, the product of the war's other great scientific effort. As early as 1939, Albert Einstein had written to FDR about the possibility of such a weapon and the danger of falling behind the Germans. In late 1941, Roosevelt established the **Manhattan Project**. By December 2, 1942, scientists proved that it was possible to create and control a sustained nuclear reaction.

The Manhattan Project moved from theory to practice in 1943. The physicist J. Robert Oppenheimer directed the young scientists at Los Alamos in designing a nuclear-fission bomb. The Manhattan Project ushered in the age of atomic energy. The first bomb was tested on July 16, 1945. The explosion astonished even the physicists; Oppenheimer quoted from Hindu scriptures in trying to comprehend the results: "Now I am become Death, destroyer of worlds."

MEN AND WOMEN IN THE MILITARY

World War II required a more than thirtyfold expansion of the U.S. armed forces from their 1939 level of 334,000 soldiers, sailors, and Marines. By 1945, 8.3 million men and women were on active duty in the army and army air forces and 3.4 million in the navy and Marine Corps, totals exceeded only by the Soviet Union. In total, some 350,000 women and more than 16 million men served in the armed forces; 292,000 died in battle, 100,000 survived prisoner-of-war camps, and 671,000 returned wounded.

Native Americans in the Military. Twenty-five thousand American Indians served in the armed forces. Most were in racially integrated units, and Harvey Natcheez, of the Ute tribe, was the first American to reach the center of conquered Berlin. Because the Navajo were one of the few tribes that had not been studied by German anthropologists, the Army Signal Corps decided that their language would be unknown to the Axis armies. Roughly 400 members of the tribe were "code-talkers" who served in Marine radio combat-communication teams in the Pacific theater, transmitting vital information in Navajo.

African Americans in the Military. Approximately 1 million African Americans served in the armed forces during World War II. African American leaders had pressed for a provision in the Selective Service Act to bar discrimination "against any person on account of race or color." But as it had since the Civil War, the army organized black soldiers in segregated units and often assigned them to the menial jobs, such as construction work, and excluded them from combat until manpower shortages forced changes in policy.

The average black soldier encountered discrimination on and off the base. Towns adjacent to army posts were sometimes open to white soldiers but off-limits to blacks. At some southern bases, German prisoners of war watched movies from the first rows along with white GIs while African American soldiers watched from the back. Military courts were quick to judge and harshly punish black GIs. It took racially based riots at army bases in North Carolina and Georgia to open up equal (although segregated) access to base recreation facilities.

Despite the obstacles, all-black units, such as the 761st Tank Battalion and the 99th Pursuit Squadron, earned distinguished records. More broadly, the war experience helped to invigorate postwar efforts to achieve equal rights, as had also been true after World War I.

African Americans served in the military in large numbers during World War II. Here a signals company has set up operations in the ruins of an ancient temple in southern Italy.

Women in the Military. The nation had a different—but also mixed—reaction to the women who joined the armed forces as army and navy nurses and as members of the WACS (Women's Army Corps), WAVES (Navy), SPARS (Coast Guard), and Marine Corps Women's Reserve. The armed services tried not to change established gender roles. Military officials told Congress that women in uniform could free men for combat. Many of the women hammered at typewriters, worked switchboards, inventoried supplies. Others, however, worked close to combat zones as photographers, code analysts, weather forecasters, radio operators, and nurses. WAC officers battled the tendency of the popular press to call females in the service "girls" rather than "women" or "soldiers" yet emphasized that military service promoted "poise and charm."

THE HOME FRONT

The war inexorably penetrated everyday life. Residents in war-production cities had to cope with throngs of new workers. Especially in 1941 and 1942, many were unattached males—young men waiting for their draft call and older men without their families. Military and defense officials worried about sexually transmitted diseases and pressured cities to shut down their vice districts. At the same time, college officials scrambled to fill their classrooms, especially after the draft age dropped to 18 in 1942. Many colleges and universities responded to federal requests with special training programs for future officers and engineering and technical training for military personnel.

FAMILIES IN WARTIME

Many Americans put their lives on fast forward. Men ad women often decided to beat the clock with instant matrimony. Couples who had postponed marriage because of the depression could afford to marry as the economy picked up. War intensified casual romances and heightened the appeal of marriage as an anchor in troubled times. Altogether, the war years brought 1.2 million "extra" marriages, compared to the rate for the period 1920–1939.

The war's impact on families was gradual. The draft started with single men, then called up married men without children, and finally tapped fathers in 1943. Left at home were millions of "service wives," whose compensation from the government was $50 per month.

The war had mixed effects on children. "Latchkey children" of working mothers often had to fend for themselves, but middle-class kids whose mothers stayed home could treat the war as an interminable scout project, with salvage drives and campaigns to sell war bonds. In the rural Midwest children picked milkweed pods to stuff life jackets; in coastal communities, they participated in blackout drills. Seattle high schools set aside one class period a day for the High School Victory Corps, training boys as messengers for air-raid wardens, while girls knitted sweaters and learned first aid.

LEARNING ABOUT THE WAR

The federal government tried to keep civilians of all ages committed to the war. It encouraged scrap drives and backyard victory gardens and created colorful posters to warn against espionage, inspire women to join the effort, and promote rationing and car-pooling. The government also managed news about the fighting. Censors screened soldiers' letters. Early in the war, they blocked publication of most photographs of war casualties, although magazines such as *Life* were full of strong and haunting images. Worried about flagging commitment, censors later authorized photographs of enemy atrocities to motivate the public.

War films revealed the nation's racial attitudes, often drawing distinctions between "good" and "bad" Germans but uniformly portraying Japanese as subhuman and repulsive. The most successful films dramatized the courage of the Allies.

WOMEN IN THE WORKFORCE

As draft calls took men off the assembly line, women changed the composition of the industrial workforce. The war gave them new job opportunities that were embodied in the image of Rosie the Riveter. Women made up one-quarter of West Coast shipyard workers and nearly half of Dallas and Seattle aircraft workers. Most women in the shipyards were clerks and general helpers. The acute shortage of welders and other skilled workers, however, opened thousands of lucrative journeyman positions to them. Aircraft companies, which compounded the labor shortage by stubborn "whites only" hiring, developed new power tools and production techniques to accommodate the smaller average size of women workers, increasing efficiency for everyone on the production line.

By July 1944, 19 million women held paid jobs, up 6 million in four years. Women's share of government jobs increased from 19 to 38 percent; they typed and filed in offices, but they also wrote propaganda for the Office of War Information and analyzed intelligence data for the office of Strategic Service. Women's share of manufacturing jobs went from 22 to 33 percent, many of them as W.O.W.s or Woman Ordnance Workers. Mirroring the sequence in which the military draft took men, employers recruited single women before turning to married women in 1943 and 1944. The federal government assisted female entry into the labor force by funding daycare programs that

As millions of men entered the armed forces, millions of women went to work. By 1943, federal agencies were actively recruiting women workers. Those who took production-line jobs received the greatest attention, like this worker at the Lockheed Aircraft Corporation plant in Burbank, California, which produced thousands of P-38 "Lightning" fighter planes.

served 600,000 children. Some women worked out of patriotism. Many others, however, needed to support their families and already had years of experience in the workforce. As one of the workers recalled of herself and a friend, "We both had to work, we both had children, so we became welders, and if I might say so, damn good ones."

Americans did not know how to respond to the growing numbers of working women. The country needed their labor, but many worried that their employment would undermine families. Employment recruitment posters showed strong, handsome women with rolled-up sleeves and wrenches in hand, but *Life* magazine reassured readers that women in factories could retain their sex appeal. Men and women commonly assumed that women would want to return to the home after victory.

ETHNIC MINORITIES IN THE WAR EFFORT

Mexican American workers made special contributions to the war effort. As defense factories and the military absorbed workers, western farms and railroads faced an acute shortage of workers. In the 1930s, western states had tried to deport Mexican nationals who were competing for scarce jobs. In 1942, however, the United States and Mexico negotiated the *bracero* program, under which the Mexican government recruited workers to come to the United States on six-to-twelve month contracts. More than 200,000 Mexicans worked on U.S. farms under the program, and more than 100,000 worked for western railroads. Although *bracero* workers still faced discrimination, the U.S. government tried to improve working conditions because it wanted to keep public opinion in Latin America favorable to the Allied cause.

The war was a powerful force for the assimilation of Native Americans. Forty thousand moved to off-reservation jobs; they were a key labor force for military supply depots throughout the West. The average cash income of Indian households tripled during the war. Many stayed in cities at its end. The experience of the war accelerated the fight for full civil rights. Congress had made Indians citizens in 1924, in part to recognize their contributions in World War I, but several states continued to deny them the vote. Activists organized the National Congress of American Indians in 1944 and began the efforts that led the U.S. Supreme Court in 1948 to require states to grant voting rights.

African Americans too, found economic advancement through war jobs. Early in the mobilization, labor leader A. Philip Randolph of the Brotherhood of Sleeping Car Porters worked with Walter White of the NAACP to plan a "Negro March on Washington" to protest racial discrimination by the federal government. To head off a major embarrassment, Roosevelt issued Executive Order 8802 in June 1941, barring racial discrimination in defense contracts and creating the **Fair Employment Practices Committee (FEPC)**; the order coined a phrase that reverberated powerfully through the coming decades: "No discrimination on grounds of race, color, creed, or national origin."

The FEPC's small staff resolved fewer than half of the employment-discrimination complaints, and white resistance to black coworkers remained strong. In Mobile, New Orleans, and Jacksonville, agreements between shipyards and segregated unions blocked skilled black workers from high-wage jobs. Nevertheless, African American membership in labor unions doubled, and wartime prosperity raised the average black income from 41 percent of the white average in 1939 to 61 percent by 1950, particularly because labor shortages raised farm wages.

Outside the workplace, African American women found that many voluntary service groups were racially segregated. In response, they formed the Women's Army for National Defense. They did their part by selling war bonds, helping with civil defense, and organizing USO clubs for black soldiers.

Many African Americans saw themselves as engaged in a "Double V" effort for victory against tyranny abroad and victory over racism at home. Economic gains helped. So did the fact that many were able to vote for the first time, either because they had moved to northern states where voting was not racially limited or because they were servicemen serving overseas. The economic and political changes helped to build a base for the civil rights movement that gained momentum in the postwar decades.

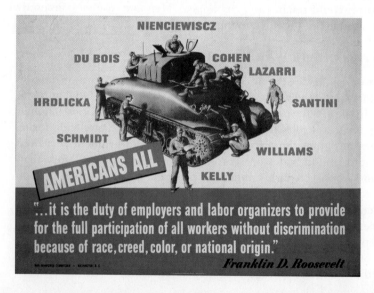

The government encouraged Americans of different nationalities to support the war effort in this poster with a quotation against discrimination by Franklin D. Roosevelt.

CLASHING CULTURES

As men and women migrated in search of work, they also crossed or collided with traditional boundaries of religion, region, and race. Some of the most troublesome conflicts arose from the acceleration of African American migration out of the South in the early 1940s. Many of the migrants headed for well-established black neighborhoods in northern cities. Others created new African American neighborhoods in western cities. White southerners and black northerners with different ideas of racial etiquette found themselves side by side in West Coast shipyards. In the Midwest, black migrants from the South and white migrants from Appalachia crowded into cities such as Cincinnati and Chicago, competing for the same high-wage jobs and scarce apartments.

Tensions between black and white residents exploded in at least 50 cities in 1943 alone. New York's Harlem neighborhood erupted in a riot after rumors of attacks on black servicemen. In Detroit, the issue was the boundary between white and black territory. In June 1943, an argument over the use of Detroit's Belle Isle Park set off three days of violence: Twenty-five black people and nine white people died in the most serious racial riot of the war.

Tensions were simultaneously rising between Mexican Americans and Anglos. As the Mexican community in Los Angeles swelled to an estimated 400,000, newspapers published anti-Mexican articles. On June 6, 1943, off-duty sailors and soldiers attacked Latinos on downtown streets and invaded Mexican American neighborhoods. The main targets were so-called *pachucos*—young Chicanos who wore flamboyant "zoot suits" with long, wide-shouldered jackets and pleated, narrow-cuffed trousers, whom the rioters considered delinquents or draft dodgers. The attacks dragged on for a week of sporadic violence against black people and Filipinos as well as Latinos. The assaults were poignantly ironic because 750,000 Mexican Americans served in the armed forces and were the most decorated group relative to their numbers.

INTERNMENT OF JAPANESE AMERICANS

On February 19, 1942, President Roosevelt authorized the secretary of war to define restricted areas and remove civilian residents who were threats to national security. The primary targets were 112,000 Japanese Americans in California and parts of Washington, Oregon, and Arizona. Japanese immigrants and their children in the western states had experienced 40 years of hostility because of racial prejudice, fear of the growing power of Japan, and jealousy of their business success. The outbreak of war triggered anti-Japanese hysteria and gave officials an excuse to take action against enemy aliens (immigrants who retained Japanese citizenship) and their American-born children.

Most West Coast Japanese were unable to leave because of ties to families and businesses. At the end of April 1942, Japanese in the coastal states were given a week to organize their affairs and report to assembly centers at fairgrounds and armories, where they were housed for several weeks before being moved again to ten internment camps in isolated locations in the western interior (see American Views: Internment of Japanese Americans in 1942). Here, they were housed in tarpaper barracks, hemmed in by barbed-wire fences, and guarded by military police. The victims reacted to the hardship and stress of their forced journeys in different ways. Several thousand second-generation Japanese Americans renounced their citizenship in disgust. But many others demonstrated their loyalty by cooperating with the authorities, finding sponsors who would help them move to other parts of the country, or joining the 442nd Regimental Combat Team, the most decorated American unit in the European war.

Although the U.S. Supreme Court sanctioned the removals in *Korematsu v. United States* (1944), the nation officially recognized its liability for lost property with the Japanese Claims Act of 1948. The nation acknowledged its broader moral responsibility in 1988, when Congress approved redress payments to each of the 60,000 surviving evacuees.

The internment of West Coast Japanese contrasted with the situation of German Americans and Italian Americans. The government interned approximately 11,000 German nationals and German Americans who were explicitly seen as individual threats. Until November 1942, it imposed curfews and travel restrictions on Italians and Italian Americans on the West Coast, but it interned fewer than 2,000. Both numbers were tiny fractions of the total populations.

THE END OF THE NEW DEAL

Roosevelt's New Deal ran out of steam in 1938. The war had reinvigorated his political fortunes by focusing national energies on foreign policy, over which presidents have the greatest power. After the 1942 election left Congress in the hands of Republicans and conservative southern Democrats, lawmakers ignored proposals that war emergency housing be used to improve the nation's permanent housing stock, abolished the National Resources Planning Board, curtailed rural electrification, and crippled the Farm Security Administration. Roosevelt himself declared, at a 1943 press conference, that "Dr. Win-the-War" had replaced "Dr. New Deal."

The presidential election of 1944 raised few new issues of substance. The Republicans nominated Governor Thomas Dewey of New York, who had made his reputation as a crime-fighting district attorney. The Democrats renominated Roosevelt for a fourth term. Missouri Senator Harry S Truman, a tough investigator of American military preparedness, replaced liberal New Dealer Henry Wallace as Roosevelt's running mate. The move appeased southern Democrats and moved the ticket toward the political center.

The most important issue was a fourth term for Roosevelt. Supporters argued that the nation could not afford to change leaders in the middle of a war, but Dewey's vigor and relative youth (he was 20 years younger than FDR) pointed up the president's failing health and energy. Voters gave Roosevelt 432 electoral votes to 99, but the narrowing gap in the popular vote—54 percent for Roosevelt and 46 percent for Dewey—made the Republicans eager for 1948.

In 1942, the federal government removed Japanese Americans from parts of four western states and interned them in isolated camps scattered through the West.

WAR AND PEACE

In January 1943, the U.S. War Department completed the world's largest office building, the Pentagon. The building housed 23,000 workers along 17.5 miles of corridors.
The building provided the space in which military planners could coordinate the tasks
of raising and equipping the armed forces that would strike directly at Germany and
Japan. Indeed, while Congress was chipping away at federal programs, the war effort was
massively expanding the government presence in American life. The gray walls of the
Pentagon symbolized a U.S. government that was outgrowing its prewar roots.

TURNING THE TIDE IN EUROPE

The unanswered military question of 1942 and 1943 was when the United States and
Britain would open a second front against Germany by attacking across the English
Channel. U.S. leaders wanted to justify massive mobilization with a war-winning cam-
paign and to strike across Europe to occupy the heart of Germany. Stalin needed a full-
scale invasion of western Europe to divert German forces from the Eastern Front, where
Soviet troops were inflicting 90 percent of German battle casualties.

The Allies spent 1943 hammering out war aims and strategies. Meeting in Casablanca
in January 1943, Roosevelt and Churchill demanded the unconditional surrender of
Italy, Germany, and Japan. The phrase meant that there would be no deals that kept the
enemy governments or leaders in power and was an effort to avoid the mistake of ending
World War I with Germany intact. Ten months later, the Allied leaders huddled again. At
Tehran, the United States and Britain promised to invade France within six months. "We
leave here," said the three leaders, "friends in fact, in spirit, in purpose."

The superficial harmony barely survived the end of the war. The Soviets had shouldered the brunt of the war for nearly two and a half years, suffering millions of casualties and seeing their nation devastated. Stalin and his generals scoffed at the small scale
of early U.S. efforts. Roosevelt's ideal of self-determination for all peoples, embodied in
the Atlantic Charter, seemed naive to Churchill, who wanted the major powers to carve
out realistic spheres of influence in Europe. Stalin wanted control of eastern Europe to
protect the Soviet Union against future invasions and assumed that realistic statesmen
would understand.

The Campaign in North Africa. The United States entered the ground war in Europe
with Operation TORCH. Soon after the British victory at El Alamein, British and American troops under General Dwight Eisenhower landed in French Morocco and Algeria
on November 8, 1942, against little opposition (see Map 26–2). These were territories
that the Germans had left under a puppet French government after the French military
collapse in 1940. German troops that remained in North Africa taught U.S. forces hard
lessons in tactics and leadership, but their stubborn resistance ended in May 1943, leaving all of Africa in Allied hands.

The Invasion of Italy. The central Mediterranean remained the focus of U.S. and British
action for the next year, despite the fact that the hard-pressed Soviets were desperate
for their allies to attack the heart of German power in northern Europe. However, the
British feared military disaster from a premature landing across the English Channel
and proposed strikes in southern Europe, which Churchill inaccurately called the "soft

AMERICAN VIEWS

THE INTERNMENT OF JAPANESE AMERICANS IN 1942

*I**n the spring of 1942, the U.S. army ordered Japanese Americans in four western states relocated to internment camps distant from the Pacific Coast. Monica Itoi Sone describes the experience of her Seattle family as they were transferred to temporary quarters—at the state fairgrounds, renamed "Camp Harmony" by the military—before they were moved again to Idaho.*

- **How** do the expectations of *issei* (immigrants who had been born in Japan) differ from those of *nisei* (their American-born children, including the author of this memoir)?
- **Why** did the U.S. army wait five months after Pearl Harbor before beginning the internment?
- **Does** the management of the assembly and internment suggest anything about stereotypes of Japanese Americans?

General DeWitt kept reminding us that E day, evacuation day, was drawing near. "E day will be announced in the very near future. If you have not wound up your affairs by now, it will soon be too late."

... On the twenty-first of April, a Tuesday, the general gave us the shattering news. "All the Seattle Japanese will be moved to Puyallup by May 1. Everyone must be registered Saturday and Sunday between 8 A.M. and 5 P.M."

Up to that moment, we had hoped against hope that something or someone would intervene for us. Now there was no time for moaning. A thousand and one details must be attended to in this one week of grace. Those seven days sputtered out like matches struck in the wind, as we rushed wildly about. Mother distributed sheets, pillowcases and blankets, which we stuffed into seabags. Into the two suitcases, we packed heavy winter overcoats, plenty of sweaters, woolen slacks and skirts, flannel pajamas and scarves. Personal toilet articles, one tin plate, tin cup and silverware completed our luggage. The one seabag and two suitcases apiece were going to be the backbone of our future home, and we planned it carefully.

Henry went to the Control Station to register the family. He came home with twenty tags, all numbered "10710," tags to be attached to each piece of baggage, and one to hang from our coat lapels. From then on, we were known as Family \ #10710. [On the day set for relocation] we climbed into the truck.... . As we coasted down Beacon Hill bridge for the last time, we fell silent, and stared out at the delicately flushed, morning sky of Puget Sound. We drove through bustling Chinatown, and in a few minutes arrived on the corner of Eighth and Lane. This area was ordinarily lonely and deserted but now it was gradually filling up with silent, labeled Japanese....

Finally at ten o'clock, a vanguard of Greyhound busses purred in and parked themselves neatly along the curb. The crowd stirred and murmured. The bus doors opened and from each, a soldier with rifle in hand stepped out and stood stiffly at attention by the door....

Newspaper photographers with flash-bulb cameras pushed busily through the crowd. One of them rushed up to our bus, and asked a young couple and their little boy to step out and stand by the door for a shot. They were reluctant, but the photographers were persistent and at length they got out of the bus and posed, grinning widely to cover their embarrassment. We saw the picture in the newspaper shortly after and the caption underneath it read, "japs good-natured about evacuation." Our bus quickly filled to capacity.... The door closed with a low hiss. We were now the Wartime Civil Control Administration's babies.

About noon we crept into a small town ... and we noticed at the left of us an entire block filled with neat rows of low shacks, resembling chicken houses. Someone commented on it with awe, "Just look at those chicken houses. They sure go in for poultry in a big way here." Slowly the bus made a left turn, drove through a wire-fenced gate, and to our dismay, we were inside the oversized chicken farm....

The apartments resembled elongated, low stables about two blocks long. Our home was one room, about 18 by 20 feet, the size of a living room. There was one small window in the wall opposite the one door. It was bare except for a small, tinny wood-burning stove crouching in the center....

I stared at our little window, unable to sleep. I was glad Mother had put up a makeshift curtain on the window for I noticed a powerful beam of light sweeping across it every few seconds. The lights came from high towers placed around the camp where guards with Tommy guns kept a twenty-four hour vigil. I remembered the wire fence encircling us, and a knot of anger tightened in my breast. What was I doing behind a fence like a criminal? If there were accusations to be made, why hadn't I been given a fair trial? Maybe I wasn't considered an American anymore. My citizenship wasn't real, after all. Then what was I? I was certainly not a citizen of Japan as my parents were. On second thought, even Father and Mother ... had little tie with their mother country. In their twenty-five years in America, they had worked and paid their taxes to their adopted government as any other citizen.

Of one thing I was sure. The wire fence was real. I no longer had the right to walk out of it. It was because I had Japanese ancestors. It was also because some people had little faith in the ideas and ideals of democracy.

Source: Monica Itoi Sone, *Nisei Daughter* (Seattle: University of Washington Press, 1979).

MAP 26–2 • **World War II in Europe, 1942–1945** Nazi Germany had to defend its conquests on three fronts. Around the Mediterranean, American and British forces pushed the Germans out of Africa and southern Italy, while guerrillas in Yugoslavia pinned down many German troops. On the Eastern Front, Soviet armies advanced hundreds of miles to drive the German Army out of the Soviet Union and eastern Europe. In June 1944, U.S. and British landings opened the Western Front in northern France for a decisive strike at the heart of Germany.

▶ **What were** the turning points in the war in Europe?

underbelly" of Hitler's empire. U.S. Army Chief of Staff George Marshall and President Roosevelt agreed to invade Italy in 1943, in part so that U.S. troops could participate in the ground fighting in Europe. Allied forces overran Sicily in July and August, but the Italian mainland proved more difficult. When Sicily fell, the Italian king and army forced Mussolini from power and began to negotiate peace with Britain and America (but not the Soviet Union). In September, the Allies announced an armistice with Italy, and Eisenhower's troops landed south of Naples on September 9. Germany responded by occupying the rest of Italy.

Just as American military planners had feared, the Italian campaign soaked up Allied resources. The mountainous Italian peninsula was one long series of defensive positions, and the Allies repeatedly bogged down. The Allies only managed to gain control of two-thirds of Italy before German resistance crumbled in the final weeks of the war.

Soviet advances and the Battle of Kursk. Meanwhile, the Soviets recruited, rearmed, and upgraded new armies, despite enormous losses. They learned to outfight the Germans in tank warfare and rebuilt munitions factories beyond German reach. They also made good use of 17.5 million tons of U.S. lend-lease assistance. As Soviet soldiers recaptured western Russia and Ukraine, they marched in 13 million pairs of American-made boots and ate U.S. rations. They traveled in 78,000 jeeps and 350,000 Studebaker, Ford, and Dodge trucks.

The climactic battle of the German-Soviet war erupted on July 5, 1943. The Germans sent 3,000 tanks against the Kursk salient, a huge wedge that the Red Army had pushed into their lines. In 1941 and 1942, such a massive attack would have forced the Soviets to retreat, but now Soviet generals had prepared a defense with 3,000 tanks of their own. With 1 million men actively engaged on each side for more than two weeks, Kursk was the largest pitched battle of the war. It marked the end of the last great German offensive, leaving Germany capable of a fighting retreat but too weak to have any hope of winning the war and expecting an American and British attack across the English Channel.

OPERATION OVERLORD

On **D-Day**—June 6, 1944—American, British, and Canadian forces landed on the coast of Normandy in northwestern France. The landings were the largest amphibious operation ever staged. Six divisions went ashore from hundreds of attack transports carrying 4,000 landing craft. Dozens of warships and 12,000 aircrafts provided support. One British and two American airborne divisions dropped behind German positions. When the sun set on the "longest day," the Allies had a tenuous toehold in France.

The next few weeks brought limited success. The Allies secured their beachheads and poured more than a million men and hundreds of thousands of vehicles ashore in the first six weeks. Although the Germans had concentrated forces further north where they expected the attack, the German defenders kept the Allies pinned for weeks along a narrow coastal strip. **Operation OVERLORD**, the code name for the entire campaign across northern France, met renewed success in late July and August. U.S. troops improved their fighting skills through "experience, sheer bloody experience." They finally broke through the German lines around the town of St.-Lô and then drew a ring around the Germans that slowly closed on the town of Falaise. The Germans lost a quarter of a million troops.

The German command chose to regroup closer to Germany rather than fight in France. The Allies liberated Paris on August 25; Free French forces (units that had never surrendered to the Nazis) led the entry. The drive toward Germany was the largest U.S. operation of the war. The only impediments appeared to be winter weather and pushing forward enough supplies for the rapidly advancing armies.

The story was similar on the Eastern Front, where the Soviets relentlessly battered one section of the German lines after another. By the end of 1944, the Red Army had entered the Balkans and reached central Poland. The Soviets had suffered as many as 24 million military and civilian deaths and sustained by far the heaviest burden in turning back Nazi tyranny (see Table 26–1).

VICTORY AND TRAGEDY IN EUROPE

In the last months of 1944, massive air strikes finally began to reduce German war production, which had actually increased during 1943 and much of 1944. The Americans flew daylight raids from air bases in Britain with heavily armed B-17s ("Flying Fortresses") and B-24s ("Liberators") to destroy factories with precision bombing. On August 17, 1943,

Table 26.1 Military and Civilian Deaths in World War II

24 million	Soviet Union
10–20 million	China
6–7 million	Germany and Austria
5.8 million	Poland
3–4 million	Indonesia
2.7 million	Japan
1–2 million	French Indochina (Vietnam, Laos, Cambodia) India Yugoslavia
500,000–1 million	France Greece Hungary Philippines Romania
300,000–500,000	Czechoslovakia Great Britain Italy Korea Lithuania The Netherlands United States

however, Germans shot down or damaged 19 percent of the bombers that attacked the aircraft factories of Regensburg and the ball-bearing factories of Schweinfurt. The Americans had to seek easier targets.

Gradually, however, the balance shifted. P-51 escort fighters helped B-17s overfly Germany in relative safety after mid-1944. Thousand-bomber raids on railroads and oil facilities began to cripple the German economy. The raids forced Germany to devote 2.5 million workers to air defense and damage repair and to divert fighter planes from the front lines. The air raids cut German military production by one-third through 1944 and destroyed the transportation system.

The Battle of the Bulge and the Collapse of Germany. Even as the air bombardment intensified, Hitler struck a last blow. Stripping the Eastern Front of armored units, he launched 25 divisions against thinly held U.S. positions in the Ardennes Forest of Belgium on December 16, 1944. He hoped to split U.S. and British forces by capturing the Belgian port of Antwerp. The attack surprised the Americans, and taking advantage of snow and fog that grounded Allied aircraft, the Germans drove a 50-mile bulge into U.S. lines. Although the Americans took substantial casualties, the German thrust literally ran out of gas beyond the town of Bastogne. The Battle of the Bulge never seriously threatened the outcome of the war, but pushing the Germans back through the snow-filled forest gave GIs a taste of the conditions that marked the war in the Soviet Union.

One of the war's most controversial actions came in February 1945, when British and American bombers attacked the historic city of Dresden. The raid triggered a firestorm that killed 25,000 people, many of them civilian refugees displaced by the Soviet advance. Because the Soviet army was less than a hundred miles from Berlin but the western allies had yet to cross the Rhine, critics have seen the raid as a purely political gesture by the British and Americans against a nonmilitary target. However, Dresden did have suburban factories producing for the military, and the city was a junction of major rail and telephone lines whose disruption created another obstacle to Germany's last-ditch resistance.

The Nazi empire collapsed in the spring of 1945. American and British divisions crossed the Rhine in March and enveloped Germany's industrial core. The Soviets drove through eastern Germany toward Berlin. On April 25, American and Soviet troops met on the Elbe River. Hitler committed suicide on April 30 in his concrete bunker deep under devastated Berlin, which surrendered to the Soviets on May 2. The Nazi state formally capitulated on May 8.

The Holocaust. The defeat of Germany revealed appalling evidence of the evil at the heart of the Nazi ideology of racial superiority. After occupying Poland in 1939, the Nazis had transformed concentration camps into forced-labor camps, where overwork, starvation, and disease killed hundreds of thousands of Jews, Gypsies, Poles, Russians, and others the Nazis classed as subhuman. As many as 7 million labor conscripts from eastern and western Europe provided forced labor in fields, factories, mines, and repair crews, often dying on the job from overwork and starvation.

The "final solution" to what Hitler thought of as the "Jewish problem" went far beyond slave labor. The German army in 1941 had gained practice with death by slaughtering hundreds of thousands of Jews and other civilians as it swept across Russia.

The Nazi regime sent slave laborers too weak to continue working on its V-2 rocket project to the Nordhausen concentration camp to die of starvation. When U.S. troops liberated the camp in April 1945, they found more than 3,000 corpses.

In the fall of that year, Hitler decided on the total elimination of Europe's Jews. The elite SS, Hitler's personal army within the Nazi Party, in 1942 set out to do his bidding. At Auschwitz, Treblinka, and several other death camps, the SS organized the efficient extermination of up to 6 million Jews and 1 million Poles, Gypsies, and others who failed to fit the Nazi vision of the German master race. Prisoners arrived by forced marches and cattle trains. Those who were not worked or starved to death were herded into gas chambers and then incinerated in huge crematoriums.

The evidence of genocide—systematic racial murder—is irrefutable. Allied officials had begun to hear reports of mass murder midway through the war, but memories of the inaccurate propaganda about German atrocities in World War I made many skeptical. Moreover, the camps were located in the heart of German-controlled territory, areas that Allied armies did not reach until 1945. At Dachau in southwestern Germany, American forces found 10,000 bodies and 32,000 prisoners near death through starvation. Soviet troops who overran the camps in Poland found even more appalling sights—gas chambers as big as barns, huge ovens, the dead stacked like firewood. For more than half a century, the genocide that we now call the **Holocaust** has given the world its most vivid images of inhumanity.

THE PACIFIC WAR

In the Pacific, as in Europe, the United States used 1943 to probe enemy conquests and to build better submarines, bigger aircraft carriers, and superior planes. Washington divided responsibilities in the Pacific theater. General Douglas MacArthur operated in the islands that stretched between Australia and the Philippines. Admiral Chester Nimitz commanded in the central Pacific. The Allies planned to isolate Japan from its southern conquests. The British moved from India to retake Burma. The Americans advanced along the islands of the southern Pacific to retake the Philippines. With Japan's army still tied down in China, the Americans then planned to bomb Japan into submission.

Racial hatred animated both sides in the Pacific war and fueled a "war without mercy." Americans often characterized Japanese soldiers as vermin. Political cartoons showed Japanese as monkeys or rats, and some Marines had "Rodent Exterminator" stenciled on their helmets. In turn, the Japanese depicted themselves as the "leading race" with the duty to rule the rest of Asia. Japan treated Chinese, Filipinos, and other conquered peoples with contempt and brutality, and the record of Japanese atrocities is substantial. Japanese viewed Americans as racial mongrels and called them demons. Each side expected the worst of the other and frequently lived up to expectations.

The Pacific campaigns of 1944 are often called **island hopping**. Planes from American carriers controlled the air, allowing the navy and land forces to isolate and capture the most strategically located Japanese-held islands while bypassing the rest.

MacArthur used a version of the bypass strategy in the Solomon Islands and New Guinea, leapfrogging past Japanese strong points. The invasion of the Philippines repeated the approach by landing on Leyte, in the middle of the island chain. The Philippine campaign also destroyed the last offensive capacity of the Japanese fleet in the Battle of Leyte Gulf. The Japanese home islands were left with no defensive screen against an expected invasion.

During 1943 and 1944, the United States also savaged the Japanese economy. Submarines choked off food, oil, and raw materials bound for Japan and island bases. By 1945, imports to Japan were one-eighth of the 1940 level. Heavy bombing of Japan began in early 1944, using the new long-range B-29. Japan's dense wooden cities were more vulnerable than their German counterparts, and Japanese air defenses were much weaker. A fire-bomb raid on Tokyo on the night of March 9, 1945, killed 124,000 people and left 1 million homeless; it was perhaps the single biggest mass killing of all time. Overall, conventional bombing destroyed 42 percent of Japan's industrial capacity. By the time the United States captured the islands of Iwo Jima and Okinawa in fierce fighting (April–June 1945) and neared the Japanese home islands, Japan's position was hopeless.

SEARCHING FOR PEACE

At the beginning of 1945, the Allies sensed victory. Conferring from February 4 to 11 in the Ukrainian town of Yalta, Roosevelt, Stalin, and Churchill planned for the postwar world. The most important American goal was to enlist the Soviet Union in finishing off the Pacific war. Americans hoped that a Soviet attack on Manchuria would tie down enough Japanese troops to reduce U.S. casualties in invading Japan. Stalin repeated his intent to declare war on Japan within three months of victory in Europe, in return for a free hand in Manchuria.

In Europe, the Allies had decided in 1944 to divide Germany and Austria into French, British, American, and Soviet occupation zones and to share control of Berlin. The Red Army already controlled Bulgaria, Romania, and Hungary, countries that had helped the Germans; Soviet officials were installing sympathetic regimes there. Soviet armies also controlled Poland. The most that Roosevelt could coax from Stalin was a vague pledge to allow participation of non-communists in coalition governments in eastern Europe. Stalin also agreed to join a new international organization, the United Nations (UN), whose foundations were laid at a conference in San Francisco in the spring of 1945. The new organization was intended to correct the mistakes of World War I, when the United States had stayed aloof from the League of Nations and had relied on international treaties without mechanisms of enforcement. American leaders wanted the UN to provide a framework through which the United States could coordinate collective security against potential aggressors while retaining its own military strength as the primary means to preserve the peace.

Conservative critics later charged that the western powers "gave away" eastern Europe at the **Yalta Conference**. In fact, the Soviet Union gained little that it did not already control. In East Asia as well, the Soviets could seize the territories the agreement granted them. Roosevelt may have overestimated his ability to charm Stalin, but the Yalta agreements were realistic diplomacy that could not undo the results of four years of fighting by the Soviet Army.

Truman and Potsdam. On April 12, two months after Yalta, Roosevelt died of a cerebral hemorrhage. Harry Truman, the new president, was a shrewd politician, but his experience was limited; Roosevelt had not even told him about the Manhattan Project. Deeply distrustful of the Soviets, Truman first ventured into personal international diplomacy in July 1945 at a British-Soviet-American conference at Potsdam, near Berlin. Most of the sessions debated the future of Germany. The leaders endorsed the expulsion of ethnic Germans from eastern Europe and moved the borders of Poland 100 miles west into historically German territory. Truman also made it clear that the United States expected to dominate the occupation of Japan. Its goal was to democratize the Japanese political system and reintroduce Japan into the international community, a policy that succeeded. The **Potsdam Declaration** on July 26 summarized U.S. policy and gave Japan an opening for surrender. However, the declaration failed to guarantee that Emperor Hirohito would not be tried as a war criminal. The Japanese response was so cautious that Americans read it as rejection.

The Atomic Bomb. Secretary of State James Byrnes now urged Truman to use the new atomic bomb, tested just weeks earlier. Japan's ferocious defense of Okinawa had confirmed American fears that the Japanese would fight to the death. Thousands of suicide missions by kamikaze pilots who tried to crash their planes into U.S. warships seemed additional proof of Japanese fanaticism. Prominent Americans were wondering if unconditional surrender was worth another six or nine months of bitter fighting. In contrast, using the bomb to end the conflict quickly would ensure that the United States could occupy Japan without Soviet participation, and the bomb might intimidate Stalin (see Overview, The Decision to Use the Atomic Bomb). In short, a decision not to use atomic weapons was never a serious alternative in the summer of 1945.

In early August, the United States dropped two of the three available nuclear bombs on Japan. On August 6, at Hiroshima, the first bomb killed at least 80,000 people and poisoned thousands more with radiation. A second bomb, three days later at Nagasaki, took another 40,000 lives. Japan ceased hostilities on August 14 and surrendered formally on September 2. The world has wondered ever since whether the United States might have defeated Japan without resorting to atomic bombs, but recent research shows that the bombs were the shock that allowed the emperor and peace advocates to overcome military leaders who wanted to fight to the death.

HOW THE ALLIES WON

The Allies won with economic capacity, technology, and military skill. The ability to outproduce the enemy made victory certain in 1944 and 1945, but it was the ability to outthink and outmaneuver the Axis powers that staved off defeat in 1942 and 1943.

In the spring of 1942, an unbroken series of conquests had given the Axis powers control of roughly one-third of the world's production of industrial raw materials, up from only 5 percent in 1939. But while Germany and Japan struggled to turn these resources into military strength, the Soviet Union accomplished wonders in relocating and rebuilding its manufacturing capacity after the disasters of 1941. The United States, meanwhile, rearmed with astonishing swiftness, accomplishing in one year what Germany had thought would take three. By 1944, the United States was outproducing all of its enemies combined; over the course of the war, it manufactured two-thirds of all the war materials used by the Allies.

The United States and the Soviet Union not only built more planes and tanks than the Axis nations, but they also built better ones. The Soviets developed and mass-produced the T-34, the world's most effective tank. American aircraft designers soon jumped ahead of the Germans. The United States and Britain gained the lead in communication systems, radar, code-breaking capability, and, of course, atomic weapons. Even behind the lines the Allies had the technical advantage. The U.S. and British forces that invaded France were fully motorized, and Soviet forces increasingly so, while the German army still depended on horses to draw supply wagons and artillery.

The Allies learned hard lessons from defeat and figured out how to outfight the Axis. Hitler's generals outsmarted the Soviet military in 1941, Japan outmaneuvered the British and Americans in the first months of the Pacific war, and the German navy came close to squeezing the life from Great Britain in 1942. In 1943 and 1944, the tables were turned. The Russians reexamined every detail of their military procedures and devised new tactics that kept the vast German armies off guard and on the defensive. New ways to fight U-boats in the Atlantic devastated the German submarine service and staved

OVERVIEW THE DECISION TO USE THE ATOMIC BOMB

Americans have long argued about whether the use of atomic bombs on the Japanese cities of Hiroshima and Nagasaki was necessary to end the war. Several factors probably influenced President Truman's decision to use the new weapon.

Military necessity	After the war, Truman argued that the use of atomic bombs was necessary to avoid an invasion of Japan that would have cost hundreds of thousands of lives. Military planners expected Japanese soldiers to put up the same kind of suicidal resistance in defense of the home islands as they had to American landings in the Philippines, Iwo Jima, and Okinawa. More recently, historians have argued that the Japanese military was near collapse and an invasion would have met far less resistance than feared.
Atomic diplomacy	Some historians believe that Truman used atomic weapons to overawe the Soviet Union and induce it to move cautiously in expanding its influence in Europe and East Asia. Truman and his advisers were certainly aware of how the bomb might influence the Soviet leadership.
Domestic politics	President Roosevelt and his chief military advisers had spent billions on the secret atomic bomb project without the full knowledge of Congress or the American public. The managers of the Manhattan Project may have believed that only proof of its military value would quiet critics and justify the huge cost.
Momentum of war	The United States and Britain had already adopted wholesale destruction of German and Japanese cities as a military tactic. Use of the atomic bomb looked like a variation on fire bombing, not the start of a new era of potential mass destruction. In this context, some historians argue, President Truman's choice was natural and expected.

off defeat. Americans in the Pacific utilized the full capacity of aircraft carriers, while Japanese admirals still dreamed of confrontations between lines of battleships.

Finally, the Allies had the appeal of democracy and freedom. The Axis nations were clearly the aggressors. Germany and Japan made bitter enemies by exploiting and abusing the people of the countries they conquered, from Yugoslavia and France to Malaya and the Philippines, and incited local resistance movements. The Allies were certainly not perfect, but they fought for the ideals of political independence and were welcomed as liberators as they pushed back the Axis armies.

CONCLUSION

The United States ended the war as the world's overwhelming economic power. It had put only 12 percent of its population in uniform, less than any other major combatant. For every American who died, 20 Germans and dozens of Soviets perished. Having suffered almost no direct destruction, the United States was able to dictate a postwar economic trading system that favored its interests.

Nevertheless, the insecurities of the war years influenced the United States for decades. A nation's current leaders are often shaped by its last war. Churchill had directed strategy, and Hitler, Mussolini, and Truman had all fought in World War I and carried its memories into World War II. The lessons of World War II would similarly influence the thinking of presidents from Dwight Eisenhower in the 1950s to George H. W. Bush in the 1990s. Even though the United States ended 1945 with the world's mightiest navy, biggest air force, and only atomic bomb, memories of the instability that had followed World War I made its leaders nervous about the shape of world politics.

One result in the postwar era was conflict between the United States and the Soviet Union, whose only common ground had been a shared enemy. After Germany's defeat, their wartime alliance gave way to hostility and confrontation in the Cold War. At home, international tensions fed the pressure for social and political conformity. The desire to enjoy the fruits of victory after 15 years of economic depression and sacrifice made the postwar generation sensitive to perceived threats to steady jobs and stable families. For the next generation, the unresolved business of World War II would haunt American life.

REVIEW QUESTIONS

1. What motivated German, Italian, and Japanese aggression in the 1930s? How did Great Britain, the USSR, and other nations respond to the growing conflict?

2. What arguments did Americans make against involvement in the war in Europe, and how deep was anti-intervention sentiment? Why did President Roosevelt and many others believe it necessary to block German and Japanese expansion? What steps did Roosevelt take to increase U.S. involvement short of war?

3. What was the military balance in early 1942? What were the chief threats to the United States and its allies? Why did the fortunes of war turn in late 1942?

4. Assess how mobilization for World War II altered life in the United States. How did the war affect families? How did it shift the regional balance of the economy? What opportunities did it open for women?

5. Did World War II help or hinder progress toward racial equality in the United States? How did the experiences of Japanese Americans, African Americans, and Mexican Americans challenge American ideals?

6. What factors were decisive in the defeat of Germany? How important were Soviet efforts on the Eastern Front, the bomber war, and the British-American landings in France?

7. What was the U.S. strategy against Japan, and how well did it work? What lay behind President Truman's decision to use atomic bombs against Japanese cities?

8. What role did advanced science and technology play in World War II? How did the scientific lead of the United States affect the war's outcome?

PEARSON myhistorylab CONNECTIONS

Reinforce what you learned in this chapter by studying the many documents, images, maps, review tools, and videos available at **www.myhistorylab.com.**

READ AND REVIEW

✔● Study and Review on **myhistorylab.com** STUDY PLAN: CHAPTER 26

📖● Read the Document on **myhistorylab.com**

> *A. Philip Randolph, "Why Should We March" (1942)*
>
> *Albert Einstein, Letter to President Roosevelt (1939)*
>
> *Charles Lindbergh, Radio Address (1941)*
>
> *Executive Order 8802 (1941)*
>
> *Jim Crow in the Army Camps, 1940 and Jim Crow Army (1941)*
>
> *Manhattan Project Notebook (1945)*

🔍● View the Map on **myhistorylab.com**

> *World War II, European Theater*
>
> *World War II, Pacific Theater*

RESEARCH AND EXPLORE

📖● Read the Document on **myhistorylab.com**

> *Personal Journeys Online*
>
> *From Then to Now Online: Nuclear Weapons*

((●● Listen on **myhistorylab.com**

> *Pearl Harbor performed by New York, Georgia Singers*
>
> *War Song*
>
> *Obey the Ration Laws*

👁● Watch the Video on **myhistorylab.com**

> *Hitler and Roosevelt*
>
> *Atomic Bomb at Hiroshima*
>
> *Atomic Age Begins*
>
> *The Desegregation of the Military and Blacks in Combat*
>
> *Truman on the End of World War II*
>
> *Rosie the Riveter*

((●● Listen on **myhistorylab.com**

Hear the audio files for Chapter 26 at
www.myhistorylab.com.

27

The Cold War at Home and Abroad •• 1946–1952

Kidde
Kokoon

CANNED

CANNED WATER

Hear the audio files for Chapter 27 at **www.myhistorylab.com.**

FOCUS QUESTIONS

WHAT WAS the catalyst for the economic boom that began in 1947?

HOW WAS Harry Truman able to win the 1948 presidential election?

WHAT WERE the origins of the Cold War?

HOW DID the Korean War shape American domestic politics?

WHY DID fear of Communism escalate in the years following World War II?

As international tensions rose with the onset of the Cold War, many families stocked extra food and water and bought a battery-powered radio. Some actually installed backyard bomb shelters like the one being tested by this family.

ONE AMERICAN JOURNEY

Veterans wake up! Your dream home is here.

Dreaming of the good life? Beautiful Lakewood is more than owning a home … It is a new and better way of living.

Advertisements like these for the new Los Angeles County community of Lakewood in 1950 aimed at families hungry for a place of their own after the privations of World War II. "Owning your own home … to have a place of our own was very, very special," remembered Jackie Rynerson.

The ads tried to make it sound easy, showing a young boy saying: We just bought a slock two-bedroom home for $43 a month and NO DOWN PAYMENT because Pop's a veteran! Even so, June Tweedy recalled that it was still a big step to become a suburban homeowner. "When you put your little check down for your down payment, it was like signing away your life. It seemed like a lot in those days."

From The Lakewood Story: History, Tradition, Values (Copyright 2004 by City of Lakewood, California).

LAKEWOOD'S NEW FAMILIES were moving into one of the most successful of the giant subdivisions that blossomed in the postwar decade. Like Levittown, New York in the same years, it attracted a flood of buyers desperate for a home of their own. On the first day of sales on Palm Sunday, 1950, 25,000 people lined up in front of the sales office, and 7200 houses sold in the first ten months, most before they were actually built.

Lakewooders were part of the first wave in the suburbanization of postwar America. Over the next decades, the families who made the journey from city's neighborhoods to thousands of new subdivisions would start the baby boom and rekindle the economy with their purchases of automobiles, appliances, and televisions.

This compelling desire to enjoy the promise of American life after years of sacrifice helps explain why Americans reacted so fiercely to new challenges and threats. They watched as congressional conservatives and President Truman fought over the fate of New Deal programs. More worrisome was the confrontation with the Soviet Union that was soon being called the **Cold War**. Triggered by the Soviet Union's imposition of Communist regimes throughout eastern Europe, the Cold War grew into a global contest in which the United States tried to counter Soviet influence around the world. The Cold War would shape the United States and the world for a generation.

LAUNCHING THE GREAT BOOM

When World War II ended, Americans feared that demobilization would bring a rerun of the inflation and unemployment that had followed World War I. Indeed, in the first 18 months of peace, rising prices, strife between labor and management, and shortages of everything from meat to automobiles confirmed their anxiety. But in fact, 1947 and 1948 ushered in an economic expansion that lasted for a quarter-century. The resulting prosperity would finance a military buildup and an activist foreign policy. It also supported continuity in domestic politics from the late 1940s to the mid-1960s.

RECONVERSION CHAOS

Japan's sudden surrender took the United States by surprise. The Pentagon, already scaling back defense spending, canceled $15 billion in war contracts in the first two days after the Japanese surrendered. Public pressure demanded that the military release the nation's 12 million service personnel as rapidly as possible. GIs in Europe and the South Pacific waited impatiently for their turn on slow, crowded troop ships. Even at the rate of 25,000 discharges a day, it took a year to get all of them back to civilian life.

Veterans came home to shortages of food and consumer goods. High demand and short supply meant inflationary pressure, checked temporarily by continuing the Office of Price Administration until October 1946. Meanwhile, producers, consumers, and retailers scrambled to evade price restrictions and scarcities.

A wave of strikes made it hard to retool factories for civilian products. Inflation squeezed factory workers, who had accepted wage controls during the war effort. Since 1941, prices had risen twice as fast as base wages. In the fall of 1945, more and more workers went on strike to redress the balance; the strikes interrupted the output of products from canned soup to copper wire. By January 1946, some 1.3 million auto, steel, electrical, and packinghouse workers were off the job. Strikes in these basic industries shut other factories down for lack of supplies. Presidential committees crafted settlements that allowed steel and auto workers to make up ground lost during the war, but they also allowed corporations to pass on higher costs to consumers.

ECONOMIC POLICY

The economic turmoil of 1946 set the stage for two major and contradictory efforts to deal more systematically with peacetime economic readjustment. The Employment Act of 1946 and the Taft-Hartley Act of 1947 represented liberal and conservative approaches to the peacetime economy.

The Employment Act was an effort by congressional liberals to ward off economic crisis by fine-tuning government taxation and spending. It started as a proposal for a full-employment bill that would ensure everyone's "right to a useful and remunerative job." Watered down in the face of business opposition, it still defined economic growth and high employment as national goals. It also established the **Council of Economic Advisers** to assist the president.

In the short term, the Employment Act aimed at a problem that did not materialize. Economists had predicted that the combination of returning veterans and workers idled by canceled defense work would bring depression-level unemployment of 8 to 10 million. In fact, more than 2 million women provided some slack by leaving the labor force outright. In addition, a savings pool of $140 billion in bank accounts and war bonds created a huge demand for consumer goods and workers to produce them. Total employment rose rather than fell with the end of the war, and unemployment in 1946–1948 stayed below 4 percent.

From the other end of the political spectrum, the **Taft-Hartley Act** climaxed a ten-year effort by conservatives to reverse the gains made by organized labor in the 1930s. The act passed in 1947 because of anger about continuing strikes. Many middle-class Americans were convinced that organized labor needed to be curbed.

In November 1946, Republicans capitalized on the problems of reconversion chaos, labor unrest, and dissatisfaction with Truman. Their election slogan was simple: "Had

CHRONOLOGY

1944   Servicemen's Readjustment Act (GI Bill) is passed.

1945   United Nations is established.

1946   Employment Act creates Council of Economic Advisers.
George Kennan sends his "long telegram."
Winston Churchill delivers his "iron curtain" speech.

1947   Truman Doctrine is announced.
Truman establishes a federal employee loyalty program.
Kennan explains containment policy in an anonymous article in
Foreign Affairs.
Marshall Plan begins providing economic aid to Europe.
HUAC holds hearings on Hollywood.
Taft-Hartley Act rolls back gains of organized labor.
National Security Act creates National Security Council and Central
Intelligence Agency.

1948   Communists stage coup in Czechoslovakia.
Berlin airlift overcomes Soviet blockade.
Truman orders desegregation of the armed forces.
Selective Service is reestablished.
Truman wins reelection.

1949   North Atlantic Treaty Organization is formed.
Communist Chinese defeat Nationalists.
Soviet Union tests an atomic bomb.
Department of Defense is established.

1950   Senator McCarthy begins his Red hunt.
Alger Hiss is convicted of perjury.
Internal Security Act (McCarran Act).
NSC-68 is drafted and accepted as U.S. policy.
Korean War begins.

1951   Senate Internal Security Subcommittee begins hearings.
Truman relieves MacArthur of his command.
Julius and Ethel Rosenberg are convicted of conspiring to commit
espionage.
Truce talks begin in Korea.

1952   United States tests the hydrogen bomb.
Eisenhower is elected president.

With the flood of veterans seeking college degrees after World War II, universities had to improvise to find adequate housing. On this Rhode Island campus, war surplus quonset huts made do as housing for married students.

enough?" The GOP won control of Congress for the first time since the election of 1928, continuing the political trend toward the right that had been apparent since 1938.

Adopted by the now firmly conservative Congress, the Taft-Hartley Act was a serious counterattack by big business against large unions. It outlawed several union tools as "unfair labor practices." It barred the closed shop (the requirement that all workers hired in a given company or plant be union members) and blocked secondary boycotts (strikes against suppliers or customers of a targeted business). The federal government could postpone a strike by imposing a cooling-off period, which gave companies time to stockpile their products. Officers of national unions had to swear that they were not Communists or Communist sympathizers, even though corporate executives had no similar obligation. The bill passed over Truman's veto.

The GI Bill

Another landmark law for the postwar era passed Congress without controversy. The Servicemen's Readjustment Act of 1944 was designed to ease veterans back into the civilian mainstream. Popularly known as the **GI Bill of Rights**, it was one of the federal government's most successful public assistance programs. Rather than pay cash bonuses to veterans, as after previous wars, Congress tied benefits to specific public goals. The GI Bill guaranteed loans of up to $2,000 for buying a house or farm or starting a business, a substantial sum at a time when a new house cost $6,000. The program encouraged veterans to attend college with money for tuition and books plus monthly stipends.

The GI Bill democratized American higher education by making college degrees accessible to men with working-class backgrounds. It brought far more students into higher education than could otherwise have enrolled. In the peak year of 1947, veterans made up half of all college students. Veterans helped convert the college degree, once available primarily to the socially privileged, into a basic business and professional credential. However, the GI tide unfortunately crowded women out of classrooms. Women's share of bachelor's degrees dropped from 40 percent in 1940 to 25 percent in 1950.

ASSEMBLY-LINE NEIGHBORHOODS

Americans faced a housing shortage after the war. In 1947, fully 3 million married couples were unable to set up their own households. Most doubled up with relatives while they waited for the construction industry to respond. Hunger for housing was fierce. Eager buyers lined up for hours and paid admission fees to tour model homes or to put their names in drawings for the opportunity to buy.

The solution started with the federal government and its Veterans Administration (VA) mortgage program. By guaranteeing repayment, the VA allowed veterans to get home-purchase loans from private lenders without a down payment. Neither the VA program nor the New Deal–era Federal Housing Administration (FHA) mortgage insurance program, however, could do any good unless there were houses to buy. Eyeing the mass market created by the federal programs, innovative private builders devised their own solution. In 1947, William Levitt, a New York builder who had developed defense housing projects, built 2,000 houses for veterans on suburban Long Island. His basic house had 800 square feet of living space in two bedrooms, living room, kitchen, and bath, a 60-by-100-foot lot, and an unfinished attic waiting for the weekend handyman. There were 6,000 Levittown houses by the end of 1948 and more than 17,000 by 1951.

Other successful builders worked on the same scale. They bought hundreds of acres of land, put in utilities for the entire tract, purchased materials by the carload, and kept specialized workers busy on scores of identical houses.

From 1946 through 1950, the federal government backed $20 billion in VA and FHA loans, approximately 40 percent of all home-mortgage debt. Housing starts neared 2 million in the peak year of 1950. By the end of the 1940s, 55 percent of American households owned their homes. The figure continued to climb until the 1980s, broadening access to the dream of financial security for many families. All during this time, the suburban population grew much faster than the population of central cities, and the population outside of metropolitan areas actually declined.

Isolation and Discrimination. Unfortunately, the suburban solution to the housing shortage came with costs. The vast new housing tracts tended to isolate women and children from traditional community life. Moreover, they were of little benefit to African Americans. As the migration of black workers and their families to northern and western cities continued after the war, discrimination excluded them from new housing. Federal housing agencies and private industry worsened the problem by **redlining** older neighborhoods, which involved withholding home-purchase loans and insurance coverage from inner-city areas that were deemed too risky as investments. Thus public and private actions kept African Americans in deteriorating inner-city ghettos.

Jackie Robinson, the first black player in modern major league baseball, joined the Brooklyn Dodgers in 1947. He was both personally courageous and an outstanding player. Here he steals home against the Chicago Cubs in 1952.

STEPS TOWARD CIVIL RIGHTS

The urgent need for decent housing helped to motivate African Americans to demand full rights as citizens. The wartime experience of fighting for freedom abroad while suffering discrimination at home steeled a new generation of black leaders to close the gap between America's ideal of equality and its performance. As had also been true after World War I, some white Americans held the opposite view, hoping to reaffirm racial segregation. A wave of racist violence surged across the South after the war; special targets were black veterans who tried to register to vote. However, many white Americans felt uneasy about the contradiction between a crusade for freedom abroad and racial discrimination at home.

In this era of rapid change and racial tension, the Truman administration recognized the importance of upholding civil rights for all Americans. Caught between pressure from black leaders and the fear of alienating southern Democrats, the president in 1946 appointed the Committee on Civil Rights, whose report developed an agenda for racial justice that would take two decades to put into effect. The NAACP had already begun a campaign of anti-segregation lawsuits, which the Justice Department now began to support. The administration ordered federal housing agencies to modify their racially restrictive policies and prohibited racial discrimination in federal employment. Federal committees began to push for desegregation of private facilities in the symbolically important city of Washington, DC. In an important decision in the case of *Shelley v. Kraemer* (1948), the Supreme Court held that clauses in real estate deeds that forbid selling or renting to minorities could not be enforced in the courts.

The president also ordered "equality of treatment and opportunity" in the armed services in July 1948. The army in particular dragged its feet, hoping to limit black enlistees to 10 percent of the total. Manpower needs and the record of integrated units in the war in Korea from 1950 to 1953 persuaded the reluctant generals. Over the next generation, African Americans would find the military an important avenue for career opportunities.

Changes in national policy were important for ending racial discrimination, but far more Americans were interested in lowering racial barriers in professional team sports. Americans had applauded individual black champions, such as boxer Joe Louis and sprinter Jesse Owens, but team sports required their members to travel, practice, and play together. The center of attention was Jack Roosevelt ("Jackie") Robinson, a gifted African American athlete, who opened the 1947 baseball season as a member of the Brooklyn Dodgers. Robinson broke the color line that had reserved the modern major leagues for white players. His ability to endure taunting and hostility and still excel on the ball field opened the door for other African Americans and Latinos. In the segregated society of the 1940s, Robinson found himself a powerful symbol of racial change.

CONSUMER BOOM AND BABY BOOM

The housing boom was a product of both pent-up demand and a postwar "family boom." Americans celebrated the end of the war with weddings; the marriage rate in 1946 surpassed even its wartime high. Many women who left the labor force opted for marriage, and at increasingly younger ages. By 1950, the median age at which women married would be just over 20 years—lower than at any previous time in the twentieth century. The United States ended the 1940s with 7 million more married couples than at the decade's start.

New marriages jumpstarted the "baby boom," as did already married couples who decided to catch up after postponing childbearing during the war. In the early 1940s, an average of 2.9 million children per year were born in the United States; in 1946–1950, the average was 3.6 million. Those 3.5 million "extra" babies needed diapers, swing sets, lunch boxes, bicycles, and schoolrooms.

Fast-growing families also needed to stock up on household goods. Out of an average household income of roughly $4,000 in 1946 and 1947, a family of four had $300 to $400 a year for furnishings and appliances. A couple might equip its new suburban kitchen with a Dripolator coffee maker for $2.45 and a Mirro-Matic pressure cooker for $12.95. The thrifty family could get along with a Motorola table radio for under $30; for $100, it could have a massive radio-phonograph combination in a 4-foot console as the centerpiece of a well-equipped living room.

TRUMAN, REPUBLICANS, AND THE FAIR DEAL

From new products to new homes to new jobs, the economic gains of the postwar years propelled Americans toward the political center. After 15 years of economic crisis and world war, they wanted to enjoy prosperity.

Recognizing this attitude, Harry Truman and his political advisers tried to define policies acceptable to moderate Republicans as well as to Democrats. This meant creating a bipartisan coalition to block Soviet influence in Western Europe and defending the core of the New Deal's social and economic agenda at home.

This political package is known as the strategy of the "vital center," after the title of a 1949 book by Arthur Schlesinger, Jr. The book linked anti-Communism in foreign policy with efforts to enact inclusive social and economic policies to extend freedom abroad and at home. The vital center reflected the political reality of the Cold War years, when Democrats had to prove that they were tough on Communism before they could enact domestic reforms. The approach defined the heart of the Democratic Party for 20 years and found full expression in the administrations of John Kennedy (1961–1963) and Lyndon Johnson (1963–1969).

TRUMAN'S OPPOSITION

Truman had unexpected luck in his campaign for a full term as president in 1948. Besides the Republicans, he faced new fringe parties on the far right and far left that allowed him to position himself in the moderate center.

Harry Truman greets supporters and railroad workers in Pittsburgh at the start of an eighteen-state campaign tour in June 1948. Truman's grassroots campaign and down-home style helped him pull out an unexpected victory in November 1948.

Truman's opponents represented the left-leaning American Progressive Party, the **Dixiecrats** (officially the States' Rights Democrats), and the Republicans. The Progressive candidate was Henry Wallace, who had been FDR's vice president from 1941 to 1945, before being dumped in favor of Truman; more recently, he had been Truman's secretary of commerce. The Dixiecrat, Governor Strom Thurmond of South Carolina, had bolted the Democratic Party over civil rights. The most serious challenger was the Republican, Thomas Dewey, who had run against Roosevelt in 1944.

Tom Dewey had a high opinion of himself. He had been an effective governor of New York and represented the moderate eastern establishment within the Republican Party. Fortunately for Truman, Dewey lacked the common touch. Smooth on the outside, he alienated people who should have been his closest supporters. He was a bit of a snob and was an arrogant campaigner, refusing to interrupt his morning schedule to talk to voters.

Dewey was also saddled with the results of the Republican-controlled "do-nothing" 80th Congress (1947–1948). Truman used confrontation with Congress to rally voters who had supported the New Deal. He introduced legislation that he knew would be ignored, and he used his veto even when he knew Congress would override it. All the while he was building a list of campaign issues by demonstrating that the Republicans were obstructionists. Vote for me, Truman argued, to protect the New Deal, or vote Republican to bring back the days of Herbert Hoover.

WHISTLE-STOPPING ACROSS AMERICA

The 1948 presidential campaign mixed old and new. For the last time, a major candidate crisscrossed the nation by rail and made hundreds of speeches from the rear platforms of trains. For the first time, national television broadcast the two party conventions, although the primitive cameras showed the handful of viewers little more than talking heads.

Truman ran on both character and issues. He was a widely read and intelligent man who cultivated the image of a backslapper. He covered 31,700 miles in his campaign train and gave ten speeches a day. Republicans belittled the small towns and cities he visited, calling them "whistle stops." Democrats made the term a badge of pride for places like Laramie, Wyoming, and Pocatello, Idaho.

Truman brought the campaign home to average Americans. He tied Dewey to inflation, housing shortages, and fears about the future of Social Security (an issue that Democrats would continue to use into the next century). In industrial cities, he hammered at the Taft-Hartley Act. In the West, he pointed out that Democratic administrations had built dams and helped to turn natural resources into jobs. He called the Republicans the party of privilege and arrogance. The Democrats, he said, offered opportunity for farmers, factory workers, and small business owners.

Truman got a huge boost from Dewey's unwillingness to fight. Going into the fall with a huge lead in the public opinion polls, Dewey sought to avoid mistakes. Wallace and Thurmond each took just under 1.2 million votes. Dewey received nearly 22 million popular votes and 189 electoral votes, but Truman won more than 24 million popular votes and 303 electoral votes (see Map 27–1).

TRUMAN'S FAIR DEAL

Truman hoped to build on the gains of the New Deal. In his State of the Union address in January 1949, he called for a Fair Deal for all Americans. He promised to extend

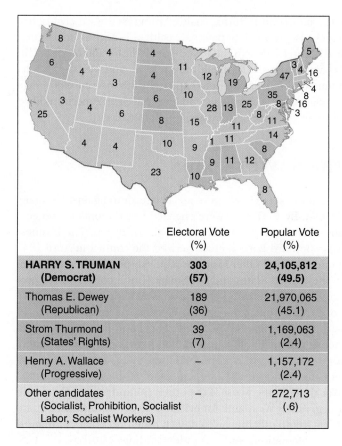

MAP 27–1 • **The Election of 1948** Harry Truman won a narrow victory in the presidential election of 1948 by holding many of the traditionally Democratic states of the South and West and winning key industrial states in the Middle West. His success depended on the coalition of rural and urban interests that Franklin Roosevelt had pulled together in the 1930s.

▶ *Why do* you think industrial states in the Midwest supported Harry S. Truman in the 1948 presidential election?

	Electoral Vote (%)	Popular Vote (%)
HARRY S. TRUMAN (Democrat)	**303** **(57)**	**24,105,812** **(49.5)**
Thomas E. Dewey (Republican)	189 (36)	21,970,065 (45.1)
Strom Thurmond (States' Rights)	39 (7)	1,169,063 (2.4)
Henry A. Wallace (Progressive)	–	1,157,172 (2.4)
Other candidates (Socialist, Prohibition, Socialist Labor, Socialist Workers)	–	272,713 (.6)

the New Deal and ensure "greater economic opportunity for the mass of the people." Over the next four years, however, conservative Republicans and southern Democrats forced Congress to choose carefully among Truman's proposals, accepting those that expanded existing programs but rejecting new departures. The result was a set of disconnected measures rather than the consistent program that Truman had advocated.

With the Housing Act of 1949, the federal government reaffirmed its concern about families who had been priced out of the private market. The act provided money for local housing agencies to buy, clear, and resell land for housing. The intent was to clear "substandard and blighted areas" and replace them with affordable modern apartments. The program never worked as intended because of scanty appropriations, poor design of the replacement housing, and local decisions that concentrated public housing in segregated minority neighborhoods, but it established the goal of decent housing for all Americans.

In 1950, Congress revitalized the weak Social Security program. Benefits went up by an average of 80 percent, and 10.5 million additional people received old-age and survivors' insurance. Most of the new coverage went to rural and smalltown people, thus consolidating the broad support that has made it politically difficult to change Social Security ever since, even in the face of projected shortages in the twenty-first century.

Congress rejected other Fair Deal proposals that would remain on the national agenda for decades. A Senate filibuster killed a permanent Fair Employment Practices

Commission to fight racial discrimination in hiring, halting progress toward civil rights. The medical establishment blocked a proposal for national health insurance as "socialistic," leaving the issue to be revisited in the 1960s with the passage of Medicare and Medicaid, in the 1990s with Bill Clinton's failed proposals for healthcare reform, and with the Obama administration's long and ultimately successful fight to expand health insurance coverage in 2009–2010. The overall message from Truman's second term was clear: Americans liked what the New Deal had given them but were hesitant about new initiatives.

CONFRONTING THE SOVIET UNION

In 1945, the United States and the Soviet Union were allies, victorious against Germany and planning the defeat of Japan. By 1947, they were engaged in a diplomatic and economic confrontation and soon came close to war over the city of Berlin. The business tycoon and presidential adviser Bernard Baruch characterized the conflict in April 1947 as a "cold war," and newspaper columnist Walter Lippmann quickly popularized the term.

Over the next 40 years, the United States and the Soviet Union contested for economic, political, and military influence around the globe. The heart of Soviet policy was to control eastern Europe as a buffer zone against Germany. The centerpiece of American policy was to link the United States, Western Europe, and Japan into an alliance of overwhelming economic power. For the United States, the Cold War was simultaneously an effort to promote democracy in Europe, maintain a favorable military position in relation to the Soviet Union, and preserve its leadership of the world economy.

Each side in the Cold War thought the worst of the other. Behind the conflicts were Soviet insecurity about an aggressive West and American fear of Communist expansionism. Americans and Soviets frequently interpreted each other's actions in the most threatening terms, turning miscalculations and misunderstandings into crises. A U.S. public that had suffered through nearly two decades of economic depression and war reacted to international problems with frustration and anger. The emotional burdens of the Cold War warped and narrowed a generation of American political life around the requirements of anti-Communism.

THE END OF THE GRAND ALLIANCE

The Yalta Conference of February 1945 had recognized military realities by marking out rough spheres of influence. The Western allies had the better of the bargain. Defeated Italy and Japan, whose reconstruction was firmly in Western hands, had far greater economic potential than Soviet-controlled Bulgaria, Romania, or Hungary. In addition, the Allies had divided Germany into four occupation zones. The British, French, and American zones in western Germany held more people and industrial potential than the Russian zone in eastern Germany.

As the victorious powers tried to put their broad agreements into operation, they argued bitterly about Germany and eastern Europe. Was the Soviet Union to dominate eastern Europe as its protective buffer, or was the region to be open to Western economic and political influence? For Poland, Truman and his advisers claimed that Yalta had assumed open elections on the American model. The Soviet Union claimed that Yalta had ensured that any Polish government would be friendly to Soviet interests and acted to guarantee that this would be so.

Facing Soviet intransigence over eastern Europe, Truman decided that the United States should "take the lead in running the world in the way the world ought to be run." One technique was economic pressure. The State Department "mislaid" a Soviet request for redevelopment loans. The United States and Britain objected to Soviet plans to take industrial equipment and raw materials from the western occupation zones in Germany, compensation that the Soviets thought they had been promised.

The United States also tried to involve the Soviet Union and eastern Europe in new international organizations. The Senate approved American membership in the newly organized United Nations (UN) with only two opposing votes, a sharp contrast to its rejection of the League of Nations in 1920. The Washington-based **International Monetary Fund (IMF)** and the **World Bank** were designed to revive international trade. The IMF stabilized national currencies against the short-term pressures of international trade. The World Bank drew on the resources of member nations to make economic development loans to governments for such projects as new dams or agricultural modernization. These organizations ensured that the reviving world economy would revolve around the industrial and technological power of the United States, and they continue to dictate the economic policy of many developing nations into the twenty-first century.

In 1946, the United States presented a plan in the United Nations to control atomic energy. Bernard Baruch suggested that an international agency should oversee all uranium production and research on atomic explosives. The Baruch plan emphasized enforcement and inspections that would have opened the Soviet nuclear effort to American interference, an unacceptable prospect for a nation trying to catch up with the United States by building its own atomic bombs.

While UN delegates debated the future of atomic energy, American leaders were becoming convinced of Soviet aggressiveness. In February 1946, George Kennan, a senior American diplomat in Moscow, sent a "long telegram" to the State Department. He depicted a Soviet Union driven by expansionist Communist ideology. The Soviets, he argued, would constantly probe for weaknesses in the capitalist world. The best response was firm resistance to protect the Western heartlands.

The British encouraged the same tough stand. Lacking the strength to shape Europe on its own, Great Britain repeatedly nudged the United States to block Soviet influence. Speaking at Westminster College in Missouri in March 1946, Winston Churchill warned that the Soviet Union had dropped an "iron curtain" across the middle of Europe and urged a firm Western response.

Churchill's speech matched the mood in official Washington. Truman's foreign-policy advisers shared the belief in an aggressive Soviet Union, and the president himself saw the world as a series of either-or choices. Added to military apprehension were worries about political and economic competition. Communist parties in war-ravaged Europe and Japan were exploiting discontent. In Asia and Africa, the allegiance of nationalists who were fighting for independence from European powers remained in doubt. America's leaders worried that much of the Eastern Hemisphere might fall under Soviet control.

Were Truman and his advisers right about Soviet intentions? The evidence is mixed. In their determination to avoid another Munich, Truman and his foreign-policy circle ignored examples of Soviet caution and conciliation. The Soviets withdrew troops from Manchuria in northern China and acquiesced in America's control of defeated Japan. They allowed a neutral but democratic government in Finland and technically free elections in Hungary and Czechoslovakia (although it was clear that

Communists would do well there). They demobilized much of their huge army and reduced their forces in eastern Europe.

However, the Soviet regime also acted to justify American fears. The Soviet Union could not resist exerting influence in the Middle East. It pressured Turkey to give it partial control of the exit from the Black Sea. It retained troops in northern Iran until warned out by the United States. The Soviets were ruthless in support of Communist control in eastern Europe in 1946 and 1947; they aided a Communist takeover in Bulgaria, backed a coup in Romania, and undermined the last non-Communist political opposition in Poland. U.S. policymakers read these Soviet actions as a rerun of Nazi aggression and determined not to let a new totalitarian threat undermine Western power.

THE TRUMAN DOCTRINE AND THE MARSHALL PLAN

Whatever restraint the Soviet Union showed was too late or too little. Early in 1947, Truman and his advisers acted decisively. The British could no longer afford to back the Greek government that was fighting a civil war against Communists, and U.S. officials feared that a Communist takeover in Greece would threaten the stability of Italy, France, and the Middle East. Truman coupled his case for intervention in Greece with an appeal for aid to neighboring Turkey, which lived under the shadow of the Soviet Union. On March 12, he told Congress that the United States faced a "fateful hour" and requested $400 million to fight Communism in Greece and Turkey and secure the free world. Congress agreed, and the United States became the dominant power in the eastern Mediterranean.

Framing the specific request was a sweeping declaration that became to be known as the **Truman Doctrine.** The president pledged to use U.S. economic power to help free nations everywhere resist internal subversion or aggression. "It must be the policy of the United States," he said, "to support free peoples who are resisting attempted subjugation by armed minorities or by outside pressures.… . I believe that our help should be primarily through economic and financial aid, which is essential to economic stability and orderly political processes."

Meanwhile, Europe was sliding toward chaos. Germany was close to famine after the bitter winter of 1946–1947. Western European nations were bankrupt and unable to import raw materials for their factories. Overstressed medical systems could no longer control tuberculosis and other diseases. Communist parties had gained in Italy, France, and Germany.

The U.S. government responded with unprecedented economic aid. Secretary of State George C. Marshall announced the European Recovery Plan on June 5, 1947. What the press quickly dubbed the **Marshall Plan** committed the United States to help rebuild Europe. The United States invited Soviet and eastern European participation, but under terms that would have reduced Moscow's control over its satellite economies. The Soviets refused, fearing that the United States wanted to undermine its influence, and instead organized their eastern European satellites in their own association for Mutual Economic Assistance, or Comecon, in 1949. In Western Europe, the Marshall Plan was a success. Aid totaled $13.5 billion over four years. It met many of Europe's economic needs and quieted class conflict. The Marshall Plan expanded American influence through cooperative efforts. Because Europeans spent much of the aid on U.S. goods and machinery, and because economic recovery promised markets for U.S. products, business and labor both supported it. In effect, the Marshall

Plan created an "empire by invitation," in which Americans and Europeans jointly planned Europe's recovery.

U.S. policy in Japan followed the pattern set in Europe. As supreme commander of the Allied Powers, General Douglas MacArthur acted as Japan's postwar dictator. He tried to change the values of the old war-prone Japan through social reform, democratization, and demilitarization. At the end of 1947, however, the United States decided that democracy and pacifism could go too far. Policymakers were fearful of economic collapse and political chaos, just as in Europe. The "reverse course" in occupation policy aimed to make Japan an economic magnet for other nations in East Asia, pulling them toward the American orbit and away from the Soviet Union.

George Kennan summed up the new American policies in the magazine *Foreign Affairs* in July 1947. Kennan argued that the Soviet leaders were committed to a long-term strategy of expanding Communism. The proper posture of the United States, he said, should be an equally patient commitment to "firm and vigilant **containment** of Russian expansive tendencies." Kennan warned that the emerging Cold War would be a long conflict, with no quick fixes.

Soviet Reactions

The bold American moves in the first half of 1947 put the Soviet Union on the defensive. In response, Soviet leaders orchestrated strenuous opposition to the Marshall Plan by French and Italian Communists. East of the Iron Curtain, Hungarian Communists expelled other political parties from a coalition government. Bulgarian Communists shot opposition leaders. Romania, Bulgaria, and Hungary signed defense pacts with the Soviet Union.

In early 1948, the Soviets targeted Czechoslovakia. For three years, a neutral coalition government there on the model of Finland had balanced trade with the West with a foreign policy friendly to the Soviet Union. In February 1948, while Russian forces assembled on the Czech border, local Communists took advantage of political bumbling by other members of the governing coalition. Taking control through a technically legal process, they pushed aside Czechoslovakia's democratic leadership and turned the nation into a dictatorship and Soviet satellite within a week.

The climax of the Soviet reaction came in divided Berlin, located 110 miles inside the Soviet Union's East German occupation zone. The city was divided into four sectors: one controlled by the Soviets and the others by the United States, Britain, and France. On June 4, 1948, Soviet troops blockaded surface traffic into Berlin, cutting off the U.S., British, and French sectors. The immediate Soviet aim was to block Western plans to merge their three German occupation zones into an independent federal republic (West Germany). Rather than abandon 2.5 million Berliners or shoot their way through, the Western nations responded to the **Berlin blockade** by airlifting supplies to the city. Stalin decided not to intercept the flights. After 11 months, the Soviets abandoned the blockade, making the Berlin airlift a triumph of American resolve.

American Rearmament

The coup in Czechoslovakia and the Berlin blockade shocked American leaders and backfired on the Soviets. The economic assistance strategy of 1947 now looked inadequate. Congress responded in 1948 by reinstating the military draft and increasing defense spending.

The United States had already begun to modernize and centralize its national security apparatus, creating the institutions that would run foreign policy in the second half of the century. The National Security Act of July 1947 created the **Central Intelligence Agency (CIA)** and the **National Security Council (NSC).** The CIA handled intelligence gathering and covert operations. The NSC assembled top diplomatic and military advisers in one committee. In 1949, legislation also created the Department of Defense to oversee the army, navy, and air force (independent from the army since 1947). The civilian secretary of defense soon began to exercise influence on foreign policy equal to that of the secretary of state.

In April 1949, ten European nations, the United States, and Canada signed the North Atlantic Treaty as a mutual defense pact. American commitments to the **North Atlantic Treaty Organization (NATO)** included military aid and the deployment of U.S. troops in Western Europe. After 1955, its counterpart would be the Warsaw Pact for mutual defense among the Soviet Union and its European satellites.

Two years later, the United States signed similar but less comprehensive agreements in the western Pacific: the ANZUS Pact with Australia and New Zealand and a new treaty with the Philippines. Taken together, peacetime rearmament and mutual defense pacts amounted to a revolution in American foreign policy.

COLD WAR AND HOT WAR

The first phase of the Cold War reached a crisis in the autumn of 1949. Two key events seemed to tilt the world balance against the United States and its allies. In September, Truman announced that the Soviet Union had tested its own atomic bomb. A month later, the Communists under Mao Zedong (Mao Tse-tung) took power in China. The following summer, civil war in Korea sucked the United States into a fierce war with Communist North Korea and China.

THE NUCLEAR SHADOW

Experts in Washington had known that the Soviets were working on an A-bomb, but the news dismayed the average citizen. As newspapers and magazines scared their readers with artists' renditions of the effects of an atomic bomb on New York or Chicago, the shock tilted U.S. nuclear policy toward military uses. In 1946, advocates of civilian control had won a small victory when Congress established the Atomic Energy Commission (AEC). The AEC tried to balance research on atomic power with continued testing of new weapons. Now Truman told the AEC to double the output of fissionable uranium and plutonium for "conventional" nuclear weapons. A more momentous decision soon followed. Truman decided in January 1950 to authorize work on the "super" bomb—the thermonuclear fusion weapon that would become the hydrogen bomb (H-bomb).

Nuclear weapons proliferated in the early 1950s. The United States repeatedly tested nuclear fission weapons in Nevada and exploded the first hydrogen bomb in the South Pacific in November 1952. Releasing 100 times the energy of the Hiroshima bomb, the detonation tore a mile-long chasm in the ocean floor. Great Britain became the third nuclear power in the same year. The Soviet Union tested its own hydrogen bomb only nine months after the United States.

Berlin was still a devastated city in 1948. When the Soviet Union closed off ground access to the British, French, and American occupation zones, the city became a symbol of the West's Cold War resolve. Allied aircraft lifted in food, fuel, and other essentials for West Berliners for nearly a year until the Soviets ended the blockade.

The nuclear arms race and the gnawing fear of nuclear war multiplied the apprehensions of the Cold War. Under the guidance of the Federal Civil Defense Administration, Americans learned that they should always keep a battery-powered radio and tune to 640 or 1240 on the AM dial for emergency information when they heard air raid sirens. Schoolchildren learned to hide under their desks when they saw the blinding flash of a nuclear detonation.

More insidiously, nuclear weapons development generated new environmental and health problems. Soldiers were exposed to posttest radiation with minimal protection. Nuclear tests in the South Pacific dusted fishing boats with radioactivity and forced islanders to abandon contaminated homes. Las Vegas promoted tests in southern Nevada as tourist attractions, but radioactive fallout contaminated large sections of the West and increased cancer rates among "downwinders" in Utah. Weapons production and atomic experiments contaminated vast tracts in Nevada, Washington, and Colorado and left huge environmental costs for later generations.

THE COLD WAR IN ASIA

Communist victory in China's civil war was as predictable as the Soviet nuclear bomb but no less controversial. The collapse of Jiang Jieshi's Nationalist regime was nearly inevitable, given its corruption and narrow support. Nevertheless, Americans looked for a scapegoat when Jiang's anti-Communist government and remnants of the Nationalist army fled to the island of Taiwan off China's southern coast.

Advocates for Jiang, mostly conservative Republicans from the Midwest and West, were certain that Truman's administration had done too little. Critics looked for scapegoats. Foreign Service officers who had honestly analyzed the weakness of the Nationalists were accused of Communist sympathies and hounded from their jobs. The results were tragedy for those unfairly branded as traitors and damage to the State Department, a weakness that would haunt the United States as it became entangled in Southeast Asia in the 1950s and 1960s.

Mao's victory expanded a deep fissure in U.S. foreign policy. During and after World War II, the United States had made Europe its first priority. Strong voices, however, had argued that America's future lay with China, Japan, and the Pacific nations. Influential senators claimed that the "loss of China" was the disastrous result of putting the needs of England and France above the long-term interests of the United States.

NSC-68 AND AGGRESSIVE CONTAINMENT

The turmoil of 1949 led to a comprehensive statement of American strategic goals. In April 1950, the State Department prepared a sweeping report known as **National Security Council Paper 68 (NSC-68)**. The document described a world divided between the forces of "slavery" and "freedom" and assumed that the Soviet Union was actively aggressive, motivated by greed for territory and a "fanatic faith" in Communism. To defend civilization itself, said the experts, the United States should use as much force as needed to resist Communist expansion anywhere and everywhere.

The authors of NSC-68 intended to extend the Truman Doctrine and convince Americans of the threat of the Cold War. They also thought in terms of military solutions. In the original containment policy, Truman and his advisers had hoped to contain the Soviets by diplomacy and by integrating the economies of Europe and Japan with that of the United States. Now that the Soviets had the atomic bomb, however, the American atomic shield might be neutralized. Instead, NSC-68 argued that the United States needed to press friendly nations to rearm and make its former enemies into military allies. It also argued that the nation needed expensive conventional forces to defend Europe on the ground and to react to crises as a "world policeman." NSC-68 thus advocated nearly open-ended increases in the defense budget (which, in fact, tripled between 1950 and 1954).

The thinking behind the report led the United States to approach the Cold War as a military competition and to view political changes in Africa and Asia as parts of a Soviet plan. The need for a flexible military response became the centerpiece of a U.S. policy of active intervention that led eventually to the jungles of Vietnam in the 1960s. And the report's implied strategy of bankrupting the Communists through competitive defense spending helped destroy the Soviet Union at the end of the 1980s.

United Nation forces in Korea fought the weather as well as Communist North Koreans and Chinese. Baking summer heat alternated with fierce winters. Snow and cold were a major help to the Chinese when they surprised United States forces in November 1950 and drove American troops such as these southward.

WAR IN KOREA, 1950–1953

The success of Mao and the Chinese Communists forced the Truman administration to define national interests in eastern Asia and the western Pacific. Most important was Japan, still an industrial power despite its devastating defeat. The United States had denied the Soviet Union any part in the occupation of Japan in 1945 and had shaped a more democratic nation that would be a strong and friendly trading partner. Protected by American armed forces, Japan would be part of a crescent of offshore strong points that included Alaska, Okinawa, the Philippines, Australia, and New Zealand.

Two questions remained at the start of 1950. One was the future of Taiwan and the remnants of Jiang's regime. Some American policymakers wanted to defend Jiang against the Communists. Others assumed that his tattered forces would collapse and

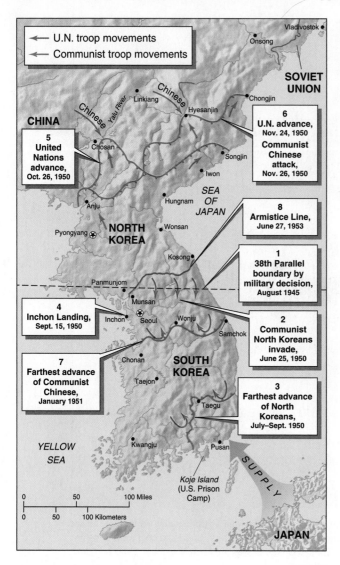

MAP 27–2 • The Korean War
After rapid reversals of fortune in 1950 and early 1951, the war in Korea settled into stalemate. Most Americans agreed with the need to contain Communist expansion but found it deeply frustrating to fight for limited objectives rather than total victory.

▶ **Was a** *stalemate the inevitable end to the Korean War? Why or why not?*

allow Mao to complete the Communist takeover of Chinese territory. The other question was Korea, whose own civil war would soon bring the world to the brink of World War III.

The Korean peninsula is the closest point on the Asian mainland to Japan. With three powerful neighbors—China, Russia, and Japan—Korea had always had to fight for its independence. From 1910 to 1945, it was an oppressed colony of the Japanese Empire. As World War II ended, Soviet troops moved down the peninsula from the north and American forces landed in the south, creating a situation similar to that in Germany. The 38th parallel, which Russians and Americans set as the dividing line between their zones of occupation, became a *de facto* border. The United States in 1948 recognized an independent South Korea, with its capital at Seoul, under a conservative government led by Syngman Rhee. Rhee's support came from large landowners and from a police force trained by the Japanese before 1945. The Soviets recognized a separate North Korea, whose Communist leader, Kim Il Sung, advocated radical social and political change. Both leaders saw the 38th parallel as a temporary barrier and hoped to unify all Koreans under their own rule. Each crushed political dissent and tried to undermine the other with economic pressure and commando raids.

As early as 1947, the United States had decided that Korea was not essential to American military strategy. Planners assumed that U.S. air power in Japan could neutralize unfriendly forces on the Korean peninsula. In January 1950, Secretary of State Dean Acheson carefully excluded Korea from the primary "defensive perimeter" of the United States but kept open the possibility of international guarantees for Korean security.

On June 25, 1950, North Korea, helped by Soviet equipment and Chinese training, attacked South Korea. The invasion began the **Korean War**, which lasted until 1953 (see Map 27–2). Truman and Acheson believed that Moscow lay behind the invasion. In fact, Kim originated the invasion plan because he seemed to be losing the civil war in the south, and he spent a year persuading Stalin to agree to it. Stalin hoped that the conquest of South Korea would force Japan to sign a favorable treaty with the USSR.

American leaders thought that the explosion of a hot war after five years of world tension demanded a military response. As the South Korean army collapsed, Truman committed American ground troops from Japan on June 30. The United States also had the good fortune of securing an endorsement from the United Nations. Because the Soviet Union was boycotting the UN (hoping to force the seating of Mao's People's Republic of China in place of Jiang's government), it could not use its veto when the Security Council asked UN members to help South Korea. The Korean conflict remained officially a United Nations action. Although U.S. generals Douglas MacArthur, Matthew Ridgway, and Mark Clark ran the show as the successive heads of the UN command, 21 other nations committed military resources in a true multinational coalition.

THE POLITICS OF WAR

Fortunes in the first year of the Korean conflict seesawed three times. The first U.S. combat troops were outnumbered, outgunned, and poorly trained. They could not stop the North Koreans. By early August, the Americans clung to a narrow toehold around the port of Pusan on the tip of the Korean peninsula. As reinforcements arrived, however, MacArthur transformed the war with a daring amphibious counterattack at Inchon, 150 miles behind North Korean lines. The North Korean army was already overextended and exhausted. It collapsed and fled north.

The temptation to push across the 38th parallel and unify the peninsula under Syngman Rhee was irresistible. MacArthur and Washington officials disregarded warnings by China that it would enter the war if the United States tried to reunite Korea by force. U.S. and South Korean troops rolled north, drawing closer and closer to the boundary between North Korea and China.

Chinese forces attacked MacArthur's command in late October but then disappeared. MacArthur dismissed the attacks as a token gesture. In fact, they were a final warning. On November 26, the Chinese struck the overextended American columns. They had massed 300,000 troops without detection by American aviation. Their assault drove the UN forces into a two-month retreat that again abandoned Seoul.

Despite his glaring mistake, MacArthur remained in command until he publicly contradicted national policy. In March 1951, with the UN forces again pushing north, Truman prepared to offer a ceasefire that would have preserved the separate nations of South and North Korea. MacArthur tried to preempt the president by demanding that China admit defeat or suffer the consequences. He then published a direct attack on the administration's policy of limiting the Asian war to ensure the security of Europe. President Truman had no choice. To protect civilian control of the armed forces, he relieved MacArthur of his command on April 11, 1951.

In Korea itself, U.S. and South Korean forces stabilized a strong defensive line that cut diagonally across the 38th parallel. Here the conflict settled into trench warfare. What had started as a civil war was now an international conflict between the two sides in the larger Cold War.

Stabilization of the Korean front ushered in two years of truce negotiations beginning in July 1951, for none of the key actors wanted a wider war. Negotiations stalled over thousands of Chinese prisoners of war who might not want to return to China. The political decision to turn free choice for POWs into a symbol of resistance to Communism left Truman's administration bogged down in a grinding war. Nearly half of the 140,000 U.S. casualties came after the truce talks started. The war was a decisive factor behind the Republican victory in the November 1952 elections and dragged on until June 1953, when an armistice returned the peninsula roughly to its prewar political division, a situation that endured into the twenty-first century.

Consequences of the Korean War. The war in Korea was a preview of Vietnam 15 years later. American leaders propped up an undemocratic regime to defend democracy. Both North Koreans and South Koreans engaged in savage political reprisals as the battlefront shifted back and forth. American soldiers found it hard to distinguish between allied and enemy Koreans. American emphasis on massive firepower led U.S. forces to demolish entire villages to kill single snipers. The air force tried to break North Korean resistance by pouring bombs on cities, power stations, factories, and dams; General Curtis LeMay estimated that the bombings killed a million Koreans.

The Korean War had global consequences. It helped to legitimize the United Nations and set a precedent for its peacekeeping role in places like the Middle East. In Washington, it confirmed the ideas underlying NSC-68, with its call for the United States to expand its military and to lead an anti-Communist alliance. Two days after the North Korean invasion, President Truman ordered the Seventh Fleet to interpose between mainland China and the Nationalist Chinese on Taiwan, a decision that guaranteed 20 years of hostility between the United States and China. In the same month, the United States began to aid France's struggle to retain control over its Southeast Asian colony of Indochina, which included Laos, Cambodia, and Vietnam.

In Europe, the United States now pushed to rearm West Germany as part of a militarized NATO and sent troops to Europe as a permanent defense force. It increased military aid to European governments and secured a unified command for the national forces allocated to NATO, a step that made West German rearmament acceptable to other nations of Western Europe that remembered 1940. Rearmament also stimulated German economic recovery and bound West Germany to the political and economic institutions of the North Atlantic nations. In 1952, the European Coal and Steel Community marked an important step toward economic cooperation that would evolve into the European Union by the end of the century. Dwight Eisenhower, who had led the Western allies in the invasion of France and Germany, became the new NATO commander in April 1951; his appointment symbolized the American commitment to western Europe.

THE SECOND RED SCARE

The Korean War reinforced the second Red Scare, an assault on civil liberties that stretched from the mid-1940s to the mid-1950s and dwarfed the Red Scare of 1919–1920. The Cold War fanned fears of Communist subversion on American soil. Legitimate concerns about espionage mixed with suspicions that Communist sympathizers in high places were helping Stalin and Mao. The scare was also a weapon that the conservative wing of the Republican Party used against the men and women who had built Roosevelt's New Deal (see Overview, The Second Red Scare).

Efforts to root out suspected subversives operated on three tracks. National and state governments established loyalty programs to identify and fire suspect employees. The courts punished members of suspect organizations. Congressional and state legislative investigations followed the whims of committee chairs. Anti-Communist crusaders often relied on dubious evidence and eagerly believed the worst. They also threatened basic civil liberties.

THE COMMUNIST PARTY AND THE LOYALTY PROGRAM

The Communist Party in the United States was in rapid decline as a political factor after World War II. The CIO and United Auto Workers froze Communists out of leadership positions, bringing industrial unions into the American mainstream. Nevertheless, Republicans used Red-baiting as a campaign tactic. In 1946, Republican campaigners told the public that the basic choice was "between Communism and Republicanism." Starting a 30-year political career, a young navy veteran named Richard Nixon won a southern California congressional seat by hammering on his opponent's connections to supposedly Communist-dominated organizations.

President Truman responded to the Republican landslide with Executive Order 9835 in March 1947, initiating a loyalty program for federal employees. It authorized the attorney general to prepare a list of "totalitarian, Fascist, Communist, or subversive" organizations and made membership or even "sympathetic association" with such groups grounds for dismissal. The loyalty program applied to approximately 8 million Americans working for the federal government or defense contractors; similar state laws affected another 5 million.

Federal employees worked under a cloud of fear. Would the cooperative store they had once patronized or the protest group they had joined in college suddenly appear on the attorney general's list? Would someone complain that they had disloyal books on their shelves? Loyalty boards asked about religion, racial equality, and a taste for foreign films. They also tried to identify homosexuals, who were thought to be targets for blackmail by foreign agents. The loyalty program resulted in 1,210 firings and 6,000 resignations under Truman and comparable numbers during Dwight Eisenhower's first term from 1953 to 1956.

AMERICAN VIEWS

INTEGRATING THE ARMY IN KOREA

*R*acial integration of the armed forces became official policy in 1948, but President Truman's directive was not fully implemented until after the war in Korea. Two veterans of that war—white G.I. Harry Summers and black officer Beverly Scott—recall some of the steps toward integration.

- What do these recollections say about the pervasiveness of racism in midcentury American life?
- How has the experience of minority soldiers changed from the 1950s to the 1990s?

Harry Summers: When they first started talking about integration, white soldiers were aghast. They would say, How can you integrate the army? How do you know when you go to the mess hall that you won't get a plate or a knife or a spoon that was used by a Negro? Or when you go to the supply room and draw sheets, you might get a sheet that a Negro had slept on? . . .

I remember a night when your rifle company was scheduled to get some replacements. I was in a three-man foxhole with one other guy, and they dropped this new replacement off at our foxhole. The other guy I was in the foxhole with was under a poncho, making coffee. It was bitterly cold. And pitch dark. He got the coffee made, and he gave me a drink, and he took a drink, and then he offered some to this new replacement, who we literally couldn't see, it was that dark.

And the guy said, "No, I don't want any."

"What the hell are you talking about, you don't want any? You got to be freezing to death. Here, take a drink of coffee."

NAMING NAMES TO CONGRESS

Congress was even busier than the executive branch. The congressional hunt for subversives had its roots in 1938, when Congressman Martin Dies, a Texas Democrat, created the Special Committee on Un-American Activities. Originally intended to ferret out pro-Fascists, the Dies Committee evolved into the permanent **House Un-American Activities Committee (HUAC)** in 1945. It investigated "un-American propaganda" that attacked constitutional government.

One of HUAC's juiciest targets was Hollywood. Hollywood's reputation for loose morals, foreign-born directors, Jewish producers, and left-leaning writers aroused the suspicions of many congressmen. HUAC sought to make sure that no un-American messages were being peddled through America's most popular entertainment.

When the hearings opened in October 1947, studio executives Jack Warner of Warner Brothers and Louis B. Mayer of MGM assured HUAC of their anti-Communism. So did the popular actors Gary Cooper and Ronald Reagan. By contrast, eight screenwriters and two directors—the so-called Hollywood Ten—refused to discuss their past political associations, citing the free-speech protections of the First Amendment to the Constitution. HUAC countered with citations for contempt of Congress. The First Amendment defense

"Well," he said, "you can't tell it now, but I'm black. And tomorrow morning when you find out I was drinking out of the same cup you were using, you ain't gonna be too happy."

Me and this other guy kind of looked at each other.

"You silly son of a bitch," we told him, "here, take the goddam coffee."

Beverly Scott: The 24th Regiment was the only all-black regiment in the division, and as a black officer in an all-black regiment commanded by whites I was always super sensitive about standing my ground. Being a man. Being honest with my soldiers . . . .

Most of the white officers were good. Taken in the context of the times, they were probably better than the average white guy in civilian life. But there was still that patronizing expectation of failure. White officers came to the 24th Regiment knowing or suspecting or having been told that this was an inferior regiment.

[In September 1951, members of the regiment were integrated into other units.]

I was transferred to the 14th [Regiment] and right away I experienced some problems. People in the 14th didn't want anybody from the 24th. I was a technically qualified communications officer, which the 14th said they needed very badly, but when I got there, suddenly they didn't need any commo officers.

Then their executive officer said, "We got a rifle platoon for you. Think you can handle a rifle platoon?"

What the hell do you mean, can I handle a rifle platoon? I was also trained as an infantry officer. He know that. I was a first lieutenant, been in the army six years . . . . If I had been coming in as a white first lieutenant the question never would have been asked.

SOURCE: Rudy Tomedi, *No Bugles, No Drums: An Oral History of the Korean War* (New York: John Wiley, 1993).

failed when it reached the Supreme Court, and the Ten went to jail in 1950. Other actors, writers, and directors found themselves on the Hollywood blacklist, banned from jobs where they might insert Communist propaganda into American movies.

At the start of 1951, the new Senate Internal Security Subcommittee went into action. The McCarran Committee, named for the Nevada senator who chaired it, targeted diplomats, labor union leaders, professors, and schoolteachers. Both committees turned their investigations into rituals. The real point was not to force personal confessions from witnesses but to badger them into identifying friends and associates who might have been involved in suspect activities.

State legislatures imitated Congress by searching for "Reducators" among college faculty in such states as Oklahoma, Washington, and California. Harvard apparently used its influence to stay out of the newspapers, cutting a deal in which the FBI fed it information about suspect faculty, whom the university quietly fired. More common was the experience of the economics professor fired from the University of Kansas City after testifying before the McCarran Committee. He found it hard to keep any job once his name had been in the papers. A local dairy fired him because it thought its customers might be uneasy having a radical handle their milk bottles.

OVERVIEW THE SECOND RED SCARE

Type of Anti-Communist Effort	Key Tools	Results
Employee loyalty programs	U.S. attorney general's list of subversive organizations Executive orders by Truman and Eisenhower	Thousands of federal and state workers fired, careers damaged
Congressional investigations	HUAC McCarran Committee Army-McCarthy hearings	Employee blacklists, investigation of writers and intellectuals, Hollywood Ten
Criminal prosecutions	Trials for espionage and conspiracy to advocate violent overthrow of the U.S. government	Convictions of Communist Party leaders (1949), Alger Hiss (1950), and Rosenbergs (1951)
Restrictions on Communist Party	Internal Security Act (1950) Communist Control Act (1954)	Marginalizing of far left in politics and labor unions

SUBVERSION TRIALS

In 1948, the Justice Department indicted the leaders of the American Communist Party under the Alien Registration Act of 1940. Eleven men and women were convicted in 1949 of conspiring to advocate the violent overthrow of the United States government through their speech and publications.

The case of Alger Hiss soon followed. In 1948, a former Communist, Whittaker Chambers, named Hiss as a Communist with whom he had associated in the 1930s. Hiss, who had held important posts in the State Department, first denied knowing Chambers but then admitted to having known him under another name. He continued to deny any involvement with Communists and sued Chambers for slander. As proof, Chambers revealed microfilms that he had hidden inside a pumpkin on his Maryland farm, and Congressman Richard Nixon quickly announced the discovery. Tests seemed to show that the "pumpkin papers" were State Department documents that had been copied on a typewriter Hiss had once owned. With the new evidence, the Justice Department indicted Hiss for perjury—lying under oath. A first perjury trial ended in deadlock, but a second jury convicted Hiss in January 1950.

Hiss was a potent symbol as well as a spy. To his opponents, he stood for every wrong turn the nation had taken since 1932. His supporters found a virtue in every trait his enemies hated, from his refined tastes to his degree from Harvard Law School. Many supporters believed he had been framed. However, the weight of evidence from Soviet archives and American intelligence intercepts confirms that he did indeed spy for the Soviets.

Another important case was that of Julius and Ethel Rosenberg. In 1950, the British arrested nuclear physicist Klaus Fuchs, who confessed to passing atomic secrets to the Soviets when he worked at Los Alamos in 1944 and 1945. The "Fuchs spy ring" soon implicated the Rosenbergs, New York radicals of strong beliefs but limited sophistication. Convicted in 1951 on the vague charge of conspiring to commit espionage, they were sent to the electric chair in 1953 after refusing to buy a reprieve by naming other spies.

As with Alger Hiss, the government had a plausible but not airtight case. After their trial, the Rosenbergs became a cause for international protest. Their small children became pawns and trophies in political demonstrations, an experience recaptured in E. L. Doctorow's novel *The Book of Daniel* (1971). There is no doubt that Julius Rosenberg was part of a successful Soviet spy ring, but Ethel Rosenberg's involvement was limited. In the words of FBI director J. Edgar Hoover, the government charged her "as a lever" to pressure her husband into naming his confederates.

SENATOR MCCARTHY ON STAGE

The best-remembered participant in the second Red Scare was Senator Joseph McCarthy of Wisconsin. Crude, sly, and ambitious, McCarthy had ridden to victory in the Republican landslide of 1946. He burst into national prominence on February 9, 1950. In a rambling speech in Wheeling, West Virginia, he latched onto the issue of Communist subversion. Although no transcript of the speech survives, he supposedly stated, "I have here in my hand a list of 205 that were known to the Secretary of State as being members of the Communist Party and who, nevertheless, are still working and shaping the policy of the State Department." In the following days, the 205 Communists changed quickly to 57, to 81, to 10, to 116. McCarthy's rise to fame climaxed with an incoherent six-hour speech to the Senate. Over the next several years, his speeches were aimed at moving targets, full of multiple untruths. He threw out so many accusations, true or false, that the facts could never catch up.

The Senate disregarded McCarthy, but the public heard only the accusations, not the lack of evidence. Senators treated McCarthy as a crude outsider in their exclusive club, but voters in 1950 turned against his most prominent opponents. Liberal politicians ran for cover; conservatives were happy for McCarthy to attract media attention away from HUAC and the McCarran Committee. In 1951, McCarthy even called George Marshall, then serving as secretary of defense, an agent of Communism. The idea was ludicrous. Marshall was one of the most upright Americans of his generation, the architect of victory in World War II, and a key contributor to the stabilization of Europe. Nevertheless, McCarthy was so popular that the Republicans featured him at their 1952 convention and their presidential candidate, Dwight Eisenhower, conspicuously failed to defend Marshall, who had been chiefly responsible for Eisenhower's fast-track career.

McCarthy's personal crudeness made him a media star but eventually undermined him. Given control of the Senate Committee on Government Operations in 1953, he investigated dozens of agencies from the Government Printing Office to the Army Signal Corps. Early in 1954, he investigated an army dentist with a supposedly subversive background. The back-and-forth confrontation led to two months of televised hearings. The cameras brought political debates into living rooms and put McCarthy's bullying style on trial. "Have you no decency?" asked the army's lawyer, Joseph Welch, at one point.

The end came quickly. McCarthy's "favorable" rating in the polls plummeted. The U.S. Senate finally voted 67 to 22 in December 1954 to condemn McCarthy for conduct "unbecoming a Member of the Senate." When he died in 1957, he had been repudiated by the Senate and ignored by the media that had built him up.

UNDERSTANDING MCCARTHYISM

The anti-subversive campaign that everyone now calls **McCarthyism,** however, died a slower death. It had actually originated with the Truman administration, and laws, such as the Internal Security Act (1950) and the Immigration and Nationality Act (1952), remained as tools of political control during the Eisenhower administration. HUAC continued to mount investigations as late as the 1960s.

In retrospect, at least four factors made Americans afraid of Communist subversion. One was the legitimate concern about atomic spies. The Soviet Union had developed an extensive espionage network in the early 1940s. More than a few U.S. officials passed on secret information, although there was not the vast interlocking conspiracy that some critics feared. A second was an undercurrent of anti-Semitism and nativism, for many labor organizers and Communist Party members (like the Rosenbergs) had Jewish and eastern European backgrounds. Third was southern and western resentment of the nation's Ivy League elite. Most general, finally, was a widespread fear that the world was spinning out of control. Many people sought easy explanations for global tensions. It was basically reassuring if Soviet and Chinese Communist successes were the result of American traitors rather than of Communist strengths.

Partisan politics mobilized the fears and resentments into a political force. From 1946 through 1952, the conservative wing of the Republican Party used the Red Scare to attack New Dealers and liberal Democrats. HUAC, the McCarran Committee, and

Senator Joe McCarthy used press releases and carefully managed congressional committee hearings to attack suspected Communists, although he had almost no hard information. At the Army-McCarthy hearings in June 1954, he clashed with attorney Joseph Welch. Here Welch listens as McCarthy points to Oregon on a map that supposedly showed Communist Party organization in the United States.

McCarthy were all tools for bringing down the men and women who had been moving the United States toward a more active government at home and abroad. The Republican elite used McCarthy until they won control of the presidency and Congress in 1952, and then abandoned him.

The broader goal of the second Red Scare was conformity of thought. Many of the professors and bureaucrats targeted for investigation had indeed been Communists or interested in Communism, usually in the 1930s and early 1940s. Most saw it as a way to increase social justice, and they sometimes excused the failures of Communism in the Soviet Union. Unlike the handful of real spies, however, they were targeted not for actions but for ideas. The investigations and loyalty programs were efforts to ensure that Americans kept any left-wing ideas to themselves.

CONCLUSION

The United States emerged from the Truman years remarkably prosperous despite the turmoil and injustice of the second Red Scare and deep worries about nuclear war. It was also more secure from international threats than many nervous Americans appreciated. The years from 1946 to 1952 set the themes for a generation that believed that the United States could do whatever it set its mind to: end poverty, land an astronaut on the moon, thwart Communist revolutions in other countries. There was a direct line from Harry Truman's 1947 declaration that the United States would defend freedom around the world to John Kennedy's 1961 promise that the nation would bear any burden necessary to protect free nations from Communism. As the world moved slowly toward greater stability in the 1950s, Americans were ready for a decade of confidence.

REVIEW QUESTIONS

1. As described in the opening of the chapter, what housing choices were available after World War II? How did these choices reshape American cities? How did the postwar readjustment create a suburban society?

2. What were the key differences between Harry Truman and congressional Republicans about the legacy of the New Deal? Why did regulating labor unions become a central domestic issue in the late 1940s? Why did Truman manage to win the presidential election of 1948 despite starting as an underdog?

3. How did the postwar years expand opportunity for veterans and members of the working class? How did they limit opportunities for women? How did they begin to challenge racial inequities in American society?

4. What foreign policy priorities did the United States set after 1945? To what extent did the United States achieve its most basic objectives? How did mutual mistrust fuel and deepen the Cold War?

5. How did the character of the Cold War change in 1949 and 1950? What were key actions by the Soviet Union and China, and how did the United States respond? What was the effect of the chaotic fighting in Korea on U.S. domestic politics and diplomacy?

6. What factors motivated an increasingly frantic fear of domestic subversion in the late 1940s and early 1950s? Who were the key actors in the second Red Scare? What was its long-term impact on American society?

7. How did the continuation and expansion of the nation's global commitments after 1945 affect life in the United States?

PEARSON myhistorylab CONNECTIONS

Reinforce what you learned in this chapter by studying the many documents, images, maps, review tools, and videos available at **www.myhistorylab.com**.

READ AND REVIEW

✔• **Study** and **Review** on **myhistorylab.com** STUDY PLAN: CHAPTER 27

 **Read** the **Document** on **myhistorylab.com**

Kenneth MacFarland, "The Unfinished Work" (1946)

National Security Council Memorandum Number 68 (1950)

Ronald Reagan, Testimony before the House Un-American Activities Committee (1947)

Joseph R. McCarthy, from Speech Delivered to the Women's Club of Wheeling, West Virginia (1950)

Senator Joseph McCarthy's telegram to President Truman following the Wheeling [W. Va.] Speech (1950)

Executive Order 9981: Desegregation of the Armed Forces (1948)

George F. Kennan, "The Long Telegram" (1946)

George Marshall, The Marshall Plan (1947)

Senate Resolution 301: Censure of Senator Joseph McCarthy (1954)

Servicemen's Readjustment Act (1944)

Truman Doctrine (1947)

🔍 **View** the **Map** on **myhistorylab.com**

Population Shifts, 1940–1950

The Korean War, 1950–1953

Research and Explore

Read the **Document** on **myhistorylab.com**

Personal Journeys Online

From Then to Now Online: The Automobile Industry

Exploring America: The Truman Doctrine

Listen on **myhistorylab.com**

Joseph P. McCarthy Speech

Watch the **Video** on **myhistorylab.com**

The Desegregation of the Military and Blacks in Combat

President Truman and the Threat of Communism

((•— Listen on myhistorylab.com

Hear the audio files for Chapter 27 at
www.myhistorylab.com.

28 The Confident Years • •1953–1964

((•─ Listen on myhistorylab.com
Hear the audio files for Chapter 28 at **www.myhistorylab.com.**

FOCUS QUESTIONS

HOW DID the "Decade of Affluence" alter social and religious life in America?

WHAT IMPACT did Dwight Eisenhower's foreign policy have on U.S. relations with the Soviet Union?

WHAT WAS John F. Kennedy's approach to dealing with the Soviet Union?

WHAT WAS the significance of *Brown v. Board of Education of Topeka*?

HOW DID Lyndon B. Johnson continue the domestic agenda inherited from the Kennedy administration? In what ways did he depart from it?

Singer Elvis Presley sings Hillbilly Heartbreak on stage in Hollywood, California during a performance in 1956.

ONE AMERICAN JOURNEY

The first day I was able to enter Central High School [in Little Rock, Arkansas, September 23, 1957, what I felt inside was terrible, wrenching, awful fear. On the car radio I could hear that there was a mob. I knew what a mob meant and I knew that the sounds that came from the crowd were very angry. So we entered the side of the building, very, very fast. Even as we entered there were people running after us, people tripping other people. There has never been in my life any stark terror or any fear akin to that. I'd only been in the school a couple of hours and by that time it was apparent that the mob was just overrunning the school. Policemen were throwing down their badges and the mob was getting past the wooden sawhorses because the police would no longer fight their own in order to protect us. So we were all called into the principal's office, and there was great fear that we would not get out of this building. We were trapped. And I thought, Okay, so I'm going to die here, in school. . . . Even the adults, the school officials, were panicked, feeling like there was no protection. . . . [A] gentleman, who I believed to be the police chief, said. . . "I'll get them out." And we were taken to the basement of this place. And we were put into two cars, grayish blue Fords. And the man instructed the drivers, he said, "Once you start driving, do not stop." And he told us to put our heads down. This guy revved up his engine and he came up out of the bowels of this building, and as he came up, I could just see hands reaching across this car, I could hear the yelling, I could see guns, and he was told not to stop. "If you hit somebody, you keep rolling, 'cause the kids are dead." And he did just that, and he didn't hit anybody, but he certainly was forceful and aggressive in the way he exited this driveway, because people tried to stop him and he didn't stop. He dropped me off at home. And I remember saying, "Thank you for the ride," and I should've said, "Thank you for my life."

Melba Patillo Beals, in Henry Hampton and Steve Frayer, eds., *Voices of Freedom: An Oral History of the Civil Rights Movement from the 1950s through the 1980s* (New York: Bantam, 1990).

MELBA PATTILLO was one of the nine African American students who entered previously all-white Central High in the fall of 1957. Her enrollment in the high school, where she managed to last through a year of harassment and hostility, was a symbolic step in the journey toward greater racial equality in U.S. society.

The struggle for full civil rights for all Americans was rooted in national ideals, but it was also shaped by the continuing tensions of the Cold War. President Dwight Eisenhower acted against his own inclinations and sent federal troops to keep the peace in Little Rock in part because he worried about public opinion in other nations. As the United States and the Soviet Union maneuvered for influence in Africa and Asia, domestic events sometimes loomed large in foreign relations.

Melba Pattillo's life after Little Rock also reveals something about the increasing geographical mobility and economic opportunities available to most Americans. She graduated from San Francisco State University, earned a master's degree from Columbia University, and worked as a television reporter and writer. The prosperous years from 1953 to 1964 spread the economic promise of the 1940s across American society. Young couples could afford large families and new houses. Labor unions grew conservative because cooperation with big business offered immediate gains for their members.

Despite challenges at home and abroad, Americans were fundamentally confident during the decade after the Korean War. They expected corporations to use scientific research to craft new products for eager customers and medical researchers to conquer diseases. When the USSR challenged U.S. preeminence and launched the first artificial space satellite in 1957, Americans responded with shock followed by redoubled efforts to regain what they considered their rightful world leadership in science and technology.

A Decade of Affluence

Americans in the 1950s believed in the basic strength of the United States. Television's *General Electric Theater* was third in the ratings in 1956–1957. Every week, its host, Ronald Reagan, a popular Hollywood lead from the late 1930s, stated, "At General Electric, progress is our most important product." It made sense to his viewers. Large, technologically sophisticated corporations were introducing new marvels: Orlon sweaters and Saran Wrap, long-playing records, and Polaroid cameras. As long as the United States defended free enterprise, Reagan told audiences on national speaking tours, the sky was the limit.

What's Good for General Motors

Dwight Eisenhower presided over the prosperity of the 1950s. Both Democrats and Republicans had courted him as a presidential candidate in 1948. Four years later, he picked the Republicans because he wanted to make sure that the party remained committed to NATO and collective security in Europe rather than retreat into isolationism. He easily defeated the Democratic candidate, Adlai Stevenson, the moderately liberal governor of Illinois.

Eisenhower and the Politics of the Middle. Over the next eight years, Eisenhower claimed the political middle for Republicans. Satisfied with postwar America, Eisenhower accepted much of the New Deal but saw little need for further reform. In a 1959 poll, liberals considered him a fellow liberal and conservatives thought him a conservative. Eisenhower's first secretary of defense, "Engine Charlie" Wilson, had headed General Motors. At his Senate confirmation hearing, he proclaimed, "For years, I thought what was good for the country was good for General Motors and vice versa." Wilson's statement captured a central theme of the 1950s. Not since the 1920s had Americans been so excited about the benefits of big business.

The New Prosperity. The economy in the 1950s gave Americans much to like. Between 1950 and 1964, output grew by a solid 3.2 percent per year. American workers in the 1950s had more disposable income than ever before. Their productivity, or output per worker, increased steadily. Average compensation per hour of work rose faster than consumer prices in nine of eleven years from 1953 to 1964. Rising productivity made it easy for corporations to share gains with large labor unions. In turn, labor leaders lost interest in making radical changes in American society. In 1955 the older and more conservative American Federation of Labor absorbed the younger Congress of Industrial Organizations. The new AFL CIO positioned itself as a partner in prosperity and a foe of Communism at home and abroad. It was a quiet consensus that seemed to benefit

CHRONOLOGY

1953   CIA-backed coup returns Shah Reza Pahlavi to power in Iran.
Soviet Union detonates hydrogen bomb.

1954   Vietnamese defeat the French; Geneva conference divides Vietnam.
United States and allies form SEATO.
Supreme Court decides *Brown v. Board of Education of Topeka*.
CIA overthrows the government of Guatemala.
China provokes a crisis over Quemoy and Matsu.

1955   Salk polio vaccine is announced.
Black citizens boycott Montgomery, Alabama, bus system.
Soviet Union forms the Warsaw Pact.
AFL and CIO merge.

1956   Interstate Highway Act is passed.
Soviets repress Hungarian revolt.
Israel, France, and Britain invade Egypt.

1957   U.S. Army maintains law and order in Little Rock after violent resistance
to integration of Central High School.
Soviet Union launches *Sputnik*, world's first artificial satellite.

1958   United States and Soviet Union voluntarily suspend nuclear tests.

1959   Fidel Castro takes power in Cuba.
Nikita Khrushchev visits the United States.

1960   U-2 spy plane shot down over Russia.
Sit-in movement begins in Greensboro, North Carolina.

1961   Bay of Pigs invasion fails.
Kennedy establishes the Peace Corps.
Vienna summit fails.
Freedom rides are held in the Deep South.
Berlin crisis leads to construction of the Berlin Wall.

1962   John Glenn orbits the earth.
Cuban missile crisis brings the world to the brink of nuclear war.
Michael Harrington publishes *The Other America*.

1963   Civil rights demonstrations rend Birmingham.
Civil rights activists march in Washington.
Betty Friedan publishes *The Feminine Mystique*.
Limited Test Ban Treaty is signed.
Ngo Dinh Diem is assassinated in South Vietnam.
President Kennedy is assassinated.

1964   Civil Rights Act is passed.
Freedom Summer is organized in Mississippi.
Office of Economic Opportunity is created.
Gulf of Tonkin Resolution is passed.
Wilderness Act marks new direction in environmental policy.

1965   Medical Care Act establishes Medicare and Medicaid.
Elementary and Secondary Education Act extends direct federal aid
to local schools.
Selma-Montgomery march climaxes era of nonviolent civil rights
demonstrations.
Voting Rights Act suspends literacy tests for voting.

everyone—workers who could afford new consumer goods and corporations that could sell to them. The United States increasingly became a "consumer's republic" that defined mass consumption as the solution to social and economic problems.

For members of minority groups with regular industrial and government jobs, the 1950s could also be economically rewarding. Detroit, Dayton, Oakland, and other industrial cities offered them factory jobs at wages that could support a family. Black people worked through the Urban League, the National Association of Colored Women, and other race-oriented groups to secure fair-employment laws and jobs with large corporations. Many Puerto Rican migrants to New York found steady work in the Brooklyn Navy Yard. Mexican American families in San Antonio benefited from maintenance jobs at the city's military bases. Steady employment allowed black people and Latinos to build strong community institutions and vibrant neighborhood business districts.

However, there were never enough family-wage jobs for all of the African American and Latino workers who continued to move to northern and western cities. Many Mexican Americans were still migrant farm laborers and workers in nonunionized sweatshops. Minority workers were usually the first to suffer from the erosion of some industrial jobs and the shift of other jobs to new suburban factories that were isolated from minority neighborhoods. Black unemployment crept upward to twice the white rate, laying the seeds of frustration that would burst forth in the 1960s.

Native Americans faced equally daunting prospects. To cut costs and accelerate assimilation, Congress pushed the policy of termination between 1954 and 1962. The government sold tribal land and assets, distributed the proceeds among tribal members, and terminated its treaty relationship with the tribe. Applied to such tribes as the Klamaths in Oregon and the Menominees in Wisconsin, termination gave thousands of Indians one-time cash payments but cut them adrift from the security of tribal organizations.

RESHAPING URBAN AMERICA

If Eisenhower's administration opted for the status quo on many issues, it nevertheless reshaped U.S. cities around an agenda of economic development. In 1954, Congress

Daly City, south of San Francisco, typified the mass-produced suburbs that housed the growing postwar middle class. It was the inspiration for the satirical song, "Little Boxes."

transformed the public housing program into urban renewal. Cities used federal funds to replace low-rent businesses and run-down housing on the fringes of their downtowns with new hospitals, civic centers, sports arenas, office towers, and luxury apartments. Urban renewal temporarily revitalized older cities in the Northeast and Midwest that were already feeling the competition of the fast-growing South and West.

Only a decade later, the same cities would be urban crisis spots, in part because of accumulating social costs from urban renewal. The bulldozers often leveled minority neighborhoods in the name of downtown expansion. Urban renewal displaced Puerto Ricans in New York, African Americans in Atlanta and Norfolk, and Mexican Americans in Denver. In Los Angeles, Dodger Stadium replaced a lively Latino community.

The Eisenhower administration also revolutionized American transportation. By the early 1950s, Americans were fed up with roads designed for Model A Fords: They wanted to enjoy their new V-8 engines and the 50 million new cars sold between 1946 and 1955. The solution was the **Federal Highway Act of 1956**, creating a national system of 41,000 miles of interstate and defense highways.

Although the first interstate opened in Kansas in 1956, most of the mileage came into use in the 1960s and 1970s. Interstates halved the time of city-to-city travel. They were good for General Motors, the steel industry, and the concrete industry, requiring the construction equivalent of 60 Panama Canals. The highways promoted long-distance trucking at the expense of railroads. They also wiped out hundreds of homes per mile when they plunged through large cities. As with urban renewal, the bulldozers most often plowed through African American or Latino neighborhoods, where land was cheap and white politicians could ignore protests. Some cities, such as Miami, used the highways as barriers between white and black neighborhoods.

AMERICAN VIEWS

THE SUBURBAN ROOTS OF ENVIRONMENTAL ACTIVISM

As new subdivisions ate up the rural landscape in the 1950s and 1960s, suburbanites found that they were bringing old environmental problems with them and creating new ones. Leapfrog development often destroyed the very landscapes that attracted people out of cities in the first place. Overburdened roads created traffic jams and air pollution. Septic tanks in high-density developments leaked sewage that fouled rural streams. Orange groves, corn fields, and wooded hills disappeared beneath the blades of bulldozers. Environmentalism was certainly about preserving the wilderness, but it was also about keeping suburbia from fouling its own nest. Journalist William H. Whyte played a leading role in identifying the suburban environmental crisis and making the case for preserving open space and natural areas as metropolitan areas grew.

- **Does** Whyte argue against all suburban growth, or against certain types of growth?
- **How** does knowledge of Whyte's efforts change our understanding of environmentalism?

Over the next three or four years Americans will have a chance to decide how decent a place this country will be to live in, and for generations to come. Already huge patches of once green countryside have been turned into vast, smog-filled deserts that are neither city, suburb, nor country, and each day—at a rate of some 3,000 acres a day—more countryside is being bulldozed under. You can't stop progress, they say, yet much more of this kind of progress and we shall have the paradox of prosperity lowering our real standard of living.

With characteristic optimism, most Americans still assume that there will be plenty of green space on the other side of the fence. But this time there won't be... . Flying from Los Angeles to San Bernardino—an unnerving lesson in man's infinite capacity to mess up his environment—the traveler can see a legion of bulldozers gnawing into the last remaining tract of green between the two cities. ... On the outer edge of the present Philadelphia metropolitan area, where there will be one million new people in the ten years ending 1960, some of the loveliest countryside in the world is being irretrievably fouled, and the main body of suburbanites has yet to arrive... .

The problem is the pattern of growth—or, rather, the lack of one... . [W]e are ruining the whole metropolitan area of the future. In the townships just beyond today's suburbia there is little planning, and development is being left almost entirely in the hands of the speculative builder. Understandably, he follows the line of least resistance and in his wake is left a hit-or-miss pattern of development... .

Sprawl is bad aesthetics; it is bad economics. Five acres are being made to do the work of one, and do it very poorly. This is bad for the farmers, it is bad for communities, it is bad for industry, it is bad for utilities, it is bad for the railroads, it is bad for the recreation groups, it is bad even for developers.

And it is unnecessary. In many suburbs the opportunity has vanished, but it is not too late to lay down sensible guidelines for the communities of the future. Most important of all, it is not too late to reserve open space while there is still some left—land for parks, for landscaped industrial districts, and for just plain scenery and breathing opportunities.

The Editors of *Fortune, The Exploding Metropolis* (Garden City, NY: Doubleday and Co., 1958), pp. 133–135.

Interstates accelerated suburbanization. The beltways or perimeter highways that began to ring most large cities made it easier and more profitable to develop new subdivisions and factory sites than to reinvest in city centers. Federal grants for sewers and other basic facilities further cut suburban costs. Continuing the pattern of the late 1940s, suburban growth added a million new single-family houses per year.

COMFORT ON CREDIT

Prosperity transformed spending habits. The 1930s had taught Americans to avoid debt. The 1950s taught them to buy on credit. The value of consumer debt, excluding home mortgages, tripled from 1952 to 1964.

New forms of marketing facilitated credit-based consumerism. The first large-scale suburban shopping center was Northgate in Seattle, which assembled all the elements of the full-grown mall—small stores facing an interior corridor between anchor department stores and surrounded by parking. By the end of the decade, developers were building malls with 1 million square feet of shopping floor. At the start of the 1970s, the universal credit card (Visa, MasterCard) made shopping even easier.

Surrounding the new malls were the servants and symbols of America's car culture. Where cities of the early twentieth century had been built around public transportation—streetcars and subways—those of the 1950s depended on private automobiles. Interstate highways sucked retail business from small-town main streets to interchanges on the edge of town. Nationally franchised motels and fast-food restaurants sprang up along suburban shopping strips. By shopping along highways rather than downtown, suburban whites also opted to minimize contact with people of other races.

The spread of automobiles contributed to increased leisure travel. The tacit pact between large corporations and labor unions meant that more workers had two-week vacations and time to take their families on the road. Between 1954 and 1963, the number of visits to National Parks doubled to more than 100 million and visits to National Forests nearly tripled. On television from 1956 to 1963, variety show hostess Dinah Shore tied the nation's best-selling car to the appeal of vacationing as she belted out the jingle "Drive your Chevrolet through the USA, America's the greatest land of all."

THE NEW FIFTIES FAMILY

Family life in the Eisenhower years departed from historic patterns. Prosperity allowed children to finish school and young adults to marry right after high school. Young women faced strong social pressure to pursue husbands rather than careers. In a decade when the popular press worried about "latent homosexuality," single men were suspect. The proportion of single adults reached its twentieth-century low in 1960. At all social levels, young people married quickly and had an average of three children spaced closely together, adding to the number of baby boomers whose needs would influence American society into the twenty-first century. Strong families, said experts, defended against Communism by teaching American values.

The Impact of Television. Television was made to order for the family-centered fifties. By 1960, fully 87 percent of households had sets. Popular entertainment earlier had been a communal activity; people saw movies as part of a group, cheered baseball teams as part of a crowd. TV was watched in the privacy of the home.

Middle-class women in the 1950s faced conflicting pressures and messages. The popular media idealized the woman whose life revolved around her house and family. As this magazine cover suggests, however, that image was as much a myth as a reality. Despite real limitations on available careers, increasing numbers of women entered the labor force and made necessary contributions to their families' incomes—while daydreaming about getting help with never-ending household tasks. Day Dreaming by Constantin Alajalov. © 1959 SEPS; Licensed by Curtis Publishing Co., Indianapolis, Ind. All rights reserved. www.curtispublishing.com

Situation comedies were the most successful programs. Viewers liked continuing characters who resolved everyday problems in half an hour. Most successful shows depicted the ideal of family togetherness. The families on *The Adventures of Ozzie and Harriet* (1952–1966), *Father Knows Best* (1954–1962), and *Leave It to Beaver* (1957–1962) were white, polite, and happy.

Stay-at-Home Moms and Working Women. The 1950s extended the stay-at-home trend of the postwar years. Women gave up some of their earlier educational gains. Their share of new college degrees and professional jobs fell. Despite millions of new electrical appliances, the time spent on housework increased. Magazines proclaimed that proper families maintained distinct roles for dad and mom, and mom was urged to find fulfillment in a well-scrubbed house and children.

In fact, far from allowing women to stay home as housewives, family prosperity in the 1950s often depended on their earnings. The number of employed women reached new highs. By 1960, nearly 35 percent of all women held jobs, including 7.5 million mothers with children under 17. The pressures of young marriages, large families, and economic needs interacted to erode some of the assumptions behind the idealized family and laid the groundwork for dramatic social changes in the 1960s and 1970s.

INVENTING TEENAGERS

Teenagers in the 1950s joined adults as consumers of movies, clothes, and automobiles. Advertisers tapped and expanded the growing youth market by promoting a distinct "youth culture," an idea that became omnipresent in the 1960s and 1970s. Many cities matched their high schools to the social status of their students: college-prep curricula for middle-class neighborhoods, vocational and technical schools for future factory workers, and separate schools or tracks for African Americans and Latinos. In effect, the schools trained some children to be doctors and officers and others to be mechanics and enlisted men.

All teenagers shared rock-and-roll, a new music of the mid-1950s that adapted black urban rhythm-and-blues for a white mass market. Rhythm-and-blues was the hard-edged and electrified offspring of traditional blues and gospel music. In turn, rock music augmented its black roots by drawing vitality from poor white southerners familiar with country and western music (Buddy Holly, Elvis Presley), Hispanics (Richie Valens), and, in the 1960s, the British working class (the Beatles). Record producers played up the association between rock music and youthful rebellion.

Technological changes helped rock split off from adult pop music. Portable phonographs and 45-rpm records let kids listen to rock-and-roll in their own rooms. Car radios and transistor radios (first marketed around 1956) let disc jockeys reach teenagers outside the home. The result was separate music for young listeners and separate advertising for teenage consumers, the roots of the teenage mall culture of the next generation.

TURNING TO RELIGION

Leaders from Dwight Eisenhower to FBI Director J. Edgar Hoover advocated churchgoing as an antidote for Communism. Regular church attendance grew from 48 percent of the population in 1940 to 63 percent in 1960. *Newsweek* talked about the "vast resurgence of Protestantism," and *Time* claimed that "everybody knows that church life is booming in the U.S."

The situation was more complex. Growing church membership looked impressive at first, but the total barely kept pace with population growth. In some ways, the so-called return to religion was new. Congress created new connections between religion and government when it added "under God" to the Pledge of Allegiance in 1954 and required currency to bear the phrase "In God We Trust" in 1955.

Another strand in the religious revival was found in the revitalized evangelical and fundamentalist churches. During the 1950s, the theologically and socially conservative Southern Baptists passed the Methodists as the largest Protestant denomination. The evangelist Billy Graham continued the grand American tradition of the mass revival meeting.

African American churches were community institutions as well as religious organizations. With limited options for enjoying their success, the black middle class joined prestigious churches. Black congregations in northern cities swelled in the postwar years. Prestigious black churches thrived and often supported extensive social service programs. In southern cities, churches were centers for community pride and training grounds for the emerging civil rights movement.

Other important changes to come in American religion had their roots in the 1950s and early 1960s. Boundaries between many Protestant denominations blurred as church leaders emphasized national unity, paving the way for the ecumenical movement and denominational mergers. Supreme Court decisions sowed the seeds for later political activism among evangelical Christians. In *Engel v. Vitale* (1962), the Court ruled that public schools could not require children to start the school day with group prayer. *Abington Township v. Schempp* (1963) prohibited devotional Bible reading in the schools. Such decisions alarmed many evangelicals; within two decades, school prayer would be a central issue in national politics.

THE GOSPEL OF PROSPERITY

At times in these years, production and consumption outweighed democracy in the American message to the world. Officially, Americans argued that abundance was a natural by-product of a free society. In fact, it was easy to present prosperity as a goal in itself, as Vice President Richard Nixon did when he represented the United States at a technology exposition in Moscow in 1959. The U.S. exhibit included 21 models of automobiles and a complete six-room ranch house. In its "miracle kitchen," Nixon engaged Soviet Communist Party chairman Nikita Khrushchev in a carefully planned "kitchen debate." The vice president claimed that the "most important thing" for Americans was "the right to choose": "We have so many different manufacturers and many different kinds of washing machines so that the housewives have a choice."

THE UNDERSIDE OF AFFLUENCE

The most basic criticism of the ideology of prosperity was the simplest—that affluence concealed vast inequalities. Michael Harrington had worked among the poor before writing *The Other America* (1962). He reminded Americans about the "underdeveloped nation" of 40 to 50 million poor people who had missed the last two decades of prosperity.

If Harrington found problems at the bottom of U.S. society, C. Wright Mills found dangers in the way that the Cold War distorted American society at the top. *The Power Elite* (1956) described an interlocking alliance of big government, big business, and the military. The losers in a permanent war economy, said Mills, were economic and political democracy. His ideas would reverberate in the 1960s during the Vietnam War.

Other critics targeted the alienating effects of consumerism and the conformity of homogeneous suburbs. Although much of the antisuburban rhetoric was based on intellectual snobbery rather than research, it represented significant dissent from the praise of affluence.

There was far greater substance to the increasing dissatisfaction among women, who faced conflicting images of the perfect woman in the media. On one side was the comforting icon of Betty Crocker, the fictional spokeswoman for General Mills who made housework and cooking look easy. On the other side were sultry sexpots like Marilyn Monroe and the centerfold women of *Playboy* magazine, which first appeared in 1953. Women wondered how to be both Betty and Marilyn. In 1963, Betty Friedan's book *The Feminine Mystique* recognized that thousands of middle-class housewives were seething behind their picture windows. It followed numerous articles in *McCall's, Redbook,* and the *Ladies' Home Journal* about the unhappiness of college-educated women who were expected to find total satisfaction in kids and cooking. Friedan repackaged the message of the women's magazines along with the results of a survey of her Smith College classmates, who were then entering their forties. What Friedan called "the problem that has no name" was a sense of personal emptiness.

On July 7, 1959, Vice-president Richard Nixon, accompanied by the Soviet leader, Nikita Khrushchev, made an official visit to the American pavilion at an exhibit in Moscow. Moments later, the two leaders staged their famous "kitchen debate," arguing over the merits of their respective systems of government. The debate was one of the dramatic moments of the Cold War. National Archives and Records Administration.

FACING OFF WITH THE SOVIET UNION

Americans got a reassuring new face in the White House in 1953, but not new policies toward the world. As had been true since 1946, the nation's leaders weighed every foreign policy decision for its effect on the Cold War. The United States pushed ahead in an arms race with the Soviet Union, stood guard on the borders of China and the Soviet empire, and judged political changes in Latin America, Africa, and Asia for their effect on the global balance of power.

WHY WE LIKED IKE

In the late twentieth century, few leaders were able to master both domestic policy and foreign affairs. Some presidents, such as Lyndon Johnson, were more adept at social problems than diplomacy. By contrast, Richard Nixon and George H. W. Bush were more interested in the world outside the United States.

Dwight Eisenhower was also a "foreign-policy president." As a general, he had understood that military power should serve political ends. He had helped to hold together the alliance that defeated Nazi Germany and built NATO into an effective force in 1951–1952. He then sought the Republican nomination, he said, to ensure that the United States would keep its international commitments. He sealed his victory in 1952 by emphasizing his foreign-policy expertise, telling a campaign audience that "to bring the Korean war to an early and honorable end... requires a personal trip to Korea. I shall make that trip... I shall go to Korea."

What makes Eisenhower's administration hard to appreciate is that many of its accomplishments were things that did not happen. Eisenhower refused to dismantle the social programs of the New Deal. He exerted American political and military power around the globe but avoided war. Preferring to work behind the scenes, he knew how to delegate authority and keep disagreements private.

In his "hidden-hand" presidency, Eisenhower sometimes masked his intelligence. It helped his political agenda if Americans thought of him as a smiling grandfather. He was the first president to have televised news conferences and knew how to manipulate them. The "Ike" whose face smiled from "I Like Ike" campaign buttons and who gave rambling, incoherent answers at White House press conferences knew exactly what he was doing—controlling information and keeping the opposition guessing. He was easily reelected in 1956, when Americans saw no reason to abandon competent leadership.

A BALANCE OF TERROR

The backdrop for U.S. foreign policy was the growing capacity for mutual nuclear annihilation. The rivalry between the United States and the USSR was played out within a framework of deterrence, the knowledge that each side could launch a devastating nuclear attack. The old balance of power had become a balance of terror.

The Eisenhower administration's doctrine of **massive retaliation** took advantage of America's superior technology while economizing on military spending. Eisenhower and his advisers worried that matching the land armies of China and the Soviet Union would inflate the role of the federal government in American society. Eisenhower compared uncontrolled military spending to crucifying humankind on a "cross of iron." "Every gun that is fired," he warned, "every warship launched, every rocket fired signifies... a theft from those who hunger and are not fed, those who are cold and not clothed." The administration concentrated military spending where the nation already had the greatest advantage—on atomic weapons. In response to any serious attack, the United States would direct maximum force against the homeland of the aggressor.

The massive-retaliation doctrine treated nuclear weapons as ordinary or even respectable. It put European and American cities on the frontline in the defense of Germany, for it meant that the United States would react to a Soviet conventional attack on NATO by dropping nuclear bombs on the Soviet Union, which would presumably retaliate in kind. The National Security Council in 1953 made reliance on "massive retaliatory damage" by nuclear weapons official policy.

The doctrine grew even more fearful as the Soviet Union developed its own hydrogen bombs. The chairman of the Atomic Energy Commission terrified the American people by mentioning casually that the Soviets could now obliterate New York City. Dozens of nuclear weapons tests in the late 1950s made the atomic threat immediate.

The Soviet Union added to the worries about atomic war by launching the world's first artificial satellite. On the first Sunday of October 1957, Americans discovered that *Sputnik*—Russian for "satellite"—was orbiting the earth. Soviet propagandists claimed that their technological "first" showed the superiority of Communism, and Americans wondered if the United States had lost its edge. Schools beefed up science courses and began to introduce the "new math," Congress passed the National Defense Education Act to expand college and postgraduate education, and the new **National Aeronautics and Space Administration (NASA)** took over the satellite program in 1958.

CONTAINMENT IN ACTION

Someone who heard only the campaign speeches in 1952 might have expected sharp foreign-policy changes under Eisenhower, but there was more continuity than change. John Foster Dulles, Eisenhower's secretary of state, had attacked the Democrats as defeatists and appeasers. He demanded that the United States liberate eastern Europe from Soviet control and encourage Jiang Jieshi to attack Communist China. Warlike language continued after the election. In 1956, Dulles proudly claimed that tough-minded diplomacy had repeatedly brought the United States to the verge of war. "We walked to the brink and looked it in the face," he famously commented.

In fact, Eisenhower viewed the Cold War in the same terms as Truman. He worried about the "sullen weight of Russia" pushing against smaller nations and saw a world caught between the incompatible values of freedom and Communism, but caution replaced campaign rhetoric about "rolling back" Communism. Around the periphery of the Communist nations, from eastern Asia to the Middle East to Europe, the United States accepted the existing sphere of Communist influence but attempted to block its growth, a policy most Americans accepted.

The U.S. worldview assumed both the right and the need to intervene in the affairs of other nations, especially countries in Latin America, Asia, and Africa. Policymakers saw these nations as markets for U.S. products and sources of vital raw materials. When political disturbances arose in these states, the United States blamed Soviet meddling to

Schoolchildren in the 1950s regularly practiced taking cover in case of atomic attack. If there was warning, they were to file into interior hallways, crouch against the walls, and cover their heads with their jackets as protection against flying glass. If they saw the blinding flash of an atomic explosion without warning, they were to "duck and cover" under their school desks.

justify U.S. intervention. If Communism could not be rolled back in eastern Europe, the CIA could still undermine anti-American governments in the third world. The Soviets themselves took advantage of local revolutions even when they did not instigate them; in doing so they confirmed Washington's belief that the developing world was a game board on which the superpowers carried on their rivalry by proxy.

Along with economic motivations and military concerns, religious belief played an important role in shaping the Cold War. When national leaders decried "godless communism," they were voicing a widely shared concern rather than mouthing a slogan. Roman Catholic leaders and laypeople worried about the restricted freedom of religious practice in Poland, Hungary, and other Soviet satellites. Members of the nation's political elite often had ties or sympathy with missionary work in China, which was effectively halted after 1949, making them deeply suspicious of the new Communist regime. At the top, strong religious convictions influenced the way that Harry Truman, Dwight Eisenhower, and John Foster Dulles viewed the confrontation with China and the USSR in moral as well as practical terms.

Twice during Eisenhower's first term, the CIA subverted democratically elected governments that seemed to threaten U.S. interests. In Iran, which had nationalized British and U.S. oil companies in an effort to break the hold of Western corporations, the CIA in 1953 backed a coup that toppled the government and helped the young shah, as the reigning monarch was called, to gain control. The shah then cooperated with the United States, but his increasingly repressive regime would lead to his overthrow in 1979 and deep Iranian resentment of the United States. In Guatemala, the leftist government was threatening the United Fruit Company. When the Guatemalans accepted weapons from the Communist bloc in 1954, the CIA imposed a regime friendly to U.S. business.

For most Americans in 1953, democracy in Iran was far less important than ending the war in Korea and stabilizing relations with China. Eisenhower declined to escalate the Korean War by blockading China and sending more U.S. ground forces. Instead, he positioned atomic bombs on Okinawa, only 400 miles from China. The nuclear threat, along with the continued cost of the war on both sides, brought the Chinese to a truce that left Korea divided into two nations.

Halfway around the world, there was a new crisis when three U.S. friends—France, Britain, and Israel—ganged up on Egypt. France was angry at Egyptian support for revolutionaries in French Algeria. Britain was even angrier at Egypt's nationalization of the British-dominated Suez Canal. And Israel wanted to weaken its most powerful Arab enemy. On October 29, 1956, Israel attacked Egypt. A week later, British and French forces attempted to seize the canal.

Although the United States had been the first nation to recognize Israel in 1948, the relationship was much less close than it would become. The United States forced a quick cease-fire, partly to maintain its standing with oil-producing Arab nations. Because Egypt blocked the canal with sunken ships, the war left Britain and France dependent on American oil that Eisenhower would not provide until they left Egypt. Resolution of the crisis involved one of the first uses of peacekeeping troops under the United Nations flag.

In Europe, Eisenhower accepted the status quo because conflicts there could result in nuclear war. In 1956, challenges to Communist rule arose in East Germany, Poland, and Hungary and threatened to break up the Soviet empire. The Soviets replaced liberal Communists in East Germany while accepting a more liberal leader in Poland. In Hungary, however, reformers took the fatal step of proposing to quit the Warsaw Pact.

Open warfare broke out when the Soviet army rolled across the border to preserve the Soviet empire. Hungarian freedom fighters in Budapest used rocks and firebombs against Soviet tanks for several days, while pleading in vain for Western aid. NATO would not risk war with the USSR. Tens of thousands of Hungarians died, and 200,000 fled when the Soviets crushed the resistance.

GLOBAL STANDOFF

The Soviet Union, China, and the United States and its allies were all groping in the dark as they maneuvered for influence in the 1950s and 1960s. In one international crisis after another, each player misinterpreted the other's motivations and diplomatic signals. Now that documents from both sides of the Cold War are becoming available, historians have realized what dangerously different meanings the two sides gave to their confrontations between 1953 and 1964.

A good example is the U-2 spy plane affair of 1960, which derailed progress toward nuclear disarmament. The Kremlin was deeply worried that West Germany and China might acquire nuclear bombs. Washington wanted to reduce military budgets and nuclear fallout. Both countries voluntarily suspended nuclear tests in 1958 and pre-pared for a June 1960 summit meeting in Paris, where Eisenhower intended to negoti-ate a test ban treaty. But on May 1, 1960, Soviet air defenses shot down an American U-2 aircraft over the heart of Russia and captured the pilot, Francis Gary Powers. The cover story for the U-2 was weather research, but the frail-looking black plane was a CIA operation. Designed to soar above the range of Soviet antiaircraft missiles, U-2s had obtained information that assured American officials there was no missile gap.

When Moscow trumpeted the news of the plane's downing, Eisenhower took per-sonal responsibility in hopes that Khrushchev would accept the U-2 as an unpleasant reality of international espionage. Unfortunately, the planes meant something very dif-ferent to the Soviets, touching their festering sense of inferiority. They had stopped pro-testing the flights in 1957, because they saw complaints as demeaning. The Americans thought their silence signaled acceptance. Khrushchev had staked his future on good relations with the United States; when Eisenhower refused to apologize in Paris, Khrushchev stalked out. Disarmament was set back for years because the two sides had such different understandings of the same events.

The most important aspect of Eisenhower's foreign policy was continuity. Despite militant rhetoric, the administration pursued containment as defined under Truman. The Cold War consensus, however, prevented the United States from seeing the nations of the developing world on their own terms. By viewing every independence move-ment and social revolution as part of the competition with Communism, U.S. leaders created unnecessary problems. In the end, Eisenhower left troublesome and unresolved issues—upheaval in Latin America, civil war in Vietnam, tension in Germany, the nuclear arms race—for his successor, John Kennedy, who wanted to confront interna-tional Communism even more vigorously.

JOHN F. KENNEDY AND THE COLD WAR

John Kennedy was a man of contradictions. A Democrat who promised to get the coun-try moving again, he presided over policies whose direction was set under Eisenhower. Despite stirring rhetoric about leading the nation toward a **New Frontier** of scientific and social progress, he recorded his greatest failures and successes in the continuing Cold War.

THE KENNEDY MYSTIQUE

Kennedy won the presidency over Richard Nixon in a cliff-hanging election that was more about personality and style than about substance (see Map 28–1). Television was crucial to the outcome. The campaign featured the first televised presidential debates. In the first session, Nixon actually gave better replies, but his nervousness and a bad makeup job turned off millions of viewers, who admired Kennedy's energy. Nixon never overcame the setback, but the race was tight, with tiny margins in crucial states giving Kennedy the victory. His televised inauguration was the perfect setting for an impassioned plea for national unity: "My fellow Americans," he challenged, "ask not what your country can do for you—ask what you can do for your country."

Kennedy brought dash to the White House. His beautiful and refined wife, Jackie, made sure to seat artists and writers next to diplomats and businessmen at White House dinners. Kennedy's staff and large family played touch football, not golf. No president had shown such verve since Teddy Roosevelt. People began to talk about Kennedy's "charisma," his ability to lead by sheer force of personality. In fact, the image of a fit, vigorous man concealed the reality that he was battling severe physical ailments that demanded constant medical attention and often left him with debilitating pain.

KENNEDY'S MISTAKES

Kennedy and Khrushchev perpetuated similar problems. Talking tough to satisfy their more militant countrymen, they repeatedly pushed each other into a corner, continuing the problems of mutual misunderstanding that had marked the 1950s. When Khrushchev promised, in January 1961, to support "wars of national liberation," he was really fending off Chinese criticism. But Kennedy overreacted in his first State of the Union address by asking for more military spending.

Three months later, Kennedy fed Soviet fears of American aggressiveness by sponsoring an invasion of Cuba. At the start of 1959, Fidel Castro had toppled the corrupt dictator Fulgencio Batista, who had made Havana infamous for Mafia-run gambling and prostitution. Castro then nationalized American investments, and thousands of Cubans fled to the United States.

When 1,400 anti-Castro Cubans landed at Cuba's **Bay of Pigs** on April 17, 1961, they were following a plan prepared by the Eisenhower administration. The CIA had trained and armed the invaders and convinced Kennedy that the landing would trigger spontaneous uprisings. But when Kennedy refused to commit U.S. armed forces to support them, Cuban forces captured the attackers.

Kennedy followed the Bay of Pigs debacle with a hasty and ill-thought-out summit meeting with Khrushchev in Vienna in June. Poorly prepared and nearly incapacitated by agonizing back pain, Kennedy made little headway. Coming after Kennedy's refusal to salvage the Bay of Pigs by military intervention, the meeting left the Soviets with the impression that the president was weak and dangerously erratic.

To exploit Kennedy's perceived vulnerability, the Soviet Union renewed tension over Berlin, deep within East Germany. The divided city served as an escape route from Communism for hundreds of thousands of East Germans. Khrushchev now threatened

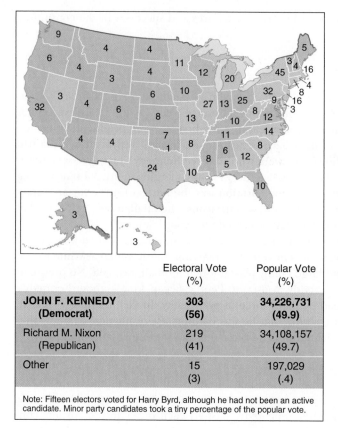

MAP 28–1 • **The Election of 1960**The presidential election of 1960 was one of the closest in American history. John Kennedy's victory depended on his appeal in northern industrial states with large Roman Catholic populations and his ability to hold much of the traditionally Democratic South. Texas, the home state of his vice-presidential running mate, Lyndon Johnson, was vital to the success of the ticket.

◀ *In what parts of the country was Kennedy strongest? How does this map help explain Kennedy's tepidness on civil rights once elected president?*

	Electoral Vote (%)	Popular Vote (%)
JOHN F. KENNEDY (Democrat)	**303 (56)**	**34,226,731 (49.9)**
Richard M. Nixon (Republican)	219 (41)	34,108,157 (49.7)
Other	15 (3)	197,029 (.4)

Note: Fifteen electors voted for Harry Byrd, although he had not been an active candidate. Minor party candidates took a tiny percentage of the popular vote.

to transfer the Soviet sector in Berlin to East Germany, which had no treaty obligations to France, Britain, or the United States. If the West had to deal directly with East Germany for access to Berlin, it would have to recognize a permanently divided Germany. Kennedy sounded the alarm: He doubled draft calls, called up reservists, and warned families to build fallout shelters.

Rather than confront the United States directly, however, the Soviets and East Germans on August 13, 1961, built a wall around the western sectors of Berlin while leaving the access route to West Germany open. The **Berlin Wall** thus isolated East Germany without challenging the Western allies in West Berlin itself. In private, Kennedy accepted the wall as a clever way to stabilize a dangerous situation. However, Berlin remained a point of East-West tension until East German Communism collapsed in 1989 and Berliners tore down the hated wall.

GETTING INTO VIETNAM

U.S. involvement in Vietnam, located in Southeast Asia on the southern border of China, dated to 1949–1950. After World War II ended, France had fought to maintain its colonial rule there against rebels who combined Communist ideology with fervor for national independence under the leadership of Ho Chi Minh. Although the United States supported independence of most other European colonies, the triumph

For many Americans in the early 1960s, John and Jacqueline Kennedy and their two children represented the ideal family, although the carefully posed pictures with happy smiles concealed the president's severe health problems and deep rifts in the marriage.

of Mao Zedong in China and the Korean War caused policymakers to see Vietnam as another Cold War conflict. The United States picked up three-quarters of the costs. Nevertheless, the French military position collapsed in 1954 after Vietnamese forces overran the French stronghold at Dien Bien Phu. The French had enough, and President Eisenhower was unwilling to join another Asian war. A Geneva peace conference "temporarily" divided Vietnam into a Communist north and a non-Communist south and scheduled elections for a single Vietnamese government.

The United States then replaced France as the supporter of the pro-Western Vietnamese in the south. Washington's client was Ngo Dinh Diem, an anti-Communist from South Vietnam's Roman Catholic elite. U.S. officials encouraged Diem to put off the elections and backed his efforts to construct an independent South Vietnam. Ho meanwhile consolidated the northern half as a Communist state that claimed to be the legitimate government for all Vietnam. The United States further reinforced containment in Asia by bringing Thailand, the Philippines, Pakistan, Australia, New Zealand, Britain, and France together in the **Southeast Asia Treaty Organization (SEATO)** in 1954.

Another indirect consequence of the Vienna summit was the growing U.S. entanglement in South Vietnam, where Kennedy saw a chance to take a firm stand and reassert America's commitment to containment. In the countryside, Communist insurgents known as the **Viet Cong** were gaining strength. Diem controlled the cities with the help of a large army and a Vietnamese elite that had worked with the French. The United States stepped up its supply of weapons and sent advisers (Green Berets).

U.S. aid did not work. Despite overoptimistic reports and the help of 16,000 U.S. troops, Diem's government by 1963 was losing the loyalty—the "hearts and minds"—of many South Vietnamese. North Vietnamese support for the Viet Cong canceled the effect of U.S. assistance. Diem courted a second civil war by violently crushing opposition from Vietnamese Buddhists. Kennedy's administration tacitly approved a coup on November 1 that killed Diem and his brother and installed an ineffective military junta.

MISSILE CRISIS: A LINE DRAWN IN THE WAVES

The escalating tensions of 1961 in Southeast Asia, the Caribbean, and Germany were a prelude to the crisis that came closest to triggering a nuclear war. On October 15, 1962, reconnaissance photos revealed Soviets at work on launching sites in Cuba from which nuclear missiles could hit the United States. Top officials spent five exhausting and increasingly desperate days sorting through the options. A full-scale invasion of Cuba was not feasible on short notice, and "surgical" air strikes were technically impossible. Either sort of military operation would kill hundreds of Soviet personnel and force Moscow to react. Secretary of Defense Robert McNamara suggested demanding removal of the missiles and declaring a naval "quarantine" against the arrival of further offensive weapons. A blockade would buy time for diplomacy.

Kennedy imposed the blockade on Monday, October 22. While Khrushchev hesitated, Soviet ships circled outside the quarantine line. On Friday, Khrushchev offered to withdraw the missiles in return for a U.S. pledge not to invade Cuba. On Saturday, a second communication nearly dashed this hopeful opening by raising a new complaint about U.S. missiles on the territory of NATO allies. The letter was the result of pressure by Kremlin hard-liners and Khrushchev's own wavering. Kennedy decided to accept the first letter and ignore the second. The United States pledged not to invade Cuba and secretly promised to remove obsolete Jupiter missiles from Turkey. Khrushchev accepted these terms on Sunday, October 28.

Why did Khrushchev risk the Cuban gamble? One reason was to protect Castro as a symbol of Soviet commitment to anti-Western regimes in the developing world. Kennedy had tried to preempt Castroism in 1961 by launching the **Alliance for Progress**, an economic-development program for Latin America that tied aid to social reform. However, the United States had also orchestrated the Bay of Pigs invasion and funded a CIA campaign to sabotage Cuba. High U.S. officials were not contemplating a full-scale invasion, but Castro and Khrushchev had reason to fear the worst.

Khrushchev also hoped to redress the strategic balance. As Kennedy discovered on taking office, the United States actually led the world in the deployment of strategic missiles. The strategic imbalance had sustained NATO during the Berlin confrontation, but 40 launchers in Cuba with two warheads each would have doubled the Soviet capacity to strike at the United States.

Soviet missiles in Cuba thus flouted the Monroe Doctrine and posed a real military threat. Kennedy and Khrushchev had also backed each other into untenable positions. In September, Kennedy had warned that the United States could not tolerate Soviet offensive weapons in Cuba, never dreaming that they were already there.

Had Khrushchev acted openly (as the United States had done when it placed missiles in Turkey), the United States would have been hard pressed to object under international law. By acting in secret and breaking previous promises, the Soviets outsmarted themselves. When the missiles were discovered, Kennedy had to act.

In the end, both sides were cautious. Khrushchev backed down rather than fight. Kennedy fended off hawkish advisers who wanted to destroy Castro. The world had trembled, but neither nation wanted war over "the missiles of October."

SCIENCE AND FOREIGN AFFAIRS

The two superpowers competed through science as well as diplomacy. When Kennedy took office, the United States was still playing catch-up in space technology. Kennedy committed the United States to placing a U.S. astronaut on the moon by 1970. The decision narrowed a multifaceted scientific and military program to a massive engineering project that favored the economic capacity of the United States.

The Soviet Union and the United States were also fencing about nuclear weapons testing. After the three-year moratorium, both resumed tests in 1961–1962. Both nations worked on multiple-targetable warheads, antiballistic missiles, and other innovations that might destabilize the balance of terror.

After the missile crisis showed his toughness, however, Kennedy had enough political maneuvering room to respond to pressure from liberal Democrats and groups like Women Strike for Peace and the Committee for a Sane Nuclear Policy by giving priority to disarmament. In July 1963, the United States, Britain, and the USSR signed the **Limited Test Ban Treaty**, which outlawed nuclear testing in the atmosphere, in outer space, and under water, and invited other nations to join in. France and China, the other nuclear powers, refused to sign, and the treaty did not halt weapons development, but it was the most positive achievement of Kennedy's foreign policy and a step toward later disarmament treaties.

RIGHTEOUSNESS LIKE A MIGHTY STREAM: THE STRUGGLE FOR CIVIL RIGHTS

Supreme Court decisions are based on abstract principles, but they involve real people. One was Linda Brown of Topeka, Kansas, a third-grader whose parents were fed up with sending her past an all-white public school to attend an all-black school a mile away. The Browns volunteered to help the NAACP challenge Topeka's school segregation by trying to enroll Linda in their neighborhood school, beginning a legal case that reached the Supreme Court. On May 17, 1954, the Court decided **Brown v. Board of Education of Topeka,** opening a new civil rights era. Led by the persuasive power of the new chief justice, Earl Warren, the Court unanimously reversed the 1896 case of *Plessy v. Ferguson* by ruling that sending black children to "separate but equal" schools denied them equal treatment under the Constitution.

GETTING TO THE SUPREME COURT

The *Brown* decision climaxed a 25-year campaign to reenlist the federal courts on the side of equal rights (see Overview, Civil Rights: The Struggle for Racial Equality). The work began in the 1930s when Charles Hamilton Houston, dean of Howard University's law school, trained a corps of civil rights lawyers. Working on behalf of the NAACP, he hoped to erode *Plessy* by suits focused on interstate travel and professional graduate schools (the least defensible segregated institutions, because states seldom provided alternatives). In 1938, Houston's student Thurgood Marshall, a future Supreme Court justice, took over the NAACP job. He and other NAACP lawyers such as Constance Baker Motley risked personal danger crisscrossing the South to file civil rights lawsuits wherever a local case emerged. In 1949, Motley was the first black lawyer to argue a case in a Mississippi courtroom since Reconstruction.

Efforts in the 1940s and early 1950s, often fueled by the experience of World War II soldiers, had important successes. In *Smith v. Allwright* (1944), the Supreme Court invalidated the all-white primary, a decision that led to increased black voter registration in many southern communities. With new political power, and often with the cooperation of relatively progressive white leaders, blacks fought for specific improvements, such as equal pay for teachers or the hiring of black police officers.

The *Brown* case combined lawsuits from Delaware, Virginia, South Carolina, the District of Columbia, and Kansas. In each instance, students and families braved community pressure to demand equal access to a basic public service. Chief Justice Earl Warren brought a divided Court to unanimous agreement. Viewing public education as central for the equal opportunity that lay at the heart of American values, the Court weighed the consequences of segregated school systems and concluded that separate meant unequal. The reasoning fit the temper of a nation that was proud of making prosperity accessible to all.

Brown also built on efforts by Mexican Americans in the Southwest to assert their rights of citizenship. After World War II, Latino organizations such as the League of United Latin American Citizens battled job discrimination and ethnic segregation. In 1946, Mexican American parents sued five Orange County, California, school districts that systematically placed their children in separate schools. In the resulting case of *Mendez v. Westminster,* federal courts prohibited segregation of Mexican-American children in California schools as a violation of the equal protection clause of the Fourteenth Amendment. Eight years later, the Supreme Court forbade Texas from excluding Mexican Americans from juries. These cases provided precedents for the Court's decision in *Brown* and subsequent civil rights cases.

DELIBERATE SPEED

Racial segregation by law was largely a southern problem, the legacy of Jim Crow laws (see Chapter 17). The civil rights movement therefore focused first on the South, allowing Americans elsewhere to think of racial injustice as a regional issue.

Southern responses to *Brown* revealed regional differences. Few southern communities desegregated schools voluntarily, for to do so undermined the entrenched principle of a dual society. Their reluctance was bolstered in 1955 when the Supreme Court allowed segregated states to carry out the 1954 decision "with all deliberate speed" rather than immediately.

The following year, 101 southern congressmen and senators issued the **Southern Manifesto**, which asserted that the Court decision was unconstitutional. President Eisenhower privately deplored the desegregation decision, which violated his sense of states' rights and upset Republican attempts to gain southern votes. At the same time,

OVERVIEW CIVIL RIGHTS: THE STRUGGLE FOR RACIAL EQUALITY

Area of Concern	Key Actions	Results
Public school integration	Federal court cases	*Mendez v. Westminster* (1946) *Brown v. Board of Education of Topeka* (1954) Enforcement by presidential action, Little Rock (1957) Follow-up court decisions, including mandatory busing programs in 1970s
Equal access to public facilities	Montgomery bus boycott (1955) Lunch counter sit-ins (1960) Freedom rides (1961) Birmingham demonstrations (1963) March on Washington (1963)	Civil Rights Act of 1964
Equitable voter registration	Voter registration drives, including Mississippi Summer Project (1964) Demonstrations and marches, including Selma to Montgomery march (1965)	Elimination of all-white primary elections with *Smith v. Allwright* Voting Rights Act of 1965 Voting Rights Act Amendments and Extension of 1975

many in Washington knew that racial discrimination offered, in the worlds of Dean Acheson, "the most effective kind of ammunition" for Soviet propaganda.

Eisenhower's distaste for racial integration left the Justice Department on the sidelines. Courageous parents and students had to knock on schoolhouse doors, often carrying court orders. Responses varied: school districts in border states, such as Maryland, Kentucky, and Oklahoma, desegregated relatively peacefully; farther south, African American children often met taunts and violence.

The first crisis came in Little Rock, Arkansas, in September 1957. The city school board admitted nine African Americans, including Melba Pattillo, to Central High, while segregationist groups, such as the White Citizens Council, stirred up white fears. Claiming he feared violence, Governor Orval Faubus surrounded Central High with the National Guard and turned the new students away. Under intense national pressure, Faubus withdrew the Guard. The black students entered the school, but a howling mob forced the police to sneak them out after two hours. Fuming at the governor's defiance of federal authority, Eisenhower reluctantly nationalized the National Guard and sent in the 101st Airborne Division to keep order.

Students from North Carolina A&T, an all-black college, began the lunch-counter sit-in movement in February 1960. Here four students sit patiently in the Greensboro Woolworth's without being served. Participants wore their best clothes and suffered politely through days of verbal and sometimes physical abuse.

Virginians in 1958–1959 tried avoidance rather than confrontation. Massive resistance was a state policy that required local school districts to close rather than accept black students. When court orders to admit 19 black students triggered the shutdown of four high schools and three junior highs in Norfolk, white parents tried to compensate with private academies and tutoring, but it was soon apparent that a modern community could not dismantle public education.

The breakthrough in school integration did not come until the end of the 1960s, when the courts rejected further delays, and federal authorities threatened to cut off education funds. As late as 1968, only 6 percent of African American children in the South attended integrated schools. By 1973, the figure was 90 percent. Attention thereafter shifted to northern communities, whose schools were segregated, not by law, but by the divisions between white and black neighborhoods and between white suburbs and multiracial central cities, a situation known as *de facto* segregation.

PUBLIC ACCOMMODATIONS

The civil rights movement also sought to integrate public accommodations. Most southern states separated the races in bus terminals and movie theaters. They required black riders to take rear seats on buses. They labeled separate restrooms and drinking fountains for "colored" users. Hotels denied rooms to black people, and restaurants refused them service.

The struggle to end segregated facilities started in Montgomery, Alabama. On December 1, 1955, Rosa Parks, a seamstress who worked at a downtown department store, refused to give up her bus seat to a white passenger and was arrested. Parks acted spontaneously, but she was part of a network of civil rights activists who wanted to challenge segregated buses and was the secretary of the Montgomery NAACP. As news of her action spread, the community institutions that enriched southern black life went into action. The Women's Political Council, a group of college-trained black women, initiated a mass boycott of the privately owned bus company. Martin Luther King Jr. a 26-year-old pastor led the boycott. He galvanized a mass meeting with a speech that quoted the biblical prophet Amos: "We are determined here in Montgomery to work and fight until justice runs down like water, and righteousness like a mighty stream."

Montgomery's African Americans organized their boycott in the face of white outrage. A car pool substituted for the buses despite police harassment. As the boycott survived months of pressure, the national media began to pay attention. After nearly a year, the Supreme Court agreed that the bus segregation law was unconstitutional.

Victory in Montgomery depended on steadfast African American involvement. Success also revealed the discrepancy between white attitudes in the Deep South and national opinion. For white southerners, segregation was a local concern best defined as a legal or constitutional matter. For other Americans, it was increasingly an issue of the South's deviation from national moral norms.

The Montgomery boycott won a local victory and made King famous, but it did not propel immediate change. King formed the **Southern Christian Leadership Conference (SCLC)** and sparred with the NAACP about community-based versus court-based civil rights tactics, but four African American college students in Greensboro, North Carolina, started the next phase of the struggle. On February 1, 1960, they put on jackets and ties and sat down at the segregated lunch counter in Woolworth's, waiting through the day without being served. Their patient courage brought more demonstrators; within two days, 85 students packed the store. Nonviolent sit-ins spread throughout the South.

The sit-ins had both immediate and long-range effects. In such comparatively sophisticated border cities as Nashville, Tennessee, sit-ins integrated lunch counters. Elsewhere, they precipitated white violence and mass arrests. King welcomed nonviolent confrontation. SCLC leader Ella Baker, one of the movement's most important figures, helped the students form a new organization, the **Student Nonviolent Coordinating Committee (SNCC)**.

The year 1961 brought "freedom rides" to test the segregation of interstate bus terminals. The idea came from James Farmer of the **Congress of Racial Equality (CORE)**, who copied a little-remembered 1947 Journey of Reconciliation that had tested the integration of interstate trains. Two buses carrying black and white passengers met only minor problems in Virginia, the Carolinas, and Georgia, but Alabamians burned one of the buses and attacked the riders in Birmingham, where they beat demonstrators senseless and clubbed a Justice Department observer. The governor and police refused to protect the freedom riders. The riders traveled into Mississippi under National Guard protection but were arrested at the Jackson bus terminal. Despite Attorney General Robert Kennedy's call for a cooling-off period, freedom rides continued through the summer. The rides proved that African Americans were in charge of their own civil rights revolution.

THE MARCH ON WASHINGTON, 1963

John Kennedy was a tepid supporter of the civil rights movement and entered office with no civil rights agenda. He appointed segregationist judges to mollify southern congressmen and would have preferred that African Americans stop disturbing the fragile Democratic Party coalition.

In the face of the slow federal response, the SCLC concentrated for 1963 on rigidly segregated Birmingham. April began with sit-ins and marches that aimed to integrate lunch counters, restrooms, and stores and secure open hiring for some clerical jobs. Birmingham's commissioner of public safety, Bull Connor, used fire hoses to blast demonstrators against buildings and roll children down the streets. When demonstrators fought back, his men chased them with dogs. Continued marches brought the arrest of hundreds of children.

The Birmingham demonstrations were inconclusive. White leaders accepted minimal demands on May 10 but delayed enforcing them. Antiblack violence continued, including a bomb that killed four children in a Birmingham church. Meanwhile, the events in Alabama had forced President Kennedy to board the freedom train with an eloquent June 11 speech and to send a civil rights bill to Congress.

On August 28, 1963, a rally in Washington transformed African American civil rights into a national cause. A quarter of a million people, black and white, marched to the Lincoln Memorial. The day gave Martin Luther King Jr. a national pulpit. His call for progress toward Christian and American goals had immense appeal. Television cut away from afternoon programs for his "I Have a Dream" speech.

The March on Washington drew on activism in the North as well as the South. African Americans in northern states and cities did not face the legal segregation of the South, but they had unequal access to jobs and housing because of private discrimination. They fought back with demands for fair housing and fair employment laws, sometimes with success and sometimes triggering white backlash. A New York law against employment discrimination, for example, was one of the factors that had pushed the Brooklyn Dodgers to sign Jackie Robinson.

RELIGIOUS BELIEF AND CIVIL RIGHTS

Although *Brown* and other civil rights court decisions drew on the secular Constitution, much of the success of the southern civil rights movement came from grassroots Christianity. A century earlier, the abolitionist crusade had drawn much of its power from evangelistic revival movements. Now in the 1950s and 1960s, black southerners drew on prophetic Christianity to forge and act on a vision of a just society. Religious conviction and solidarity provided courage in the face of opposition.

At the same time, most white Christians understood that segregation contradicted the message of the Bible. The two largest religious groups in the South, the Presbyterian Church of the United States and the Southern Baptist Convention, took public stands in favor of desegregation in the mid-1950s. Revival leader Billy Graham shared a pulpit with Martin Luther King Jr. in 1957 and insisted against local laws that his revival services be integrated. The opponents of civil rights thus lacked the moral support of the South's most fundamental cultural institutions.

In this context, it was no accident that black churches were organizing centers for civil rights work. King named his organization the Southern Christian Leadership Conference with clear intent and purpose.

On August 28, 1963, Rev. Martin Luther King Jr. delivered his famous "I Have a Dream" speech to the March on Washington for Jobs and Freedom. The address was a climactic moment in the civil rights movement, encapsulating the optimism of decades of struggle, but the March on Washington also papered over emerging divisions that would become apparent later in the 1960s.

"LET US CONTINUE"

The two years that followed King's speech mingled despair and accomplishment. The optimism of the March on Washington shattered with the assassination of John Kennedy in November 1963. In 1964 and 1965, however, President Lyndon Johnson pushed through Kennedy's legislative agenda and much more in a burst of government activism unmatched since the 1930s. Federal legislation brought victory to the first phase of the civil rights revolution, launched the **War on Poverty**, expanded health insurance and aid to education, and opened an era of environmental protection.

DALLAS, 1963

In November 1963, President Kennedy visited Texas to raise money and patch up feuds among Texas Democrats. On November 22, the president's motorcade took him near the Texas School Book Depository building in Dallas, where Lee Harvey Oswald had stationed himself at a window on the sixth floor. Acting on his own, Oswald fired three shots that wounded Texas Governor John Connally and killed the president. Vice President Lyndon Johnson took the oath of office as president on Air Force One while the blood-spattered Jacqueline Kennedy looked on. Two days later, as Oswald was being led from one jail cell to another, Jack Ruby, a Texas nightclub owner, killed him with a handgun in full view of TV cameras.

WAR ON POVERTY

Five days after the assassination, Lyndon Johnson claimed Kennedy's progressive aura for his new administration. "Let us continue," he told the nation, promising to implement Kennedy's policies. In fact, Johnson was vastly different from Kennedy. He was a professional politician who had reached the top through Texas politics and congressional infighting. As Senate majority leader during the 1950s, he had built a web of political obligations and friendships. Johnson's upbringing in rural Texas shaped a man who was endlessly ambitious, ruthless, and often personally crude, but also deeply committed to social equity. He had entered public life with the New Deal in the 1930s and believed in its principles. Johnson, not Kennedy, was the true heir of Franklin Roosevelt.

Johnson inherited a domestic agenda that the Kennedy administration had defined but not enacted. Kennedy's farthest-reaching initiative was rooted in the acknowledgment that poverty was a persistent U.S. problem. Michael Harrington's study *The Other America* became an unexpected bestseller. As poverty captured public attention, Kennedy's economic advisers devised a community action program that emphasized education and job training, a national service corps, and a youth conservation corps. They prepared a package of proposals to submit to Congress in 1964 that focused on social programs intended to alter behaviors that were thought to be passed from generation to generation, thus following the American tendency to attribute poverty to the personal failings of the poor.

Johnson made Kennedy's antipoverty package his own. Adopting Cold War rhetoric, he declared "unconditional war on poverty." The core of Johnson's program was the **Office of Economic Opportunity (OEO)**. Established under the direction of Kennedy's brother-in-law R. Sargent Shriver in 1964, the OEO operated the Job Corps for school dropouts, the Neighborhood Youth Corps for unemployed teenagers, the Head Start program to prepare poor children for school, and VISTA (Volunteers in Service to America) to send volunteers into America's poorest communities. OEO's biggest effort went to Community Action Agencies. By 1968, more than 500 such agencies provided health and educational services. Despite flaws, the War on Poverty improved life for millions of Americans.

CIVIL RIGHTS, 1964–1965

Johnson's passionate commitment to economic betterment accompanied a commitment to civil rights. In Johnson's view, segregation not only deprived African Americans of access to opportunity but also distracted white southerners from their own poverty and underdevelopment.

One solution was the **Civil Rights Act of 1964**, which Kennedy had introduced but which Johnson got it enacted. The law prohibited segregation in public accommodations, such as hotels, restaurants, gas stations, theaters, and parks, and outlawed employment discrimination on federally assisted projects. It also created the Equal Employment Opportunity Commission (EEOC) and included gender in the list of categories protected against discrimination, a provision whose consequences were scarcely suspected in 1964.

Even as Congress was debating the 1964 law, **Freedom Summer** moved political power to the top of the civil rights agenda. Organized by SNCC, the Mississippi Summer Freedom Project was a voter-registration drive that sent white and black volunteers to the small towns and back roads of Mississippi. The target was a political system that used rigged literacy tests and intimidation to keep black southerners from voting. In Mississippi in 1964, only 7 percent of eligible black citizens were registered voters. Local black activists had laid the groundwork for a registration effort with years of courageous effort through the NAACP and voter leagues. Now an increasingly militant SNCC took the lead. The explicit goal was to increase the number of African American voters. The tacit intention was to attract national attention by putting middle-class white college students in the line of fire. Freedom Summer gained 1,600 new voters and taught 2,000 children in SNCC-run Freedom Schools at the cost of beatings, bombings, church arson, and the murder of three project workers.

Another outgrowth of the SNCC effort was the Mississippi Freedom Democratic Party (MFDP), a biracial coalition that bypassed Mississippi's all-white Democratic Party, followed state party rules, and sent its own delegates to the 1964 Democratic convention. To preserve party harmony, President Johnson refused to expel the "regular" Mississippi Democrats and offered instead to seat two MFDP delegates and enforce party rules for 1968. The MFDP walked out, seething with anger.

Freedom Summer and political realities both focused national attention on voter registration. Lyndon Johnson and Martin Luther King Jr. agreed on the need for federal voting legislation when King visited the president in December 1964 after winning the Nobel Peace Prize. For King, power at the ballot box would help black southerners to take control of their own communities. For Johnson, voting reform would fulfill the promise of American democracy. It would also benefit the Democratic Party by replacing with black voters the white southerners who were drifting toward the anti-integration Republicans.

The target for King and the SCLC was Dallas County, Alabama, where only 2 percent of eligible black residents were registered, compared with 70 percent of white residents. Peaceful demonstrations started in January 1965. By early February, jails in the county seat of Selma held 2,600 black people whose offense was marching to the courthouse to demand the vote. The campaign climaxed with a march from Selma to the state capital of Montgomery.

On Sunday, March 7, 500 marchers crossed the bridge over the Alabama River, to meet a sea of state troopers. The troopers gave them two minutes to disperse and then attacked on foot and horseback "as if they were mowing a big field." The attack drove the demonstrators back in bloody confusion while television cameras rolled.

As violence continued, Johnson addressed a joint session of Congress to demand a voting-rights law. By opening the political process to previously excluded citizens, the Voting Rights Act was as revolutionary and far-reaching as the Nineteenth Amendment, which guaranteed women the right to vote, and the Labor Relations Act of 1935, which recognized labor unions as the equals of corporations.

Johnson signed the **Voting Rights Act** on August 6, 1965. The law outlawed literacy tests and provided for federal voting registrars in states where registration or turnout in 1964 was less than 50 percent of the eligible population. It applied initially in seven southern states. Black registration in these states jumped from 27 percent to 55 percent within the first year. In 1975, Congress extended coverage to Hispanic voters in the Southwest. The Act required new moderation from white leaders, who had to satisfy black voters, and it opened the way for black and Latino candidates to win positions at every level of state and local government. In the long run, the Voting Rights Act climaxed the battle for civil rights and shifted attention to the continuing problems of economic opportunity and inequality.

WAR, PEACE, AND THE LANDSLIDE OF 1964

Lyndon Johnson was the peace candidate in 1964. Johnson had maintained Kennedy's commitment to South Vietnam. On the advice of such Kennedy holdovers as Defense Secretary Robert McNamara, he stepped up commando raids and naval shelling of North Vietnam, on the assumption that North Vietnam controlled the Viet Cong. On August 2, North Vietnamese torpedo boats attacked the U.S. destroyer *Maddox* in the Gulf of Tonkin while it was eavesdropping on North Vietnamese military signals. Two days later, the *Maddox* and the *C. Turner Joy* reported another torpedo attack (probably false sonar readings). Johnson ordered a bombing raid in reprisal and asked Congress to authorize "all necessary measures" to protect U.S. forces and stop further aggression. Congress passed the **Gulf of Tonkin Resolution** with only two nay votes, effectively authorizing the president to wage undeclared war.

Johnson's militancy paled beside that of his Republican opponent. Senator Barry Goldwater of Arizona represented the new right wing of the Republican Party, which was drawing strength from the South and West. Johnson looked moderate when Goldwater declared that "extremism in the defense of liberty is no vice." In contrast, Johnson pledged not "to send American boys nine or ten thousand miles from home to do what Asian boys ought to be doing for themselves" while Goldwater proposed an all-out war.

The election was a landslide. Johnson's 61 percent of the popular vote was the greatest margin ever recorded in a presidential election. Democrats racked up two-to-one majorities in Congress. For the first time in decades, liberal Democrats could enact their domestic program without begging votes from conservative southerners or Republicans, and Johnson could achieve his goal of a **Great Society** based on freedom and opportunity for all.

The result was a series of measures that Johnson pushed through Congress before the Vietnam War eroded his political standing and distracted national attention. The National Endowment for the Arts and the National Endowment for the Humanities seemed uncontroversial at the time but would later become the focus of liberal and conservative struggles over the character of American life. The Wilderness Act (1964), which preserved 9.1 million acres from development, would prove another political battlefield in the face of economic pressures in the next century.

The goal of increasing opportunity for all Americans stirred the president most deeply. The Elementary and Secondary Education Act was the first general federal aid program for public schools, allocating $1.3 billion for textbooks and special education. The Higher Education Act funded low-interest student loans and university research facilities. The Medical Care Act created **Medicare**, federally funded health insurance for the elderly, and **Medicaid**, which helped states offer medical care to the poor. The Appalachian Regional Development Act funded economic development in the depressed mountain counties of 12 states from Georgia to New York and proved a long-run success.

It is sometimes said that the United States declared war on poverty and lost. In fact, the nation came closer to winning the war on poverty than it did the war in Vietnam. New or expanded social insurance and income-support programs, such as Medicare, Medicaid, Social Security, and food stamps, cut the proportion of poor people from 22 percent of the American population in 1960 to 13 percent in 1970. Infant mortality dropped by a third because of improved nutrition and better access to healthcare for mothers and children. Taken together, the political results of the 1964 landslide moved the United States much closer to the vision of an end to poverty and racial injustice.

CONCLUSION

The era commonly remembered as the 1950s stretched from 1953 to 1964. Consistent goals guided U.S. foreign policy through the entire period, including vigilant anti-Communism and the confidence to intervene in trouble spots around the globe. At home, the Supreme Court's *Brown* decision introduced a decade-long civil rights revolution that reached its emotional peak with the March on Washington and its political climax with the Civil Rights Act (1964) and Voting Rights Act (1965). However, many patterns of personal behavior and social relations remained unchanged. Women faced similar expectations from the early fifties to the early sixties. Churches showed more continuity than change.

But the consistency and stability of the 1950s were fragile. The national consensus would splinter after 1964. What had seemed like a common road to the future soon divided into many different paths. Some members of minority groups turned their backs on integration. Some younger Americans dropped out of mainstream society to join the aptly named counterculture. Others sought the security of religious commitment and community. Perhaps most divisively, "hawks" battled "doves" over Vietnam. If civil rights and Cold War had been the defining issues for the fifties, Vietnam would define the sixties, which stretched from 1965 to 1974.

REVIEW QUESTIONS

1. What were the sources of prosperity in the 1950s and 1960s? How did prosperity shape cities, family life, and religion? What opportunities did it create for women and for young people? How did it affect the American role in the world? Why did an affluent nation still need a war on poverty in the 1960s?

2. What assumptions about the Soviet Union shaped U.S. foreign policy? What assumptions about the United States shaped Soviet policy? What did American leaders think was at stake in Vietnam, Berlin, and Cuba?

3. Who initiated and led the African American struggle for civil rights? What role did the federal government play? What were the goals of the civil rights movement? Where did it succeed, and in what ways did it fall short?

4. How did the growth of nuclear arsenals affect international relations? How did the nuclear shadow affect U.S. politics and society?

5. In what new directions did Lyndon Johnson take the United States? Were there differences between the goals of the New Frontier and the Great Society?

6. Why was school integration the focus of such strong conflict? How did the work of Mexican Americans and African Americans support the same goal of equal access to education?

7. How did religious belief shape American society in the Eisenhower and Kennedy years?

myhistórylab CONNECTIONS

Reinforce what you learned in this chapter by studying the many documents, images, maps, review tools, and videos available at www.myhistorylab.com.

READ AND REVIEW

✓●─Study and Review on myhistorylab.com STUDY PLAN: CHAPTER 28

▭●─Read the Document on myhistorylab.com

Ladies Home Journal, "Young Mother" (1956)

Brown v. Board of Education of Topeka, Kansas (1954)

Life Magazine Identifies the New Teenage Market (1959)

John F. Kennedy, Cuban Missile Crisis Address (1962)

Student Nonviolent Coordinating Committee, Statement of Purpose (1960)

Test Ban Treaty (1962)

Lyndon Johnson, "The War on Poverty" (1964)

Executive Discussions on the Cuban Missile Crisis (1962)

Executive Order 10730: Desegregation of Central High School (1957)

Fannie Lou Hammer, Voting Rights in Mississippi, 1962–1964

Jo Ann Gibson Robinson, Bus BoycottJulian Bond, Sit-ins and the Origins of SNCC (1960)

🔍─View the Map on myhistorylab.com

Civil Rights Movement

RESEARCH AND EXPLORE

▭●─Read the Document on myhistorylab.com

Personal Journeys Online

From Then to Now Online: Medical Research on Polio and AIDS

Exploring America: The Consumer Society: 1950–1960

((●─Listen on myhistorylab.com

Mass Meeting speech by Martin Luther King, Jr.

Watch the **Video** on **myhistorylab.com**

Ike for President: Eisenhower Campaign Ad, 1952

Duck and Cover

President John F. Kennedy and the Cuban Missile Crisis

How Did the Civil Rights Movement Change American Schools?

Eisenhower's Special Message to Congress on the Middle East, 1957

Rev. Dr. Martin Luther King, Jr.'s Speech at the March on Washington, August, 1963

──────── **Listen** on **myhistorylab.com** ────────

Hear the audio files for Chapter 28 at
www.myhistorylab.com.

Hear the audio files for Chapter 29 at **www.myhistorylab.com.**

FOCUS QUESTIONS

WHY DID the national consensus of the 1950s and early 1960s unravel?

WHAT CHALLENGES did cities face in the late 1960s and 1970s?

HOW DID the Tet Offensive change American public opinion about the war in Vietnam?

WHAT WAS the legacy of Richard Nixon's presidency?

WHAT FACTORS limited Jimmy Carter's effectiveness as president?

Peace protesters lean in close to the barrels of guns held by
the military police during an anti-Vietnam War protest outside
the Pentagon in Arlington, Virginia, in 1967.

ONE AMERICAN JOURNEY

The strike [against California grape growers] broke out in September of 1965.... The whole boycott is a nonviolent tool. It's an economic sanction, so to speak but it's a way that people can participate. One thing about nonviolence is that it opens the doors for everyone to participate, the women, the children. And women being involved on the picket lines made it easier for the men then to accept nonviolence.... I consider nonviolence to be a very strong spiritual force because it's almost like an energy that goes out and touches people.

Most of them [the farmworkers] were either first generation Mexican-Americans or recent immigrants. To get them to accept the whole philosophy that you can create a movement with nonviolence was not easy. It was not easy. To get them to understand that—and this you could see happening in people, that they would become transformed. They would actually become stronger through practicing nonviolence.

I gave a speech [at Northern Illinois University] and this one young man came up to me afterwards and he said, "My mother works in the fields. She's an onion picker" He says, "and I was always ashamed of my mother until today."... We have to get farmworkers the same types of benefits, the same type of wages, the respect that they deserve because they do the most sacred work of all. They feed our nation every day.

Dolores Huerta, interview with Vincent Harding at The Veterans of Hope Project, http://www.veteransofhope.org/show.php?vid551&tid546&sid577

From the early 1960s, **DOLORES HUERTA** was a co-worker with Cesar Chavez in organizing the United Farm Workers union (UFW). Her personal journey took her from her birthplace in the state of New Mexico to Stockton, California, where she grew up in a multiracial neighborhood, and then to every corner of the United States as a spokesperson for the UFW. In this interview she reflected on the power of nonviolent approaches such as the national boycott of table grapes that was the UFW's most successful tactic.

Dolores Huerta's story speaks to the importance of grassroots action and to the role of churches as sources of social change, but also to the depth of economic and cultural divisions within the United States in the later 1960s and 1970s. At the same time that groups like the UFW worked to build social movements across ethnic differences, many minority Americans responded to slow progress toward racial equality by advocating separation rather than integration, helping to plunge the nation's cities into crisis, while other Americans began to draw back from some of the objectives of racial integration. The failure to win an easy victory in Vietnam eroded the nation's confidence and fueled bitter divisions about the nation's goals. Stalemate in Southeast Asia, political changes in third-world countries, and an oil supply crisis in the 1970s challenged U.S. influence in the world. Political scandals, summarized in three syllables, "Watergate," undercut faith in government. Fifteen years of turmoil forced a grudging recognition of the limits to American military power, economic capacity, governmental prerogatives, and even the ideal of a single American dream.

The End of Consensus

Pleiku is a town in Vietnam 240 miles north of Saigon (now Ho Chi Minh City). In 1965, Pleiku was the site of a South Vietnamese army headquarters and U.S. military base. At 2:00 A.M. on February 7, Viet Cong attacked the U.S. base, killing eight Americans and wounding a hundred. President Johnson ordered retaliatory airstrikes. A month later, Johnson ordered a full-scale air offensive code-named Rolling Thunder. The official reason for the bombing was to pressure North Vietnam to negotiate an end to the war. In the back of President Johnson's mind were the need to prove his toughness and the mistaken assumption that China was aggressively backing North Vietnam.

The air strikes pushed the United States over the line from propping up the South Vietnamese government to leading the war effort. A president who desperately wanted a way out of Southeast Asia kept adding U.S. forces. Eventually, the war in Vietnam would distract the United States from the goals of the Great Society and drive Johnson from office. It hovered like a shadow over the next two presidents, set back progress toward global stability, and divided the American people.

Deeper into Vietnam

Lyndon Johnson faced limited options in Vietnam (see Map 29–1). The pervasive American determination to contain Communism and Kennedy's previous commitments there hemmed Johnson in. Advisers persuaded him that controlled military escalation—a middle course between withdrawal and all-out war—could secure Vietnam. They failed to understand the extent of popular opposition to the official government in Saigon and the willingness of North Vietnam to sacrifice to achieve national unity.

Rolling Thunder put the United States on the up escalator to war. Because an air campaign required ground troops to protect bases in South Vietnam, U.S. Marines landed on March 8. Over the next four months, William Westmoreland, the commander of U.S. forces in South Vietnam, wore away Johnson's desire to contain U.S. involvement. More bombs, a pause, an offer of massive U.S. aid—nothing brought North Vietnam to the negotiating table. On July 28, he finally gave Westmoreland doubled draft calls and an increase in U.S. combat troops from 75,000 to 275,000 by 1966. Johnson's decision turned a South Vietnamese war into a U.S. war. At the end of 1967, U.S. forces in South Vietnam totaled 485,000; they reached their maximum of 543,000 in August 1969.

The U.S. strategy on the ground was **search and destroy**. As conceived by Westmoreland, sophisticated surveillance and heavily armed patrols were used to locate enemy detachments, which could then be destroyed by air strikes, artillery, and reinforcements carried in by helicopter. The approach made sense when the opposition consisted of North Vietnamese troops and large Viet Cong units.

However, most opponents were not North Vietnamese divisions but South Vietnamese guerrillas. The Viet Cong avoided set-piece battles. Instead, they forced the United States to make repeated sweeps through farms and villages. The enemy was difficult for Americans to recognize among farmers and workers, making South Vietnamese society itself the target. The U.S. penchant for massive firepower killed thousands of Vietnamese and made millions refugees. Because the South Vietnamese government was unable to secure areas after American sweeps, the Viet Cong often reappeared after the Americans had crashed through a district.

CHRONOLOGY

1962   Rachel Carson publishes *Silent Spring*.
Port Huron Statement launches Students for a Democratic Society.
Supreme Court limits vocal prayer in schools in *Engel v. Vitale*.

1965   Congress approves Wilderness Act.
Malcolm X is assassinated.
Residents of Watts neighborhood in Los Angeles riot.
Immigration Reform Act allows increased immigration from outside Europe.

1967   African Americans riot in Detroit and Newark.

1968   Viet Cong launches Tet Offensive.
James Earl Ray kills Martin Luther King Jr.
Lyndon Johnson declines to run for reelection.
SDS disrupts Columbia University.
Sirhan Sirhan kills Robert Kennedy.
Peace talks start between the United States and North Vietnam.
Police riot against antiwar protesters during the Democratic National
Convention in Chicago.
Richard Nixon is elected president.

1969   Neil Armstrong and Buzz Aldrin walk on the moon.

1970   United States invades Cambodia.
National Guard units kill students at Kent State and Jackson State universities.
Earth Day is celebrated.
Environmental Protection Agency is created.

1971   *New York Times* publishes the secret Pentagon Papers.
President Nixon freezes wages and prices.
Plumbers unit is established in the White House.

1972   Nixon visits China.
United States and Soviet Union adopt SALT I.
Operatives for Nixon's reelection campaign break into Democratic
headquarters in the Watergate complex in Washington, DC.

1973   Paris accords end direct U.S. involvement in South Vietnamese war.
United States moves to all-volunteer armed forces.
Watergate burglars are convicted.
Senate Watergate hearings reveal the existence of taped White House
conversations.
Spiro Agnew resigns as vice president, is replaced by Gerald Ford.
Arab states impose an oil embargo after the third Arab-Israeli War.

1974   Nixon resigns as president, is succeeded by Gerald Ford.

1975   Communists triumph in South Vietnam.
United States, USSR, and European nations sign the Helsinki Accords.

1976	Jimmy Carter defeats Gerald Ford for the presidency.
1978	Carter brings the leaders of Egypt and Israel to Camp David for peace talks.
	U.S. agrees to transfer control of the Panama Canal to Panama.
1979	SALT II agreement is signed but not ratified.
	OPEC raises oil prices.
	Three Mile Island nuclear plant comes close to disaster.
	Iranian militants take U.S. embassy hostages.
1980	Iranian hostage rescue fails.
	Soviet troops enter Afghanistan.
	Ronald Reagan defeats Jimmy Carter for the presidency.

The U.S. air war also had limited results. Pilots dropped a vast tonnage of bombs on the Ho Chi Minh Trail, a network of supply routes from North Vietnam to South Vietnam through the mountains of neighboring Laos. Despite the bombing, thousands of workers converted rough paths into roads that were repaired as soon as they were damaged. The air assault on North Vietnam itself remained "diplomatic," intended to force North Vietnam to stop intervening in the South Vietnamese civil war. Since North Vietnam's leadership considered North and South to be one country, the American goal was unacceptable. Attacking North Vietnam's poorly developed economy, the United States soon ran out of targets.

VOICES OF DISSENT

At home, protest against the war quickly followed the commitment of U.S. combat forces. The first national antiwar march took place in Washington on April 17, 1965. Twenty-five thousand people picketed the White House, assembled at the Washington Monument for speeches by Senator Ernest Gruening of Alaska (one of the two dissenting votes on the Gulf of Tonkin Resolution) and African American leaders, and walked up the Mall to the Capitol.

Martin Luther King Jr. offered one of the strongest condemnations of the war in a speech at New York's Riverside Church on April 4, 1967. He decried the diversion of resources from domestic programs to the military, the impact of the war on the people of Vietnam, and what he saw as the poisonous effects of warfare on the soul of America. The speech was a deeply Christian argument for policies of negotiation and reconciliation in place of war.

From Protest to Confrontation. In 1966 and 1967, antiwar activity changed from respectful protest to direct confrontations with what protesters called the war machine. Much of the anger was directed at the military draft administered by the **Selective Service System.** As the name implies, the Selective Service supposedly picked the young men who could best serve the nation as soldiers and deferred induction of those with vital skills.

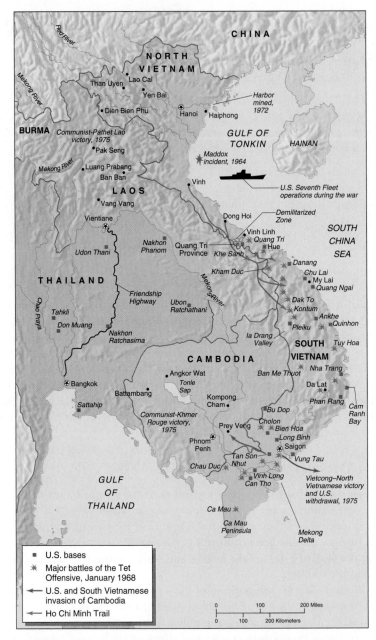

Map 29–1 • The War in Vietnam The United States attacked North Vietnam with air strikes but confined large-scale ground operations to South Vietnam and Cambodia. In South Vietnam, U.S. forces faced both North Vietnamese army units and Viet Cong rebels, all of whom received supplies by way of the so-called Ho Chi Minh Trail, named for the leader of North Vietnam. The coordinated attacks on cities and towns throughout South Vietnam during the Tet Offensive in 1968 surprised the United States.

▶ *Take a look at the targets of the Tet Offensive. What do the facts that there were so many of them and that they were spread out across South Vietnam tell you about the nature of the war?*

The city of Hue suffered severe damage in the Tet Offensive and its aftermath. Here refugees return to the rubble of bombed-out houses. Getty Images Inc.–Hulton Archive Photos.

As the war expanded, the administration tried to hold the allegiance of the middle class by finding ways to exempt their sons from service in Vietnam. Full-time college enrollment was good for a deferment; so was the right medical diagnosis from the right doctor. As a result, draftees and enlistees tended to be small-town and working-class youth. The resentment created by the draft was an important wedge that began to erode the long-standing alliance between working-class Americans and the Democratic Party.

Military service also deepened the gap between blacks and whites. The black community supplied more than its share of combat soldiers. In 1965, when African Americans made up 11 percent of the nation's population, 24 percent of the soldiers who died in Vietnam were black. This disparity forced the Defense Department to revise its combat assignments so that the racial impact was more equal in later years.

Draft resistance provided a direct avenue for protest against the war. Some young men burned the small paper cards that indicated their selective service classification, causing Congress to enact steep penalties for the act. Several thousand moved to Canada, to spend a decade or more in exile. Thousands of others described their religious and ethical opposition to war in applications for conscientious-objector classification. Much smaller numbers went to jail for refusing to cooperate in any way with the Selective Service System.

New Left and Community Activism

The antiwar movement was part of a growing grassroots activism that took much of its tone from the university-based **Students for a Democratic Society (SDS)**. SDS tried to harness youthful disillusionment about consumerism, racism, and imperialism. It wanted to counter the trends that seemed to be turning Americans into tiny cogs in the machinery of big government, corporations, and universities. SDS thought of itself as a "New Left" that was free from the doctrinal squabbles that hampered the old left of the 1930s and 1940s.

Many of the original SDS leaders were also participants in the civil rights movement. The same was true of Mario Savio, founder of the **Free Speech Movement (FSM)** at the University of California at Berkeley in 1964. Savio hoped to build a multi-issue "community of protest" around the idea of "a free university in a free society." FSM protests climaxed with a December sit-in that led to 773 arrests and stirred protest on other campuses.

What SDS wanted to do with its grassroots organizing resembled the federal community-action programs associated with the war on poverty. The **Model Cities Program** (1966) invited residents of poor neighborhoods to write their own plans for using federal funds to improve local housing, education, health services, and job opportunities. Model Cities assemblies challenged the racial bias in programs like urban renewal and helped train community leaders.

In the 1970s and 1980s, when SDS was long gone and the Model Cities Program was fading, the lessons of grassroots reform would still be visible in alternative organizations and political movements that strengthened democracy from the bottom up. Activists staffed food cooperatives, free clinics, women's health groups, and drug-counseling centers across the country. Community-based organization was a key element in self-help efforts by African Americans, Asian Americans, and Latinos. Neighborhood associations and community-development corporations that provided affordable housing and jobs extended the "backyard revolution" into the 1980s and beyond. Social conservatives, such as antiabortionists, used the same techniques on behalf of their own agendas.

Youth Culture and Counterculture

The popular context for the serious work of the New Left was the growing youth culture and **counterculture**. Millions of young people in the second half of the 1960s expressed their alienation from American society by sampling drugs or chasing the rainbow of a youth culture. The middle-aged and middle-class dubbed the rebellious young "hippies."

The youth culture took advantage of the nation's prosperity. It was consumerism in a tie-dyed t-shirt. A high point was the 1969 Woodstock rock festival in New York State. But Woodstock was an excursion, not a life-altering commitment. Members of the Woodstock Generation were consumers in a distinct market niche, dressing but not living like social reformers or revolutionaries.

Within the youth culture was a smaller and more intense counterculture that added Eastern religion, social radicalism, and evangelistic belief in the drug LSD. San Francisco's Haight-Ashbury district became a national mecca for hippies in 1967's "Summer of Love," and hippie districts sprang up around university campuses across the country.

The cultural rebels of the late 1950s and early 1960s had been trying to combine personal freedom with new social arrangements. Many hippies were more interested in altering their minds with drugs than with politics or poetry. Serious exploration of societal alternatives was left for the minority who devoted themselves to the political work of the New Left, communal living, women's liberation, and other movements.

Writer Ken Kesey and the self-defined Merry Pranksters toured the country in a brightly painted bus, parked here in San Francisco's Golden Gate Park. They sometimes threw open parties where they served punch laced with psychedelic drugs in the hope of inciting radical social change.

SOUNDS OF CHANGE

The youth culture was shaped by films and philosophers, by pot and poets, but above all by music. Many changes in American society are mirrored in the abrupt shift from the increasingly complacent rock-and-roll of the early 1960s to the more provocative albums of mid-decade. The songs were still aimed at popular success, but the musicians were increasingly self-conscious of themselves as artists and social critics.

At the start of the decade, the African American roots of rock-and-roll were unmistakable, but there was no social agenda. Elvis Presley and the Everly Brothers kept the messages personal. Music that criticized American society initially found a much smaller audience through the folk-music revival in a few big cities and university campuses. Singers like Pete Seeger and Joan Baez drew on white country music and old labor-organizing songs to keep alive dissenting voices.

Then, in an artistic revolution, the doors opened to a new kind of rock music. The Beatles capitalized on their immense popularity to begin a career of artistic experimentation. They also opened the way for such hard-edged British bands as the Rolling Stones and The Who to introduce social criticism and class consciousness into rock lyrics. San Francisco's new psychedelic-rock scene took its name from drugs, such as LSD, and centered on shows at the Fillmore Auditorium and performers such as the Grateful Dead, Jefferson Airplane, and Janis Joplin.

Bob Dylan, a folksinger with an acoustic guitar, "went electric" at the Newport, Rhode Island, folk festival in 1965 and further transformed the music scene. Dylan's music was musically exciting and socially critical in a way that expressed much of the discontent of American young people.

COMMUNES AND CULTS

Out of the half-secular, half-spiritual vision of the counterculture came people who not only dropped out of mainstream institutions but also tried to drop into miniature societies built on new principles. Thousands of Americans in the late 1960s and 1970s formed "intentional communities" or "communes." Upper New England, the Southwest, and the West Coast were commune country where members usually tried to combine individual freedom and spontaneity with cooperative living.

A number of communes were serious endeavors. Some tried to follow spiritual leadings from Christianity or Buddhism. Others studied *The Whole Earth Catalog* (1968) to learn how to live off the land. Thousands of smaller and less conspicuous urban communes whose members occupied large old houses pursued experiments in socialism, environmentalism, or feminism. Such efforts helped to spread the ideas of organic farming, cooperative land ownership, and low-consumption environmentalism that would move into the mainstream.

THE FEMINIST CRITIQUE

The growing dissatisfaction of many women with their domestic roles helped set the stage for a revived feminism that was another result of the ferment of the 1960s. Important steps in this revival included the Presidential Commission on the Status of Women in 1961; the addition of gender as one of the categories protected by the Civil Rights Act of 1964 (see Chapter 28), and creation of the National Organization for Women (NOW) in 1966.

Mainstream feminism targeted unequal opportunity in the job market. Throughout the mid-1960s and 1970s, activists battled to open job categories to women and for equal pay for everyone with equal qualifications and responsibilities.

Changes in sexual behavior paralleled efforts to equalize treatment in the workplace. More reliable methods of contraception, especially birth-control pills introduced in the early 1960s, gave women greater control over childbearing. In some ways a replay of ideas from the 1920s, a new sexual revolution eroded the double standard that expected chastity of women but tolerated promiscuity among men. One consequence was a singles culture that accepted sexual activity between unmarried men and women.

More radical versions of the feminist message came from women who had joined the civil rights and antiwar movements only to find themselves working the copy machine and the coffeemaker while men plotted strategy. Radicals caught the attention of the national media with a demonstration against the 1968 Miss America pageant. Protesters crowned a sheep as Miss America and encouraged women to make a statement by tossing their bras and makeup in the trash.

Women's liberation took off as a social and political movement in 1970 and 1971. Within a few years, millions of women had recognized events and patterns in their lives as discrimination based on gender. The feminist movement, and specific policy measures related to it, put equal rights and the fight against sexism (a word no one knew before 1965) on the national agenda and gradually changed how Americans thought about the relationships between men and women. Feminists focused attention on rape as a crime of violence and called attention to the burdens the legal system placed on rape victims. In the 1980s and 1990s, they also challenged sexual harassment in the workplace, gradually refining the boundaries between acceptable and unacceptable behavior.

OVERVIEW WHY WERE WE IN SOUTH VIETNAM?

U.S. leaders offered a number of justifications for U.S. military involvement in Vietnam. Here are some of the key arguments, with points that supported or questioned the explanation.

To Prop Up a Domino:	Communist success in South Vietnam would undermine pro-American regimes in adjacent nations, which would topple like a row of dominoes.
Pro	The firm U.S. stand contributed to an anti-Communist coup in Indonesia in 1965 and encouraged pro-American interests in Thailand and the Philippines.
Con	Detailed knowledge of each nation in Southeast Asia shows that their own histories and internal issues were far more important in determining their futures than was American action in Vietnam.
To Contain China:	China's Communist regime wanted to expand its control throughout Asia.
Pro	The People's Republic of China was hostile to the United States, as shown in the Korean War, and had a long history of trying to control Vietnam.
Con	North Vietnam had closer ties to the Soviet Union than to China and played the two Communist nations against each other to preserve its independence from China.
To Defeat Aggression:	South Vietnam was an independent nation threatened by invasion.
Pro	The major military threat to South Vietnam after 1965 came from the growing presence of the North Vietnamese army, and U.S. military intervention was necessary to counter that invasion.
Con	The conflict in South Vietnam originated as a civil war within South Vietnam. Moreover, South and North Vietnam were a single nation, artificially divided in 1954, so that North Vietnam was trying to reunify rather than invade South Vietnam.
To Protect Democracy:	South Vietnam was a democratic nation that deserved U.S. support.
Pro	South Vietnam had an emerging middle class and an opportunity to develop democratic institutions.
Con	South Vietnam was never a true democracy, ruled first by civilian dictator Ngo Dinh Diem and then a series of military strongmen.

COMING OUT

The new militancy among gay men and lesbians drew on several of the social changes of the late 1960s and 1970s. Willingness to acknowledge and talk about nonstandard sexual behavior was part of a change in public values. Tactics of political pressure came from the antiwar and civil rights movements.

Gay activism spread from big cities to small communities, from the coasts to Middle America. New York police had long harassed gay bars and their customers. When police raided Manhattan's Stonewall Inn in June 1969, however, patrons fought back in a weekend of disorder. The **Stonewall Rebellion** was a catalyst for homosexuals to assert themselves as a political force. San Francisco also became a center of gay life.

With New Yorkers and San Franciscans as examples, more and more gay men and lesbians "came out," or went public about their sexual orientation. They published newspapers, organized churches, and lobbied politicians for protection of basic civil rights such as equal access to employment, housing, and public accommodations. They staged "gay pride" days and marches. In 1974, the American Psychiatric Association eliminated homosexuality from its official list of mental disorders.

CITIES UNDER STRESS

In the confident years after World War II, big cities had an upbeat image. By the 1970s, however, slums and squalid back streets dominated popular imagery. Movies and television reinforced the message that cities had become places of random and frequent violence.

DIAGNOSING AN URBAN CRISIS

The nation entered the 1960s with the assumption that urban problems were growing pains. Exploding metropolitan areas needed money for streets, schools, and sewers. Politicians viewed the difficulties of central cities as by-products of exuberant suburban growth, which left outmoded downtowns in need of physical redevelopment.

Central cities had a special burden in caring for the domestic poor. Baltimore, for example, had 27 percent of the Maryland population in 1970 but 66 percent of the state's welfare recipients.

Many urban problems were associated with the "second ghettos" created by the migration of 2.5 million African Americans from southern farms to northern and western cities in the 1950s and 1960s. By 1970, one-third of all African Americans lived in the 12 largest cities, crowding into ghetto neighborhoods dating from World War II.

At the end of their journeys, postwar black migrants found systems of race relations that limited their access to decent housing, the best schools, and many unionized jobs. Many families arrived just in time to face the consequences of industrial layoffs and plant closures in the 1970s and 1980s. Already unneeded in the South because of the mechanization of agriculture, the migrants found themselves equally unwanted in the industrial North, caught in decaying neighborhoods and victimized by crime.

Central cities faced additional financial problems unrelated to poverty and race. Many of their roads, bridges, fire stations, and water mains were 50 to 100 years old by the 1960s and 1970s, and they were wearing out. Decay of urban utility and transportation systems was a by-product of market forces and public policy. Private developers often borrowed money saved through northeastern bank accounts, insurance policies, and pension funds to finance new construction in sunbelt suburbs. The defense budget pumped tax dollars from the old industrial cities into the South and West.

CONFLICT IN THE STREETS

African Americans and Hispanics who rioted in city streets in the mid-1960s were fed up with the lack of job opportunities, with substandard housing, and with crime. Riots in Rochester, Harlem, and Brooklyn in July 1964 opened four years of racial violence. Before they subsided, the riots had scarred most big cities and killed 200 people, most of them African Americans.

The explosion of the Watts neighborhood in Los Angeles fixed the danger of racial unrest in the public mind. Trouble started on August 11, 1965, when a white highway-patrol officer arrested a young African American for drunken driving. Loud complaints drew a crowd, and the arrival of Los Angeles police turned the bystanders into an angry mob that attacked passing cars. The primary targets were symbols of white authority and businesses with reputations for exploiting their customers, a conclusion reached by the National Advisory Commission on Civil Disorders. Rioting, looting, and arson spread through Watts for two days until the National Guard cordoned off the trouble spots and occupied the neighborhood on August 14 and 15. After Watts, Americans expected "long hot summers" and got them. Scores of cities suffered riots in 1966, including a riot by Puerto Ricans in Chicago that protested the same problems blacks faced. The following year, the worst violence was in Newark, New Jersey, and in Detroit, where 43 deaths and blocks of blazing buildings stunned television viewers.

Few politicians wanted to admit that African Americans and Hispanics had serious grievances. Their impulse was to blame riffraff and outside agitators. This theory was wrong. Almost all participants were neighborhood residents. Except that they were younger, they were representative of the African American population, and their violence came from the frustration of rising expectations. Despite the political gains of the civil rights movement, unemployment remained high, and the police still treated all blacks as potential criminals. The urban riots were political actions to force the problems of African Americans onto the national agenda.

MINORITY SELF-DETERMINATION

Minority separatism and demands for self-determination tapped the same anger that fueled the urban riots. Drawing on a long heritage of militancy (such as armed resistance during racial riots), activists challenged the central goal of the civil rights movement, which sought full integration and participation in American life. The phrase **Black Power**, popularized by SNCC leader Stokely Carmichael, summed up the new alternative.

The slogans of Black Power, Brown Power, and Red Power spanned goals that ran from civil rights to cultural pride to revolutionary separatism. They were all efforts by minorities to define themselves through their own heritage and backgrounds, not simply by looking in the mirror of white society.

Expressions of Black Power. Black Power translated many ways—control of one's own community through the voting machine, celebration of the African American heritage, creation of a parallel society that shunned white institutions.

Black Power also meant increased interest in the **Nation of Islam**, or Black Muslims, who combined a version of Islam with radical separatism. They called for self-discipline, support of black institutions and businesses, and total rejection of whites. The Nation of Islam appealed to blacks who saw no future in integration and was strongest in northern cities where it offered an alternative to the life of the streets.

In the early 1960s, Malcolm X emerged as a leading Black Muslim. Growing up as Malcolm Little, he was a street-wise criminal until he converted to the Nation of Islam in prison. After his release, Malcolm preached that blacks should stop letting whites set the terms by which they judged their appearance, communities, and accomplishments. He emphasized the African cultural heritage and economic self-help and proclaimed himself an extremist for black rights. In the last year of his life, however, he returned from a pilgrimage to Mecca willing to consider limited acceptance of whites. Rivals within the movement assassinated him in February 1965, but his ideas lived on in *The Autobiography of Malcolm X.*

The **Black Panthers** pursued similar goals. Bobby Seale and Huey Newton grew up in the Oakland, California, area and met as college students. They saw African American ghettos as internal colonies in need of self-determination and asserted their equality. They shadowed police patrols to prevent mistreatment of African Americans and carried weapons into the California State Legislature in May 1967 to protest gun control. The Panthers also promoted community-based self-help efforts, such as a free-breakfast program for school children and medical clinics, and ran political candidates.

In contrast to the rioters in Watts, the Panthers had a political program, if not the ability to carry it through. Panther chapters imploded when they attracted shakedown artists as well as visionaries. Nevertheless, they survived as a political organization into the 1970s, and former Panther Bobby Rush entered Congress in 1992.

Members of the Black Panthers assemble outside the Alameda County Courthouse in Oakland, California, on July, 15, 1968, as Panther leader Huey Newton goes on trial for killing a police officer.

Hispanic Activism in the Southwest. Latinos in the Southwest developed their own Brown Power movement in the late 1960s. Led by Reies López Tijerina, Hispanics in rural New Mexico demanded the return of lands that had been lost to Anglo Americans despite the guarantees of the Treaty of Guadalupe Hidalgo in 1848. Mexican Americans in the 1970s organized for political power in southern Texas communities where they were a majority.

The best-known Hispanic activism combined social protest with the crusading spirit of earlier labor union organizing campaigns. Cesar Chavez organized the multiracial United Farm Workers (UFW) among Mexican American agricultural workers in California in 1965. Chavez was committed both to nonviolent action for social justice and to the labor movement. UFW demands included better wages and safer working conditions, such as less exposure to pesticides. Because farmworkers were not covered by the National Labor Relations Act, there was no established mechanism to force growers to recognize the union as a bargaining agent. Chavez supplemented work stoppages with national boycotts against table grapes, making *la huelga* ("the strike") a cause for urban liberals.

Native Americans Assert Their Identity. Native Americans also fought both for equal access to American society and to preserve cultural traditions through tribal institutions. Like efforts to secure rights and opportunities for African Americans and Latinos, the "Red Power" movement had deep roots in efforts to reverse the termination policy of the 1950s and to secure economic improvements for reservations. Indians in cities like Los Angeles and Portland came together across tribal lines to develop social and

Armed confrontation between militant Indians and state and federal law enforcement at Wounded Knee, South Dakota, in 1973 recalled the decades of warfare between Plains tribes and the U.S. Army in the previous century.

cultural services. One result of this political work came in 1968, when Congress restored the authority of tribal law on reservations. Three years later the Alaska Native Claims Settlement Act granted native Alaskans 44 million acres and $963 million to settle claims for their ancestral lands. Legally sophisticated tribes sued for compensation and enforcement of treaty provisions, such as fishing rights in the Pacific Northwest. Larger tribes established their own colleges, such as Navajo Community College (1969) and Oglala Lakota College (1971).

A second development was media-oriented protests that asserted Red Power. One of the earliest was a series of "fish-ins" in which Indians from Washington state, helped by the multitribal National Indian Youth Council, exercised treaty-based fishing rights in defiance of state regulations. Native American students gained national attention by seizing the abandoned Alcatraz Island for a cultural and educational center (1969–1971). Indians in Minneapolis created the **American Indian Movement (AIM)** in 1968 to increase economic opportunity and stop police mistreatment. AIM participated in the cross-country Broken Treaties Caravan, which climaxed by occupying the Bureau of Indian Affairs in Washington in 1972. AIM also allied with Sioux traditionalists on the Pine Ridge Reservation in South Dakota against the tribe's elected government. In 1973, they took over the village of Wounded Knee, where the U.S. Army in 1890 had massacred 300 Indians. They held out for 70 days before leaving peacefully.

SUBURBAN INDEPENDENCE: THE OUTER CITY

In the mid-1960s, the United States became a suburban nation. The 1970 census found more people living in the suburban counties of metropolitan areas (37 percent) than in central cities (31 percent) or in small towns and rural areas (31 percent). Just after World War II, most new suburbs had been bedroom communities that depended on the jobs, services, and shopping of central cities. By the late 1960s, suburbs were evolving into "outer cities," whose inhabitants had little need for the old central city.

Suburban Economic Growth and Political Influence. Suburbs captured most new jobs, leaving the urban poor with few opportunities for employment. In the 15 largest metropolitan areas, the number of central city jobs fell by 800,000 in the 1960s, while the number of suburban jobs rose by 3.2 million. Suburban rings gained a growing share of public facilities intended to serve the entire metropolitan area. As pioneered in California, community colleges served the suburban children of the baby boom.

Suburban political power grew along with economic clout. In 1962, the Supreme Court handed down a landmark decision in the case of *Baker v. Carr*. Overturning laws that treated counties or other political subdivisions as the units to be represented in state legislatures, *Baker* required that legislative seats be apportioned on the basis of population. The principle of "one person, one vote" broke the stranglehold of rural counties on state governments, but the big beneficiaries were not older cities, but fast-growing suburbs. By 1975, suburbanites held the largest block of seats in the House of Representatives. Reapportionment in 1982, based on the 1980 census, produced a House that was even more heavily suburban.

School Busing Controversies. School integration controversies in the 1970s reinforced a tendency for suburbanites to separate themselves from city problems. In *Swann v. Charlotte-Mecklenburg Board of Education* (1971), the U.S. Supreme Court held that crosstown busing was an acceptable solution to the de facto segregation that resulted from residential patterns within a single school district. When school officials around the country failed to achieve racial balance, federal judges ordered their own busing plans. Although integration through busing occurred peacefully in dozens of cities, many white people resented the practice. Working-class students in cities like Boston who depended on public schools found themselves on the front lines of integration, while many middle-class families switched to private education.

Because the Supreme Court also ruled that busing programs normally stopped at school-district boundaries, suburbs with independent districts escaped school integration. One result was to make busing self-defeating, for it led white families to move out of the integrating school district. Others placed their children in private academies, as happened frequently in the South. The political separation of suburbs from city thus allowed white suburbanites to think of themselves as defending local control rather than privilege.

THE YEAR OF THE GUN, 1968

Some years are turning points that force society to reconsider its basic assumptions. In 1914, the violence of World War I undermined Europe's belief in progress. In 1933, Americans had to rethink the role of government. In 1968, mainstream Americans increasingly turned against the war in Vietnam, student protest and youth counterculture turned ugly, and political consensus shattered.

THE TET OFFENSIVE

At the end of 1967, U.S. officials were overconfidently predicting victory. Then, at the beginning of Tet, the Vietnamese New Year, the Viet Cong attacked 36 of 44 provincial capitals and the national capital, Saigon. They hit the U.S. embassy and reached the

GIs evacuate a wounded comrade from fighting near the border between Vietnam and Cambodia.

runways of Tan Son Nhut air base. If the United States was winning, the Tet Offensive should not have been possible.

As a military effort, the attacks failed. U.S. and South Vietnamese troops repulsed the attacks and cleared the cities. But the offensive was a psychological blow that convinced the American public that the war was quicksand. Television coverage of the Tet battles made the bad publicity worse. At least until Tet, the commentary from network news anchors had supported the U.S. effort, but the pictures undermined civilian morale. A handful of images stayed in people's memories—a Buddhist monk burning himself to death in protest; a child with flesh peeled off by napalm; a South Vietnamese official executing a captive on the streets of Saigon.

In the wake of the Tet crisis, General Westmoreland's request for 200,000 more troops forced a political and military reevaluation. Clark Clifford, a dedicated Cold Warrior, was the new secretary of defense. Now he had second thoughts. Twenty "wise men"—the big names of the Cold War—told the president that the war was unwinnable on terms acceptable to America's allies and to many Americans. The best option, the wise men told LBJ, was disengagement.

LBJ's Exit

The president was already in political trouble. After other prominent Democrats held back, Minnesota's liberal senator Eugene McCarthy had decided to challenge Johnson in the presidential primaries. Because he controlled the party organizations in two-thirds of the states, Johnson did not need the primary states for renomination and ignored the first primary in New Hampshire. McCarthy won a startling 42 percent of the popular vote and 20 of 24 delegates in the New Hampshire primary. The vote was a protest against Johnson's Vietnam policy rather than a clear mandate for peace. Nevertheless, the vote proved that the political middle would no longer hold. By showing Johnson's vulnerability, New Hampshire also drew Robert Kennedy into the race. The younger brother of JFK, Kennedy could be arrogant and abrasive, but he was more successful than other mainstream politicians in touching the hearts of Hispanic and African American voters.

Facing political challenges and an unraveling war, on March 31, 1968, Johnson announced a halt to most bombing of North Vietnam, opening the door for peace negotiations that formally began in May 1969. He then astounded the country by withdrawing from the presidential race. It was a statesmanlike act by a man who had been consumed by a war he did not want, had never understood, and could not end.

VIOLENCE AND POLITICS: KING, KENNEDY, AND CHICAGO

Johnson's dramatic withdrawal was followed by the violent disruption of U.S. politics through assassination and riot. On April 4, 1968, an ex-convict, James Earl Ray, shot and killed Martin Luther King Jr. as he stood on the balcony of a Memphis motel. King was in Memphis to support striking city workers, an example of his increasing emphasis on economic justice and equality as well as civil rights. King's death was the product of pure racial hatred, and it triggered a climactic round of violence in black ghettos. Fires devastated the West Side of Chicago and downtown Washington, DC. The army guarded the steps of the Capitol, ready to protect Congress from its fellow citizens.

The shock of King's death was still fresh when another political assassination stunned the nation. On June 5, Robert Kennedy won California's primary election. He was still behind Vice President Hubert Humphrey in the delegate count but coming on strong. As Kennedy walked out of the ballroom at his headquarters in the Ambassador Hotel in Los Angeles, a Jordanian immigrant named Sirhan Sirhan put a bullet in his brain. Sirhan may have wanted revenge for America's tilt toward Israel in that country's victorious Six-Day War with Egypt and Jordan in 1967.

Kennedy's death ensured the Democratic nomination for Humphrey, a liberal who had loyally supported Johnson's war policy. After his nomination, Humphrey faced the Republican Richard Nixon and the Independent George Wallace. Nixon positioned himself as the candidate of the political middle. Wallace appealed to southern whites and working-class northerners who feared black militancy and hated "the ivory-tower folks with pointy heads."

Both got great help from the Democratic Convention, held in Chicago on August 26–29. While Democrats feuded among themselves, Chicago Mayor Richard Daley and his police department monitored antiwar protesters. The National Mobilization Committee to End the War in Vietnam drew from the New Left and from older peace activists—sober and committed people who had fought against nuclear weapons in the 1950s and the Vietnam War throughout the 1960s. They wanted to embarrass the Johnson-Humphrey administration by marching to the convention hall on nomination night. Mixed in were the Yippies, an informal group who planned to attract young people to Chicago with the promise of street theater, media events, and confrontation that would

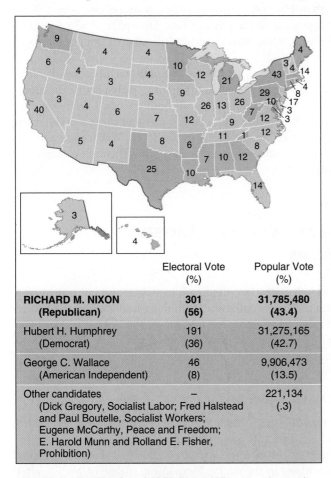

	Electoral Vote (%)	Popular Vote (%)
RICHARD M. NIXON (Republican)	**301** **(56)**	**31,785,480** **(43.4)**
Hubert H. Humphrey (Democrat)	191 (36)	31,275,165 (42.7)
George C. Wallace (American Independent)	46 (8)	9,906,473 (13.5)
Other candidates (Dick Gregory, Socialist Labor; Fred Halstead and Paul Boutelle, Socialist Workers; Eugene McCarthy, Peace and Freedom; E. Harold Munn and Rolland E. Fisher, Prohibition)	–	221,134 (.3)

MAP 29–2 • The Election of 1968 Richard Nixon won the presidency with the help of George Wallace, the American Independent Party candidate. Wallace won several southern states, offering an alternative to white southerners unhappy with the Democratic Party but not yet prepared to vote Republican. He also drew northern working-class votes away from Hubert Humphrey and thus helped Nixon to take several midwestern states.

▶ *How does this map help explain the shift of the South to the Republican Party over the course of the 1970s?*

puncture the pretensions of the power structure. To the extent they had a program, it was to use the youth culture to attract converts to radical politics.

The volatile mix was ready for a spark. On August 28, the same night that Democratic delegates were nominating Humphrey, tensions exploded in a police riot. Protesters and Yippies had congregated in Grant Park, across Michigan Avenue from downtown hotels. Undisciplined police waded into the crowds with clubs and tear gas. Young people fought back with rocks and bottles. Television caught the hours of violence that ended when the National Guard separated police from demonstrators. For Humphrey, the convention was a catastrophe, alienating liberal Democrats and associating Democrats with disorder in the public mind.

The election was closer than Humphrey had any right to hope (see Map 29–2). Election day gave Wallace 13.5 percent of the popular vote, Humphrey 42.7 percent of the popular vote and 191 electoral votes, and Nixon 43.4 percent of the popular vote and 301 electoral votes.

The Wallace candidacy was a glimpse of the future. The national media saw Wallace in terms of bigotry and a backlash against civil rights, getting only part of the story. Many of Wallace's northern backers were unhappy with both parties. Liberal on economic issues but conservative on family and social issues, many of these working-class voters evolved into "Reagan Democrats" by the 1980s. In the South, Wallace was a transitional choice for conservative voters who would eventually transfer their allegiance from the Democratic to the Republican Party.

NIXON, WATERGATE, AND THE CRISIS OF THE EARLY 1970S

The new president was an unlikely politician, ill at ease in public and consumed by a sense of inferiority. His painful public presence and dishonesty have tended to obscure his administration's accomplishments. He reduced tensions in the Cold War. He reluctantly upgraded civil rights enforcement, set goals for minority hiring by federal contractors, and presided over impressive environmental legislation.

GETTING OUT OF VIETNAM, 1969–1975

After 1968, things got worse in Southeast Asia before they got better. Despite his claims during the campaign, Nixon had no secret plan to end the war. Opposition intensified with the revelation that U.S. soldiers in March 1968 had slaughtered hundreds of men, women, and children in the South Vietnamese village of My Lai after failing to find any Viet Cong. This crime accentuated the dehumanizing power of war and showed how far the United States was straying from its ideals. Protests at home culminated in 1969 with the Vietnam Moratorium on October 15, when 2 million protesters joined rallies across the country.

Disaffection also mounted in Vietnam. Racial tensions sapped morale on the front lines. Troops lost discipline, took drugs, and hunkered down waiting for their tours of duty to end, and the high command had to adapt its code of justice to keep an army on the job.

Nixon and Vice President Spiro Agnew responded by trying to isolate the antiwar opposition, but Nixon also reduced the role of U.S. ground forces. Nixon claimed that his policies represented "the great silent majority of my fellow Americans." The administration arranged for a "spontaneous" attack by construction workers on antiwar protesters in New York. The hard-hat counterattack was a cynically manipulated symbol, but Nixon and Agnew tapped genuine anger about failure in Asia and rapid change in U.S. society.

"Vietnamization" and the Secret War Against Cambodia. Nixon's secretary of defense, Melvin Laird, responded to the antiwar sentiment with "Vietnamization," withdrawing U.S. troops as fast as possible without undermining the South Vietnamese government. In July 1969, the president announced the **Nixon Doctrine**. The United States would help other countries fight their wars with weapons and money but not with soldiers. The policy substituted machines for men. Americans rearmed and enlarged the South Vietnamese army and surreptitiously bombed Communist bases in neutral Cambodia.

The secret war against Cambodia culminated on April 30, 1970, with an invasion. The aim was to smash Viet Cong and North Vietnamese bases to allow time to rebuild the South Vietnamese army. Americans who had hoped that the war was fading away were outraged. At Kent State University in Ohio, the National Guard was called in to maintain order. Taunts, tossed bottles, and the recent record of violence put them on edge. On May 4, one unit fired on a group of young people and killed four of them. At Jackson State University in Mississippi, two students were killed when troops fired on their dormitory.

Stalemate and Cease-fire. The Cambodian "incursion" extended the military stalemate in Vietnam to U.S. policy. Beginning in December 1969, a new lottery system for determining the order of draft calls by birthdate let two-thirds of young men know they would not be drafted. In December 1970, Congress repealed the Gulf of Tonkin Resolution and prohibited the use of U.S. ground troops outside South Vietnam. Cambodia, however, was already devastated. The U.S. invasion had destabilized its government and opened the way for the bloodthirsty Khmer Rouge, who killed millions of Cambodians in the name of a working-class revolution. Vietnamization continued; only 90,000 U.S. ground troops were still in Vietnam by early 1972. A final air offensive in December smashed Hanoi into rubble and helped to force four and a half years of peace talks to a conclusion.

The cease-fire began on January 27, 1973. It confirmed U.S. withdrawal from Vietnam. North Vietnamese and Viet Cong forces would remain in control of the territory they occupied in South Vietnam, but they were not to be reinforced or substantially reequipped. The United States promised not to increase its military aid to South Vietnam. There were no solid guarantees for the South Vietnamese government. Immediately after coming to terms with North Vietnam, Nixon suspended the draft in favor of an all-volunteer military.

In 1975, South Vietnam collapsed. Only the U.S. presence had kept its political, ethnic, and religious factions together. For the first two years after the Paris agreement, North Vietnam quietly rebuilt its military capacity. In the spring of 1975, it opened an offensive, and South Vietnamese morale evaporated. Resistance crumbled so rapidly that the United States had to evacuate its embassy in Saigon by helicopter while frantic Vietnamese tried to join the flight.

NIXON AND THE WIDER WORLD

To his credit, Richard Nixon took U.S. foreign policy in new directions even while he was struggling to escape from Vietnam and Cambodia. Like Dwight Eisenhower before him, Nixon's reputation as an anti-Communist allowed him to improve relations with China and the Soviet Union. Indeed, he hoped to distract the American people from frustration in Southeast Asia with accomplishments elsewhere.

One of the first triumphs was a legacy from previous administrations. On July 20, 1969, Buzz Aldrin and Neil Armstrong successfully landed on the moon. Their *Apollo 11* expedition combined science and Cold War politics. The American flag that they planted on the lunar surface represented victory in one phase of the space race between the United States and the Soviet Union. The National Aeronautics and Space Administration had been working since 1961 to meet John F. Kennedy's goal of a manned trip to the moon before the end of the decade.

Closer to home, Nixon and Henry Kissinger, his national security adviser (and later secretary of state), shared what they considered a realistic view of foreign affairs. For both men, foreign policy was not about crusades or moral stands. It was about the balance of world economic and military power. With the United States weakened by the Vietnam War and the Soviets worried by the rise of China, the time was ripe to move toward a new balance among the three nations.

Since 1950, the United States had acted as if China did not exist, refusing economic relations and insisting that the Nationalist regime on Taiwan was the legitimate Chinese government. But the People's Republic of China was increasingly isolated within the Communist world. In 1969, it almost went to war with the Soviet Union. Nixon was eager to take advantage of Chinese-Soviet tension. Secret talks led to an easing of the American trade embargo in April 1971 and a tour of China by a U.S. table-tennis team. Henry Kissinger, Nixon's national security adviser, then arranged for Nixon's startling visit to Mao Zedong in Beijing in February 1972.

Playing the "China card" helped to improve relations with the Soviet Union. The Soviets needed increased trade with the United States and a counterweight to China, the United States was looking for help in getting out of Vietnam, and both countries wanted to limit nuclear armaments. Protracted negotiations led to the **Strategic Arms Limitation Treaty (SALT)** that Nixon signed in Moscow in May 1972. The agreements blocked the creation of extensive antiballistic missiles systems (ABMs) but failed to limit bombers, cruise missiles, or multiple independently targeted warheads on single missiles.

Diplomats used the French word *détente* to describe the new U.S. relations with China and the Soviet Union. *Détente* means an easing of tensions, not friendship or alliance. It facilitated travel between the United States and China. It allowed U.S. farmers to sell wheat to the Soviets. More broadly, *détente* implied that the United States and China recognized mutual interests in Asia and that the United States acknowledged the Soviet Union as an equal in world affairs. *Détente* made the world safer.

COURTING MIDDLE AMERICA

Nixon designed domestic policy to help him win reelection. His goal was to solidify his "Middle American" support. The strategy targeted the growing populations of the South and the suburbs, as well as blue-collar voters who were ready to abandon the Democrats for law-and-order Republicans.

The Nixon White House preferred to ignore troubled big cities. Instead, Nixon tilted federal assistance to the suburbs. The centerpiece of his **New Federalism** was General Revenue Sharing (1972), which passed federal funds directly to local governments with no limits on use. By 1980, it had transferred more than $18 billion to the states and more than $36 billion to local governments. Revenue sharing was a suburban-aid program. Its no-strings grants supplemented the general funds of every full-service government, whether a city of 2 million or a suburban town of 500.

Nixon hoped to move cautiously in enforcing school desegregation, but a task force led by Secretary of Labor George Shultz crafted an approach that allowed substantial desegregation. In this instance, as elsewhere with his domestic policies, Nixon was inflammatory in speeches but moderate in action, increasing the funding of federal civil rights agencies.

OIL, OPEC, AND STAGFLATION

One of the most troublesome domestic issues was inflation. The cost of living began to outpace wages in the late 1960s. One of the causes was LBJ's decision to fight in Vietnam without tax increases until 1968. An income tax cut in 1969, supported by both parties, made the situation worse. Inflation eroded the value of savings and pensions. It also made U.S. goods too expensive for foreign buyers and generated a trade deficit that placed pressures on the international value of the dollar.

The U.S. economy took another hit from inflation in 1973–1974. The main cause was the sharp increase in the price of energy, an input to every product and service. Angry at U.S. support for Israel in the Arab-Israeli War of October 1973, Arab nations imposed an embargo on oil exports that lasted from October 1973 to March 1974. The shortages eased when the embargo ended, but the **Organization of Petroleum Exporting Countries (OPEC)** had challenged the ability of the industrial nations to dictate world economic policy.

While Nixon searched for short-term political advantage, underlying problems of the U.S. economy went untreated. After 30 years at the top, the United States could no longer dominate the world economy by itself. The newly found power of OPEC was obvious. Just as important was the surging industrial capacity of Germany and Japan, which now had economies as modern as that of the United States. Declining rates of saving and investment in industrial capacity seemed to put the United States in danger of following the British road to economic obsolescence and second-level status. Indeed, a new term entered the popular vocabulary in 1971: *Stagflation* was the painful combination of stagnant economic growth, high unemployment, and inflation that matched no one's economic theory but everyone's daily experience.

AMERICANS AS ENVIRONMENTALISTS

In the turbulent 1970s, Americans found one issue they could agree on. In the 1970s, resource conservation grew into a multifaceted environmental movement.

After the booming 1950s, Americans had started to pay attention to "pollution," a catchall for the damage that advanced technologies and industrial production did to natural systems. Rachel Carson's *Silent Spring* in 1962 pushed pollution onto the national agenda. Carson, a well-regarded science writer, described the side effects of DDT and other pesticides on animal life. Her book resonated with many suburbanites, who realized that urban sprawl provided housing and shopping centers at the cost of

Tanks full of toxic chemical waste were buried within a stone's throw of homes in the Love Canal neighborhood of Niagara Falls, New York, forcing homeowners to abandon their houses.

bulldozed forests and farms, polluted streams, and smog-choked skies. (See American Views: The Suburban Roots of Environmental Activism, Chapter 28.)

Environmentalism gained strength among Americans in 1970. On April 22, 10,000 schools and 20 million other people took part in Earth Day, an occasion first conceived by Wisconsin senator Gaylord Nelson. Earth Day gained a grassroots following in towns and cities across the country. New York closed Fifth Avenue to automobiles for the day. Companies touted their environmental credentials. The event helped to transform the technical field of pollution control into a broadly based movement.

The American establishment had been looking for a safe and respectable crusade to divert the idealism and discontent of the 1960s. Now the mainstream media discovered the ravaged planet. So did a politically savvy president. An expedient pro-environmental stance might attract some of the antiwar constituency. Nixon had already signed the National Environmental Policy Act on January 1, 1970, and later in the year created the **Environmental Protection Agency (EPA)** to enforce environmental laws. The rest of the Nixon administration brought legislation on clean air, clear water, pesticides, hazardous chemicals, and endangered species (see Overview, The Environmental Decades) that made environmental management and protection part of governmental routine.

As Americans became more aware of human-caused environmental hazards, they realized that minority and low-income communities had more than their share of problems. Landfills and waste disposal sites were frequently located near minority neighborhoods. In Buffalo, white working-class residents near the Love Canal industrial site discovered in 1978 that an entire neighborhood was built on land contaminated by decades of chemical dumping. Activists sought to understand the health effects and force compensation, paving the way for Superfund cleanup legislation (see American Views: Grassroots Community Action).

OVERVIEW THE ENVIRONMENTAL DECADES

Administration	Focus of Concern	Legislation
Johnson	Wilderness and wildlife	Wilderness Act (1964) National Wildlife Refuge System (1966) Wild and Scenic Rivers Act (1968)
Nixon	Pollution control and endangered environments	National Environmental Policy Act (1969) Environmental Protection Agency (1970) Clean Air Act (1970) Occupational Safety and Health Act (1970) Water Pollution Control Act (1972) Pesticide Control Act (1972) Coastal Zone Management Act (1972) Endangered Species Act (1973)
Ford	Energy and hazardous materials	Toxic Substances Control Act (1976) Resource Conservation and Recovery Act (1976)
Carter	Energy and hazardous materials	Energy Policy and Conservation Act (1978) Comprehensive Emergency Response, Compensation, and Liability Act (Superfund) (1980)
	Parks and wilderness	Alaska National Interest Lands Conservation Act (1980)

FROM DIRTY TRICKS TO WATERGATE

The **Watergate** crisis pivoted on Richard Nixon's character. Despite his solid political standing, Nixon saw enemies everywhere and overestimated their strength. Subordinates learned during his first administration that the president would condone dishonest actions—"dirty tricks"—if they stood to improve his political position. In 1972 and 1973, dirty tricks grew from a scandal into a constitutional crisis when Nixon abused the power of his office to cover up wrongdoing and hinder criminal investigations.

The chain of events that undermined Nixon's presidency started with the **Pentagon Papers**. In his last year as secretary of defense, Robert McNamara had commissioned a report on the U.S. road to Vietnam. The documents showed that the country's leaders had planned to expand the war even while they claimed to be looking for a way out. In June 1971, one of the contributors to the report, Daniel Ellsberg, leaked it to the *New York Times*. Its publication infuriated Nixon.

In response, the White House compiled a list of journalists and politicians who opposed Nixon. As one White House staffer, John Dean, put it, the president's men could then "use the available federal machinery [Internal Revenue Service, FBI] to screw our political enemies." Nixon set up a special investigations unit in the White House. Two former CIA employees, E. Howard Hunt and G. Gordon Liddy, became the chief "plumbers," as the group was known because its job was to prevent leaks of information.

Early in 1972, Hunt went to work for CREEP—the Committee to Re-Elect the President—while Liddy took another position on the presidential staff. CREEP had already raised millions and was hatching plans to undermine Democrats with rumors and pranks. Then, on June 17, 1972, five inept burglars hired with CREEP funds were caught breaking into the Democratic National Committee office in Washington's Watergate apartment building. The people involved knew that an investigation would lead back to the White House. Nixon felt too insecure to ride out what would probably have been a small scandal. Instead, he initiated a coverup. On June 23, he ordered his assistant H. R. Haldeman to warn the FBI off the case with the excuse that national security was involved. Nixon compounded this obstruction of justice by arranging a $400,000 bribe to keep the burglars quiet.

The coverup worked in the short run. As mid-level officials from the Justice Department pursued their investigation, the public lost interest in what looked more like slapstick than a serious crime. Nixon's opponent in the 1972 election was South Dakota Senator George McGovern, an impassioned opponent of the Vietnam War. McGovern was honest, intelligent, and well to the left of center on such issues as the defense budget and legalization of marijuana. He did not appeal to the white southerners and blue-collar northerners whom Nixon and Agnew were luring from the Democrats. An assassination attempt that took George Wallace out of national politics also helped Nixon win in a landslide.

The coverup began to come apart with the trial of the Watergate burglars in January 1973. Federal Judge John Sirica used the threat of heavy sentences to pressure one burglar into a statement that implied that higher-ups had been involved. Meanwhile, the *Washington Post* was linking Nixon's people to dirty tricks and illegal campaign contributions. Nixon was aware of many of the actions that his subordinates had undertaken. He now began to coach people on what they should tell investigators, claimed his staff had lied to him, and tried to set up White House Counsel John Dean to take the fall.

In the late spring and early summer, attention shifted to the televised hearings of the Senate's Select Committee on Presidential Campaign Activities. The real questions, it became obvious, were what the president knew and when he knew it. It seemed to be John Dean's word against Richard Nixon's.

A bombshell turned the scandal into a constitutional crisis. A mid-level staffer told the committee that Nixon had made tape recordings of his White House conversations. Both the Senate and the Watergate special prosecutor, Archibald Cox, subpoenaed the tapes. Nixon refused to give them up, citing executive privilege and the separation of powers. In late October, after he failed to cut a satisfactory deal, he fired his attorney general and the special prosecutor. This "Saturday-night massacre" caused a storm of protest, and many Americans thought that it proved that Nixon had something to hide. In April 1974, he finally released edited transcripts of the tapes, with foul language deleted and key passages missing; he claimed that his secretary had accidentally erased crucial material. Finally, on July 24, 1974, the U.S. Supreme Court ruled unanimously that Nixon had to deliver 64 tapes to the new special prosecutor.

Opposition to the president now spanned the political spectrum from Barry Goldwater to liberal Democrats, and Congress began impeachment proceedings. On July 27, the House Judiciary Committee took up the specific charges. Republicans joined Democrats in voting three articles of impeachment: for hindering the criminal investigation of the Watergate break-in, for abusing the power of the presidency by using federal agencies to deprive citizens of their rights, and for ignoring the committee's subpoena for the tapes. Before the full House could vote on the articles of impeachment and send them to the Senate for trial, Nixon delivered the tapes. One of them contained the "smoking gun," direct evidence that Nixon had participated in the coverup on June 23, 1972, and had been lying ever since. On August 8, he announced his resignation, effective the following day.

Watergate was two separate but related stories. On one level, it was about individuals who deceived or manipulated the American people. Nixon and his cronies wanted to win too badly to play by the rules and repeatedly broke the law. Nixon paid for his overreaching ambition with the end of his political career; more than 20 others paid with jail terms. On another level, the crisis was a lesson about the Constitution. The separation of powers allowed Congress and the courts to rein in a president who had spun out of control. The Ervin Committee hearings in 1973 and the House Judiciary Committee proceedings in 1974 were rituals to assure Americans that the system still worked. Nevertheless, the sequence of political events from 1968 to 1974 disillusioned many citizens.

THE FORD FOOTNOTE

Gerald Ford was Nixon's appointee to replace Spiro Agnew, who had resigned and pleaded no contest to charges of bribery and income tax evasion in 1973 as Watergate was gathering steam. Ford was competent but unimaginative. His first major act was his most controversial—the pardon of Nixon for "any and all crimes" committed while president. Since Nixon had not yet been indicted, the pardon saved him from future prosecution. To many Americans, the act looked like a payoff.

Ford's administration presided over the collapse of South Vietnam in 1975, but elsewhere in the world, *détente* continued. U.S. diplomats joined the Soviet Union and 30 other European nations in the capital of Finland to sign the **Helsinki Accords**. The agreements called for increased commerce between the Eastern and Western blocs and for human-rights guarantees. They also legitimized the national boundaries that had been set in eastern Europe in 1945. At home, the federal government did little new during Ford's two and a half years in office.

Ford beat back Ronald Reagan for the 1976 Republican presidential nomination, but he was clearly vulnerable. His Democratic opponent was a political enigma. James Earl Carter Jr. had been a navy officer, a farmer, and the governor of Georgia. He was one of several new-style politicians who transformed southern politics in the 1970s. Carter and the others left race-baiting behind to talk like modern New Dealers, emphasizing that whites and blacks both needed better schools and economic growth. He appealed to Democrats as someone who could reassemble LBJ's political coalition and return the South to the Democratic Party. In his successful campaign, Carter presented himself as an alternative to party hacks and Washington insiders.

American Views

Grassroots Community Action

*I*n the 1950s, a major chemical company closed a waste dump in Niagara Falls, New York. The site, known as Love Canal, was soon surrounded by a park, school, and hundreds of modest homes. Residents put up with noxious odors and seepage of chemical wastes until 1978, when they learned that the state health department was concerned about the health effects on small children and pregnant women. Over the next two years, residents battled state and federal bureaucracies and reluctant politicians for accurate information about the risks they faced and then for financial assistance to move from the area (often their homes represented their only savings). In October 1980, President Carter signed a bill to move all of the families permanently from the Love Canal area.

One of the leaders of the grassroots movement was housewife Lois Gibbs. The following excerpts from her story show her increasing sophistication as a community activist, starting by ringing doorbells in 1978 and ending with national television exposure in 1980. Although the Love Canal case itself was unusual, community-based organizations in all parts of the country learned the tactics of effective action in the 1960s and 1970s.

- What public programs in the 1960s and 1970s gave citizens experience in grassroots action?
- How might the Internet change the tactics of community organizing?

KNOCKING ON DOORS

I decided to go door-to-door with a petition. It seemed like a good idea to start near the school, to talk to the mothers nearest it. I had already heard that a lot of the residents near the school had been upset about the chemicals for the past couple of years. I thought they might help me. I had never done anything like this. . . . I was afraid a lot of doors would be slammed in my face, that people would think I was some crazy fanatic. But I decided to do it anyway . . . and knocked on my first door. There was no answer. I just stood there, not knowing what to do. It was an unusually warm June day and I was perspiring. I thought: What am I doing here? I must be crazy. People are going to think I am. Go home, you fool! And that's just what I did.

Jimmy Carter: Idealism and Frustration in the White House

Jimmy Carter took office with little room to maneuver. Watergate bequeathed him a powerful and self-satisfied Congress and a combative press. OPEC oil producers, Islamic fundamentalists, and Soviet generals followed their own agendas. The American people themselves were fractionalized and quarrelsome, uneasy with the new advocacy of equality for women, uncertain as a nation whether they shared the same values and goals.

It was one of those times when I had to sit down and face myself. I was afraid of making a fool of myself, I had scared myself, and I had gone home. When I got there, I sat at the kitchen table with my petition in my hand, thinking. Wait. What if people do slam doors in your face? People may think you're crazy. But what's more important—what people think or your child's health? Either you're going to do something or you're going to have to admit you're a coward and not do it. . . . The next day, I went out on my own street to talk to people I knew. It was a little easier to be brave with them. If I could convince people I knew—friends— maybe it would be less difficult to convince others. . . . I went to the back door, as I always did when I visited a neighbor. Each house took about twenty or twenty-five minutes. . . .

PHIL DONAHUE AND POLITICAL ACTION

The *Phil Donahue Show* called. They wanted us to appear on their June 18 show. The reaction in the office was different this time, compared to the show in October 1978. In October, everyone was excited. "Phil Donahue—wow!" Now, residents reacted differently. "Donahue. That's great press. Now we'll get the politicians to move!" . . . Now our people looked at the show as a tool to use in pushing the government to relocate us permanently. By this time we understood how politicians react to public pressure, how to play the political game. We eagerly agreed to go, and found forty other residents to go with us. . . . [After arriving in Chicago] We then planned how we would handle the *Phil Donahue Show*. . . . We had to get the real issues across. Each resident was assigned an issue. One told of the chromosome tests. Another was to concentrate on her multiple miscarriages. Another was to ask for telegrams from across the country to the White House in support of permanent relocation. I coached them to get their point in, no matter the question asked. For example, if Donahue asked what you thought of the mayor, and your assignment was to discuss miscarriages, you should answer: "I don't like the mayor because I have had three miscarriages and other health problems, and he won't help us." Or: "My family is sick, and the mayor won't help us. That's why we need people to send telegrams to the White House for permanent relocation." . . . The residents were great! Each and every one followed through with our plan.

Source: Lois Marie Gibbs, as told to Murray Levine, *Love Canal: My Story* (Albany: State University of New York Press, 1982), pp. 12–13, 161–64.

CARTER, ENERGY, AND THE ECONOMY

Carter's approach to politics reflected his training as an engineer. He liked to break a problem into logical parts and was better at working with details than broad goals. He failed to understand the importance of personalities or the rules of Washington politics, losing friends even in his own party.

The biggest domestic problem remained the economy, which slid into another recession in 1978. Another jump in oil prices helped make 1979 and 1980 the worst years for inflation in the postwar era. Interest rates surged past 20 percent as the Federal Reserve tried to reduce inflation by squeezing business and consumer credit. Carter himself was a fiscal conservative whose impulse was to cut federal spending. This course worsened unemployment and alienated liberal Democrats, who wanted to revive the Great Society.

Carter simultaneously proposed a comprehensive energy policy. He asked Americans to make energy conservation the moral equivalent of war—to accept individual sacrifices for the common good. Congress created the Department of Energy but refused to raise taxes on oil and natural gas to reduce consumption. However, the Energy Policy and Conservation Act (1978) did encourage alternative energy sources to replace foreign petroleum.

Antinuclear activism blocked one obvious alternative to fossil fuels. The antinuclear movement had started with concern about the ability of the Atomic Energy Commission to monitor the safety of nuclear-power plants and about the disposal of spent fuel rods. In the late 1970s, activists staged sit-ins at the construction sites of nuclear plants. A near-meltdown at the Three Mile Island nuclear plant in Pennsylvania in March 1979 stalemated efforts to expand nuclear-power capacity.

CLOSED FACTORIES AND FAILED FARMS

Ford and Carter both faced massive problems of economic transition that undercut their efforts to devise effective government programs. Industrial decay stalked such "gritty cities" as Allentown, Pennsylvania; Trenton, New Jersey; and Gary, Indiana. Communities whose workers had made products in high volume for a mass market found that technological revolutions made them obsolete. Critics renamed the old manufacturing region of the Northeast and Midwest the Rustbelt in honor of its abandoned factories.

Stories of **deindustrialization** were similar in small cities like Springfield, Ohio, and large cities like Cleveland. As high-paying jobs in unionized industries disappeared, sagging income undermined small businesses and neighborhoods. Falling tax revenue brought Cleveland to the verge of bankruptcy in 1978; bankers forced public service cuts and tax increases, which meant further job losses.

Plant closures were only one facet of business efforts to increase productivity by substituting machinery for employees. Between 1947 and 1977, American steelmakers doubled output while cutting their workforce from 600,000 to 400,000. High interest rates and a strong dollar made U.S. exports too expensive and foreign imports cheap, forcing American manufacturers to cut costs or perish.

Parallel to the decline of heavy industry was the continuing transformation of American agriculture from small family enterprises to corporate agribusinesses. Agriculture was a national success story in the aggregate, but one accompanied by many human and environmental costs. The early 1970s brought an unexpected boom in farming. Crop failures and food shortages around the world in 1972 and 1973 expanded markets and pushed up prices for U.S. farm products. For a few years, agriculture looked like the best way for the United States to offset the high cost of imported oil. But the boom was over by the 1980s, when global commodity prices slumped. Farmers found themselves with debts they could not cover.

The boom of the 1970s was thus a brief interruption in the long-term transformation of U.S. agriculture. The number of farms slid from 4 million in 1960 to 2.4 million in 1980 and 1.9 million in 2000. Many farmers sold out willingly, glad to escape from drudgery and financial insecurity. Others could not compete in an agricultural system that favored large-scale production by demanding large amounts of capital for equipment and fertilizer. By 2000, fewer than 2 percent of American workers made their living from farming.

BUILDING A COOPERATIVE WORLD

Despite troubles on the home front, Carter's first two years brought foreign policy successes that reflected a new vision of a multilateral world. As a relative newcomer to international politics, Carter was willing to work with African, Asian, and Latin American nations on a basis of mutual respect. Carter appointed Andrew Young—an African American from Georgia with long experience in the civil rights movement—as ambassador to the United Nations, where he worked effectively to build bridges to third-world nations. Carter convinced the Senate in 1978 to approve treaties to transfer control of the Panama Canal to Panama by 2000, removing a sore point in relations with Latin America.

Carter's strong religious beliefs and moral convictions were responsible for a new concern with human rights around the globe. He criticized the Soviet Union for prohibiting free speech and denying its citizens the right to emigrate, angering Soviet leaders, who did not expect the human rights clauses of the Helsinki Accords to be taken seriously. Carter was also willing to criticize some (but not all) American allies. He withheld economic aid from South Africa, Guatemala, Chile, and Nicaragua, which had long records of human rights abuses. In Nicaragua, the change in policy helped left-wing Sandinista rebels topple the Somoza dictatorship.

Carter had several successes. He completed the Nixon initiative by normalizing diplomatic relations with China. He also risked his reputation and credibility in September 1978 to bring Egyptian President Anwar al-Sadat and Israeli Prime Minister Menachem Begin together at Camp David, the presidential retreat. He refused to admit failure and dissuaded the two leaders from walking out. A formal treaty known popularly as the **Camp David Agreement** was signed in Washington on March 26, 1979. The pact normalized relations between Israel and its most powerful neighbor and led to Israel's withdrawal from the Sinai Peninsula. It was a vital prelude to further progress toward Arab-Israeli peace in the mid-1990s.

NEW CRISES ABROAD

In the last two years of Carter's administration, the Cold War sprang back to life around the globe and smothered the promise of a new foreign policy. The Soviets ignored the human-rights provisions of the Helsinki Accords. Soviet advisers or Cuban troops intervened in African civil wars. At home, Cold Warriors who had never accepted détente found it easier to attack Carter than Nixon.

The Failure of SALT II. Carter inherited negotiations for SALT II—a strategic arms limitation treaty that would have reduced both the U.S. and Soviet nuclear arsenals—from the Ford administration. SALT II met stiff resistance in the Senate. Opponents claimed it would create a "window of vulnerability" in the 1980s that would invite the Soviets to launch a nuclear first strike. Carter tried to counter criticism by stepping up defense spending, starting a buildup that would accelerate under Ronald Reagan.

Hopes for SALT II vanished on December 24, 1979, when Soviet troops entered Afghanistan, a technically neutral Muslim nation on the southern border of the Soviet

Union. A pro-Soviet government had fallen into factional strife, while tribespeople, unhappy with modernization, were mounting increasing resistance. One of the factions invited intervention by the Soviets, who quickly installed a client government. The situation resembled the U.S. involvement in South Vietnam. Similar, too, was the inability of Soviet forces to suppress the Afghan guerrillas, who had American weapons and controlled the mountains. In the end, it took the Soviets a decade to find a way out.

The Iranian Hostage Crisis. The final blow to Carter's foreign policy came in Iran. Since 1953, the United States had strongly backed Iran's monarch, Shah Reza Pahlavi. The shah modernized Iran's economy, but his feared secret police jailed and tortured political opponents. U.S. aid and oil revenues helped him build a large army, but the Iranian middle class despised his authoritarianism, and Muslim fundamentalists opposed the Westernizing influence of modernization. A revolution toppled the shah at the start of 1979.

The upheaval installed a nominally democratic government, but the Ayatollah Ruhollah Khomeini, a Muslim cleric who hated the United States, exercised real power. Throughout 1979, Iran grew increasingly anti-American. After the United States allowed the exiled shah to seek medical treatment in New York, a mob stormed the U.S. embassy in Tehran on November 4, 1979, and took more than 60 Americans hostage. They demanded that Carter surrender the shah. The administration tried economic pressure and diplomacy, but Khomeini had no desire for accommodation. When Iran announced in April 1980 that the hostages would remain in the hands of the militants

The Iran hostage crisis reflected intense anti-American feelings in Iran and provoked an equally bitter anti-Iranian reaction in the United States. Fifty-two of the more than 60 U.S. embassy employees first seized were held for 444 days, giving the United States a painful lesson about the limits on its ability to influence events around the world.

rather than be transferred to the government, Carter ordered an airborne rescue. Even a perfectly managed effort would have been difficult. The hostages were held in the heart of a city of 4 million hostile Iranians, hundreds of miles from the nearest aircraft carrier and thousands of miles from U.S. bases. Hampered by lack of coordination among the military services, the attempt turned into a fiasco that added to the national embarrassment and a feeling of powerlessness. The United States and Iran finally reached agreement on the eve of the 1980 election. The hostages gained their freedom after 444 days, at the moment Ronald Reagan took office as the new president.

The hostage crisis consumed Jimmy Carter the way that Vietnam had consumed Lyndon Johnson. It gripped the public and stalemated other issues. Carter's tragedy was that "his" Iranian crisis was the fruit of policies hatched by the Eisenhower administration and pursued by every president since then, all of whom had overlooked the shah's despotic government because of his firm anti-Communism.

CONCLUSION

In the mid-1970s, Americans encountered real limits to national capacity. From 1945 to 1973, they had enjoyed remarkable prosperity. That ended in 1974. Long lines at gas stations showed that prosperity was fragile. Cities and regions felt the costs of obsolete industries. Environmental damage caused many Americans to reconsider the goal of economic expansion.

The nation also had to recognize that it could not run the world. American withdrawal from Vietnam in 1973 and the collapse of the South Vietnamese government in 1975 were defeats; the United States ended up with little to show for a long and painful war. SALT I stabilized the arms race, but it also recognized that the Soviet Union was an equal. The American nuclear arsenal might help deter a third world war, but it could not prevent the seizure of hostages in Iran.

These challenges came amid deep economic and social changes in the United States. The ways Americans made their livings and the range of opportunities they faced were in flux. Farm laborers had better working conditions, but auto workers had fewer jobs. The nation finished the 1970s more egalitarian than it had been in the early 1960s but also more divided. More citizens had the opportunity to advance economically and to seek political power, but there were deepening fissures between social liberals and cultural conservatives, old and new views about roles for women, rich and poor, whites and blacks. In 1961, John Kennedy had called on his fellow citizens to "bear any burden, pay any price" to defend freedom. By 1980, the nation had neither the economic capacity to pay any price nor the unity to agree on what burdens it should bear.

REVIEW QUESTIONS

1. Why did the United States fail to achieve its objectives in Vietnam? What factors limited President Johnson's freedom of action there? How did the Tet Offensive affect U.S. policy? How did antiwar protests in the United States influence national policy?

2. How did racial relations change between 1965 and 1970? What were the relationships between the civil rights movement and minority separatism? What were the similarities and differences between African American, Latino, and Native American activism?

3. In what ways was 1968 a pivotal year for U.S. politics and society? How was it influenced by global events?

4. What were the implications of *détente*? Why did the Cold War reappear in the late 1970s? How and why did U.S. influence over the rest of the world change during the 1970s?

5. How did Richard Nixon's political strategy respond to the growth of the South and West? How did it respond to the shift of population from central cities to suburbs?

6. How did the backgrounds of Presidents Johnson, Nixon, and Carter shape their successes and failures as national leaders?

7. What political and constitutional issues were at stake in the Watergate scandal? How did it change American politics?

8. Why was the space race important for the United States? How did it strengthen the alliance between American science, government, and industry?

myhistorylab CONNECTIONS

Reinforce what you learned in this chapter by studying the many documents, images, maps, review tools, and videos available at **www.myhistorylab.com**.

READ AND REVIEW

✔•─|Study and **Review** on **myhistorylab.com** STUDY PLAN: CHAPTER 29

☐•─|Read the **Document** on **myhistorylab.com**

Cesar Chavez, "He Showed Us the Way" (1978)

Donald Wheeldin, "The Situation in Watts Today" (1967)

Stokely Carmichael and Charles V. Hamilton, from Black Power: The Politics of Liberation in America (1967)

Students for a Democratic Society, The Port Huron Statement (1962)

The Gay Liberation Front, Come Out (1970)

Jimmy Carter, The "Malaise" Speech (1979)

Roe v. Wade (January 22, 1973)

The Civil Rights Act of 1964

Toi Derricotte, Black in a White Neighborhood, 1977–1978

Voting Literacy Test (1965)

View the **Map** on **myhistorylab.com**

Vietnam War

RESEARCH AND EXPLORE

Read the **Document** on **myhistorylab.com**

Personal Journeys Online

From Then to Now Online: Energy Worries

Exploring America: American Indian Movement

Exploring America: Rachel Carson

Listen on **myhistorylab.com**

Angela Davis interview from prison

liberation/poem by Sonia Sanchez

Message to the Grassroots by Malcolm X, excerpt

Watch the **Video** on **myhistorylab.com**

Civil Rights March on Washington

Richard Nixon, "I am not a crook"

Malcolm X

The Vietnam War

Protests Against the Vietnam War

Jimmy Carter and the "Crisis of Confidence"

―――――――― **Listen** on **myhistorylab.com** ――――――――
Hear the audio files for Chapter 29 at
www.myhistorylab.com.

30

The Reagan Revolution and a Changing World •• 1981–1992

Hear the audio files for Chapter 30 at **www.myhistorylab.com.**

FOCUS QUESTIONS

WHAT WAS revolutionary about the Reagan revolution?

HOW AND why did the Cold War come to an end?

HOW DID growth in the Sunbelt shape national politics in the 1980s and 1990s?

WHAT KEY social and cultural issues divided Americans in the 1980s and 1990s?

Ronald Reagan and his wife, Nancy, celebrate his inauguration as president.

ONE AMERICAN JOURNEY

The Khmer Rouge marched into the city [Phnom Penh, the capital of Cambodia], dressed in black. Young Khmer Rouge [Marxist revolutionary] soldiers, eight or ten years old, were dragging their rifles, which were taller than them. The whole city, more than two million people was forced out of their homes into the streets. My family walked until we reached Mao Tse-Tung Boulevard, the main boulevard in Phnom Penh. All the population of the city was gathered there. The Khmer Rouge were telling everyone to leave the city.

Although my two middle children were safe in France, my oldest and youngest daughters were close beside me. Párika was only seven. Mealy, who was nineteen, carried her infant son. I kept my children huddled together. As soon as a parent let go, a child would be lost in the huge crowd. And the Khmer Rouge kept ordering everybody, "You must go forward." They shot their guns in the air. Even during the middle of the night the procession was endless. . . .

Each night, when we came back to the village from working in the fields, Mom would say, "Children, let's all go to sleep." She would quietly warn me that the wood had eyes and ears. She'd say, "It's nine o'clock now. Go to sleep. There is nothing else to do but work. All the men are gone in our family." Mom was actually saying for the Khmer Rouge spies to hear, "They are only girls. Don't kill them. We are the only members left of the family." We were lying to them about our identity. It was a horrible game.

If you hid your identity, that meant you wanted your past forgotten. We had changed from people who were intellectual, who used to think independently. You became humiliated, allowed to live only as a slave. We were accepted into the United States thanks to my husband's military service. My daughters and I flew to the United States on July 4, 1979. As we landed, I thought, "This is real freedom."

I've found that America is a country where people have come from all over the world. You do your job, you get paid like anybody else, and you're accepted. But Cambodians I know in France, like my sister, feel differently. People are not accepted if they are not French. But in America you're part of the melting pot. In 1983, I came to Los Angeles for my daughter Monie's wedding. I decided to stay. Long Beach has the largest concentration of Cambodians in the country. I called the community center in Long Beach. They said they had no job openings. So I decided to get involved in running a store. Donut shops are very American.

All that refugees have is our work, our dreams. Do I still hurt from what happened in the past? When I opened my mouth to tell you my story, I don't know where my tears came from. My daughters don't like to talk about the past in Cambodia. They want to forget and think about their future. They ask me why I would talk about the past with anybody. I said, "The past cannot be erased from my memory."

Celia Noup, in Al Santoli, *New Americans: An Oral History* (New York, 1988).

CELIA NOUP taught school for 20 years in Cambodia, which borders on South Vietnam. In 1975, after a long civil war, the Communist Khmer Rouge insurgents took over Cambodia's capital, Phnom Penh, and forced its inhabitants into the countryside to work in the fields. Four years later, Noup managed to make her way to a refugee camp in neighboring Thailand and then to the United States. Within a decade, she was working from 5:00 A.M. to 7:00 P.M. in her own donut shop near Los Angeles airport and worrying about helping her children buy houses.

Celia Noup's journey shows some of the ways that new waves of immigration from Asia, Latin America, and Africa have changed the United States over the last generation.

Immigrants fueled economic growth in the 1980s and 1990s with their labor and their drive to succeed in business. They revitalized older neighborhoods in cities from coast to coast and changed the ethnic mix of major cities. And they created new racial tensions that found their way into national political debates about immigration and into open conflict in places such as Miami and Los Angeles.

Noup's story is also a reminder of the drawn-out consequences of the U.S. involvement in Vietnam and the long shadow of the Cold War. The Cambodian civil war was fueled by reactions to the Vietnamese war and the U.S. invasion of Cambodia in 1969. American refugee policy was humanitarian but also political, opening the door to people fleeing Communist regimes but holding it shut against refugees from right-wing dictatorships. In Washington, foreign policy decisions in the 1980s started with the desire of a new administration to reaffirm American toughness after failures in Vietnam and ended with the astonishing evaporation of the Cold War.

By the end of Ronald Reagan's presidency (1981–1989), new rules governed domestic affairs as well as international relations. In the 1980s Americans decided to reverse the growth of federal government responsibilities that had marked both Republican and Democratic administrations since the 1930s. By the 1990s, the center of U.S. politics had shifted substantially to the right. The backdrop to the political changes was massive readjustments in the American economy that began in the 1970s with the decline of heavy industry and then continued to shift employment from factory jobs to service jobs in the 1980s. The ideology of unregulated markets celebrated economic success, but masked a troubling reality: a widening gap between the rich and poor. The result by 1992 was a nation that was much more secure in the world than it had been in 1980, but also more divided against itself.

REAGAN'S DOMESTIC REVOLUTION

Political change began in 1980, when Ronald Reagan and his running mate, George H. W. Bush, rode American discontent to a decisive victory in the presidential election (see Map 30–1). Building on a conservative critique of American policies and developing issues that Jimmy Carter had placed on the national agenda, Reagan presided over revolutionary changes in U.S. government and policies. The consequences of his two terms included an altered role for government, powerful but selective economic growth, and a shift of domestic politics away from bread-and-butter issues toward moral or lifestyle concerns.

REAGAN'S MAJORITY

Ronald Reagan reinvented himself several times on his unusual journey to the White House. A product of small-town Illinois, he succeeded in Hollywood in the late 1930s as a romantic lead actor while adopting the liberal politics common at the time. After World War II, he moved rapidly to the political right as a spokesman for big business. He entered politics with a rousing conservative speech at the 1964 Republican convention and then accepted the invitation of wealthy California Republicans to run for governor in 1966, serving two terms in that office.

Some of Reagan's most articulate support came from anti-Communist stalwarts of both parties, who feared that the United States was losing influence in the world. Despite Jimmy Carter's tough actions in 1979 and 1980 and increased defense spending, such conservatives had not trusted him to do enough. Soviet military buildup, charged the critics,

CHRONOLOGY

1973	*Roe v. Wade:* Supreme Court strikes down state laws banning abortion in the first trimester of pregnancy.
1980	Ronald Reagan is elected president.
1981	Economic Recovery and Tax Act, reducing personal income tax rates, is passed.
	Reagan breaks strike by air traffic controllers.
	AIDS is recognized as a new disease.
1982	Nuclear freeze movement peaks.
	United States begins to finance Contra rebels against the Sandinista government in Nicaragua.
	Equal Rights Amendment fails to achieve ratification.
1983	241 Marines are killed by a terrorist bomb in Beirut, Lebanon.
	Strategic Defense Initiative introduced.
	United States invades Grenada.
1984	Reagan wins reelection.
1985	Mikhail Gorbachev initiates economic and political reforms in the Soviet Union.
1986	Tax Reform Act is adopted.
1987	Congress holds hearings on the Iran-Contra scandal.
	Reagan and Gorbachev sign the Intermediate-Range Nuclear Forces Treaty.
1988	George H. W. Bush is elected president.
1989	Communist regimes in eastern Europe collapse; Germans tear down Berlin Wall.
	Financial crisis forces federal bailout of many savings and loans.
	United States invades Panama to capture General Manuel Noriega.
1990	Iraq invades Kuwait; and United States sends forces to the Persian Gulf.
	West Germany and East Germany reunite.
	Americans with Disabilities Act is adopted.
1991	Persian Gulf War: Operation Desert Storm drives the Iraqis from Kuwait.
	Soviet Union dissolves into independent nations.
	Strategic Arms Reduction Treaty (START) is signed.
1992	Acquittal of officers accused of beating Rodney King triggers Los Angeles riots.

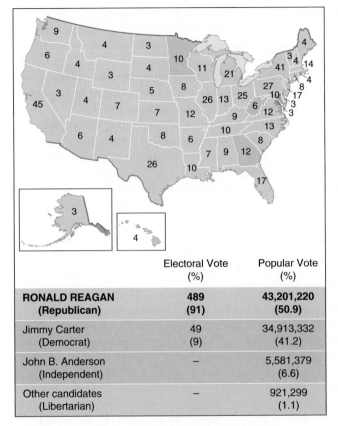

	Electoral Vote (%)	Popular Vote (%)
RONALD REAGAN (Republican)	**489 (91)**	**43,201,220 (50.9)**
Jimmy Carter (Democrat)	49 (9)	34,913,332 (41.2)
John B. Anderson (Independent)	–	5,581,379 (6.6)
Other candidates (Libertarian)	–	921,299 (1.1)

MAP 30–1 • **The Election of 1980** Ronald Reagan won in a landslide in 1980. Independent candidate John Anderson took more votes from Jimmy Carter than from Reagan, but Reagan's personal magnetism was a powerful political force. His victory confirmed the shift of the South to the Republican Party.

▶ *What political* and cultural trends were reflected in Reagan's strong performance in the South and West?

was creating a "window of vulnerability," a dangerous period when the Soviet Union might threaten the United States with a first strike by nuclear weapons.

Other Reagan voters directed their anger at government bureaucracies. Wealthy entrepreneurs from the fast-growing South and West believed that Nixon-era federal offices, such as the Environmental Protection Agency and the Occupational Safety and Health Administration, were choking their businesses in red tape. Many of these critics had amassed new fortunes in oil, real estate, and retailing and hated the taxes that funded social programs.

Christian conservatives worried that social activists were using the federal courts to alter traditional values. Jimmy Carter, a member of the Southern Baptist church, had won a clear majority among white evangelical voters in 1976, but Reagan's contrasting position on school prayer and abortion gave him the edge in 1980 and made him the overwhelming preference of conservative Christian voters in 1984.

In many ways the two groups of Reagan supporters were mismatched. Christian moralists had little in common with the high-rollers and Hollywood tycoons with whom Reagan rubbed shoulders. But both shared a distrust of the federal government.

Foreign policy activists and opponents of big government would have been unable to elect Reagan without disaffected blue-collar and middle-class voters who deserted the Democrats. Reagan's campaign hammered on the question "Are you better off than you were four years ago?" Democrats faced a special dilemma with the deepening tension between working-class white voters and black voters, a division that had roots in the expansion of African American populations and neighborhoods in cities like Detroit and Chicago during the 1950s and 1960s. Democrats needed both groups to win but found white blue-collar voters deeply alienated by affirmative action and busing for school integration.

A further Democratic challenge was Ronald Reagan's personal appeal. With a common touch that made him a favorite for a sizable segment of the public, Reagan tapped into the nostalgia for a simpler America. The new president won over many Americans by surviving a 1981 assassination attempt in fine spirits. Reagan's popularity compounded the Democrats' inability to excite younger voters. The mid-1980s consistently showed that roughly two-thirds of people in their twenties and early thirties were choosing the Republicans as the party of energy and new ideas, leaving the Democrats to the middle-aged and elderly.

In the election of 1984, Democrats sealed their fate by nominating Walter Mondale, who had been vice president under Carter. Mondale was earnest, honest, and dull. Reagan ran on the theme "It's Morning in America," with the message that a new age of pride and prosperity had begun. Mondale assumed that Americans cared enough about the exploding federal deficit that Reagan's defense spending had produced to accept an across-the-board tax increase. With the economy growing and inflation now in check, most voters did not want Mondale to remind them of long-range financial realities, and Reagan won reelection with 98 percent of the electoral votes. His election confirmed that the American public found conservative ideas increasingly attractive.

THE NEW CONSERVATISM

Reagan's approach to public policy drew on conservative intellectuals who offered a coherent critique of the New Deal—New Frontier approach to U.S. government. They feared that the antiwar movement had undermined the anti-Communist stance and that social changes were corrupting mainstream values.

Downsizing the Great Society. Worries about big government permeated the critique of domestic policy. Edward Banfield's radical ideas about the failures of the Great Society set the tone of the neoconservative analysis. In *The Unheavenly City* (1968), he questioned the basic idea of public solutions for social problems. He argued that inequality is based on human character and rooted in the basic structure of society; government action can only solve problems that require better engineering, such as pollution control, better highways, or the delivery of explosives to military targets. Government's job, said Banfield, was to preserve public order, not to right wrongs or encourage unrealistic expectations.

Free Market Utopians. Another strand of conservative argument came from free market utopians. After years of stagflation, Americans were eager to hear that unleashing free markets would trigger renewed prosperity.

The common themes of the conservative critique were simple: Free markets work better than government programs; government intervention does more harm than good; government assistance saps the initiative of the poor. In 1964, three-quarters of Americans had trusted Washington "to do what is right." By 1980, three-quarters were convinced that the federal government wasted tax money. The cumulative effect of the neoconservative arguments was to trash the word "liberal" and convince many Americans that labor unions and minorities were "special interests" but that oil tycoons, defense contractors, and other members of Reagan's coalition were not.

Conservative Political Savvy. Conservatives promoted their ideology with new political tactics. Targeted mailings raised funds and mobilized voters with emotional appeals while bypassing the mass media, with their supposed preference for mainstream or liberal policies. Conservative organizers also knew how to use radio call-in shows to spread their message. Such appeals contrasted with the Democrats' reliance on more traditional ways to get out the vote through personal contacts and labor unions. Through the 1980s, Democrats repeatedly found themselves blindsided by creative Republican campaign tactics.

REAGANOMICS: DEFICITS AND DEREGULATION

The heart of the 1980s revolution was the **Economic Recovery and Tax Act of 1981 (ERTA)**, which reduced personal income tax rates by 25 percent over three years. The explicit goal was to stimulate business activity by lowering taxes overall and slashing rates for the rich. Cutting the government's total income by $747 billion over five years, ERTA meant less money for federal programs and more money in the hands of consumers and investors to stimulate economic growth.

Reagan's first budget director, David Stockman, later revealed a second goal. ERTA would lock in deficits by "pulling the revenue plug." Because defense spending and Social Security were untouchable, Congress would find it impossible to create and fund new programs without cutting old ones. If Americans still wanted social programs, they could enact them at the local or state level, but Washington would no longer pay.

The second part of the economic agenda was to free capitalists from government regulations, in the hope of increasing business innovation and efficiency. The **deregulation** revolution built on a head start from the 1970s. A federal antitrust case had split the unified Bell System of AT&T and its subsidiaries into seven regional telephone companies and opened long-distance service to competition. Congress also deregulated air travel in 1978.

Environmental Regulation and Federal Lands. Corporate America used the Reagan administration to attack environmental legislation as "strangulation by regulation." Reagan's new budgets sliced funding for the Environmental Protection Agency. Vice President Bush headed the White House Task Force on Regulatory Relief, which delayed or blocked regulations on hazardous wastes, automobile emissions, and exposure of workers to chemicals on the job.

Most attention, however, went to the controversial appointment of a Colorado lawyer, James Watt, as secretary of the interior. Watt was sympathetic to a western movement known as the **Sagebrush Rebellion**, which wanted the vast federal land holdings in the West transferred to the states for less environmental protection and more rapid economic use. Federal resource agencies sold trees to timber companies at a loss to the Treasury, expanded offshore oil drilling, and expedited exploration for minerals.

Deregulation of the Banking Industry. The early 1980s also transformed American financial markets. Savings and loans had traditionally been conservative financial institutions that funneled individual savings into safe home mortgages. Under new rules, savings and loans began to compete for deposits by offering high interest rates and reinvesting the money in much riskier commercial real estate. By 1990, the result was a financial crisis in which bad loans destroyed hundreds of S&Ls, especially in the Southwest. American taxpayers were left to bail out depositors to the tune of hundreds of billions of dollars to prevent a collapse of the nation's financial and credit system.

With the deregulation of financial markets, corporate consolidations and mergers flourished. Corporate raiders raised money with "junk bonds"—high-interest, high-risk securities—and snapped up profitable and cash-rich companies that could be milked of profits and assets. The merger mania channeled capital into paper transactions rather than investments in new equipment and products. Another effect was to damage the economies of small and middle-sized communities by transferring control of local companies to outside managers.

In the short term, the national economy boomed in the mid-1980s. Deregulated credit, tax cuts, and massive deficit spending on defense fueled exuberant growth. The stock market mirrored the overall prosperity; the Dow Jones average of blue-chip industrial stock prices more than tripled from August 1982 to August 1987.

CRISIS FOR ORGANIZED LABOR

The flip side of the economic boom was another round in the Republican offensive against labor unions. Reagan set the tone when he fired more than 11,000 members of the Professional Air Traffic Controllers Organization for violating a no-strike clause in their hiring agreements. He claimed to be enforcing the letter of the law, but the message to organized labor was clear. For many years, corporations had hesitated to hire permanent replacements for striking workers. With Reagan's example, large companies, such as Hormel and Phelps-Dodge, chose that option, undercutting the strike as an effective union strategy.

Decline of Union Membership and Blue-Collar Jobs. Organized labor counted a million fewer members at the end of Reagan's administration in 1989 than in 1964, even though the number of employed Americans had nearly doubled. As union membership declined and unions struggled to cope with the changing economy, corporations seized the opportunity to demand wage rollbacks and concessions on working conditions as trade-offs for continued employment, squeezing workers in one plant and then using the settlement to pressure another. Workers in the 1970s and 1980s faced the threat that employers might move a factory to a new site elsewhere in the United States or overseas. Or a company might sell out to a new owner, who could close a plant and reopen without a union contract.

Another cause for shrinking union membership was the overall decline of blue-collar jobs, from 36 percent of the American workforce in 1960 to roughly 25 percent at the end of the 1990s. Unionization of white-collar workers made up only part of the loss from manufacturing. Unions were most successful in recruiting government workers, such as police officers, teachers, and bus drivers. By the late 1980s, the American Federation of State, County, and Municipal Employees had twice the membership of the United Steel Workers.

Impact of Economic Restructuring. In the 1950s and 1960s, increasing productivity, expanding markets for U.S. goods, and strong labor unions had made it possible for factory workers to enter the middle class. In an era of deindustrialization, however, companies replaced blue-collar workers with machinery or shifted production to nonunion plants. The corporate merger mania of the 1980s added to instability when takeover specialists loaded old companies with new debt, triggering efforts to cut labor costs, sell off plants, or raid pension funds for cash to pay the interest. Manufacturing employment in the 1980s declined by nearly 2 million jobs, with the expansion of high-tech manufacturing concealing much higher losses in traditional industries.

AN ACQUISITIVE SOCIETY

The new prosperity fueled lavish living by the wealthy and a fascination with the "lifestyles of the rich and famous." Prime-time soap operas flourished, bringing to the small screen stories of intrigue among the rich folks. With a few exceptions, even the "middle class" in television sitcoms enjoyed lives available only to the top 20 percent of Americans.

The national media in the early 1980s discovered yuppies, or young urban professionals, who were both a marketing category and a symbol of social change. These

"They're museum quality!"

This 1993 cartoon contrasting a yuppie couple and a family dressed as hippies makes two points. While highlighting the rapid changes in American styles and tastes from the 1970s to the 1990s, it also satirizes the supposed yuppie tendency to value everything as a commodity or "collectible." © Edward Koren/The New Yorker Collection/www.cartoonbank.com.

upwardly mobile professionals supposedly defined themselves by elitist consumerism. Middle-line retailers like Sears had clothed Americans for decades and furnished their homes. With the help of catalog shopping, status-seeking consumers now flocked to such upscale retailers as Neiman-Marcus and Bloomingdale's.

Far richer than even such atypical yuppies were wheeler-dealers who made themselves into media stars of finance capitalism. The autobiography of Lee Iacocca, who had helped revive the fortunes of the Chrysler Corporation, was a bestseller in 1984, portraying the corporate executive as hero. *Forbes* magazine began to publish an annual list of the nation's 400 richest people. Long before his television show, real-estate developer Donald Trump made himself a celebrity with a well-publicized personal life and a stream of projects crowned with his name: office tower, hotel, casino. New movements in popular music reacted to the acquisitive 1980s. Punk rock pared rock-and-roll to its basics, lashing out at the emptiness of 1970s disco sound. Hip-hop originated among African Americans and Latinos in New York, soon adding the angry and often violent lyrics of rap. Rap during the 1980s was about personal power and sex, but it also dealt with social inequities and deprivation and tapped some of the same anger and frustration that had motivated black power advocates in the 1960s. When it crossed into mainstream entertainment, it retained a hard-edged "attitude" that undercut any sense of complacency about an inclusive American society.

MASS MEDIA AND FRAGMENTED CULTURE

On June 1, 1980, CNN Cable News Network gave television viewers their first chance to watch news coverage 24 hours a day. CNN made a global reputation with live reporting on the pro-democracy protests of Chinese students in Beijing in 1989. When American bombs began to fall on Baghdad in January 1991, White House officials watched CNN to find out how their war was going.

CNN, MTV, and the rest of cable television reflected both the fragmentation of American society in the 1980s and 1990s and the increasing dependence on instant communication. As late as 1980, ordinary Americans had few choices for learning about their nation and world: virtually identical newscasts on NBC, CBS, and ABC and similar stories in *Time* and *Newsweek* helped to create a common understanding. Fifteen years later, they had learned to surf through dozens of cable channels in search of specialized programs and were beginning to explore the amazing variety of the World Wide Web (see Chapter 31).

POVERTY AMID PROSPERITY

Federal tax and budget changes had different effects on the rich and poor. Those in the top fifth increased their share of after-tax income relative to everyone else during the 1980s, and the richest 1 percent saw their share of all privately held wealth grow from 31 percent to 37 percent. The 1981 tax cuts also came with sharp increases in the Social Security tax, which hit lower-income workers the hardest. The tax changes meant that the average annual income of households in the bottom 20 percent *declined* and that many actually paid higher taxes.

Cities and their residents absorbed approximately two-thirds of the cuts in the 1981–1982 federal budget. Provisions for accelerated depreciation (tax write-offs) of factories and equipment in the 1981 tax act encouraged the abandonment of center-city factories in favor of new facilities in the suburbs. One result was a growing jobs-housing mismatch. There were often plenty of jobs in the suburbs, but the poorer people who most needed the jobs were marooned in city slums and dependent on public transit that seldom served suburban employers.

Federal tax and spending policies in the 1980s decreased the security of middle-class families. As the economy continued to struggle through deindustrialization, average wage rates fell in the 1980s when measured in real purchasing. The squeeze put pressure on traditional family patterns and pushed into the workforce women who might otherwise have stayed home. Many Americans no longer expected to surpass their parents' standard of living.

Corporate Downsizing and White-Collar Jobs. Lower-paying office jobs fell under the same sorts of pressure as factory jobs with the increasing reliance of banks, telephone companies, and credit card companies on automation. Increasing numbers of clerical and office workers in organizations of all sorts, from corporations to universities, were "temps" who shifted from job to job. The shift toward temporary and part-time workers not only kept wages low but also allowed less spending on health insurance and other benefits.

The chill of corporate downsizing hit white-collar families most heavily toward the end of the 1980s. Big business consolidations delivered improved profits by squeezing the ranks of middle managers as well as assembly-line workers. With fewer workers to supervise and with new technologies to collect and distribute information, companies could complete their cost cutting by trimming administrators.

Increase in the Poverty Rate.   At the lower end of the economic ladder, the proportion of Americans living in poverty increased. After declining steadily from 1960 to a low of 11 percent in 1973, the poverty rate climbed back to the 13 to 15 percent range. Although the economy in the 1980s created lots of new jobs, half of them paid less than poverty-level wages. Most of the nation's millions of poor people lived in households with employed adults. In 1992, fully 18 percent of all full-time jobs did not pay enough to lift a family of four out of poverty, a jump of 50 percent over the proportion of underpaid jobs in 1981.

The Wage Gap and the Feminization of Poverty.   Nor could most women, even those working full-time, expect to earn as much as men. In the 1960s and 1970s, the average working woman earned just 60 percent of the earnings of the average man. Only part of the wage gap could be explained by measurable factors, such as education or experience. The gap narrowed in the 1980s and 1990s, with women's earnings rising to 75 percent of men's by 2003. About half of the change was the result of bad news—the decline of earnings among men as high-wage factory jobs disappeared. The other half was the positive result of better-educated younger women finding better jobs. Indeed, women would earn 57 percent of four-year college degrees awarded in 2002 compared to 38 percent in 1960, and they earned 47 percent of first professional degrees, up from 3 percent.

Nevertheless, the low earning capacity of women with limited educations meant that women were far more likely than men to be poor. Women constituted nearly two-thirds of poor adults at the end of the 1980s. Only 6 percent of married-couple households were below poverty level, but 32 percent of households headed by a woman without a husband present were poor. The feminization of poverty and American reliance on private support for child rearing also meant that children had a higher chance of living in poverty than adults and that poor American children were worse off than their peers in other advanced nations.

Homelessness in America.   Falling below even the working poor were growing numbers of homeless Americans. In the 1980s, several factors made homelessness more visible and pressing. A new approach to the treatment of the mentally ill reduced the population of mental hospitals from 540,000 in 1960 to only 140,000 in 1980. Deinstitutionalized patients were supposed to receive community-based treatment, but many ended up on the streets and in overnight shelters. New forms of self-destructive drug abuse, such as crack addiction, joined alcoholism. A boom in downtown real estate destroyed old skid-row districts with their bars, missions, and dollar-a-night hotels.

These factors tripled the number of permanently homeless people during the early and middle 1980s, from 200,000 to somewhere between 500,000 and 700,000. Twice or three times that many may have been homeless for part of a given year. For every person in a shelter on a given night, two people were sleeping on sidewalks, in parks, in cars, and in abandoned buildings.

CONSOLIDATING THE REVOLUTION: GEORGE BUSH

In 1988 George H. W. Bush, Reagan's vice president for eight years, won the presidential election with 56 percent of the popular vote and 40 out of 50 states. Bush's view of national and world politics reflected a background in which personal connections counted. He was raised as part of the New England elite, built an oil business in Texas, and then held a series of high-level federal appointments.

Homeless people huddle over a heating grate outside the Commerce Department building in Washington, waiting until shelters open at night. In the 1980s, rising home prices and the closure of most mental hospitals pushed many Americans onto the streets. Estimates of the number of homeless in the late 1980s ranged from 300,000 to 3 million, depending on the definition of homelessness and the political goals of the estimator.

Michael Dukakis, the Democratic nominee in 1988, was a dry-as-dust, by-the-numbers manager who offered the American people "competence." The Bush campaign director, Lee Atwater, looked for hot-button issues that could fit onto a three-by-five card. Pro-Bush advertisements tapped into real worries among the voters—fear of crime, racial tension, eroding social values—and attached them to Dukakis. George Bush, despite his background in prep schools and country clubs, came out looking tough as nails, while the Democrats looked inept.

The ads locked Bush into a rhetorical war on crime and drugs that was his major domestic policy. Americans had good cause to be worried about public safety, but most were generally unaware that the likelihood of becoming the target of a violent crime had leveled off and would continue to fall in the 1990s or that crime was far worse in minority communities than elsewhere, in part due to gang- and drug-related activities. Bush tripled the federal drug control budget and stepped up efforts to stop the flow of illegal drugs across the border. Longer sentences and mandatory jail time meant that half of federal prison inmates in 1990 were in for drug crimes.

George Bush believed that Americans wanted government to leave them alone. He ignored a flood of new ideas from entrepreneurial conservatives, such as HUD Secretary Jack Kemp. The major legislation from the Bush administration was a transportation bill that shifted federal priorities from highway building toward mass transit and the **Americans with Disabilities Act** (1990) to prevent discrimination against people with physical handicaps. In the areas of crime and healthcare, however, Bush's lack of leadership left continuing problems.

The same attitude produced weak economic policies. The national debt had amounted to 50 percent of personal savings in 1980 but swelled to 125 percent by 1990. The massive budget deficits of the 1980s combined with growing trade deficits to turn the United States from an international creditor to a debtor nation. After pledging no new taxes in his campaign, Bush backed into a tax increase in 1990. A stronger leader might have justified the taxes to the nation, but voters found it hard to forget the president's attempts to downplay the importance of his decision.

The most conspicuous domestic event of the Bush administration—the "Rodney King riot" of April 1992 in Los Angeles—was a reminder of the nation's inattention to the problems of race and poverty. Rodney King was a black motorist who had been savagely clubbed and kicked by police officers while being arrested after a car chase on March 3, 1991. A nearby resident captured the beating on videotape from his apartment. Early the next year, the four officers stood trial for unjustified use of force before a suburban jury. The televised trial and the unexpected verdict of not guilty on April 29 stirred deep anger that escalated into four days of rioting.

The disorder revealed multiple tensions among ethnic groups and was far more complex than the Watts outbreak of 1965 (see Chapter 29). African Americans from south-central Los Angeles participated, but so did Central American and Mexican immigrants in adjacent districts, who accounted for about one-third of the 12,000 arrests. The disorder spread south to Long Beach and north to the edge of upscale neighborhoods in Westwood and Beverly Hills. Rioters assaulted the downtown police headquarters, city hall, and the *Los Angeles Times* building. As in 1965, some targets were white passers-by and symbols of white authority. But members of competing minority groups were also victims as angry black people targeted hundreds of Korean-owned and Vietnamese-owned shops as symbols of economic discrimination. Four days of disorder left 58 people dead, mostly African Americans and Latinos.

THE CLIMAX OF THE COLD WAR

Ronald Reagan entered office determined to reassert U.S. leadership in world affairs and not to lose the Cold War. He considered the Soviet Union not a coequal nation with legitimate world interests but an "evil empire." After the era of *détente*, global tensions had started to mount in the late 1970s. They were soon higher than they had been since the 1960s. But by the end of Reagan's two terms, unexpected changes were rapidly bringing the Cold War to an end, and George Bush faced a radically new set of foreign policy issues.

CONFRONTING THE SOVIET UNION

Who renewed the Cold War after Nixon's diplomacy of *détente* and Carter's early efforts at negotiation? The Soviets had pursued military expansion in the 1970s, triggering the fear that they might stage a nuclear Pearl Harbor. The Soviet Union in 1980 was supporting Marxist regimes in civil wars in Angola, Ethiopia, Nicaragua, and especially Afghanistan, where its 1980 intervention led to a decade of costly and futile military occupation. Were these actions parts of a careful plan? Or did they result from the Cold War inertia of a rudderless nation that reacted to situations one at a time? Given the aging Soviet leadership and the economic weaknesses revealed in the late 1980s, it makes more sense to see the Soviets as muddling along rather than executing a well-planned global strategy.

On the American side, Reagan's readiness to confront "the focus of evil in the modern world" reflected the views of many conservative supporters that the Soviet Union was a monolithic and ideologically motivated foe bent on world conquest. In hindsight, some Reaganites claim that the administration's foreign policy and massive increases in defense spending were part of a deliberate and coordinated scheme to check a Soviet offensive and bankrupt the Soviet Union by pushing it into a new arms race. It is just as likely, however, that the administration's defense and foreign policy initiatives were a set of discrete but effective decisions.

The Reagan administration reemphasized central Europe as the focus of superpower rivalry, just as it had been in the 1950s and early 1960s. To counter improved Soviet armaments, the United States began to place cruise missiles and mid-range Pershing II missiles in Europe in 1983. NATO governments approved the action, but it frightened millions of their citizens.

Escalation of the nuclear arms race reinvigorated the antiwar and antinuclear movement in the United States as well as Europe. Drawing on the experience of the antiwar movement, the nuclear-freeze campaign caught the imagination of many Americans in 1981 and 1982. It sought to halt the manufacture and deployment of new atomic weapons by the great powers. Nearly a million people turned out for a nuclear-freeze rally in New York in 1982. Hundreds of local communities endorsed the freeze or took the symbolic step of declaring themselves nuclear-free zones.

In response, Reagan announced the **Strategic Defense Initiative (SDI)**, or Star Wars program, in 1983. SDI was to deploy new defenses that could intercept and destroy ballistic missiles as they rose from the ground and arced through space. Few scientists thought that SDI could work. Many arms control experts thought that defensive systems were dangerous and destabilizing, because strong defenses suggested that a nation might be willing to risk a nuclear exchange.

RISKY BUSINESS: FOREIGN POLICY ADVENTURES

The same administration that sometimes seemed reckless in its grand strategy also took risks to assert U.S. influence in global trouble spots to block or roll back Soviet influence. Reagan asserted America's right to intervene anywhere in the world to support local groups fighting against Marxist governments. The assumption underlying this assertion, which later became to be known as the **Reagan Doctrine**, was that Soviet-influenced governments in Asia, Africa, and Latin America needed to be eliminated if the United States was to win the Cold War.

Nevertheless, Reagan kept the United States out of a major war and backed off in the face of serious trouble. Foreign interventions were designed to achieve symbolic victories rather than change the global balance of power. The exception was the Caribbean and Central America, the "backyard" where the United States had always claimed an overriding interest and where left-wing action infuriated Reagan's conservative supporters.

Intervention and Covert Activities in Central America. The Reagan administration attributed political turmoil in Central America to Soviet influence and to arms and agitators from Soviet-backed Cuba. Between 1980 and 1983, the United States sent more military aid to conservative governments and groups in Central America than it had during the previous 30 years. Indeed, Central America became the focus of a secret foreign policy operated by the CIA and then by National Security Council (NSC) staff, since a Democratic Congress was not convinced of the danger. The CIA and the NSC engaged not just in espionage but in direct covert operations. The chief target was Nicaragua, the Central American country where leftist Sandinista rebels had overthrown the Somoza dictatorship in 1979. In the early 1980s, Reagan approved CIA plans to arm and organize approximately 10,500 so-called Contras, from the remnants of Somoza's National Guard. From bases in Honduras, the Contras harassed the Sandinistas with sabotage and raids.

The Reagan administration bent the law to support its covert effort to overthrow the Sandinista regime. An unsympathetic Congress blocked U.S. funding for the Contras. In response, CIA director William Casey directed Lieutenant Colonel Oliver North of the National Security Council staff to illegally organize aid from private donors. The arms pipeline operated until a supply plane was shot down in 1986. The Contras failed as a military effort, but the civil war and international pressure persuaded the Sandinistas to allow free elections that led to a democratic, centrist government.

The War Against Drugs. The American war against drugs was simultaneously shaping U.S. policy in the Caribbean and straining relations with Latin America. As president, George Bush parlayed the war on drugs into war on Panama during his first year in office, extending the American tradition of ousting uncooperative governments around the Caribbean. General Manuel Noriega, the Panamanian strongman, had once been on the CIA payroll. He had since turned to international drug sales in defiance of United States anti-smuggling efforts. On December 20, 1989, American troops invaded Panama, hunted down Noriega, and brought him back to stand trial in the United States on drug-trafficking charges. A handful of Americans and thousands of Panamanians died, many of them civilians caught in the crossfire.

Intervention in the Middle East. If the results of intervention in Nicaragua and Panama were mixed, intervention in the Middle East was a failure. In 1982 Israel invaded Lebanon, a small nation to its north, to clear Palestinian guerrillas from its borders and set up a friendly Lebanese government. The Israeli army bogged down in a civil war between Christian Arabs and Muslims. Reagan sent U.S. Marines to preserve the semblance of a Lebanese state and provide a face-saving exit for Israel. In October 1983, a terrorist car bomb killed 241 Marines in their barracks. The remainder were soon gone, confirming the Syrian observation that Americans were "short of breath" when it came to Middle East politics. The debacle in Lebanon undermined U.S.-backed peace initiatives in the Middle East.

The Iran-Contra Affair. Even less effective were the Reagan administration's secret efforts to sell weapons to Iran in return for Iranian help in securing the release of Americans held hostage by pro-Iranian Islamic radicals in Lebanon. The United States in 1985 joined Israel in selling 500 antitank missiles to Iran, then embroiled in a long, bitter war with Iraq. The deal followed stern public pronouncements that the United States would never negotiate with terrorists and considered Iran's religious leaders to be backers of international terrorism. It also violated the official trade embargo against Iran, which had been in place since the U.S. embassy seizure in 1979. In May 1986, National Security adviser Robert McFarlane flew to Iran for more arms-for-hostages talks, carrying a chocolate cake and a Bible autographed by Reagan to present to the Iranian leader Ayatollah Khomeini.

When the deals came to light in 1986 and congressional hearings were held in the summer of 1987, Americans were startled to learn that Colonel North had funneled millions of dollars from the arms sales to the Nicaraguan Contras in a double evasion of the law.

As had been true with Watergate, the Iran-Contra affair was a two-sided scandal. First was the blatant misjudgment of operating a secret, bumbling, and unlawful foreign policy that depended on international arms dealers and ousted Nicaraguan military officers. Second was a concerted effort to cover up the illegal and unconstitutional actions. North shredded relevant documents and lied to Congress. In his final report in 1994, Special Prosecutor Lawrence Walsh found that President Reagan and Vice President Bush were aware of much of what had gone on and had participated in efforts to withhold information and mislead Congress.

U.S. Policy in Asia.   American policy in Asia was a refreshing contrast with practices in Central America and the Middle East. In the Philippines, American diplomats helped push corrupt President Ferdinand Marcos out and opened the way for a popular uprising to put Corazon Aquino in office. In South Korea, the United States similarly helped ease out an unpopular dictator by firmly supporting democratic elections that brought in a more popular but still pro-American government.

EMBRACING *PERESTROIKA*

Thaw in the Cold War started in Moscow as Soviet leaders sought to salvage a system under severe economic stress. Mikhail Gorbachev became general secretary of the Communist Party in 1985, when the Soviet Union was trapped in the sixth year of its failed attempt to control Afghanistan. Gorbachev startled Soviet citizens by urging *glasnost,* or political openness, with free discussion of issues and relaxation of controls on the press. He followed by setting the goal of *perestroika,* or restructuring of the painfully bureaucratic Soviet economy that was falling behind capitalist nations. His hope was that market-oriented reforms would help the Soviet Union keep up with the United States.

Gorbachev decided that he needed to reduce the crushing burden of Soviet defense spending if the Soviet Union was to have any chance of modernizing. During Reagan's second term, the Soviets offered one concession after another in a drive for arms control.

Reagan had the vision (or audacity) to embrace the new Soviet position. He cast off decades of belief in the dangers of Soviet Communism and had the political courage to take Gorbachev seriously. One of his reasons for SDI had been his belief that the abolition of nuclear weapons was better than fine-tuning the balance of terror. Now he was willing to forget his own rhetoric. He frightened his own staff when he met with Gorbachev in the summer of 1986 and accepted the principle of deep cuts in strategic forces. Reagan explained that when he railed against the evil empire, he had been talking about Brezhnev and the bad old days; Gorbachev and *glasnost* were different.

In the end, Reagan negotiated the **Intermediate-Range Nuclear Forces Treaty (INF)** over the strong objections of the CIA and the Defense Department. INF was the first true nuclear-disarmament treaty (see Overview, Controlling Nuclear Weapons: Four Decades of Effort). Previous agreements had only slowed the growth of nuclear weapons; they were "speed limits" for the arms race. The new pact matched Soviet SS-20s with U.S. cruise missiles as an entire class of weapons that would be destroyed, with on-site inspections for verification.

CRISIS AND DEMOCRACY IN EASTERN EUROPE

The wall that divided East from West Berlin from 1962 to 1989 was a hated symbol of the Cold War. When the Communist government of East Germany collapsed in November 1989, jubilant Berliners celebrated the opening of the wall and the reuniting of the divided city.

Reagan's successor, President Bush, acted on his belief in personal diplomacy, basing much of his foreign policy on his changing attitudes toward Mikhail Gorbachev. He started lukewarm, talking tough to please the Republican right wing. Bush feared that Gorbachev, by instituting reforms that challenged the entrenched Communist Party leaders, was being imprudent: one of the worst things he could say about another leader. Before 1989 was over, however, the president had decided that Gorbachev was OK. For the next two years, the United States pushed the prodemocratic transformation of eastern Europe while being careful not to gloat in public or damage Gorbachev's position at home.

The End of Communist Regimes in Eastern Europe. The people of eastern Europe overcame both U.S. and Soviet caution. Instead of the careful economic liberalization Gorbachev envisioned, the Warsaw Pact system collapsed. Poland held free elections in June 1989, Hungary adopted a democratic constitution in October, and prodemocracy demonstrations then forced out Communist leaders in other eastern European countries. When East Germans began to flee westward through Hungary, the East German regime bowed to mounting pressure and opened the Berlin Wall on November 9. By the end of 1989, there were new democratic or non-Communist governments in Czechoslovakia, Romania, Bulgaria, and East Germany. These largely peaceful revolutions destroyed the military and economic agreements that had harnessed the satellites to the Soviet economy (the Warsaw Pact and Comecon). The Soviet Union swallowed hard, accepted the loss of its satellites, and slowly withdrew its army from eastern Europe.

German Reunification and the Dissolution of the Soviet Union. Events in Europe left German reunification as a point of possible conflict. Soviet policy since 1945 had sought to prevent the reemergence of a strong, united Germany that might again threaten its neighbors. West German Chancellor Helmut Kohl removed one obstacle when he reassured Poland and Russia that Germany would seek no changes in the boundaries drawn after World War II. By July 1990, the United States and the Soviet Union had agreed that a reunited Germany would belong to NATO. The decision satisfied France and Britain that

OVERVIEW CONTROLLING NUCLEAR WEAPONS: FOUR DECADES OF EFFORT

Limiting the testing of nuclear weapons	Limited Test Ban Treaty (1963)	Banned nuclear testing in the atmosphere, ocean, and outer space.
	Comprehensive Test Ban Treaty (1996)	Banned all nuclear tests, including underground tests; rejected by U.S. Senate in 1999.
Halting the spread of nuclear weapons	Nuclear Non-Proliferation Treaty (1968)	Pledged five recognized nuclear nations (United States, Soviet Union, Britain, France, China) to pursue disarmament in good faith, and 140 other nations not to acquire nuclear weapons.
	Strategic Arms Limitation Treaty (SALT I, 1972)	Limited the number of nuclear-armed missiles and bombers maintained by the United States and Soviet Union. Closely associated with U.S.-Soviet agreement to limit deployment of antiballistic missile systems to one site each.
	Strategic Arms Limitation Treaty (SALT II, 1979)	Further limited the number of nuclear-armed missiles and bombers. Not ratified but followed by Carter and Reagan administrations.
Reducing the number of nuclear weapons	Intermediate-Range Nuclear Forces Treaty (1987)	Required the United States to eliminate 846 nuclear armed cruise missiles, and the Soviet Union to eliminate 1,846 SS-20 missiles.
	Strategic Arms Reduction Treaty (START I, 1991)	By July 1999, led to reductions of approximately 2,750 nuclear warheads by the United States and 3,725 warheads by the nations of the former USSR. Expired December 2009.
	Strategic Arms Reduction Treaty (START II, 1993)	Set further cuts in nuclear arsenals. Ratified by Russia in April 2000. Russia withdrew in 2002 after the U.S. abandoned the Anti-Ballistic Missile Treaty.
	Strategic Offensive Reductions (2002)	Russia and the United States each agree to deploy no more than 1,700–2,200 strategic nuclear warheads.

Data Source: Arms Control Association.

a stronger Germany would still be under the influence of the Western allies. In October, the two Germanies completed their political unification, although it would be years before their mismatched economies functioned as one. Reunification was the last step in the diplomatic legacy of World War II.

The final act in the transformation of the Soviet Union began with a failed coup against Mikhail Gorbachev in August 1991. The Soviet Union had held free elections

OVERVIEW WHY DID THE COLD WAR END?

Commentators have offered a number of explanations for the rapid failure of the USSR and the collapse of Soviet power at the end of the 1980s. All of these factors made contributions to the complex unraveling of the Cold War.

Economic exhaustion:	The United States in the late 1970s embarked on a great modernization and expansion of its military forces. The USSR exhausted its economy and revealed its technical backwardness by trying to keep pace. Gorbachev's policy of *perestroika* was an attempt to reduce the bureaucratic inertia of the economy.
Failure of leadership:	The Soviet Union in the 1970s and early 1980s was governed by unimaginative bureaucrats. A closed elite that thought only of preserving their privileges and authority could not adapt to a changing world. The policy of *glasnost* was an effort to encourage new ideas.
Intervention in Afghanistan:	The disastrous intervention in Afghanistan revealed the limits of Soviet military power. It alienated the large Muslim population of the USSR and brought disillusionment with the incompetence of Soviet leaders.
Triumph of democratic ideas:	As political discussion became more free, the appeal of democratic ideas took on its own momentum, especially in eastern European satellite nations such as East Germany, Czechoslovakia, and Poland.
Power of nationalism:	The collapse of the Soviet empire was triggered by the resurgence of national sentiments throughout the Soviet empire. National sentiments fueled the breakaway of the eastern European satellite nations such as Hungary, Romania, and Poland. Nationalism also broke up the USSR itself as 14 smaller socialist republics declared independence from the Russian-dominated Union.

in 1989. Now Gorbachev scheduled a vote on a new constitution that would decrease the power of the central government. Old-line Communist bureaucrats who feared the change arrested Gorbachev in his vacation house and tried to take over the government apparatus in Moscow. Boris Yeltsin, president of the Russian Republic, organized the resistance. Muscovites flocked to support Yeltsin and defied tank crews in front of the Russian parliament building. Within three days, the plotters themselves were under arrest.

The coup hastened the fragmentation of the Soviet Union. Before the month was out, the Soviet parliament banned the Communist Party. Gorbachev soon resigned. Previously suppressed nationalist feelings caused all 15 component republics of the Soviet Union to declare their independence. The superpower Union of Soviet Socialist Republics ceased to exist. Russia remained the largest and strongest of the new states, followed by Ukraine and Kazakhstan. (See Overview, Why Did the Cold War End?)

THE PERSIAN GULF WAR

On August 2, 1990, President Saddam Hussein of Iraq seized the small neighboring oil-rich country of Kuwait. The quick conquest gave Iraq control of 20 percent of the world's oil production and reserves. President Bush demanded unconditional withdrawal, enlisted European and Arab allies in an anti-Iraq coalition, and persuaded Saudi Arabia to accept substantial U.S. forces to protect it against Iraqi invasion.

The background for Iraq's invasion was a simmering dispute over border oil fields and islands in the Persian Gulf. Iraq was a dictatorship that had just emerged from an immensely costly eight-year war with Iran. Saddam Hussein had depended on help from the United States and Arab nations in this war, but Iraq was now economically exhausted. Kuwait was a small, rich nation whose ruling dynasty enjoyed few friends but plenty of oil royalties. The U.S. State Department had signaled earlier in 1990 that it might support some concessions by Kuwait in its dispute with Iraq. Saddam Hussein read the signal as an open invitation to do what he wanted; having been favored in the past by the United States, he probably expected denunciations but no military response.

The Iraqis gave George Bush a golden opportunity to assert America's world influence. The Bush administration was concerned that Iraq might target oil-rich Saudi Arabia. The importance of Middle Eastern oil helped to enlist France and Britain as military allies and to secure billions of dollars from Germany and Japan. Iraq had antagonized nearly all its neighbors. The collapse of Soviet power and Gorbachev's interest in cooperating with the United States meant that the Soviets would not interfere with U.S. plans.

Bush and his advisers offered a series of justifications for U.S. actions. First, and most basic, were the desire to punish armed aggression and the presumed need to protect Iraq's other neighbors. In fact, there was scant evidence of Iraqi preparations against Saudi Arabia. The buildup of U.S. air power plus effective economic sanctions would have accomplished both protection and punishment. Sanctions and diplomatic pressure might also have brought withdrawal from most or all of Kuwait. However, additional American objectives—to destroy Iraq's capacity to create nuclear weapons and to topple Saddam's regime—would require direct military action.

Bush probably decided on war in October, eventually increasing the number of American troops in Saudi Arabia to 580,000. The United States stepped up diplomatic pressure by securing a series of increasingly tough United Nations resolutions that culminated in November 1990 with Security Council Resolution 678, authorizing "all necessary means" to liberate Kuwait. The president convinced Congress to agree to military action under the umbrella of the UN. The United States ignored compromise plans floated by France and last-minute concessions from Iraq.

The Persian Gulf War began one day after the UN's January 15 deadline for Iraqi withdrawal from Kuwait. **Operation Desert Storm** opened with massive air attacks on command centers, transportation facilities, and Iraqi forward positions. The air war destroyed 40 to 50 percent of Iraqi tanks and artillery by late February. The attacks also seriously hurt Iraqi civilians by disrupting utilities and food supplies.

The 40-day rain of bombs was the prelude to a ground attack (see Map 30–2). On February 24, 1991, allied forces swept into Iraq. Americans, Saudis, Syrians, and Egyptians advanced directly to liberate Kuwait. A cease-fire came 100 hours after the start of the ground war. Allied forces suffered only 240 deaths in action, compared to perhaps 100,000 for the Iraqis.

Bush directed Desert Storm with the "Vietnam syndrome" in mind, believing that Americans were willing to accept war only if it involved overwhelming U.S. force and ended quickly. The United States hoped to replace Saddam Hussein without disrupting Iraqi society. Instead, the 100-hour war incited armed rebellions against Saddam in southern Iraq by Shiites, a group within the Muslim religion whose adherents comprise a majority in Iraq, and in the north by the ethnically distinct Kurds. Because Bush and his advisers were unwilling to get embroiled in a civil war or commit the United States to occupy all of Iraq, they

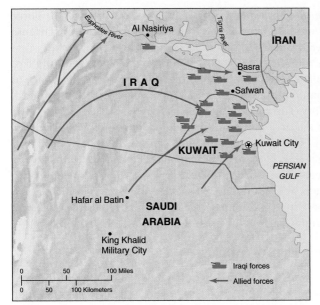

MAP 30–2 • **The Persian Gulf War** Ground operations against Iraq in the Persian Gulf War followed six weeks of aerial bombardment. The ground attack, which met quick success, was a multinational effort by the United States, Britain, France, Saudi Arabia, and other Arab nations threatened by an aggressive Iraq. The war freed Kuwait from Iraqi occupation but stopped before forcing a change in Iraq's government.

▶ **What was** the U.S. strategy in the Persian Gulf War? How was it shaped by America's experience in Vietnam?

stood by while Saddam crushed the uprisings. In one sense, the U.S. won the war but not the peace. Saddam Hussein became a hero to many in the Islamic world simply by surviving.

GROWTH IN THE SUNBELT

The rise of the **Sunbelt**, which is anchored by Florida, Texas, and California, reflected the leading economic trends of the 1970s and 1980s, including military spending, immigration from Asia and Latin America, and recreation and retirement spending. Corporations liked the business climate of the South, which had weak labor laws, low taxes, and generally low costs of living and doing business.

New factories dotted the southern landscape, often in smaller towns rather than cities. General Motors closed factories in Flint, Michigan, but invested in a new Saturn plant in Spring Hill, Tennessee. In contrast to troubled industrial cities in the Northeast and Midwest, cities like Orlando, Charlotte, Atlanta, Dallas, and Phoenix enjoyed head-long prosperity. Houston, with sprawling growth, business spinoffs from NASA, and purr-ing air-conditioners, epitomized the booming metropolitan areas of the South and West.

THE DEFENSE ECONOMY

The Vietnam buildup and reinvestment in the military during the Carter (1977–1981) and Reagan (1981–1989) administrations fueled the growth of the Sunbelt. Over the 40 years from the Korean conflict to the Persian Gulf War, the United States made itself the mightiest military power ever known. Military bases and defense contractors remolded the economic landscape, as mild winters and clear skies for training and operations helped the South and West attract more than 75 percent of military payrolls.

Big cities and small depended on defense spending. Southern California thrived on more than 500,000 jobs in the aircraft industry. A thousand miles away, visitors to

Colorado Springs could drive past sprawling Fort Carson and visit the new Air Force Academy, opened in 1958. Sunk deep from view was the North American Air Defense Command headquarters beneath Cheyenne Mountain west of the city.

Defense spending underwrote the expansion of American science and technology. Nearly one-third of all engineers worked on military projects. Large universities, such as MIT, the University of Michigan, the California Institute of Technology, and Stanford, were leading defense contractors. The modern electronics business started in New York, Boston, and the San Francisco Bay area with research and development for military uses, such as guided-missile controls. California's Silicon Valley grew with military sales long before it turned to consumer markets. The space component of the aerospace industry was equally reliant on the defense economy, with NASA spending justified by competition with the Soviet Union. NASA's centers were scattered across the South: launch facilities at the Kennedy Space Center in Cape Canaveral, Florida; research labs at Huntsville, Alabama; and Houston's Manned Spacecraft Center as the control center for space exploration.

AMERICANS FROM AROUND THE WORLD

Few Americans anticipated the effects of the **Immigration and Nationality Act of 1965,** which transformed the ethnic mix of the United States and helped to stimulate the Sunbelt boom. The new law initiated a change in the composition of the American people by abolishing the national quota system in effect since 1924. Quotas had favored immigrants from western Europe and limited those from other parts of the world. The old law's racial bias contradicted the self-proclaimed role of the United States as a defender of freedom, and immigration reform was part of the propaganda battle of the Cold War. The new law gave preference to family reunification and welcomed immigrants from all nations equally. The United States also accepted refugees from Communism outside the annual limits.

Immigration reform opened the doors to Mediterranean Europe, Latin America, and Asia. Legal migration to the United States surged from 1.1 million in 1960–1964 to nearly 4 million for 1990–1994. Nonlegal immigrants may have doubled the total number of newcomers in the 1970s and early 1980s. Not since World War I had the United States absorbed so many new residents.

Immigration changed the nation's ethnic mix. Members of officially defined ethnic and racial minorities accounted for 25 percent of Americans in 1990 and 30 percent in 2000 (see Table 30-1). Roughly 28 million Americans, or 10.4 percent of the population, had been born in other countries according to the 2000 census.

The largest single group of new Americans came from Mexico. The long border has facilitated easy movement from south to north. Especially in the border states of

TABLE 30-1 Major Racial and Ethnic Minorities in the United States

	1960 Population (in millions)	Percentage of Total	2000 Population (in millions)	Percentage of Total
American Indians	0.5	0.3	2.5	0.9
Asians and Pacific Islanders	1.1	0.6	10.6	3.7
African Americans	18.9	10.5	34.7	12.3
Hispanics	not available		35.3	12.5

Texas, New Mexico, Arizona, and California, permanent immigrants have mingled with tourists, family members on visits, temporary workers, and other workers without legal permission to enter the United States. Mexican Americans were the largest minority group in many southwestern and western states in the later twentieth century.

The East Coast has especially welcomed migrants from the West Indies and Central America. Many Puerto Ricans, who hold U.S. citizenship, came to Philadelphia and New York in the 1950s and 1960s.

Another great immigration has occurred eastward across the Pacific. Chinese, Filipinos, Koreans, Samoans, and other Asians and Pacific Islanders constituted only 6 percent of newcomers to the United States in 1965 but nearly half of all arrivals in 1990. The number of ethnic Chinese in the United States jumped from a quarter of a million in 1965 to 1,645,000 in 1990.

The most publicized Asian immigrants were refugees from Indochina after the Communist victory in 1975. The first arrivals tended to be highly educated professionals who had worked with the Americans. Another 750,000 Vietnamese, Laotians, and Cambodians arrived after 1976 by way of refugee camps in Thailand, as did Celia Noup. Most settled on the West Coast.

In addition to Southeast Asians, political conflicts and upheavals sent other waves of immigrants to the United States. Many Iranians fled the religious regime that took power in their country in the late 1970s, at the same time that Ethiopians were fleeing a nation shattered by drought, civil war, and doctrinaire Marxism. To escape repression in the Soviet Union, Jews and conservative Christians came to the United States in the 1980s, and the collapse of Communism in the Soviet Union opened the door for more Russians, Ukrainians, Romanians, and other eastern Europeans.

Recent immigrants have found both economic possibilities and problems. On the negative side, legal and illegal immigration has added to the number of nonunion workers. By one estimate, two-thirds of the workers in the Los Angeles garment trade were undocumented immigrants. Most worked for small, nonunion firms in basements and storefronts, without health insurance or pensions. But a positive contrast was the abundance of opportunities for talent and ambition in the expanding economy of the mid-1980s and 1990s. The 130,000 Vietnamese immigrants of 1975 now have an average income above the national figure. Asians and Pacific Islanders by 2000 constituted 22 percent of the students in California's public universities. Like earlier European immigrants, many newcomers have opened groceries, restaurants, and other businesses that serve their own group before expanding into larger markets.

OLD GATEWAYS AND NEW

The new immigration from Asia, Latin America, and the Caribbean had its most striking effects in coastal and border cities. New York again became a great mixing bowl of the U.S. population. By 1990, some 28 percent of the population of New York City was foreign-born, compared to 42 percent at the height of European immigration in 1910.

Just as important was the transformation of southern and western cities into gateways for immigrants from Latin America and Asia. Los Angeles emerged as "the new Ellis Island" that rivaled New York's historic role in receiving immigrants. The sprawling neighborhoods of East Los Angeles make up the second-largest Mexican city in the world. New ethnic communities appeared in Los Angeles suburbs: Iranians in Beverly Hills, Chinese in Monterey Park, Japanese in Gardena, Thais in Hollywood, Samoans in

Carson, Cambodians in Lakewood. One hundred languages are spoken among students entering Los Angeles schools.

New York and Los Angeles are world cities as well as immigrant destinations. Like London and Tokyo, they are capitals of world trade and finance, with international banks and headquarters of multinational corporations. They have the country's greatest concentrations of international lawyers, accounting firms, and business consultants. The deregulation of international finance and the explosive spread of instant electronic communication in the 1980s confirmed their importance as global decision centers (see Table 30-2).

Similar factors have turned Miami into an economic capital of the Caribbean. A quarter-million Cuban businessmen, white-collar workers, and their families moved to the United States between 1959 and 1962 to escape Castro's socialist government. By the late 1970s Cubans owned about one-third of the area's retail stores and many of its other businesses. Their success in business made Miami a major Latino market and helped to attract millions of Latin American tourists and shoppers. Access to the Caribbean and South America also made Miami an international banking and commercial center with hundreds of offices for corporations engaged in U.S.–Latin American trade.

Cross-border communities in the Southwest, such as El Paso, Texas, and Juarez, Mexico, or San Diego, California, and Tijuana, Mexico, are "Siamese twins joined at the cash register." Employees with work permits commute from Mexico to the United States. American popular culture flows southward. Bargain hunters and tourists pass in both directions.

Both nations have promoted the cross-border economy. The Mexican government in the mid-1960s began to encourage a "platform economy" by allowing companies on the Mexican side of the border to import components and inputs duty-free as long as 80 percent of the items were re-exported and 90 percent of the workers were Mexicans. The intent was to encourage U.S. corporations to locate assembly plants south of the border. Such *maquila* industries were able to employ lower-wage workers and avoid strict antipollution laws (leading to serious threats to public health on both sides of

---

TABLE 30-2 Global Cities

Ranked by Population in 2007 (population in millions)	Ranked as Economic Decision Centers
Tokyo, Japan 35.7	1. London
New York 19.4	2. New York
Ciudad de Mexico 19.0	3. Hong Kong
Mumbai, India 19.0	4. Paris
Sao Paulo, Brazil 18.8	5. Tokyo
Delhi, India 15.9	6. Singapore
Shanghai, China 15.0	7. Chicago
Kolkata, India 14.8	8. Milan
Dhaka, Bangladesh 13.5	9. Los Angeles
Buenos Aires, Argentina 12.8	10. Toronto
Los Angeles 12.5	11. Madrid
Karachi, Pakistan 12.1	12. Amsterdam

SOURCES: UN Department of Economic and Social Affairs/Population Division, *World Urbanization Prospects*: The 2007 Revision; Peter J. Taylor and Robert Lang, "U.S. Cities in the 'World City Network,'" The Brookings Institution, February 2005.

the border). From the Gulf of Mexico to the Pacific Ocean, 1,800 *maquiladora* plants employed half a million workers. North of the border, U.S. factories supplied components under laws that meshed with the Mexican regulations.

The Graying of America

Retirees were another factor contributing to the growth of the Sunbelt. Between 1965 and 2000, the number of Americans aged 65 and over jumped from 18.2 million to 35 million, or 12.4 percent of the population.

Older Americans have become a powerful voice in public affairs. They tend to vote against local taxes but fight efforts to slow the growth of Social Security, even though growing numbers of the elderly are being supported by a relatively smaller proportion of working men and women. By the 1990s, observers noted increasing resentment among younger Americans, who fear that public policy is biased against the needs of those in their productive years. In turn, the elderly fiercely defend the programs of the 1960s and 1970s that have kept many of them from poverty.

Retired Americans changed the social geography of the United States. Much growth in the South and Southwest has been financed by money earned in the Northeast and Midwest and transferred by retirees. Florida in the 1980s got nearly 1 million new residents aged 60 or older, and California, Arizona, Texas, and the Carolinas also attracted many retirees.

Values in Collision

In 1988, two very different religious leaders sought a presidential nomination. Pat Robertson's campaign for the Republican nomination tapped deep discontent with the changes in American society since the 1960s. A television evangelist, Robertson used the mailing list from his *700 Club* program to mobilize conservative Christians and push the Republican Party further to the right on family and social issues. Jesse Jackson, a civil rights leader and minister from Chicago, mounted a grassroots campaign with the opposite goal of moving the Democratic Party to the left on social and economic policy. Drawing on his experience in the black civil rights movement, he assembled a "Rainbow Coalition" that included labor unionists, feminists, and others whom Robertson's followers feared.

In diagnosing social ills, Robertson pointed to the problems of individual indulgence, while Jackson pointed to racism and economic inequality. Their sharp divergence expressed differences in basic values that divided Americans in the 1980s and beyond. In substantial measure, the conflicts were rooted in the social and cultural changes of the 1960s and 1970s that had altered traditional institutions.

Women's Rights and Public Policy

The women's liberation movement of the 1960s achieved important gains when Congress wrote many of its goals into law in the early 1970s. Title IX of the Educational Amendments (1972) to the Civil Rights Act prohibited discrimination by sex in any educational program receiving federal aid. The legislation expanded athletic opportunities for women and slowly equalized the balance of women and men in faculty positions. In the same year, Congress sent the Equal Rights Amendment (ERA) to the states for ratification. The amendment read, "Equal rights under the law shall not be denied or abridged by the United States or by any state on account of sex." More than 20 states ratified in the first few months. As conservatives who wanted to preserve traditional family patterns rallied strong opposition, however, the next dozen states ratified only after increasingly tough battles in state legislatures. The ERA then stalled, three states short, until the time limit for ratification expired in 1982.

Abortion Rights and the Conservative Backlash. In January 1973, the U.S. Supreme Court expanded the debate about women's rights with the case of *Roe v. Wade*. Voting 7 to 2, the Court struck down state laws forbidding abortion in the first three months of pregnancy and set guidelines for abortion during the remaining months. Drawing on the earlier decision of *Griswold v. Connecticut*, which dealt with birth control, the Court held that the Fourteenth Amendment includes a right to privacy that blocks states from interfering with a woman's right to terminate a pregnancy.

These changes came in the context of increasingly sharp conflict over the feminist agenda. Both the ERA and *Roe* stirred impassioned support and equally passionate opposition that pushed the two major political parties in opposite directions. Behind the rhetoric were male fears of increased job competition during a time of economic contraction and concern about changing families. Also fueling the debate was a deep split between the mainstream feminist view of women as fully equal individuals and the contrary conservative belief that women had a special role as anchors of families, an updating of the nineteenth-century idea of separate spheres. The arguments tapped such deep emotion that the two sides could not even agree on a common language, juxtaposing a right to life against rights to privacy and freedom of choice.

Women in the Workforce. The most sweeping change in the lives of American women did not come from federal legislation or court cases, but from the growing likelihood that a woman would work outside the home. In 1960, some 32 percent of married women were in the labor force; 40 years later, 61 percent were working or looking for work (along with 69 percent of single women). Federal and state governments slowly responded to the changing demands of work and family with new policies, such as a federal childcare tax credit.

More women entered the workforce as inflation in the 1970s and declining wages in the 1980s eroded the ability of families to live comfortable lives on one income. A second reason for the increase in working women from 29 million in 1970 to 66 million in 2000 was the broad shift from manufacturing to service jobs, reducing demand for factory workers and manual laborers and increasing the need for such "women's jobs" as data-entry clerks, reservation agents, and nurses. Indeed, the U.S. economy still divides job categories by sex. There was some movement toward gender-neutral hiring in the 1970s because of legal changes and the pressures of the women's movement. Women's share of lawyers more than quadrupled, of economists more than tripled, and of police detectives more than doubled. Nevertheless, job types were more segregated by sex than by race in the 1990s.

AIDS AND GAY ACTIVISM

After the increasing openness about sexual orientation in the 1970s, the character of life in gay communities took an abrupt turn in the 1980s when a new worldwide epidemic emerged. Scientists identified a new disease pattern, **acquired immune deficiency syndrome (AIDS)**, in 1981. The name described the symptoms resulting from infection by the human immunodeficiency virus (HIV), which destroys the body's ability to resist disease. HIV is transferred through blood and semen. In the 1980s, the most frequent

The AIDS Quilt, displayed in Washington in October 1992, combined individual memorials to AIDS victims into a powerful communal statement. The quilt project reminded Americans that AIDS had penetrated every American community.

American victims were gay men and intravenous drug users.

A decade later, it was clear that HIV/AIDS was a national and even global problem. By the end of 2005, AIDS had been responsible for 550,000 deaths in the United States, and transmission to hetero-sexual women was increasing. The U.S. Centers for Disease Control and Prevention estimated roughly 40,000 new cases of HIV infection per year at the beginning of the twenty-first century, bringing the total of infected Americans to around 1,200,000. Once a problem of big cities, HIV infection had spread to every American community and had helped to change American attitudes about the process of dying through the spread of hospices for the care of the terminally ill. Meanwhile, the toll of AIDS deaths in other parts of the world, particularly eastern Africa, dwarfed that in the United States and made it a world health crisis.

By the 1990s, Americans were accustomed to open discussion of gay sexuality, if not always accepting of its reality. Television stars and other entertainers could "come out" and retain their popularity. So could politicians in certain districts. On the issue of gays in the military, however, Congress and the Pentagon were more cautious, accepting a policy that made engaging in homosexual acts, though not sexual orientation itself, grounds for discharge.

CHURCHES IN CHANGE

Americans take their search for spiritual grounding much more seriously than do citizens of other industrial nations. Roughly half of privately organized social activity (such as charity work) is church related. In the mid-1970s, 56 percent of Americans said that religion was "very important" to them, compared to only 27 percent of Europeans. Moreover, religious belief is an important source of political convictions and basis for political action (see American Views: The Religious Imperative in Politics).

Nonetheless, the mainline Protestant denominations that traditionally defined the center of American belief were struggling after 1970. The United Methodist Church, the Presbyterian Church U.S.A., the United Church of Christ, and the Episcopal Church battled internally over the morality of U.S. foreign policy, the role of women in the ministry, and the reception of gay and lesbian members. They were strengthened by an ecumenical impulse that united denominational branches divided by ethnicity or regionalism. However, they gradually lost their position among American churches, perhaps because ecumenism diluted the certainty of their message. Liberal Protestantism has historically been strongest in the slow-growing Northeast and Midwest.

By contrast, evangelical Protestant churches have benefited from the direct appeal of their message and from strong roots in the booming Sunbelt. Members of evangelical churches (25 percent of white Americans) now outnumber the members of mainline Protestant churches (20 percent). Major evangelical denominations include Baptists, the Church of the Nazarene, and the Assemblies of God. Fundamentalists, defined by a belief in the literal truth of the Bible, are a subset of evangelicals. So are 8 to 10 million Pentecostals and charismatics, who accept "gifts of the spirit," such as healing by faith and speaking in tongues.

Outsiders knew evangelical Christianity through "televangelists," such as Oral Roberts and Pat Robertson. Spending on religious television programming rose from $50 million to $600 million by 1980. The "electronic church" built on the radio preaching and professional revivalism of the 1950s. By the 1970s it reached 20 percent of American households.

Evangelical churches emphasized religion as an individual experience focused on personal salvation. Unlike many of the secular and psychological avenues to fulfillment, however, they also offered communities of faith that might stabilize fragmented lives. The conservative nature of their theology and social teaching in a changing society offered certainty that was especially attractive to many younger families.

Another important change in national religious life has been the continuing Americanization of the Roman Catholic Church following the Second Vatican Council in 1965, in which church leaders sought to respond to postwar industrial society. In the United States, Roman Catholicism moved toward the center, helped by the popularity of John Kennedy and by worldly success that made Catholics the economic peers of Protestants. Even as the tight connection between Catholicism and membership in European immigrant communities gradually faded, Asian and Latino immigrants brought new vigor to many parishes, and many inner-city churches have been centers for social action. Church practice lost some of its distinctiveness; celebrating Mass in English rather than Latin was an important move toward modernization, but it also sparked a conservative counter-effort to preserve the traditional liturgy. Traditional and nontraditional Catholics also disagree about whether priests should be allowed to marry and other adaptations to American culture.

The new globalization of American society simultaneously increased the nation's religious diversity and confirmed the dominant position of Christianity. Many immigrants from Asia and Africa have come with their native religious beliefs. There are now hundreds of Hindu temples and thousands of Buddhist centers. More than a million Muslims now worship in mosques that are found in every major city. In total, the proportion of Americans who identify themselves with non-Christian religions grew from 3 percent in 1990 to 4 percent in 2001. Over the same period, however, the proportion identifying with a Christian group or denomination grew from 86 to 87 percent. Indeed, many recent immigrants are Christians: Roman Catholics from Vietnam and the Philippines, Protestants from Korea, evangelicals from the former Soviet Union, Catholics and evangelicals from Latin America.

CULTURE WARS

In the 1950s and 1960s, Americans argued most often over foreign policy, racial justice, and the economy. Since the 1980s, they have also quarreled over beliefs and values, especially as the patterns of family life have become more varied. In the course of

In December 1993, the U.S. Supreme Court heard arguments on whether states could require protesters to remain a certain distance from abortion clinics. These antiabortion and proabortion protesters revealed the deep divisions over this and other issues in the culture wars.

these quarrels, religious belief has heavily influenced politics as individuals and groups try to shape America around their own, and often mutually conflicting, ideas of the godly society. Americans who are undogmatic in religion are often liberal in politics as well, hoping to lessen economic inequities and strengthen individual social freedom. Religious and political conservatism also tend to go together.

The division on social issues is related to theological differences within Protestantism. The "conservative" emphasis on personal salvation and the literal truth of the Bible expresses itself in a desire to restore "traditional" social patterns. Conservatives worry that social disorder occurs when people follow personal impulses and pleasures. In contrast, the "liberal" or "modern" emphasis on the universality of the Christian message restates the Social Gospel with its call to build the Kingdom of God through social justice and may recognize divergent pathways toward truth. Liberals worry that greed in the unregulated marketplace creates disorder and injustice.

The cultural conflict also transcends the historic three-way division of Americans among Protestants, Catholics, and Jews. Instead, the conservative-liberal division now cuts through each group. For example, Catholic reformers, liberal Protestants, and Reform Jews may find agreement on issues of cultural values despite theologies that are worlds apart. The same may be true of conservative Catholics, fundamentalist Protestants, and Orthodox Jews.

Conservatives initiated the culture wars, trying to stabilize what they fear is an American society spinning out of control because of lack of self-discipline and sexual indulgence. In fact, the evidence on the sexual revolution is mixed. Growing numbers of teenagers reported being sexually active in the 1970s, but the rate of increase tapered off in the 1980s. The divorce rate began to drop after 1980. Births to teenagers dropped after 1990, and the number of two-parent families increased. There was, however, an astonishing eagerness to talk about sex in the 1990s, a decade when soap-opera story lines and talk shows covered everything from family violence to exotic sexual tastes.

The explosion of explicit attention to sexual behavior set the stage for religiously rooted battles over two sets of issues. One cluster revolved around so-called family values, questioning the morality of access to abortion, the acceptability of homosexuality, and the roles and rights of women. A second set of concerns has focused on the supposed role of public schools in undermining morality through sex education, unrestricted reading matter, nonbiblical science, and the absence of prayer. The Supreme

AMERICAN VIEWS

THE RELIGIOUS IMPERATIVE IN POLITICS

The strong religious faith of many Americans frequently drives them to different stands on politi-cal issues. The first of these two documents, a letter by Jerry Falwell to potential supporters of the Moral Majority, reflects the politically conservative outlook of many evangelical Christians. Falwell was pastor of the Thomas Road Baptist Church in Lynchburg, Virginia. He founded the Moral Majority, a conservative religious lobbying and educational organization, in 1979 and served as its president until 1987, the year he wrote the letter reprinted here. The organization was especially impor-tant for voter registration efforts among conservative Christians. The second document, from an open letter issued by the Southside United Presbyterian Church in Tucson in 1982, expresses the conviction of other believers that God may sometimes require civil disobedience to oppose oppressive government actions. The letter explains the church's reasons for violating immigration law to offer sanctuary to refugees from repressive Central American regimes supported by the United States.

■ How do Falwell and the Southside Presbyterian Church define the problems that demand a religious response?
■ Are there any points of agreement?
■ How does each statement balance the claims of God and government?

FROM THE REVEREND JERRY FALWELL:

I believe that the overwhelming majority of Americans are sick and tired of the way that amoral liberals are trying to corrupt our nation from its commitment to free-dom, democracy, traditional morality, and the free enterprise system. And I believe

that the majority of Americans agree on the basic moral values which this nation was founded upon over 200 years ago.

Today we face four burning crises as we continue in this Decade of Destiny—the 1980s—loss of our freedom by giving in to the Communists; the destruction of the family unit; the deterioration of the free enterprise system; and the crumbling of basic moral principles which has resulted in the legalizing of abortion, wide-spread pornography, and a drug problem of epi-demic proportions.

That is why I went to Washington, D.C., in June of 1979, and started a new

Court decisions in 1962 and 1963 that prohibited vocal prayer and devotional Bible reading in public schools were targets for many.

A culturally conservative issue with great popular appeal in the early 1990s was an effort to prevent states and localities from protecting homosexuals against discrimination. Under the slogan "No special rights," antigay measures passed in Cincinnati, Colorado, and communities in Oregon in 1993 and 1994, only to have the Supreme Court overturn the Colorado law in *Romer v. Evans* (1996). It is important to note that public support for lesbian and gay civil rights varies with different issues (strong support for equal employment opportunity, much less for making marriage available to same-sex couples) and whether the issues are framed in terms of specified rights for gays or in terms of the right of everyone to be free from government interfer-ence with personal decisions, such as living arrangements and sexual choices.

organization, The Moral Majority. Right now you may be wondering: "But I thought Jerry Falwell was the preacher on the Old-Time Gospel Hour television program?"

You are right. For over twenty-four years I have been calling the nation back to God from the pulpit on radio and television. But in recent months I have been led to do more than just preach. I have been compelled to take action.

I have made the commitment to go right into the halls of Congress and fight for laws that will save America.

I will still be preaching every Sunday on the Old-Time Gospel Hour and I still must be a husband and father to my precious family in Lynchburg, Virginia.

But as God gives me the strength, I must do more. I must go into the halls of Congress and fight for laws that will protect the grand old flag for the sake of our children and grandchildren.

FROM SOUTHSIDE UNITED PRESBYTERIAN CHURCH:

We are writing to inform you that Southside Presbyterian Church will publicly violate the Immigration and Nationality Act, Section 274 (A).

We take this action because we believe the current policy and practice of the United States Government with regard to Central American refugees is illegal and immoral. We believe our government is in violation of the 1980 Refugee Act and international law by continuing to arrest, detain, and forcibly return refugees to the terror, persecution, and murder in El Salvador and Guatemala.

We believe that justice and mercy require the people of conscience to actively assert our God-given right to aid anyone fleeing from persecution and murder.

We beg of you, in the name of God, to do justice and love mercy in the administration of your office. We ask that "extended voluntary departure" be granted to refugees from Central America and that current deportation proceedings against these victims be stopped.

Until such time, we will not cease to extend the sanctuary of the church. Obedience to God requires this of us all.

Sources: Gary E. McCuen, ed., *The Religious Right* (Hudson, WI, G. E. McCuen, 1989); Ann Crittenden, *Sanctuary* (New York, Weidenfeld & Nicolson, 1988).

CONCLUSION

Taken as a whole, the years from 1981 through 1992 brought transformations that redirected the course of American life. Because many changes were associated with national policy choices, it is fair to call this the era of the Reagan revolution. The astonishing collapse of the Soviet Union ended 40 years of Cold War. New political leadership in Washington reversed the 50-year expansion of federal government programs to deal with economic and social inequities. Prosperity alternated with recessions that shifted the balance between regions. Economic inequality increased after narrowing for a generation at the same time that more and more leaders proclaimed that unregulated markets could best meet social needs. Middle-class Latinos and African Americans made substantial gains, while many other minority Americans sank deeper into poverty.

At the same time, it is important to recognize that every revolution has its precursors. Intellectuals have been clarifying the justifications for Reagan administration actions since the 1960s. The Reagan-Bush years extended changes that began in the 1970s, particularly the conservative economic policies and military buildup of the troubled Carter administration. Intervention in the Persian Gulf amplified U.S. policies that had been in place since the CIA intervened in Iran in 1953. The outbreak of violence in Los Angeles after the Rodney King verdict showed that race relations remained tense, complicated by the growing numbers of Latinos and immigrants from Asia who competed with African Americans for economic advancement.

In 1992, the United States stood as the undisputed world power. Its economy was poised for a surge of growth at the same time that rivals such as Japan were mired in economic crisis. It was the leader in scientific research and the development of new technologies. Its military capacities far surpassed those of any rival and seemed to offer a free hand in shaping the world—capacities that would be tested and utilized in the new century.

REVIEW QUESTIONS

1. Is it accurate to talk about a Reagan Revolution in U.S. politics? Did Reagan's presidency change the economic environment for workers and business corporations? How did economic changes in the 1980s affect the prospects of the richest and poorest Americans?

2. How did American ideas about the proper role of government change during the 1980s? What was the basis of these changes?

3. What caused the breakup of the Soviet Union and the end of the Cold War? Did U.S. foreign policy under Reagan and Bush contribute significantly to the withdrawal of Soviet power from eastern Europe? Did the collapse of the USSR show the strength of the United States and its allies or the weakness of Soviet Communism?

4. How did the United States use military force during the Reagan and Bush administrations? Did military actions achieve the expected goals?

5. What were some of the important economic trends that shifted American growth toward the Sunbelt (South and West)? How has immigration from other nations affected the different American regions?

6. What changes in family roles and sexual behavior became divisive political issues? How have churches responded to cultural changes? What are some of the ways in which churches and religious leaders have tried to influence political decisions?

7. How did U.S. military involvement in Southeast Asia in the 1960s continue to affect American society for decades to come?

PEARSON myhistorylab CONNECTIONS

Reinforce what you learned in this chapter by studying the many documents, images, maps, review tools, and videos available at **www.myhistorylab.com.**

READ AND REVIEW

✓●—|Study and **Review** on **myhistorylab.com** STUDY PLAN: CHAPTER 30

📖●—|Read the **Document** on **myhistorylab.com**

George H. W. Bush, Inaugural Address (1989)

Patricia Morrisroe, "Yuppies — The New Class" (1985)

Paul Craig Roberts, The Supply-Side Revolution (1984)

Ronald Reagan, First Inaugural Address (1981)

T. Boone Pickens, "My Case for Reagan" (1984)

George Bush, Allied Military Action in the Persian Gulf (1991)

Cecelia Rosa Avila, Third Generation Mexican American (1988)

Jesse Jackson, Common Ground (1988)

Ronald Reagan, Iran Contra Address (March 4, 1987)

Ronald Reagan, The Air Traffic Controllers Strike (1981)

William Julius Wilson, The Urban Underclass (1980)

🔍—|View the **Map** on **myhistorylab.com**

America's Move to the Sunbelt, 1970–1981

The Middle East in the 1980s and 1990s

RESEARCH AND EXPLORE

📖●—|Read the **Document** on **myhistorylab.com**

Personal Journeys Online

From Then to Now Online: Women and Office Work

Exploring America: Growing Inequality

👁—|Watch the **Video** on **myhistorylab.com**

George Bush Presidential Campaign Ad: The Revolving Door

Oliver North Hearing

Evangelical Religion and Politics, Then and Now

President Bush on the Gulf War

Ronald Reagan on the Wisdom of Tax Cuts

———————— ((●—|Listen on **myhistorylab.com** ————————

Hear the audio files for Chapter 30 at
www.myhistorylab.com.

31

Complacency, Crisis, and Global Reengagement • • 1993–2010

((•─Listen on **myhistorylab.com**

Hear the audio files for Chapter 31 at **www.myhistorylab.com.**

FOCUS QUESTIONS

WHAT ISSUES did Bill Clinton capitalize on in his 1992 presidential campaign?

WHAT ROLE did new information technology play in the economic boom of the 1990s?

WHAT GAINS did women and minorities make in national politics in the 1990s?

WHAT WERE the key elements of George W. Bush's agenda?

HOW DID the government and the American people respond to the enormous challenges of the first decade of the twenty-first century?

Survivors of Hurricane Katrina struggle to reach temporary safety at the Louisiana Superdome in New Orleans on August 30, 2005.

ONE AMERICAN JOURNEY

When Katrina came and left, we started clapping.... I looked out the window and I said, "Lord, look at this here. We got to roll up our sleeves and start cleaning up."... I had this little storm tracker radio ... I'm listening, and I'm looking at our automobile, and it was being submerged every minute that went by. I'm saying, "Something is wrong, because this water should be receding, but it's coming in faster."... I heard the man on the radio say, "If you're held up anywhere in New Orleans, you need to try your best to make it to the Superdome or convention center, because the levees have been breached and we can't stop the water."

The Superdome was about half a mile away.... we had a few light things like a toothbrush and your driver's license. So we had to walk through the water to about our waist. At the time there was just a lot of stuff from the automobiles like gas, oil, and stuff like that in the water. We saw some dead bodies as we were walking ... We left about 10:00, and we got there about 11:00 or 12:00.

We thought we was going to a shelter, but it was more of a prison. Outside the Superdome, we was searched by the military.... Soon as we got in there, I knew something wasn't right.... There wasn't no effort to try and get us out, but they constantly was bringing more people into the Superdome.

You could count the white people in the rest of the Superdome on one hand. I say 99 percent was black and poor. I know everybody else feels like we weren't in a major city in America, our country.

Kevin Owens, in D'Ann R. Penner and Keith C. Ferdinand, *Overcoming Katrina: African American Voices from the Crescent City and Beyond* (Palgrave Macmillan, 2008).

KEVIN OWENS was among the tens of thousands of New Orleans residents who were flooded out of their homes in August 2005 when levees failed in the aftermath of Hurricane Katrina. Like many others, his first Katrina journey took him and his family to temporary safety in the Louisiana Superdome, where overcrowding and lack of food and sanitation meant days of misery. His second Katrina journey came when federal officials evacuated Superdome refugees to Texas and his third when he and his family left Texas for a job in Birmingham, Alabama. He has returned to New Orleans to assess the damage to his house and told his interviewer that he'd like to be part of the rebuilding process. He felt in the meanwhile "like I've been robbed of everything I love." As of 2009, the city's population was still down 130,000, 30 percent, from the pre-Katrina total.

The disaster of Hurricane Katrina struck many Americans as proof that the nation was in trouble. It followed the terrorist attacks of September 11, 2001, and a war in Iraq where the United States seemed unable to consolidate its early victories, while the inadequate emergency response in New Orleans showed deep problems at home. The events in these first years of the twenty-first century ended a decade of prosperity at home and complacency about the place of the United States in the world. In the new century Americans struggled to cope with deeply partisan politics, to cope with a fast-changing and troubled economy, and to understand their changing place in the world.

Politics of the Center

In the race for president in 1992, Bill Clinton promised economic leadership and attention to everyday problems. He promised to reduce government bureaucracy and the deficit, touted the value of stable families, and talked about healthcare and welfare reform. His message revealed an insight into the character of the United States in the 1990s. What mattered most were down-to-earth issues, not the distant problems of foreign policy, which seemed to have little urgency after the end of the Cold War. Bill Clinton's election, first term, and reelection in 1996 showed the attraction of pragmatic policies and the political center in a two-party system.

The Election of 1992: A New Generation

The mid-1990s brought a new generation into the political arena. The members of "Generation X" came of voting age with deep worries about the foreclosing of opportunities. They worried that previous administrations had ignored growing economic divisions and let the competitive position of the United States deteriorate. The range of suggested solutions differed widely—individual moral reform, a stronger labor movement, leaner competition in world markets—but the generational concern was clear.

This generational change made 1992 one of the most volatile national elections in decades. A baby boomer and successful governor of Arkansas who was not widely known nationally, Democrat Bill Clinton decided that George H. W. Bush was vulnerable when more senior Democrats opted to pass on the contest. Clinton made sure that the Democrats fielded a full baby boomer (and southern) ticket by choosing as his running mate the equally youthful Tennessean Albert Gore Jr.

Bush, the last politician of the World War II generation to gain the White House, won renomination by beating back the archconservative Patrick Buchanan,

Despite personal flaws, Bill Clinton was enormously effective as a political campaigner.

CHRONOLOGY

1969   First version of Internet (ARPAnet) launched.

1980   CNN begins broadcasting.

1991   World Wide Web launched.

1992   Bill Clinton elected president.

1993   Congress approves the North American Free Trade Agreement (NAFTA).
Congress adopts Family Leave Act.

1994   Independent Counsel Kenneth Starr begins investigation of Bill and Hillary
Clinton. Paula Jones files sexual harassment lawsuit against Bill Clinton.
Republicans sweep to control of Congress.
Federal government temporarily shuts down for lack of money.

1995   United States sends peacekeeping troops to Bosnia.

1996   Clinton wins a second term as president.

1998   Paula Jones lawsuit dismissed.
House of Representatives impeaches Clinton.

1999   Senate acquits Clinton of impeachment charges.
United States leads NATO intervention in Kosovo.

2000   George W. Bush defeats Al Gore in nation's closest presidential election.

2001   Congress passes massive ten-year tax reduction.
United States refuses to agree to Kyoto Treaty to limit global warming.
Terrorists crash airliners into World Trade Center and Pentagon.
U.S. military operations oust Taliban regime in Afghanistan.
Congress passes U.S. PATRIOT Act to combat domestic terror.

2002   United States and Russia agree to cut number of deployed nuclear warheads.
Congress creates Department of Homeland Security.
United Nations Security Council passes resolution requiring Iraq to allow open
inspections of weapons systems.

2003   U.S. and British troops invade Iraq and topple government of Saddam Hussein.
Supreme Court allows limited forms of affirmative action in university
admissions.

2004   George W. Bush reelected as president.

2005   Hurricane Katrina devastates New Orleans.
Iraq adopts new constitution.

2006   Democrats regain narrow edge in Congress.

2008   Barack Obama elected president.
United States recommits to military presence in Afghanistan while reducing
its role in Iraq.

who claimed that the last 12 years had been a long betrayal of true conservatism. The Republican National Convention in Houston showed how important cultural issues had become to the Republican Party. The party platform conformed to the beliefs of the Christian right.

The wild card was the Texas billionaire Ross Perot, whose independent campaign started with an appearance on a television talk show. Perot loved flip charts, distanced himself from professional politicians, and claimed to talk sense to the American people. He also tried to occupy the political center. In May, Perot outscored both Bush and Clinton in opinion polls, but his behavior became increasingly erratic. He withdrew from the race and then reentered after floating stories that he was the target of dark conspiracies.

Bush campaigned as a foreign policy expert. He expected voters to reward him for the end of the Cold War, but he ignored anxieties about the nation's direction at home. His popularity had surged immediately after the Persian Gulf War, only to fall as the country became mired in a recession. Clinton hammered away at economic concerns, appealing to swing voters, such as suburban independents and blue-collar Reagan Democrats. He presented himself as the leader of new, pragmatic, and livelier Democrats.

Election day gave the Clinton-Gore ticket 43 percent of the popular vote, Bush 38 percent, and Perot 19 percent. Clinton held the Democratic core of northern and midwestern industrial states and loosened the Republican hold on the South and West (see Map 31–1).

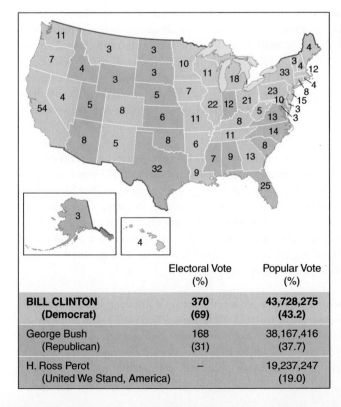

	Electoral Vote (%)	Popular Vote (%)
BILL CLINTON **(Democrat)**	**370** **(69)**	**43,728,275** **(43.2)**
George Bush (Republican)	168 (31)	38,167,416 (37.7)
H. Ross Perot (United We Stand, America)	–	19,237,247 (19.0)

MAP 31–1 · The Election of 1992 Bill Clinton defeated George H. W. Bush in 1992 by reviving the Democratic Party in the industrial Northeast and enlisting new Democratic voters in the western states, where he appealed both to Hispanic immigrants and to people associated with fast-growing high-tech industries. He won reelection in 1996 with the same pattern of support. However, the coalition was an unstable combination of "Old Democrats," associated with older industries and labor unions, and "New Democrats," favoring economic change, free trade, and globalization.

▶ *What explains Bill Clinton's strength in the South and the West? How would you explain his victories in Georgia and Louisiana?*

POLICING THE WORLD

Although Clinton was much more interested in domestic policies, he inherited a confused expectation that the United States could use its military and economic power to keep the world on an even keel and counter ethnic hatred without incurring serious risks to itself. During the administration's first years, U.S. diplomats helped broker an Israel-PLO accord that gave Palestinians self-government in Gaza and the West Bank, only to watch extremists on both sides undermine the accords and plunge Israel into a near–civil war by 2002. The world also benefited from a gradual reduction of nuclear arsenals and from a 1996 treaty to ban the testing of nuclear weapons.

Bosnia and Kosovo. Clinton reluctantly committed the United States to a multinational effort to end the bloody civil war in ethnically and religiously divided Bosnia in 1995. In the early 1990s, the former Communist nation of Yugoslavia, in southeastern Europe, fragmented into five independent nations: Slovenia, Macedonia, Croatia, Bosnia, and Yugoslavia (the name retained by the predominantly Serbian nation with its capital at Belgrade). Bosnia, divided both ethnically and religiously between Christians and Muslims, erupted in bitter civil war. Christian Serbs, supported by Belgrade, engaged in massacres and deportations of Muslim Bosnians with the goal of creating "ethnically clean" Serbian districts. Too late to stop most bloodshed, NATO troops after 1995 enforced a brittle peace accord and a division of territory into Bosnian and Serb sectors under a shaky federated government.

The U.S. military revisited the same part of Europe in 1999, when the United States and Britain led NATO's intervention in Kosovo. The overwhelming majority of people in this Yugoslav province were ethnic Albanians who had chafed under the control of the Serb-controlled Yugoslav government. When a Kosovar independence movement began a rebellion, Yugoslav president Slobodan Milosevic responded with brutal repression that threatened to drive over 1 million ethnic Albanians out of the province. To protect the Kosovars, NATO in March 1999 began a bombing campaign that targeted Yugoslav military bases and forces in Kosovo. In June, Yugoslavia agreed to withdraw its troops and make way for a multinational NATO peacekeeping force, marking a measured success for U.S. policy.

The Reinvention of NATO. To satisfy Russia, the peacekeeping force that entered Kosovo in June was technically a U.S. operation, but it was a reinvented NATO that negotiated with Yugoslavia. The new NATO is a product of the new Europe of the 1990s. A key step was expansion into the former Soviet sphere in eastern Europe. In 1999, NATO formally admitted Poland, Hungary, and the Czech Republic over the objections of Russia. Three years later, NATO agreed to give Russia a formal role in discussions about a number of its policy decisions, further eroding the barriers of the Cold War, and it added another nine nations of eastern Europe in 2004 and 2009.

Clinton's Neoliberalism. Domestic policy attracted Clinton's greatest interest, and his first term can be divided into two parts. In 1993–1994, he worked with a slim Democratic majority in Congress to modernize the U.S. economy, taking advantage of an economic upturn that lasted for most of the decade. In 1995 and 1996, however, he faced solid Republican majorities, the result of an unanticipated Republican tide in the November 1994 elections.

The heart of Clinton's agenda was an effort to make the United States economy more equitable domestically and more competitive internationally. These goals marked Clinton as a **neoliberal** who envisioned a partnership between a leaner government and a dynamic private sector. Steps to "reinvent" government cut federal employment below Reagan administration levels. A new tax bill reversed some of the inequities of the 1980s by increasing taxes on the wealthiest 1.2 percent of households. In early 1993, Clinton pushed through the Family and Medical Leave Act, which provided up to 12 weeks of unpaid leave for workers with newborns or family emergencies and had been vetoed twice by George H. W. Bush.

Clinton's biggest setback was the failure of comprehensive healthcare legislation. The goals seemed simple at first: containment of healthcare costs and extension of basic medical insurance from 83 percent of Americans under age 65 to 100 percent. In the abstract, voters agreed that something needed to be done.

Clinton appointed his wife, Hillary Rodham Clinton, to head the healthcare task force. Many found this an inappropriate role for a first lady. The plan that emerged from the White House ran to 1,342 pages of complex regulations, with something for everyone to dislike. Thus the reform effort went nowhere.

CONTRACT WITH AMERICA AND THE ELECTION OF 1996

Conservative political ideology and personal animosity against the Clintons were both part of the background for an extraordinary off-year election in 1994, in which voters defeated dozens of incumbents and gave Republicans control of Congress. For most of 1995, the new speaker of the House, Newt Gingrich of Georgia, dominated political headlines as he pushed the **Contract with America**, the official Republican campaign platform for the 1994 elections, which called for a revolutionary reduction in federal responsibilities.

Clinton lay low and let the new Congress attack environmental protections, propose cuts in federal benefits for the elderly, and try to slice the capital-gains tax to help the rich. As Congress and president battled over the budget, congressional Republicans refused to authorize interim spending and forced the federal government to shut down for more than three weeks between November 1995 and January 1996. Gingrich was the clear loser in public opinion, both for the shutdowns and for his ideas. Democrats painted Gingrich and his congressional allies as a radical fringe who wanted to gut Medicare and Medicaid, undermine education, punish legal immigrants, and sell off national parks—core values and programs that most Americans wanted to protect.

After the budget confrontations, 1996 brought a series of measures to reward work—a centrist position acceptable to most Americans. The minimum wage increased. Congress made pension programs easier for employers to create and made health insurance portable when workers changed jobs. After tough negotiations, Clinton signed bipartisan legislation to "end welfare as we know it." **Temporary Assistance for Needy Families (TANF)** replaced Aid to Families with Dependent Children (AFDC). TANF had strict requirements that aid recipients be seeking work or be enrolled in schooling, and it set a time limit on assistance. By 2001, the number of public-assistance recipients had declined 58 percent from its 1994 high, but there are doubts that many of the former recipients have found jobs adequate to support their families.

Clinton's reelection in 1996 was a virtual replay of 1992. His opponent, Robert Dole, represented the World War II generation of politicians. Because the nation was prosperous and at peace, and because Clinton had claimed the political center and sounded like Dwight Eisenhower, the results were never in doubt. Clinton became the first Democratic president to be elected to a second term since Franklin Roosevelt. The Clinton-Gore ticket took 70 percent of the electoral votes and 49 percent of the popular vote (versus 41 percent for Dole and 9 percent for a recycled Ross Perot). Clinton easily won the Northeast, the industrial Midwest, and the Far West; Hispanic voters alienated by anti-immigrant rhetoric from the Republicans helped Clinton also take the usually Republican states of Florida and Arizona.

The election confirmed that voters liked the pragmatic center. They were cautious about the free-market advocates on the extreme right, showing little interest in having Republicans actually enact the Contract with America. They were equally unimpressed by liberal advocates of entitlements on the European model. What voters wanted was to continue the reduction of the federal role in domestic affairs that had begun in the 1980s without damaging social insurance programs.

THE DANGERS OF EVERYDAY LIFE

Part of the background for the sometimes vicious politics of mid-decade was a sense of individual insecurity and fear of violence that coexisted with an economy that was booming in some sectors but still leaving many Americans behind.

Random Violence and Domestic Terrorism. One after another, headlines and news flashes in the 1990s proclaimed terrifying random acts of violence. The greatest losses of life came in Waco, Texas, and in Oklahoma City. On April 19, 1993, federal agents raided the fortified compound of the Branch Davidian cult outside Waco after a 51-day siege. The raid triggered a fire, probably set from inside, that killed more than 80 people. On the second anniversary of the Waco raid, Timothy McVeigh packed a rented truck with explosive materials and detonated it in front of the federal office building in downtown Oklahoma City, presumably as revenge against what he considered an oppressive government. The blast collapsed the entire front of the nine-story building and killed 169 people. In April 1999, two high school students in Littleton, Colorado, took rifles and pipe bombs into Columbine High School to kill 12 classmates, a teacher, and themselves; schools in Arkansas and Oregon experienced similar terror from gun-wielding students.

Gun Control. Workplace assassins, schoolroom murders, and domestic terrorism invigorated efforts to monitor access to firearms. The Brady Handgun Violence Prevention Act, passed in 1994, took its name from James Brady, President Reagan's first press secretary, who was seriously injured in the 1981 attempt to kill the president. The act set up a waiting period and background checks for purchases of firearms from retailers, pawnshops, and licensed firearm dealers.

Gun control was political dynamite, for Americans have drastically differing understandings of the Second Amendment, which states: "A well regulated militia, being necessary to the security of a free State, the right of the people to keep and bear arms, shall not be infringed." The powerful National Rifle Association, the major lobby for gun owners and manufacturers, now argued that the amendment establishes an absolute individual right. Federal courts for many decades interpreted the Second Amendment to apply to the possession of weapons in connection with citizen service in a government-organized militia. In June 2008, however, the Supreme Court in *District of Columbia v. Heller* struck down the ban in Washington, DC, on the ownership or possession of handguns. The majority in the 5-4 decision argued that the Second Amendment implied an individual right to own firearms. At the same time, it left most state and federal firearms laws intact by allowing restrictions on individual categories of weapons and regulations on acquisition and use that fall short of prohibitions.

Crime and the War on Drugs. Conservatives, including many gun-ownership advocates, put their faith in strict law enforcement as the best route to public security. The 1990s saw numerous states adopt "three-strike" measures that drastically increased penalties for individuals convicted of a third crime. The number of people serving sentences of a year or longer in state and federal prisons grew from 316,000 in 1980 to 740,000 in 1990 and 1,422,000 in 2004, with another 714,000 being held for shorter periods in local jails. By 2007, more than one in every 100 adults was behind bars.

The war on drugs, begun in the 1980s, was the biggest contributor to the prison boom. As the drug war dragged on through the 1990s, the federal government poured billions of dollars into efforts to stop illegal drugs from crossing the Mexican border or from landing by boat or airplane. The United States intervened in South American nations that produced cocaine, particularly Peru and Colombia, aiding local military efforts to uproot crops and battle drug lords. Meanwhile, aggressive enforcement of domestic laws against drug possession or sales filled U.S. prison cells. The antidrug campaign fell most heavily on minorities.

In fact, crime fell steadily for a decade after reaching a peak in the early 1990s. The rate of violent crime as reported by the FBI (murder, rape, robbery, aggravated assault) fell by 37 percent from 1993 to 2007, including a 40 percent drop in the number of murders. The rate of major property crimes (burglary, larceny-theft, and motor vehicle theft) fell by 31 percent over the same period. Easing fears combined with escalating costs to cause some states to rethink the reliance on prison terms.

Debating the Death Penalty. Governor George Ryan of Illinois was elected in 1998 as a conservative Republican. In January 2003, this small-town businessman emptied death row in the Illinois prison system by commuting the death sentences of 167 convicted murderers to prison terms of life or less. He asserted that his review of individual cases had led him to doubt the justice of the death-penalty system as a whole, which he said is "haunted by the demons of error—error in determining guilt and error in determining who among the guilty deserves to die."

Discussion of flaws in the application of the death penalty reveals basic disagreements about the best approach to public order. Thirty-eight of the 50 states impose the death penalty, although sixteen states have not carried out an execution since 1976. The majority of Americans have accepted capital punishment as a flawed but necessary defense for society.

In contrast, a passionate minority thinks that capital punishment is a tool so bent and blunted as to be worse than useless. They point out that the deterrent effect of capital punishment is weak at best; murder rates are often higher in death-penalty states than in similar states without the penalty. They note that African Americans and Latinos receive the death penalty far more often than whites charged with the same crimes. The nation's Roman Catholic bishops in 1999 condemned the death penalty, and in *Atkins v. Virginia* (2002) the Supreme Court forbade the execution of mentally retarded persons. The debate about capital punishment exemplifies the fault lines that divide Americans as they try to balance the demands of justice and public order.

MORALITY AND PARTISANSHIP

If the economy was the fundamental news of the later 1990s, Bill Clinton's personal life was the hot news. Years of rumors, innuendos, and lawsuits culminated in 1999 in the nation's second presidential impeachment trial. President Clinton's problems began in 1994 with the appointment of a special prosecutor to investigate possible fraud in the **Whitewater** development, an Arkansas land promotion in which Bill and Hillary Clinton had invested in the 1980s. The probe by Kenneth Starr, the independent counsel, however, expanded into a wide-ranging investigation that encompassed the firing of the White House travel-office staff early in 1993, the suicide of White House aide Vincent Foster, and the sexual behavior of the president. Meanwhile, Paula Jones had brought a lawsuit claiming sexual harassment by then-governor Clinton while she was a state worker in Arkansas. The investigation of Whitewater brought convictions of several friends and former associates of the Clintons, but no evidence pointing decisively at either Bill or Hillary Clinton.

The legal landscape changed in January 1998, with allegations about an affair between the president and Monica Lewinsky, a former White House intern. Lewinsky admitted to the relationship privately and then to Starr's staff after the president had denied it in a sworn deposition for the Paula Jones case. This opened Clinton to charges of perjury and obstruction of justice.

In the fall of 1998, the Republican leaders who controlled Congress decided that Clinton's statements and misstatements justified initiating the process of impeachment. In December, the majority on the House Judiciary Committee recommended four articles of impeachment, or specific charges against the president, to the House of Representatives. By a partisan vote, the full House approved two of the charges and forwarded them to the Senate. The formal trial of the charges by the Senate began in January 1999 and ended on February 12. Moderate Republicans joined Democrats to ensure that the Senate would fall far short of the two-thirds majority required for conviction and removal from office.

A NEW ECONOMY?

Within months of the impeachment trial, Americans had a new worry. In the closing months of 1999, many people stocked up on canned food and kerosene, powdered milk, ammunition, and cash. They were preparing to survive, not foreign invasion or natural disaster, but rather the possible collapse of the global computer network. Early programs had used only two digits for years in dates because memory space was precious, leading to fears that old programs would treat 2000 as 1900 or choke in electronic confusion. Europeans called the problem the "millennium bug," Americans the "Y2K" problem (for Year 2000). In fact, almost nothing happened.

In larger perspective, the Y2K worries illustrate how much the American economy had changed in the preceding decade, and how mysterious the changes seemed. More than ever, it was a global economy. And, unlike any time in the past, it was an economy that depended on electronic computing to manage and transmit vast quantities of data.

The impact of the electronic revolution was still being absorbed into the structures and routines of everyday life as Americans put Y2K behind them and looked to a new century.

THE PROSPEROUS 1990S

From 1992 through 2000, Americans enjoyed nine years of continuous economic expansion. Unemployment dropped from 7.2 percent in 1992 to 4.0 percent at the start of 2000 as American businesses created more than 12 million new jobs. Key states like California rebounded from economic recession with new growth driven by high-tech industries, entertainment, and foreign trade. The stock market soared during the nineties; rising demand for shares in established blue-chip companies and new **Internet** firms swelled the value of individual portfolios, retirement accounts, and pension funds. The rate of home ownership rose after declining for 15 years. Prosperity also trickled down to Americans at the bottom of the economic ladder. The proportion of Americans in poverty dropped to 12 percent in 1999, and the gap between rich and poor began to narrow (slightly) for the first time in two decades.

The economic boom was great news for the federal budget. Tight spending and rising personal income turned perennial deficits into surpluses for 1998, 1999, and 2000. Reduced borrowing by the U.S. Treasury resulted in low interest rates, which further fueled corporate expansion and consumer spending. In 1997, Clinton signed a deficit-reduction bill that seemed to promise fiscal stability.

Behind the statistics were substantial gains in the efficiency of the U.S. economy. International rivals, especially Japan, experienced severe economic slumps in the mid-1990s. In the United States, in contrast, by the end of the decade the productivity of manufacturing workers was increasing more than 4 percent per year, the highest rate in a generation. Part of the gain was the payoff from the painful business restructuring and downsizing of the 1970s and 1980s. Another cause was improvements in efficiency from the full incorporation of personal computers and electronic communication into everyday life and business practice. In the later 1990s, fast-growing information-based industries seemed to be jump-starting another era of prosperity. However, many individual technology companies failed in 2001 and 2002 in a "dotcom bust" that dragged down the stock market for several years, and the real estate bubble that followed diverted investment from productive uses, leaving the United States weaker rather than stronger in relation to rising nations like China.

THE SERVICE ECONOMY

At the beginning of the twenty-first century, the United States was an economy of services. As fewer Americans drove tractors and toiled on assembly lines, more became service workers. The service sector includes everyone not directly involved in producing and processing physical products. Service workers range from lawyers to hair stylists, from police officers who write traffic tickets to theater employees who sell movie tickets. In 1965, services already accounted for more than half of American jobs. By the end of the 1990s, their share rose to more than 75 percent.

Service work varies greatly. At the bottom of the scale are minimum-wage jobs held mostly by women, immigrants, and the young, such as cleaning people, childcare workers, hospital orderlies, and fast-food workers. These positions offer little in terms of advancement, job security, or benefits. In contrast, many of the best new jobs are in information industries. Teaching, research, advertising, mass communications, and professional consulting depend on producing and manipulating information. All of these fields have grown. They add to national wealth by creating and applying new ideas rather than by supplying standardized products and services.

The information economy flourishes in large cities with libraries, universities, research hospitals, advertising agencies, and corporate headquarters. New York's bankers and stockbrokers made Manhattan an island of prosperity in the 1980s. Pittsburgh, with major universities and corporate headquarters, made the transition to the information economy even while its steel industry failed.

The rise of the service economy had political consequences. Rapid expansion of jobs in state and local government triggered popular revolts against state taxes that started in 1978 with passage of California's Proposition 13, which limited property taxes, and continued into the 1990s. Another growth industry was healthcare. Spending on medical and health services amounted to 15 percent of the gross domestic product in 2000, up from 5 percent in 1960. The need to share this huge expense fairly was the motivation for Medicare and Medicaid in the 1960s and the search for a national health insurance program in the 1990s and beyond.

THE HIGH-TECH SECTOR

The epitome of the "sunrise" economy was electronics, which grew hand-in-glove with the defense budget. The first computers in the 1940s were derived in part from wartime code-breaking efforts. Employment in computer manufacturing rose in the mid-1960s with the expansion of mainframe computing. Large machines from IBM, Honeywell, NCR, and other established corporations required substantial support facilities and staff and were used largely by universities, government agencies, and corporations. In the 1970s, new companies began to build smaller, specialized machines for such purposes as word processing. One cluster of firms sprang up outside Boston around Route 128, benefiting from proximity to MIT and other Boston-area universities. California's **Silicon Valley**, north of San Jose, took off with corporate spinoffs and civilian applications of military technologies and benefited from proximity to Stanford University.

Extraordinary improvements in computing capacity drove the electronics boom. At the start of the microcomputer era, Intel co-founder Gordon Moore predicted that the number of transistors on a microchip would double every 18 months, with consequent increases in performance and drops in price. "Moore's Law" worked at least through the opening of the new century as producers moved from chips with 5,000 transistors to ones with 50,000,000. The practical result was a vast increase in the capacities and portability of computers, with personal computers and consumer electronics becoming part of everyday life in the 1990s.

AN INSTANT SOCIETY

The spread of consumer electronics helped to create an "instant society." Americans in the 1990s learned to communicate by e-mail and to look up information on the **World Wide Web**. The United States was increasingly a society that depended on instant information and expected instant results.

The Internet grew out of concerns about defense and national security. Its prototype was ARPAnet (for Advanced Research Projects Administration of the Defense Department), intended to be a communication system that could survive nuclear attack. As the Internet evolved into a system that connected universities and national weapons laboratories, the Pentagon gave up control in 1984 (when there were only 1,000 Internet-connected devices rather than the billion of 2008). Through the 1980s, it was used mainly by scientists and academics to share data and communicate by e-mail. The World Wide Web, created in 1991, expanded the Internet's uses by allowing organizations and companies to create websites that placed political and commercial information only a few clicks away from wired consumers.

Instant satisfaction was one of the principles behind the boom of dotcom businesses in 1998, 1999, and 2000. Many were services that repackaged information for quick access. Others were essentially on-line versions of mail order catalogs, but capable of listing hundreds of thousands of items. Still others were instant-delivery services designed to save consumers a trip to the video store or minimart.

Mobile telephones, or cell phones, were part of the same instant society. They exploited underutilized radio bands and communication satellites to allow wireless conversations among cells—geographic areas linked by special microwave broadcasting towers. Technological changes again drove demand. The chunky car phone built into a vehicle gave way to sleek handheld devices the size of *Star Trek* communicators and then to personal digital assistants like the iPhone and BlackBerry. Wireless phone companies originally sold their phones as emergency backups and business necessities, just as wired telephones had been sold in the first years of the twentieth century. The 5 million American cell phone subscribers of 1990 had exploded to 255 million in 2007.

Meanwhile the twenty-first century Internet had become another inescapable method of communication. Direct travel reservation sites pushed travel agencies out of business. Young people found and kept friends with MySpace and Facebook. Columns of classified ads in newspapers shrank as craigslist expanded. Listings on eBay competed with face-to-face garage sales, and businesses invested in websites rather than Yellow Pages display ads.

IN THE WORLD MARKET

Instant access to business and financial information accelerated the globalizing of the American economy. Expanding foreign commerce had become a deliberate goal of national policy with the General Agreement on Tariffs and Trade (GATT) in 1947. GATT regularized international commerce after World War II and helped to secure one of the goals of World War II by ensuring that world markets remained open to American industry. The Trade Expansion Act in 1962 authorized President Kennedy to make reciprocal trade agreements to cut tariffs by up to 50 percent so as to keep American companies competitive in the new European Common Market.

With the help of national policy and booming economies overseas, the value of U.S. imports and exports more than doubled, from 7 percent of the gross domestic product in 1965 to 16 percent in 1990—the largest percentage since World War I. Americans in the 1970s began to worry about a "colonial" status, in which the United States exported food, lumber, and minerals and imported automobiles and television sets. By the 1980s, foreign economic competitiveness and trade deficits, especially with Japan, became issues of national concern that continued into the new century, when China and India were emerging as the newest competitors.

The effects of international competition were more complex than "Japan-bashers" acknowledged. Mass-production industries, such as textiles and aluminum, suffered from cheaper and sometimes higher-quality imports, but many specialized industries and services, such as Houston's oil equipment and exploration firms, thrived. Globalization also created new regional winners and losers. In 1982, the United States began to do more business with Pacific nations than with Europe.

The Politics of Trade. More recent steps to expand the global reach of the U.S. economy were the **North American Free Trade Agreement (NAFTA)** in 1993 and a new worldwide General Agreement on Tariffs and Trade (GATT) approved in 1994. Negotiated by Republican George Bush and pushed through Congress in 1993 by Democrat Bill Clinton, NAFTA combined 25 million Canadians, 90 million Mexicans, and 250 million U.S. consumers in a single "common market" similar to that of western Europe. This enlarged free-trade zone was intended to open new markets and position the United States to compete more effectively against the European Community and Japan. The agreement may have been a holdover from the Bush years, but it matched Clinton's ideas about reforming the American economy.

NAFTA was a hard pill for many Democrats, and it revived the old debate between free traders and protectionists. Support was strongest from businesses and industries that sought foreign customers, including agriculture and electronics. Opponents included organized labor, communities already hit by industrial shutdowns, and environmentalists worried about lax controls on industrial pollution in Mexico. In contrast to the nineteenth-century arguments for protecting infant industries, new industries now looked to foreign markets, whereas uncompetitive, older firms hoped for protected domestic markets. The readjustments from NAFTA have produced obvious pain in the form of closed factories or farms made unprofitable by cheaper imports, while its gains are less visible—a new job here, larger sales there.

The **World Trade Organization (WTO)**, which replaced GATT in 1996, became the unexpected target of a global protest movement. Seattle officials, committed to promoting Seattle as a world-class city, lobbied hard to get the 1999 WTO meeting. With finance and foreign affairs ministers and heads of government expected to attend, it would give Seattle world attention. Instead, it gave the city a headache. Fifty thousand protesters converged on the meeting, held from November 30 to December 4, 1999.

Protesters were convinced that the WTO is a tool of transnational corporations that flout local labor and environmental protections in the name of "free trade" that benefits only the wealthy nations and their businesses. WTO defenders pointed to the long-term effects of open trade in raising net production in the world economy and thereby making more wealth available for developing nations. Opponents asserted, in turn, that such wealth never reaches the workers and farmers in those nations. American opponents demanded that U.S. firms, such as sportswear companies, that make their products overseas make sure that their overseas workers have decent living conditions and wages.

BROADENING DEMOCRACY

Closely related to the changes in the American economy were the changing composition of the American people and the continued emergence of new participants in U.S. government. Bill Clinton's first cabinet, in which three women and four minority men balanced seven white men, recognized the makeup of the American population and marked the maturing of minorities and women as distinct political constituencies. The

**Table 31.1 Immigrants 1991–2007, by Continent and by Twenty Most
                Important Countries of Origin**

Total	16,301,000	**Europe**	2,352,000
North America	6,410,000	Poland	261,000
Mexico	3,450,000	Ukraine	260,000
Dominican Republic	535,000	Russia	241,000
El Salvador	412,000	United Kingdom	246,000
Cuba	375,000	**South America**	1,157,000
Haiti	323,000	Colombia	302,000
Jamaica	323,000	**Africa**	909,000
Canada	261,000	**Oceania**	90,000
Guatemala	225,000		
Asia	5,363,000		
Philippines	920,000		
China	872,000		
India	856,000		
Vietnam	636,000		
Korea	318,000		
Pakistan	222,000		

SOURCE: *Statistical Abstract of the United States.*

first cabinet appointed by George W. Bush in 2001 included four minority men and four women, one of whom was Asian American. In both administrations, the new prominence of women and minorities in the national government followed years of growing success in cities and states.

AMERICANS IN 2000

The federal census for the year 2000 found 281,400,000 Americans in the 50 states, District of Columbia, and Puerto Rico (and probably 2–3 million more residents were not counted). The increase from 1990 was 13.2 percent, or 32,700,000. It was the largest ten-year population increase in U.S. history, evidence of the nation's prosperity and its attractiveness for immigrants. More than 12 percent of Americans had been born in other countries, the highest share since 1920 (Table 31–1). One-third of all Americans lived in four states: California, Texas, New York, and Florida. These were the key prizes in presidential elections.

The West grew the fastest. Fast growth implies young populations, and the states with the lowest average age were all western: Utah, Alaska, Idaho, and Texas. The Southwest and South also had the fastest growing metropolitan areas. Among large metro areas with over 500,000 people in 2000, all 20 of the fastest growing were in the West and Southeast.

In contrast, parts of the American midlands grew slowly. Rural counties continued to empty out in Appalachia and across the Great Plains as fewer and fewer Americans

AMERICAN VIEWS

RELIEF WORK IN AFRICA

*I*n the early twenty-first century, thousands of Americans work in other countries for relief and reconstruction organizations such as the Peace Corps, CARE, and Mercy Corps, and thousands more do similar work under the sponsorship of religious groups. In 2003, Peggy Senger Parsons, an evangelical Quaker minister and trauma counselor from "far off Planet America" spent several months in the small African nation of Burundi, trying to help residents develop strategies for dealing with the impacts of civil war and endemic criminal violence. Here are some excerpts from her blog.

■ What does Peggy Parsons's experience suggest about the spread of American culture around the world?

■ How does the level of personal safety in a nation such as Burundi compare to that in the United States?

■ What questions does Parsons's experience raise about the challenges of building peace and democracy in troubled and divided nations?

■ How might religiously based work in other countries differ from efforts sponsored by the U.S. government, such as with the Peace Corps? How might it be the same?

We function in Swahili and French, mine bad and hers good.... I have been in the company of four children who have been giving me language and cultural tutorials, which I exchanged for introducing them to the Beatles.

Pavement is a subjective concept in Burundi. Traffic is extremely real. We fly in a zig zag pattern through cars, trucks, bicycles, and lots of little children. If you notice a lack of angels in America, it is because they are all in Burundi keeping the babies from being killed on the road.... And in four days I am totally immune to the sight of guys with automatic weapons. My host says that he cannot tell a rebel from a Burundi soldier and sometimes neither can they.

We have a night watchman... we live in a walled compound and he is there to keep us safe. His only weapon is a whistle.

were needed for mining and farming or for the small towns associated with those industries.

Another important trend was increasing ethnic and racial diversity. Hispanics were the fastest growing group in the U.S. population. Although immigrants concentrated in the coastal and border states, Hispanics and Asian Americans were also spreading into interior states. Asians and Hispanics who had been in the United States for some time showed substantial economic success. Non-Hispanic whites are now a minority in California at 47 percent, in the District of Columbia, in Hawaii, and in New Mexico.

The changing ethnicity of the American people promises to be increasingly apparent in coming decades. Immigrants tend to be young adults who are likely to form families, and birth rates have been high among Hispanics and Asian Americans. The result is a sort of multiethnic baby boom. Over the coming decades, the effects of ethnic

The children tell me that if there is trouble he whistles, and all the nearby watchmen whistle and then come running to help. Then I met Gadi the moneychanger. He walks around with rolls of money as big as softballs in every pocket and he does not carry a gun. He has a quiet gentle confidence that reminds me of every wiseguy I ever met in Chicago. I do not know what happens if you jump a moneychanger—but it must be bad enough that nobody tries. Some things are very familiar.

My traumatology students are amazing. They have come from great distances and at great sacrifice to study with me.... Many of the terms I need to use have no equivalent. I have learned the face that my translator makes when I give her a hard one. She signals for me to stop, and the students confer and when a consensus is reached about a newly coined phrase someone shouts *Voila!* And we have a new psychological term. My students were interviewed on Burundi National Radio. The reporter came on the second day to do a quick filler piece and stayed all afternoon and then asked to join the class. He carries a huge reel-to-reel recorder. The voices of these students went out to 22 million listeners this morning in Burundi, Congo, Rwanda, and Tanzania. They were fabulous explaining the effects of trauma and how they themselves had been helped in the class. On Friday my class thanked me for telling them the truth and for bringing them the best of myself. They compared me to a Jonah "who did not run away but ran towards her call," can't get better pay than that.

I was not prepared for the fact that my trauma class students would be such recent victims [many bearing fresh wounds from beatings or torture]. Thursday there was a bit of shooting outside of the teaching compound. I had to be told what it was—a "thump" and then a "tat, tat, tat." But it was quiet after that and we resume. After a long morning of brain physiology and learning about the left brain functions, my translator said, "Peggy have mercy on them—they say they need to sing." And so they did, all Christian music. I taught them "We Shall Overcome" and told them about Dr. King and we marched around the room singing that "I do believe, deep in my heart, that Burundi will have peace one day."

change will be apparent not only in schools but also in the workplace, popular culture, and politics.

WOMEN FROM THE GRASSROOTS TO CONGRESS

The increasing prominence of women and family issues in national politics was a steady, quiet revolution that bore fruit in the 1990s, when the number of women in Congress more than doubled. In 1981, President Reagan appointed Arizona judge Sandra Day O'Connor to be the first woman on the United States Supreme Court. In 1984, Walter Mondale chose New York Congresswoman Geraldine Ferraro as his vice presidential candidate. In 1993 Clinton appointed the second woman to the Supreme Court, U.S. Appeals Court judge Ruth Bader Ginsburg. Clinton appointee

Janet Reno was the first woman to serve as attorney general, and Madeleine K. Albright the first to serve as secretary of state. George W. Bush continued to break new ground by naming Condoleezza Rice as his national security advisor in 2001 and as secretary of state in 2005.

Political gains for women at the national level reflected their growing importance in grassroots politics. The spreading suburbs of postwar America were "frontiers" that required concerted action to solve immediate needs like adequate schools and decent parks. Because pursuit of such community services was often viewed as "woman's work" (in contrast to the "man's work" of economic development), postwar metropolitan areas offered numerous opportunities for women to engage in volunteer civic work, learn political skills, and run for local office. Moreover, new cities and suburbs had fewer established political institutions, such as political machines and strong parties; their politics were open to energetic women. Most women in contemporary politics have been more liberal than men—a difference that political scientists attribute to women's interest in the practical problems of schools, neighborhoods, and two-earner families. But women's grassroots mobilization, especially through evangelical churches, has also strengthened groups committed to conservative social values.

Regional differences have affected women's political gains. The West has long been the part of the country most open to women in state and local government and in business. Westerners have been more willing than voters in the East or South to choose women as mayors of major cities and as members of state legislatures. Many of the skills learned from politics were also useful as women played a growing role in professional and managerial occupations.

In 1991, the nomination of Judge Clarence Thomas, an African American, to the U.S. Supreme Court had ensured that everyone knew that the terms of U.S. politics were changing. Because of his conservative positions on social and civil rights issues, Thomas was a controversial nominee. Controversy deepened when law professor Anita Hill accused Thomas of harassing her sexually while she served on his staff at the Equal Employment Opportunity Commission. The accusations led to riveting hearings before a U.S. Senate committee. Critics tried to discredit Hill with vicious attacks on her character, and the committee failed to call witnesses who could have supported her claims. The public was left with Hill's plausible but unproved allegations and Thomas's equally vigorous but unproved denials. The Senate confirmed Thomas to the Supreme Court. Partisans on each side continued to believe the version that best suited their preconceptions and agendas.

Whatever the merits of her charges, Hill's badgering by skeptical senators angered millions of women. In the shadow of the hearings, women made impressive gains in the 1992 election, which pushed women's share of seats in the 50 state legislatures above 20 percent. The number of women in the U.S. Senate jumped from two to seven (and grew further to seventeen Democrats and four Republicans in 2007). The number of women serving as federal judges grew from 48 in 1981 to more than 200—roughly a quarter of the total.

Women have influenced national politics as voters as well as candidates and cabinet members. Since the 1980s, voting patterns have shown a gender gap. Women in the 1990s identified with the Democratic Party and voted for its candidates at a higher rate than men. The reasons include concerns about the effect of government spending cuts and interest in measures to support families rather than in conservative rhetoric. This gender gap has helped keep Democrats competitive and dampened the nation's conservative swing on social issues.

MINORITIES AT THE BALLOT BOX

The changing makeup of the American populace also helped black and Latino candidates for public office to increased success. After the racial violence of the 1960s, many black people turned to local politics to gain control of their own communities. The first black mayor of a major twentieth-century city was Carl Stokes in Cleveland in 1967. The 1973 election brought victories for Tom Bradley in Los Angeles, Maynard Jackson in Atlanta, and Coleman Young in Detroit. By 1983, three of the nation's four largest cities had black mayors. In 1989, Virginia made Douglas Wilder the first black governor in any state since Reconstruction.

The election of a minority mayor was sometimes more important for its symbolism than for the transfer of real power. Efforts to restructure the basis of city council elections, however, struck directly at the balance of power.

Most mid-sized cities stopped electing city councils by wards or districts during the first half of the twentieth century. Voting at large shifted power away from geographically concentrated ethnic groups. It favored business interests that claimed to speak for the city as a whole but could assign most of the costs of economic growth to older and poorer neighborhoods.

In the 1970s, minority leaders and community activists realized that a return to district voting could convert neighborhood segregation from a liability to a political resource. As amended in 1975, the federal Voting Rights Act allowed minorities to use the federal courts to challenge at-large voting systems that diluted the impact of their votes. Blacks and Mexican Americans used the act to reestablish city council districts in the late 1970s and early 1980s in city after city across the South and Southwest.

At the national level, minorities gradually increased their representation in Congress. Ben Nighthorse Campbell of Colorado, a Cheyenne, brought a Native American voice to the U.S. Senate in 1992. The number of African Americans in the House of Representatives topped 40 after 1992, with the help of districts drawn to concentrate black voters. Even after a series of Supreme Court cases invalidated districts drawn with race as the "predominant

In November 2002, Linda Sanchez (left) and Loretta Sanchez celebrate Linda's election to Congress from Los Angeles County. Loretta had won a congressional seat from Orange County in 1996, and Linda's victory made them the first sisters to serve simultaneously in the House of Representatives.

factor," however, African Americans held most of their gains, while the number of Latino members of Congress rose to 30 by 2009.

In struggling for political influence, recent immigrants have added new panethnic identities to their national identities. Hispanic activists revived the term "Chicano" to bridge the gap between recent Mexican immigrants and Latinos whose families had settled in the Southwest before the American conquest in 1848. Great gaps of experience and culture separated Chinese, Koreans, Filipinos, and Vietnamese, but they gained political recognition and influence if they dealt with other Americans as "Asians." Native Americans have similarly downplayed tribal differences in efforts to secure better opportunities for Indians as a group.

RIGHTS AND OPPORTUNITIES

The increasing presence of Latinos and African Americans in public life highlighted a set of troublesome questions about the proper balance between equal rights and equal opportunities. The debates at the end of the twentieth century replayed many of the questions that European immigration raised at the century's beginning.

Illegal Immigration and Bilingual Education. One issue is the economic impact of illegal immigration. Advocates of tight borders assert that illegal immigrants take jobs away from legal residents and eat up public assistance. Many studies, however, find that illegal immigrants fill jobs that nobody else wants. Over the long run, high employment levels among immigrants mean that their tax contributions through sales taxes and Social Security taxes and payroll deductions more than pay for their use of welfare, food stamps, and unemployment benefits, which illegal immigrants are often afraid to claim for fear of calling attention to themselves. Nevertheless, high immigration can strain local government budgets even if it benefits the nation as a whole. Partly for this reason, 60 percent of California voters approved **Proposition 187** in 1994, cutting off access to state-funded public education and healthcare for illegal immigrants.

A symbolic issue was the degree to which American institutions should accommodate non–English speakers. Referendums in Alaska (1996) and Utah (2000) raised to 26 the number of states that declared English their official language. California voters in 1998 banned bilingual public education, a system under which children whose first language was Spanish or another "immigrant" tongue were taught for several years in that language before shifting to English-language classrooms. Advocates of bilingual education claimed that it eased the transition into American society, but opponents said that it blocked immigrant children from fully assimilating into American life.

The issue of illegal immigration simmered in the 1990s, but exploded in the new century. As the total of undocumented immigrants reached 11 to 12 million by best estimates, many Americans became increasingly concerned about a porous southern border. Unlike early eras of concern about immigration that had usually coincided with economic downturns, the new immigration worries came in an era of economic prosperity. In 2007, the president and leaders in both political parties were blindsided when a carefully constructed compromise over immigration policy failed because of public outcry over provisions that many voters interpreted as amnesty for rule-breaking.

Affirmative Action. An equally divisive issue was a set of policies that originated in the 1960s as **affirmative action**, a phrase that first appeared in executive orders issued by Presidents Kennedy and Johnson. The initial goal was to require businesses that received federal contracts to "take affirmative action to ensure that applicants are employed, and that employees are treated during employment without regard for their race, creed, color, or national origin." By the 1970s, many states and cities had adopted similar policies for hiring their own employees and choosing contractors and extended affirmative action to women as well as minorities. Colleges and universities used affirmative-action policies in recruiting faculty and admitting students.

As these efforts spread, the initial goal of nondiscrimination evolved into expectations and requirements for active ("affirmative") efforts to achieve greater diversity among employees, students, or contractors. Government agencies began to set aside a small percentage of contracts for woman-owned or minority-owned firms. Cities actively worked to hire more minority police officers and firefighters. Colleges made special efforts to attract minority students. The landmark court case about affirmative action was *University of California v. Bakke* (1978). Alan Bakke was an unsuccessful applicant to the medical school at the University of California at Davis. He argued that the university had improperly set aside 16 of 100 places in its entering class for minority students, thereby engaging in reverse discrimination against white applicants. In a narrow decision, the U.S. Supreme Court ordered Bakke admitted because the only basis for his rejection had been race. At the same time, the Court stated that race or ethnicity could legally be one of several factors considered in college and university admissions as long as a specific number of places were not reserved for minorities.

In 1996, California voters took grassroots action, approving a ballot measure to eliminate state-sponsored affirmative action. One effect was to prohibit state-funded colleges and universities from using race or ethnicity as a factor in deciding which applicants to admit. In the same year, the Supreme Court let stand a lower-court ruling in *Hopwood v. Texas,* which had forbidden the University of Texas to consider race in admission decisions. The number of black freshmen in the University of Texas dropped by half in 1997 and the number of blacks and Hispanics among first-year law students by two-thirds. The results were similar at the University of California at Berkeley, where the number of blacks among entering law students dropped from twenty to one.

In 2003, the Supreme Court affirmed the basic principle of affirmative action in two cases involving admission to the University of Michigan. Aided by supporting statements filed by major corporations and by members of the U.S. military, the Court found that promoting ethnic and racial diversity among students constitutes a compelling state interest, and it approved narrowly tailored affirmative-action programs that weigh race and ethnicity along with other admissions criteria on an individual basis. But four years later, a different majority on the Court rejected public school plans in Lexington, Kentucky, and Seattle that took race into account in deciding how to match students and schools, leaving the larger issue for further court cases.

EDGING INTO A NEW CENTURY

On the evening of November 7, 2000, CBS-TV made the kind of mistake that journalists dread. Relying on questions put to a sample of voters after they cast their ballots in the presidential contest between Albert Gore Jr. and George W. Bush, the CBS newsroom first projected that Gore would win Florida and likely the election, then reversed itself and called the election for Bush, only to find that it would be days or even weeks before the votes in several pivotal states, including Florida, could be certified.

The inability to predict the outcome in 2000 was an indication of the degree to which Americans were split down the middle in their political preferences and their visions for the future. The United States entered the twenty-first century both divided and balanced, with extremes of opinion revolving around a center of basic goals and values.

THE 2000 ELECTION

On November 8, 2000, the day after their national election, Americans woke up to the news that neither Republican George W. Bush nor Democrat Albert Gore Jr. had a majority of votes in the electoral college. Although Gore held a lead in the popular vote (about 340,000 votes out of more than 100 million cast), both candidates needed a majority in Florida to win its electoral votes and the White House. After protracted protests about voting irregularities and malfunctioning voting equipment, politically divided Floridians engaged in an on-again off-again recount in key counties. The U.S. Supreme Court finally preempted the state process and ordered a halt to recounting on December 12 by the politically charged margin of 5 to 4. The result was to make Bush the winner in Florida by a few hundred votes and the winner nationwide by 271 electoral votes to 267 (see Map 31–2).

Both Bush, governor of Texas and son of President George H. W. Bush (1989–93), and Gore, vice president for the previous eight years, targeted their campaigns at middle Americans. Each offered to cut taxes, downsize the federal government, and protect

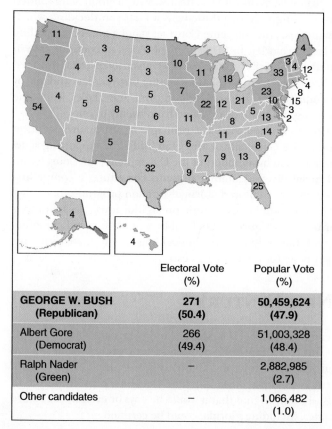

MAP 31–2 • The Election of 2000 In the nation's closest presidential election, Democrat Al Gore was most successful in the Northeast and Far West, while George W. Bush swept the South and won most of the Great Plains states. Green Party candidate Ralph Nader took most of his votes from Gore, in an ironic twist, helping to swing the election to Bush.

▶ *Compare this* map of the 2000 election results with Map 31–1: The Election of 1992. What states did George W. Bush win that Bill Clinton won in 1992? Why was Bush able to capture these states for the Republicans?

	Electoral Vote (%)	Popular Vote (%)
GEORGE W. BUSH (Republican)	**271 (50.4)**	**50,459,624 (47.9)**
Albert Gore (Democrat)	266 (49.4)	51,003,328 (48.4)
Ralph Nader (Green)	–	2,882,985 (2.7)
Other candidates	–	1,066,482 (1.0)

Social Security, differing in the details rather than the broad goals. In trying to claim the political middle, they reflected the successful political message of the Clinton administration. Voters also shaved the Republican control of Congress to razor-thin margins, further undermining any chance of radical change in either a conservative or a liberal direction. To those on the political left and right who had hoped for new directions for the nation, it looked like a formula for paralysis; for the majority of Americans, it looked like stability.

REAGANOMICS REVISITED

Despite the message of stability, the Bush administration took the Republican return to executive power as an opportunity to tilt domestic policy abruptly to the right. Following the example of Ronald Reagan, Bush made massive tax cuts the centerpiece of his first months in office. By starting with proposals for ten-year cuts so large that two generations of federal programs were threatened, Bush and congressional Republicans forced the Democrats to "compromise" on reductions far higher than the economy could probably support. The resulting cuts to income taxes and estate taxes were projected to total $1,350 billion over the decade, with one-third of the benefits going to families earning more than $200,000. The federal budget quickly plunged into the red, undoing the careful political balancing and fiscal discipline of the Clinton administration. Deficits were $375 billion in 2003, $413 billion in 2004, $319 billion in 2005, and $248 billion in 2006, with more of the same forecast for the rest of the decade.

The Bush team also moved quickly to deregulate the economy. It opened many of the environmental and business regulations of the last two decades to reconsideration—from arsenic standards in drinking water to protection for wetlands to the pollution controls required of electric utilities. In many cases, the administration proposed to rely on the market through voluntary compliance and incentives to replace regulations. Vice President Dick Cheney developed a new production-oriented energy policy in consultation with energy companies but not with environmental or consumer groups. The collapse of the energy-trading company Enron in a hailstorm of criticism over deceptive accounting and shady market manipulations to create an energy crisis in California in early 2000 slowed the push to deregulate. In turn, Enron proved to be the first of many companies that had to restate earnings in 2002, depressing the stock market and raising questions about the ethics of big business and business accounting practices. Stock market declines and the evaporation of retirement savings for many workers raised doubts about the solidity of the 1990s boom and helped to hold down economic growth for a third year.

Education policy, a centerpiece of Bush's image as an innovator from his service as governor of Texas, was another legislative front. Tough battles with Congress resulted in compromise legislation, reminiscent of the 1990s, that included national testing standards, as Bush wanted, balanced by more federal funding. More important for both education and religion was the narrow decision by the Supreme Court in *Zelman v. Simmons-Harris* (2002) to uphold the use of taxpayer-funded assistance, or vouchers, to help students attend religious schools. By declaring that both religious and secular institutions can compete for government money as long as it is channeled through individuals who made "true private choices" about how to spend it, the court continued a two-decade trend to narrow the constitutional prohibition on the "establishment of religion."

DOWNSIZED DIPLOMACY

Strong conservatives had long criticized subordinating U.S. authority and freedom of action to international agreements. The new Bush administration heeded this criticism and brought a revolutionary approach to foreign affairs. The administration repeatedly adopted unilateral or bilateral policies in preference to the complexities of negotiations with an entire range of nations.

In his first 18 months, Bush opted out of a series of treaties and negotiations on global issues, sometimes despite years of careful bargaining. In each case he pointed to specific flaws or problems, but the goal was to reduce restrictions on U.S. business and its military. The administration undercut efforts to implement the Convention on Biological Warfare because of possible adverse effects on drug companies. It refused to sign on to efforts to reduce the international trade in armaments, declined to acknowledge a new International Criminal Court that is designed to try war criminals, and ignored an international compact on the rights of women in deference to cultural conservatives. Most prominently, it refused to accept the Kyoto Agreement, aimed at combating the threat of massive environmental change through global warming resulting from the carbon dioxide released by fossil fuels, dismissing a growing scientific consensus on the problem.

In the field of arms control, Bush entered office with the intention of ending the 1972 treaty that had limited the deployment of antimissile defenses by the United States and Russia in order to stabilize the arms race. The treaty had been a cornerstone of national security policy. Despite the objection of Russia, Bush formally withdrew from the treaty in December 2001. In its place he revived Ronald Reagan's idea of a Strategic Defense Initiative with proposals for new but unproven technologies to protect the United States against nuclear attacks by "rogue states." This argument was supported in 2002 by North Korea's revelation that it was pursuing a nuclear weapons program, even though it had agreed not to do so in 1994. Bush also decided not to implement the START II treaty, which had been one of the major accomplishments of his father's term as president. In its place, he worked directly to improve relations with Russia and negotiated a bilateral agreement to reduce substantially the number of nuclear warheads that Russia and the United States actively deploy (while pressing for the development of new tactical nuclear weapons). A new U.S. policy that explicitly claimed the right to act militarily to preempt potential threats confirmed the go-it-alone approach.

PARADOXES OF POWER

The United States in the twenty-first century faced the paradox of power: the enormous economic, military, and technological capacity that allowed it to impose its will on other nations did not extend to an ability to prevent anti-American actions by deeply enraged individuals.

In the 1990s, the U.S. economy had surged while Japan stagnated, Europe marked time, and Russia verged on economic collapse. The U.S. economy in the early twenty-first century was twice the size of Japan's; California alone had economic capacity equal to France or Britain. America's lead was nurtured by research and development spending equal to that of the next six countries combined. The U.S. military budget exceeded the total military spending of the next dozen nations. The United States had the world's only global navy and a huge edge in military technology.

But the United States remained vulnerable. Huge trade deficits, massive oil imports, and a falling dollar in the early years of the new century underlined its economic vulnerability. Overseas, terrorist attacks by Islamic radicals killed 19 American soldiers at military housing in Saudi Arabia in 1996 and 17 sailors on the destroyer *Cole* while in port in the Arab nation of Yemen in 2000. Bombs at the U.S. embassies in Kenya and Tanzania in 1998 killed more than 200 people. These bombings followed the detonation of explosives in the basement garage of the World Trade Center in New York in February 1993, killing six people. New acts of terror remained a constant threat—realized in an appalling manner on September 11, 2001.

SEPTEMBER 11, 2001

On September 11, 2001, terrorists hijacked four commercial jetliners. They crashed one plane into the Pentagon and one into each of the twin towers of the World Trade Center. Passengers on the fourth plane fought the hijackers and made sure that it crashed in the Pennsylvania mountains rather than hit a fourth target. Altogether, 479 police officers, firefighters, and other emergency workers died in the collapse of the towers. Thousands of volunteers rushed to assist rescue efforts or contribute to relief efforts. The total confirmed death toll was 2,752 in New York, 184 at the Pentagon, and 40 in Pennsylvania. A Saudi Arabian businessman who had turned against the United States because of its military presence in the Middle East and its support for Israel Osama bin Laden was probably

the brains behind the attacks on the U.S. military and on diplomats overseas and the earlier blast at the World Trade Center. Operating from exile in Afghanistan, he now masterminded the new and spectacular assault.

The events of September 11 were an enormous shock to the American people, but worries about escalating terrorism were not new. Security specialists such as Defense Secretary William Cohen had been sounding the alarm through the 1990s. The U.S. Commission on National Security/21st Century, appointed by President Clinton, had included detailed warnings in its

Flames shoot from the South Tower of the World Trade Center in New York as it is struck by hijacked United Airlines Flight 15 on the morning of September 11, 2001. Smoke pours from the North Tower which had been hit sixteen minutes earlier by another hijacked aircraft.

February 2001 report, although the new administration had ignored its recommendations to reorganize federal homeland security. The problem, however, had been to connect broad concerns to specific threats. It is always enormously difficult to separate and correlate key points in the vast flood of information that flows through law-enforcement and intelligence agencies. It is much easier to read the warnings after an event has occurred than to pick out the essential data before the unexpected happens—something as true about the attack on Pearl Harbor, for example, as about the attack of 9/11.

SECURITY AND CONFLICT

On September 12, President George W. Bush called the Pentagon and World Trade Center attacks "acts of war." Three days later, Congress passed a Joint Resolution that gave the president sweeping powers "to use all necessary and appropriate force against those nations, organizations, or persons he determines planned, authorized, committed, or aided the terrorist attacks that occurred on September 11, 2001." Only one member voted against the resolution—the same level of agreement that the nation showed after December 7, 1941.

The government response in the United States was a hodge-podge of security measures and arrests. Federal agents detained more than 1,000 terrorist suspects, mostly men from the Middle East, releasing some but holding hundreds without charges, evidence, or legal counsel. President Bush also declared that "enemy combatants" could be tried by special military tribunals, although domestic and international protest caused the administration to agree to more legal safeguards than originally planned. Congress passed the **PATRIOT Act** (Providing Appropriate Tools Required to Intercept and Obstruct Terrorists) in late October, which gave federal authorities substantial new capacity to conduct criminal investigations, in most provisions for the next three to five years. These included the power to request "roving" wiretaps of individuals rather than single telephones, obtain nationwide search warrants, tap information in computerized records, and detain foreigners without filing charges for up to a week. These measures raised a number of concerns about the protection of civil liberties, as noted by the several dozen members of Congress who voted against the act. The law would be renewed in 2006 with a few added provisions to protect basic constitutional and political rights.

In November 2002, Congress approved a massive reorganization of the federal government to improve security at home. The new Department of Homeland Security includes the Immigration and Naturalization Service, Customs Service, Coast Guard, Secret Service, and Transportation Security Administration. It is the second-largest federal agency, after the Defense Department. In 2004 Congress adopted a package of reforms to improve intelligence gathering and analysis, creating the position of director of national intelligence to oversee the CIA and report directly to the president.

In contrast to the suppression of dissent during World War I or the internment of Japanese Americans during World War II, Americans in 2001 and 2002 were careful on the home front. The leaders and supporters of the War on Terror reacted to dissenting voices, particularly those from a pacifist tradition, with caustic remarks rather than repression. Censorship consisted of careful management of the news and stonewalling of requests under the Freedom of Information Act rather than direct censorship of speech and the press. Violations of civil liberties have affected individuals rather than entire groups. President Bush made an important gesture soon after September 11 by appearing at a mosque and arguing against blanket condemnation of Muslims. Ethnic profiling has resulted in heightened suspicion and surveillance of Muslims, selective enforcement of immigration laws on visitors from 20 Muslim nations, and detention of several hundred U.S. residents of Middle Eastern origin, rather than incarceration of entire ethnic groups.

In the months after 9/11, the military response overseas focused on Afghanistan, where the ruling Taliban regime was harboring bin Laden. Afghanistan had been wracked by civil war since the invasion by the Soviet Union in 1979. The Taliban, who came to power after the Soviet withdrawal and civil war, were politically and socially repressive rulers with few international friends. U.S. bombing attacks on Taliban forces began in early October 2001, and internal opposition groups in Afghanistan threw the Taliban out of power by December. bin Laden, however, escaped with the aid of mountainous terrain and the confusion of war. The United States and NATO allies were left with an uncertain commitment to rebuild a stable Afghanistan, which remained an active war zone where resurgent Taliban activity in 2007 and 2008 threatened previous gains. On May 2, 2011, Osama bin Laden was found inside a private residence in Abbottabad, Pakistan and shot and killed by U.S. forces.

IRAQ AND CONFLICTS IN THE MIDDLE EAST

Even while the United States was intervening in Afghanistan, the administration was extending its attention to other nations that supported or condoned anti-American terrorists or had the potential to produce chemical, biological, or nuclear weapons of mass destruction. George Bush named North Korea, Iran, and Iraq as an "axis of evil" for these reasons, and then focused on Iraq. After the Gulf War, Iraq had grudgingly accepted a United Nations requirement that it eliminate weapons of mass destruction, but gradually made UN inspections impossible. This resistance caused Bush to make the overthrow of Iraq's ruthless dictator, Saddam Hussein, the center of foreign policy. In effect, he declared one small, possibly dangerous nation to be the greatest menace the United States faced.

In addition to the direct fallout from the Persian Gulf War, the background to the deep-seated tensions in the Middle East included U.S. support of Israel amidst the deterioration of relations between Israel and the Arab Palestinians in territories occupied by Israel since 1967. The United States has consistently backed Israel since the 1960s. The cornerstones of U.S. policy have been the full endorsement of Israel's right to exist with secure borders and agreement on the right of Palestinians to a national state—in effect, a policy of coexistence. The United States helped to broker an Israel-Egypt peace agreement in 1977 and agreements pointing toward an independent Palestinian state in the 1990s. But hard-line Israeli governments have repeatedly taken advantage of U.S. support from the 1980s in Lebanon (see Chapter 30) to the present.

In 2001–2002, the United States watched from the sidelines as the Israeli-Palestinian agreements for transition to a Palestinian state fell apart. Palestinian extremists and suicide bombers and an Israeli government that favored military responses locked each other into a downward spiral that turned into civil war. As a result, many Arabs identify the United States as an enemy of Arab nations and peoples. Israel's decision in 2005 to withdraw from the Gaza Strip and transfer authority there to the Palestinian government was a step toward resolution that unfortunately led to radical takeover there in 2007–08. The deep and long-unsolvable Israeli-Palestinian conflict helps to explain anti-American terrorism among Arabs, and sometimes other Muslims.

In the spring and summer of 2002, the administration escalated threats of unilateral intervention to change the Iraqi regime and began preparations for a second war in the Persian Gulf region. On October 10, Congress authorized preemptive military action against Iraq. However, international pressure from unenthusiastic allies and from other Arab nations persuaded Bush to put diplomacy ahead of war and devote two months to making his case at the United Nations. On November 8, the UN Security Council unanimously adopted a compromise resolution that gave Iraq three and a half months to allow full and open inspections before military action might be considered. In the following months, UN inspectors searched Iraqi military sites while the United States built up forces in the Middle East in preparation for war. On March 17, 2003, Bush suspended further diplomatic efforts, and on March 19 a full scale U.S.-British invasion of Iraq began.

The war to overthrow Saddam Hussein was a success as a large-scale military operation. On May 1, 2003, President Bush declared "mission accomplished"—that U.S. and British forces now controlled Iraq and major combat operations in Iraq were over.

Peace proved far more difficult than war. Reconstruction of damaged bridges, roads, water systems, and electrical systems took far longer than expected and many basic services were still fragile or nonexistent four years after the U.S. invasion. Meanwhile, American troops and relief workers were the continuing targets of car bombs, booby-trapped highways, mortar attacks, and similar guerrilla resistance. At the end of 2009, more than 4,300 U.S. soldiers had died in Iraq, over 90 percent of them after the president declared victory.

By 2007, a consensus had emerged among both critics of the war and realistic supporters that the United States had overthrown Saddam without any clear plan for next steps. Because of decisions by Secretary of Defense Donald Rumsfeld, the occupation force was inadequate in size from the start—a deficiency that a "surge" of additional U.S. forces in 2007 could not fully remedy. Early on, U.S. officials dismantled the Iraqi army and police, putting 650,000 unemployed but armed men onto the streets. The decision to shut down state industries and purge members of Saddam's political party from low-level government jobs like schoolteachers created massive unemployment. The result was the decimation of Iraq's middle class, a collapse of living standards, and the creation of roughly two million refugees who fled Iraq's new chaos for neighboring nations. However, the surge in 2007 did help to stabilize Iraq and reduce the level of violence by 2008, paving the way for gradual transfer of authority to the reconstructed Iraqi government over the next years.

The aftermath of the war also created political problems for George Bush. A systematic search found no active production facilities or stockpiles for chemical, nuclear, or biological weapons of mass destruction. In October 2004, the final report of the U.S. bomb hunters concluded that Saddam had disbanded his chemical and nuclear weapons efforts after 1991, refuting one of the basic justifications for the war. The continuing necessity to mobilize National Guard and reserve units met heavy criticism. The need to keep an occupying army in Iraq stretched the military close to the breaking point at exactly the same time that the Taliban showed renewed strength in Afghanistan.

HURRICANE AND FINANCIAL STORM

Wars past and present were the pivotal issue in the 2004 election. George W. Bush argued for staying the course with the same administration. Democratic candidate John Kerry had a liberal voting record as a Massachusetts senator and decorations for meritorious service in Vietnam, but central to the Republican campaign were attacks on the veracity of his war record. A wild card was the issue of same sex marriage. Courts in Massachusetts and politicians in Oregon and San Francisco decided that legal marriage could not be denied to same sex couples. Their actions mobilized religious and cultural conservatives and led to successful ballot measures banning same sex marriage in 11 states. Bush won a solid although not overwhelming victory that helped Republicans extend their lead in Congress.

After the election, Bush reaffirmed his commitment to a U.S. presence in Iraq, where a deeply divided nation held elections for a new government early in 2005. Kurds from northern Iraq and Shiite Muslims from southern Iraq voted in large numbers and formed a coalition government. Participation was much lower among Sunni Muslims in central Iraq, who had benefited most from Saddam Hussein's regime and who were the heart of continued guerrilla resistance to the United States occupation forces. The same divisions were evident in October when Iraqis approved a new constitution that met Shiite and Kurdish desires for greater autonomy but left many Sunnis dissatisfied. Those tensions played into the hands of militants who kept the level of violence among Iraqis high. Meanwhile, U.S. coalition allies such as Britain were quietly packing and leaving Iraq to its American conquerors. Nevertheless, Iraq did have a functioning government by the end of the Bush administration, opening the possibility of scaling down the U.S. military presence.

As the nation worried about the open-ended commitment in Iraq, it received a devastating reminder of vulnerability when Hurricane Katrina devastated the Gulf Coast at the end of August 2005. The storm first seemed to spare New Orleans, much of which lies below sea level, but its backlash breached levees that protected the city.

Much of the city and its surroundings flooded. Tens of thousands of residents who had not evacuated found themselves trapped in homes or huddled in overcrowded shelters. The slowness and inadequacy of the emergency response raised serious doubts about the effectiveness of the Department of Homeland Security and its Federal Emergency Management Agency and revealed the deep fault lines that still separate the poor from the larger society—exacerbated in New Orleans by the fact that most of the poor residents were African American.

Iraq and Katrina combined to deal Republicans a blow in the 2006 congressional elections, in which Democrats regained effective control of Congress for the first time in 12 years. Through 2007, as candidates of both parties jockeyed for presidential nominations, important domestic issues like immigration policy, health insurance, and the future of Social Security remained unresolved. Federal courts began to cautiously consider the basic issues of civil liberties raised by the PATRIOT Act and, even more, by the unilateral actions of the Bush administration in claiming free rein to deal with persons suspected as terrorists.

The Crash of 2008 upended the political jockeying with a series of stunning financial blows. The national economy began to weaken in 2007 because of pressure on housing prices. Especially in the Southwest and Southeast, housing values had inflated beyond the actual level of demand as buyers counted on the ability to resell at a high price. So-called subprime mortgage lending added to the bubble as lenders abandoned conservative practices to make incautious loans to buyers without adequate incomes and resources. Bundling these loans together and reselling them as "black box" investments added further instability. Through 2007 and into 2008, mortgage defaults increased and housing prices plummeted, knocking out one of the main props of extraordinarily high stock market indexes.

By mid-2008, declining real estate values and rising unemployment threatened the banking system, because many banks held now worthless mortgages as part of their required assets. Big investment banks and insurance companies tottered or failed and stock market indexes dropped by close to 50 percent from their highs (including a plunge of 22 percent during the second week of October), wiping out individual nest eggs and retirement accounts. Only a huge influx of government cash and guarantees saved banking from the effects of "toxic" assets, largely through the **Troubled Asset Relief Program (TARP)**, which Congress approved in October 2008. TARP authorized up to $700 billion for government purchase or guarantee of illiquid and difficult-to-value mortgages and other bank assets. The federal government also used TARP funds to buy preferred stock in major banks as an additional way to shore them up.

The banking system stabilized in 2009 and the stock market regained about half of its losses. However, the succession of financial crises and the virtual shutdown of private construction plunged the United States into a deep recession. Small businesses found it hard to secure credit, major automobile makers declared bankruptcy, and unemployment peaked above 10 percent in October 2009 before a slow economic recovery began in 2010.

THE OBAMA PHENOMENON

In this context that favored Democrats, Americans in 2008 faced a presidential election campaign with two improbable candidates. The Republicans nominated John McCain, an Arizona senator who had been a prisoner of war during the Vietnam War and who cultivated a reputation as a maverick. Democrats had a hard-fought contest between Hillary Rodham Clinton, who hoped to be the first woman nominated for president by a major party, and Barack Obama, an Illinois senator who became the first African American nominee. Although Obama won the nomination with surprising ease, Democrats would have made history with either candidate.

Democrats capitalized on Republican problems with the more effective campaign. McCain divided his potential supporters by choosing Alaskan governor Sarah Palin as his vice-presidential running mate. A conservative suburban politician, Palin's short political resume and home state gave her populist appeal but left her unprepared for the national spotlight. Obama meanwhile generated enthusiasm among younger, often

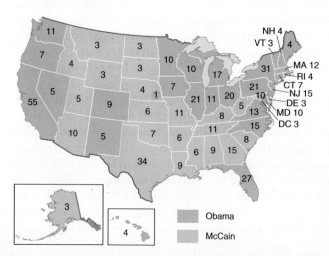

MAP 31–3 • The Election of 2008 In 2008, Barack Obama won the presidency by holding the reliably Democratic Northeast and Pacific Coast and winning swing states in the Rocky Mountains (Colorado, New Mexico), the Midwest (Ohio, Indiana, Iowa), and the Southeast (Virginia, North Carolina, Florida).

▶ *Which southern states voted for Barack Obama in 2008? Does the election of 2008 indicate that Republican dominance in the South may be coming to an end?*

first-time voters as well as middle-class independents. (See Overview, Core Support for Republicans and Democrats in 2008.) The result was a solid victory in which Democrats added swing states like Virginia, North Carolina, Iowa, and Colorado to their northern and West Coast strongholds (see Map 31–3).

The United States passed a tremendously important step in its national maturity by electing an African American as president, but the enthusiasm of Obama's inauguration was not enough to overcome the realities of political deadlock. Obama secured a substantial economic stimulus package to fight the deep recession, his administration began to reinvigorate protections for workers and the environment, and he tapped Sonia Sotomayor to be the first Latina on the Supreme Court. He showed his pragmatic approach by carefully assessing the situation in Afghanistan and authorizing a cautious expansion of the U.S. commitment there. The most bruising battle for the new administration came over healthcare reform, where Republicans dug in their heels against a larger federal role while Democrats tried to reconcile their liberal and conservative wings. After a year of bitter debate inside and outside Congress, President Obama in March 2010 signed a bill that promised to extend health insurance to 32 million previously uninsured Americans. It represents the greatest expansion of the federal government's social safety net since the creation of Medicare and Medicaid in 1965.

In 2010, the American people were tired of Foreign Wars, battered by lost retirement accounts, homes, and jobs, and impatient with a recovery that seemed to benefit bankers more than working people. They wanted someone to shake up the system, but they also feared losing what security they had. They desperately wanted change, but they showed no willingness to trust anyone to deliver it—neither Democrats nor Republicans, federal government nor corporate America. it was an enormous challenge for anyone who hoped to lead the nation into the second decade of the new century.

The Obama family brought youthful energy to the White House reminiscent of the Kennedy family in the 1960s and Theodore Roosevelt's family in the first years of the twentieth century.

OVERVIEW CORE SUPPORT FOR REPUBLICANS AND DEMOCRATS IN 2008

	Republicans	Democrats
Age	60 and older	18–29 years old
Religion	White Protestants Evangelicals Regular church-goers	Jews
Education		Less than high school Postgraduate education
Family income		Under $50,000
Sex		Women
Race and Ethnicity	Whites	African Americans Latinos Asian Americans
Geography	South Central states Appalachian states	Pacific Coast Northeast Great Lakes states
Size of Community	Rural areas and small towns	Large cities

CONCLUSION

If there was a dominant theme that ran through the changes and challenges of the 1990s and the new century, it was interconnection. The Internet, e-mail, and cell phones brought instant communication. Corporate mismanagement affected far more people than before because of pensions and savings invested in the stock market. Whether by television or Twitter, information—and sometimes real news—traveled faster than ever before.

Despite what some might have wished, Americans also found that they could not always isolate the nation from the problems and conflicts that wracked much of the rest of the world. The Clinton administration joined international peacekeeping efforts in Bosnia and Kosovo. The Bush administration chose to ignore several international agreements, but still sought the cover of United Nations approval for action against Iraq (although it largely disregarded international opinion in its pursuit of the war).

Beyond its growing military commitments, the United States in the first years of the twenty-first century was deeply connected to the world. Travel, work and study abroad—and foreign tourists, workers, and students in the United States—improved American understanding of other nations. However, the ease and volume of travel and trade also brought problems and fears. The nation's growing diversity—closely connected to its internationalized economy—was reflected in the political gains of African Americans and Hispanics, as well as women, but the same diversity fueled battles over affirmative action and language politics. Many Americans had long worried that the United States was being flooded by illegal immigrants, and the revelation that some of the 9/11 terrorists had learned to fly in U.S. training schools compounded fears of a porous border.

International connection had other economic and environmental implications. Americans enjoyed the benefits of open trade and cheap imports, but a ballooning national debt and fast-growing trade deficits reduced the purchasing power of the dollar and made the economy dependent on investment from abroad. Hovering in the background were global environmental concerns such as global warming caused or accelerated by the massive use of fossil fuels whose combustion adds carbon dioxide to the atmosphere.

Americans have seldom made their personal journeys in isolation. We have depended on our communities and seen the consequences when the failure of community support throws us on our own, as happened to some in New Orleans in 2005. We welcome refugees from tyranny and journey across oceans to help others. In the coming decades, our community will increasingly span the entire globe as we face the challenges of economic, environmental, and political change. We—the authors of this book—look forward to learning and writing about these new journeys in the years to come.

REVIEW QUESTIONS

1. Was the U.S. political system more polarized and divided in 1992 than in 1980? How did religiously conservative Americans understand issues of foreign relations and economic policy? How did religiously liberal Americans understand the same issues? What was the gender gap in national politics in the 1990s? Why were Republicans unable to appeal to most black and Hispanic voters in 1992?

2. What were Bill Clinton's major policy accomplishments? Do these represent liberal, moderate, or conservative positions?

3. What was the Contract with America? What are other examples of a conservative political trend in the 1990s?

4. What issues were involved in Clinton's impeachment? How does the impeachment compare with the challenges to presidents Andrew Johnson and Richard Nixon?

5. Did the U.S. economy undergo fundamental changes in the 1990s? What has been the impact of the computer revolution? Of the growing importance of world markets?

6. What new directions did George W. Bush establish for U.S. domestic and foreign policy?

7. How did the terrorist attacks of September 11, 2001, change life in the United States? How did ordinary Americans respond at the time and since the attacks?

8. What are some of the reasons the experience of the United States in reconstructing Iraq after 2003 has differed from its experience in Japan and Germany after World War II?

9. What factors contributed to Democratic Party victories in the 2008 election?

PEARSON
myhistorylab CONNECTIONS

Reinforce what you learned in this chapter by studying the many documents, images, maps, review tools, and videos available at **www.myhistorylab.com.**

READ AND REVIEW

✔•⎯ **Study** and **Review** on **myhistorylab.com** STUDY PLAN: CHAPTER 31

📖•⎯ **Read** the **Document** on **myhistorylab.com**

Republican Contract with America (1994)

U.S. v. Timothy James McVeigh (1997)

Articles of Impeachment against William Jefferson Clinton (1998)

Bill Clinton, Answers to the Articles of Impeachment (1998)

Clinton Health Care Reform Proposals (1993)

Illegal Immigration Reform and Immigrant Responsibility Act (1996)

George W. Bush, Address to Congress (2001)

George W. Bush, Address to the Nation on the Iraq Invasion (2003)

Nancy Pelosi, Inaugural Address (2007)

Al Gore, Global Warming (2006)

Dirty Politics in the 2008 Election (2007)

🔍⎯ **View** the **Map** on **myhistorylab.com**

Settlement of the United States, c. 1998

Present-day Africa and the Middle East

Present-day Europe

Present-day World

RESEARCH AND EXPLORE

📖•⎯ **Read** the **Document** on **myhistorylab.com**

Personal Journeys Online

From Then to Now Online: America's Mission to the World

Exploring America: Globalization

((•⎯ **Listen** on **myhistorylab.com**

The Audacity of Hope by Barack Obama, excerpt

👁⎯ **Watch** the **Video** on **myhistorylab.com**

Bill Clinton First Inauguration

Bill Clinton Sells Himself to America: Presidential Campaign Ad, 1992

The Historical Significance of the 2008 Presidential Election

⎯⎯⎯ ((•⎯ **Listen** on **myhistorylab.com** ⎯⎯⎯

Hear the audio files for Chapter 31 at
www.myhistorylab.com.

APPENDIX

The Constitution of the United States of America

We the people of the United States, in order to form a more perfect union, establish justice, insure domestic tranquillity, provide for the common defense, promote the general welfare, and secure the blessings of liberty to ourselves and our posterity, do ordain and establish this Constitution for the United States of America.

ARTICLE I

SECTION 1. All legislative powers herein granted shall be vested in a Congress of the United States, which shall consist of a Senate and House of Representatives.

SECTION 2. 1 The House of Representatives shall be composed of members chosen every second year by the people of the several States, and the electors in each State shall have the qualifications requisite for electors of the most numerous branch of the State legislature.

2. No person shall be a representative who shall not have attained to the age of twenty-five years, and been seven years a citizen of the United States, and who shall not, when elected, be an inhabitant of that State in which he shall be chosen.

3. Representatives and direct taxes[1] shall be apportioned among the several States which may be included within this Union, according to their respective numbers, which shall be determined by adding to the whole number of free persons, including those bound to service for a term of years, and excluding Indians not taxed, three fifths of all other persons.[2] The actual enumeration shall be made within three years after the first meeting of the Congress of the United States, and within every subsequent term of ten years, in such manner as they shall by law direct. The number of representatives shall not exceed one for every thirty thousand, but each State shall have at least one representative; and until such enumeration shall be made, the State of New Hampshire shall be entitled to choose three, Massachusetts eight, Rhode Island and Providence Plantations one, Connecticut five, New York six, New Jersey four, Pennsylvania eight, Delaware one, Maryland six, Virginia ten, North Carolina five, South Carolina five, and Georgia three.

4. When vacancies happen in the representation from any State, the executive authority thereof shall issue writs of election to fill such vacancies.

5. The House of Representatives shall choose their speaker and other officers; and shall have the sole power of impeachment.

SECTION 3. 1. The Senate of the United States shall be composed of two senators from each State, chosen by the legislature thereof,[3] for six years; and each senator shall have one vote.

2. Immediately after they shall be assembled in consequence of the first election, they shall be divided as equally as may be into three classes. The seats of the senators of the first class shall be vacated at the expiration of the second year, of the second class at the expiration of the fourth year, and of the third class at the expiration of the sixth year, so that one third may be chosen every second year; and if vacancies happen by resignation, or otherwise, during the recess of the legislature of any State, the executive thereof may make temporary appointments until the next meeting of the legislature, which shall then fill such vacancies.[4]

3. No person shall be a senator who shall not have attained to the age of thirty years, and been nine years a citizen of the United States, and who shall not, when elected, be an inhabitant of that State for which he shall be chosen.

4. The Vice President of the United States shall be President of the Senate, but shall have no vote, unless they be equally divided.

5. The Senate shall choose their other officers, and also a president pro tempore, in the absence of the Vice President, or when he shall exercise the office of the President of the United States.

6. The Senate shall have the sole power to try all impeachments. When sitting for that purpose, they shall be on oath or affirmation. When the President of the United States is tried, the chief justice shall preside: and no person shall be convicted without the concurrence of two thirds of the members present.

7. Judgment in cases of impeachment shall not extend further than to removal from office, and disqualification to hold and enjoy any office of honor, trust or profit under the United States: but the party convicted shall nevertheless be liable and subject to indictment, trial, judgment and punishment, according to law.

SECTION 4. 1. The times, places, and manner of holding elections for senators and representatives, shall be prescribed in each State by the legislature thereof; but the Congress may at any time by law make or alter such regulations, except as to the places of choosing senators.

2. The Congress shall assemble at least once in every year, and such meeting shall be on the first Monday in December, unless they shall by law appoint a different day.

SECTION 5. 1. Each House shall be the judge of the elections, returns and qualifications of its own members, and a majority of each shall constitute a quorum to do business; but a smaller

---

[1] See the Sixteenth Amendment.
[2] See the Fourteenth Amendment.
[3] See the Seventeenth Amendment.
[4] See the Seventeenth Amendment.

number may adjourn from day to day, and may be authorized to compel the attendance of absent members, in such manner, and under such penalties as each House may provide.

2. Each House may determine the rules of its proceedings, punish its members for disorderly behavior, and, with the concurrence of two thirds, expel a member.

3. Each House shall keep a journal of its proceedings, and from time to time publish the same, excepting such parts as may in their judgment require secrecy; and the yeas and nays of the members of either House on any question shall, at the desire of one fifth of those present, be entered on the journal.

4. Neither House, during the session of Congress, shall, without the consent of the other, adjourn for more than three days, nor to any other place than that in which the two Houses shall be sitting.

SECTION 6. 1 The senators and representatives shall receive a compensation for their services, to be ascertained by law, and paid out of the Treasury of the United States. They shall in all cases, except treason, felony, and breach of the peace, be privileged from arrest during their attendance at the session of their respective Houses, and in going to and returning from the same; and for any speech or debate in either House, they shall not be questioned in any other place.

2. No senator or representative shall, during the time for which he was elected, be appointed to any civil office under the authority of the United States, which shall have been created, or the emoluments whereof shall have been increased, during such time; and no person holding any office under the United States shall be a member of either House during his continuance in office.

SECTION 7. 1. All bills for raising revenue shall originate in the House of Representatives; but the Senate may propose or concur with amendments as on other bills.

2. Every bill which shall have passed the House of Representatives and the Senate, shall, before it become a law, be presented to the President of the United States; If he approves he shall sign it, but if not he shall return it, with his objections, to that House in which it shall have originated, who shall enter the objections at large on their journal, and proceed to reconsider it. If after such reconsideration two thirds of that House shall agree to pass the bill, it shall be sent, together with the objections, to the other House, by which it shall likewise be reconsidered, and if approved by two thirds of that House, it shall become a law. But in all such cases the votes of both Houses shall be determined by yeas and nays, and the names of the persons voting for and against the bill shall be entered on the journal of each House respectively. If any bill shall not be returned by the President within ten days (Sundays excepted) after it shall have been presented to him, the same shall be a law, in like manner as if he had signed it, unless the Congress by their adjournment prevent its return, in which case it shall not be a law.

3. Every order, resolution, or vote to which the concurrence of the Senate and the House of Representatives may be necessary (except on a question of adjournment) shall be presented to the President of the United States; and before the same shall take effect, shall be approved by him, or being disapproved by him, shall be repassed by two thirds of the Senate and House of Representatives, according to the rules and limitations prescribed in the case of a bill.

SECTION 8. 1. The Congress shall have the power.

1. To lay and collect taxes, duties, imposts, and excises, to pay the debts and provide for the common defense and general welfare of the United States; but all duties, imposts, and excises shall be uniform throughout the United States.

2. To borrow money on the credit of the United States;

3. To regulate commerce with foreign nations, and among the several States, and with the Indian tribes;

4. To establish a uniform rule of naturalization, and uniform laws on the subject of bankruptcies throughout the United States;

5. To coin money, regulate the value thereof, and of foreign coin, and fix the standard of weights and measures;

6. To provide for the punishment of counterfeiting the securities and current coin of the United States;

7. To establish post offices and post roads;

8. To promote the progress of science and useful arts, by securing for limited times to authors and inventors the exclusive right to their respective writings and discoveries;

9. To constitute tribunals inferior to the Supreme Court;

10. To define and punish piracies and felonies committed on the high seas, and offenses against the law of nations;

11. To declare war, grant letters of marque and reprisal, and make rules concerning captures on land and water;

12. To raise and support armies, but no appropriation of money to that use shall be for a longer term than two years;

13. To provide and maintain a navy;

14. To make rules for the government and regulation of the land and naval forces;

15. To provide for calling forth the militia to execute the laws of the Union, suppress insurrections and repel invasions;

16. To provide for organizing, arming, and disciplining the militia, and for governing such part of them as may be employed in the service of the United States, reserving to the States respectively, the appointment of the officers, and the authority of training the militia according to the discipline prescribed by Congress;

17. To exercise exclusive legislation in all cases whatsoever, over such district (not exceeding ten miles square) as may, by cession of particular States, and the acceptance of Congress, become the seat of the government of the United States, and to exercise like authority over all places purchased by the consent of the legislature of the State in which the same shall be, for the erection of forts, magazines, arsenals, dockyards, and other needful buildings; and

18. To make all laws which shall be necessary and proper for carrying into execution the foregoing powers, and all other powers vested by this Constitution in the government of the United States, or any department or officer thereof.

SECTION 9. 1. The migration or importation of such persons as any of the States now existing shall think proper to admit, shall not be prohibited by the Congress prior to the year one thousand eight hundred and eight, but a tax or duty may be imposed on such importation, not exceeding ten dollars for each person.

2. The privilege of the writ of habeas corpus shall not be suspended, unless when in cases of rebellion or invasion the public safety may require it.

3. No bill of attainder or ex post facto law shall be passed.

4. No capitation, or other direct, tax shall be laid, unless in proportion to the census or enumeration hereinbefore directed to be taken.[5]

5. No tax or duty shall be laid on articles exported from any State.

6. No preference shall be given by any regulation of commerce or revenue to the ports of one State over those of another: nor shall vessels bound to, or from, one State be obliged to enter, clear, or pay duties in another.

7. No money shall be drawn from the treasury, but in consequence of appropriations made by law; and a regular statement and account of the receipts and expenditures of all public money shall be published from time to time.

8. No title of nobility shall be granted by the United States: and no person holding any office of profit or trust under them, shall, without the consent of the Congress, accept of any present, emolument, office, or title, of any kind whatever, from any king, prince, or foreign State.

SECTION 10. 1. No State shall enter into any treaty, alliance, or confederation; grant letters of marque and reprisal; coin money; emit bills of credit; make any thing but gold and silver coin a tender in payment of debts; pass any bill of attainder, ex post facto law, or law impairing the obligation of contracts, or grant, any title of nobility.

2. No State shall, without the consent of the Congress, lay any imposts or duties on imports or exports, except what may be absolutely necessary for executing its inspection laws: and the net produce of all duties and imposts laid by any State on imports or exports, shall be for the use of the treasury of the United States; and all such laws shall be subject to the revision and control of the Congress.

3. No State shall, without the consent of the Congress, lay any duty of tonnage, keep troops, or ships of war in time of peace, enter into any agreement or compact with another State, or with a foreign power, or engage in war, unless actually invaded, or in such imminent danger as will not admit of delay.

ARTICLE II

SECTION 1. 1. The executive power shall be vested in a President of the United States of America. He shall hold his office during the term of four years, and, together with the Vice President, chosen for the same term, be elected, as follows:

2. Each State shall appoint, in such manner as the legislature thereof may direct, a number of electors, equal to the whole number of senators and representatives to which the State may be entitled in the Congress: but no senator or representative, or person holding any office of trust or profit under the United States, shall be appointed an elector.

The electors shall meet in their respective States, and vote by ballot for two persons, of whom one at least shall not be an inhabitant of the same State with themselves. And they shall make a list of all the persons voted for, and of the number of votes for each; which list they shall sign and certify, and transmit sealed to the seat of the government of the United States, directed to the president of the Senate. The president of the Senate shall, in the presence of the Senate and House of Representatives, open all the certificates, and the votes shall then be counted. The person having the greatest number of votes shall be the President, if such number be a majority of the whole number of electors appointed; and if there be more than one who have such majority, and have an equal number of votes, then the House of Representatives shall immediately choose by ballot one of them for President; and if no person have a majority, then from the five highest on the list the said House shall in like manner choose the President. But in choosing the President, the votes shall be taken by States, the representation from each State having one vote; a quorum for this purpose shall consist of a member or members from two thirds of the States, and a majority of all the States shall be necessary to a choice. In every case after the choice of the President, the person having the greatest number of votes of the electors shall be the Vice President. But if there should remain two or more who have equal votes, the Senate shall choose from them by ballot the Vice President.[6]

3. The Congress may determine the time of choosing the electors, and the day on which they shall give their votes; which day shall be the same throughout the United States.

4. No person except a natural born citizen, or a citizen of the United States, at the time of the adoption of this Constitution, shall be eligible to the office of President; neither shall any person be eligible to the office who shall not have attained to the age of thirty-five years, and been fourteen years a resident within the United States.

5. In case of the removal of the President from office, or of his death, resignation, or inability to discharge the powers and duties of the said office, the same shall devolve on the Vice President, and the congress may by law provide for the case of removal, death, resignation or inability, both of the President and Vice President, declaring what officer shall then act as President, and such officer shall act accordingly until the disability be removed, or a President shall be elected.

6. The President shall, at stated times, receive for his services a compensation which shall neither be increased nor diminished during the period for which he shall have been elected, and he shall not receive within that period any other emolument from the United States, or any of them.

7. Before he enter on the execution of his office, he shall take the following oath or affirmation:—"I do solemnly swear (or affirm) that I will faithfully execute the office of President of the United States, and will to the best of my ability, preserve, protect and defend the Constitution of the United States."

---

[5]See the Sixteenth Amendment.

[6]Superseded by the Twelfth Amendment.

SECTION 2. 1. The President shall be commander in chief of the army and navy of the United States, and of the militia of the several States, when called into the actual service of the United States; he may require the opinion in writing, of the principal officer in each of the executive departments, upon any subject relating to the duties of their respective offices, and he shall have power to grant reprieves and pardons for offenses against the United States, except in cases of impeachment.

2. He shall have power, by and with the advice and consent of the Senate, to make treaties, provided two thirds of the senators present concur; and he shall nominate, and by and with the advice and consent of the Senate, shall appoint ambassadors, other public ministers and consuls, judges of the Supreme Court, and all other officers of the United States, whose appointments are not herein otherwise provided for, and which shall be established by law; but the Congress may by law vest the appointment of such inferior officers, as they think proper, in the President alone, in the courts of laws, or in the heads of departments.

3. The President shall have power to fill up all vacancies that may happen during the recess of the Senate, by granting commissions which shall expire at the end of their next session.

SECTION 3. He shall from time to time give to the Congress information of the state of the Union, and recommend to their consideration such measures as he shall judge necessary and expedient; he may, on extraordinary occasions, convene both Houses, or either of them, and in case of disagreement between them with respect to the time of adjournment, he may adjourn them to such time as he shall think proper; he shall receive ambassadors and other public ministers; he shall take care that the laws be faithfully executed, and shall commission all the officers of the United States.

SECTION 4. The President, Vice President, and all civil officers of the United States, shall be removed from office on impeachment for, and conviction of, treason, bribery, or other high crimes and misdemeanors.

ARTICLE III

SECTION 1. The judicial power of the United States shall be vested in one Supreme Court, and in such inferior courts as the Congress may from time to time ordain and establish. The judges, both of the Supreme and inferior courts, shall hold their offices during good behavior, and shall, at stated times, receive for their services, a compensation, which shall not be diminished during their continuance in office.

SECTION 2. 1. The judicial power shall extend to all cases, in law and equity, arising under this Constitution, the laws of the United States, and treaties made, or which shall be made, under their authority;—to all cases of admiralty and maritime jurisdiction;—to controversies to which the United States shall be a party;[7]—to controversies between two or more States;—between a State and citizens of another State;—between citizens of different States;—between citizens of the same State claiming lands under grants of different States, and between a State, or the citizens thereof, and foreign States, citizens or subjects.

2. In all cases affecting ambassadors, other public ministers and consuls, and those in which a State shall be party, the Supreme Court shall have original jurisdiction. In all the other cases before mentioned, the Supreme Court shall have appellate jurisdiction, both as to law and fact, with such exceptions, and under such regulations as the Congress shall make.

3. The trial of all crimes, except in cases of impeachment, shall be by jury; and such trial shall be held in the State where the said crimes shall have been committed; but when not committed within any State, the trial shall be such place or places as the congress may by law have directed.

SECTION 3. 1. Treason against the United States shall consist only in levying war against them, or in adhering to their enemies, giving them aid and comfort. No person shall be convicted of treason unless on the testimony of two witnesses to the same overt act, or on confession in open court.

2. The Congress shall have power to declare the punishment of treason, but no attainder of treason shall work corruption of blood, or forfeiture except during the life of the person attained.

ARTICLE IV

SECTION 1. Full faith and credit shall be given in each State to the public acts, records, and judicial proceedings of every other State. And the Congress may by general laws prescribe the manner in which such acts, records and proceedings shall be proved, and the effect thereof.

SECTION 2. 1. The citizens of each State shall be entitled to all privileges and immunities of citizens in the several States.[8]

2. A person charged in any State with treason, felony, or other crime, who shall flee from justice, and be found in another State, shall on demand of the executive authority of the State from which he fled, be delivered up to be removed to the State having jurisdiction of the crime.

3. No person held to service or labor in one State under the laws thereof, escaping into another, shall, in consequence of any law or regulation therein, be discharged from such service or labor, but shall be delivered up on claim of the party to whom such service or labor may be due.[9]

SECTION 3. 1. New States may be admitted by the Congress into this Union; but no new State shall be formed or erected within the jurisdiction of any other State, nor any State be formed by the junction of two or more States, or parts of States, without the consent of the legislatures of the States concerned as well as of the Congress.

2. The Congress shall have power to dispose of and make all needful rules and regulations respecting the territory or other property belonging to the United States; and nothing in this Constitution shall be so construed as to prejudice any claims of the United States, or of any particular State.

[7]See the Eleventh Amendment.

[8]See the Fourteenth Amendment, Sec. 1.
[9]See the Thirteenth Amendment.

SECTION 4. The United States shall guarantee to every State in this Union a republican form of government, and shall protect each of them against invasion; and on application of the legislature, or of the executive (when the legislature cannot be convened) against domestic violence.

ARTICLE V

The Congress, whenever two thirds of both Houses shall deem it necessary, shall propose amendments to this Constitution, or, on the application of the legislatures of two thirds of the several States, shall call a convention for proposing amendments, which in either case shall be valid to all intents and purposes, as part of this Constitution, when ratified by the legislatures of three fourths of the several States, or by conventions in three fourths thereof, as the one or the other mode of ratification may be proposed by the Congress; Provided that no amendment which may be made prior to the year one thousand eight hundred and eight shall in any manner affect the first and fourth clauses in the ninth section of the first article; and that no State, without its consent, shall be deprived of its equal suffrage in the Senate.

ARTICLE VI

1. All debts contracted and engagements entered into, before the adoption of this Constitution, shall be as valid against the United States under this Constitution, as under the Confederation.[10]

2. This Constitution, and the laws of the United States which shall be made in pursuance thereof; and all treaties made, or which shall be made, under the authority of the United States, shall be the supreme law of the land; and the judges in every State shall be bound thereby, any thing in the Constitution or laws of any State to the contrary notwithstanding.

3. The senators and representatives before mentioned, and the members of the several State legislatures, and all executive and judicial officers, both of the United States and of the several States, shall be bound by oath or affirmation to support this Constitution; but no religious test shall ever be required as a qualification to any office or public trust under the United States.

ARTICLE VII

The ratification of the conventions of nine States shall be sufficient for the establishment of this Constitution between the States so ratifying the same.

Done in Convention by the unanimous consent of the States present the seventeenth day of September in the year of our Lord one thousand seven hundred and eighty-seven, and of the independence of the United States of America the twelfth. In witness whereof we have hereunto subscribed our names.
[Signatories' names omitted]

Articles in addition to, and amendment of, the Constitution of the United States of America, proposed by Congress,

and ratified by the legislatures of the several States, pursuant to the fifth article of the original Constitution.

Amendment I

[First ten amendments ratified December 15, 1791]
Congress shall make no law respecting an establishment of religion, or prohibiting the free exercise thereof; or abridging the freedom of speech, or of the press; or the right of the people peaceably to assemble, and to petition the government for a redress of grievances.

Amendment II

A well regulated militia, being necessary to the security of a free State, the right of the people to keep and bear arms, shall not be infringed.

Amendment III

No soldier shall, in time of peace be quartered in any house, without the consent of the owner, nor in time of war, but in a manner to be prescribed by law.

Amendment IV

The right of the people to be secure in their persons, houses, papers, and effects, against unreasonable searches and seizures, shall not be violated, and no warrants shall issue, but upon probable cause, supported by oath or affirmation, and particularly describing the place to be searched, and the persons or things to be seized.

Amendment V

No person shall be held to answer for a capital or otherwise infamous crime, unless on a presentment or indictment of a grand jury, except in cases arising in the land or naval forces, or in the militia, when in actual service in time of war or public danger; nor shall any person be subject for the same offense to be twice put in jeopardy of life or limb; nor shall be compelled in any criminal case to be a witness against himself, nor be deprived of life, liberty, or property, without due process of law; nor shall private property be taken for public use, without just compensation.

Amendment VI

In all criminal prosecutions, the accused shall enjoy the right to a speedy and public trial, by an impartial jury of the State and district wherein the crime shall have been committed, which district shall have been previously ascertained by law, and to be informed of the nature and cause of the accusation; to be confronted with the witnesses against him; to have compulsory process for obtaining witnesses in his favor, and to have the assistance of counsel for his defense.

Amendment VII

In suits at common law, where the value in controversy shall exceed twenty dollars, the right of trial by jury shall be preserved, and no fact tried by a jury shall be otherwise reexamined in any court of the United States, than according to the rules of the common law.

---

[10]See the Fourteenth Amendment, Sec. 4.

Amendment VIII

Excessive bail shall not be required, nor excessive fines imposed, nor cruel and unusual punishments inflicted.

Amendment IX

The enumeration in the Constitution of certain rights shall not be construed to deny or disparage others retained by the people.

Amendment X

The powers not delegated to the United States by the Constitution, nor prohibited by it to the States, are reserved to the States respectively, or to the people.

Amendment XI [January 8, 1798]

The judicial power of the United States shall not be construed to extend to any suit in law or equity, commended or prosecuted against one of the United States by citizens of another State, or by citizens or subjects of any foreign State.

Amendment XII [September 25, 1804]

The electors shall meet in their respective States, and vote by ballot for President and Vice President, one of whom, at least, shall not be an inhabitant of the same State with themselves; they shall name in their ballots the person voted for as President, and in distinct ballots, the person voted for as Vice President, and they shall make distinct lists of all persons voted for as President and of all persons voted for as Vice President, and of the number of votes for each, which lists they shall sign and certify, and transmit sealed to the seat of the government of the United States, directed to the President of the Senate;—The President of the Senate shall, in the presence of the Senate and House of Representatives, open all the certificates and the votes shall then be counted;—The person having the greatest number of votes for President, shall be the President, if such number be a majority of the whole number of electors appointed; and if no person have such majority, then from the persons having the highest numbers not exceeding three on the list of those voted for as President, the House of Representatives shall choose immediately, by ballot, the President. But in choosing the President, the votes shall be taken by States, the representation from each State having one vote; a quorum for this purpose shall consist of a member or members from two thirds of the States, and a majority of all the States shall be necessary to a choice. And if the House of Representatives shall not choose a President whenever the right of choice shall devolve upon them, before the fourth day of March next following, then the Vice President shall act as President, as in the case of the death or other constitutional disability of the President. The person having the greatest number of votes as Vice President shall be the Vice President, if such number be a majority of the whole number of electors appointed, and if no person have a majority, then from the two highest numbers on the list, the Senate shall choose the Vice President; a quorum for the purpose shall consist of two thirds of the whole number of Senators, and a majority of the whole number

shall be necessary to a choice. But no person constitutionally ineligible to the office of President shall be eligible to that of Vice President of the United States.

Amendment XIII [December 18, 1865]

SECTION 1. Neither slavery nor involuntary servitude, except as a punishment for crime whereof the party shall have been duly convicted, shall exist within the United States, or any place subject to their jurisdiction.

SECTION 2. Congress shall have power to enforce this article by appropriate legislation.

Amendment XIV [July 28, 1868]

SECTION 1. All persons born or naturalized in the United States, and subject to the jurisdiction thereof, are citizens of the United States and of the State wherein they reside. No State shall make or enforce any law which shall abridge the privileges or immunities of citizens of the United States; nor shall any State deprive any person of life, liberty, or property, without due process of law; nor deny to any person within its jurisdiction the equal protection of the laws.

SECTION 2. Representatives shall be apportioned among the several States according to their respective numbers, counting the whole number of persons in each State, excluding Indians not taxed. But when the right to vote at any election for the choice of electors for President and Vice President of the United States, representatives in Congress, the executive and judicial officers of a State, or the members of the legislature thereof, is denied to any of the male inhabitants of such State, being twenty-one years of age, and citizens of the United States, or in any way abridged, except for participating in rebellion, or other crime, the basis of representation there shall be reduced in the proportion which the number of such male citizens shall bear to the whole number of male citizens twenty-one years of age in such State.

SECTION 3. No person shall be a senator or representative in Congress, or elector of President and Vice President, or hold any office, civil or military, under the United States, or under any State, who having previously taken an oath, as a member of Congress, or as an officer of the United States, or as a member of any State legislature, or as an executive or judicial officer of any State, to support the Constitution of the United States, shall have engaged in insurrection or rebellion against the same, or given aid or comfort to the enemies thereof. But Congress may by a vote of two thirds of each House, remove such disability.

SECTION 4. The validity of the public debt of the United States, authorized by law, including debts incurred for payment of pensions and bounties for services in suppressing insurrection or rebellion; shall not be questioned. But neither the United States nor any State shall assume or pay any debt or obligation incurred in aid of insurrection or rebellion against the United States, or any claim for the loss or emancipation of any slave; but all such debts, obligations, and claims shall be held illegal and void.

SECTION 5. The Congress shall have the power to enforce, by appropriate legislation, the provisions of this article.

Amendment XV [March 30, 1870]

SECTION 1. The right of citizens of the United States to vote shall not be denied or abridged by the United States or by any State on account of race, color, or previous condition of servitude.

SECTION 2. The Congress shall have power to enforce this article by appropriate legislation.

Amendment XVI [February 25, 1913]

The Congress shall have power to lay and collect taxes on incomes, from whatever source derived, without apportionment among the several States, and without regard to any census or enumeration.

Amendment XVII [May 31, 1913]

The Senate of the United States shall be composed of two senators from each State, elected by the people thereof, for six years; and each senator shall have one vote. The electors in each State shall have the qualifications requisite for electors of the most numerous branch of the State legislature.

When vacancies happen in the representation of any State in the Senate, the executive authority of such State shall issue writs of election to fill such vacancies: Provided, That the legislature of any State may empower the executive thereof to make temporary appointments until the people fill the vacancies by election as the legislature may direct.

This amendment shall not be so construed as to affect the election or term of any senator chosen before it becomes valid as part of the Constitution.

Amendment XVIII[11] [January 29, 1919]

After one year from the ratification of this article, the manufacture, sale, or transportation of intoxicating liquors within, the importation thereof into, or the exportation thereof from the United States and all territory subject to the jurisdiction thereof for beverage purposes is thereby prohibited.

The Congress and the several States shall have concurrent power to enforce this article by appropriate legislation.

This article shall be inoperative unless it shall have been ratified as an amendment to the Constitution by the legislatures of the several States, as provided in the constitution, within seven years from the date of the submission hereof to the States by Congress.

Amendment XIX [August 26, 1920]

The right of citizens of the United States to vote shall not be denied or abridged by the United States or by any State on account of sex.

Congress shall have the power to enforce this article by appropriate legislation.

Amendment XX [January 23, 1933]

SECTION 1. The terms of the President and Vice President shall end at noon on the 20th day of January and the terms of Senators and Representatives at noon on the 3rd day of January, of the years in which such terms would have ended if this article had not been ratified; and the terms of their successors shall then begin.

SECTION 2. The Congress shall assemble at least once in every year, and such meeting shall begin at noon on the 3rd day of January, unless they shall by law appoint a different day.

SECTION 3. If, at the time fixed for the beginning of the term of President, the President-elect shall have died, the Vice President-elect shall become President. If a President shall not have been chosen before the time fixed for the beginning of his term, or if the President-elect shall have failed to qualify, then the Vice President-elect shall act as President until a President shall have qualified; and the Congress may by law provide for the case wherein neither a President-elect nor a Vice President-elect shall have qualified, declaring who shall then act as President, or the manner in which one who is to act shall be selected, and such person shall act accordingly until a President or Vice President shall have qualified.

SECTION 4. The Congress may by law provide for the case of the death of any of the persons from whom, the House of Representatives may choose a President whenever the right of choice shall have devolved upon them, and for the case of the death of any of the persons from whom the Senate may choose a Vice President whenever the right of choice shall have devolved upon them.

SECTION 5. Sections 1 and 2 shall take effect on the 15th day of October following the ratification of this article.

SECTION 6. This article shall be inoperative unless it shall have been ratified as an amendment to the Constitution by the legislatures of three-fourths of the several States within seven years from the date of its submission.

Amendment XXI [December 5, 1933]

SECTION 1. The Eighteenth Article of amendment to the Constitution of the United States is hereby repealed.

SECTION 2. The transportation or importation into any State, Territory, or possession of the United States for delivery or use therein of intoxicating liquors in violation of the laws thereof, is hereby prohibited.

SECTION 3. This article shall be inoperative unless it shall have been ratified as an amendment to the Constitution by conventions in the several States, as provided in the Constitution, within seven years from the date of the submission thereof to the States by the Congress.

Amendment XXII [March 1, 1951]

No person shall be elected to the office of the President more than twice, and no person who has held the office of President, or acted as President, for more than two years of a

---

[11]Repealed by the Twenty-first Amendment.

term to which some other person was elected President shall be elected to the office of the President more than once.

But this article shall not apply to any person holding the office of President when this article was proposed by the Congress, and shall not prevent any person who may be holding the office of President, or acting as President, during the term within which this article becomes operative from holding the office of President or acting as President during the remainder of such term.

This article shall be inoperative unless it shall have been ratified as an amendment to the Constitution by the legislatures of three-fourths of the several States within seven years from the date of its submission to the States by the Congress.

Amendment XXIII [March 29, 1961]

SECTION 1. The District constituting the seat of Government of the United States shall appoint in such manner as the Congress may direct.

A number of electors of President and Vice President equal to the whole number of Senators and Representatives in Congress to which the District would be entitled if it were a State, but in no event more than the least populous State; they shall be in addition to those appointed by the States, but they shall be considered, for the purposes of the election of President and Vice President, to be electors appointed by a State; and they shall meet in the District and perform such duties as provided by the twelfth article of amendment.

SECTION 2. The Congress shall have power to enforce this article by appro4riate legislation.

Amendment XXIV [January 23, 1964]

SECTION 1. The right of citizens of the United States to vote in any primary or other election for President or Vice President, for electors for President or Vice President, or for Senator or Representative in Congress, shall not be denied or abridged by the United States or any State by reason of failure to pay any poll tax or other tax.

SECTION 2. The Congress shall have power to enforce this article by appropriate legislation.

Amendment XXV [February 10, 1967]

SECTION 1. In case of the removal of the President from office or of his death or resignation, the Vice President shall become President.

SECTION 2. Whenever there is a vacancy in the office of the Vice President, the President shall nominate a Vice President who shall take office upon confirmation by a majority of both Houses of Congress.

SECTION 3. Whenever the President transmits to the President pro tempore of the Senate and the Speaker of the House of Representatives his written declaration that he is unable to discharge the powers and duties of his office, and until he transmits to them a written declaration to the contrary, such powers and duties shall be discharged by the Vice President as Acting President.

SECTION 4. Whenever the Vice President and a majority of either the principal officers of the executive departments or of such other body as Congress may by law provide, transmit to the President pro tempore of the Senate and the Speaker of the House of Representatives their written declaration that the President is unable to discharge the powers and duties of his office, the Vice President shall immediately assume the powers and duties of the office as Acting President.

Thereafter, when the President transmits to the President pro tempore of the Senate and the Speaker of the House of Representatives his written declaration that no inability exists, he shall resume the powers and duties of his office unless the Vice President and a majority of either the principal officers of the executive departments or of such other body as Congress may by law provide, transmit within four days to the President pro tempore of the Senate and the Speaker of the House of Representatives their written declaration that the President is unable to discharge the powers and duties of his office. Thereupon Congress shall decide the issue, assembling within forty-eight hours for that purpose if not in session. If the Congress, within twenty-one days after receipt of the latter written declaration, or, if Congress is not in session, within twenty-one days after Congress is required to assemble, determines by two-thirds vote of both Houses that the President is unable to discharge the powers and duties of his office, the Vice President shall continue to discharge the same as Acting President; otherwise, the President shall resume the powers and duties of his office.

Amendment XXVI [June 30, 1971]

SECTION 1. The right of citizens of the United States who are eighteen years of age or older to vote shall not be denied or abridged by the United States or by any State on account of age.

SECTION 2. The Congress shall have power to enforce this article by appropriate legislation.

Amendment XXVII [12] [May 7, 1992]

No law, varying the compensation for services of the Senators and Representatives, shall take effect until an election of Representatives shall have intervened.

---

[12]James Madison proposed this amendment in 1789 together with the ten amendments that were adopted as the Bill of Rights, but it failed to win ratification at the time. Congress, however, had set no deadline for its ratification, and over the years—particularly in the 1980s and 1990s—many states voted to add it to the Constitution. With the ratification of Michigan in 1992 it passed the threshold of three-fourths of the states required for adoption, but because the process took more than 200 years, its validity remains in doubt.

PRESIDENTIAL ELECTIONS

Year	Number of States	Candidates	Party	Popular Vote*	Electoral Vote†	Percentage of Popular Vote
1789	11	GEORGE WASHINGTON	No party designations		69	
		John Adams			34	
		Other Candidates			35	
1792	15	GEORGE WASHINGTON	No party designations		132	
		John Adams			77	
		George Clinton			50	
		Other Candidates			5	
1796	16	JOHN ADAMS	Federalist		71	
		Thomas Jefferson	Democratic-Republican		68	
		Thomas Pinckney	Federalist		59	
		Aaron Burr	Democratic-Republican		30	
		Other Candidates			48	
1800	16	THOMAS JEFFERSON	Democratic-Republican		73	
		Aaron Burr	Democratic-Republican		73	
		John Adams	Federalist		65	
		Charles C. Pinckney	Federalist		64	
		John Jay	Federalist		1	
1804	17	THOMAS JEFFERSON	Democratic-Republican		162	
		Charles C. Pinckney	Federalist		14	
1808	17	JAMES MADISON	Democratic-Republican		122	
		Charles C. Pinckney	Federalist		47	
		George Clinton	Democratic-Republican		6	
1812	18	JAMES MADISON	Democratic-Republican		128	
		DeWitt Clinton	Federalist		89	
1816	19	JAMES MONROE	Democratic-Republican		183	
		Rufus King	Federalist		34	
1820	24	JAMES MONROE	Democratic-Republican		231	
		John Quincy Adams	Independent-Republican		1	
1824	24	JOHN QUINCY ADAMS	Democratic-Republican	108,740	84	30.5
		Andrew Jackson	Democratic-Republican	153,544	99	43.1
		William H. Crawford	Democratic-Republican	46,618	41	13.1
		Henry Clay	Democratic-Republican	47,136	37	13.2

*Percentage of popular vote given for any election year may not total 100 percent because candidates receiving less than 1 percent of the popular vote have been omitted.
†Prior to the passage of the Twelfth Amendment in 1904, the electoral college voted for two presidential candidates; the runner-up became Vice-President. Data from Historical Statistics of the United States, Colonial Times to 1957 (1961), pp. 682–683, and The World Almanac.

PRESIDENTIAL ELECTIONS

Year	Number of States	Candidates	Party	Popular Vote*	Electoral Vote†	Percentage of Popular Vote
1828	24	ANDREW JACKSON	Democrat	647,286	178	56.0
		John Quincy Adams	National Republican	508,064	83	44.0
1832	24	ANDREW JACKSON	Democrat	687,502	219	55.0
		Henry Clay	National Republican	530,189	49	42.4
		William Wirt	Anti-Masonic	33,108	7	2.6
		John Floyd			11	
1836	26	MARTIN VAN BUREN	Democrat	765,483	170	50.9
		William H. Harrison	Whig ⎱	739,795	73 26 14	49.1
		Hugh L. White	Whig		11	
		Daniel Webster	Whig ⎰			
		W. P. Mangum	Whig			
1840	26	WILLIAM H. HARRISON	Whig	1,274,624	234	53.1
		Martin Van Buren	Democrat	1,127,781	60	46.9
1844	26	JAMES K. POLK	Democrat	1,338,464	170	49.6
		Henry Clay	Whig	1,300,097	105	48.1
		James G. Birney	Liberty	62,300		2.3
1848	30	ZACHARY TAYLOR	Whig	1,360,967	163	47.4
		Lewis Cass	Democrat	1,222,342	127	42.5
		Martin Van Buren	Free Soil	291,263		10.1
1852	31	FRANKLIN PIERCE	Democrat	1,601,117	254	50.9
		Winfield Scott	Whig	1,385,453	42	44.1
		John P. Hale	Free Soil	155,825		5.0
1856	31	JAMES BUCHANAN	Democrat	1,832,955	174	45.3
		John C. Frémont	Republican	1,339,932	114	33.1
		Millard Fillmore	American ("Know Nothing")	871,731	8	21.6
1860	33	ABRAHAM LINCOLN	Republican	1,865,593	180	39.8
		Stephen A. Douglas	Democrat	1,382,713	12	29.5
		John C. Breckinridge	Democrat	848,356	72	18.1
		John Bell	Constitutional Union	592,906	39	12.6
1864	36	ABRAHAM LINCOLN	Republican	2,206,938	212	55.0
		George B. McClellan	Democrat	1,803,787	21	45.0
1868	37	ULYSSES S. GRANT	Republican	3,013,421	214	52.7
		Horatio Seymour	Democrat	2,706,829	80	47.3
1872	37	ULYSSES S. GRANT	Republican	3,596,745	286	55.6
		Horace Greeley	Democrat	2,843,446	*	43.9

*Because of the death of Greeley, Democratic electors scattered their votes.

PRESIDENTIAL ELECTIONS (CONTINUED)

Year	Number of States	Candidates	Party	Popular Vote*	Electoral Vote†	Percentage of Popular Vote
1876	38	RUTHERFORD B. HAYES	Republican	4,036,572	185	48.0
		Samuel J. Tilden	Democrat	4,284,020	184	51.0
1880	38	JAMES A. GARFIELD	Republican	4,453,295	214	48.5
		Winfield S. Hancock	Democrat	4,414,082	155	48.1
		James B. Weaver	Greenback-Labor	308,578		3.4
1884	38	GROVER CLEVELAND	Democrat	4,879,507	219	48.5
		James G. Blaine	Republican	4,850,293	182	48.2
		Benjamin F. Butler	Greenback-Labor	175,370		1.8
		John P. St. John	Prohibition	150,369		1.5
1888	38	BENJAMIN HARRISON	Republican	5,447,129	233	47.9
		Grover Cleveland	Democrat	5,537,857	168	48.6
		Clinton B. Fisk	Prohibition	249,506		2.2
		Anson J. Streeter	Union Labor	146,935		1.3
1892	44	GROVER CLEVELAND	Democrat	5,555,426	277	46.1
		Benjamin Harrison	Republican	5,182,690	145	43.0
		James B. Weaver	People's	1,029,846	22	8.5
		John Bidwell	Prohibition	264,133		2.2
1896	45	WILLIAM MCKINLEY	Republican	7,102,246	271	51.1
		William J. Bryan	Democrat	6,492,559	176	47.7
1900	45	WILLIAM McKINLEY	Republican	7,218,491	292	51.7
		William J. Bryan	Democrat; Populist	6,356,734	155	45.5
		John C. Woolley	Prohibition	208,914		1.5
1904	45	THEODORE ROOSEVELT	Republican	7,628,461	336	57.4
		Alton B. Parker	Democrat	5,084,223	140	37.6
		Eugene V. Debs	Socialist	402,283		3.0
		Silas C. Swallow	Prohibition	258,536		1.9
1908	46	WILLIAM H. TAFT	Republican	7,675,320	321	51.6
		William J. Bryan	Democrat	6,412,294	162	43.1
		Eugene V. Debs	Socialist	420,793		2.8
		Eugene W. Chafin	Prohibition	253,840		1.7
1912	48	WOODROW WILSON	Democrat	6,296,547	435	41.9
		Theodore Roosevelt	Progressive	4,118,571	88	27.4
		William H. Taft	Republican	3,486,720	8	23.2
		Eugene V. Debs	Socialist	900,672		6.0
		Eugene W. Chafin	Prohibition	206,275		1.4

PRESIDENTIAL ELECTIONS

Year	Number of States	Candidates	Party	Popular Vote*	Electoral Vote†	Percentage of Popular Vote
1916	48	WOODROW WILSON	Democrat	9,127,695	277	49.4
		Charles E. Hughes	Republican	8,533,507	254	46.2
		A. L. Benson	Socialist	585,113		3.2
		J. Frank Hanly	Prohibition	220,506		1.2
1920	48	WARREN G. HARDING	Republican	16,143,407	404	60.4
		James M. Cox	Democrat	9,130,328	127	34.2
		Eugene V. Debs	Socialist	919,799		3.4
		P. P. Christensen	Farmer-Labor	265,411		1.0
1924	48	CALVIN COOLIDGE	Republican	15,718,211	382	54.0
		John W. Davis	Democrat	8,385,283	136	28.8
		Robert M. La Follette	Progressive	4,831,289	13	16.6
1928	48	HERBERT C. HOOVER	Republican	21,391,993	444	58.2
		Alfred E. Smith	Democrat	15,016,169	87	40.9
1932	48	FRANKLIN D. ROOSEVELT	Democrat	22,809,638	472	57.4
		Herbert C. Hoover	Republican	15,758,901	59	39.7
		Norman Thomas	Socialist	881,951		2.2
1936	48	FRANKLIN D. ROOSEVELT	Democrat	27,752,869	523	60.8
		Alfred M. Landon	Republican	16,674,665	8	36.5
		William Lemke	Union	882,479		1.9
1940	48	FRANKLIN D. ROOSEVELT	Democrat	27,307,819	449	54.8
		Wendell L. Willkie	Republican	22,321,018	82	44.8
1944	48	FRANKLIN D. ROOSEVELT	Democrat	25,606,585	432	53.5
		Thomas E. Dewey	Republican	22,014,745	99	46.0
1948	48	HARRY S. TRUMAN	Democrat	24,105,812	303	49.5
		Thomas E. Dewey	Republican	21,970,065	189	45.1
		J. Strom Thurmond	States' Rights	1,169,063	39	2.4
		Henry A. Wallace	Progressive	1,157,172		2.4
1952	48	DWIGHT D. EISENHOWER	Republican	33,936,234	442	55.1
		Adlai E. Stevenson	Democrat	27,314,992	89	44.4
1956	48	DWIGHT D. EISENHOWER	Republican	35,590,472	457*	57.6
		Adlai E. Stevenson	Democrat	26,022,752	73	42.1
1960	50	JOHN F. KENNEDY	Democrat	34,227,096	303†	49.9
		Richard M. Nixon	Republican	34,108,546	219	49.6
1964	50	LYNDON B. JOHNSON	Democrat	42,676,220	486	61.3
		Barry M. Goldwater	Republican	26,860,314	52	38.5

PRESIDENTIAL ELECTIONS (CONTINUED)

Year	Number of States	Candidates	Party	Popular Vote*	Electoral Vote†	Percentage of Popular Vote
1968	50	RICHARD M. NIXON	Republican	31,785,480	301	43.4
		Hubert H. Humphrey	Democrat	31,275,165	191	42.7
		George C. Wallace	American Independent	9,906,473	46	13.5
1972	50	RICHARD M. NIXON‡	Republican	47,165,234	520**	60.6
		George S. McGovern	Democrat	29,168,110	17	37.5
1976	50	JIMMY CARTER	Democrat	40,828,929	297***	50.1
		Gerald R. Ford	Republican	39,148,940	240	47.9
		Eugene McCarthy	Independent	739,256		
1980	50	RONALD REAGAN	Republican	43,201,220	489	50.9
		Jimmy Carter	Democrat	34,913,332	49	41.2
		John B. Anderson	Independent	5,581,379		
1984	50	RONALD REAGAN	Republican	53,428,357	525	59.0
		Walter F. Mondale	Democrat	36,930,923	13	41.0
1988	50	GEORGE H. W. BUSH	Republican	48,901,046	426****	53.4
		Michael Dukakis	Democrat	41,809,030	111	45.6
1992	50	BILL CLINTON	Democrat	43,728,275	370	43.2
		George Bush	Republican	38,167,416	168	37.7
		H. Ross Perot	United We Stand, America	19,237,247		19.0
1996	50	BILL CLINTON	Democrat	45,590,703	379	49.0
		Robert Dole	Republican	37,816,307	159	41.0
		H. Ross Perot	Reform	7,866,284		8.0
2000	50	GEORGE W. BUSH	Republican	50,459,624	271	47.9
		Albert Gore, Jr.	Democrat	51,003,328	266	49.4
		Ralph Nader	Green	2,882,985		2.7
2004	50	GEORGE W. BUSH	Republican	62,040,610	286*****	50.7
		John F. Kerry	Democrat	59,028,444	251	48.3
2008	50	BARACK H. OBAMA	Democrat	69,456,897	365	52.9
		John McCain	Republican	59,934,814	173	45.7

*Walter B. Jones received 1 electoral vote.
†Harry F. Byrd received 15 electoral votes.
‡Resigned August 9, 1974: Vice President Gerald R. Ford became President.
**John Hospers received 1 electoral vote.
***Ronald Reagan received 1 electoral vote.
****Lloyd Bentsen received 1 electoral vote.
*****John Edwards received 1 electoral vote.

GLOSSARY

Abolitionist movement A radical antislavery crusade committed to the immediate end of slavery that emerged in the three decades before the Civil War.

Act for Religious Toleration The first law in America to call for freedom of worship for all Christians. It was enacted in Maryland in 1649 to quell disputes between Catholics and Protestants, but it failed to bring peace.

Actual representation The practice whereby elected representatives normally reside in their districts and are directly responsive to localinterests.

Acquired immune deficiency syndrome (AIDS) Acomplex of deadly pathologies resulting from infection with the human immunodeficiency virus (HIV).

Affirmative Action A set of policies to open opportunities in business and education for members of minority groups and women by allowing race and sex to be factors included in decisions to hire, award contracts, or admit students to higher education programs.

Age of Enlightenment Major intellectual movement occurring in Western Europe in the late seventeenth and early eighteenth centuries. Inspired by recent scientific advances, thinkers emphasized the role of human reason in understanding the world and directing its events. Their ideas placed less emphasis on God's role in ordering worldly affairs.

Alamo Franciscan mission at San Antonio, Texas, that was the site in 1836 of a siege and massacre of Texans by Mexican troops.

Albany Plan of Union Plan put forward in 1754 by Massachusetts governor William Shirley, Benjamin Franklin, and other colonial leaders, calling for an intercolonial union to manage defense and Indian affairs. The plan was rejected by participants at the Albany Congress.

Albany Regency Popular name after 1820 for the state political machine in New York headed by Martin Van Buren.

Alien Friends Act Law passed by Congress in 1798 authorizing the president during peacetime to expel aliens suspected of subversive activities; one of the **Alien and Sedition Acts.**

Alliance for Progress Program of economic aid to Latin America during the Kennedy administration.

Allies In World War I, Britain, France, Russia, and other belligerent nations fighting against the **Central Powers** but not including the United States, which insisted upon being merely an associated nation. In World War II, the Allies fighting the **Axis Powers** included the United States as well as the Soviet Union, Great Britain, France, China, and other nations.

American Anti-Slavery Society The first national organization of abolitionists, founded in 1833.

American Colonization Society Organization, founded in 1817 by antislavery reformers, that called for gradual emancipation and the removal of freed blacks to Africa.

American Federation of Labor (AFL) Union formed in 1886 that organized skilled workers along craft lines and emphasized a few workplace issues rather than a broad social program.

American Female Moral Reform Society Organization founded in 1839 by female reformers that established homes of refuge for prostitutes and petitioned for state laws that would criminalize adultery and the seduction of women.

American Indian Movement (AIM) Group of Native American political activists who used confrontations with the federal government to publicize their case for Indian rights.

Americans with Disabilities Act Legislation in 1992 that banned discrimination against physically handicapped persons in employment, transportation, and public accommodations.

American System The program of government subsidies favored by Henry Clay and his followers to promote American economic growth and protect domestic manufacturers from foreign competition.

American system of manufacturing A technique of production pioneered in the United States in the first half of the nineteenth century that relied on precision manufacturing with the use of interchangeable parts.

American Temperance Society National organization established in 1826 by evangelical Protestants that campaigned for total abstinence from alcohol and was successful in sharply lowering per capita consumption of alcohol.

Anarchist A person who believes that all government interferes with individual liberty and should be abolished by whatever means.

Anglican Of or belonging to the Church of England, a Protestant denomination.

Anglo–American Accords Series of agreements reached in the British–American Convention of 1818 that fixed the western boundary between the United States and Canada at the 49th parallel, allowed for the joint occupation of the Oregon Country, and restored to Americans fishing rights off Newfoundland.

Annapolis Convention Conference of state delegates at Annapolis, Maryland, that issued a call in September 1786 for a convention to meet at Philadelphia in May 1787 to consider fundamental changes to the **Articles of Confederation.**

Antifederalist An opponent of the **Constitution** in the debate over its ratification.

Anti-Masons Third party formed in 1827 in opposition to the presumed power and influence of the Masonic order.

Appeal to the Colored Citizens of the World Pamphlet published in 1829 by David Walker, a Boston free black, calling for slaves to rise up in rebellion.

Articles of Confederation Written document setting up the loose confederation of states that comprised the first national government of the United States from 1781 to 1788.

Atlanta Compromise Booker T. Washington's policy accepting segregation and **disfranchisement** for African Americans in exchange for white assistance in education and job training.

Atlantic Charter Statement of common principles and war aims developed by President Franklin Roosevelt and British Prime Minister Winston Churchill at a meeting in August 1941.

Australian ballot Secret voting and the use of official ballots rather than party tickets.

Axis Powers The opponents of the United States and its allies in World War II. The Rome–Berlin Axis was formed between Germany and Italy in 1936 and included Japan after 1940.

Aztecs A warrior people who dominated the Valley of Mexico from about 1100 until their conquest in 1519–21 by Spanish soldiers led by Hernán Cortés.

Bacon's Rebellion Violent conflict in Virginia (1675–1676), beginning with settler attacks on Indians but culminating in a rebellion led by Nathaniel Bacon against Virginia's government.

Baker v. Carr U.S. Supreme Court decision in 1962 that allowed federal courts to review the apportionment of state legislative districts and established the principle that such districts should have roughly equal populations ("one person, one vote").

Bank War The political struggle between President Andrew Jackson and the supporters of the **Second Bank of the United States.**

Battle of New Orleans Decisive American **War of 1812** victory over British troops in January 1815 that ended any British hopes of gaining control of the lower Mississippi River Valley.

Battle of Plattsburg American naval victory on Lake Champlain in September 1814 in the **War of 1812** that thwarted a British invasion from Canada.

Battle of Put-in-Bay American naval victory on Lake Erie in September 1813 in the **War of 1812** that denied the British strategic control over the Great Lakes.

Battle of the Atlantic The long struggle between German submarines and the British and U.S. navies in the North Atlantic from 1940 to 1943.

Battle of the Little Bighorn Battle in which Colonel George A. Custer and the Seventh Cavalry were defeated by the Sioux and Cheyennes under Sitting Bull and Crazy Horse in Montana in 1876.

Battles of Lexington and Concord The first two battles of the American Revolution which resulted in a total of 273 British soldiers dead, wounded, and missing and nearly 100 Americans dead, wounded, and missing.

Bay of Pigs Site in Cuba of an unsuccessful landing by 1,400 anti-Castro Cuban refugees in April 1961.

Beaver Wars Series of bloody conflicts, occurring between 1640s and 1680s, during which the Iroquois fought the French and their Indian allies for control of the fur trade in eastern North America and the Great Lakes region.

Benevolent empire Network of reform associations affiliated with Protestant churches in the early nineteenth century dedicated to the restoration of moral order.

Berlin blockade Three-hundred-day Soviet blockade of land access to United States, British, and French occupation zones in Berlin, 1948–1949.

Berlin Wall Wall erected by East Germany in 1961 and torn down in 1989 that isolated West Berlin from the surrounding areas in Communist-controlled East Berlin and East Germany.

Bill of Rights A written summary of inalienable rights and liberties.

Black codes Laws passed by states and municipalities denying many rights of citizenship to free blacks before the Civil War. Also, during the Reconstruction era, laws passed by newly elected southern state legislatures to control black labor, mobility, and employment.

Black Hawk's War Short 1832 war in which federal troops and Illinois militia units defeated the Sauk and Fox Indians led by Black Hawk.

Black Panthers Political and social movement among black Americans, founded in Oakland, California, in 1966 and emphasizing black economic and political power.

Black Power Philosophy emerging after 1965 that real economic and political gains for African-Americans could come only through self-help, **self-determination,** and organizing for direct political influence. Latinos and Native Americans developed their own versions as Brown Power and Red Power, respectively.

"Bleeding Kansas" Violence between pro- and antislavery forces in Kansas Territory after the passage of the **Kansas-Nebraska Act** in 1854.

Blitzkrieg German war tactic in World War II ("lightning war") involving the concentration of air and armored firepower to punch and exploit holes in opposing defensive lines.

Bolshevik Member of the communist movement in Russia that established the Soviet government after the 1917 Russian Revolution; hence, by extension, any radical or disruptive person or movement seeking to transform economic and political relationships.

Bonus Army A group of unemployed veterans who demonstrated in Washington for the payment of service bonuses, only to be dispersed violently by the U.S. Army in 1932.

Boston Massacre After months of increasing friction between townspeople and the British troops stationed in the city, on March 5, 1770, British troops fired on American civilians in Boston.

Boston Tea Party Incident that occurred on December 16, 1773, in which Bostonians, disguised as Indians, destroyed $9,000 worth of tea belonging to the British East India Company in order to prevent payment of the duty on it.

British Constitution The principles, procedures, and precedents that governed the operation of the British government. These could be found in no single written document

Brook Farm A utopian community and experimental farm established in 1841 near Boston.

Brown v. Board of Education of Topeka Supreme Court decision in 1954 that declared that "separate but equal" schools for children of different races violated the **Constitution.**

Bureau of Reclamation Federal agency established in 1902 providing public funds for irrigation projects in arid regions; played a major role in the development of the West by constructing dams, reservoirs, and irrigation systems, especially beginning in the 1930s.

Cahokia Located near modern St. Louis, this was one of the largest urban centers created by Mississippian peoples, containing perhaps 30,000 residents in 1250.

Californios Persons of Spanish descent living in California.

Camp David Agreement Agreement to reduce points of conflict between Israel and Egypt, hammered out in 1977 with the help of U.S. president Jimmy Carter.

Carpetbaggers Pejorative term to describe northern transplants to the South, many of whom were Union soldiers who stayed in the South after the war.

Central Intelligence Agency (CIA) Agency that coordinates the gathering and evaluation of military and economic information on other nations, established in 1947.

Central Powers Germany and its World War I allies Austria, Turkey, and Bulgaria.

Chain migration Process common to many immigrant groups whereby one family member brings over other family members, who in turn bring other relatives and friends and occasionally entire villages.

Charles River Bridge v. Warren Bridge Supreme Court decision of 1837 that promoted economic competition by ruling that the broader rights of the community took precedence over any presumed right of monopoly granted in a corporate charter.

Cherokee War Conflict (1759–1761) on the southern frontier between the Cherokee Indians and colonists from Virginia southward. It caused South Carolina to request the aid of British troops and resulted in the surrender of more Indian land to white colonists.

Chesapeake Incident Attack in 1807 by the British ship *Leopard* on the American ship *Chesapeake* in American territorial waters that nearly provoked an Anglo-American war.

Chisholm Trail The route followed by Texas cattle raisers driving their herds north to markets at Kansas railheads.

Church of Jesus Christ of Latter-day Saints See **Mormon Church.**

Civil Rights Act of 1866 Law that defined national citizenship and specified the civil rights to which all national citizens were entitled.

Civil Rights Act of 1875 Law that prohibited racial discrimination in jury selection, public transportation, and public accommodations; declared unconstitutional by the U.S. Supreme Court in 1883.

Civil Rights Act of 1964 Federal legislation that outlawed discrimination in public accommodations and employment on the basis of race, skin color, sex, religion, or national origin.

Claims club A group of local settlers on the nineteenth-century frontier who banded together to prevent the price of their land claims from being bid up by outsiders at public land auctions.

Coercive Acts Legislation passed by Parliament in 1774; included the Boston Port Act, the Massachusetts Government Act, the Administration of Justice Act, and the **Quartering Act** of 1774.

Cold War The political and economic confrontation between the Soviet Union and the United States that dominated world affairs from 1946 to 1989.

Collective bargaining Representatives of a union negotiating with management on behalf of all members.

Colored Farmers' Alliance An organization of southern black farmers formed in Texas in 1886 in response to the **Southern Farmers' Alliance,** which did not accept black people as members.

Columbian exchange The transatlantic exchange of plants, animals, and diseases that occurred after the first European contact with the Americas.

Committees of Correspondence Committees formed in Massachusetts and other colonies in the pre-Revolutionary period to keep Americans informed about British measures that would affect the colonies.

Committee of Safety Any of the extralegal committees that directed the Revolutionary movement and carried on the functions of government at the local level in the period between the breakdown of royal authority and the establishment of regular governments under the new state constitutions. Some Committees of Safety continued to function throughout the Revolutionary War.

Committee on Public Information (CPI) Government agency during World War I that sought to shape public opinion in support of the war effort through newspapers, pamphlets, speeches, films, and other media.

Communism A social structure based on the common ownership of property.

Compromise of 1850 The four-step compromise which admitted California as a free state, allowed the residents of the New Mexico and Utah territories to decide the slavery issue for themselves, ended the slave trade in the District of Columbia, and passed a new fugitive slave law to enforce the constitutional provision stating that a slave escaping into a free state shall be delivered back to the owner.

Compromise of 1877 The congressional settling of the 1876 election which installed Republican Rutherford B. Hayes in the White House and gave Democrats control of all state governments in the South.

Conciliatory Proposition Plan proposed by Lord North and adopted by the House of Commons in February 1775 whereby Parliament would "forbear" taxation of Americans in colonies whose assemblies imposed taxes considered satisfactory by the British government. The Continental Congress rejected this plan on July 31, 1775.

Confederate States of America Nation proclaimed in Montgomery, Alabama, in February 1861 after the seven states of the Lower South seceded from the United States.

Confiscation Act of 1862 Second confiscation law passed by Congress, ordering the seizure of land from disloyal Southerners and the emancipation of their slaves.

Congressional Reconstruction Name given to the period 1867–1870 when the Republican-dominated Congress controlled **Reconstruction era** policy. It is sometimes known as Radical Reconstruction, after the radical faction in the **Republican Party.**

Congress of Industrial Organizations (CIO) An alliance of industrial unions that spurred the 1930s organizational drive among the mass-production industries.

Congress of Racial Equality (CORE) Civil rights group formed in 1942 and committed to nonviolent civil disobedience, such as the 1961 "freedom rides."

Conservation The efficient management and use of natural resources, such as forests, grasslands, and rivers, as opposed to **preservation** or uncontrolled exploitation.

Constitutional Convention Convention that met in Philadelphia in 1787 and drafted the **Constitution of the United States.**

Constitutional Union party National party formed in 1860, mainly by former **Whigs,** that emphasized allegiance to the Union and strict enforcement of all national legislation.

Constitution of the United States The written document providing for a new central government of the United States, drawn up at the **Constitutional** Convention in 1787 and ratified by the states in 1788.

Containment The policy of resisting further expansion of the Soviet bloc through diplomacy and, if necessary, military action, developed in 1947–48.

Continental Army The regular or professional army authorized by the Second Continental Congress and commanded by General George Washington during the Revolutionary War. Better training and longer service distinguished its soldiers from the state militiamen.

Continental Association Agreement, adopted by the **First Continental Congress** in 1774 in response to the **Coercive Acts,** to cut off trade with Britain until the objectionable measures were repealed. Local committees were established to enforce the provisions of the association.

Contract theory of government The belief that government is established by human beings to protect certain rights—such as life, liberty, and property—that are theirs by natural, divinely sanctioned law and that when government protects these rights, people are obligated to obey it. But when government violates its part of the bargain (or contract) between the rulers and the ruled, the people are no longer required to obey it and may establish a new government that will do a better job of protecting them. Elements of this theory date back to the ancient Greeks; John Locke used it in his *Second Treatise on Government* (1682), and Thomas Jefferson gave it memorable expression in the Declaration of Independence, where it provides the rationale for renouncing allegiance to King George III.

Contract with America Platform on which many Republican candidates ran for Congress in 1994. Associated with House Speaker Newt Gingrich, it proposed a sweeping reduction in the role and activities of the federal government.

Copperheads A term Republicans applied to northern war dissenters and those suspected of aiding the Confederate cause during the Civil War.

Council of Economic Advisers Board of three professional economists established in 1946 to advise the president on economic policy.

Counterculture Various alternatives to mainstream values and behaviors that became popular in the 1960s, including experimentation with psychedelic drugs, communal living, a return to the land, Asian religions, and experimental art.

Country (Real Whig) ideology Strain of thought first appearing in England in the late seventeenth century in response to the growth of governmental power and a national debt. Main ideas stressed the threat to personal liberty posed by a standing army and high taxes and emphasized the need for property holders to retain the right to consent to taxation.

Coureurs de bois French for "woods runner," an independent fur trader in New France.

Covenant A formal agreement or contract.

Coxey's Army A protest march of unemployed workers, led by Populist businessman Jacob Coxey, demanding inflation and a public works program during the depression of the 1890s.

Cult of domesticity The belief that women, by virtue of their sex, should stay home as the moral guardians of family life.

culture areas Geographical regions inhabited by peoples who share similar basic patterns of subsistence and social organization.

*Dartmouth College v. Woodward*Supreme Court decision of 1819 that prohibited states from interfering with the privileges granted to a private corporation.

Dawes Act An 1887 law terminating tribal ownership of land and allotting some parcels of land to individual Indians with the remainder opened for white settlement.

D-Day June 6, 1944, the day of the first paratroop drops and amphibious landings on the coast of Normandy, France, in the first stage of **Operation OVERLORD** during World War II.

Declaration of Independence The document by which the Second Continental Congress announced and justified its decision (reached July 2, 1776) to renounce the colonies' allegiance to the British government. Drafted mainly by Thomas Jefferson and adopted by Congress on July 4, the declaration's indictment of the king provides a remarkably full catalog of the colonists' grievances, and Jefferson's eloquent and inspiring statement of the **contract theory of government** makes the document one of the world's great state papers.

Declaration of London Statement drafted by an international conference in 1909 to clarify international law and specify the rights of neutral nations.

Declaration of Rights and Grievances Resolves, adopted by the **Stamp Act Congress** at New York in 1765, asserting that the **Stamp Act** and other taxes imposed on the colonists without their consent, given through their colonial legislatures, were unconstitutional.

Declaration of Sentiments The resolutions passed at the **Seneca Falls. Convention** in 1848 calling for full female equality, including the right to vote.

Declaration of the Causes and Necessity of Taking Up Arms Document, written mainly by John Dickinson of Pennsylvania and adopted on July 6, 1775, by which the Second Continental Congress justified its armed resistance against British measures.

Declaratory Act Law passed in 1766 to accompany repeal of the **Stamp Act** that stated that Parliament had the authority to legislate for the colonies "in all cases whatsoever." Whether "legislate" meant tax was not clear to Americans.

Deindustrialization The process of economic change involving the disappearance of outmoded industries and the transfer of factories to new low-wage locations, with devastating effects in the Northeast and Middle West, especially in the 1970s and 1980s.

Deism Religious orientation that rejects divine revelation and holds that the workings of nature alone reveal God's design for the universe.

Democratic Party Political party formed in the 1820s under the leadership of Andrew Jackson; favored states' rights and a limited role for the federal government, especially in economic affairs.

Denmark Vesey's Conspiracy The most carefully devised slave revolt, named after its leader, a free black in Charleston. The rebels planned to seize control of Charleston in 1822 and escape to freedom in Haiti, a free black republic, but they were betrayed by other slaves, and seventy-five conspirators were executed.

Deregulation Reduction or removal of government regulations and encouragement of direct competition in many important industries and economic sectors.

Détente A lessening of tension, applied to improved American relations with the Soviet Union and China in the mid-1970s.

Disfranchisement The use of legal means to bar individuals or groups from voting.

Dixiecrats Southern Democrats who broke from the party in 1948 over the issue of civil rights and ran a presidential tickets as the States' Rights Democrats.

Dollar diplomacy The U.S. policy of using private investment in other nations to promote American diplomatic goals and business interests.

Dominion of New England James II's failed plan of 1686 to combine eight northern colonies into a single large province, to be governed by a royal appointee (Sir Edmund Andros) with an appointed council but no elective assembly. The plan ended with James's ouster from the English throne and rebellion in Massachusetts against Andros's rule.

Dred Scott **decision** Supreme Court ruling, in a lawsuit brought by Dred Scott, a slave demanding his freedom based on his residence in a free state and a free territory with his master, that slaves could not be U.S. citizens and that Congress had no jurisdiction over slavery in the territories.

Eastern Front The area of military operations in World War II located east of Germany in eastern Europe and the Soviet Union.

Economic Recovery and Tax Act of 1981 (ERTA) A major revision of the federal income tax system.

Eighteenth Amendment Constitutional revision, ratified in 1919 and repealed in 1933, that prohibited the manufacture or sale of alcohol in the United States.

Emancipation Proclamation Decree announced by President Abraham Lincoln in September 1862 and formally issued on January 1, 1863, freeing slaves in all Confederate states still in rebellion.

Embargo Act of 1807 Act passed by Congress in 1807 prohibiting American ships from leaving for any foreign port.

Empresario An agent who received a land grant from the Spanish or Mexican government in return for organizing settlements.

Encomienda In the Spanish colonies, the grant to a Spanish settler of a certain number of Indian subjects, who would pay him tribute in goods and labor.

Enumerated products Items produced in the colonies and enumerated in acts of Parliament that could be legally shipped from the colony of origin only to specified locations, usually England and other destinations within the British Empire.

Environmental Protection Agency (EPA) Federal agency created in 1970 to oversee environmental monitoring and cleanup programs.

Era of Good Feelings The period from 1817 to 1823 in which the disappearance of the **Federalists** enabled the **Republicans** to govern in a spirit of seemingly nonpartisan harmony.

Espionage Act Law whose vague prohibition against obstructing the nation's war effort was used to crush dissent and criticism during World War I.

Fair Employment Practice Committee (FEPC) Federal agency established in 1941 to curb racial discrimination in war production jobs and government employment.

Farmers' Alliance A broad mass movement in the rural South and West during the late nineteenth century, encompassing several organizations and demanding economic and political reforms; helped create the **Populist Party.**

Fascist Government Subscribing to a philosophy of governmental dictatorship that merges the interests of the state, armed forces, and big business; associated with the dictatorship of Italian leader Benito Mussolini between 1922 and 1943 and also often applied to Nazi Germany.

Federal Deposit Insurance Corporation (FDIC) Government agency that guarantees bank deposits, thereby protecting both depositors and banks.

Federal Highway Act of 1956 Measure that provided federal funding to build a nationwide system of interstate and defense highways.

Federalism The sharing of powers between the national government and the states.

Federalist A supporter of the **Constitution** who favored its ratification.

Federal Reserve Act The 1913 law that revised banking and currency by extending limited government regulation through the creation of the Federal Reserve System.

Federal Trade Commission (FTC) Government agency established in 1914 to provide regulatory oversight of business activity.

Field Order No. 15 Order by General William T. Sherman in January 1865 to set aside abandoned land along the southern Atlantic coast for forty-acre grants to freedmen; rescinded by President Andrew Johnson later that year.

Fifteenth Amendment Passed by Congress in 1869, guaranteed the right of American men to vote, regardless of race.

Fireside chats Speeches broadcast nationally over the radio in which President Franklin Roosevelt explained complex issues and programs in plain language, as though his listeners were gathered around the fireside with him.

First Continental Congress Meeting of delegates from most of the colonies held in 1774 in response to the **Coercive Acts.** The Congress endorsed the Suffolk Resolves, adopted the **Declaration of Rights and Grievances,** and agreed to establish the **Continental Association** to put economic pressure on Britain to repeal its objectionable measures. The Congress also wrote addresses to the king, the people of Britain, and the American people.

Fletcher v. Peck Supreme Court decision of 1810 that overturned a state law by ruling that it violated a legal contract.

Fort Sumter Begun in the late 1820s to protect Charleston, South Carolina, it became the center of national attention in April 1861 when President Lincoln attempted to provision federal troops at the fort, triggering a hostile response from on-shore Confederate forces, opening the Civil War.

Fourierist communities Short-lived utopian communities in the 1840s based on the ideas of economic cooperation and self-sufficiency popularized by the Frenchman Charles Fourier.

Fourteenth Amendment Constitutional amendment passed by Congress in April 1866 incorporating some of the features of the **Civil Rights Act of 1866.** It prohibited states from violating the civil rights of its citizens and offered states the choice of allowing black people to vote or losing representation in Congress.

Frame of Government William Penn's 1682 plan for the government of Pennsylvania, which created a relatively weak legislature and strong executive. It also contained a provision for religious freedom.

Franco-American Accord of 1800 Settlement reached with France that brought an end to the **Quasi-War** and released the United States from its 1778 alliance with France.

Freedmen's Bureau Agency established by Congress in March 1865 to provide social, educational, and economic services, advice, and protection to former slaves and destitute whites; lasted seven years.

Freedom Summer Voter registration effort in rural Mississippi organized by black and white civil rights workers in 1964.

Free silver Philosophy that the government should expand the money supply by purchasing and coining all the silver offered to it.

Free Speech Movement (FSM) Student movement at the University of California, Berkeley, formed in 1964 to protest limitations on political activities on campus.

French and Indian War The last of the Anglo-French colonial wars (1754–1763) and the first in which fighting began in North America. The war (which merged with the European conflict known as the Seven Years' War) ended with France's defeat and loss of its North American empire.

Fugitive Slave Act Law, part of the Compromise of 1850, that required authorities in the North to assist southern slave catchers and return runaway slaves to their owners.

Fundamental Constitutions of Carolina A complex plan for organizing the colony of Carolina, drafted in 1669 by Anthony Ashley Cooper and John Locke. Its provisions included a scheme for creating a hierarchy of nobles who would own vast amounts of land and wield political power; below them would be a class of freedmen and slaves. The provisions were never implemented by the Carolina colonists.

Fundamentalists Religious conservatives who believe in the literal accuracy and divine inspiration of the Bible; the name derives from an influential series of pamphlets, *The Fundamentals* (1909–1914).

Gabriel Prosser's Rebellion Slave revolt that failed when Gabriel Prosser, a slave preacher and blacksmith, organized a thousand slaves for an attack on Richmond, Virginia, in 1800. A thunderstorm upset the timing of the attack, and a slave informer alerted the whites. Prosser and twenty-five of his followers were executed.

Gag rule Procedural rule passed in the House of Representatives that prevented discussion of antislavery petitions from 1836 to 1844.

Gang system The organization and supervision of slave field hands into working teams on southern plantations.

Gentlemen's Agreement A diplomatic agreement in 1907 between Japan and the United States curtailing but not abolishing Japanese immigration.

GI Bill of Rights Legislation in June 1944 that eased the return of veterans into American society by providing educational and employment benefits.

Gibbons v. Ogden Supreme Court decision of 1824 involving coastal commerce that overturned a steamboat monopoly granted by the state of New York on the grounds that only Congress had the authority to regulate interstate commerce.

Gilded Age Term applied to late-nineteenth-century America that refers to the shallow display and worship of wealth characteristic of the period.

Glasnost Russian for "openness," applied to Mikhail Gorbachev's encouragement of new ideas and easing of political repression in the Soviet Union.

Glorious Revolution Bloodless revolt that occurred in England in 1688 when parliamentary leaders invited William of Orange, a Protestant, to assume the English throne and James II fled to France. James's ouster was prompted by fears that the birth of his son would establish a Catholic dynasty in England.

Gospel of Wealth Thesis that hard work and perseverance lead to wealth, implying that poverty is a character flaw.

Grandfather clause Rule that required potential voters to demonstrate that their grandfathers had been eligible to vote; used in some southern states after 1890 to limit the black electorate, as most black men's grandfathers had been slaves.

Grand Settlement of 1701 Separate peace treaties negotiated by Iroquois diplomats at Montreal and Albany that marked the beginning of Iroquois neutrality in conflicts between the French and the British in North America.

Grange The National Grange of the Patrons of Husbandry, a national organization of farm owners formed after the Civil War.

Granger laws State laws enacted in the Midwest in the 1870s that regulated rates charged by railroads, grain elevator operators, and other middlemen.

Great Awakening Tremendous religious revival in colonial America. Sparked by the tour of the English evangelical minister George Whitefield, the Awakening struck first in the Middle Colonies and New England in the 1740s and eventually spread to the southern colonies by the 1760s.

Great Compromise Plan proposed by Roger Sherman of Connecticut at the 1787 **Constitutional Convention** for creating a national bicameral legislature in which all states would be equally represented in the Senate and proportionally represented in the House.

Great Depression The nation's worst economic crisis, extending throughout the 1930s, producing unprecedented bank failures, unemployment, and industrial and agricultural collapse and prompting an expanded role for the federal government.

Great League of Peace and Power Confederation of five Iroquois nations – the Mohawks, Oncidas, Onodagas, Cayugas, and Senecas – formed in the fifteenth century to diminish internal conflict and increase collective strength against their enemies.

Great Migration The mass movement of African Americans from the rural South to the urban North, spurred especially by new job opportunities during World War I and the 1920s.

Great Society Theme of Lyndon Johnson's administration, focusing on poverty, education, and civil rights.

Great Uprising Unsuccessful railroad strike of 1877 to protest wage cuts and the use of federal troops against strikers; the first nationwide work stoppage in American history.

Greater East Asia Co-Prosperity Sphere Japanese goal of an East Asian economy controlled by Japan and serving the needs of Japanese industry.

Greenback Party A third party of the 1870s and 1880s that garnered temporary support by advocating currency inflation to expand the economy and assist debtors.

Gulf of Tonkin Resolution Congressional resolution in August 1964 that authorized the president to take all necessary measures to protect South Vietnam, adopted after reports of North Vietnamese attacks on U.S. navy ships in the Gulf of Tonkin off North Vietnam.

Halfway Covenant Plan adopted in 1662 by New England clergy to deal with the problem of declining church membership. It allowed adults who had been baptized because their parents were church members but who had not yet experienced conversion to have their own children baptized. Without the Halfway Covenant, these third-generation children would remain unbaptized until their parents experienced conversion.

Harlem Renaissance A new African-American cultural awareness that flourished in literature, art, and music in the 1920s.

Headright system A system of land distribution during early colonial era that granted settlers fifty acres for themselves and another fifty for each "head" (or person) they brought to the colony.

Helsinki Accords Agreement in 1975 among NATO and Warsaw Pact members that recognized European national boundaries as set after World War II and included guarantees of human rights.

Holocaust The systematic murder of millions of European Jews and others deemed undesirable by Nazi Germany.

Homestead Act Law passed by Congress in 1862 providing 160 acres of land free to anyone who would live on the plot and farm it for five years.

Hooverville Shantytown, sarcastically named after President Hoover, in which unemployed and homeless people lived in makeshift shacks, tents, and boxes. Hoovervilles cropped up in many cities in 1930 and 1931.

Horatio Alger Stories A series of best-selling tales about young rags-to-riches heroes first published in 1867 stressing the importance of neat clothes, cleanliness, thrift, and hard work. The books also highlighted the importance of chance in getting ahead and the responsibility of those better off to serve as positive role models.

Horizontal integration The merger of competitors in the same industry.

House Committee on Un-American Activities Congressional Committee (1938-1975) that investigated suspected Nazi and Communist sympathizers.

House of Burgesses The legislature of colonial Virginia. First organized in 1619, it was the first institution of representative government in the English colonies.

Hull House Chicago **settlement house** that became part of a broader neighborhood revitalization and immigrant assistance project led by Jane Addams.

Immigration and Nationality Act of 1965 Federal legislation that replaced the national quota system for immigration with overall limits of 170,000 immigrants per year from the Eastern Hemisphere and 120,000 per year from the Western Hemisphere.

Imperialism   The policy and practice of exploiting nations and peoples for the benefit of an imperial power either directly through military occupation and colonial rule or indirectly through economic domination of resources and markets.

Impressment   The British policy of forcibly enlisting American sailors into the British navy.

Indentured servant   An individual—usually male but occasionally female— who contracted to serve a master for a period of four to seven years in return for payment of the servant's passage to America. Indentured servitude was the primary labor system in the Chesapeake colonies for most of the seventeenth century.

Independent Treasury System   Fiscal arrangement first instituted by President Martin Van Buren in which the federal government kept its money in regional vaults ("pet banks") and transacted its business entirely in hard money.

Indian Removal Act   Legislation passed by Congress in 1830 that provided funds for removing and resettling eastern Indians in the West. It granted the president the authority to use force if necessary.

Initiative   Procedure by which citizens can introduce a subject for legislation, usually through a petition signed by a specific number of voters.

Intermediate Nuclear Force Agreement (INF)   Disarmament agreement between the United States and the Soviet Union under which an entire class of missiles would be removed and destroyed and on-site inspections would be permitted for verification.

International Monetary Fund (IMF)   International organization established in 1945 to assist nations in maintaining stable currencies.

Internet   The system of interconnected computers and servers that allows the exchange of e-mail, posting of websites, and other means of instant communication.

Interstate and Defense Highways   Federal legislation in 1956 committed the federal government to finance more than 40,000 miles of new limited access freeways to criss-cross the United States.

Interstate Commerce Act   The 1887 law that expanded federal power over business by prohibiting pooling and discriminatory rates by railroads and establishing the first federal regulatory agency, the **Interstate Commerce Commission.**

Interstate Commerce Commission (ICC)   The first federal regulatory agency, established in 1887 to oversee railroad practices.

Intolerable Acts   American term for the **Coercive Acts** and the **Quebec Act.**

Irreconcilables   Group of U.S. senators adamantly opposed to ratification of the **Treaty of Versailles** after World War I.

Island hopping   In the Pacific Theater during World War II, the strategy in which U.S. forces seized selected Japanese-held islands while bypassing and isolating other islands held by Japan.

Jacksonian Democrats   See **Democratic Party.**

Jay's Treaty   Treaty with Britain negotiated in 1794 in which the United States made major concessions to avert a war over the British seizure of American ships.

Jazz Age   The 1920s, so called for the popular music of the day as a symbol of the many changes taking place in the mass culture.

Jim Crow law s Segregation laws that became widespread in the South during the 1890s, named for a minstrel show character portrayed satirically by white actors in blackface.

John Brown's Raid   New England abolitionist John Brown's ill-fated attempt to free Virginia's slaves with a raid on the federal arsenal at Harpers Ferry, Virginia, in 1859.

Joint-stock company   Business enterprise in which a group of stockholders pooled their money to engage in trade or to fund colonizing expeditions. Joint-stock companies participated in the founding of the Virginia, Plymouth, and Massachusetts Bay colonies.

Judicial review   A power implied in the **Constitution** that gives federal courts the right to review and determine the constitutionality of acts passed by Congress and state legislatures.

Judiciary Act of 1789   Act of Congress that implemented the judiciary clause of the **Constitution** by establishing the Supreme Court and a system of lower federal courts.

Kansas-Nebraska Act   Law passed in 1854 creating the Kansas and Nebraska Territories but leaving the question of slavery open to residents, thereby repealing the **Missouri Compromise.**

Kellogg-Briand Pact   1928 international treaty that denounced aggression and war but lacked provisions for enforcement.

King George's War   The third Anglo-French war in North America (1744–1748), part of the European conflict known as the War of the Austrian Succession. During the North American fighting, New Englanders captured the French fortress of Louisbourg, only to have it returned to France after the peace negotiations.

King Philip's War   Conflict in New England (1675–1676) between Wampanoags, Narragansetts, and other Indian peoples against English settlers; sparked by English encroachments on native lands.

King William's War   The first Anglo-French conflict in North America (1689–1697), the American phase of Europe's War of the League of Augsburg. Ended in negotiated peace that reestablished the balance of power.

Knights of Labor   Labor union that included skilled and unskilled workers irrespective of race or gender; founded in 1869, peaked in the 1880s, and declined when its advocacy of the eight-hour workday led to violent strikes in 1886.

Know-Nothing Party   Anti-immigrant party formed from the wreckage of the **Whig Party** and some disaffected northern Democrats in 1854.

Korean War   War between North Korea and South Korea (1950–1953) in which the People's Republic of China fought on the side of North Korea and the United States and other nations fought on the side of South Korea under the auspices of the United Nations.

Ku Klux Klan Perhaps the most prominent of the vigilante groups that terrorized black people in the South during **Reconstruction Era,** founded by Confederate veterans in 1866.

Laissez-faire The doctrine that government should not intervene in the economy, especially through regulation.

Land Grant College Act Law passed by Congress in July 1862 awarding proceeds from the sale of public lands to the states for the establishment of agricultural and mechanical (later engineering) colleges. Also known as the Morrill Act, after its sponsor, Congressman Justin Morrill of Vermont.

Land Ordinance of 1785 Act passed by Congress under the **Articles of Confederation** that created the grid system of surveys by which all subsequent public land was made available for sale.

League of Nations International organization created by the **Versailles Treaty** after World War I to ensure world stability.

League of Women Voters Group formed in 1920 from the National American Woman Suffrage Association to encourage informed voting and social reforms.

Lecompton Constitution Proslavery draft written in 1857 by Kansas territorial delegates elected under questionable circumstances; it was rejected by two governors, supported by President Buchanan, and decisively defeated by Congress.

Lend-Lease Act Program begun in 1941 through which the United States transferred military equipment to Britain and other World War II allies.

Liberal Republicans Members of a reform movement within the **Republican Party** in 1872 that promoted measures to reduce government influence in the economy and restore control of southern governments to local white elites.

Liberty Bonds Interest-bearing certificates sold by the U.S. government to finance the American World War I effort.

Liberty Party The first antislavery political party, formed in 1840.

Limited Test Ban Treaty Agreement in 1963 between the United States, Britain, and the Soviet Union to halt atmospheric and underwater tests of nuclear weapons.

Lincoln-Douglas debates Series of debates in the 1858 Illinois senatorial campaign during which Democrat Stephen A. Douglas and Republican Abraham Lincoln staked out their differing opinions on the issue of slavery in the territories.

Lost Cause The phrase many white southerners applied to their Civil War defeat. They viewed the war as a noble cause but only a temporary setback in the South's ultimate vindication.

Lynching Execution, usually by a mob, without trial.

Mahanism The ideas advanced by Alfred Thayer Mahan, stressing U.S. naval, economic, and territorial expansion.

Manhattan Project The effort, using the code name Manhattan Engineer District, to develop an atomic bomb under the management of the U.S. Army Corps of Engineers during World War II.

Manifest Destiny Doctrine, first expressed in 1845, that the expansion of white Americans across the continent was inevitable and ordained by God.

Marbury v. Madison Supreme Court decision of 1803 that created the precedent of judicial review by ruling as unconstitutional part of the **Judiciary Act of 1789.**

Marshall Plan The European Recovery Program (1949), which provided U.S. economic assistance to European nations; named for Secretary of State George Marshall.

Massive retaliation Popular name for the military doctrine adopted in the 1950s, whereby the United States promised to respond to any attack on itself or its allies with massive force, including nuclear weapons.

McCarthyism Anticommunist attitudes and actions associated with Senator Joe McCarthy in the early 1950s, including smear tactics and innuendo.

McCulloch v. Maryland Supreme Court decision of 1819 upholding the constitutionality of the Second Bank of the United States and the exercise of federal powers within a state.

Medicaid Supplementary medical insurance for the poor, financed through the federal government; program created in 1965.

Medicare Basic medical insurance for the elderly, financed through the federal government; program created in 1965.

Mercantilism Economic system whereby the government intervenes in the economy for the purpose of increasing national wealth. Mercantilists advocated possession of colonies as places where the mother country could acquire raw materials not available at home.

Mexican Cession of 1848 The land ceded to the U.S. by Mexico in the Treaty of Guadalupe Hidalgo.

Middle Passage The voyage between West Africa and the New World slave colonies.

Minute Men Special companies of militia formed in Massachusetts and elsewhere beginning in late 1744. These units were composed of men who were to be ready to assemble with their arms at a minute's notice.

Missouri Compromise Sectional compromise in Congress in 1820 that admitted Missouri to the Union as a slave state and Maine as a free state and prohibited slavery in the **Louisiana Purchase** territory above 36°309 north latitude.

Model Cities Program Effort to target federal funds to upgrade public services and economic opportunity in specifically defined urban neighborhoods between 1966 and 1974.

Molly Maguires Secret labor organization of mostly Irish miners in the Pennsylvania anthracite coal region in the decade after the Civil War. Named after a woman who led a massive protest against landlords in Ireland in the 1840s, the Maguires carried out selective murders of coal company officials until an infiltrator exposed the group in 1877 and its leaders were arrested, tried, and executed.

Monroe Doctrine Declaration by President James Monroe in 1823 that the Western Hemisphere was to be closed off to further European colonization and that the United States would not interfere in the internal affairs of European nations.

Mormon Church (Church of Jesus Christ of Latter-day Saints) Church founded in 1830 by Joseph Smith and based on the revelations in a sacred book he called the Book of Mormon.

Muckraking Journalism exposing economic, social, and political evils, so named by Theodore Roosevelt for its "raking the muck" of American society.

Mugwumps Elitist and conservative reformers who favored **sound money** and limited government and opposed tariffs and the **spoils system.**

Multinational corporation Firm with direct investments, branches, factories, and offices in a number of countries.

National Aeronautics and Space Administration (NASA) Federal agency created in 1958 to manage American space flights and exploration.

National American Woman Suffrage Association The organization, formed in 1890, that coordinated the ultimately successful campaign to achieve women's right to vote.

National Association for the Advancement of Colored People (NAACP): An interracial organization founded in 1910 dedicated to restoring African American political and social rights.

Nationalists Group of leaders in the 1780s who spearheaded the drive to replace the **Articles of Confederation** with a stronger central government.

National Origins Act A 1924 law sharply restricting immigration on the basis of immigrants' national origins and discriminating against southern and eastern Europeans and Asians.

National Security Council (NSC) The formal policymaking body for national defense and foreign relations, created in 1947 and consisting of the president, the secretary of defense, the secretary of state, and others appointed by the president.

National Security Council Paper 68 (NSC-68) Policy statement that committed the United States to a military approach to the **Cold War.**

Nation of Islam Religious movement among black Americans that emphasizes self-sufficiency, self-help, and separation from white society.

Nativist/Nativism Favoring the interests and culture of native-born inhabitants over those of immigrants.

Nat Turner's Rebellion Uprising of slaves in Southampton County, Virginia, in the summer of 1831 led by Nat Turner that resulted in the death of fifty-five whites.

Natural rights Political philosophy that maintains that individuals have an inherent right, found in nature and preceding any government or written law, to life and liberty.

Neoliberal Advocate of or participant in the effort to reshape the **Democratic Party** for the 1990s around a policy emphasizing economic growth and competitiveness in the world economy.

New Deal The economic and political policies of the Roosevelt administration in the 1930s.

New Federalism President Richard Nixon's policy to shift responsibilities for government programs from the federal level to the states.

New Freedom Woodrow Wilson's 1912 program for limited government intervention in the economy to restore competition by curtailing the restrictive influences of trusts and protective tariffs, thereby providing opportunities for individual achievement.

New Frontier John F. Kennedy's domestic and foreign policy initiatives, designed to reinvigorate a sense of national purpose and energy.

New Harmony Short-lived utopian community established in Indiana in 1825, based on the socialist ideas of Robert Owen, a wealthy Scottish manufacturer.

New Jersey Plan Proposal of the New Jersey delegation at the 1787 **Constitutional Convention** for a strengthened national government in which all states would have equal representation in a **unicameral legislature.**

New Lights People who experienced conversion during the revivals of the **Great Awakening.**

New Nationalism Theodore Roosevelt's 1912 program calling for a strong national government to foster, regulate, and protect business, industry, workers, and consumers.

New York Draft Riot A mostly Irish-immigrant protest against conscription in New York City in July 1863 that escalated into class and racial warfare that had to be quelled by federal troops.

Niagara Movement African-American group organized in 1905 to promote racial integration, civil and political rights, and equal access to economic opportunity.

Nineteenth Amendment Constitutional revision that in 1920 established women citizens' right to vote.

Nisei U.S. citizens born of immigrant Japanese parents.

Nixon Doctrine In July, 1969, President Nixon described a new American policy toward Asia, in which the United States would honor treaty commitments but would gradually disengage and expect Asian nations to handle military defense on their own.

Nonimportation Movement A tactical means of putting economic pressure on Britain by refusing to buy its exports to the colonies. Initiated in response to the taxes imposed by the **Sugar** and **Stamp Acts,** it was used again against the **Townshend duties** and the **Coercive Acts.** The nonimportation movement popularized resistance to British measures and deepened the commitment of many ordinary people to a larger American community.

North American Free Trade Agreement (NAFTA) Agreement reached in 1993 by Canada, Mexico, and the United States to substantially reduce barriers to trade.

North Atlantic Treaty Organization (NATO) Military alliance of the United States, Canada, and European nations created in 1949 to protect Europe against possible Soviet aggression.

Northwest Ordinance of 1787 Legislation passed by Congress under the **Articles of Confederation** that prohibited slavery in the Northwest Territories and provided the model for the incorporation of future territories into the Union as coequal states.

Nullification A constitutional doctrine holding that a state has a legal right to declare a national law null and void within its borders.

Nullification crisis Sectional crisis in the early 1830s in which a **states' rights** party in South Carolina attempted to nullify federal law.

Office of Economic Opportunity (OEO) Federal agency that coordinated many programs of the **War on Poverty** between 1964 and 1975.

Oligopoly An industry, such as steel making or automobile manufacturing, that is controlled by a few large companies.

Olive Branch Petition Petition, written largely by John Dickinson and adopted by the Second Continental Congress on July 5, 1775, as a last effort of peace that avowed America's loyalty to George III and requested that he protect it from further aggressions. Congress continued military preparations, and the king never responded to the petition.

Omaha Platform The 1892 platform of the **Populist Party** repudiating laissez-faire and demanding economic and political reforms to aid distressed farmers and workers.

Oneida Community Utopian community established in upstate New York in 1848 by John Humphrey Noyes and his followers.

Open Door American policy of seeking equal trade and investment opportunities in foreign nations or regions.

Open shop Factory or business employing workers whether or not they are union members; in practice, such a business usually refuses to hire union members and follows antiunion policies.

Operation Desert Storm Code name for the successful offensive against Iraq by the United States and its allies in the Persian Gulf War (1991).

Operation OVERLORD U.S. and British invasion of France in June 1944 during World War II.

Oregon Trail Overland trail of more than 2,000 miles that carried American settlers from the Midwest to new settlements in Oregon, California, and Utah.

Organization of Petroleum Exporting Countries (OPEC) Cartel of oil-producing nations in Asia, Africa, and Latin America that gained substantial power over the world economy in the mid- to late 1970s by controlling the production and price of oil.

Ostend Manifesto Message sent by U.S. envoys to President Pierce from Ostend, Belgium, in 1854, stating that the United States had a "divine right" to wrest Cuba from Spain.

Pan-American Union International organization originally established as the Commercial Bureau of American Republics by Secretary of State James Blaine's first Pan-American Conference in 1889 to promote cooperation among nations of the Western Hemisphere through commercial and diplomatic negotiations.

Panic of 1857 Banking crisis that caused a credit crunch in the North; it was less severe in the South, where high cotton prices spurred a quick recovery.

Pan-Indian resistance movement Movement calling for the political and cultural unification of Indian tribes in the late eighteenth and early nineteenth centuries.

PATRIOT Act Federal legislation adopted in 2001, in response to the terrorist attacks of September 11, intended to facilitate antiterror actions by federal law enforcement and intelligence agencies.

Peace of Paris Treaties signed in 1783 by Great Britain, the United States, France, Spain, and the Netherlands that ended the Revolutionary War. First in a preliminary agreement and then in the final treaty with the United States, Britain recognized the independence of the United States, agreed that the Mississippi River would be its western boundary, and permitted it to fish in some Canadian waters. Prewar debts owed by the inhabitants of one country to those of the other were to remain collectible, and Congress was to urge the states to return property confiscated from Loyalists. British troops were to evacuate United States territory without removing slaves or other property. In a separate agreement, Britain relinquished its claim to East and West Florida to Spain.

Pendleton Civil Service Act A law of 1883 that reformed the **spoils system** by prohibiting government workers from making political contributions and creating the Civil Service Commission to oversee their appointment on the basis of merit rather than politics.

Pentagon Papers Classified Defense Department documents on the history of the U.S. involvement in Vietnam, prepared in 1968 and leaked to the press in 1971.

People's Party See **Populist Party**.

Pequot War Conflict between English settlers (who had Narragansett and Mohegan allies) and Pequot Indians over control of land and trade in eastern Connecticut. The Pequots were nearly destroyed in a set of bloody confrontations, including a deadly English attack on a Mystic River village in May 1637.

Perestroika Russian for "restructuring," applied to Mikhail Gorbachev's efforts to make the Soviet economic and political systems more modern, flexible, and innovative.

Persian Gulf War War (1991) between Iraq and a U. S.-led coalition that followed Iraq's invasion of Kuwait and resulted in the expulsion of Iraqi forces from that country.

Pietists Protestants who stress a religion of the heart and the spirit of Christian living.

Pilgrims Settlers of Plymouth Colony, who viewed themselves as spiritual wanderers.

Platt Amendment A stipulation the United States had inserted into the Cuban constitution in 1901 restricting Cuban autonomy and authorizing U.S. intervention and naval bases.

Plessy v. Ferguson U.S. Supreme Court decision in 1896 affirming the constitutionality of racial segregation by law.

Pogroms Government-directed attacks against Jewish citizens, property, and villages in tsarist Russia beginning in the 1880s; a primary reason for Russian Jewish migration to the United States.

Poll tax A tax imposed on voters as a requirement for voting. Most southern states imposed poll taxes after 1900 as a way to disfranchise black people; the measures also restricted the white vote.

Pontiac's War Indian uprising (1763–1766) led by Pontiac of the Ottawas and Neolin of the Delawares. Fearful of their fate at the hands of the British after the French had been driven out of North America, the Indian nations of the Ohio River Valley and the Great Lakes area united to oust the British from the Ohio-Mississippi Valley. They failed and were forced to make peace in 1766.

Popular Sovereignty A solution to the slavery crisis suggested by Michigan senator Lewis Cass by which territorial residents, not Congress, would decide slavery's fate.

Populist Party A major third party of the 1890s, also known as the **People'sParty.**Formed on the basis of the **Southern Farmers' Alliance** and other reform organizations, it mounted electoral challenges against the Democrats in the South and the Republicans in the West.

Potsdam Declaration Statement issued by the United States during a meeting of U.S. president Harry Truman, British Prime Minister Winston Churchill, and Soviet premier Joseph Stalin held at Potsdam, near Berlin, in July 1945 to plan the defeat of Japan and the future of Eastern Europe and Germany. In it, the United States declared its intention to democratize the Japanese political system and reintroduce Japan into the international community and gave Japan an opening for surrender.

Predestination The belief that God decided at the moment of Creation which humans would achieve salvation.

Preparedness Military buildup in preparation for possible U.S. participation in World War I.

Preservation Protecting forests, land, and other features of the natural environment from development or destruction, often for aesthetic appreciation.

Proclamation of 1763 Royal proclamation setting the boundary known as the **Proclamation Line.**

Progressive Era The period of the twentieth century before World War I when many groups sought to reshape the nation's government and society in response to the pressures of industrialization and urbanization.

Prohibition A ban on the production, transportation and sale of liquor, achieved temporarily through state laws and the Eighteenth Amendment.

Prohibition Party A venerable third party still in existence that has persistently campaigned for the abolition of alcohol but has also introduced many important reform ideas into American politics.

Proposition 187 California legislation adopted by popular vote in California in 1994, which cuts off state-funded health and education benefits to undocumented or illegal immigrants.

Proprietary colony A colony created when the English monarch granted a huge tract of land to an individual or group of individuals, who became "lords proprietor." Many lords proprietor had distinct social visions for their colonies, but these plans were hardly ever implemented. Examples of proprietary colonies are Maryland, Carolina, New York (after it was seized from the Dutch), and Pennsylvania.

Protestants Europeans who supported reform of the Catholic Church in the wake of Martin Luther's critique of the Church.

Pueblo Revolt Rebellion in 1680 of Pueblo Indians in New Mexico against their Spanish overlords, sparked by religious conflict and excessive Spanish demands for tribute.

Puritans Individuals who believed that Queen Elizabeth's reforms of the Church of England had not gone far enough in improving the church, particularly in ensuring that church members were among the saved. Puritans led the settlement of Massachusetts Bay Colony.

Putting-out system System of manufacturing in which merchants furnished households with raw materials for processing by family members.

Quakers Members of the Society of Friends, a radical religious group that arose in the mid-seventeenth century. Quakers rejected formal theology and an educated ministry, focusing instead on the importance of the "Inner Light," or Holy Spirit that dwelt within them. Quakers were important in the founding of Pennsylvania.

Quartering Acts Acts of Parliament requiring colonial legislatures to provide supplies and quarters for the troops stationed in America. Americans considered this taxation in disguise and objected. None of these acts passed during the pre-Revolutionary controversy required that soldiers be quartered in an occupied house without the owner's consent.

Quasi-War Undeclared naval war of 1797 to 1800 between the United States and France.

Quebec Act Law passed by Parliament in 1774 that provided an appointed government for Canada, enlarged the boundaries of Quebec southward to the Ohio River, and confirmed the privileges of the Catholic Church. Alarmed Americans termed this act and the **Coercive Acts** the **Intolerable Acts.**

Queen Anne's War American phase (1702–1713) of Europe's War of the Spanish Succession. At its conclusion, England gained Nova Scotia.

Radical Republicans A shifting group of Republican congressmen, usually a substantial minority, who favored the abolition of slavery from the beginning of the Civil War and later advocated harsh treatment of the defeated South.

Reagan Doctrine The policy assumption that Soviet-influenced governments in Asia, Africa, and Latin America needed to be eliminated if the United States was to win the Cold War.

Recall The process of removing an official from office by popular vote, usually after using petitions to call for such a vote.

Reconquista The long struggle (ending in 1492) during which Spanish Christians reconquered the Iberian Peninsula from Muslim occupiers, who first invaded in the eighth century.

Reconstruction Era The era (1865–1877) when the resolution of two major issues—the status of the former slaves and the terms of the Confederate states' readmission into the Union—dominated political debate.

Redeemers Southern Democrats who wrested control of governments in the former Confederacy, often through electoral fraud and violence, from Republicans beginning in 1870.

Redemptioners Similar to **indentured servants,** except that redemptioners signed labor contracts in America rather than in Europe, as indentured servants did. Shipmasters sold redemptioners into servitude to recoup the cost of their passage if they could not pay the fare upon their arrival.

Redlining Restricting mortgage credit and insurance to properties in neighborhoods defined as being high risk.

Red Scare Post–World War I public hysteria over **Bolshevik** influence in the United States directed against labor activists, radical dissenters, and some ethnic groups.

Referendum Submission of a law, proposed or already in effect, to a direct popular vote for approval or rejection.

Reformation Sixteenth-century movement to reform the Catholic Church that ultimately led to the founding of new Protestant Christian religious groups.

Regulators Vigilante groups active in the 1760s and 1770s in the western parts of North and South Carolina. The South Carolina Regulators attempted to rid the area of outlaws; the North Carolina Regulators sought to protect themselves against excessively high taxes and court costs. In both cases, westerners lacked sufficient representation in the legislature to obtain immediate redress of their grievances. The South Carolina government eventually made concessions; the North Carolina government suppressed its Regulator movement by force.

Repartimiento In the Spanish colonies, the assignment of Indian workers to labor on public works projects.

Republicanism A complex, changing body of ideas, values, and assumptions, closely related to **country ideology,** that influenced American political behavior during the eighteenth and nineteenth centuries. Derived from the political ideas of classical antiquity, Renaissance Europe, and early modern England, republicanism held that self-government by the citizens of a country, or their representatives, provided a more reliable foundation for the good society and individual freedom than rule by kings. The benefits of monarchy depended on the variable abilities of monarchs; the character of republican government depended on the virtue of the people. Republicanism therefore helped give the American Revolution a moral dimension. But the nature of republican virtue and the conditions favorable to it became sources of debate that influenced the writing of the state and federal constitutions as well as the development of political parties.

Republican Party Party that emerged in the 1850s in the aftermath of the bitter controversy over the **Kansas-Nebraska Act,** consisting of former **Whigs,** some northern Democrats, and many **Know-Nothings.**

Republican Party (Jeffersonian) Party headed by Thomas Jefferson that formed in opposition to the financial and diplomatic policies of the **Federalist Party;** favored limiting the powers of the national government and placing the interests of farmers and planters over those of financial and commercial groups; supported the cause of the French Revolution.

Rescate Procedure by which Spanish colonists would pay ransom to free Indians captured by rival natives. The rescued Indians then became workers in Spanish households.

Reservationists Group of U.S. senators favoring approval of the **Treaty of Versailles,**the peace agreement after World War I, after amending it to incorporate their reservations.

Rhode Island system During the industrialization of the early nineteenth century, the recruitment of entire families for employment in a factory.

Roe v. Wade U.S. Supreme Court decision in 1973 that disallowed state laws prohibiting abortion during the first three months (trimester) of pregnancy and established guidelines for abortion in the second and third trimesters.

Roosevelt Corollary President Theodore Roosevelt's policy asserting U.S. authority to intervene in the affairs of Latin American nations; an expansion of the **Monroe Doctrine.**

Rush–Bagot Agreement Treaty of 1817 between the United States and Britain that effectively demilitarized the Great Lakes by sharply limiting the number of ships each power could station on them.

Sabbatarian movement Reform organization founded in 1828 by Congregationalist and Presbyterian ministers that lobbied for an end to the delivery of mail on Sundays and other Sabbath violations.

"Sack of Lawrence" Vandalism and arson committed by a group of pro-slavery men in Lawrence, the free-state capital of Kansas Territory.

Sagebrush Rebellion Political movement in the western states in the early 1980s that called for easing of regulations on the economic use of federal lands and the transfer of some or all of those lands to state ownership.

Sand Creek Massacre The near annihilation in 1864 of Black Kettle's Cheyenne band by Colorado troops under Colonel John Chivington's orders to "kill and scalp all, big and little."

Santa Fe Trail Overland trial across the southern plains from St. Louis to New Mexico that funneled American traders and goods to Spanish-speaking settlements in the Southwest.

Scalawags Southern whites, mainly small landowning farmers and well-off merchants and planters, who supported the southern **Republican Party** during

Reconstruction for diverse reasons; a disparaging term.

Search and destroy U.S. military tactic in South Vietnam, using small detachments to locate enemy units and then massive air, artillery, and ground forces to destroy them.

Second Bank of the United States A national bank chartered by Congress in 1816 with extensive regulatory powers over currency and credit.

Second Continental Congress An assemblage of delegates from all the colonies that convened in May 1775 after the outbreak of fighting in Massachusetts between British and American forces. It became the national government that eventually declared independence and conducted the Revolutionary War.

Second Great Awakening Series of religious revivals in the first half of the nineteenth century characterized by great emotionalism in large public meetings.

Securities and Exchange Commission (SEC) Federal agency with authority to regulate trading practices in stocks and bonds.

Sedition Act of 1918 Broad law restricting criticism of America's involvement in World War I or its government, flag, military, taxes, or officials.

Segregation A system of racial control that separated the races, initially by custom but increasingly by law during and after **Reconstruction.**

Selective Service Act of 1917   The law establishing the military draft for World War I.

Selective Service System   Federal agency that coordinated military conscription before and during the Vietnam War.

Self-determination   The right of a people or nation to decide on its own political allegiance or form of government without external influence.

Seneca Falls Convention   The first convention for women's equality in legal rights, held in upstate New York in 1848. **See also Declaration of Sentiments.**

Separatists   Members of an offshoot branch of Puritanism. Separatists believed that the Church of England was too corrupt to be reformed and hence were convinced that they must "separate" from it to save their souls. Separatists helped found Plymouth Colony.

Settlement house   A multipurpose structure in a poor neighborhood that offered social welfare, educational, and homemaking services to the poor or immigrants; usually under private auspices and directed by middle-class women.

Seventeenth Amendment   Constitutional change that in 1913 established the direct popular election of U.S. senators.

Shakers   The followers of Mother Ann Lee, who preached a religion of strict celibacy and communal living.

Sharecropping   Labor system that evolved during and after **Reconstruction** whereby landowners furnished laborers with a house, farm animals, and tools and advanced credit in exchange for a share of the laborers' crop.

Shays's Rebellion   An armed movement of debt-ridden farmers in western Massachusetts in the winter of 1786–1787. The rebellion shut down courts and created a crisis atmosphere, strengthening the case of **nationalists** that a stronger central government was needed to maintain civil order in the states.

Sheppard-Towner Maternity and Infancy Act of 1921   The first federal social welfare law; funded infant and maternity health care programs in local hospitals.

Sherman Antitrust Act   The first federal antitrust measure, passed in 1890; sought to promote economic competition by prohibiting business combinations in restraint of trade or commerce.

Silicon Valley   The region of California between San Jose and San Francisco that holds the nation's greatest concentration of electronics firms.

Sixteenth Amendment   Constitutional revision that in 1913 authorized a federal income tax.

Slaughterhouse **cases**   Group of cases resulting in one sweeping decision by the U.S. Supreme Court in 1873 that contradicted the intent of the **Fourteenth Amendment** by decreeing that most citizenship rights remained under state, not federal, control.

Slave codes   Sometimes known as "black codes." A series of laws passed mainly in the southern colonies in the late seventeenth and early eighteenth centuries to define the status of slaves and codify the denial of basic civil rights to them. Also, after American independence and before the Civil War, state laws in the South defining slaves as property and specifying the legal powers of masters over slaves.

Slave Power   A key concept in abolitionist and northern antislavery propaganda that depicted southern slaveholders as the driving force in a political conspiracy to promote slavery at the expense of white liberties.

Social Darwinism   The application of Charles Darwin's theory of biological evolution to society, holding that the fittest and the wealthiest survive, the weak and the poor perish, and government action is unable to alter this "natural" and beneficial process.

Social Gospel movement: An effort by leading Protestants to apply religious ethics to industrial conditions and thereby alleviate poverty, slums, and labor exploitation.

Socialism   A social order based on government ownership of industry and worker control over corporations as a way to prevent worker exploitation.

Solid South   The one-party (Democratic) political system that dominated the South from the 1890s to the 1950s.

Songhai empire   A powerful West African state that flourished between 1450 and 1591, when it fell to a Moroccan invasion.

Sons of Liberty   Secret organizations in the colonies formed to oppose the

Stamp Act   From 1765 until independence, they spoke, wrote, and demonstrated against British measures. Their actions often intimidated stamp distributors and British supporters in the colonies.

Sound money   Misleading slogan that referred to a conservative policy of restricting the money supply and adhering to the gold standard.

Southeast Asia Treaty Organization (SEATO)   Mutual defense alliance signed in 1954 by the United States, Britain, France, Thailand, Pakistan, the Philippines, Australia, and New Zealand.

Southern Christian Leadership Conference (SCLC)   Black civil rights organization founded in 1957 by Martin Luther King Jr., and other clergy.

Southern Farmers' Alliance   The largest of several organizations that formed in the post-Reconstruction South to advance the interests of beleaguered small farmers.

Southern Homestead Act   Largely unsuccessful law passed in 1866 that gave black people preferential access to public lands in five southern states.

Southern Manifesto   A document signed by 101 members of Congress from southern states in 1956 that argued that the Supreme Court's decision in *Brown v. Board of Education of Topeka* itself contradicted the **Constitution.**

Southwest Ordinance of 1790   Legislation passed by Congress that set up a government with no prohibition on slavery in U.S. territory south of the Ohio River.

Sovereignty   The supreme authority of the state, including both the right to take life and to tax.

Specie Circular   Proclamation issued by President Andrew Jackson in 1836 stipulating that only gold or silver could be used as payment for public land.

Spheres of Influence   A region dominated and controlled by an outside power.

Spoils system The awarding of government jobs to party loyalists.

Stamp Act Law passed by Parliament in 1765 to raise revenue in America by requiring taxed, stamped paper for legal documents, publications, and playing cards. Americans opposed it as "taxation without representation" and prevented its enforcement. Parliament repealed it a year after its enactment.

Stamp Act Congress October 1765 meeting of delegates sent by nine colonies, held in New York City, that adopted the **Declaration of Rights and Grievances** and petitioned against the **Stamp Act.**

States' rights Favoring the rights of individual states over rights claimed by the national government.

Stonewall Rebellion On June 27, 1969, patrons fought back when police raided the gay Stonewall Inn in New York; the name refers to that event and to the increase in militancy by gay Americans that it symbolizes.

Stono Rebellion Uprising in 1739 of South Carolina slaves against whites; inspired in part by Spanish officials' promise of freedom for American slaves who escaped to Florida.

Strategic Arms Limitation Treaty (SALT) Strategic Arms Limitation Treaty signed in 1972 by the United States and the Soviet Union to slow the nuclear arms race.

Strategic Defense Initiative (SDI) President Reagan's program, announced in 1983, to defend the United States against nuclear missile attack with untested weapons systems and sophisticated technologies; also known as "Star Wars."

Student Nonviolent Coordinating Committee (SNCC) Black civil rights organization founded in 1960 and drawing heavily on younger activists and college students.

Students for a Democratic Society (SDS) The leading student organization of the New Left of the early and mid-1960s.

Subtreasury plan A program promoted by the **Southern Farmers' Alliance** in response to low cotton prices and tight credit. Farmers would store their crop in a warehouse (or "subtreasury") until prices rose, in the meantime borrowing up to 80 percent of the value of the stored crops from the government at a low interest rate.

Suffolk Resolves Militant resolves adopted in September 1774 in response to the **Coercive Acts** by representatives from the towns in Suffolk County, Massachusetts, including Boston. They termed the **Coercive Acts** unconstitutional, advised the people to arm, and called for economic sanctions against Britain. The **First Continental Congress** endorsed these resolves.

Suffrage The right to vote in a political election.

Sugar Act Law passed in 1764 to raise revenue in the American colonies. It lowered the duty from 6 pence to 3 pence per gallon on foreign molasses imported into the colonies and increased the restrictions on colonial commerce.

Sunbelt The states of the American South and Southwest.

Sussex Pledge Germany's pledge during World War I not to sink merchant ships without warning, on the condition that Britain also observe recognized rules of international law.

Swann v. Charlotte-Mecklenburg Board of Education U.S. Supreme Court decision in 1971 that upheld cross-city busing to achieve the racial integration of public schools.

Sweatshops Small, poorly ventilated shops or apartments crammed with workers, often family members, who pieced together garments.

Taft-Hartley Act Federal legislation of 1947 that substantially limited the tools available to labor unions in labor–management disputes.

Tammany Hall New York City's **Democratic Party** organization, dating from well before the Civil War, that evolved into a powerful political machine after 1860, using patronage and bribes to maintain control of the city administration.

Taos Revolt Uprising of Pueblo Indians in New Mexico that broke out in January 1847 over the imposition of American rule during the Mexican War; the revolt was crushed within a few weeks.

Tariff Act of 1789 Apart from a few selected industries, this first tariff passed by Congress was intended primarily to raise revenue and not protect American manufacturers from foreign competition.

Tariff Act of 1798 Law placing a duty of 5 percent on most imported goods, designed primarily to generate revenue and not to protect American goods from foreign competition.

Tea Act of 1773 Act of Parliament that permitted the East India Company to sell tea through agents in America without paying the duty customarily collected in Britain, thus reducing the retail price. Americans, who saw the act as an attempt to induce them to pay the Townshend duty still imposed in the colonies, resisted this act through the **Boston Tea Party** and other measures.

Tejano A person of Spanish or Mexican descent born in Texas.

Teller Amendment A congressional resolution adopted in 1898 renouncing any American intention to annex Cuba.

Temperance Reform movement originating in the 1820s that sought to eliminate the consumption of alcohol.

Temporary Assistance for Needy Families (TANF) Federal program created in 1996 to replace earlier welfare programs to aid families and children; it involves explicit work requirements for receiving aid and places a time limit on benefits.

Tenement Four- to six-story residential dwelling, once common in New York and certain other cities, built on a tiny lot without regard to providing ventilation or light.

Tennessee Valley Authority (TVA) Federal regional planning agency established to promote **conservation,** produce electric power, and encourage economic development in seven southern states.

Tenure of Office Act Passed by the Republican controlled Congress in 1867 to limit presidential interference with its policies, the act prohibited the president from removing certain officeholders without the Senate's consent. President Andrew Johnson, angered at which he believed as an unconstitutional attack on presidential authority, deliberately violated the act by firing Secretary of War Edwin M. Stanton. The House responded by approving articles of impeachment against a president for the first time in American history.

Thirteenth Amendment   Constitutional amendment ratified in 1865 that freed all slaves throughout the United States.

Tories   A derisive term applied to loyalists in America who supported the king and Parliament just before and during the American Revolution. The term derived from late-seventeenth-century English politics when the Tory party supported the duke of York's succession to the throne as James II. Later the Tory party favored the Church of England and the crown over dissenting denominations and Parliament.

Townshend Duty Act of 1967   Act of Parliament, passed in 1767, imposing duties on colonial tea, lead, paint, paper, and glass. Designed to take advantage of the supposed American distinction between internal and external taxes, the Townshend duties were to help support government in America. The act prompted a successful colonial nonimportation movement.

Trail of Tears   The forced march in 1838 of the Cherokee Indians from their homelands in Georgia to the Indian Territory in the West; thousands of Cherokees died along the way.

Transcendentalism   A philosophical and literary movement centered on an idealistic belief in the divinity of individuals and nature.

Trans-Continental Treaty of 1819   Treaty between the United States and Spain in which Spain ceded Florida to the United States, surrendered all claims to the Pacific Northwest, and agreed to a boundary between the Louisiana Purchase territory and the Spanish Southwest.

Treaty of Fort Laramie   The treaty acknowledging U.S. defeat in the Great Sioux War in 1868 and supposedly guaranteeing the Sioux perpetual land and hunting rights in South Dakota, Wyoming, and Montana.

Treaty of Ghent   Treaty signed in December 1814 between the United States and Britain that ended the **War of 1812.**

Treaty of Greenville   Treaty of 1795 in which Native Americans in the Old Northwest were forced to cede most of the present state of Ohio to the United States.

Treaty of Lancaster   Negotiation in 1744 whereby Iroquois chiefs sold Virginia land speculators the right to trade at the Forks of the Ohio. Although the Iroquois had not intended this to include the right to settle in the Ohio Country, the Virginians assumed that it did. Ohio Valley Indians considered this treaty a great grievance against both the English and the Iroquois.

Treaty of San Lorenzo   See **Pinckney's Treaty.**

Treaty of Tordesillas   Treaty negotiated by the pope in 1494 to resolve the territorial claims of Spain and Portugal. It drew a north–south line approximately 1,100 miles west of the Cape Verde Islands, granting all lands west of the line to Spain and all lands east of the line to Portugal. This limited Portugal's New World empire to Brazil but confirmed its claims in Africa and Asia.

Treaty of Versailles   The treaty ending World War I and creating the **League of Nations.**

Transportation revolution   Dramatic improvements in transportation that stimulated economic growth after 1815 by expanding the range of travel and reducing the time and cost of moving goods and people.

Troubled Asset Relief Program (TARP)   Federal program in 2008 to purchase or guarantee shaky bank assets to protect the economy from widespread bank failures.

Truman Doctrine   President Harry Truman's statement in 1947 that the United States should assist other nations that were facing external pressure or internal revolution; an important step in the escalation of the **Cold War.**

Trusts   In late 19th- and early-20th-century usage, refers to monopolies that eliminated competition and fixed prices and wages in a given industry. Increasing numbers of Americans viewed these entities as threats to the free enterprise system.

Underground Railroad   Support system set up by antislavery groups in the Upper South and the North to assist fugitive slaves in escaping the South.

Underwood-Simmons Tariff Act   The 1913 reform law that lowered tariff rates and levied the first regular federal income tax.

Unicameral legislature   A legislative body composed of a single house.

Union League   A **Republican Party** organization in northern cities that became an important organizing device among freedmen in southern cities after 1865.

United States v. Cruikshank   Supreme Court ruling of 1876 that overturned the convictions of some of those responsible for the Colfax Massacre, ruling that the Enforcement Act applied only to violations of black rights by states, not individuals.

University of California v. Bakke   U.S. Supreme Court case in 1978 that allowed race to be used as one of several factors in college and university admission decisions but made rigid quotas unacceptable.

Valley Forge   Area of Pennsylvania approximately twenty miles northwest of Philadelphia where General George Washington's continental troops were quartered from December 1777 to June 1778 while British forces occupied Philadelphia during the Revolutionary War. Approximately 2,500 men, about a quarter of those encamped there, died of hardship and disease.

Vertical integration   The consolidation of numerous production functions, from the extraction of the raw materials to the distribution and marketing of the finished products, under the direction of one firm.

Viet Cong   Communist rebels in South Vietnam who fought the pro-American government established in South Vietnam in 1954.

Virginia Plan   Proposal of the Virginia delegation at the 1787 **Constitution Convention** calling for a national legislature in which the states would be represented according to population. The national legislature would have the explicit power to veto or overrule laws passed by state legislatures.

Virtual representation   The notion, current in eighteenth-century England, that parliamentary members represented the interests of the nation as a whole, not those of the particular district that elected them.

Volstead Act The 1920 law defining the liquor forbidden under the Eighteenth Amendment and giving enforcement responsibilities to the Prohibition Bureau of the Department of the Treasury.

Voting Rights Act Legislation in 1965 that overturned a variety of practices by which states systematically denied voter registration to minorities.

Waltham system During the industrialization of the early nineteenth century, the recruitment of unmarried young women for employment in factories.

War Hawks Members of Congress, predominantly from the South and West, who aggressively pushed for a war against Britain after their election in 1810.

War Industries Board (WIB) The federal agency that reorganized industry for maximum efficiency and productivity during World War I.

War of 1812 War fought between the United States and Britain from June 1812 to January 1815 largely over British restrictions on American shipping.

War on Poverty Set of programs introduced by Lyndon Johnson between 1963 and 1966 designed to break the cycle of poverty by providing funds for job training, community development, nutrition, and supplementary education.

Warsaw Pact Military alliance of the Soviet Union and Communist nations of Eastern Europe from 1955 to 1989.

Watergate A complex scandal involving attempts to cover up illegal actions taken by administration officials and leading to the resignation of President Richard Nixon in 1974.

Webster–Ashburton Treaty Treaty signed by the United States and Britain in 1842 that settled a boundary dispute between Maine and Canada and provided for closer cooperation in suppressing the African slave trade.

Welfare capitalism A paternalistic system of labor relations emphasizing management responsibility for employee well-being. While providing some limited benefits, its function was primarily to forestall the formation of unions or public intervention.

Whig Party Political party, formed in the mid-1830s in opposition to the Jacksonian Democrats, that favored a strong role for the national government in promoting economic growth.

Whigs The name used by advocates of colonial resistance to British measures during the 1760s and 1770s. The Whig party in England unsuccessfully attempted to exclude the Catholic duke of York from succession to the throne as James II; victorious in the **Glorious Revolution,** the Whigs later stood for religious toleration and the supremacy of Parliament over the crown.

Whiskey Rebellion Armed uprising in 1794 by farmers in western Pennsylvania who attempted to prevent the collection of the excise tax on whiskey.

Whitewater Arkansas real estate development in which Bill and Hillary Clinton were investors; several fraud convictions resulted from investigations into Whitewater, but evidence was not found that the Clintons were involved in wrongdoing.

Wide Awakes Group of red-shirted, black-caped young men who paraded through city streets in the North extolling the virtues of the **Republican Party** during the 1860 presidential election campaign.

Wilmot Proviso The amendment offered by Pennsylvania Democrat David Wilmot in 1846 which stipulated that "as an express and fundamental condition to the acquisition of any territory from the Republic of Mexico . . . neither slavery nor involuntary servitude shall ever exist in any part of said territory."

Wobblies Popular name for the members of the Industrial Workers of the World (IWW).

Woman's Christian Temperance Union (WCTU) National organization formed after the Civil War dedicated to prohibiting the sale and distribution of alcohol.

Workingmen's movement Associations of urban workers who began campaigning in the 1820s for free public education and a ten-hour workday.

World Bank Officially the International Bank for Reconstruction and Development, an international organization established in 1845 that assists governments around the world in economic development efforts.

World Trade Organization International organization that sets standards and practices for global trade, and the focus of international protests over world economic policy in the late 1990s.

World Wide Web Since 1991, the Web has expanded the use of the Internet by allowing organizations and companies to create websites that place political and commercial information only a few clicks away from wired consumers.

Wounded Knee Massacre The U.S. Army's brutal winter massacre in 1890 of at least two hundred Sioux men, women, and children as part of the government's assault on the tribe's Ghost Dance religion.

XYZ Affair Diplomatic incident in 1798 in which Americans were outraged by the demand of the French for a bribe as a condition for negotiating with American diplomats.

Yalta Conference Meeting of U.S. president Franklin Roosevelt, British Prime Minister Winston Churchill, and Soviet premier Joseph Stalin held in February 1945 to plan the final stages of World War II and postwar arrangements.

Yellow-dog contracts Employment agreements binding workers not to join a union.

Yellow press A deliberately sensational journalism of scandal and exposure designed to attract an urban mass audience and increase advertising revenues.

CREDITS

INDEX